G000098855

200675663

WAVELL

THE LIFE AND TIMES OF
AN IMPERIAL SERVANT

BY THE SAME AUTHOR

Prof: The Life and Times of Frederick Lindemann

WAVELL

THE LIFE AND TIMES OF
AN IMPERIAL SERVANT

ADRIAN FORT

JONATHAN CAPE
LONDON

Published by Jonathan Cape 2009

2 4 6 8 10 9 7 5 3 1

Copyright © Adrian Fort 2009

Adrian Fort has asserted his right under the Copyright, Designs
and Patents Act 1988 to be identified as the author of this work

This book is sold subject to the condition that it shall not,
by way of trade or otherwise, be lent, resold, hired out,
or otherwise circulated without the publisher's prior
consent in any form of binding or cover other than that
in which it is published and without a similar condition,
including this condition, being imposed
on the subsequent purchaser.

First published in Great Britain in 2009 by
Jonathan Cape
Random House, 20 Vauxhall Bridge Road,
London SW1V 2SA

www.rbooks.co.uk

Addresses for companies within The Random House Group Limited can be found at:
www.randomhouse.co.uk/offices.htm

The Random House Group Limited Reg. No. 954009

ISBN 9780224076784

A CIP catalogue record for this book
is available from the British Library

The Random House Group Limited supports The Forest Stewardship
Council (FSC), the leading international forest certification organisation. All our titles
that are printed on Greenpeace-approved FSC certified paper carry the FSC logo. Our
paper procurement policy can be found at www.rbooks.co.uk/environment

Mixed Sources
Product group from well-managed
forests and other controlled sources
www.fsc.org Cert no. TT-COC-2139
© 1996 Forest Stewardship Council
FSC

Typeset in Ehrhardt MT Rg by Palimpsest Book Production Limited,
Grangemouth, Stirlingshire

Printed and bound in Great Britain by
CPI Mackays, Chatham, Kent ME5 8TD

In memory of my beloved parents
Richard and Angela Fort.

WEST SUSSEX COUNTY LIBRARY SERVICE	
200675663	
Askews	27-Jan-2009
B WAV	

CONTENTS

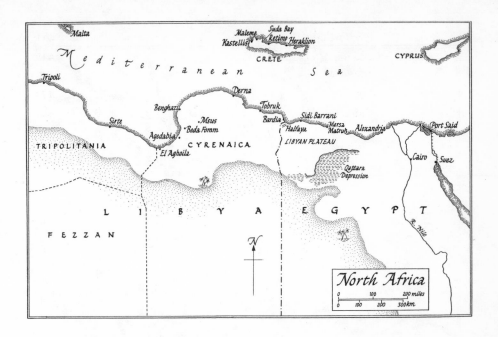

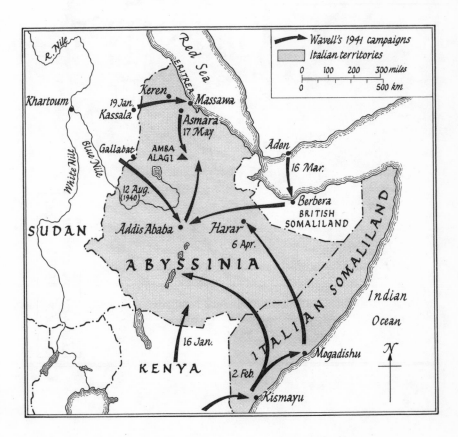

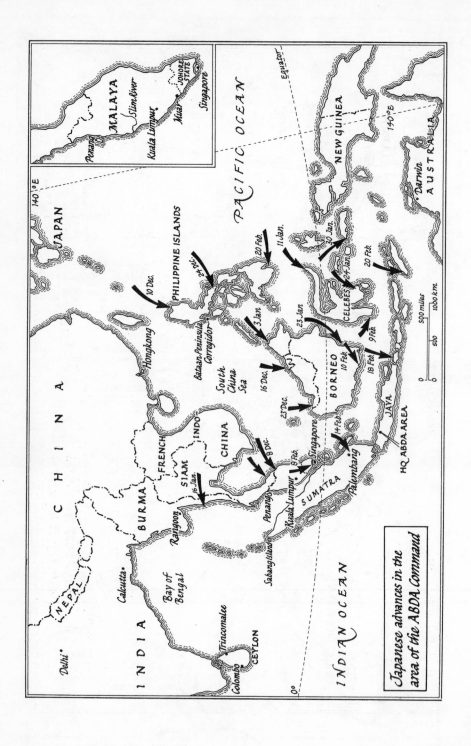

Japanese advances in the area of the ABDA Command

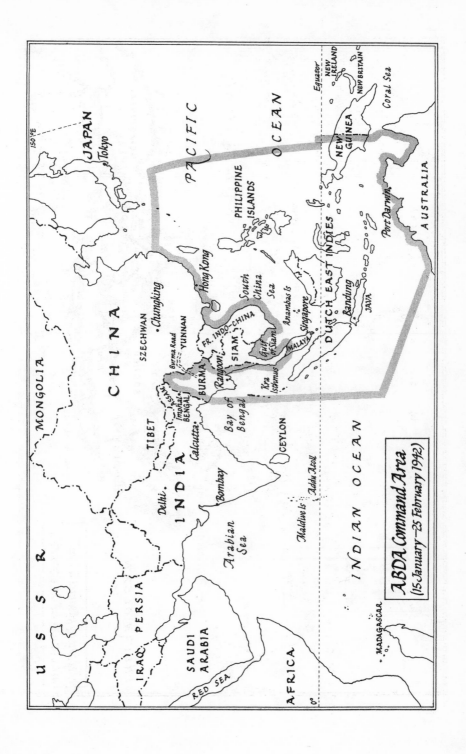

ABDA Command Area
(15 January—25 February 1942)

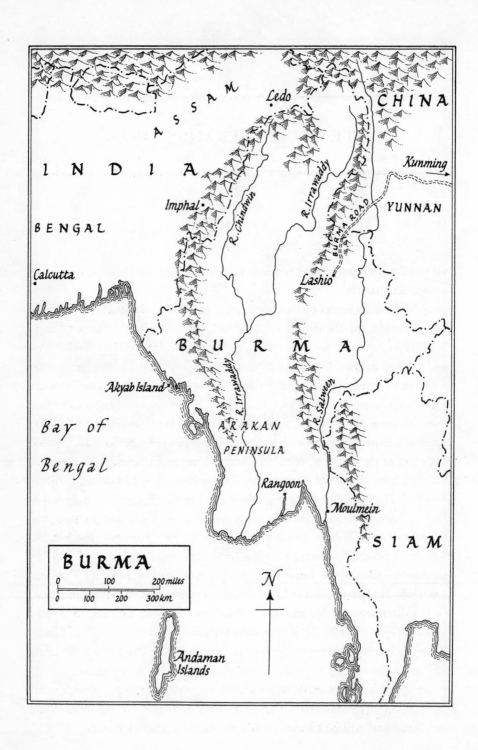

TEXTUAL PERMISSIONS

Grateful acknowledgement is made to the following for their permission to reproduce material:
Archibald Wavell letters by kind permission of the Wavell Estate; material from the papers of Lord Allenby, Sir Robert Brook-Popham, Sir John Burnett-Stuart, Sir Philip Chetwode, Sir John Dill, Sir Thomas Hutton, Sir Basil Liddell Hart and General Richard O'Connor by kind permission of the Liddell Hart Centre for Military Archives; Extract from *Forty Years On* by Alan Bennett (Faber and Faber, 1973) copyright Alan Bennett reprinted by permission of Faber and Faber; material from Sir Henry Channon's papers by kind permission of Henry Channon; material reproduced with permission of Curtis Brown Ltd, London on behalf of the Estate of Winston Churchill, copyright Winston S. Churchill; material from the Royal Archives by the permission of Her Majesty Queen Elizabeth II © 2009; material from the Peter Fleming Papers, by kind permission of Kate Grimond; Material from the Haldane Diary and Letters from Wavell to Dover Wilson, by kind permission of the Trustees of the National Library of Scotland; material from the Irwin Papers and the Percival Papers, by kind permission of the Imperial War Museum; material from the Lampson Diaries by kind permission of Lord Killearn; Letters from Wavell to Freya Stark by kind permission of Mr and Mrs Murray; material from the diary of William Walker, *The Red Hackle*, by Private John Gethins and letters from Wavell to Sir Henry Jackson by kind permission of the Trustees of The Black Watch Museum.

Every effort has been made to obtain the necessary permissions with reference to copyright material. The publishers apologise for any inadvertent omissions and will be pleased to rectify them in future editions.

ILLUSTRATIONS

1 Young Archibald Wavell (by kind permission of the Wavell Estate); 2 Wavell as a Young Lieutenant, 1914 (by kind permission of the Wavell Estate); 3 Wavell on the front cover of *Time* magazine, reprinted through the courtesy of the Editors of TIME Magazine © 2008 Time Inc.; 4 Joan Bright Astley (by kind permission of Joan Bright Astley); 5 Wavell in Egypt, 1940 (Peter Coats' Photographic Archive); 6 Wavell in Calcutta, 1943 (Peter Coats' Photographic Archive); 7 Peter Coats (Peter Coats' Photographic Archive); 8 Henry Channon (Henry Channon); 9 Lady Mary Herbert (Peter North); 10 Wavell in Singapore, 1942 (Peter Coats' Photographic Archive); 11 Wavell and Bernard Montgomery, 1943 (Peter Coats' Photographic Archive); 12 Wavell and horse, 1940 (Peter Coats' Photographic Archive); 13 'We do our duty', 1945 (© Hindustan Times); 14 Wavell on the cover of *Illustrated* (*Illustrated*, 1945); 15 Jinnah, Alexander, Pethick-Lawrence and Cripps (Getty); 16 Wavell, Felicity and Lady Wavell, 1943 (Peter Coats' Photographic Archive); 17 Cripps and Gandhi (Peter Coats' Photographic Archive); 18 Wavell and Rajagopalachari, 1945 (Peter North); 19 Wavell and Joe Stillwell 1942 (Getty); 20 Churchill, Sikandar Hiyat Khan and Wavell, 1941 (Peter Coats' Photographic Archive); 21 Cartoon of Lady Wavell reproduced with permission of Punch Ltd., *www.punch.co.uk*; 22 Lady Wavell in Gown (Peter Coats' Photographic Archive); 23 Archie John Wavell (Peter North Folder); 24 Wavell's three daughters (Peter Coats' Photographic Archive); 25 Golf at Simla (Peter Coats' Photographic Archive); 26 Wavell with Cecil Beaton and Bruce Fortune, 1944 (The Cecil Beaton Studio Archive at Sotheby's); 27 Wavell in his office (Getty); 28 Lord and Lady Mountbatten (Getty); 29 Portrait of Wavell (The Cecil Beaton Studio Archive at Sotheby's); 30 Wavell and ducks (Peter Coats' Photographic Archive).

Maps by Reginald Piggott.

INTRODUCTION

ON 7 February 1941 the remnants of Mussolini's once-proud legions in the Western Desert laid down their weapons before General Wavell's British Army of the Nile. Their surrender brought to a conclusion a series of glorious victories which cheered a country that since the beginning of the Second World War had suffered only reverses, the threat of invasion and fears that the war might be lost. Archibald Wavell's astonishing successes in North Africa brought him worldwide fame and the plaudits of the nation. Yet Wavell had reached the pinnacle of his military career on the eve of the fall of the British Empire, its swift demise opening the floodgates to much of the disorder and uncertainty that besets us in the twenty-first century.

The passage of time has shown that although Wavell and many of his contemporaries reached positions of power at a time when the Empire seemed almost an eternal verity, his generation allowed it to crumble and collapse in a few short years.

How, and why, did that come to pass? These men had been raised on the enduring merits of classical civilisation, and had been taught to see the might of Ancient Rome reflected in the modern British Empire, which in Wavell's day spanned nearly a quarter of the Earth's land surface. The failure of Wavell's generation to preserve the Empire when they were entrusted with its management raises the question of whether their education and formative influences were, after all, equal to the task. Wavell's own actions while holding the highest military and civil offices demonstrate how he, like many British leaders at the time, did not at heart endorse the imperialism that had made Great Britain the world's pre-eminent nation.

During three short years, between 1940 and 1943, when Wavell commanded the Empire's forces in the Middle East and then in the Far East, the prospects for continued British hegemony anywhere in those huge regions were fading beyond recall. Over the following three years, while Wavell was Viceroy of India, the fate of the Empire's principal component – India – was sealed. Within six months of Wavell's dismissal as Viceroy, the Union Jack had been hauled down all over the subcontinent, heralding the end not only of the entire British Empire, but also of the centuries-old empires of Holland and France.

In Wavell's time it was axiomatic that the British Empire would long endure and help sustain world peace and prosperity, until some distant time when its mantle might safely be handed on to the grateful natives. Yet, as it turned out, an embattled Wavell found that his role was instead to defend, regain or attempt to preserve huge areas of Africa, the Middle East and the Far East in which imperialism was no longer welcome. That duty conflicted with his instinctive sympathy with those who yearned for independence and for the passing of colonial rule, presumably heedless of the mayhem that might ensue.

How Wavell squared that circle, aided by an outstanding intellect and an imperturbable character, is assessed here. The passage of time has exposed much new information about Wavell and his struggles, both as general and Viceroy. Although there have been previous books on the subject, some are so uncritical as to do Wavell little justice, and most are now very out of date, both in their presentation and in the light of recent assessments of modern, post-imperial developments. Despite its being hardly possible to present a full picture of Wavell without considering his career both as a soldier and as Viceroy of India, until now there has been only one account that covers both.

The custom of former days precluded too close an examination of a subject's private life, with the result that previous portraits of Wavell have failed to address or dispel the rumours about him. The truth is that, besides being an outstanding soldier and an enlightened imperial administrator in wild, exceptional times, he was a cultured man of letters, relishing a bohemian atmosphere and companions as much as, if not more than, the more prosaic company of soldiers and officials that many highly placed people thought appropriate for him. There seems little reason to deny the modern reader a glimpse of this aspect of a great man.

SHAPING UP

Winchester College, July 1900. On a cool summer evening a group of boys had gathered to mark the ending of their schooldays. In long-sleeved black waistcoats and pinstripe trousers, shrouded in ankle-length gowns, they assembled in a quiet garden bordered by a stream. Above them, tall plane-trees in full leaf shaded ancient grey walls, enclosing an atmosphere of ritual, tradition and quiet calm. Nearby stood the chapel of St Mary-at-Winchester, and at the toll of its bell the group moved slowly into a stone courtyard, climbing well-worn steps into a gloomy, pew-filled hall. Shuffling forward to their places, they awaited the arrival of the Reverend Dr Fearon, the school's formidable Head Master, who would ascend a dais to address them, for the last time in their schoolboy careers.

In the quiet countryside of southern England, Winchester lay at the core of an Empire on which, it was proudly said, the sun never set. Britain ruled not just the waves, but one-fifth of the Earth's land surface, on which lived a quarter of mankind, under the Union Jack. But in Winchester that evening the flag was flying for Domum, the end of the College's year, when speeches and ancient ceremony, Latin songs and the award of medals, and formal dinner with warden and Head Master briefly usurped the long routine of learning. It was the day when boys who had run the course of their years at school took their leave – some with sorrow, others with relief.

Among those departing was Archie Wavell. At seventeen he was a stocky self-contained boy, blending in quietly with his colleagues as he took part in the ceremonies. He showed no great distinction from his fellow-leavers; he did not stand out from the crowd. Yet within the calm boy who took his place in the hall lay innate qualities which, refined and nurtured by his upbringing and education, were, forty years on, to make him for a brief time Britain's best-known and most successful soldier, and then Viceroy of India at a crucial moment in the history of that country, the keystone of the British Empire.

His family originated in France, inhabiting land around the Cherbourg peninsula. At the turn of the thirteenth century one of his ancestors had come over to England after fighting for King John, in his ill-fated attempt to entrench English power in Normandy. Rebuffed in France, the King withdrew to England, and some of his soldiers followed their master. Among them was Sir Richard de Vauville, who abandoned his native land and crossed over the sea to Sussex.

His descendants migrated westwards, anglicising their name to Wavell. Some of them settled in Hampshire, and over time the family developed a close connection with Winchester, the county town. Archie was the tenth Wavell to be educated at its famous school, and by the time he left it, with a well-developed feeling for history, it was almost exactly 700 years since his family had first arrived in England.

Archie's father was a soldier. At twenty he had joined what became the Norfolk Regiment, and had campaigned in Africa, fighting in the Zulu War. In 1883 he was forty, a major, and had been married for three years. On 5 May that year, in a large Victorian house in Colchester, where the regiment was stationed, his wife Lillie gave birth to their first son. He was christened Archibald, after his father, and Percival, his mother's maiden name.

The army was in the family's blood; many of Archie's forebears had been soldiers, including a grandfather whose vivid military life had led him to many exotic scenes of action, in Europe and India, Mexico and South America. From his earliest days Archie inhabited a military landscape, filled with bustle, movement and order, and the atmosphere in Colchester reflected the sights and sounds of a garrison town – the colours of uniforms; the smell of leather and polish; the clatter of hooves; the rumble of wagons; the call of bugles; the shouts of command; and the swing of marching soldiers.

Within these noisy surroundings his parents maintained a quiet, conventional household, regulated with late-Victorian formality in which the natural love of parents for their offspring found little expression. Archie's mother, who came from Cheshire, appears to have been retiring by nature, sweet-natured but plagued by arthritis, and kept rather in the shadow of her husband. The fact that Archie's father was middle-aged by the time his son was born reinforced a certain distance between the two, which may also have existed between husband and wife. Yet in many families at the Wavells' level of society that was the custom, and, deep down, relations between father and son were close.

Lillie Wavell does not seem to have made a deep or long-lasting mark on her son's development, with one significant exception: she developed the habit – common enough in those days – of having her son brought down to the drawing-room to be shown off to friends and visitors. The poor child hated these occasions, having to perform or speak to the assembled guests, and they soon extinguished his desire, and then even his ability, to talk in an easy manner just because he was expected to do so. These ordeals were to affect him in an extraordinary way, curtailing for ever his ability to indulge in small-talk or casual conversation. In later life he ascribed his silences, for which he became notorious, to his mother parading him before her friends. It was an impediment that was to cause him great difficulty at crucial moments in his career.

When Archie was five years old his father's regiment was ordered to India, uprooting the child from the surroundings he had known since birth. So he embarked on a new adventure with his parents and sisters – Florence Anne, a year older than he, and Lillian Mary a year younger. The family set off on a long sea voyage to a bright and different land, and Archie left behind the only home he had known, he found instead the excitement of new sensations, of taste and smell, sight and sound.

It was Rudyard Kipling who so clearly evoked the intensity of a child's early years in the India of that time, and who, after formative years in India, became the muse of the British Empire in its period of decline. Wavell was to be partic-ularly drawn to the prose and poetry of Kipling,[1] whose childhood memories of India were similar to his own, and the atmosphere and images that the famous author described played their part in nurturing a sense of the poetry in life that became one of Wavell's distinguishing characteristics.

'My first impression,' Kipling wrote of India, 'is of daybreak, light and colour, and golden and purple fruits at the level of my shoulder', and he was always to remember 'far-going Arab Dhows on the pearly waters, and gaily dressed Parsees wading out to worship the sunset'. 'I have always felt,' Kipling wrote, 'the menacing darkness of tropical eventides, as I have loved the voices of night-winds through palm or banana trees, and the song of the tree-frogs.'[2]

The young Archie Wavell also heard the song of the East, as for three impressionable years he absorbed the colourful life of an army cantonment in southern India, a vivid contrast to his earliest memories of Colchester.

Soon there was another upheaval. In 1891 his father made what was, for a professional soldier in peacetime, the unusual decision to transfer to another regiment. An opening had arisen for him in the Royal Highlanders,[3] to command its second battalion. Major Wavell grasped the opportunity: it enabled him to avoid moving on to Burma where the Norfolk Regiment had been ordered, and instead to return home to Britain.

For an eight-year-old boy it was another huge change, but an exciting one, as Archie found himself once more in new surroundings. His father was promoted to colonel and posted to Limerick. There the family lived for twelve months, before leaving behind the soft rain and green hills of Ireland and moving to Glasgow, to the Black Watch's barracks at Maryhill.

It was not long before Archie was confronted with yet another new prospect. In 1893, when he was ten years old, his parents sent him away to boarding-school, at Summer Fields, in Oxfordshire, one of the foremost of the preparatory schools lately established to train boys for the proving-ground of the British Empire, the public school. His trunks were packed, and he turned from the sights and sounds of home, the companionship of parents and sisters, and set off on the long road south. There, for much of the next few years, a colder, more remote authority would control his daily life.

Of schools that were grim, bleak and harsh; where discipline was fierce; where the teaching was erratic; and where boys were beaten, bullied, ill fed and comprehensively subdued, parents had at that time a wide choice. But Archie Wavell was lucky: his parents had the insight to choose a school that was not only a leader in the field of education, but where, relatively at least, the regime was tolerant, the surroundings attractive and the atmosphere benign; an institution with a culture infused by uncharacteristically artistic origins, that was to play its part in schooling the mind and outlook of generations of servants and leaders of the British Empire.

Until quite recently, let alone in the harsher climate of Victorian times, most children of a tender age were not at all happy to leave home and parents, to spend long weeks at a time in a distant school. However, Archie had already become rather quiet and reserved, and when the moment came for parting from his parents, he did not display any visible signs of minding very much. The ten-year-old Wavell – Christian names were abandoned on passing through the portals of a prep school – appears to have been quite happy, within a short time of being introduced to the other boys in his new surroundings, to release his parents from any obligation to stay.

From its beginnings the school aimed to cultivate what it called 'the family feeling and life', and perhaps the essence lingering from the enlightened and artistic circumstances of the school's origins helped to foster in Wavell the love of lyrics and poetry that would blossom as he grew older, and lend an engaging touch of lightness to his intellect – but which would also draw him to slightly unconventional and bohemian company, causing him difficulty at an important moment in his career.

Despite the wisp of artiness, the school had a rigorous scholastic regime, steeped in the Classics, which, for the ten or so years of their schooling, formed the main diet of the generations that were to run the Empire in its final decades. Wavell was at Summer Fields from the age of ten to thirteen, a time when the mind expands quickly. The school's first scholarship to Eton had been won in 1868; at that time the boys were 'expected to compose both Latin and Greek prose and verse, and to be able to construe from the following formidable list: St Mark's Gospel and part of the Acts in the Greek Testament; the *Ajax* of Sophocles; three books of the *Odyssey*; one book of Xenophon and one of Herodotus; one book of Livy, two of the *Aeneid*, two of Ovid and four of Horace'.[4] A fine regime for boys of prep-school age.

The syllabus and timetable had not evolved much by the time Wavell arrived at the school some twenty-five years later. The working day lasted from 7.00 in the morning until 9.00 at night, with almost eight hours of study, including prayers, chapel and Bible reading. Leisure, so called, included music, in which Wavell was never greatly interested, games and drill. Of the thirty-eight hours' work each week, nearly 60 per cent comprised lessons in Latin and Greek. This mental training turned out to be perfectly suited to Wavell, and it was at Summer Fields that it first became clear he had a particularly good brain, something for which he was to gain a wide reputation, especially in military circles where competition from rival thinkers was not invariably keen.

His intellectual ability was most obvious from his memory. From when he was quite young it had become apparent that he had an exceptional ability to learn by heart, certainly verse that rhymed easily. In *Other Men's Flowers*, his acclaimed anthology of poetry, he later recorded that the first major poem that he learnt was 'Horatius', from *The Lays of Ancient Rome*, by that pillar of the Indian Empire, Lord Macaulay. However easy the *Lays* may be to read, they are 561 lines long and take a good twenty minutes to recite. For a young child to do this from start to finish is quite an achievement. It was also in those strict days an unusual privilege – although Archie may not have thought so – for a child to be allowed to recite and take centre stage for such a long period. He did not comment on his parents' view of the matter, but he did explain, engagingly, that 'admiring aunts used to give me threepence for reciting it from beginning to end; a wiser uncle gave me sixpence for a promise to do nothing of the kind'.[5]

Many of Wavell's fellow-pupils had also inherited intelligence and natural ability, which were to enable them in due course to occupy posts of high importance at home and in the Empire, but even in their company the 'clear-headed and inventive' Wavell was noticed by the school authorities. His paramount asset was his good memory, but he was also a fast worker, careful and accurate, remembering what he was told – all qualities of value to a future soldier.

The arid diet of Greek, Latin, maths and Bible reading was a little moistened by a well-stocked library of books – which the boys were expected to read – mainly uplifting adventures about the far corners of the world. Many had Empire-building themes, from authors such as Robert Louis Stevenson, Rider Haggard and Rudyard Kipling. The titles of the sort of fare on the school reading list in Wavell's time tell their own story: *Lion Hearted*; *To Punish the Czar*; *Deeds That Won the Empire*; *Fights for the Flag*; *Facing Fearful Odds*; *With Rifle and Bayonet*; and *Brave Men in Action* – a welcome contrast to long tracts from Livy, Virgil and Euclid.

Predominant among the books on offer were those by G.A. Henty, with stirring titles such as *Held Fast for England*; *By Sheer Pluck*; *Tales of Daring and Danger*; and *By Conduct and Courage*. Forming part of the 'literature of blood-stained fiction' pioneered by Rider Haggard, and filled with the brightest imperial sentiments, such books reflected the prevailing public mood and the Victorian belief in 'character' as the foundation of national strength. Sustained by the tales of adventure in the Summer Fields school library, and quietly mastering the dusty reams of Latin prose and Greek syntax, Wavell proved his ability by his results: after a year at the school he was top of the class in Greek, Latin translation, Latin composition, maths and English, and second in French.

Wavell's early prowess did not necessarily imply that he had more than what could be achieved by a particularly good memory. Nor, looking to the future, that he had the type of spatial intelligence needed to deal not so much with problems for which solutions have previously been rehearsed, as with unlearnt, unseen difficulties – like the surprises that develop on a battlefield, especially when fighting new and different enemies such as, in Wavell's case, the Japanese. Of the seven distinct types of intelligence now identified by the medical world, it would seem that Wavell's was the linguistic and logical type – that most suited to learning and school-work.

He also demonstrated 'pluck' – a term greatly in vogue at the time – on the playing field: 'Good cricketer,' said his report (he captained the school's second XI); 'very good at football; most determined tackler; an indefatigable player and a pleasure to watch'. Although this was a report addressed to the boy's parents, who paid the fees, it was clear that in this case the Head Master meant what he said. Young Archie was developing qualities that would be of great value to him as a soldier, although, significantly, his report also referred to 'a formidable natural reserve'.

When he was thirteen the time came for him to move on to public school. Summer Fields had done its job well: that year twelve of its pupils won open scholarships to public schools. In keeping with family tradition, it was decided that Wavell should try for Winchester. For him it was less of a trial than for most: despite the rigour of the exams, the high standard required and the presence of sixty-nine competitors, he sailed through. Winchester was then the most intellectually demanding school in the land, and of its 400 or so boys the seventy scholars were the cleverest; even so, Wavell was placed seventh of the new intake of twenty scholars.

In the autumn of 1896, after a long summer holiday spent at home near the barracks in Glasgow, and with cousins in Hampshire and in Ireland, Wavell arrived at Winchester, the paramount source of personnel for the top ranks of the professions that played a vital part in the orderly running of the Empire.

From the start it was a strict classical training, with an emphasis on memorising text: 100 lines of Virgil and eighty of Sophocles were handed out at regular intervals, and over time the boys had to learn thousands of lines by heart. Wavell found this relatively simple, and he was later to comment that for anyone who learnt easily, it was a slight and even enjoyable task, and that, for him, having to learn verse by heart at 'Morning Lines' at Winchester laid a foundation on which his memory ever since had been building and furnishing. History was largely confined to classical history, the dons glossing over the fact – if they were even aware of it – that much of it was make-believe. There was a little maths and some modern history – but not too modern: instruction ground to a halt shortly after the Battle of Waterloo.

It was Greek that took pride of place. Wavell and his fellows had to learn by heart fifty of the pages of a manual for Greek instruction, which was made no easier to follow by the fact that the explanations of the text were written in Latin.

Whether or not he thought much about it at the time, with hindsight he was scathing about these teaching methods:

> Xenophon was the first book I ever read, and I found him incredibly dull because none of my masters ever told me the story of that march, they were interested only in irregular verbs, and syntax . . . It was many years later, when I had seen most of the ground, that I realised how interesting it might have been, and how the young imagination might have been stirred to adventure.[6]

'Homer,' he wrote, 'was the one exception to the distaste with which I regarded Greek.'

His syllabus incorporated some rather inadequate teaching of modern languages and an hour or two of science; it included geology, but in those days that too was treated with caution: it made the authorities nervous, and at Eton, for example, it was decided that the subject could 'not be received by mere boys without a violent disturbance of their religious belief'.[7] Perhaps the purpose of the boys' education was best summarised by Dr Warre, Head Master of Eton, who stated that they were to acquire moral health so that they would grow up to be 'honest secretaries of state, open-handed village squires, broad-minded bishops'.

Although in due course he was to lead a modern army, with all its scientific aids, Wavell admitted to being 'abysmally ignorant of science', and never shook free of some rather basic uncertainties:

> My school education was severely classical; and the only scientific facts I remember being taught were that light and sound both travelled at incredible speeds, but one of them (I am pretty sure it was light) was a good deal the faster.[8]

And so the Empire prospered.

For the boys, the dons' moral earnestness was not wholly persuasive, and in Wavell's time at Winchester temptation sometimes proved hard to resist. Such lapses greatly upset the Head Master. Raymond Asquith, famous among the Great War's 'lost generation', was four years senior to Wavell, who 'fagged' for him, and recalled the Head Master addressing the boys about an abominable crime, urging them:

> . . . with passionate fervour to prefer every known form of prostitution and bestiality to the sin of Sodom. He told us in confidence that the Headmasters, in league with the Government, were proposing to increase the legal penalty from two to fourteen years; whereat a perceptible shudder ran through the audience – of whom some eighty-five per cent – by the lowest estimate – were legally liable to incarceration on that charge. The bolder spirits muttered that the law was not altered yet, and registered a mental vow to make the best of the lucid interspace . . .[9]

Wavell was now passing from boyhood to youth; he remained slightly below average height – (as an adult he was five foot nine inches), but seemed quite unperturbed by that. As he matured his self-confidence grew, and he appeared quiet and friendly, though with a certain air of detachment.

Away from the Classics divisions, where both his brainpower and his determination were praised by his teachers, he did not thrust himself forward. Nor did he volunteer for Winchester's Cadet Corps. In that matter, however, superior forces – principally in the form of his father – prevailed, and he was at length compelled to join up.

In time he learnt to appreciate the value of all these activities, despite not excelling at any of them. There was plenty to do outside the classroom. Debates arranged by the boys were often on subjects that mixed youthful idealism with precocity, and many would be surprisingly topical today: 'whether smoking is a pernicious habit'; 'whether museums and picture-galleries should be open on Sundays'; 'whether the railways ought to be in the hands of the State'; 'whether the police ought to have fire-arms'; 'whether the Elgin Marbles should be returned'.

The young minds were filled with sound imperial ideas, of the sort expressed in a school address by a visiting Member of Parliament:

> For the last century in the great continent of Africa which we are gradually making our own, England is the only country which has never failed to turn an attentive ear to the cries of the downtrodden and oppressed, and for that purpose she has poured out not only treasure but the blood of the noblest of her sons, like water. I do lay stress upon

the fact that it is our rule in India and our rule alone which stands between countless millions and every kind of oppression, tyranny and wrong.[10]

On that point there was soon to develop an alternative view.

As Wavell's schooldays neared their end, the question arose as to his future career. There was not a long discussion. The army had played an important part in the family's history, and Colonel Wavell was a devoted soldier, still serving, with limited knowledge of the alternatives, and he determined that his son should follow family tradition. Surprisingly, his son expressed no special interest in a soldier's life, despite childhood influences when, as he later said, 'he used to run about the barracks and revel in the glories of the regiment'. A near-contemporary at Winchester, Hugh Dowding, later head of RAF Fighter Command during the Battle of Britain, found himself at the same age in similar circumstances. In the words of his biographer:

> There were other careers he might have followed, but they were alike in demanding a sense of vocation which he did not feel . . . the army, on the other hand, asked nothing outwardly that any upright youth whose tastes were as yet unfixed was not prepared to give. It promised a pleasant life: the choice of a soldier's trade could arouse no opposition. If Dowding was stirred by no compelling reason to join the army, at least he could say truthfully that he knew of nothing he would like better.[11]

The Winchester dons had other ideas. They thought that their favoured pupil could easily go on to university, and in fact should do so before embarking on an altogether worthier civil career. That was the fixed opinion of the Head Master: he wrote to Colonel Wavell, pointing out the error of his ways: 'I regret to see you are sending your son to the Army Class, and I hasten to assure you this desperate step is not necessary.' It was an opinion that was rather lost on the colonel, and as Wavell showed no particular bent towards any other profession, and took the line of least resistance, the matter was settled.

Although in the Army Class he was taught a broader spread of subjects, Wavell's education was still considerably narrower and less balanced than that of the German and Italian contemporaries against whom he would have to lead British forces forty years on. Compared with Germany, for example, the language teaching in English schools was very weak – perhaps because, as was often said, 'The German always had to learn languages: the army never knew where it might be going.'

Although the type of education received by Wavell strengthened and disciplined the mind, it was curiously narrow. In the whole of Wavell's time at Summer Fields and Winchester there was nothing, or next to nothing, in the syllabus about civilisations beyond the Western world, nor any enquiry into European life in the centuries that followed the fall of Rome.

Having learnt a lot about a little, Wavell came to the end of his schooldays. He had begun to develop the quiet confidence and stubborn determination that were to characterise his successes and failures as a soldier in war and peace, and his political role as Viceroy of India. He also seemed, for a time, to have overcome the disadvantages of shyness in an animated community such as an English school, a microcosm of the adult world that he would soon enter. He was characteristically circumspect about the impression he had made, claiming that he was not popular with his contemporaries, and rather lonely. His quiet persona seemed to have prevented him from making many close friends, but he was genial with those that he had. Some were to be friends for life, and would remain in touch with him as they also reached influential positions high in the Empire's firmament.

In August 1900 he was admitted to the Royal Military College, Sandhurst. The subjects for study were military administration, military history, military topography, fortification, law, geography and French. The Classics, after ten years in the front rank, seemed to have fled the field.

II

FIRST BLOOD

EDUCATED to the highest standard, his mind stretched and disciplined, Wavell now emerged from the cocoon of youth, harsh though it had felt from time to time. He did not at once have to cope with the freedoms and uncertainties that follow schooldays: his advance was gradual. Like a university, the Royal Military College, Sandhurst, was in practice and atmosphere a staging-post between youth and adulthood.

Maintaining his glowing schoolboy record, Wavell was placed fourth in the college's entrance examination. The majority of his fellow-cadets came from public schools, with a sprinkling of exotic foreigners of princely blood or whose families were of high importance in their own countries, and it was assumed that the 360 cadets were already gentlemen. The atmosphere exuded spit and polish, precision and brisk organisation, and the college's purpose was to provide the cadets with the rudiments and basic skills of general military knowledge. Then they would be handed on to absorb the ways and traditions of their chosen regiments – in the British Army of that time the regiment was deemed to be of paramount importance – the unit best able to inspire loyalty and courage in fighting conditions; it was a concept that Wavell came very strongly to support.

It was an axiom that an officer should be 'fit for service', and there was plenty of daily exercise, including gymnastics, swimming, marching, riding and sword-drill. Prowess on a horse was a requirement, encouraged by foxhunting, which was promoted as being good for learning to take risks and to read a landscape.

By contrast, a school atmosphere pervaded the classrooms, where professors taught the drier side of soldiering: military law, history and administration. As his career progressed, Wavell took to heart lessons from military history – he was frequently to cite them in his own lectures – and when he became a senior officer he placed great store on administrative support for the fighting soldier. Camaraderie was encouraged after the day's work, in the mess and at gatherings called 'Smokers', which featured lusty singing, both solo and communal; a favourite ditty was 'The Noisy Johnnie', which the authorities took as proof that the cadets' spirits were not crushed by excessive study. At Sandhurst, however, as at Winchester, Wavell was distinguished not only by intellect, but also by shyness, so it is unlikely that he relished the singing, and he would probably have sooner died than give a solo performance.

While Wavell was at Winchester great excitement had arisen over Queen Victoria's Diamond Jubilee, when a festive spirit had infused the nation, and up and down the country parades and parties in honour of the revered Queen-Empress marked what, in hindsight, was probably the apex of the imperial age. Benign, envied, admired and all-powerful, Britannia's rule was celebrated by the naval review off Spithead, on 26 June 1897. The British Empire, at least in the opinion of its rulers, was worthy of the mantle of Ancient Rome, and its power and hopes for future aggrandisement excited a generation of imperialists who were now becoming influential in the army, in politics and in business. One such was Cecil Rhodes, who had clearly painted his vision for Britain:

> The idea dancing and gleaming before one's eyes, like a will-of-the-wisp, at last frames itself into a plan. Why should we not form a secret society with but one object – the furtherance of the British Empire and the bringing of the whole uncivilised world under British rule; for the recovery of the United States; for making the Anglo-Saxon race but one Empire? What a dream, but yet it is probable; it is possible.[1]

By 1897 Rhodes' seductive dream seemed attainable: Britain held sway from the Arctic to the Antarctic, and in parts of every continent on the planet; its Empire contained more than 370 million subjects and spread across eleven million square miles.

Yet even as the old century closed, in one part of the world the mighty British lion had received a challenge. In South Africa trouble had arisen in the wake of the discovery in 1886 of immense deposits of gold in the Transvaal. Although the country was not an imperial possession, the prospect of riches had drawn to it many British entrepreneurs and businessmen, and a large number of chancers of a fairly rough stamp. It had also attracted some of the millionaires who had made fortunes in the recently discovered diamond deposits at Kimberley. Among them were Alfred Beit and Cecil Rhodes, new-minted tycoons who soon began to establish a power base in Johannesburg and to introduce an element of commercial organisation into the haphazard diggings that had begun to deface the fabulous gold reef.[2]

However, the gold was firmly in Afrikaner territory, which was a cause of anxiety for Britain. The Boers had a long history of discord with the British in southern Africa, and in order to maintain their independence large numbers had moved north from the Cape in the Great Trek of 1834. By the end of the nineteenth century their descendants were firmly settled in the Orange Free State, to the north-west of Cape Colony, and in the South African Republic in the Transvaal, further north still, stretching all the way to Portuguese East Africa. There were also large numbers of Boers – or 'Afrikaners' – in Natal, although that was a British colony. Imperial sensibilities were further offended by the existence of German South-West Africa, an enormous territory directly to the north-east of Cape Colony, particularly since German hostility to British pretensions in Africa had been made dramatically clear in the famous 'Kruger Telegram' of 1895.[3]

There were two main reasons for Britain's distrust of the situation in southern Africa. One was that Boer hostility was frustrating Britain's desire to amalgamate her own colonies in the region with the Boer republics, and so to form a single union under the British flag. The other was that the geographical situation of the Boer republics blocked imperial dreams of extending the Empire north through Africa, as described by Cecil Rhodes.[4] The British also perceived an internal threat: not only were there two independent republics on the borders of British South Africa, but there were also large communities of Boers in Natal and in Cape Colony itself, where about two-thirds of the white population comprised Boers or fellow-travellers. All these tensions were greatly increased by the discovery of gold in the Transvaal, which very soon made that republic by far the richest country in the whole of Africa, enabling it to buy – from industrialised nations united in a growing jealousy of the British Empire and a fondness for cash – large amounts of modern armaments to improve its defences against its imperial neighbour. Rifles, heavy guns and ammunition streamed into the Transvaal in quantities easily sufficient to arm both republics and the Dutch further south as well.

Despite their new-found wealth, the dour and sombre Boers, wedded to a pastoral way of life, greatly resented the brash and colourful adventurers flocking to the gold diggings, and known by the host government as 'Uitlanders' – outsiders. For a time they were grudgingly tolerated, partly because their activities generated large tax payments, of which a considerable amount chanced to find its way into the pockets of the Transvaal leaders. However, as the immense commercial significance of the gold reef became clearer, the Transvaal government became altogether more wary, especially when the Uitlanders began to demand political rights and a voice in the government.

When the War Office ordered the army to South Africa the tension rapidly increased, and early in October 1899 the Boers delivered an ultimatum to the British asking them to remove their troops from Natal. The demand was spurned, and the result was war.

The Black Watch was among the regiments sent out to South Africa while Wavell was at Sandhurst; soon after its arrival it became involved in a disastrous engagement at Magersfontein, in which a significant part was played by the battalion formerly commanded by Wavell's father, and which included several of Wavell's acquaintances and family friends. Perhaps his close connection with a regiment that was fighting in South Africa reinforced the thoroughness of his work at the Royal Military College, for, despite the predominance of physical over mental work, in both his first and second terms he came first in the passing-out examination, his character being marked with the highest grade: 'Exemplary'.

In only a short time his knowledge was of practical use, at war in the service of the Empire. The growing need for officers to lead the forces fighting the Boers curtailed Wavell's time at Sandhurst, and he left after two terms instead of three. On 8 May 1901, less than a year after leaving school, he was gazetted to the 1st Battalion, the Black Watch. He was just eighteen. Before joining up, he went to Dublin to stay with his father, then on the staff of the Duke of Connaught, the commander-in-chief in Ireland. After brief training courses at the musketry school at Hythe and at regimental headquarters – where he inhabited 'a single bleak room at the very summit of Edinburgh Castle, through which all of the winds of Scotland whistled in their due season'[5] – he was ordered to South Africa. At the end of September, the 'Dolly Gray' draft (as it became known) marched from its barracks to Edinburgh's Waverley Station. Crowds lined the route and sang, and bands played 'Auld Lang Syne' in a final emotional farewell. Many of those in the crowds were wives or sweethearts, tearfully proud of their men leaving for battle. Among young officers of Wavell's class, girls were a rarer commodity: the code of behaviour was strict, and relations with the opposite sex were formal. In any case, by his own account Wavell was rather gauche in the presence of women. It seemed that he was going to the wars, from which he might never come back alive, without ever having had a girlfriend.

Yet it was a heady prospect: newly commissioned and responsible for a group of tough Scotsmen he hardly knew, he was leaving familiar surroundings for a far-away country where many British soldiers had already been wounded or killed. He had parted from his parents and sisters; he didn't know for how long he would be away; and although he could not be sure what mental or physical endurance would be required of him, he realised that he might take part in great events. He knew also that he was clever, that he had mastered what had so far been asked of him and that he had no reason to doubt himself. For a young man embarking on a soldier's life, which was in his blood, it was an exciting start. He was not an emotional or high-spirited man, yet the cheers of the crowds and the sound of the pipes would have been a stirring send-off for any eighteen-year-old.

The draft consisted of 115 men and two young officers besides Wavell. After several weeks they landed at Durban and set off by train for Standerton, in remote territory half-way between Johannesburg and the notorious Majuba Hill, where in 1881 a severe defeat had been inflicted on British arms. There, on 2 November 1901, they joined up with battalion headquarters.

It was almost two years since his regiment had fought its first dramatic action, at Magersfontein, and the war had now moved on to a very different phase. From fewer than 10,000 in the run-up to the war, the British garrison in South Africa had grown to nearly 250,000 – by the war's end 450,000 British soldiers would have served there – yet the main leaders of the Boer forces, Botha, De Wet, Smuts and De la Rey, were still at large. They commanded an estimated 20,000 men in the field, and their death or capture was now the chief objective of the British forces on the veld.

For some time it had been realised that the war would not end while Boer forces were armed and free: living off the land, their farms serving as store-houses, shelters and intelligence agencies combined, they might continue the fight indefinitely. As long as the enemy could find food and water for themselves and their horses, rest in some safety and be informed of British troop movements, they might roam the country and attack at will. The army's strategy was therefore to establish 'protected areas' and clear them of Boer fighters, whom they hoped to reduce to the status of guerrillas; within those protected areas they hoped gradually to reintroduce normal civilian life.

Under its new commander-in-chief, General Sir Herbert Kitchener, the army had achieved considerable success, and by the time Wavell reached South Africa about 14,000 square miles of the former war zone had been declared 'absolutely clear'.

Now the high command began to implement the second phase of its plan: the blockhouse system, whose purpose was to divide the territory into manageable areas which could be caged in by a system of fortified block-houses linked by impenetrable wire, or by natural barriers. By the end of 1901 thousands of blockhouses stretched in lines through the country – eventually there would be 8,000, covering 3,400 miles – and the strategy was beginning to pay dividends. By the time Wavell arrived on the scene, an average of 2,000 Boers a month were being trapped and made captive. It was a strategy in which the Black Watch was to play a part, and Wavell's draft joined a column formed by Colonel Michael Rimington. This legendary fighter had earned his spurs early in the war when he commanded a highly successful corps of scouts, known as Rimington's Tigers. Tall, spare and muscular, dark and grim, his frame battered by countless riding accidents, he had 'the general air of the devil about him'.[6] He was the type of cunning and daring individualist whom in later life Wavell would engage for his own purposes – men such as Orde Wingate, Ralph Bagnold and Peter Fleming.

It was a swift baptism for Wavell: fresh from Sandhurst, wearing the sand-coloured kilt of a Scottish regiment although he himself was not Scottish, in a remote part of Africa, and in charge of men to whom their surround-ings would have been as strange as to himself. He had not yet proved himself, but he was joining a force that had seen a considerable amount of action, and from which he would hear at first hand of the dangers and excitements of war. The enemy were masters of surprise, and the terrain, known as the highveld, was hard fighting; much of it was flat and there were few trees, except willows along streams and river banks, and gum trees planted for shade around farmhouses and cattle crushes. In November, when Wavell arrived, the days were long and hot, and shade extremely scarce. The great undulating slopes of veld seemed to merge with one another, making it hard to read a map and easy to fall behind or become lost. Ambushes were a constant threat, and the Boers did not shrink from using expanding bullets, which caused appalling wounds.

Wavell's solid, dogged nature was suited to his new surroundings. It was a heady atmosphere: they were all professional soldiers and had volunteered for the army; it was the life that most of them wanted, and they were keen to encounter the enemy. They had been told that the Boers were demoralised, tired of fighting and running short of provisions. In fact those still in the field were hard men, skilled fighters and merciless. With expert knowledge of the ground, able to live for long periods on dried meat and mealie rusks, which they carried on their saddles, they could cover great distances and continually elude the British.

At least Wavell's force had numbers on its side. Within two days its head-quarters column – Rimington's Inniskilling Dragoons and a hundred men of the Black Watch – had been joined by six other Black Watch companies. They all met up at Standerton, with detachments from the Royal Artillery Mounted Rifles, the New South Wales Mounted Rifles and a bloodthirsty contingent of Canadian Scouts, known to 'take no prisoners'. Each man had a rifle, and the officers had swords and pistols. There was a pom-pom and four other guns, and nearly 2,000 troops, many of them seasoned in action.

Rimington had been ordered to co-operate with Sir Henry Rawlinson, another highly successful column commander, who was moving west through the Transvaal towards the Vaal River, which ran past Standerton. The prize was the capture of the charismatic Boer leader, Christiaan de Wet. A burly, ruthless man in his early forties, he wore tinted spectacles and hated the British. Kitchener, and the British Government, believed that De Wet was now the linchpin keeping the enemy in the field, and that if he were captured his followers would lose heart and the war would end.

Rimington planned a series of drives with mounted troops locating and attacking the Boer *kommandos*, while infantry detachments protected bases, guns and transport, keeping as close as possible to the mobile columns wher-ever the action took them. Wavell and his draft had three days in which to acclimatise and learn their part in the scheme, so that before each drive started every soldier would understand the nature and importance of his objective. Wavell was now to have the chance of adding practical soldiering to the theories he had so recently learnt at Sandhurst.

He did not come under fire during these operations, but spent the following weeks in long hard slogs, searching the veld for an enemy that seemed in-visible, and in danger of attack at any time. When there was no contact with the enemy, it was, as Wavell wrote, 'not very exciting work but it taught a young officer his job on active service, how to handle and look after his men, and himself'.[7]

At the beginning of the new year they embarked on an exhaustive series of marches, averaging thirteen miles a day. They had some successes, and on 31 January 1902 captured twenty-one Boers and thirteen wagons. Besides searching for armed Boers, the column carried out the scorched-earth policy imposed from on high. It was unedifying, but the best way of wearing down an elusive enemy:

> Farm burning goes merrily on, and our course through the country is marked as in prehistoric ages, by pillars of smoke by day and fires by night. We usually burn from six to a dozen farms by day; these being about all that in this sparsely-inhabited country we encounter. I do not gather that any special reason or cause is alleged or proved against the farms burnt . . . The people are disconcertingly like English, especially the girls and children – fair and big and healthy looking. These folk we invite out on to the veldt or into the little garden in front, where they huddle together in their cotton frocks and big cotton sun-bonnets, while our men set fire to the house . . . The fire bursts out of windows and doors with a loud roaring, and black volumes of smoke roll over-head. Standing round are a dozen or two of men holding horses. The women, in a little group, cling together, comforting each other or hiding their faces in each other's laps.[8]

Still the war dragged on. In order to force a conclusion, Kitchener decided on a new tactic: to assemble large numbers of troops and send them forward to sweep and scour huge rectangles of country, driving the Boers ahead of them like birds on a shoot, until finally forcing them up against the block-house lines. Penned in by wire, pressed forward by lines of British soldiers, they would be herded into a funnel in the south-east of the country, where the blockhouse barrier met the Drakensberg Mountains, its passes sealed tight by troops.

This was the blueprint for the 'new model drive'. Single unbroken lines of troops would roll inexorably across the veld, a trooper every thirty yards or so, the last file of one column touching the first of the next, the net being dragged over forty or fifty miles. Wavell could have remembered his Greek lessons at Winchester, such a short time ago, and learning from Herodotus how Darius and his Persians subdued Lesbos and other Greek islands, and how the soldiers of antiquity advanced with linked hands to form an armed chain that stretched from the north to the south of each island.

Wavell's contingent was to start at Reitz and to sweep the country for about eighty miles towards Wolvehoek, in the north-west corner of the rectangle, where the blockhouse line met a railway that was ceaselessly patrolled by seven armoured trains. Together with columns to the north and south they would form a giant piston, designed to force the *kommandos* against the sides and end of the piston block.

Yet the line was often pierced as a result of human weakness: some command posts employed African nightwatchmen, known to the Tommies as the 'Black Watch', but most were manned only by an NCO and six privates, for whom there was nothing to do when off-duty but talk, smoke or gamble. Bored and off their guard, they would often be taken by surprise by Boer detachments galloping up to the blockhouses without warning and firing shotguns into the loopholes while their comrades cut the fences.

After three days Wavell's column reached the railway; nearly 300 of the enemy had been killed or wounded, but that was only one-sixth of the number that had been seen or reported. They were given a few days' rest before moving off once more, reversing direction and heading east to Heilbron, before wheeling south towards Harrismith and the Drakensberg.

The probing British columns, spread wide across the country, at last began to force the enemy into a contracting circle, pushing the Boers before them as they approached the end of the funnel. The conclusion of the campaign was in sight, and on 27 February, 'almost hand in hand', the British had one of the largest catches of the campaign, 'snaffling' (as Wavell described it) more than 1,100 Boers. Then they marched into Harrismith, their final 'RV'.

With recurrent anxiety, arduous trekking and the occasional scent of danger, it was an exhilarating time for Wavell. He was fit, working day and night with his comrades, fighting a mobile war under the wide African sky. He was playing his part in a great plan, serving Queen and country, and final success was near. For a young officer straight from Sandhurst and recently still in the schoolroom, it was a fine introduction to the life of a soldier.

Now his battalion was relieved by another that had just arrived from India, and his days of action against the Boers were over. The next three months were spent on garrison duty in Harrismith, an anticlimax that kindled a desire in many of the men to put South Africa behind them just as soon as they could. For Wavell there were a few diversions, such as partridge shooting and polo: 'I sometimes hit the ball now,' he wrote to one of his sisters, with what was becoming characteristic self-deprecation, 'which I never used to before.' Yet the days hung heavy, and in July he suffered acute discomfort when he broke his shoulder in a game of football between officers and sergeants. Immobile, he was detained at Harrismith, in what he felt was aptly called 'Number 19 Stationary Hospital'. There he grew increasingly bored, until eventually he was granted sick leave.

He had done well, earning the Queen's South African Medal and four clasps – 'quite up to the average', as his commanding officer laconically commented in his Confidential Report – but now he had had enough. With relief the young soldier embarked for home, setting sail from Durban. It was almost a year to the day since he had left England.

The beauty of South Africa had been an uplifting background to the often exhausting days of soldiering, and had touched the artist in Wavell; long afterwards he would recite with pleasure Kipling's images of the land:

> *Rivers at night that cluck and jeer,*
> *Plains which the moonshine turns to sea,*
> *Mountains that never let you near,*
> *And stars to all eternity.*[9]

He was one of twelve Black Watch officers, including his colonel, Carthew Yorstoun, who had served with Rimington's column. He had come through unscathed, but had endured long, hard days and nights, limited to thirty-five pounds of kit, living in the open save for a bivouac into which he 'crawled each night like a tired puppy'. He had known life with soldiers on active service, and learnt the importance of keeping to a plan, especially if attacked. In cold and rain, heat and dust, he had worked with his men under the stress of constant vigilance. It was the best kind of training.

III

OUTPOSTS OF EMPIRE

THE signing of the Treaty of Vereeniging, at the end of May 1902, brought the Boer War to an end. The Boer republics were promised eventual self-government, but in the meantime they became British colonies, setting the bounds of the Empire wider still. On the surface this continued to seem the natural order of things, but with a new monarch, a new century and the soldiers coming home, a slight but perceptible change had entered the atmosphere. For the first time doubts began to arise about the moral worth of the Empire, and more specifically about its economic value – money being closer than morals to most people's hearts. In later life Wavell would say that the Boer War marked the moment when the British people began to lose faith in their imperial destiny. Soon the debate about the Empire's purpose and value moved beyond South Africa, and the spotlight travelled across the map to India, where the imperial sun shone more brightly than anywhere else.

Yet for a time the Jubilee spirit prevailed. The importance of India, the main plank in the imperial structure, was soon to be affirmed by Lord Curzon, erstwhile Viceroy and one of the foremost satraps of imperialism, in a celebrated speech in Birmingham in which he defended the creed of Empire. As it happened, he showed remarkable foresight:

> As America has gone so might Canada, Australia, and South Africa go . . .
> A sheaf of popular arguments could easily be found for casting off the Indian problem . . . When India has gone and the great Colonies have gone, do you suppose that we can stop there? Your ports and coaling stations, your fortresses and dockyards, your Crown Colonies and protectorates will go too . . . what would be the fate of our home population?

24

England, from having been the arbiter, would sink at best into the inglorious playground, of the world. Our antiquities, our natural beauties, our relics of a once mighty sovereignty, our castles and cathedrals, our mansion houses and parks, would attract a crowd of wandering pilgrims. People would come to see us just as they climb the Acropolis at Athens or ascend the waters of the Nile. A congested population, ministering to our reduced wants, and unsustained by enormous demand from India and the Colonies, would lead a sordid existence . . . with no aspiration but a narrow and selfish materialism . . . England would become a sort of glorified Belgium.[1]

And it was to India, where in October 1902 his battalion had been sent from South Africa, that Wavell prepared to travel. First, however, he was to take several months' sick leave in England. It was an attractive prospect, considering how much of his life had been spent away from home: from the ages of ten to seventeen he had spent two-thirds of the year at boarding-school; after that came Sandhurst, and from there, after a brief interval, he had been sent across the world to fight in South Africa. Now he was faced with further exile from his family. His battalion was due to remain in India for the next fifteen or so years, which meant that in the normal course of events he would be away (apart from occasional home leave) until he was over thirty, by which time both his parents would be approaching old age.

Most officers were inured to being uprooted from home, having at an early age been sent away to school; but the practice hardly made for close family relations. Wavell's case was no exception: the shy child had turned into a young man with a distant, if dutiful, relationship with his parents, warmer it seems with his father than his mother. Overall, his affection for his family – especially for his two sisters – remained intact, but it was now encased in a slightly detached and introspective shell.

While they looked for somewhere suitable for the general's retirement, his parents had been renting a house near Ascot, an area close to the army's soul. For Wavell, it could not have been a greater contrast to South Africa, and there, in a Berkshire that was not yet suburban, the young soldier back from the wars spent a snowy winter with his family. Although he managed to ride and go out hunting, his injured shoulder prevented him taking much exercise; but it gradually healed, and he was warmed by the presence of his parents and sisters, in the surroundings of a quiet English county.

At the end of February 1903, after four months' rest, he set sail to rejoin his battalion, now at Ambala, in the Punjab, the area in the north of India that provided the most warlike of the soldiers who served the Empire. There, and at Peshawar, where the regiment in due course moved, Wavell settled into the agreeable, if monotonous, routine of regimental life.

In one respect a young officer in India led a claustrophobic existence: the complement of officers in a battalion, from colonel to subalterns, was quite small, and further restricted by a rigid hierarchy and strict rules of conduct. The number of people with whom an officer of Wavell's age and rank could have free and easy relationships was very limited. In such close confinement the character of the senior officer made quite a difference. In Wavell's case the battalion commander was Colonel 'Chumpy' Maxwell who, though shrewd, was a genial man. Wavell described him as 'fat, heavy and barely mobile' – not obvious qualities for a soldier in the Punjab – but he created an amiable atmosphere for the battalion to work in. Not that the duties in the Punjab were oppressive: it was, as Wavell described it, 'an easy-going business', and on most days the work was over by lunchtime; Thursdays were an exception – they were a holiday.

For two years Wavell's battalion, some 700 strong, remained at Ambala. The country around was as 'flat as a billiard-table', with scattered groves and trees and a mixture of wasteland, sandhills and cultivated patches stretching south for more than 700 miles. Its arid reaches were littered with the remains of animals that had died of thirst, and with humans dead from a bubonic plague which during 1903 and 1904 claimed as many as 250 lives a day, a source of resentment among the natives, who believed that the British authorities made the plague to keep down the population.[2]

In due course the regiment moved to Peshawar, the main military centre in north-west India, and the launch-pad for many an expedition to restore a semblance of peace along the unruly frontier. The battalion's duties were light, but there was plenty of sport with which to fill the gaps left in the day – chiefly polo, but also cricket, tennis, shooting, fishing, hunting and pig-sticking, which was regarded as a test of skill and bravery not only for soldiers but also for 'civilians', as political officers and others in government service were known. The trout and mahseer in the mountain rivers and lakes provided some of the best fishing in the world, but that sport did not appeal to Wavell, although he was keen on most of the others. He did not have very much money, but hunting and polo (then as now) were much cheaper for army officers than for civilians, and Wavell, who rode well, took to them enthusi-astically. He managed to buy a particularly fast pony on which he won several 'steeplechases', setting a hot pace across terraced fields and steep ravines, startling jackals, monkeys and vultures from the wild ground baked in the 100-degree heat. He was not a graceful or fearless rider, but he was determined and able to control such fear as he did feel.

Like so many officers in those days, he put a great deal of time and thought into shooting expeditions, for which India was fertile ground. There were many types of bird and beast – large and small, ferocious and harmless – to stalk and kill: leopards and bears in the hills, and wolves and jackals on the plains. The mountain air and natural beauty of Kashmir and the other frontier provinces leading up to the Himalayas provided the perfect setting for weeks of exhilarating sport when an officer could be spared from military duty. Wavell took as much advantage as he could of this regime. Yet sporting expeditions also helped him improve his soldierly skills, first properly developed when chasing the Boers. He often went off on his own, and it taught him to be, in the words of his commanding officer, a good scout: his military ability could only benefit from the stamina and fitness that he developed by trudging around the mountainous terrain; from the honing of gamekeeper instincts; from the shooting practice that was needed if the bag were to be filled; and from the detailed planning that was necessary for good sport – and to avoid injury, running out of essential supplies or getting completely lost.

There was also boxing and amateur theatricals. Other Ranks played football, cricket and hockey, and Wavell liked to join in their games as well. He took seriously the duty of a platoon commander to know and look after his soldiers – and football provided a means of doing so. One of the privates in his platoon described Wavell's zeal:

A good sport was Wavell. He was fitba' daft. We used to get a loan of a rupee from the company sports fund after every game. That bought you a gallon of beer. Wavell was keen to get a game. So I stood down to let him play outside-right. He gave me a rupee for that. He wanted to play in nearly every match, so I said: 'You can ha'e my place ony time, but it'll cost you a rupee.'[3]

Such sports were not only fun, but provided an outlet for pent-up energy and a release from periodic boredom. Another abiding source of pleasure was Wavell's already exceptional knowledge of poetry, and in the evenings, on the pillared verandah outside his whitewashed brick bungalow, he and his long-standing friend C.R.B. Henderson could be heard quoting verse after verse at each other.

Warmer forms of social life were rather scarce: senior officers had their wives, but to their juniors connubial bliss was a luxury denied. Instead they were offered the varied allures of the 'fishing fleet' – girls out from England, supposedly in search of a husband. Cynics regarded them as ladies whose physical or financial charms were not quite up to landing them a desirable catch back in England, but, plain, poor or otherwise, they provided a welcome tonic, and healthy young officers starved of female company could not afford to be fastidious. Even so, demand outstripped supply, and although overt relations with Indians were out of the question natural thoughts aroused by local beauty could hardly be quelled for long, and discreet arrangements beyond the cantonments were, by custom, permitted.

For Wavell, the lack of feminine company seemed not to be a problem. However engaging and attractive his inner nature, he had not yet mastered the art of relaxing in a lively, carefree or casual manner. 'I took no part in social activities,' he recorded, 'I was shy and gauche, and had not the least wish to meet any of the ladies in the station.' In that respect he had not advanced much from his Sandhurst days, and on the whole did not share his brother-officers' relish for the noise and sparkle of parties in the mess, where there was often a lively atmosphere, even if it was not justified by the fare:

> One arrived in the Mess about half-past seven, dressed in full regi-mentals – stiff shirt, skin-tight trousers, skin-tight jacket and all the rest of it. One had a glass of sherry and as soon as dinner was ready the mess sergeant or mess havildar saluted the senior officer and announced that dinner was served. Then we trooped into the dining room in order of rank . . .
>
> . . . although we were living in fairly primitive surroundings we always had a most elaborate dinner. You invariably started with what was called a first toast. This was generally a sardine or half a boiled egg on a piece of soggy toast. You then went on to tinned fish. Then you had a joint and then pudding and a savoury, which was more or less the same as the first course and was called the second toast . . .[4]

Then glasses would be raised to the King-Emperor, followed by a Gaelic toast, after which the pipers would march around the dining-table, deafening hosts and guests impartially. After dinner, there would be a variety of high-spirited behaviour, depending upon regimental custom.

'Conversation was informal but a certain protocol was observed: it was assumed automatically that a captain was more intelligent than a lieutenant, and a major more than a captain, and so on. As for expressing an opinion which differed from the general point of view, that was almost unheard of.'[5] It might be thought that for someone of Wavell's intellect such customs would be hard to observe with sustained enthusiasm, but the very power of his intelligence enabled him to accept it all with good nature.

> The picture that his company commander of those days gives of him is not what one would call normal for a young subaltern. It is of a very young officer so absorbed either in some book on military history or of the language which he was at the moment learning, as to be completely oblivious to conversations going on around him in the common sitting-room after dinner, and literally deaf even to a question addressed directly to him.[6]

He may have felt more at ease with some of the civilians whom he began to meet on guest nights, usually young members of the Indian Civil Service, or those working in other branches of the Government of India. They were generally the more intelligent products of the universities and public schools, in particular Winchester, and Haileybury, with its roots in the East India Company. They were usually classical scholars who did not question too deeply the future of the imperial vision that they had absorbed in their formative years:

> They saw the empire romantically as a great instrument of civilisation and enlightenment, a successor to Greece and Rome; and their own rôle in the empire in idealistic terms of service in its civilising mission. They had been educated in fact to think of themselves as super-prefects, administering the empire justly and efficiently in the interests of the governed.[7]

Punch magazine captured the spirit succinctly, on the occasion of yet another imperial conquest:

> *'Peccavi – I've Scinde' wrote Lord Ellen so proud.*
> *More briefly Dalhousie wrote 'Vovi – I've Oude'.*[8]

For many of those in the Indian Civil Service life was very agreeable – and much cheaper than back in England – and they could feel that they were serving a noble purpose, which they had been taught was something to aspire

to. Kipling, ever keen to speak up for the Indian Empire, reacted energetic-
ally when his sister questioned whether Englishmen had the welfare of the
natives at heart:

> What else are we working in the country for? For what else do the best
> men of the Commission die from overwork, and disease, if not to keep
> the people alive in the first place and healthy in the second? We spend
> our best men in the country like water, and if ever a foreign country was
> made better through 'the blood of the martyrs' India is that country . . .[9]

This was a sentiment that he expressed more memorably in verse:

> *Some beneath the further stars*
> *Bear the greater burden*
> *Set to serve the lands they rule*
> *(Save he serve, no man may rule)*
> *Serve and love the lands they rule;*
> *Seeking praise nor guerdon.*[10]

When Wavell was a subaltern the entire subcontinent, with its population
of nearly 300 million people, was administered by the 1,250 men of the
Indian Civil Service. It was quite common for one comparatively young man
to combine a whole range of offices, such as deputy commissioner, superin-
tendent of police, district judge, chief engineer of public works, district
agricultural officer and district inspector of schools. However, a crucial ingredient in the ability to manage civil affairs with so few people was the
belief of the native population, not least the Indian troops, that Britain could
deploy sufficient force to resist both attack from outside and rebellion from
within. A vital tool for maintaining that confidence was the provision of the
highest standards of administrative efficiency, which was achieved by
recruiting the finest intellects from Britain's public schools and universities.
Yet although behind the façade lay 70,000 or 80,000 British and about 300,000
Indian soldiers, their active use was politically undesirable, extremely expensive and viewed with great disfavour by the home government. It fell instead
to civilian administrators to maintain peace and harmony, and they were only
able to do so with the support of the Indians, who were greatly influenced
by the prestige of their British rulers, some of which they gained for themselves when awarded government posts.

On the surface Wavell could pass for just another subaltern, but he was in fact more in tune with the rather earnest and intellectual civilian dinner guests than with many of his brother-officers: some he would have known at school, and he would have recognised the Platonic ideals of their training, and their objectives in ruling their districts. From the 'civilians' Wavell began to learn about India's history and the state of its politics, and Britain's vision for the country. The knowledge was to prove very useful forty years later, when he returned as Viceroy.

It was only to be expected that among the large number of young men who joined the army out of family loyalty, or for enjoyment, or for lack of the ability to do anything else, there would be some who became deeply interested in their profession, determined to master its detail and to make the most of its opportunities. It was clear that Wavell was such a one. He had learnt as much as any of his contemporaries about the tools of his trade, and his knowledge had been refined by active service against the Boers. Keen as he was to play a full part in the regiment's recreations, he now put his heart into the many extra courses that were provided – a few of which were compulsory – for those wanting to make a mark with their career.

All officers had to learn and be examined in Urdu,[11] the lingua franca of northern India. Unsurprisingly, Wavell sailed through both the Lower and Higher Urdu exams. In one way they were a continuation of what he had learnt at school: although it was hardly explained or even understood, through the ignorance of Western schoolmasters, centuries of migration to Europe from the Middle East and India, and vice versa, had in fact resulted in many similarities between Eastern languages and the Greek and Latin taught in England. Construing such delights caused little difficulty to the bright young subaltern: when a friend came upon him reading a French novel during one of his Urdu lessons, Wavell explained that it was the only way he could remain sufficiently awake to listen to his Indian instructor. His prowess in Urdu and Pushtu, and in Persian, of which he also learnt the basic elements, helped him communicate with Indians both on- and off-duty, and added to the success he was already making of his career.

In the spring of 1905 he managed to escape the crowded schedule of his regimental duties and sail home for six months' leave. When at length he returned to Peshawar he took the first of three steps that were to distinguish him from his brother-officers, after which he would begin to be noticed by higher authority and to be spoken of as a 'coming man'.

The first of these initiatives was his application to be placed on a transport course. It duly led to an attachment to the Chitral Relief Column, to which he was appointed Transport Officer. He was placed in charge of an Indian mountain battery due to set out on the five-week journey to a remote region in the far north of the country, between the Indus and Afghanistan. Chitral was the capital of a province the size of Wales, about sixty miles on the Indian side of the Hindu Kush. Between it and Peshawar lay fast-flowing rivers and several mountain ranges of up to 20,000 feet. It had recently been the centre of a great drama, when in 1895 an army of more than 10,000 furious rebels had converged on the town volubly expressing their intention to slaughter its British occupants, who were surrounded and besieged until a hastily assembled relief force marched to their rescue. Since then a British presence in Chitral had been maintained, and once a year a column was sent up with supplies, and to replace the weary garrison.

When Wavell joined the relief column, Chitral had regained a degree of surface calm, and on this occasion no fighting was anticipated. It was already typical of him that he should volunteer for the expedition instead of remaining behind with his brother-officers and their sporting pursuits. He set about the task of organising transport, collecting horses, mules and camels, and enough barley, grain and bran to keep them on their feet if they could not find grazing on the way. He had then to find a route that would lead them past water supplies in case of need. Although a Transport Officer's work was unglamorous, it required careful planning and reinforced the lesson that he had learnt in South Africa, and was never to forget, that efficient transport and supplies were of vital importance to the success of a campaign.

Meanwhile, on a larger stage, the Russo-Japanese War had broken out,'[12] causing consternation in Britain and in other leading countries when Japan inflicted a comprehensive and totally unexpected defeat on Russia. The conflict had soon become an important topic for senior soldiers, and for discussion at the army's Staff College; but its effect was also debated in wider circles, as recorded by Alfred Zimmern, Wavell's friend and Winchester contemporary, by then a don at Oxford:

I went into my class and told them that I was going to lay aside Greek history for that morning, 'because', I said, 'I feel I must speak to you about the most important historical event that has happened, or is likely to happen, in our lifetime, the victory of a non-white people over a white people'.[13]

In India as well as elsewhere in the East, the legend of European invincibility was suddenly held up to question, heralding a new and disturbing impact on British prestige.

Britain certainly felt that the Empire had to remain invincible, above all in the northern outposts of India. Imperial policy for the defence of the subcontinent, for which the army was the willing tool, was complicated not only by the frontier being inhabited by tribes for whom murder, arson, theft and torture were an agreeable feature of daily life, but also because beyond the high passes lay the remote, brooding and strategically important state of Afghanistan:

> The English had inherited from the Sikhs a line at which the administration stopped short; up to that line there were districts of the Punjab administered by Deputy Commissioners. Beyond that line there were wild tribes where the Queen's Writ did not run. Beyond them again came the Amir of Kabul, but where exactly his jurisdiction ended or began, no one could say.[14]

The real threat to the Empire, according to long-held beliefs in British governing circles, came from the north, where, beyond the wild passes and plains of Afghanistan, lay Russia.

Russia was out of sympathy with Britain because of its aversion to the liberal ideas (even if still expressing benevolent despotism) for which Britain prided herself in her dealings with the Empire. Russia was mistrusted by almost all the other great powers because of her size and power, her own taste for empire-building, and her ultimate desire to expand both south towards the Persian Gulf and east towards China.

Britain felt that a friendly Afghanistan was an essential requirement for preventing Russia from sweeping over her border and threatening the North-West Frontier. However, the arguments for Britain continuing to pay the bribes necessary to keep the friendship of Afghanistan, and to maintain expensive garrisons in northern India, had become fused with the idea that India was fundamental to the existence of the British Empire, and essential to Britain's international influence. The possession of an Empire was felt to confirm Great Power status; it was a necessity, regardless of the increasing costs and commitments that it brought:

> First and foremost India means Empire. Because we hold India and govern three hundred millions of another race, we are without a near

33

rival among the nations of the world. Take India from us, and we will sink to the level of a trade competitor with Germany and the United States.[15]

However, these cherished tenets were beginning to be challenged, and the circular theory that because we had an Indian Empire, it had to be maintained was no longer taken as read:

Without India we should not be a Continental power, and should have no need to keep 80,000 British soldiers locked up in an unhealthy climate, waiting for an attack which may never come. Without India we should be rid of possible imbroglios with Russia, Persia, Afghanistan and China. A fortiori, we should be quit of Egypt also: the Mediterranean and the Suez Canal would no longer be a supreme concern to us.[16]

At the beginning of 1908 there was a particularly sharp and unwelcome increase in the threats that swirled more or less permanently around the North-West Frontier. Yet although far below the surface the anchors of imperial policy were threatening to drag, the governments both in Delhi and London remained determined to meet renewed trouble in the north with the time-honoured remedy of a punitive expedition.

In this case the Empire's mailed fist was to be aimed at the Zakka Khel, a tribe of fierce, treacherous and skilful Pathan warriors who lived in remote tribal territory beyond the lands administered by Britain, and who maintained a violent and precarious existence in the Bazar Valley, a forbidding part of the Hindu Kush, just west of the Khyber Pass.

Wavell now took a second step in furthering his career, by arranging to take part in the expedition himself. His chance to do so came about as an indirect result of a difference of opinion with his father, which had arisen when Wavell proposed to apply for a transfer away from India altogether. He had become firmly attracted to the sporting delights to be found in the outposts of Empire, for which Peshawar had a particularly good name, and he was therefore dismayed when, at the end of 1907, the Black Watch were ordered to leave Peshawar and move to Sialkot, a small and less appealing encampment on the border of Kashmir. Looking around for an alternative posting, he settled on the idea of a tour with the King's African Rifles, a regiment stationed in Somaliland, at that time a lion-hunter's paradise of which he had heard glowing accounts.

He was now twenty-four, but he remained a dutiful son and probably slightly in awe of a parent who, although far away in England, was not only forty years older than he, but a general. So he asked his father for his advice, if not his permission, on the idea of a move to Africa. The response was cool. The general had fixed opinions, and had lately been making persistent suggestions to his son that he should apply for the Staff College at Camberley, an essential rung for those aiming to reach the top of the military ladder. Far better, the general thought, for his son to return to the regiment's depot in Perth, where he could read for the Staff College exams and, equally to the point, see more of his family. Meekly or otherwise, Wavell accepted the suggestion and arrangements were made for him to leave India the following year.

A Staff College application was set in hand, and after a certain delay caused by Colonel Maxwell's total ignorance of the relevant regulations, Wavell duly received a month's posting to Divisional Headquarters at Rawalpindi, where his merits as a candidate for Camberley could be assessed. It was a chance result of this posting that enabled him to seize the opportunity to join the impending punitive expedition.

The Bazar Valley campaign was a model example of the army's active service in India; it also showed how tightly imperial policy was controlled, and how short was the chain of command between the soldiers in the field and the government in London. The trouble had started in October 1907, when Zakka Khel terrorists swept down from their valley and fell upon on a village near Peshawar, razing houses and killing a policeman before returning home. Ten more raids followed in quick succession, and news of them soon reached Westminster. In the House of Commons the Government explained that they were not:

> mere border disturbances such as are frequent on the tribal frontier. They were all serious raids organised for purposes of plunder, and executed by armed bands of Zakka Khel beyond the limits of tribal territory, and in the area under the direct administration of the Government of India.[17]

In the tribal territories the mullahs took a more supportive view, bestowing upon the exploits the blessings of religion, which in this case required that for one warrior killed in any future incident, ten British soldiers should die. The tribesmen had scented blood, their truculence grew, and in only a matter of weeks further raids took place, followed by a spate of violence. The final provocation came when gangs of Zakka Khel slipped through the walls of

Peshawar itself – murdering police and civilians, looting the Hindu quarter and making off with hoards of cash and jewels.

This outrage stung the British into action, and the Government of India swiftly took control. The Viceroy, Lord Minto, had already begun to fear that further raids might ignite a wider revolt along the entire frontier and in the tribal lands beyond. The military wheels began to turn. Army Headquarters placed Major-General Sir James Willcocks in command of three brigades – English, Scottish, Irish and Indian troops, comprising infantry, lancers, Gurkhas, sappers, miners and mountain batteries. The flow of telegrams increased, the India Office fussed about expanding bullets, and the Treasury queried the costs. Orders restricted to word-of-mouth ensured that secrecy was maintained until the last moment, while railway, transport, supply, medical and other arrangements were completed.

Wavell was in an office in Rawalpindi, far from these lively exchanges, as part of his trial for a Staff College application. One morning he was studying some administrative papers when he was handed a coded telegram to decipher. As soon as he read it, he realised that in his hands he held a golden opportunity:

> He was shown how to use the cipher and was given a telegram which proved to deal with the force which was being secretly assembled for this frontier expedition, and requested the staff to detail an officer to command an ammunition column; the only qualifications were that he should have passed an examination in Hindustani, and have done a transport course.[18]

The solution was obvious. It was a moment for a little native cunning and corner-cutting. He himself had passed the Hindustani exam, and he had also done a transport course. Lieutenant Wavell of the Black Watch was just the man required. He knew nothing of the components of an ammunition column, but he would not let that deter him. He told the weary staff officer that he could handle this minor matter himself, and telegraphed a reply submitting his own name for command of the ammunition column. The choice was approved – and when in due course the beady eye of higher authority lighted upon this irregularity, it was reluctantly conceded that he had shown enough initiative to escape a reprimand.

A short time later he set out with the Bazar Valley Field Force, ready to observe at first hand one of the typical military operations on which Britain embarked at regular intervals in order to maintain peace in the world. He had learnt enough to relate the reasons for the expedition both to the political situation that made such forays necessary and to the wider question of why, in such hostile country, there was a British presence at all. The experience would advance his career in the short term, and would also play a part in equipping him for the great political role that he was destined to play in India in due course.

So he left for Peshawar, the scene of a swift and secret assembly of guns, ammunition, swords, pistols, rifles, water, rations, horses and mules; and the noise and bustle of a force of thousands preparing to march into the hills.

The fight was expected to be short and sharp. The troops, in khaki and pith helmets, were equipped with only three days' rations, and there were to be no followers, tents, baggages, supply columns or journalists. The commanding officer was vested with full political control, ready to treat with tribal leaders in the aftermath of the expected victory. Up and down the line, from the Viceroy to the drummer-boy, the orders were rehearsed: to fall upon the Zakka Khel with a surprise attack, and to prevent revolt from spreading through the mountains to the north.

The Political Agent for the Khyber was summoned to advise the generals. They decided to converge on the enemy from different directions, forcing them into open battle. The Agent took command of a separate flying column, and, two days before the main advance began, set out with 1,000 men towards the Khyber Pass. His plan was to descend upon the Zakka Khel from the east, blocking their escape routes into Afghanistan.

The numerous colonial wars that Britain fought through the nineteenth century are frequently described as 'minor', but although in many cases 'we had got the Maxim gun and they had not', for the soldiers involved each was a heady and dangerous prospect. The Bazar Valley campaign was no exception: Wavell was joining an expedition fraught with danger and uncertainty, attempting to subdue a ferocious and well-armed enemy in a barren, sheer and rugged land, crossed with deep defiles, which the tribesmen knew far better than the British. The Zakka Khel held the high ground, overlooking the only lines of approach that the expedition could follow, just as, in Wavell's words – his mind itching with history – 'From Mount Tabor a wild rush of mountain men destroyed Sisera's labouring host in the swampy plain below.'[19]

Although the soldiers were better armed and more disciplined than the tribesmen, they were to enter difficult and little-known territory, where at every turn they might face surprise or ambush. The anxiety of some of the young troopers was heightened by stories of the fate of men in previous campaigns, and old sweats issued grim warnings about the importance of rescuing the wounded and never leaving them to the mercies of the enemy. Wavell knew by heart Kipling's 1890 poem 'The Young British Soldier', which handled the matter neatly:

> *When you're wounded and left on Afghanistan's plains,*
> *And the women come out to cut up what remains,*
> *Jest roll to your rifle and blow out your brains*
> *An' go to your Gawd like a soldier.*[20]

The third brigade remained in reserve at Nowshera, ready to march in case the tribesmen watching from the northern heights succumbed to temptation and entered the fray.

At six in the morning, in icy cold, the main force set off for the pass at the southern end of the valley. Snow covered the higher reaches, and in the distance they could see a steep peak that dominated the valley, protecting the village of Chinar, the enemy stronghold that lay at its feet. As the column emerged from the pass it divided into two. The main body, including Wavell's ammunition column, was ordered forward towards Walai, within a few miles of Chinar. They soon came under fire from riflemen hidden among the hillside boulders, and bullets began to pour into the troops doggedly winding along the valley. By seven in the evening, after marching for thirteen hours, the column entered Walai. They could go no further until dawn, so there they halted, in the freezing cold, digging pits and makeshift stone defences, surrounding the most vulnerable with their limited stock of barbed wire.

During the night the sniping intensified. The Indian warriors repeatedly approached the British bivouacs, screaming and yelling and firing into the soldiers as they rushed to within revolver range, those without guns hurling rocks and stones. Yet they failed to press home their attacks, and as each hour passed it became clearer that the British advance had taken the enemy by surprise, and would not be repulsed.

General Willcocks had received no news of the force approaching westward from the Khyber Pass, but when at length he did establish contact, he ordered the column to withdraw from its isolated and vulnerable position and to make its way south to join the main force, while he himself planned an advance in order to tempt the tribesmen back into their village and expose themselves to an open fight. Between the two forces lay three miles of steep and rocky defiles, ideal for defensive guerrilla tactics. As they moved forward, they saw that the crests that overlooked them were held by a large number of enemy, so orders were given for Sikh troops to advance and attack, and for Wavell to bring up ammunition to provide a steady rain of shrapnel on enemy clearly visible from the guns.

Reinforcements were then called up from the south, and before long the troops entered the village, securing its wood and fodder and flattening its fortifications. Seeing their shelter disintegrating, large numbers of Zakka Khel, watched by the troops on the hilltops above them, turned and fled north-west across the valley, towards Afghanistan.

During the following days the tribesmen persistently rushed the soldiers on the edges of the moving columns, attacking them at close range and greatly hampering their movement. Finally, the British moved up to the north-west ridges and succeeded in forcing a pitched battle. However, near the passes into Afghanistan the Zakka Khel had been joined by considerable numbers of other tribesmen, threatening the spread of defiance right along the frontier that the Government of India had feared.

At length the day was won, and the cheers of British soldiers, echoing against the towering hills, replaced the sounds of battle: the crash of guns, the thud of spears, the shrieks of rage and the groans of death.

With the tribesmen abandoning the attack, the second phase of the expedition began, and the army set in hand a process of systematic destruction. The Government's hope was that the time which it would take the tribesmen to rebuild their lives and villages, replace their animals and replenish their stores would give them – and their neighbours – ample scope to reflect upon the cost of challenging Britain's imperial might. Opposition was steadily growing among Liberal politicians and their supporters back in England, and among widening circles of politically minded intellectuals in India, to Britain's methods of imposing her rule, but to the soldiers it was all just part of the job.

Although the Bazar Valley campaign was brief, it was also vivid. The soldiers who took part in it felt hope and pain, heat and cold, fear and exhilaration, triumph and despair. Bullets whined, rocks flew, tribesmen yelled, mules stampeded, bugles echoed, men died and the ground shook with the reverberation of mountain guns. Wavell's own account stuck to the bare facts: 'The campaign was a short one and nothing exciting happened, but my column issued a considerable amount of ammunition and proved useful.'[21]

Others also thought that he had played a useful part. Some months later he received the 'North-West Frontier 1908' clasp, issued with the North-West Frontier of India Medal, adding to the medals and four clasps he had earned in South Africa. Campaign medals, as opposed to those for gallantry, are to some extent a matter of chance – of where a unit is posted, and whether it is ordered into any engagements. Yet by joining the Chitral and Bazar Valley expeditions Wavell had made the most of opportunity. His initiative and talent had distinguished him from his contemporaries. The gap between them would now begin to widen.

Later he recorded his sense of gratitude and pleasure for his youthful experiences in India:

> I owe much to India, where I have spent more than thirteen years of my life. As a child I played and grew up for two and a half years in the Nilgari Hills where the sun and air of a fine climate gave my body a good start in life. As a subaltern I came closest to knowledge of the common Indian people. I learnt enough of the language to speak with the villagers where I camped and shot with my Shikaris in the hills of Kashmir, where I was several times alone with them for many weeks . . .[22]

At the time, his surroundings in India seemed immutable, yet soon they were to vanish entirely. His service there as a young soldier was in many ways exactly what his upbringing and education had pointed to, as with his civilian contemporaries, who, although quite young men, were already managing huge areas of country, responsible for the lives and well-being of thousands of Indians, and accepting without question and in equal measure their duty of service and obedience to their commands. In fact, their preparation was for a role in a play that was approaching its final act, although that was hardly contemplated by English minds. When Wavell next set foot in India, its countenance was unchanged – life still moved at the pace of a bullock cart – but the whole imperial framework (political, economic, social) was beginning to loosen.

Soon after he had finished with the excitements in the Hindu Kush the army applied its customary rules of balance and he was given a year's leave, something with which in those days it – that is, the taxpayer – was surprisingly generous. Wavell habitually took full advantage of available leave, always maintaining that he was lazy, but certainly making up for it by thoroughly learning the job.

There then began a series of developments that would quickly lift him above ordinary regimental soldiering, almost for the rest of his career. In its place he would find interesting jobs and increasing responsibility, leading in due course to the highest military rank and then to the role of statesman.

In the English way of things, chance, personality and personal recommendation were all to play their part in this process – just as they were with the
reverses that were to befall him – but the force that impelled him along his
path was largely his singular intelligence.

He took the third step on this upward slope when he received permission to sit the Staff College exam. In his brief time at Divisional Headquarters
– before his successful, if unorthodox, method of joining the frontier
expedition – he had proved to senior officers that he was good staff material. He could easily have applied to the newly established Indian Staff College
at Quetta, a mirror image of the mother institution at Camberley, but one
of the reasons against that was his father's request that he should come back
and see more of his family. So he sailed for England, arriving home at the
end of March 1908, to read for the exams and to try his luck.

To most people it would have been a daunting prospect, and a very long
shot. Competing for every vacancy there were about seven officers, almost
all of whom were more mature and experienced than Wavell. In fact he
was remarkably young to make the attempt at all: in May 1908 he turned
twenty-five, whereas at that time, the average age of officers trying for
Camberley was well over thirty, and many people set aside some years for
the process, fearing the need for successive attempts. Wavell's father, anxious
that his son should succeed, pushed him hard and encouraged him to attend
a crammer, as it was the sort of exam – of eighteen papers – for which
crammers existed.

He spent the summer months with his parents at the house that they had
rented a few years previously in the village of Cranborne, in Dorset, and
which was to remain the family home until after Lillie Wavell's death in
1926. It was a lovely, stone-dressed, red-brick Georgian house, which had
been bought a few years earlier by the Marquess of Salisbury, the main
landowner in the area, as he did not like any large houses in the village not
being owned by himself. Wavell spent a happy time idling in its peaceful
garden and playing tennis at the nearby manor house, when not driven indoors
by a father concerned that he was not doing enough work for his exams.

The general need not have worried: despite being the most junior subaltern and by far the youngest applicant, and taking a more casual approach
than other candidates, Wavell passed top at his first attempt. It was a remarkable achievement, leading him directly into a fast and serious stream of army
life working with clever and determined men, most of whom were nearly
ten years his senior.

As it happened, he arrived at Camberley at a most exciting time, when a great drive for innovation and modernisation was transforming the whole direction and organisation of the army. The air was full of new ideas, and it had been decreed that 'the General Staff will be drawn from the officers of the Army who may be considered capable of forming a school of progressive military thought'.[23] As that type of thought did not often strike the average regimental officer, the main source of talent for the General Staff was the Staff College, the transit camp for the bright and ambitious.

So Wavell, with four other subalterns and a larger number of older captains and majors, joined an elite group of soldiers ready to play their part in planning a modern imperial army, albeit for an Empire whose pre-eminence was being questioned, if not yet actually threatened. In his two years at Camberley he would discover much wider aspects of the army's role than regimental soldiering, and would confirm his transformation into a soldier who, though still young, was on a path that would one day lead to high command.

He was helped by the fact that the senior instructors soon formed a high opinion of his ability, and because while he was at the Staff College it was run consecutively by two particularly able and imaginative men, both of whom took a personal interest in their youngest student. He, in return, was deeply affected by their teaching and guidance.

His first commandant was Henry Wilson, a very tall, dapper Irishman, as much interested in politics as in the army, a combination that was to bring him the rank of field-marshal, a seat in Parliament and assassination at the hands of Irish terrorists. Appointed commandant at the beginning of 1907, Wilson was gripped by the belief that a war with Germany was inexorably approaching. He duly set about inspiring his students with the idea that the War Office staff should prepare for such an event by working closely with the French, and by the preparation of comprehensive plans for sending an army into battle on the Continent.

Wilson's views on the future enemy were shared by his successor, Colonel W.R. Robertson, a former domestic servant who by the time his career ended had ascended the entire length of the army ladder, from private to Chief of the Imperial General Staff. Robertson, in contrast to Wilson, thought that Staff College students should not concern themselves with politics, although he himself was just as politically aware as Wilson, and as concerned about the increasing power of Germany. Although other countries began to exert their influence in areas that Britain regarded as her prerogative – the Russians in Persia, Tibet and Afghanistan, and the French in Egypt, Siam and Central

Africa – it was the aggressive spirit of Germany that Robertson saw as the paramount threat. The students' minds were opened to the practical link between the army and politics, but even so, with the exception of the recent Russo-Japanese War, little thought was given to the world beyond Europe, apart from exercises in Wales aimed at replicating the military situation on the North-West Frontier.

Despite the army's drive for modernisation, the syllabus hardly touched on recent conflict, a strange omission considering that in only one of Queen Victoria's sixty-three years on the throne had the British Army not been in action somewhere or other. Instead it was the Napoleonic Wars that the instructors regarded as fresh news that would repay study. Yet Wavell was in his element, responding to the encouragement of the far-sighted senior staff, even if some of his written work still bore the gravitas of the slightly earnest schoolboy. The retentive brain, furnished with data, was sent into battle, and cohorts of dates and campaigns and allusions from history marched across the pages of his submissions. Although in papers and discussions at Camberley, and for ever after, Wavell readily yielded to the temptation to salt his output with scholarly knowledge, by now he had experienced two types of warfare, and the more obvious traits of the student were fading. As the course progressed, its subjects became more interesting and relevant to operations with which, in the event, they would soon have to deal in earnest.

At Camberley, as at Winchester, he made just a few, good friends. Many of them were soon to be slaughtered on the battlefield, or to die in more unusual circumstances. Major C.B. Thomson, for example, of the Royal Engineers, was killed in the the R101 airship disaster when, as Air Minister, he was on the maiden flight that, in a flash of exploding gas and burning tarpaulin, halted all plans for passenger travel in airships.[24]

Wavell certainly impressed the men who ran the institution. One of the instructors was Colonel George Morris, who, despite arousing mixed feelings among his peers, as being too fond of gambling and not fond enough of field-sports, was considered by many to be potentially one of the best commanders in the army; in Morris' view, Wavell was one of the two ablest students of his year, with the most co-ordinated brain of any student he had taught. Further praise came from Robertson himself – not normally an expansive man – who described Wavell as by far the ablest of any of the officers who had come to his notice as commandant. Wavell had made his mark where it counted; and in 1911 he proved his academic ability once more, by passing out of the Staff College with the highest possible grade.

A PROPER WAR

WAVELL now faced the prospect of rejoining his regiment, which would mean either a return to India or a new start at the headquarters in Scotland. However, shortly before he was due to leave Camberley he was unexpectedly presented with an alternative that seemed altogether more unusual and stimulating. The prospect arose of work among the brightest of the army's intellects, in the centre of events, at the War Office. The commandant sent for him and said that he had been asked to find a student to go to Russia, learn the language and take the army interpreter's exam – and he was choosing Wavell. It was a good opportunity, with the presumption that on his return he would take on responsibility for Russian affairs at the War Office.

Wavell consistently maintained that he was attracted to regimental life, and that he regretted time on secondment, but for a man who liked to use his brains, who had developed a taste for adventure and who had just spent two years in the relatively heady atmosphere of Camberley, this offer seemed remarkably suitable. Without much hesitation he accepted.

He set off across Europe in the depths of winter 1911, travelling via Berlin and Warsaw. He had never been outside the British Empire and spoke no Russian. When he arrived in Moscow he found that he had entered a world unlike anything he had experienced before.

At that time in Russia the army was viewed with distaste by most sections of society, but the officers that France, Germany and Britain periodically sent over to learn the language were reputed to behave rather better than the average Russian officer, and so they received a cautious welcome among people whose curiosity about life beyond their country overcame their initial prejudice. Wavell found a berth with a Madame Ertel, a widow who lived in a flat near the Kremlin. Her husband, whose radical views led to his imprisonment and exile, had been a friend of Chekhov and an acquaintance of Tolstoy, and was the author of a once-admired novel called *The Lady of Volkhonsk*. Wavell was now ushered into an animated and informal family household, consisting of one Armenian student and seven women of variously uncertain ages: a daughter, sisters, cousins, aunts and grandmothers, among whose friends were writers, artists, actors and similarly bohemian types.

The quiet young Englishman was a complete novelty to these chattering members of the *intelligentsia* and they gave him a lively welcome. How he should be addressed led to an immediate debate, resulting in the selection of 'Archibald Archibaldovitch'. It did not go down well with its owner, who responded with a rather subdued 'I prefer "Mr Wavell"'. Being unable to speak Russian was a barrier at first, but learning the language was the reason for his stay, and he set to it with a will. The outlook did not seem very cheerful. He had less than a year to pass the interpreter's exam, and months of study stretched ahead of him, with long, hard days to be spent under the watchful gaze of Madame Ertel. The few relaxations on offer consisted of trudging the streets, having tea in the English atmosphere of a store called Muir and Merrilies, and playing football with a group of schoolboys and students whom he met soon after his arrival.

After a time he did manage to break off, sailing down the Volga to the Crimea and the Caucasus with two fellow-officers who were also learning Russian, but he soon had to rejoin Madame Ertel and her sisters, this time at their summer retreat in the country. There he found even fewer diversions than in Moscow, and for weeks on end, secluded on a remote estate, in the languid summer heat, he spent his days engrossed in study. After a time he became aware of a rather different sort of intensity in the party, when he began to excite the interest of one of Madame's sisters. For many men that might have been a welcome distraction, but on Wavell her charms made little impact:

> . . . to his dismay she began to make love to him. Passionate little notes were left on his pillow; long, languishing glances were cast at him across the table. This was more than he could stand; he wrote urgently to the British Military Attaché in Petrograd to ask whether he could be given permission to attend Russian Army manoeuvres.[1]

Permission was granted, which the military attaché had not expected, and with relief Wavell escaped to Moscow, to spend a week at the invitation of the Grenadier Corps and join them on their autumn manoeuvres. It proved to be a valuable opportunity to observe the Russian Army, of which the British authorities had limited knowledge. For their part, few Russian soldiers had ever seen a British officer, and Wavell's appearance in a kilt at a formal parade added considerably to their curiosity.

The months spent learning and speaking a new language in these strange surroundings left him with a strong affection for his vivid hosts, and he was always to say that he liked Russians more than any other foreigners. He returned to England just after Christmas 1911, arriving in good time to take the interpreter's paper,[2] in which, maintaining his well-established record in exams, he took a first-class.

The prospects that had earlier been held out to him by Robertson were now realised, and in March 1912 he was posted to the War Office and set to producing what was to be his first item of professional writing, a handbook on the Russian Army. He was soon transferred, as a GSO3[3] to the Training Branch of the Department of the Chief of the Imperial General Staff, which was responsible for education, training and Home Defence. There he spent some happy months and, with a look over his shoulder to his schooldays, drove around the country inspecting school training corps.

His growing reputation as a soldier with an intellect brought Wavell a commission to translate into English a book on the Russian royal family. He was also asked to contribute to a naval and military history of the Russo-Japanese War that was then being compiled by Ernest Swinton, the secretary of the Historical Section of the Committee of Imperial Defence.[4] The literary atmosphere in which this small part of his new job was conducted was enhanced by the presence of Henry Newbolt,[5] a barrister who was in charge of producing the naval section of the history. Newbolt had already made a name for himself as a writer of verse with stirring national and imperial themes, and poems such as his 'Drake's Drum' – which joined the ever-lengthening list of those that Wavell knew by heart – and 'Vitaï Lampada', published in the year of the Diamond Jubilee, were already standard schoolboy recitals:

> *The sand of the desert is sodden red,*
> *Red with the wreck of a square that broke;*
> *The Gatling's jammed and the colonel dead,*

And the regiment blind with dust and smoke.
The river of death has brimmed his banks,
And England's far, and Honour a name,
But the voice of a schoolboy rallies the ranks,
'Play up! Play up! And play the game!'[6]

On the whole, earnest Wykehamists treated the jammed Gatling and other flights of Newbolt's fancy with little enthusiasm, and Wavell for one preferred Kipling's more artistic treatment of similar themes; but working with the poet himself added zest to this part of Wavell's early work at the War Office.

He then moved to a less peripheral post, in the Military Operations Department, known as MO3, of which the overall chief was his former commandant, Henry Wilson. Wavell was assigned to a section dealing with the preparation of military information about Russia and various other countries.

It was a far cry from regimental soldiering, but it was important work to which he was well suited. The young lieutenant spent his days at a desk answering queries passed on by anyone who noticed the word 'Russia' in a document, and in communicating with the military attachés in Russia and in London. When nothing more urgent was on hand, he would spend hours going through foreign newspapers culling information that might one day come in useful.

In this slightly academic atmosphere, where officers sent minutes and memoranda to each other even if they were in adjacent rooms, he was with a group of men who were among the cleverest in the army. There he spent the next two years, except for two interludes each of several weeks when he was sent to Russia to attend army manoeuvres, first in the Caucasus, in May 1912, and the following year near Kiev, his War Office superiors noting that his reports could have been written only by an officer with exceptional powers of observation and a thorough knowledge of his profession and the Russian language. In March 1913 he was promoted to the rank of captain.

He took a flat in Pall Mall, near his work and in the centre of London. His routine precluded the high life of the Brigade of Guards or Household Cavalry on 'London Duties', in which the popular game was polo, where hunting in Leicestershire counted as a parade, and whose junior officers were automatically placed on the leading hostesses' invitation lists. Wavell was not from that type of landed family, nor was he rich enough for such a routine. Even so, he received a steady flow of invitations, and was quietly genial and sociable, even if his close friends were few. He developed a predilection for an easy-going intellectual atmosphere, and if the literary lions of Moscow had at first bewildered him, they had broadened his mind, and he had acquired a taste for bohemian situations that contrasted with the military atmosphere. He enjoyed talking to Everard Calthrop, also in MO3, whose years in the British Legation in Tokyo learning Japanese as a 'Language Officer' had left him with a certain disregard for army convention, and who often took Wavell with him to exotic shops and eating houses in Soho and other slightly louche parts of the city.

Despite the attractions of such friends and entertainments, the anchor of his life remained his family. Over the years most of his spare time had been spent with cousins or with his sisters, and more recently at his parents' house in its tranquil Dorset village. The ties binding the family seemed strong, although it is possible to gain the impression that Wavell's mother did not inspire the warmest type of love and affection, at least not in her son. Hampered by arthritis, Lillie Wavell was somewhat overshadowed by the general, who found the role of the Victorian paterfamilias an easy one to play, and who was held in some awe by his children long after they had grown up.

On the other hand, the affection between Wavell and his two sisters was strong. At some point they dropped the names with which they were christened, Florence Anne changing to Nancy and Lillian Mary to Molly. Although one was just over thirty and one just under, they had not married, and the fact that neither they nor Wavell had enlarged the family circle may have strengthened its bonds. By the time Wavell had spent a year in the War Office, and had himself passed thirty, it had become the opinion of his father, at least, that it was time to find a bride.

He himself might have felt at least a hint of pressure in the matter, but as it happened, around the time of his thirtieth birthday he did fall for, and propose to, an Irish Catholic girl, but she turned him down, although he 'bore his rejection with fortitude'.[7] Later in the year he began seeing a girl called Eugénie Quirk. Her father, Colonel John Quirk, was a gallant officer, with a DSO, who in the 1880s had commanded a battalion of the Welch Regiment; in 1875 he had married Eugénie O'Neill, a Dublin girl supposedly related to the Empress Eugénie, wife of Napoleon III. The Quirk family originated in the Isle of Man, but Eugénie's great-grandfather moved to Liverpool, where he started a shipbuilding yard and married an aunt of the future Prime Minister, W.E. Gladstone, whose family home was in that part of England.

Eugénie, or 'Queenie' as she was known in her family, was four years younger than Wavell. Being a colonel's daughter she was used to the ways of army families. By all accounts she was a lively and attractive girl, with curly, red-gold hair and turquoise eyes, and as a seventeen-year-old she had been the toast of the Dublin Season. Yet her friendship with the keen and clever captain from the War Office did not seem to be a particularly passionate affair – Wavell himself described his courtship as 'peculiar' – but whether or not he was responding in part to the pressures of convention, Wavell had his share of hot blood and through the summer months became increasingly attracted to his new friend.

Meanwhile he was drawn into the spiral of events that began with a murder in Sarajevo on the last Sunday in June 1914, which at first hardly rustled the summer leaves, but which in just over five weeks caused the eclipse of peace in Europe:

> On the idle hill of summer,
> Sleepy with the flow of streams,
> Far I hear the steady drummer
> Drumming like a noise in dreams.[8]

The descent to war was so swift that MO3 barely had time to work through its 'precautionary stage', which included distributing details of the organisation of the French and German armies, and briefing officers designated to take charge of Intelligence Sections of the Expeditionary Force. When war did break out, Wavell's section – comprising himself and one other officer – had to produce and maintain a comprehensive picture of Russian troop dispositions, and supply the Intelligence Section, MO5, with the information it needed for its daily war summary for the country's military and political leaders.

For all the preparation, when the time came, the immense undertaking of mobilisation had the force of a hurricane blowing through the War Office. The detail and complexity of the plans now tested to the full the mental and physical stamina of the elite officers whose job it was to carry them out, and the lives and well-being of enormous numbers of people depended upon their smooth execution. Wavell and his colleagues worked tirelessly as seven German armies smashed their way through France to within shelling distance of Paris. It was vital that the War Office put up a superlative performance, and even though Wavell was much younger than almost all the officers in the directorate, he brought to the job exactly the qualities required.

It is not clear where there arose the fatal optimism that the war would be over by Christmas, but during August and the early part of September it infected even the best-informed officers. Wavell, along with so many others, felt that time was short, and he quickly started searching for a means of being posted to France. But it was the senior and experienced officers who departed first, while he was kept behind as part of a depleted staff. As the war situation began to change, he was soon transferred from MO3 and put in charge of MO5, whose duties included arrangements for military censorship and others on the periphery of the secret services.[9]

It was not long before mounting casualties increased the transit of officers to France, creating vacancies at home. Some five weeks after the outbreak of war, Wavell was promoted to acting major, placed in command of the infant Intelligence Corps and ordered to embark for General Headquarters in France. Relieved and excited, he made some hurried preparations. At the same time he turned to an altogether different matter: throwing off his blanket of reserve, he proposed to Eugénie Quirk. In a later description of the event he confined himself to a characteristic, mildly humorous comment: 'I don't think I warned her of any of my failings; I wanted to marry the girl.'[10]

By the end of September he had arrived in France, just as the Germans executed their Schlieffen Plan in what was to prove the final phase of a mobile war. This Teutonic blueprint for crushing France and subjugating Europe had been devised some ten years earlier, and was based on Hannibal's defeat of the Romans at the ancient Battle of Cannae, considered an object lesson not only at Winchester and the Staff College, but also in the German High Command.

'Alas, regardless of their doom', the glittering squadrons of Uhlans and Lancers drew near extinction in the face of the machine gun, and the German and Allied armies began a final *pas de deux*, sidestepping north-west in a bid to outflank each other in what became described as 'the race to the sea'. British headquarters followed in their wake and established itself at Saint-Omer, some thirty miles behind the front line at Ypres.

Wavell did not want to be at headquarters: he wanted to be at the front. As at previous moments in his career, he appeared to be impelled by an inner force driving him towards whatever was the most serious and active part of the military setting in which he happened to be placed. It seemed as though he felt duty bound to follow the hardest and most worthy path he could. The characteristics that led him doggedly to endure the privations of the Boer War, to join the expedition to Chitral in preference to the pleasures of sport and the regimental mess, and to search for active service on the North-West

Frontier now made him feel uneasy in a headquarters far behind the lines, frustrated in a desire to share the rigours of the men at the front.

Determined to get near the fighting, he made several excursions to the battle zone, including visits to the the Black Watch trenches. In his own description of those forays he sounds faintly like a John Buchan hero, modestly accepting fearful adventures:

> I visited a friend in Messines while it was being barely held by our cavalry against repeated German attacks, and was told by the friend that I was a bloody fool to come to a place under shell fire unless I had business there. He was quite right, I had no business at the front; but the trouble was I had no real business in the rear either. Anyone could have looked after the Intelligence Corps. I knew I was regarded as a GHQ drone by the hard-pressed people I visited at the front, and I felt it. I wanted to get away to more active soldiering.[11]

Meanwhile death and injury were leading to rapidly increasing numbers of vacancies, both in the front line and among the staff some distance behind it, and his wish for more action was soon granted. It happened more or less at his own request. When he had been in France for five or six weeks he received another Intelligence appointment, as a GSO2, one rung higher than his War Office post. It was forward of GHQ, but still not in the fighting line, and, just like Buchan's Richard Hannay, he felt disappointed to be remaining with the staff and not getting directly to grips with the Hun. However, with typical resolve Wavell paid a visit to the officer whose lot it was to find suitable pegs to fill the large numbers of holes that were now opening, and persuaded him to look for an appointment that would take him closer to the battlefield.

Within days his wish was granted. On 16 November 1914 he was appointed brigade-major of the 9th Infantry Brigade, giving him the authority of a staff officer and a direct part in a brigade's activities at the front. It was not long before both his skills as a soldier and his qualities as a man were put to the ultimate test, in the chaos of full-scale battle. So far his record had been exemplary: he had passed with honours through every institution that he had attended; he had mastered the technical skills of a junior regimental officer; he had prospered as a bright young man at the War Office; and he had seen active service. Now additional qualities were required, to withstand the hell of the Western Front:

If you were hit by either a rifle or a machine-gun, the chances were that either you were killed outright, or eventually you returned to life more or less in one piece. However, in contrast to World War II, bullet wounds were the minority; the greater part of casualties were caused by the terrible effects of shell-fire . . . the crude iron of the shells (most of them many times bigger than anything used in the land battles of 1939–45) shattered into huge ragged chunks that sometimes two men would be unable to lift. The effect on the soft human carapace of impact with these whirling fragments may be imagined . . .'[12]

. . . men squashed, or cut in two, or divided from top to bottom, blown into showers by an ordinary shell, bellies turned inside out and scattered anyhow, skulls forced bodily into the chest as if by a blow with a club, and in place of the head a bit of neck, oozing currant jam of brains all over the chest and back . . .'[13]

In such conditions no one could be sure how they would behave, and it was rapidly becoming apparent that a soldier's past character or performance provided little guide to his conduct in the trenches. It had always been difficult to assess a man's 'war-value': physical courage was in general taken for granted in the army, but it was hard to predict an officer's quotient of moral courage. However, Wavell's apparent determination to be as close to the fighting as his job would allow was soon to disclose his mettle. To give him added strength, he did have one private source of pleasure and encouragement: on a fortnight's leave in England in April 1915 he had married Queenie Quirk.[14] They had a brief honeymoon, the last three days of which were spent in London, ending as a train steamed out of Victoria Station, taking one more soldier far away to war.

His journey took him to the 'Ypres Salient', the bulge of land pressing forward into the German front line in such a way that its unfortunate occupants were flanked on three sides by the enemy, who, typically, were ensconced in superior, drier and better-sited trenches than the British. Wavell recorded his view of the scene:

. . . the troops that fought in the Salient in 1915 had neither confidence of skill nor hope of gaining ground. The old army was dead; the new armies and the new equipment were not yet ready. Struggling in a muddy plain, with the enemy holding the advantage of higher ground almost everywhere, they were overlooked, outgunned, outmanoeuvred, and not a little bewildered by the new weapons of gas and liquid fire used against them. Only their obstinate courage kept a footing in that cramped semicircle and held the Germans from setting foot on the ramparts of Ypres.[15]

Now Wavell himself was one of the troops fighting in the Salient. Numerous small attacks had been ordered, with an accompanying brisk demand for stretcher-bearers. Even though Ypres had little strategic or tactical value, its defence being really only a matter of prestige, the army commanders insisted that it be held. They had reluctantly accepted plans for a new offensive devised by the French, to whom the British (whose army was much the smaller) had at that stage of the war to play second fiddle. The French High Command believed that by driving north from Champagne, storming Vimy Ridge and then driving east, they could pierce the Western Front and end the war. To help them justify this belief, the British committed themselves to a diversionary attack near Loos, just north of the proposed French advance. There were no uplifting hopes to gild this lily, such as that it might itself punch a hole in the German lines: it was just a small, local fight in an attempt to divert German reserves from the impending French attack.

It was to take place in 9th Infantry Brigade's area, and Wavell, as the brigade's chief staff officer – the crucial link between the battalion commanders at the front and the staff further back[16] – was himself to play a vital part in the plan and its execution.

On 1 June 1915 the brigade moved into trenches just south-east of Ypres. The first intimation that an attack was to be ordered came six days later when Wavell received a warning order from the headquarters of 3rd Division, of which his brigade formed a part. Their objective was to be a ridge just east of Ypres, running north from the Menin Road. Behind it was a large pond, 'l'étang de Bellewaarde', and a farm, well defended by Germans. Having received the Divisional Orders in a dugout just behind the fighting trenches, Wavell set about helping his brigadier translate the complex directives into brigade orders and issue them to battalion commanders.

In this potential for chaos the efficiency of a brigade staff officer could make a crucial difference to the preservation of the morale – and the lives – of all the men in the brigade. Wavell, to a greater extent than was then usual, would carefully reconnoitre the ground over which the troops might have to fight. He also issued very clear instructions: 'As brigade administration officer,' one of his subordinates recalled, 'I never made a mistake serious enough to draw a rebuke from him. I take no credit – there was never any ambiguity in his instructions and orders.'[17]

Having examined the ground for three days before the attack, the brigadier, brigade staff and regimental officers made their plan. It involved neatly passing battalions through each other in a system of leapfrog as they successively attacked the enemy trenches, and Wavell seemed rather pleased with it. As in countless similar attacks on the Western Front, the intention was to unleash closely grouped artillery bombardments at a series of exact times, with machine-gun attacks and infantry advances scheduled for the intervals between them, paving the way for a final onrush.

The plan had required close co-ordination for the occupation and evacuation of each target trench, but in 1915 there were no portable radio sets and officers had to rely for their information on flares, whistles, runners, pigeons or aerial observers. In this case the troop movements were ordered by whistle blasts; they did little more than add to the general noise and mayhem, with the result that the troops started advancing at the wrong pace and time. Chaos soon set in, and further havoc was caused by the cry of 'gas' that went up in an overcrowded trench; a muddle developed, and men fled back towards the British trenches in complete disorder.

For all the careful planning, the whole enterprise was ruined, mainly because in their excitement several battalions rushed forward too soon and became entangled with troops in front of them, crowding together in trenches too small to provide cover or to permit the reorganisation needed for a further advance.

As soon as he realised what was happening Wavell left the brigade dugout and set off for the battleground, which was under heavy fire, to try and restore the situation. An eye-witness wrote:

> The Brigade-Major arrived, cursing, and called upon some of our men to advance and reoccupy the trench in front. He led them himself, and they made a very fine dash across . . . I do not think more than twenty fell, and they reoccupied that trench, and, I believe, the third also, before the Huns realised that they were empty.[18]

It was conduct of extreme bravery, in an appalling situation. As the Brigade War Diary euphemistically put it, '. . . casualties by this time were considerable and very few officers were left. Units were greatly mixed, and reorganisation was necessary.'[19]

'Reorganisation', for those who had survived, was the preliminary to further punishment:

> . . . About 6.00 the worst moment of the day came. The Huns started to bombard us with a shell which was quite new to us. It sounded like a gigantic fire-cracker, with two distinct explosions. These shells came over just above the parapet, in a flood . . . after about a quarter of an hour of this sort of thing, there was a sudden crash in the trench and ten feet of the parapet, just beyond me, was blown away and everyone stood around blinded by dust. With my first glance I saw what looked like half a dozen bodies, mingled with sandbags, and then I smelt gas and realised that these were gas shells . . .
>
> The next day we had the brigadier round . . . we were congratulated and patted on the back, and told that we had done very good work, and that next time we should have a chance on our own. What luck![20]

But six out of every ten men had been lost.

As evening fell on 16 June, Wavell's own world was turned upside down. The Brigade War Diary recorded: '6.30 p.m. Capt. A.P. Wavell wounded by a shell outside HQ dugout.'

He had emerged for some fresh air during a lull in the fighting and was some way off in the open when the German shelling recommenced. He was walking back to the dugout, and had almost reached it, when he was hit in the head by a stray bullet, or a splinter of iron from a shell. It went through his left eye.

Almost at once he was in great pain, and his face swelled up around his eyes. He could walk, but hardly see, and the brigadier suggested that he head back to a dressing-station. With an orderly to help him, Wavell began the hazardous journey to the rear, through continuous shellfire, until at length they reached the Menin Gate at Ypres. There he was given injections and moved out of the battle zone. When he awoke, he was in a hospital near Boulogne.

For his bravery in the action Wavell was mentioned in despatches and was among the first to be awarded the newly created Military Cross.[21] He had come through the ordeal with great honour: the general commanding 3rd Division, Sir Aylmer Haldane, described Wavell as an excellent officer and strongly recommended him for promotion.

Haldane also recorded an incident just before 9th Brigade's attack, which illustrated the outlook of some of the high officers directing the war:

> . . . the Corps Commander, who had three times appeared at my head-quarters, handed over to me the 42nd Infantry Brigade of the Light Division – a unit of the Kitchener Army which had just arrived from home – and ordered me to throw it into the fight and secure what it was evident we had already lost. As the brigade in question would have had to pass over ground littered with dead and wounded, and under the concentrated fire of the enemy's guns, I pointed out that the only possible result must be to augment our already heavy casualties and gain nothing.
>
> He turned on me in the casemate, where I was with my staff, clerks and orderlies, and said in a loud voice: 'What the hell does that matter? There are plenty more men at home.'[22]

The corps commander in question was General Sir Edmund Allenby, whom Wavell was later to revere for his conduct of military affairs in Palestine.

The war was now distorting the pattern of military advancement, and as former high-flyers were killed, wounded or in some other manner eclipsed, hitherto unknown men were rising to the fore. The army hierarchy was in flux, and openings were arising up and down the line. While the war still raged, there could be little thought beyond the short term, but those for whom Wavell worked had not forgotten his merits. He was just thirty-two, and he had reached the point where, should he recover from his wounds and re-enter the orbit of influential soldiers, he had the prospect of making a considerable name for himself.

Before that, there was an interlude in his story: he withdrew from the field and was moved to hospital in England, where the doctors set about trying to save his sight. Almost exactly six months after being shot in the head and just escaping death or total blindness Wavell reported for duty once more, arriving at General Headquarters in France as a GSO2. He had the satisfaction of being back in the war, but he was to find his new posting dreary. GHQ was established at Montreuil, which he found a depressing place – it is nowadays twinned with Slough – and his duties were adminis-trative, even if some of them, in particular the development of Army Battle Schools designed to train new officers and NCOs, were of great importance in the preparations for the impending Battle of the Somme. He was enrolled in a branch called, somewhat cryptically, O(b), under a particularly bright and lively brigadier called Jock Burnett-Stuart, whom Wavell described as having at that time 'probably the best and quickest brain in the Army of his rank'.[23] However, even he found the work rather leaden, and his subordinates were uninspired by the routine, which mainly concerned the organisation of armaments, unit formation and the appointment and training of staff officers.

On the other hand, Wavell had reached Supreme Headquarters. He could observe at close quarters the work at the pinnacle of the military machine as a great battle was being fought some thirty miles away. The experience he gained of the ways of the top of the army hierarchy would help him climb the military ladder during the difficult peacetime years ahead.

Meanwhile, among those who had reached positions of power and patronage, and who had, in however small a way, been impressed by Wavell, was the new Chief of the Imperial General Staff, his former commandant at Camberley, General Sir William Robertson. Even in the great events of war he had not forgotten the young subaltern whom he had sent to Moscow, and in the autumn he summoned Wavell to London.

On reaching the War Office, Wavell was told that he was to go to Russia, and on 19 October 1916 he was appointed a temporary lieutenant colonel, on 'Special Duty with the Russian Army in the Caucasus'. His pre-war experience and his interpreter's qualification in Russian had proved their worth and rewarded him with a vital job, even if he was at first reluctant to move even further from the Western Front. The value of his mission lay in meeting the army's need to have accurate information about Russian troop dispositions, as part of the Allied strategy of attacking the enemy from both east and west.

In view of the importance of the Russians in the alliance against the Central Powers, and of a cross-flow of information between the eastern and western Allied armies, it seems remarkable how few Englishmen had been seconded to Russia: in the Caucasus, for example, where the Russian Army was playing a vital part in containing the Turkish armies, Wavell was the one and only British military representative.

So he set off on a typically roundabout wartime journey to Tiflis,[24] the headquarters of Grand Duke Nikolai Nikolaevitch, commander-in-chief of the Caucasus Army and Viceroy, whom Wavell thought 'the handsomest and most impressive-looking man' he had ever met.[25] The Grand Duke instructed that the English colonel should be given all the information he wanted.

The Russians had achieved considerable success against the Turks, and to be able to know whether they could continue to do so would be of great use to the War Office, because the evidence so far received showed that most of the Turkish troops withdrawn from the Russian front had in due course joined the forces opposing the British further south. Wavell's appreciation of this, and his thoughts on the condition of the Russian Army, would therefore be of great value to the General Staff in London. At first he found it difficult to prise much useful information from the secretive Russians, but he soon realised that the clue lay in noting from which Turkish regiments men were reaching the Russian lines as deserters or prisoners-of-war, and making the assumption that units that suddenly stopped providing such men had been moved away from the Russian front and would therefore in due course reappear in front of the British.

It was rather a lonely winter for Wavell, although in due course it was brightened by the arrival of his wife. She had displayed characteristic persistence in acquiring permits to travel to the Caucasus, and had made her way there with their seven-month-old son. Born the previous May, he had been christened Archibald, but was always subsequently known as 'Archie John'.

Visiting the Asia Minor front in April, Wavell heard that he was being posted to Persia, for further liaison with the Russians, but – wanting to return to the Western Front – he managed to persuade the War Office to change its mind and was instead summoned back to London, which he and his wife reached in June. On reporting to the War Office, he was interviewed by Sir Frederick Maurice, Director of Military Operations, one of his former instructors at the Staff College, and told that he was to be the liaison officer between the Chief of the Imperial General Staff (CIGS) and Sir Edmund Allenby, newly appointed commander of the Egyptian Expeditionary Force, established to oppose the Turkish armies in Palestine. Wavell had been mentioned in despatches for a second time and was now promoted to brevet lieutenant colonel.

Robertson, who had singled out Wavell for his job at the Russian headquarters, was now giving him a pivotal role as man-in-the-middle between the General Staff in London and the army headquarters in Palestine. It was still liaison, but this time at the highest level – between the army's most senior officer and the commander-in-chief of a large army in a theatre of the war that, as a result of stalemate on the Western Front, was steadily gathering importance.

Yet Wavell was not pleased. Even after three years of war he had not been given a senior staff appointment with a division, or a direct command, both of which were generally accepted as essential stepping-stones in a successful military career. On the other hand, considering the number of his contemporaries now in uniform and jostling for position, he had made remarkable progress, and his intelligence and dogged reliability had made favourable impressions, crucially on men wielding great influence in the army. At the end of June 1917 he set out for Cairo to take up his new post.

General Allenby was considered by most of the Imperial General Staff to be an energetic and able soldier, but the commander-in-chief in France, Field-Marshal Haig, disliked him as a man and did not much respect his performance in battle. For a combination of those two reasons Allenby had been selected to command in Palestine, receiving from the Government a simple but comprehensive brief: defend Egypt from external attack or internal disorder, and plan the defeat of the Turks in Palestine.

The military chiefs in London had realised that these projects were important enough to warrant a direct channel of information between the War Office and the Middle East headquarters. To provide it, they needed an officer of the approximate seniority of a major or lieutenant colonel, with a keen intelligence, sound common sense and a good command of military niceties and regulations. In the opinion of Sir William Robertson, which was what counted, these requirements pointed clearly to Lieutenant Colonel A.P. Wavell, MC.

Consequently, on 4 July 1917 Robertson addressed a letter to the commander-in-chief in Egypt:

My dear Allenby,

Lieutenant-Colonel Wavell has been appointed liaison officer between you and me. I do not know if you know him but he is quite a useful man. He is the first liaison officer I have appointed to Egypt, although I have been contemplating having one for some time past, as I have with Salonika. I wish to say, although I hope it is quite unnecessary, that he is in no way a spy. His simple duty is to help you and to help me. It is difficult to convey in telegrams or in letters exactly what one means or to give all the information that is needed. I shall be glad if you will make full use of him and see that he is given the necessary facilities to carry out his work. I think he should be useful to both of us and that is the reason I have appointed him.[26]

Wavell was duly sent off to Egypt, with the goodwill of the CIGS, and with the hope that any suspicion of spying, or resentment at his position, would soon be extinguished. Although initially uncertain as to his reception by Allenby or his staff, he need not have worried: he was immediately made welcome and at once set to work.

Allenby's own arrival in Egypt, a week earlier, had been preceded by his reputation, neatly summarised by his nickname 'The Bull':[27] he was a large man, florid when aroused, and alleged to be a martinet in matters of detail. Wavell was soon to admire him greatly, and was in due course to become his biographer,[28] but conceded that Allenby could make his feelings vigorously plain:

> His manner was often gruff and abrupt; his questions were straight and sharp; and he demanded an immediate direct reply. Any attempt at prevarication, any indefiniteness, even hesitation, might provoke a sudden explosion of anger that could shake the hardiest.[29]

Tales of Allenby had become exaggerated in the telling, and his appearance at his first conference with his General Staff was awaited with a certain foreboding. The meeting was held at the Savoy Hotel, Cairo, not far from army headquarters. Allenby fixed his immediate attention on the proximity of the base to Alexandria's fleshpots, such as the Café de Paris, a miniature of the Moulin Rouge and habitually filled with British uniforms. He thought it might be more profitable to be nearer the combat zone, an opinion that he now shared with his officers:

> Allenby turned to the Major-General commanding the Royal Artillery and said to him:
> 'Do you hear the guns?'
> The officer in question replied: 'No, Sir.'
> Whereupon Allenby repeated again: 'Do you mean to say you can't hear the guns blazing away?'
> With a bewildered look, the officer again repeated: 'No, Sir, I can't hear them.' And Lord Allenby immediately said: 'Don't you think it would be a good thing to move somewhere where we *could* hear the guns?'[30]

Whatever the hapless major-general may have thought about 'The Bull', following this brief discussion, any misgivings harboured by Wavell were soon dispelled. The chief was open and cordial in his welcome, encouraging his staff to take Wavell into their confidence. Within a short time Allenby had written to Robertson in London:

> Wavell is here, and is in touch with all matters. He accompanies me tomorrow to the Palestine front, where we shall spend a few days. I am very glad to have him and I think he will be able, when you see him, to give you a clear picture of the situation here and our state of readiness.[31]

The readiness in question referred to a remarkable plan that Allenby had devised for his forces to capture Jerusalem.

When appointing Allenby, the Prime Minister, Lloyd George, had instructed him to expel the Turks from the Holy City: it would be a Christmas present, he said, for a war-weary populace. So, having carried out a rapid but comprehensive survey of his new domain, the general had devised a master plan. The War Office had told him to ask for whatever was needed to implement it, and Wavell, less than a month after his arrival in Egypt, was sent back to London with the commander's wish list.

Although Allenby's plan was simple in its essence, the detailed case that Wavell was charged with presenting to the CIGS was complex. It involved the creation of two infantry corps, a cavalry corps, five air squadrons, and the provision of equipment including heavy artillery, anti-aircraft guns and aeroplanes. Explaining the requirements was a job that could only be done well by a man with a first-class memory and an intellect sharp enough to understand the reasons behind each of the plan's many components.

The basic idea was to carry out a deception, of the type that was to become dear to Wavell's heart when he later held high command himself. The Turkish Army, at which the ruse was aimed, was drawn up along defences stretching for twenty-six miles from Gaza, near the Mediterranean coast, inland to Beersheba, on a line some forty-five miles south of Jerusalem. Allenby planned to attack both Gaza and Beersheba in a manner that would make the Turks think the main assault was on Gaza, while the engagement at Beersheba was only a raid. The intention was to do just the opposite.

Wavell summarised the plan for the chiefs in London. His précis explained all the complications that were envisaged, and their proposed remedies. He set out the armaments required; the supplies to be provided; the construction of railways, tracks and pipelines; the corps and divisions to be used; the role of the Royal Flying Corps; the use of the navy for dummy landings on the coast; dates and times for the unfolding stages of battle; and estimates of enemy strengths and intentions. He painted a picture that was crystal-clear, although filled with detail, contained in a four-page document.

Wavell was not given a combat role in the battle, but he was to gain a much rarer experience – a first-hand view of the planning and execution of a major campaign in all its aspects. The result was to add greatly to the value with which he was already credited by the staff with whom he worked, and by the superiors whom he served.

On 31 October 1917 the British launched their attack. The deception proved entirely successful, despite fierce fighting around Gaza where the Turks were expecting an assault. Wavell produced a report on the opening of the campaign, and at the end of November the Director of Military Operations in London sent it to the War Cabinet, marked 'Very Secret'. Within a short time the Turkish armies were in full retreat, and the way to Jerusalem lay open. Just after midday on 9 December the mayor surrendered his keys: the British had taken the Holy City in under forty days, bringing to a close the Muslim rule that had begun with the surrender to Saladin 730 years earlier. 'Today,' proclaimed Allenby proudly, 'the wars of the Crusades are completed.' The victors then made a formal entry through the Jaffa gate.

Wavell was among the small band of men invited to join the ceremony. By his side walked T.E. Lawrence, called forward to savour the taste of victory. Writing some years later, Wavell seemed to have lost nothing of the emotion of that moment, his account placing Allenby on a pedestal that some of his fellow-soldiers judged as perhaps an inch or so too high:[32]

> Israelite, Assyrian, Greek, Roman, Jew, Arab, Crusader, Turk had entered Jerusalem as conquerors before the British. None of these nations can have been represented by one more impressive or worthier of his race than was Allenby, physically or morally.[33]

The general himself was presumably less inflated by such noble concepts or the need to purify Jerusalem, as he gave orders for the Ottoman authorities to carry on administering the city, just as they had before.

A few days later Wavell returned to London to present his account of the campaign to the General Staff. What happened next is a further illustration of how he was diverging from the normal path of an officer of his age and seniority, even though the careers of so many were benefiting from the fortunes of war. Robertson told him that he was now to assist, with technical support and information, the British representatives at the Supreme War Council, due to meet at the end of January 1918. Robertson's proposal might have filled most young officers with enthusiasm, but not Wavell, for he felt that it would take him further from the front line than an active soldier should want to be. Nevertheless, he duly complied with his orders and prepared for a briefing by the CIGS.

Opposing views had developed among the Allies as to how to react to the major German offensive that was now generally expected. The CIGS intended to present his opinion in person to the Supreme War Council, but he wanted the support of an intelligent officer with first-hand experience of the campaign in Palestine and who had up-to-date facts at his fingertips. His choice fell on Wavell, who on 8 January 1918 was appointed 'AA & QMG, Supreme War Council, Versailles'.

Having been briefed by the CIGS, Wavell prepared a memorandum for the General Staff. He later summarised the arguments that he put forward:

> We missed our big chance at Gallipoli, i.e. in not crushing Turkey the moment she declared herself. Once that was gone – Bulgaria in against us, Serbia overrun, Russia cut off, Greece on the fence etc. – the war *had* to be settled in the west. Salonika . . . Italy, Palestine and such like were never really possibilities of doing anything big; the war was going to be won or lost in France . . .[34]

However, the military representatives were not impressed by lucid prose from a relatively junior officer. The Prime Minister, supported by Sir Henry Wilson, proved more persuasive an advocate than Robertson and his advisers, and the council ordered an extension of the campaign in the Near East.

With the decision taken, Wavell asked to be relieved of his role amidst the politics of Versailles so as to return to the military arena. This seemingly perverse request puzzled and irritated both the CIGS and Wilson; but Wavell was adamant, determined not to be flattered by his appointment as an adviser to the political leaders and decision-makers at Versailles. Although he had demonstrated a high degree of gallantry and efficiency in the desperate conditions at Ypres, he still felt a moral obligation to fight at the front if he possibly could.

He was taking a risk with his career, as he no longer had a post to fill in the Egyptian Expeditionary Force, and he realised that he would have to take his chance in the pool of supernumerary officers; but he was prepared to do so, sure that Allenby would call on him once more. His confidence was justified: within two months, on 16 April 1918, he was appointed BGGS[35] to XX Corps. After his long period as a liaison officer, albeit at the highest levels, it was a welcome reward.

The corps commander was General Sir Philip Chetwode, Bt, a dapper, aristocratic cavalry officer who, like Wavell himself, was later to become a field-marshal and commander-in-chief in India. He immediately impressed Wavell, who would later describe him as having about the best and quickest military brain that he had ever known.

In May 1918 Wavell arrived at XX Corps, joining a staff of nine; there, as BGGS, he finally achieved what he had long wanted: an active part in developing and executing plans for an offensive campaign. The massive German assault in the west had begun in March, and, along with several other factors, had caused a postponement of Allenby's plans for a new attack on the Turkish positions. It had also meant a major reorganisation of XX Corps. Nearly 60,000 seasoned British troops had to be hurriedly transferred from Palestine and sent back to France as reinforcements. Their place was taken by Indian cavalry from France and by new units arriving from India and Mesopotamia.

Wavell now entered into the complicated work of reorganising XX Corps and training its new formations. It suited him exactly, and he soon displayed an ability to combine an intelligent appreciation of the overall objective of a plan with a mastery of the details of putting it into effect. It was not long before General Chetwode expressed himself fully satisfied with his new brigadier general, who began to make a real mark both as an efficient administrator and as a trainer of troops.

At last the preparations for what was expected to be the final offensive in Palestine were complete. It proved to be an overwhelming triumph. Victory at the Battle of Megiddo was followed by a cavalry chase that was so rapid and decisive that Wavell praised it as 'the greatest success of mobile forces in history'.[36] Despite that comprehensive accolade, it was to be the last such use of cavalry by the British Army, a fitting climax to mounted warfare as the cheering squadrons pursued the Turkish forces fleeing north across the plain of Megiddo – traditionally the site of Armageddon[37] – to Damascus and Aleppo. On 31 October 1918, four years to the day since it had entered the war, the Ottoman Empire abandoned the struggle.

Wavell had learnt much from the campaigns in Palestine, through his role in their planning, and from observing their outcome. He later recorded what

he had seen, characteristically drawing on history to illustrate the difficulties the British had faced, and suggesting lessons for the future:

> The problem really dates back to Biblical times, when the war char-
> iots of the Egyptians, Philistines and Assyrians controlled the issue of
> battles in the plains, but were powerless in the Judaean Hills, a land of
> foot warfare . . .
>
> To sum up, the campaigns show the great power which cavalry exer-
> cised by their mobility. How much more formidable, then, will be the
> power exercised by a mechanical force, with its much heavier weight
> of fire, its larger range and higher speed, and furnished, as it would
> be, with the protective armour which cavalry were for all practical
> purposes forced to discard four hundred years ago.[38]

Wavell was thirty-one when the war began. Despite active service in South
Africa and on India's wild frontier, he still retained, even by 1914 when he
was seconded to the War Office, something of the keen and obedient youth,
rather like, in a civilian business, a promising young man taken up by the
directors as a personal assistant. Nor had marriage and fatherhood given him
the quickened maturity that usually comes in their wake, because for much
of the war he had been far away from his family.

In Flanders' fields he had aged quickly, both physically and spiritually, as
befell all who spent time in the trenches. On the other hand, at his post in
Russia and as liaison officer in the Egyptian Expeditionary Force, he had
reverted to roles that by their nature imposed a certain deference to the age
and importance of the men whom he served. Perhaps it was during his time
as BGGS with General Chetwode, when he played a significant part in planning a major campaign under considerable pressure, that he finally shed the
remaining traces of youth.

His wartime career had been remarkably varied and he had acquired
considerable insight into soldiering at the highest levels. He emerged from
the war a brigadier general, older and more rugged in appearance, and
seeming altogether different from the young captain of four years earlier.
Yet the fertile mind and the pleasures and interests of the intellectual youth
had not been irretrievably battered by war, and were soon to be revived.
They were to be of considerable help in the next stages of Wavell's career.

V

REPUTATIONS

ON 11 November 1918, the day the Great War ended, the British commander-in-chief, Sir Douglas Haig, entered in his diary the single word 'Rain'. From almost everyone else, with the possible exception of those with lucrative government armaments contracts, the end of four years of bloodshed, pain and grief inspired more expansive comment. For a short time there was an economic boom fuelled in part by war gratuities for soldiers returning from the front. It did not, however, continue amid the devastation of war, and soon gave way to stagnant trade and rapidly rising unemployment.

For many of the men awaiting demobilisation, the country's economic plight raised the previously unthinkable question of whether they should actually stay on in the army, at least for a time, even though the huge majority were heartily sick of the sight of khaki. That question was itself affected by the deteriorating prospects, for all ranks, of a military career in an army the size of which was likely to be much reduced by a government forced to make savings, and conscious of a mood of apathy towards the services among a public seared by the death of so many men.

At the end of 1918 there had been some three and three-quarter million men in the army, about fifteen times as many as immediately before the war. Although the war had left so many men dead, or crippled – mentally, physically or both – there was still a glut of khaki, and limited prospects of promotion. Whether or not to stay in the army was a question relevant even to successful professional soldiers like Wavell, although he, a brigadier general at only thirty-five, could certainly be satisfied with his career so far. Yet the advent of peace and a much smaller army might mean, even in his case, an actual reduction in rank and pay, perhaps for some considerable time.

The fact that he had not had an active command in battle was also a worry for him. Even his important work at a senior level for some of the army's highest commanders might not count for much in an institution as rule-bound as the post-war army, especially if the influence of his patrons were to fade – for he was not well known beyond their circle.

With his fertile, eclectic and enquiring mind, Wavell could reasonably have addressed the possibilities of switching to a civilian career; but had he done so, he would have had to balance – against the success that he had so far made of a soldier's life – his lack of experience or practical knowledge of any profession other than the army. In any case, such considerations would probably have evaporated at his father's front door, as it would have been wholly out of character for Wavell to dispute the matter with the old general, for whom anything other than a soldier son would have been unthinkable.

Untroubled by such ideas, Wavell's parents maintained their peaceful existence at Cranborne Lodge, rejoined by Nancy and Molly, back from war service. Wavell, his wife and the infant Archie John had moved into a house just off Eaton Square, in an attractive part of central London, and a second child, Eugénie Pamela, was born in December 1918.[1]

Before long, he received orders to return to the Egyptian Expeditionary Force headquarters at Heliopolis, where a senior appointment was found for him. On 1 March 1919 he resumed his position as brigadier general, General Staff, of XX Corps, but now there was no major fighting or training men for battle, but instead the work of policing the sullen, volatile and mostly anti-British populations of Egypt and Palestine.

There followed, together with Wavell's resumption of the rank of colonel, a series of appointments and courses, all of relatively short duration, in Egypt, Germany and England, including a return to the Black Watch after an absence from regimental soldiering of more than ten years.

After eighteen months of unsettled life, Wavell was appointed GSO1 under his former boss Jock Burnett-Stuart, now Director of Military Operations and Intelligence. This new job was enlivened by various excursions, including an official tour to Canada and America, and a brief spell as a representative at the Geneva Disarmament Conference. He also became involved in various controversies about the wide strategic responsibilities involved in imperial defence. One of these concerned the establishment of a major base at Singapore, of great strategic importance. Wavell was appointed to the committee deciding the form of defence that should be established in the Far East theatre, and became thoroughly versed in all its implications.

That committee's conclusions were to prove appallingly misconceived. As Wavell later described it:

> In the end, big guns were installed at great cost, and never fired an effective round in the defence of Singapore; while the Air Force which might have saved Singapore by attack on the Japanese transports was not there at the right time, because it had to be elsewhere. So I suppose both sides had some justification for their views. The matter of the defence of the island against attack from the north never arose so far as I remember; the task of the committee was only to plan against seaward attack.[2]

At the end of 1925 Wavell's appointment expired and he went on the 'half-pay' list, a discouraging system that persisted until 1939. In practice it meant even less than its description – 'colonels were four a penny,' as Wavell put it – and he had to look to his laurels to maintain himself, a wife and (by now) four[3] children in the style to which they had become accustomed. The immediate material prospects were discomfiting, but having sold the lease on the Belgravia house, they all moved down to Dorset; Wavell's parents were glad to have the family with them, and for a few months all seemed well.

However, in June 1926 Lillie Wavell died, after forty-six years of marriage. Wavell himself spoke curiously little of his mother, at least outside the family, and in his public records and writings he hardly acknowledged her existence – when he wrote to the family, it was usually to his father or sisters. A distant relationship with a mother is not common, and always has its effects, one way or another, on a son's development. But in a formal and hierarchical upbringing such as Wavell's, perhaps a lack of warm maternal affection ceased after the earliest years to have too much consequence.

For his future career, the expiry of his appointment at the War Office had a silver lining. Two aspects of his innate ability were about to work strongly in his favour and accelerate his progress in the next few years – a period of great difficulty for army officers, or at least for those who were not rich – enabling him to emerge at length at the front of the pack.

The first followed the departure of Burnett-Stuart, who had formed a high opinion of Wavell, from the War Office to assume command of a division of particular significance in the context of the army's future development. The second was that Wavell turned his intelligence and imagination to writing. In a decade when the army was static and resistant to change, anyone who combined brains with technical knowledge of the state of Britain's defences, and who could explain his thoughts lucidly, could do the country a considerable service and might simultaneously advance his own career. Wavell now began to perform this service, sporadically at first, but more regularly as his reputation grew and brought him the influence that came with promotion.

First he had to clarify his ideas and find a vehicle for expressing them. At the War Office before 1914, and especially in his various wartime posts, Wavell had produced several succinct memoranda and lucid orders, and with the advent of peace he had for the first time been called upon to deliver lectures to adult audiences. His skill in doing so, and his capacity for original thought, now attracted to his ideas the attention of influential people.

While Wavell was at the War Office he had come to the notice of Captain Basil Liddell Hart, then military correspondent of the *Daily Telegraph*, and also military adviser to the *Encyclopaedia Britannica*, a much-respected and popular compilation of articles covering wide fields of knowledge. Liddell Hart's many publications had a considerable following in America and in Europe, and he had begun to carve out a niche as an agent for change in the British Army. He was soon to play an important role in raising Wavell's profile. His first request was for an article on the Palestine Campaigns, believing that Wavell was well informed on the matter and more able than most soldiers to produce a sensible account. Liddell Hart realised at once that here was a man who could write well and intelligently, even by the high standards which he considered graced his own output. Wavell's article appeared in a new supplement to the *Encyclopaedia* in 1927.

True to his inclinations, Wavell broadened his account beyond the military facts that had sufficed for his lectures and for a related contribution to the *Army Quarterly*,[4] and gracefully painted the story into its historical setting. For Liddell Hart it was a promising start, and was to be the first of a series of articles that Wavell would write for the *Encyclopaedia*. As Liddell Hart commented, it contained all that it should, combining 'literary style with clearness and simplicity, perfectly easy to follow and yet of value to military as well as general readers'.[5]

The attractions of writing now began to grow on Wavell, and he extended his output to book reviews, both for the *Army Quarterly* and similar service magazines, and for the esteemed *Times Literary Supplement*. His early productions suffered a little from the heavy dragoon interpretation of humour, but were refreshingly different from most of the competition, and reflected their author's deep learning. Although adhering to the standard format of a service magazine ('With Map'), his approach was more imaginative than the average contributor's. In a typical example he juxtaposed his experiences in the Palestine campaign with a similar incident in far-away biblical times, but, with an eye on the likely readership, attempted a jocular explanatory heading:

'*Night attacks are not by any to be enterprised nor taken in hand, unadvisedly, lightly or wantonly, like young subalterns that have no understanding, but reverently, discreetly, advisedly, soberly; duly considering the causes for which Night Attacks were ordained*' – (From the unpublished maxims of General Sir Hercules Cromwellington, KCB)

All that we know of Gideon, son of Joash, warrior and statesman, is contained in three chapters of the Bible . . . with the possible exception of Joshua, he was the best general and shrewdest head of the state that Israel ever brought forth.[6]

Wavell's lectures and articles were constructed for stolid fellow-soldiers, yet he could rarely stop a perceptive sense of humour from piercing the leaden surface. He was amused to discover, for example, how:

That unhumorous race, the Germans, held an investigation after the late war into the causes of morale, and attributed much of the British soldier's staying power to his sense of humour. They therefore decided to instil this sense into their own soldiers, and included in their manual an order to cultivate it.

They gave as an illustration in the manual one of Bairnsfather's pictures of 'Old Bill', sitting in a building with an enormous shell-hole in the wall. A new chum asks: 'What made that hole?' 'Mice', replies 'Old Bill'.

In the German manual a solemn footnote of explanation is added: 'It was not mice, it was a shell.'[7]

Meanwhile great changes were altering the military landscape, and they were to accelerate Wavell's progress. Even a decade after the end of the Great War the scars of battle remained deep in the nation's mind, and the feeling that another such war must never occur was the paramount influence on the policies of successive governments. Yet among soldiers and politicians alike there was a growing body of opinion that, as the goal of international disarmament seemed unattainable, the army must be maintained in a proper state of readiness, utilising for that purpose the latest scientific developments.

In August 1926 Burnett-Stuart was placed in command of 3rd Division, in Southern Command, and told that a new experimental force was to be formed. Three months later, in need of intelligent support in the new venture, he sent for Wavell, who was appointed GSO1, or chief general staff officer, to his division. Wavell was delighted to come off the half-pay list, to serve under a man he particularly liked, and to move to the one area of the army where radical views were being discussed and, he hoped, firm plans made.

At first all seemed well. In March 1927 the Government announced that 'Arrangements have been made to assemble an experimental mechanised force, composed entirely of mechanised units.' Although the basic object of mechanisation was to render the army more efficient without increased cost, vested interests in the War Office soon created difficulties, with the result that although announcements about the proposed new force were made in Parliament, no actual steps were taken to put the force together. This discovery led to a series of rows, involving the Secretary of State, the CIGS and Burnett-Stuart, each seeking the correct head – other than their own – on which to lay the blame for misleading Parliament, and the apparent discrepancy between official words (plentiful) and deeds (scarce) about the experimental development was soon exposed in the press.

As yet uninvolved in these testy military politics, Wavell's life now entered a particularly happy phase, with probably a greater semblance of normality than he had enjoyed for many years. In his work, he was full of ideas and enthusiasm for new concepts of mobile warfare – or, as he put it, describing the tank as a reincarnation of Gothic horsemen – a return to the earlier forms of mobile war that were extinguished in the trenches.

Partly because of the leaden ideas of his senior officers, it soon fell to Wavell to do the lion's share of creating and arranging schemes and training exercises for the new force. His commanding officer, Colonel Jack Collins, appeared totally bemused by the new experiments, unable to respond to the beckoning visions of fast-moving mobile forces in a new type of army, even if he saw them. Instead, he busied himself with statistics; as Wavell said: 'Jack worked like a beaver, produced masses of paper and statistics, worked out the amount of petrol required for the force per mile to several places of decimals, and the amount of parking-space to the yard . . .'[8]

In not much over a decade, contemporaries of men like Collins in the

German Army would be driving their tanks across Europe, largely untroubled by the amount of parking-space; but at least in some quarters, new ideas and training had begun to receive support.

Meanwhile Wavell continued to nourish his interest in literature and his own creative urge. On the foundation of the Kipling Society in 1927 he became a life member. In the same year he was invited to contribute more articles to the *Encyclopaedia Britannica* by Liddell Hart, who had been appointed editor of the military and military-history departments of the publication. Wavell's work for that edition included revising other authors' work, on Waterloo and the Seven Weeks' War, and several articles of his own on battles in the Russian campaigns in the Great War. As Liddell Hart said, Wavell made the stories readable for soldier and civilian alike: from a mass of detail, he set out clear pictures of the topography of the fighting, the forces involved, the progress of the battles and their results, with a nod to historical precedents and great captains of the past. He also contributed part of a major article on the army, along with the French military supremo, Ferdinand Foch. Wavell's part concentrated on the years 1870 to 1914, and was full of important facts, leavened by arcane titbits. The bibliography certainly proved the author's erudition: it contained more than sixty works, mainly from the nineteenth century, many of several volumes, in French and German as well as English, and from authors ancient and modern – from Xenophon, Caesar and Plutarch to Carlyle and Clausewitz. It was a good way for him to attract interest to his ideas, which were gradually reaching army circles wider than those immediately around him. Although he was no longer on the half-pay list, the money may also have been welcome: overall he earned from his encyclopaedia articles about £3,200 in today's money.

Encouraged by Liddell Hart, Wavell also expanded his original article on Palestine into a book, which was published in 1928.[9] He was typically circumspect about its success: 'Personally,' he said, 'I think the book is adequate for the series for which it was written, but I don't believe that it would have the least interest for the general public.'[10]

He had a wide range of work as 3rd Division's senior staff officer, but his paramount concern was the experimental force – renamed, perhaps as a gesture of hope, the 'Experimental Armoured Force'; Wavell's job was to cherish it and nurture it with a blend of original theory and efficient practice. 'I like the Plain and this job very much,' he wrote to T.E. Lawrence, then in India, 'I'm still G to the 3rd Division. The Mechanised Force helps us a bit out of the rut of ordinary peace soldiering. We ought to have an interesting time of it this year, it's a formidable weapon of war.'[11]

The initial exercises of the 'formidable weapon of war' illustrated the magnitude of the task of converting new ideas into workable practice. Basic but vital questions soon arose, such as how to use, in a co-ordinated attack, infantry, cavalry and several mechanised units, each moving at different and varying speeds. However, as the commanding officer appeared to be apathetic about even his own ideas, he received those from others with a marked lack of vigour; Wavell's contributions were to an extent hobbled, although a man more extrovert and willing to challenge authority might have stirred things up to a greater degree.

Conventional infantry or cavalry habits would not suffice. On the very first major exercise the force repeatedly got itself comprehensively jammed as 'the serpentine column, which wound its length in coils over a distance of some thirty-two miles, suffered bombing and machine-gun attack from the air, when checked by road blocks'.[12] On that occasion the troops were troubled only by umpires, blanks and a curious public lining the roads – perhaps one reason why the lessons were not studied more deeply. But it would not be too long before exactly the same thing happened in graver circumstances, with Stuka dive-bombers, German tanks and machine-gun troops bearing down at high speed on columns retreating along roads crowded with refugees.

The great experiment did not sweep all before it, mainly because the force was not used as a separate arm moving at speeds far above that of the foot soldier. In the press, Liddell Hart exposed what such a force might achieve, if given its head:

> If the enemy like to sit in positions, let them, while the Armoured Force interrupts their supplies or transfers its fire-power to fresh points . . . Once that happens a moral rot is likely to set in among the hungry and helpless occupants of ineffective positions. And the Armoured Force might achieve the ideal which was the ambition of Marshal Saxe, that connoisseur of the art of war, when he argued that a really able general might win a campaign without fighting a battle at all.[13]

To which the Germans came fairly close, when they met the French in 1940.

At the end of the 1928 training season the experimental force was disbanded, with the promise of the formation of two new groups of mechanical units – not distinct, but as an armoured reinforcement of infantry

73

divisions. The growing band of believers in armour were dismayed by this 'jam tomorrow', which they regarded as a futile approach that had been tried in the Great War.

Wavell was unperturbed. Devising and planning the first practical attempts to deploy an independent mobile force had advanced his understanding of its problems. At the same time it had brought him to the attention of others in the army who had begun to think along similar lines. Just as a broad river was soon to flow between the military ideas of a renascent Germany and those of its former conquerors, so a gulf deepened between the old guard at all levels in the British Army and the bright and energetic new thinkers, among whom Wavell was moving to the fore. His natural inclination to deference, and what he himself admitted was a certain laziness, would prevent him from going out too much on a limb, but in the rather hidebound peacetime army that was to work to his advantage. When the Staff College Conference discussed the lessons of the armoured force, Wavell was invited to address the hall, which was filled with many of the army's most senior ranks. With a few concise and powerful points, helped by memorable analogies, he caught their close attention – it was the moral effect of an armoured force that was decisive, he said, and that depended on mobility rather than armour or fire-power.

It was not Wavell's habit to be ruffled by difficulties with his work, especially as most of them arose from the refreshing atmosphere of innovation, and it was equally in his nature to relax when there was nothing essential to be done. He took all the leave he could, and made the most of the country surroundings in which the family had temporarily come to rest. His appointment to the 3rd Division carried with it the use of an attractive house in a village on Salisbury Plain, and there he and his wife settled with the children and nanny; the girls were now aged eight, seven and four, and Archie John was eleven, following in his father's footsteps at Summer Fields and shortly to proceed to Winchester.

At this stage they were a conventional happy army family, with gardener in the garden, wife picking flowers, cook in the kitchen, groom in the stables, ponies in the paddock, rows of riding kit and leather boots in the saddle-room, and general clutter and children's detritus filling odd corners. Wavell wrote a happy description of their home:

Our house on Salisbury Plain was the first, the smallest and the happiest of our official residences. It was a little farmhouse in the Avon valley,

with no pretension to distinction or beauty, but pleasant and comfortable like a buxom country lass. It had one good, walled garden, a paddock
for our horses and the children's ponies, and a tennis court. When we
had induced the engineers to add a saddle-room . . . we had almost all
that a growing family could require . . . The Plain was at our door, the
Royal Artillery Harriers sometimes met at our house, I could canter
across the Plain to my office in twenty minutes. It usually took longer
than that, through the divergencies of the hound puppies who accompanied me, and my first ten minutes or so at the office were often
devoted to organising search parties for the missing . . .

The farm buildings, if not within a literal stone's throw, were within a
moderate brassey shot of the house; so that we and the farmer, an inar-
ticulate but kind-hearted person, soon came into contact. After certain
mutual adjustments, as between children, hound puppies, and ponies on
our side, and cows, hens and hayfields on his, we became good friends.[14]

Army life is a series of punctuation marks, with movement orders arriving
at frequent, if not regular, intervals, and in June 1930 the family's relatively
rustic existence came to an end. Wavell received recognition for his pioneering
efforts with the Experimental Armoured Force and was promoted to brigadier,
in command of an infantry brigade at Aldershot. So they all upped sticks
and moved to a villa at Blackdown: 'from village maiden to stockbroker's
wife', as Wavell described it:

The new residence was reasonably comfortable; we could slip on horses
and ponies, every morning, through the garden into open riding country.
I believe the daughters occasionally did so of a summer's night, making
their exit to the paddock by balcony roof and coal-shed . . . But it had
no character and no charm. Instead of a ride of five or six miles in the
morning, I was within walking distance of my office; it would have
been madness to walk hound puppies with main roads so near; we had,
in modern official parlance, been 'deruralised' and 'suburbanised'.[15]

Although his domestic life was transposed to a less attractive setting, it
was a moment of great importance in his military career: Wavell had achieved
his first independent command.
Soon he began to demonstrate foresight and imagination as well as the

efficiency and intelligence that had led to his appointment, and, because he was dealing with a military experiment that was attracting wide attention, he gained further recognition beyond his immediate circle, not least via Liddell Hart, who was gradually increasing his contacts and influence both in the army and among politicians. However, from being a good staff officer and adviser to taking command was a quantum leap. Wavell was forty-seven, and had spent so many years 'on the staff' that he knew there were some above him who wondered if he could make the grade as a commander. He also had doubts himself:

> I started without much confidence in my capacity for command, and was not sure that I could make a success of it. I soon found to my relief that I could make up my mind and act quickly in handling my brigade, and could give them orders without hesitation, not only in the field but in the various administrative problems.[16]

With the Western world mired in economic slump, there was not a great deal of work that could be done by an army starved of funds. Although Aldershot was near the centre of the military world, and home to two divisions, in the early 1930s it was also in the grip of retrenchment:

> The barracks of corrugated iron were icy cold in winter, and so many men were serving overseas that no more than 500 were present at any one time: in practice four men and two ropes equalled one platoon. Equipment was minimal and the atmosphere was one of farce. The few Austin Sevens were driven by majors in spurs, and so unable to accelerate uphill . . . usually flags stood in for weapons.[17]

Wavell was nevertheless determined to make the most of two openings: he found increasing opportunity to develop his theories, by writing and lecturing, and to express his ideas in practice by arranging memorable and valuable army exercises, at a time when, for the troops at home in peacetime, exercises were the only chance of practising skills in anything remotely like war conditions.

Soon after his arrival at Blackdown he sent to the respected military journal of the Royal United Services Institute an article entitled 'The Army and the Prophets'. Word had it that Wavell had submitted the piece four years earlier for an essay competition set by the *Army Quarterly*, but the judges – speaking volumes for the military establishment – had turned it down as being 'too advanced and visionary for practical purposes'. The prophets to whom he was referring included three prolific military writers: Liddell Hart, Colonel J.C.C. Fuller, a deep thinker with an independent streak, and Hans von Seeckt, founder of the new German Army. By 1930 these authors had published considerably more than had been the case when Wavell first composed his article, so he now updated it for publication. He did not express his own opinions, but presented a lucid synopsis of avant-garde military thought. The article was also far-sighted. In particular he referred to the inevitability, in future wars, of industry and the civilian population being, in effect, closely involved from the start. He also discussed the widespread use of aeroplanes, and the development of small, highly mobile mechanised forces – using tanks as the principal fighting arm, with infantry and other arms as auxiliaries. The opposite, in fact, to the days of 1918.

He was given much credit for his summary of current ideas, and it added to his growing stature within the army. At this stage of his career Wavell's articles did not have a wide circulation, but they were read by the people who counted.

He now came further to the fore as a trainer of troops, arranging several brigade exercises that were praised not only for their military value, but also for the radical and rather light-hearted way in which they were conceived. Wavell had a shrewd understanding of good training methods: he wanted to encourage his men to think about what they were doing and to take an interest in it – at a time when many soldiers, despite having joined the army voluntarily, were bored by their work.

It was an entirely new approach. Wavell shared a view that would be axiomatic among Allied military leaders in the Second World War: that it was no longer possible to make the demands of troops that had formerly been commonplace. In its way stood the army's old command–control theory, whereby the 'master plan' must be adhered to unwaveringly, a concept dating in essence from the Peninsular War some 120 years earlier; it was very different from the system that was evolving in the German Army, based on the idea of *Auftragstaktik*, or Mission Command, whereby senior commanders issued general directives to subordinates who were given latitude in interpreting them, so that even the most junior soldiers were trained in the duties of ranks two or three levels above them.[18] Which of the two was the better system became apparent in the Battle of France in 1940, when 'eight or nine divisions, each of about four hundred armoured vehicles of different kinds, but carefully assorted to be complementary and divisible into small self-contained units, cut off all communications between us and the main French Armies'.[19] In North Africa in 1941 the British armies faced with the new German methods responded with a mixture of 'vagueness, Utopianism and quiet despair'.

In planning his brigade exercises, Wavell received considerable help from his brigade major, Eric Dorman-Smith. 'Chink', as he was known, was another military intellectual, believed to have been the only man to have received full marks (1000/1000) in his Staff College exams, being awarded them by the equally intelligent Colonel 'Boney' Fuller. Chink was a mercurial figure, to that extent a fitting counterpoint to Wavell, but his rushing flow of ideas included the inspired and the absurd, and needed careful filtering. Nor was he universally popular, not least for having unwisely remarked that he divided army officers into two types: 'those who were bone from the neck up, and those who were solid bone' – the sort of comment that people tend not to forget.

For Wavell, at 6th Infantry Brigade, Dorman-Smith was a successful staff officer, besides offering welcome hospitality, when leave could be snatched, on his estate in Ireland. Wavell's wife neither liked Chink nor approved of his dealings with women, and declined to accompany her husband on these trips; but for Wavell the occasional excursion to struggle, clad in old tweed clothes, through peat-bogs in search of snipe was just the sort of thing he liked:

> . . . they would pick a ruined cottage, make a fire from sticks, and cook potatoes in an iron pot. After dark they read by oil-lamps beside the library fire in silence, whiskey and soda to hand. 'They are just two men who like each other', noted Dorman-Smith's wife, 'very close.'[20]

In his training exercises Wavell aimed to present his troops with realistic situations, and tried to accustom them to the breakdown and confusion he believed they would meet in war. To do that he needed to capture their imagination, so he sought to enliven his brigade exercises by basing them on historical precedents or topical stories. One exercise drew on the Fashoda Incident of 1898, and another on Rider Haggard's *King Solomon's Mines*, which at least the officers had probably glanced at as children. Another was jocularly presented as a theatrical production – *A Stirring Drama of Love and War, in Four Acts, entitled Araminta of Antelopia, or the Non-Stop Princess*

– billed as being by the 'Blackdown and Deepcut Strollers', featuring Wavell as the director and Dorman-Smith as the producer. His exercises were certainly remembered for their 'novelty', by officers and men alike.

The training was altogether on a higher level than had been usual. Wavell introduced extras such as guerrillas, deception, aeroplane attacks, last-minute alterations, and as many ingredients as possible of the muddle of real war – 'far worse than anything that can be produced in peace,' he would say. He began regularly to outwit his opponents and win his 'battles', but he was characteristically mute about his successes – describing the dramatic four days of the *Araminta* exercise, for example, as 'quite interesting training, and I think amused the troops'. His ideas were becoming increasingly respected but, inevitably, not every exercise went without a hitch. On one occasion there was what in military parlance is called a 'complete Horlicks', at the end of which one of the participating company commanders called on Wavell to express a strong complaint and later recorded:

A bad day. All orders had gone awry. I went to see Brigade in the evening and said so to Archie Wavell. He replied, 'Have a glass of port', and insisted on me having two more as other people arrived. I felt much better afterwards, and said so.[21]

It was good man management, even if it did not quite answer the major's complaints. Wavell himself was not always enthralled by the day's work, or by the company of soldiers, and would sometimes slip out of a gathering. The wife of one of his officers recalled how he and his directing staff were having lunch at her house during an exercise, and while she was in the kitchen the brigadier came in and sat down: 'I hope you don't mind if I come and talk to you,' he said, 'I'm so bored with that lot; I'll help you lay the table.'[22]

His skill as a trainer led increasingly to his being asked to teach and lecture, often by the Staff College. He did not suppress his unorthodox streak, writing to Liddell Hart: 'I have again been detailed to lecture and set a paper to Staff College students in this Command on Military History and the principles of war . . . Military History is not a subject that should ever form part of an examination.'

One lecture brought Wavell widespread attention: in December 1932 he addressed the Staff College students on 'The Training of the Army for War', and two months later spoke on the same subject in London, this time to an audience containing many senior officers. His address is particularly interesting because, as well as being a guide to his outlook on the army, it illustrates his broader perspective. It left a clear impression on his fellow-officers, especially those senior to him, about where his ideas were leading, and it started people thinking about the possibilities for his further promotion. He was now touching fifty: either he was reaching, or as some thought passing, his peak, or he was preparing to advance to the highest levels in the army.

His London speech dealt with the training of infantry: the backbone of the army, as he put it, and the most difficult to train. It was a comprehensive lecture, touching on all the standard aspects of the physical and mental preparation of a brigade for battle – discipline, fitness, weapons training, and so on – but also questioning long-held creeds dear to the army establishment, such as the value of close-order drill. Wavell presented a swathe of radical ideas, of which few others in the room would have thought, such as establishing an Intelligence Directorate to study the psychology of British citizens; bringing the army into closer relations with civil life; 'man management' of soldiers; how most profitably to spend spare time; and encouraging flying as a sport 'to develop the qualities we require – resource, nerve, quick decision and an eye for country'.

Despite his halting delivery, it was an extremely well-ordered and wide-ranging view of the methods and purposes of training an army, but it also clearly expressed a modern approach, almost suggesting a wish for a 'People's Army', certainly for an army with a democratic core based on understanding and co-operation. The spirit he conjured up was one that would turn out to reflect the attitudes of conscripts in the Second World War, in sharp contrast to the professional attitudes of its predecessor.[23] What he said that day demonstrated a strong liberal strand in his make-up. He was far from being what today would be described as 'Thatcherite', but a man of the centre, both emotionally and politically, taking an avant-garde attitude to 'man management', and arguing for the need to explain why action should be taken, in place of the traditional approach of inculcating strict discipline, issuing orders and discouraging original thought.

This was on all fours with the spirit of his education, and reflected 1930s public opinion, which had reacted against both the carnage of the Great War and the social order that had permitted it to happen – a sea-change in attitudes that would be reinforced after the Second World War and would lead, among so many other changes, to the fall of the British Empire.

The lecture won acclaim in many quarters, but also isolated Wavell from the reactionary senior officers who filled most of the top ranks and positions of power at the War Office. A typical representative of such men, Lieutenant General Sir Harry Knox, then Director of Military Training, expressed indignant dissent from Wavell's argument, fixing first on Wavell's opinions on drill:

> ... We cannot allow the pendulum to swing too far. It is necessary to go slowly in this matter; to put ourselves in the position of the men; to consider what we are trying to make of them; and to remember that drill is a foundation for other forms of training.
>
> With regard to a text-book on psychology – God forbid we should have another book! Every regimental officer, if he is worth anything at all, has worked with men, and if he has not learnt after a year or two how to manage men he never will learn. I do not believe a book will be the slightest use . . .[24]

It was an interesting collision of attitudes, even if only in the peaceful arena of a lecture theatre. Wavell did not share the outlook or temperament of men like Knox, who exhibited what General Sir Ernest Swinton, one of the pioneers of tank development in the Great War, described as the army's tendency to 'mental crystallisation and blind adherence to tradition'.

A paramount obstacle to the change in atmosphere that Wavell sought was simple inertia. It was a product both of financial restraint and of the fact that the ranks were filled with men who had fought in the First World War and who, although they were soldiers, consequently desired peace. Government reluctance to provide funds to re-equip the army with new weaponry was also a discouragement. It was difficult to inspire soldiers by training them with flags and ropes, as frequently happened throughout the 1920s. Yet they had to be ready to fight: since the Armistice, not a single year had passed without British troops being called upon to fight somewhere in the Empire.

Wavell was beating a new and invigorating path. Yet it was also in his nature and desire to be helpful and conciliatory; for much of his army career that would be to his benefit, although it was not to help him in some of the momentous times ahead, when he was to serve politicians who did not consider a conciliatory attitude to be appropriate to the hour. At his 'Army Training' lecture in London those of his audience who had been relishing his invigorating approach were dismayed when, instead of holding his ground and developing his line, he appeared to abandon his stance. Having listened to the angry general, he replied simply: 'General Knox's knowledge and experience are, of course, far greater and far wider than mine, and if there is any point on which he and I differ he is much more likely to be right.'[25]

That might have been no more than a polite deflection of a small point, or, as so often with Wavell, a case of simply listening without responding; it also would have been out of character had he intended sarcasm. But at the time it seemed a significant and regrettable climb-down by someone who had appeared to be opening up a refreshing new approach. It reinforced the feeling, in Liddell Hart's words, that Wavell was 'inclined to defer to senior rank'. His brigade major had also noted a 'curious oscillation between originality and orthodoxy' in Wavell's make-up, suggesting only that 'a mind steeped in the Classics might be more ready than most to accept fate'.[26]

His performance as brigade commander, his lectures and his articles, however new or controversial, brought him in October 1933 promotion to major-general. The success with which he was now making his name was reflected in his Confidential Report on leaving his command. Written by his divisional commander and endorsed by the corps commander, Sir Charles Harington, it set out a long list of appointments for which he considered Wavell to be suited, and advised that he needed only more experience to become qualified for the highest appointments in the army.

Nothing was immediately available. Once again he went on the half-pay list, handing over his command in January 1934 and taking a house in Camberley, and later in the year a place in London as well, no doubt to the satisfaction of his wife and children. With time on his hands he reverted to cerebral matters, such as book reviews and setting and correcting Staff College papers – which he would take with him even on holiday. He had also been asked to rewrite two volumes of the army's Bible, *Field Service Regulations*. The invitation, bestowed by the War Office, was a great honour, but it presaged time-consuming work. While engaged on it he maintained his correspondence with Liddell Hart, whose star remained in the ascendant and who at the end of 1934 moved from the *Daily Telegraph* to become military correspondent of *The Times*, at the beginning of a period when the newspaper drew close to the Government and exerted an increasingly baleful influence on people's attitudes towards Hitler and Mussolini.

Wavell's redraft of the *FSR* emphasised the principles that he applied in his training, particularly surprise and mobility, two elements that were soon to bring him his moment of glory in the African desert. It was more pungent and readable than the previous version, and Wavell illustrated it with everyday analogies, combining an ability to write well with technical mastery of his subject. However, he was not surprised that much of what he wrote was altered by the leaden hand of the War Office.

Liddell Hart, who planned to discuss the new *FSR* in *The Times*, told Wavell that his ideas were 'a vast improvement on our past doctrine, and form a landmark in our military manuals. My chief criticism is that they don't always go far enough along the new road . . .' and questioned whether they would exert their full weight on people who had grown up in the old ways.

Wavell remained eager for intellectual sustenance; seeking relief from soldiers and soldiering, he found satisfaction in corresponding with T.E. Lawrence. In the past they had discussed the Arab Revolt in the Great War, and had exchanged letters about Lawrence's account of it in his *Seven Pillars of Wisdom*. In March 1934 Wavell combined his interest in both Liddell Hart and Lawrence by reviewing Liddell Hart's book *T.E. Lawrence in Arabia and After* for *The Listener*. The review was typical Wavell, combining an intellectual vision of its subject with a foray into Shakespearean analogy. Noting the problem of Lawrence's character, he wrote:

> Part of the explanation seems to be that he was, as he himself has said, most unwillingly a man of action. Like a Hamlet who has promptly and efficiently despatched his uncle at the beginning of Act II, he has spent the later years in repentant abdication, in writing an explanation to Horatio, and finally in retirement to a monastery . . . Lawrence's genius may be perverse, and may often be cloaked by an impish humour, but it has the unmistakable stamp of real greatness, of greatness purged of all self-seeking.[27]

During Allenby's campaigns Wavell had been greatly impressed by the use of deception and unorthodox operations. He returned to the subject in his book on the Palestine campaign. Discussing the last great offensive, in the summer of 1918, Wavell cited the fact that only 17,000 front-line combat troops were employed west of the River Jordan, facing the British, while 14,000 Turkish soldiers were in Syria and on the Hijaz railway, a further 8,000 were garrisoning the holy city of Medina, with another 3,000 in reserve nearby – all tied down by the fear of surprise attacks. 'Armies are like plants,' Lawrence had written, 'immobile as a whole, firm-rooted, nourished through long stems to the head. We might be a vapour, blowing where we listed . . .'[28]

Besides his seminal *Seven Pillars*, Lawrence had written what was probably the first treatise on the theory of guerrilla warfare.[29] Wavell was a ready listener, and it seems that Lawrence's writings and wartime career significantly influenced Wavell, who was to champion deceptive operations in the Second World War.

The two men often met at Wavell's house in the country, and Wavell subsequently posed a question that he might well have applied to himself:

How should he be judged in the end, this unwilling leader of a great adventure, this over-fastidious writer of one of the greatest masterpieces of the language, this cunning craftsman, this catholic scholar – as a man of action or a man of thought?[30]

Wavell claimed, remarkably, that on the theoretical side Lawrence had read more and thought more on military history and the military art than probably any great commander. He was particularly sad at the desert warrior's accidental death, which pre-empted an imminent meeting at Lawrence's cottage:

I discussed with him in talk and on paper his theory of irregular warfare, and of its antidotes; but on his ideas of regular warfare and the professional soldier we touched only once, and were interrupted: I had made notes on which to resume the subject with him when he had more leisure. But the date set for its discussion was a visit to him at his cottage early in June 1935.[31]

In 1934 Wavell was sent on two excursions: the first, at the request of Burnett-Stuart, by then commander-in-chief in Egypt, was to reconnoitre a route from Palestine to Baghdad (between which there were no metalled roads), in case at some future date troops at British airfields in Iraq needed rescuing. There was also the need to plan the defence of the Iraq–Haifa pipeline, which was laid above ground with pumping-stations along its route, although the significance of the immense oilfield discovered seven years earlier at Kirkuk was yet to become fully apparent. The Government had accepted the importance of developing air routes to link Britain and her Empire in the east, and the planners had noted the country's value as a staging-post. However, by the prevailing Anglo-Iraqi treaty Britain was permitted to maintain only a handful of airfields in Iraq and a very small number of troops to protect them; the one garrison of any size was at Habbaniya, west of Baghdad. Should trouble arise there, a force would have to be sent from Palestine. Wavell was ordered to find the best route, taking account of security, landing-grounds and water supplies, of which on one long stretch there were none at all. It was to prove a valuable reconnaissance.

He was also selected for a course on military affairs run by the French, and in December he set out for Paris, with two other major-generals, Sir James Marshall-Cornwall and the much-decorated New Zealander, Bernard Freyberg.[32] The purpose of the trip was to provide for the War Office a second opinion on the state of training and efficiency in the French Army, suspiciously good reports of which had been sent to the War Office by the British military attaché in Paris. Mrs Wavell and the other two wives concluded that duty called them to accompany their husbands to Paris, where they installed themselves in the Hotel Majestic. After an initial outing, *en famille*, for a picnic in the country and a look at Chartres cathedral, Wavell spent three weeks attending lectures at Versailles.

Rather to the War Office's discomfiture, the major-generals were unimpressed by the state and attitude of the French Army. Wavell thought their ideas and methods unrealistic and almost atrophied. 'The Frenchman's mind,' he said, 'is much too logical to evolve practical plans for the wholly illogical art of war.' Even if they did not foretell the disasters of 1940, Wavell, Marshall-Cornwall and Freyberg returned a unanimous and damning report. The French attitude was the opposite of Wavell's: flexibility in a commander had become one of his watchwords, along with the paramount virtues of mobility and surprise. 'A soldier wants above all things,' he told Liddell Hart, 'a flexible mind, not wedded to any particular theory. There is nothing fixed in war except a few elementary rules of commonsense . . .'[33]

On 11 March 1935, Wavell was appointed to command the 2nd Division, at Aldershot, and moved yet again, to the more imposing 'Churchill House, Marlborough Lines'. He set about further developing his talent for arranging imaginative and comprehensive exercises, which were organised to encourage thought and enthusiastic contributions from all who took part. In those prewar days annual army exercises in England were a major undertaking, often extending through several counties. By the mid-1930s the various innovations, not least with embryonic armoured and mobile forces, were attracting widespread comment – mostly in a vigorously rearming Germany, where the reports in the British press and service magazines were carefully studied.

One such exercise – so unusual that it was the subject of a leading article in *The Times* – was based on the myth of the 'Golden Fleece'; Wavell sent a copy of the story to every soldier to read in advance of the exercise, to 'put them in the picture'. He continually played up the importance of surprise, often by means of deception. On one occasion he 'salted' an attaché case with accurate plans, so that when, as Wavell had planned, it was duly captured by his opponents, they assumed the plans to be false. Wavell had taken this trick to heart after its success in the Palestine Campaign, and it was to live on, with variations, into the Second World War, being used against the Japanese by Wavell himself, and memorably in the celebrated episode of 'The Man Who Never Was'. It was perhaps not surprising that Wavell was described as not only the most original-minded commander seen on exercises in those years, but also the most open-minded.[34] 'Fit for the highest commands and appointments,' wrote the commander-in-chief in his Confidential Report.

Promoted to major-general and now in his fifties, Wavell had entered a new phase of life, finally shedding most of the attributes of the younger man – the keen and efficient soldier, on hand to support his superiors. Accustomed now to command, he had assumed a certain gravitas – and a new and larger house, on the edge of Farnborough, with an extra wing constructed by the Royal Engineers, 'into which our daughters retired, preferring seclusion to comfort'.[35] He had not shed his taciturnity, and remained tongue-tied except with close friends, with whom he was as amiable and informal as ever. For others, the awe inspired by the stocky, silent exterior was often redeemed by his quiet charm and an unexpected smile, and by respect for his skill.

From 1932 to 1933 he had served a term as ADC to the King, but his new rank brought him an ADC of his own. Bernard Fergusson was the first. He had met his new general at a Black Watch regimental dinner a few years earlier, but on that occasion the talk had not flowed freely: after some moments of silence Wavell had swivelled round to Fergusson, sitting on his blind side:

'Good evening.'
'Good evening, Sir. I think you know Major X, of the Y Regiment.'
'Yes. I don't like him.'

End of conversation. However, Fergusson did not take long to form a great liking and admiration for his new chief. He later recalled the short, silent, friendly man he had been sent to serve, sometimes irritable in the early morning, but rarely angry, and attracting those close to him with a lovable charm while appearing outwardly rugged and slightly crumpled:

'He himself was perhaps the worst-turned-out general in the Army; many a time I was fined a drink by some officers' mess or another for failing to spot some sartorial enormity which he had committed. He had a favourite pair of breeches which he used to wear entirely to annoy me. In the boot of his car he kept a hat-box with what he called his 'better hat'.[36]

Both general and ADC wore an eyeglass, and when Fergusson lost his in some leaves, Wavell was seen bending over and peering through his own, in search of his ADC's, until he ordered a file of passing soldiers to take over the hunt. Elsewhere, his appearance in his new exalted rank was the source of benevolent amusement, especially when he was in the vicinity of immaculate Guards officers.

What an astonishing contrast he was. This brilliant, imaginative brain lay behind the most expressionless poker face I have ever come across. Wavell wrote brilliantly, but never spoke at all if he could help it. On arrival young officers were warned that if they met a man who looked like a gamekeeper and said nothing, he was certain to be the divisional commander.[37]

With an ADC on hand to arrange details, the general could contemplate the day's work at his leisure. Fergusson wrote:

Wavell's ordinary day followed an easy pattern. I would appear at his house in the evening ('Give yourself some sherry'), with a map and a sheet of paper from each of the brigades, telling me what companies would be practising what form of training where and when. Wavell would select two or three which were near each other, and a rendez-vous for the grooms and horses . . . Next morning at 8.15 I would pick him up in the car and drive out to the rendez-vous; we would tell the car and grooms where to meet us, and spend a couple of hours watching troops.[38]

The climax of the 1935 training season was an exercise, on a corps, as opposed to mere division scale. It was a huge endeavour, such as had not been undertaken for a decade. Despite the numbers involved, in the conference that followed the exercise it was Wavell who was specifically praised by the commanding general, who, having blundered in his own role, took the unusual step of announcing, 'I should like it to be known that Major-General

Wavell formed an accurate appreciation of the situation and warned me of what was likely to happen.'[39]

Besides training his division, Wavell prepared an important lecture, which he delivered at the Royal United Services Institute (RUSI) in December 1935. Called 'The Higher Commander', it was a tour de force of the qualities of generals and generalship, emphasising, as with his articles, the human side of soldiering. He enlightened the audience with an eclectic display of ancient, medieval and modern history, taking in a little French philosophy along the way. He approached head-on the controversial ground that he had trodden in previous talks and articles: the need for change in the 'atmosphere, trad-itions, and spirit in which and on which the Army lives . . .' He exposed again his liberal ethos as he condemned the emphasis on spit, polish, regulations and dress. He made several proposals, considered by some as dangerously revolutionary. These included interchanging officers between the three serv-ices; officers and civilians temporarily swapping places, and training junior officers in senior ranks to which, as he suggested, vacancies left by the dead and wounded in wartime would quickly propel them. This was the innova-tive training strategy adopted by the German Army.[40] He also proposed sabbatical leave for officers to broaden their minds by travel, and urged that 'the higher commander should have a much closer acquaintance with the work and ideas of the Air Force . . .' It was a stimulating stir of the pot from a newly created divisional commander entering the higher reaches of the army, all the more so at a time when the threatening situation in Europe was begin-ning to expose the military hierarchy to public and political gaze.

A few months later Wavell further enriched the mix of man of action and man of letters by accepting the commission to write a biography of his old chief, Lord Allenby. It promised to be a congenial project: 'The Bull' had just died, so Wavell would not have the disadvantage of his subject breathing down his neck. He greatly revered Allenby, and having written a book on the campaigns in Palestine, much of the research had already been done and was stored in his mind. He had been invited to write the book by Allenby's widow, giving him a free run of the primary sources, but the field-marshal turned out to have left very few papers and no diary or memoir. However, in an age when it was not the custom to include in biographies much of a personal or private nature, that was not fatal to the project. Wavell hoped to finish the book the following year, despite the time needed for his army commitments.

As major-general commanding a division, he had occasional formal and ceremonial duties, to which he did not take naturally, although he was prepared to enter into their spirit. One such was the Jubilee Review at Aldershot in 1936, at which he had to lead his division past the King. He later wrote a wryly amusing article[41] describing the horse that had been chosen to share this honour with him: a supposedly well-bred animal, which had been sent by 'Remounts' to replace another that had, he said, 'a solemn but peculiarly stupid face' and, being apt to fall over even on the flat, had fallen out of favour. Its noble replacement had unfortunately turned out to be a 'low comedian': it would buck without warning, even while standing still, thereby unseating its high-ranking rider at embarrassing moments; it would then gaze innocently into the middle distance. At the rehearsal for the King's Jubilee parade, the horse bucked just as Wavell was performing the difficult 'salute arms mounted' in front of the commander-in-chief, who was standing in for the King; it caused its rider to bury his sword and his face in the horse's mane – 'just the sort of thing,' Wavell later wrote, 'he might have thought funny'; the commander-in-chief certainly did.

By now, the field ahead of Wavell for promotion to the highest ranks was thinning out, although, as he had himself acknowledged, there were sure to be others younger than he who would race forward in time of war. It was during 1936 that the idea of another war in Europe, which after the Armistice had been quite unthinkable, finally began to emerge as a credible prospect. Fears that it might happen were still confined to a minority of senior commanders and did not extend to the civilian population, which was largely ignorant of the state of the nation's defences. The Government itself was reluctant to contemplate the matter sufficiently to accept the need for strengthening Britain's defences: the policy of appeasement was in full swing, encouraged rather than deterred by Germany's reoccupation of the Rhineland in March 1936, by Japan's militaristic aggrandisement in the Far East and by the success of German troops in the Spanish Civil War. The supposed impossibility of fighting Germany and Italy in the west at the same time as Japan in the east led all too easily to the policy of avoiding war anywhere, more or less at any cost.

Whether the few innovators in the War Office and in the senior ranks of the army would successfully force the pace in the army's development, or whether they would be stifled by the old guard on the Army Board, was of the greatest importance to the safety of Britain. Meanwhile, changes had taken place at the top of the War Office. In 1933 Field-Marshal Milne – after two extensions as Chief of the Imperial General Staff, the second even more unpopular than the first – had finally retired. He was replaced by Sir

Archibald Montgomery-Massingberd, who in April 1936 himself stepped down as CIGS. By then Burnett-Stuart had fallen out of the race to replace him, a casualty of the frequently caustic comments that had long irritated his chief, who at one moment of exasperation had rounded on him very publicly to say: 'Take your pipe out of your mouth when speaking to a superior officer' – an order not often given to a general.

Massingberd's replacement as CIGS was Sir Cyril Deverell, more a 'safe pair of hands' than an innovator, so that as 1937 drew near there was still no resolution to the debate on whether the British Army should be shaped for imperial defence, or to provide a strong expeditionary force in case of a major war. It was the opinions of Wavell and a few other advocates of a new approach to equipment and to fighting methods that began to spread the feeling that, one way or the other, the army's redevelopment was dangerously sluggish.

In September 1936 Wavell was given the chance to observe another nation's progress when he was nominated to lead a mission to attend Soviet Army manoeuvres – another useful consequence of having learnt Russian, as senior officers who could speak the language were still scarce. He watched 1,200 tanks of various types being put successfully through arduous paces, with only three or four breaking down. The most memorable event was the finale, when 1,500 paratroopers descended on the battlefield. It might have been expected that Wavell, with his enthusiasm for surprise, mobility and innovation, would be inspired by this first sight of a new 'arm' in battle, but he did not seem particularly impressed.[42] He dismissed the event as spectacular, but of doubtful tactical value, admittedly an opinion that the German High Command was to come to share, following the bloody operation by German paratroops to capture British-held airfields in Crete in 1941, then under Wavell's command.

Meanwhile, the British Government was struggling to control events in the Middle East, whose stability was considered vital to the security of the Empire. The commanding officer in Palestine, Sir John Dill, had been appointed to Aldershot, the army's most senior command. To take his place, the CIGS fixed upon Wavell, considering that although his knowledge of Palestine was rather out of date, he probably had more military experience of the area than any other senior officer. Accordingly, at the beginning of July 1937, the Military Secretary told Wavell to make ready for another change.

VI

COUNTDOWN

WAVELL considered the impending move to Palestine highly inconvenient. Although he was accustomed to the pattern of change in army life, he did not relish the idea of once more moving house, storing furniture, finding homes for animals and generally unsettling his family. Unfortunately he did not confine this opinion to his immediate circle, and his lack of enthusiasm – focusing less on the high honour and more on the difficulties involved – reached the ears of the Secretary of State for War and left its mark. Nevertheless he dutifully consented, and on 12 September 1937 took over as General Officer-in-Command of the British Force in Palestine and Transjordan.

Wavell soon realised that his new command was in a particularly volatile state, seething with resentment, tension and discord and filled with nefarious specimens who regularly confronted the authorities with a wide variety of outrages.

The army in Palestine was at the raw end of a line of political problems which, in their acute form, had only a short history. For hundreds of years the region had lain more or less dormant, accustomed to the corrupt but generally easy-going ways of its Ottoman rulers. However, by the turn of the century the Turkish sultan's financial difficulties and the outrage caused by his periodic acts of barbarism had made his empire the 'Sick Man of Europe', some of whose territory began to interest Britain and France. Much of his power was soon transferred to a government of 'Young Turks', whose response to the empire's weakness and growing instability was to join Germany's side in 1914. Their subsequent loss of the war led to upheavals that deeply disturbed the politics of the area, and in the post-war climate there was a strong desire for change, which focused on the revolutionary leader Kemal Atatürk.

The defeat of the Turks left a power vacuum in the Middle East, which was initially filled when the League of Nations granted Britain and France mandates over the former Ottoman dominions in the area. The geographical split of power became a cause of dispute between Britain, France and assorted Arab factions, but, broadly, France was given hegemony over Syria and the Lebanon, while Britain was to rule Palestine and Iraq. The mandates were to cease when the mandated territories were judged, by the League of Nations, to be able to stand alone in the new, post-war world.

Britain's assumption of its mandate was soon bedevilled by Arab demands for it to honour successive obligations incurred during the war. Unfortunately these were contradictory. The first was the promise of independence that Britain made to the Arabs in return for their agreement to attack the Turks in what became known as the Arab Revolt. This hostage to fortune, which the British considered worth giving in view of the dangers ensuing from their defeat at Gallipoli in 1915, was enshrined in assurances given to the Arab leader Sherif Husein by Sir Henry McMahon, Britain's High Commissioner in Egypt. McMahon's undertaking was compromised soon afterwards by secret negotiations between the British and the French, which resulted in the Sykes-Picot Agreement. In this pact, the British both reserved to themselves and assured to their French allies future hegemony in territories that in effect had already been promised to the Arabs.

Britain privately determined not to cede any influence in territory essential to her for the purposes of Empire. This could not be reconciled with the belief of the Arabs that they had been promised a kingdom of their own, particularly as the lands in question included those that Britain wanted to continue to control. The tangle was tightened in 1918, when the British Government, still anxious not to lose Arab support, publicly stated that the Arabs were entitled to recognition of their separate national condition. The news led to a wave of jubilation across the Arab world: for them, the day of exultation seemed to have dawned – falsely, as it chanced. Confusion soon increased when Britain declared itself in favour of the establishment of a national home for the Jewish people in Palestine.

So although there was only a single Ottoman Empire, one and the same part of it, renamed Palestine, had effectively been reserved for three different claimants – British, Arab and Jew. Its future was further jeopardised in 1933 when Hitler became Chancellor of Germany. As a result of the development of Zionism, which had encouraged a return of Jews to the biblical homeland they had left at the Diaspora eighteen centuries earlier, there were at the end of the Great War about 55,000 Jews in Palestine, some 8 per cent of the population. The increasing exodus of Jews from Germany in the three years following Hitler's accession to power saw a further 135,000 settle in Palestine, a number that the indigenous Arabs viewed as a serious threat to their economic future. In fact, many Arabs had been happy to sell their land to incoming Jews, but their initial satisfaction turned to resentment at the success that the Jewish owners began to make of their new purchases: farming, boring wells, cultivating orange groves, importing scientific expertise, setting up technical institutions – and even developing industry, tripling in ten years the number of people working in factories. In Jewish areas of Palestine daily wages for unskilled workers were soon six times higher than they were in Egypt.

This economic revolution greatly unsettled the neighbouring Arabs, whose dissidence erupted in April 1936, when a General Strike was called and a full-scale revolt began, with attacks on communications and Jewish settlements, with the aim of halting Jewish immigration. Rapidly deploying two divisions, the British Army managed to separate the warring factions and clamp a lid on the cauldron, but they did not extinguish the fire beneath it, now stoked by the Grand Mufti of Jerusalem. This charismatic demagogue, called Haj Amin, was a former British civil servant, but now a violently anti-Semitic political schemer who had become President of the Supreme Muslim Council and head of the Arab Higher Committee, the nationalists' ruling body and a focal point of all their dreams.[1]

In the meantime Britain had set up a commission to make suggestions for a political solution to the problems in the mandated territory. The commission's report,[2] published in 1937, recommended the partition of Palestine between Arabs and Jews. The Grand Mufti appealed to neighbouring countries to support him in opposing this idea, and organised for the purpose a pan-Arab conference in Syria.

Into this lively scene now arrived General Wavell with wife, children and cocker spaniel 'Chorny'. Taking over command on 12 September, he turned to his initial task of understanding the relationship between the army and the civil authorities, in which he was helped by the fact that the High Commissioner was Sir Arthur Wauchope, his old friend, and many years earlier his colonel in the Black Watch. Beyond deploying troops for the altruistic purpose of keeping apart two communities, each of which nurtured the fixed opinion that the other should cease to exist, he had to consider the wider needs of Empire. He had to restore peace in Palestine in order to safeguard imperial communications through the Suez Canal, and so that no alien political influences should take root, to threaten the Empire's influence in Palestine itself or in neighbouring countries, some of which were becoming vitally important sources of oil.

Since the war Wavell had displayed imaginative and exemplary skill in carrying out the duties of his staff appointments, and in command first of a brigade and then of a division. Now he could show his paces in a volatile situation in which firm execution of clear and imaginative plans might make all the difference in an area vital to imperial interests. For Wavell – as for Palestine – much might turn on how order was restored and then maintained.

The flickering hopes expressed at the pan-Arab conference, that moderation might prevail and that Britain should be subjected to political rather than armed pressure, were extinguished a fortnight after Wavell's arrival, when a prominent British official was murdered in Nazareth.[3] Further trouble arose on 5 November, when two unarmed Black Watch privates, off duty and walking in Jerusalem, were shot in the back by gunmen. The forces under Wavell's command included the Black Watch, and among them was his son, Archie John. He had continued in his father's footsteps through Summer Fields and Winchester into the army, and had joined the battalion stationed in Palestine soon after his father's arrival. Wavell himself had ordered the pursuit of the murderers of the two privates, and they were traced to a hillside village. The Black Watch soldiers were in the mood for indiscriminate revenge, and Wavell worried about the international furore that might result if their discipline broke. As he recalled:

I must admit that I spent an unhappy night, as I knew I had taken a certain risk. There were a great number of people, both in Palestine and at home, who were only too ready to accuse British troops of atrocities, and I did not want my old regiment involved in what might well be a serious incident . . . I heard in the morning that all had gone well. The murderers had not been found, but the behaviour of the troops had been impeccable.[4]

The War Office had been persuaded by the temporary lull in the revolt to withdraw the two divisions that had been lent to Sir John Dill. Wavell was left with only two brigades, and smaller garrisons in Haifa and Jerusalem, whose King David Hotel housed British Headquarters. There was also an RAF squadron, equipped with armoured cars and commanded by an officer with whom Wavell established a harmonious relationship and in whose aeroplane he travelled all over the country overseeing the army's operations.

Imagination and foresight were now required. Although he had become well acquainted with Palestine during the First World War and its aftermath, and had updated his knowledge while exploring the route to Iraq in 1934, Wavell now found a very different atmosphere from that of nearly twenty years earlier. He had experienced the army's role in time of civil unrest during his brief post-war appointment in Egypt, but that had been soon contained.[5] Now he faced far deeper hostility. Both Jews and Arabs had become organised into gangs, their leaders establishing a *carte* of their requirements. The gunmen were offered a simple tariff: £5 for murdering a casual Jew; £50 (the local price of two polo ponies) for a police inspector; £200 for a prominent Arab or British official. These competitive rates meant that officers had to be armed when in public, and patrolled the streets in armoured cars, painted soft yellow and mounted with machine-guns. Everyday life was punctuated by a violence unknown in the old, tranquil days of the Turks: railway lines were mined, telephone wires cut, armoured police patrols quartered town and countryside, the frontier was closely guarded, roads were unsafe after dark, Arab villagers sought police protection, Jewish colonists slept behind barbed-wire entanglements protected by armed watchmen, and Jews and Arabs feared to enter each other's quarters. No one could tell when or where the next outrage would happen.

The number of gunmen at large had not changed much since the start of the revolt, for however many thugs were rounded up, replacements slipped into the country across the porous border with Syria, whose government the British viewed as little more than a collection of brigands. There was a development that had affected the army's task, making it in one way simpler, but in another more difficult. The gunmen had formed large gangs. When overwhelmed by army patrols, a correspondingly larger number of terrorists were killed or captured. On the other hand, they were now well organised and better armed, and under the ultimate direction of about half a dozen sheikhs who had set themselves up as 'holy warriors'.

Although the Zionist leaders, Chaim Weizmann and David Ben-Gurion, did not see the merit in partition, there was considerable support from people tired of the increasing lawlessness, and much of the Jewish colony in Palestine was vigorous, progressive and Western in outlook. Many British politicians argued that if the Jews were firmly supported, they might form a buttress for imperial interests in the Middle East. Against that had to be set the Empire's need for the friendship of the Arabs, with their oilfields and the importance of the Persian Gulf as a staging-post, who formed by far the largest part of the region's population.

Wavell's sense of history inclined him to the cause of the Arab communities, which had been settled in Palestine long before the Jews and had much better title to the land. There is no evidence that he was anti-Semitic, but he did fear that overt support for Jewish colonisation might unite the Arabs against the British. It is also likely that he harboured a high-minded, rather English feeling for the underdog, which in Palestine had within a few short years become the Arab. Yet he knew that he must resist partiality: the measure of his success would be whether his brigades worked well with each other and with the police. He had to defeat the terrorists by deploying force that was beyond the scope of the civil authorities, doing so without permanently alienating significant sections of the population. It was clear that if the terrorists could be withdrawn from the community, there remained a well of potential support for the British authorities.

His first task was to help the police defuse the tension that had arisen after the murder of the official in Nazareth, a potential trigger for renewed violence throughout the country. Wavell moved resolutely the day after the murder, sending out troops on the trail of the assassins, making thirty arrests and later detaining a further eighty gangsters. He also ordered the dissolution of the Arab Higher Committee and the arrest of its members. Although the Grand Mufti himself managed to evade capture by taking sanctuary in Jerusalem's Mosque of Omar, before escaping, disguised as a woman, to the Lebanon, Wavell ordered his dismissal from the Supreme Muslim Council, which was apparently subject to the army's writ. He established a system of summary and efficient military courts, which proved a great success; in a three-month period they heard eighty-five cases, involving 100 defendants, and passed thirty capital sentences as well as prison sentences totalling 244 years. Wavell himself had to sign the death certificates.

He was also faced with the task of reclaiming ground lost in a security lapse that had taken place shortly before his arrival, leaving rebels in control of large numbers of villages, particularly in the north of the country. He imposed a policy of firmly bearing down on the gangs: instigating thorough searches, drawing the gunmen into fire-fights and dynamiting the houses where they were found. Following the ideas he had preached in his training in England, he concentrated his limited resources at strong points, with mobile flying columns at short notice to move out to flashpoints. The troops learnt to work with the police, whom they relieved of having to operate against the larger gangs that had become adept at mining roads and railways and laying well-placed ambushes. For a time the army received a steady flow of information from villagers unhappy about their houses being commandeered as bases for terrorism, but where the gangs gained at least temporary control, their rather biblical methods of discouraging the villagers succeeded in cutting off most of the army's intelligence. The hill tracks, often nearly impassable in mist and freezing winter rains, would be patrolled by troops with Cypriot donkeys carrying wireless sets, Lewis Guns, mortars and ammunition delivered to 'roadhead' in specially adapted donkey transports.

Wavell, who loved to travel by air whenever he could, managed through a mixture of charm and clear presentation of his aims to persuade the previously jealously independent RAF command, headed by the man later to become known as Bomber Harris, to work closely with the army. Soon the troops had learnt to call for quick support from the RAF, and on locating terrorist gangs would flush them into the open so that low-flying aeroplanes could mow them down as they tried to escape.

The problems of containing the violence were complicated by Palestine's lengthy border with Syria. It was not long before the Grand Mufti had regained control of events and had begun to direct them from the Lebanon. From there he communicated with high authorities and powerful gang leaders in Syria, where the French declined to take strong measures to help the British, perhaps conscious of the fact that Syrian exports to Palestine were worth four times as much as the flow in reverse, or perhaps from simple national antipathy.

Until a largely impenetrable barbed-wire fence was rolled along the frontier, at huge expense,[6] gunmen could often escape by crossing into Syria and later re-entering Palestine unhindered. Meanwhile army patrols working with the police had to deal with indiscriminate attacks on Jews, soldiers, public transport and harmless civilians; armed robbery; abductions; bomb-throwing; damage to property; the cutting of telephone wires; and the mining of roads and railways. Even so, each week the army and police between them managed to amass piles of captured revolvers, rifles, small-arms ammunition, ammonal, gelignite, guncotton and detonators.

Wavell soon gained the confidence of both troops and police, who were encouraged to use imaginative methods of countering the gangs. It was not a very gentlemanly dispute: the enemy would lay ambushes for troops and travellers, tying camels to railway tracks. They were unsparing with booby-traps, which they often concealed in attaché cases left at railway stations, in women's shopping baskets or in the privy areas of camels themselves – necessitating 'camel searches', which the soldiers particularly disliked. Gunmen would leave primed grenades wedged in boxes or under stones that soldiers were likely to move. But the army responded firmly – for example, discouraging the sabotage of railway lines by chaining villagers to flat trucks coupled to the front of engines. The stratagem was made harsher by the fact that those on the trucks were often blown to pieces as a result of the terrorists' habit of greasing the rails, so that even if the soldiers saw traces of sabotage they were unable to stop the engines in time. Yet for all the difficulties, Wavell's forceful methods successfully discouraged at least some local co-operation with the gangs.

Certain bandit strongholds called for special measures. In southern Galilee, for instance, besides the normal outrages there were frequent attacks on the Iraq Petroleum Company's pipeline, which carried oil to a terminus on the Mediterranean coast. To protect this vital artery, Wavell ordered the deployment of specialist anti-terror groups, the brainchild of an artillery captain called Orde Wingate.

Wingate was a brave and determined man who had become a fervent Zionist, and it was at lunch with the Jewish leader Chaim Weizmann, at his house in Rehovoth, that Wavell had first met him. The young officer persuaded Wavell to establish what became known as Special Night Squads – patrols of tough but well-disciplined Jews, commanded by British offi-cers, who could challenge the Arab gangs on their own ground. It was characteristic of Wavell to accept an idea that matched his belief in the imaginative and unorthodox, and his appreciation of the value of oper-ating by night. The squads turned out to be a great success, not least because of their use of police dogs, which greatly upset the Arabs, who regarded the animals as unclean. Wingate was awarded a DSO for his part in one of the actions – a rare distinction for a junior officer in peacetime. 'I carried away in a corner of my mind,' Wavell later wrote, 'an impres-sion of a notable character who might be valuable as a leader of unorthodox enterprise in war, if I should ever have need of one.'[7] It was a need that would soon arise.

Yet Wavell's job was not all work and no play: he continued intermittently with his biography of Lord Allenby, on which he had worked when he first arrived in Jerusalem and was making the arrangements for his assumption of command. There was the occasional day's shooting near the Sea of Galilee, home to thousands of duck, snipe and coot. He sometimes managed a round of golf, although courses in Palestine were little more than stony waste nominally cleared of scrub; there was polo at Sarafand, and hunting jackals with the Ramleh Vale hounds, tearing through hedges of prickly pear and careering headlong through orange groves, sending fruit flying in all directions. The spring climate was attractive, and the occasional swim in the Dead Sea or the Mediterranean refreshed both body and soul.

Wavell impressed his soldiers and the civil authorities as a man who knew what had to be done. Quiet and steady, he would listen to proposals, sitting doodling at his desk, and at length saying quietly, 'I should do that, if I were you'; organising his troops, arranging air support for mobile columns, encouraging the police, mixing efficiency with flair.

It could not be said that the battle was won during his time in Palestine. In 1938 the violence increased, and by the end of that year many police stations had been occupied by rebels, and a number of towns were no longer served by trains. In some Arab areas gangs had gained complete control, collecting taxes and imposing their own summary courts. However, Wavell had achieved prominence in difficult circumstances, and demonstrated steady qualities commanding an army which, besides being constrained by political requirements and with barely sufficient strength for the job, was confronted by an enemy that was extremely difficult to pinpoint.

Meanwhile, back in England, far from Palestine's dust, diving aeroplanes, machine-gun fire, bombs, booby-traps, barbed wire, narrow streets, flat roofs, steel shutters, mosques, hidden gunmen, orange groves, giant spiders and South African police dogs – the War Office in London had entered a period of flux.

The chief cause of agitation was the new War Minister, Leslie Hore-Belisha, a zealous reformer whose ambitious but insensitive crusade to democratise the army had made him, in the short time since his appointment, cordially disliked by most of the country's top soldiers, who sensed a threat to their domination of the War Office. Having been installed by the Prime Minister to brush aside army resistance to mechanisation and modernisation, Belisha had lost little time in setting about it. To help him he began to rely, for a short time quite heavily, on Basil Liddell Hart, who became his unofficial adviser, inevitably arousing the enmity of senior British officers, although Liddell Hart's ideas were much admired in the German Army, especially by the exuberant Panzer commander Hans Guderian.

Differences between the War Minister and the army's old guard widened, and in due course led to questioning the whole basis of senior appointments, including that of the CIGS himself, as the Secretary of State concluded that if he was to reform the army, he would first have to purge its ruling Army Council. It was now that Wavell's name began to be considered for the very highest commands in the army, and as he was relatively close to the War Minister's new adviser, he found that to his existing qualifications for high office was added the voice of a friend at court.

Wavell's career over the past twenty years now coalesced: the quiet, clever young man of 1914; the officer selected to liaise with the Russians in 1916 and with the high commanders in 1917; the efficient BGGS; the inspired trainer of troops; the writer and lecturer; the innovative brigade and divisional commander; and finally the general in charge of an active theatre, found himself in the lists for even further promotion – initially as a candidate for the Southern Command, but in the rapidly fluctuating conditions as a possibility for the highest post of all, Chief of the Imperial General Staff.

Wavell had already come across the new War Minister:

> Our first encounters were not propitious. The first time I met him he demanded my opinion on a matter which concerned the Adjutant-General. I replied that it was for the AG to advise him. He said that he knew the AG's view but wanted mine, since he disagreed with the AG. I refused to give it. I said that the AG had the full facts, which I had not, and that it would not be fair on the AG for me to give my views behind his back. H-B was not very pleased and did not seem to see the objection.[8]

This incident illustrates the contrasts within Wavell that were to have an increasing effect as his career progressed. Conscious of what was correct in professional conduct, and with a strong feeling for fair play, he disregarded interpersonal nuances and the politics of the moment, seemingly careless of the risk to his career in being either unable or unwilling to conciliate a politician.

Requested by Hore-Belisha to submit pen-portraits of candidates for senior military appointments, Liddell Hart had done so in a briefing note entitled

'Some Noteworthy Officers', in which Wavell was described as 'Outstanding. He has not only great ability but marked originality – if inclined to the "professional" point of view. Does not impress at first sight.' Although Wavell had only just left for Palestine, at the beginning of October 1937 Liddell Hart had submitted Wavell's name to the War Minister as a possible choice for CIGS, but at that moment he was considered more suitable for Southern Command, a position of the highest importance because, should war break out, its general would be the designated commander of a corps in a British Expeditionary Force. As it happened, the incumbent CIGS had at first agreed with the proposal to appoint Wavell as his successor, but had then changed his mind on the basis that being only a major-general he was too junior for the post.

Hore-Belisha's patience now began to wear thin, and he decided that he could no longer work with his present CIGS. The natural successor was Dill, but Hore-Belisha did not like him either. There had to be someone else: 'Who would make a good CIGS?' he asked Liddell Hart: 'Is there anyone who isn't tame? I want a real gangster.' In the sense intended, a gangster was something Wavell himself was not, for all his merits and his belief in the virtues of the unorthodox and imaginative in war; further, the War Minister remembered his first, unsatisfactory meeting with the general. When Liddell Hart tried to explain that Wavell had many qualities although he did not impress at first sight, Hore-Belisha briskly replied that for CIGS it was necessary to have a man who did.

A few weeks later Hore-Belisha again asked for his advice on a new CIGS. Liddell Hart recorded:

> . . . It seemed to be a question of either Wavell or Gort. Either would be acceptable to the army, and their reputation stood high. For that reason perhaps it would be a bit awkward putting Gort over the head of Wavell, who was considerably senior. If Gort was CIGS I would like to see Wavell as Adjutant-General – or vice-versa. Wavell was the deeper thinker . . .
>
> Hore-Belisha reverted to the poor impression Wavell had made on him by his hesitation to take Palestine – he wanted so many assurances and dwelt on what he would lose by moving house etc.[9]

Lord Gort was Military Secretary, the bridge between the CIGS and the Secretary of State for War. A very rich Grenadier Guardsman, who had won the Victoria Cross in 1918, he was more positive about Wavell than was the minister, saying that he would be the best man as CIGS, that he was a first-class brain and would command ready acceptance in the army.

'Wavell's only drawback was his streak of trade-unionism, in the sense of the soldier's innate distrust of politicians, and his unimpressive manner . . .'[10] He was now approaching a level that called for political acumen as well as outstanding military ability, as the job of Chief of the Imperial General Staff stretched beyond professional soldiers and technical military matters. In Palestine, Wavell had been working closely with the High Commissioner, who represented the Government, with the RAF and with civil authorities such as the commanders of the Palestine Police. He had proved successful, and the fact that he was being considered for CIGS demonstrated how highly he was regarded in his profession.

He had proved his ability in every commission that he had received, and most recently in active command. He had avoided the personal intrigues that carpeted the floors of the War Office, and had been drawn to the fore by his skill and character; but he had slipped back again for superficial reasons, particularly his shyness and his apparent taciturnity, and was now thought too dour for the top job in the army. He was also hobbled by his unwilling-ness to present himself to politicians in a way that did not come easily to him. Hore-Belisha had told Chamberlain that 'Dill is too conventional, and Wavell, though he has more brain than Gort, is, I fancy, not without calcu-lation as to the effect of showing courage on his personal position.'[11] 'H-B had only seen me twice,' wrote Wavell, 'and then we had not hit it off. I think it was fortunate for me; I don't believe I should have been happy or successful with H-B.'[12]

Wavell was a perceptive, and on the whole dispassionate, judge of char-acter, and he was probably wise not to hitch his wagon to the star of the iconoclastic Hore-Belisha, whose career did not last long. The result of the conflict between a reforming politician and traditional soldiers was a compromise. Certain changes were grudgingly accepted by the army leaders: some cavalry regiments were re-equipped with infantry-support tanks, and others with fast tanks in which to carry out their traditional reconnaissance and screening roles. On the other hand, many regiments retained their cherished horses. It was soon to be Wavell's lot to try and forge these disparate ingredients into a weapon capable of withstanding the German Army.

In November 1937, having spent barely two months getting to grips with his job in Palestine, he was summoned home and offered the Southern Command in succession to Sir John Burnett-Stuart, due to retire the following spring. Wavell remained only a few months more in Palestine, leaving for home on 8 April 1938. One of his last engagements was to open a garden on Mount Carmel, overlooking the 'Valley of the Brook Kishon', in memory of Lord Allenby.[13]

The army's difficult and at times bloody task was brought close to home when Archie John was badly injured in the foot by a landmine. He had already shown a determined streak, and his bravery and desire to be near the action were later to be evident when he served in Burma with the Chindits, and during the Mau-Mau rebellion in Kenya, in which he was killed.

By now, the political situation in Europe was deteriorating rapidly, and the condition and leadership of the army were becoming an issue of great national importance. Wavell returned to England a few weeks after the *Anschluss* of March 1938, when German troops marched over the Austrian frontier to the delirious applause of the Austrian crowds.

The Government, however, remained set on appeasement:

The country had exchanged Lord Baldwin with his pipe for Mr Neville Chamberlain with his umbrella, but as outward and visible signs of British might, energy and efficiency there was not much to choose between these two weapons.[14]

Only in the field of air defence was there any real progress, however belated. Winston Churchill, inspired by his scientific adviser and closest friend Professor Lindemann,[15] was doing all he could to encourage the harnessing of science to war; the development of radar, at least, was advancing to the point where it would provide respite to the country and save it from extinction, while it finally started to reduce its military deficit.

By nature Wavell was rarely in grim mood, and the sharpness of the military problems about to confront him was at least slightly dulled by the 'interest', as he euphemistically described it, of the considerable task before him. He could also draw comfort from the peaceful surroundings of the family's new home in Wiltshire. Salisbury at that time lay in a fold of lush pastures, clustered under its ancient cathedral, washed by five gentle rivers, with horses and carts moving slowly through its narrow ways. Wavell wrote of their new house:

It was large and comfortable, with garden and lawn and paddock, but not in any way attractive. There was, I remember, some controversy about my selection of a study. The attitude of my family in previous houses had been: 'Poor Daddy had a lot of work to do, he must be given a really nice room for his study.' This generous policy had resulted in the room selected being so obviously the most comfortable in the house that my wife and daughters and dogs and ADCs and their friends conducted most of their affairs, by interview or telephone, in the study. At Salisbury I firmly selected as my study a very small room on an upper floor. This was condemned by my family as definitely an anti-social act, but I did get more homework done.[16]

He had now been promoted to lieutenant general. His new empire, Southern Command, stretched far beyond the verdant Wiltshire valleys: from Southampton down to Land's End, up the Atlantic coast to Bristol, and inland to Oxford and Reading, it covered seven counties. It also included major cities of commercial or naval importance, such as Plymouth, Portsmouth and Bristol. Under his command were some ambitious officers whose names were shortly to be as famous as his own: Bernard Montgomery, then a colonel, whom Wavell considered to be one of the army's most capable officers, and whom he had specially recommended for a brigade at Portsmouth and would shortly recommend for the command of 3rd Division. Also Major-General Alan Brooke, a terse Ulster Gunner whom the War Office, with its Byzantine logic, had preferred to a tank officer as commander of the newly created Mobile Division.

Wavell soon became engrossed in his command, touring it extensively, by air whenever he could, spending long days visiting units, covering large amounts of ground, and demonstrating his exceptional physical stamina. With naval bases, airfields and the RAF Army School of Co-operation within his area of command, he realised as far as he could his belief in cross-fertilising ideas between the three services. Yet there was hardly any money or the equipment needed for full-scale exercises, so Wavell was forced to complain about the lack of practical scope.

One of the few brigade exercises was held off the south coast, designed to rehearse beach landings. It was inspired and driven by Montgomery, and the invasion in question was to be at Slapton Sands, near Dartmouth, where disaster was later to befall a wartime practice for the D-Day landings. Wavell observed the proceedings from on board the admiralty yacht *Enchantress*.

Although on this occasion there was no loss of life, the performance of all three services demonstrated to the army commander how much was still to be done:

> It was a pitiful exposition of our complete neglect of landing operations. There was *one* so-called landing-craft, an experimental one made many years before and dug out of some scrap-heap for this exercise, in which I rather think it sank. For the rest the troops landed in open row-boats as they had done for the last 200 years and more. A storm came on, and the troops were unable to re-embark as had been intended . . .'[17]

With increasing aggressiveness in Germany confusing a pusillanimous government in England, it was a dispiriting time; but Wavell's roving, enquiring mind kept him sanguine and determined to inspire his troops to make the most of the equipment that they had – however inadequate. Whenever he came across some imaginative suggestion he did his best to promote it. One such was a device called the 'Projectory Infantry Anti-Tank' (PIAT), introduced to Wavell by its enterprising inventor, Colonel Blacker. It was a gun that could destroy tanks, although small enough to be carried and fired by a foot-soldier. At once Wavell realised the tremendous possibilities of this weapon: he encouraged Blacker to give demonstrations, drew it to the attention of senior officers and to the War Office, and did his best to overcome bureaucratic resistance and have it adopted by the army.

Wavell had continued intermittently with his biography of Allenby, despite the demands of his various postings, but had not found time for any other literary adventures. Now General Sir Ernest Swinton, whom he had first met long ago presiding over the writing of the official history of the Russo-Japanese War, came to stay with him in Wiltshire. During the Great War, Swinton[18] had played a leading part in the development of tanks, and had latterly been appointed Chichele Professor of Military History at Oxford. Talented but rather indolent, he was intending soon to retire, and early in May 1938 asked Wavell if he would like to be considered as his successor. It would not be a mere formality, as there was an independent selection board, but Swinton claimed to have a certain influence. The post carried a Fellowship of All Souls, almost the highest academic prize in the land. Wavell readily agreed to let his name go forward: it would be a great honour, and an emolument that would benefit him after his retirement as a soldier, now only

three years off. More importantly, it would be testimony to his deep knowledge of military history, his intellect and his record as an author.

It was a rare tribute – the number of soldiers who are Fellows of All Souls
is not noticeably large – but accepting it would preclude his becoming a
corps commander should a British Expeditionary Force be sent to the
Continent. As it turned out, the Chichele suggestion never came to fruition,
as Swinton conquered the temptation to retire and continued to sit firmly
on his learned chair.

Meanwhile, the peace of Europe was becoming increasingly fragile, despite
the relief that followed the Munich Agreement: 'What a grim and stupid
business it all is,' Wavell wrote, 'but if Hitler has cast himself for Napoleon,
I suppose the saner portions of Europe must try and find him a St Helena.'[19]

In retrospect Wavell said that he was one of those who thought Britain
should have fought Germany in September 1938, rather than sacrifice
Czechoslovakia by acceding to the Munich terms. Whether the agreement
was in the country's best interests has not finally been resolved: Wavell felt
that the Germans made more use of the ensuing twelve months than Britain.
One way or another, despite the fact that in the interim Britain took delivery
of the squadrons of Spitfires and perfected the radar arrangements that
together won the Battle of Britain, the country's honour was tarnished.

He made the most of peacetime pursuits. He rode regularly with the South
and West Wilts Hunt, together with his wife and children, the whole family
being happy in the company of dogs and horses. His daughters were now
blossoming in different ways. Pamela, tall, with long black hair, had a rather
traditional type of beauty; she was less vivacious than her sisters, and not
quite as keen as they were on riding. Felicity, known to some of her friends
as 'Fizzie', had a round, smiling face and was full of fun. Joan enjoyed time
spent with horses as much as anything else, and was accompanied wherever
possible by Chorny, the spaniel. She spent a great deal of time with her
aunts, who liked to call her Patricia, and of whom Wavell was very fond.

Neither of Wavell's two sisters had married, perhaps because – like so
many girls of their generation – their hearts had been lost to men who never
returned from Flanders' fields, or perhaps because they were just born spin-
sters. They were wholly good-natured, and shared an Edwardian house on
the edge of the New Forest. Nancy, the elder – the sisters had been known
as Nancy and Molly since childhood – was quiet, tall and slim, and, like her
brother, rather intellectual; elegant herself, she rode side-saddle on beautifully turned-out horses, a contrast with her younger sister, Molly, who was

tubby, noisy and jocular, and spent much of her time training horses for children.

When he had the chance Wavell also pursued his academic interests, and in February 1939 delivered the Lees-Knowles lectures at Cambridge. His purpose was to persuade his audience 'to a flesh-and-blood study and understanding of military history, and that war is not a matter of diagrams, principles, or rules'. In the hall were a mere two dozen or so undergraduates with military aspirations, or who had at least joined the Officers' Training Corps, and the talks were little remarked on at the time; but later, when their author had won his famous victories, they were to receive wide acclaim, and were considered to be the best lectures of their kind ever delivered; in due course they were published in *The Times* and formed part of a popular book.

In the lectures he surveyed the nature and functions of generals, their relation to their troops and to the statesmen who direct them. As befitted the surroundings of an ancient university, he illustrated his ideas with precedents from classical Greece and Rome, besides many from more recent history. He began with Socrates' words on the virtues necessary for a general, which Wavell considered to be axiomatic, and which could certainly be applied to himself: 'The general must know how to get his men their rations and every other kind of stores needed for war. He must have imagination to originate plans, practical sense and energy to carry them through.'[20]

Or, as he put it, 'There are ten military students who can tell you how Blenheim was won for one who has any knowledge at all of the administrative preparations that made the march to Blenheim possible.' In structure, content and spirit the lectures were full to the brim of technical knowledge, wisdom and common sense. Enemy ears were listening too, and they seemed to be impressed:

> In the British army today there is only one good general, but he is incomparably good. The others have no proper conception of the direction of mechanised war but this officer . . . may well prove the dominant personality in any war within the next five years.[21]

Wavell's ascent of the army ladder was chronicled by his annual Confidential Reports, records of a soldier's career intended to give to higher authority a clear picture of an officer's attainments and limitations, so that he can be placed in the position that is most advantageous to the army and, above a certain level, to the country. Wavell's Confidential Reports over the course of nearly forty years of soldiering form a litany of praise, bestowed by future generals, field-marshals and famous soldiers – Robertson, Wilson, Chetwode, Cavan, Jackson, Burnett-Stuart, Montgomery-Massingberd. All acknowledged Wavell's exceptional talent. He was described as suitable for almost any department that the army offered, whether academic, as commandant of the Imperial Defence College or of the Staff College, for which he was described as 'particularly fitted', or in high staff positions, or as a trainer and commander of troops. Faced with the official form containing a long list of categories and adjectives, in descending order of merit, with which to indicate prowess, one general wrote, 'Under all the 27 headings, with the possible exception of "smartness of appearance", the first adjective is applicable.'

His reserve was balanced by the speed of his brain. To the men who knew from experience what qualities the nation needed from its soldiers, Wavell seemed probably second to none in the army. His future tests would be as a commander-in-chief in the shock of battle, and in the worlds of diplomacy and politics; his performance in these fields was yet to be ascertained.

Meanwhile 1939 promised an increasingly active round of meetings at the War Office – area commanders were now invited to Army Council meetings, where future strategy and the development of the army itself were on the agenda. Wavell also played a significant part in further exercises, insisting, in March 1939, on holding one that required close RAF air-strike support for the army. He was no less withering about its outcome than he had been about the landing trials:

> It . . . showed conclusively that the RAF had given little or no thought to the problem of close support of ground operations, that their pilots had not been trained for this form of war, and that the results on the targets provided were extremely poor in consequence. I doubt whether the exercise occasioned even a ripple of thought about close support to pass over the minds of the Air Staff, but if I had remained in England and war had not come I intended to follow it up.[22]

The use of air attacks in close support of mobile columns had been one of the cardinal innovations of the reborn German Army – something of which British military leaders appeared to be wholly ignorant – and the lack of attention paid to it in England was to prove appallingly expensive.

For a long time in Europe there were to be no advancing British troops for the RAF to support, closely or otherwise, although battle conditions in North Africa were to offer a different opportunity. Fortunately the RAF now had another preoccupation: learning, under the guidance of Henry Tizard, chairman of the Aeronautical Research Committee, and his team of scientists, how to respond to the radar detection of approaching enemy aircraft, a skill that was for a time to prove far more valuable than close support of the army.

Wavell now received an unexpected opportunity. Early in July 1939 he was confronted with a sudden and unexpected development: the Military Secretary wrote to him on behalf of the CIGS to ask if he would be prepared to fill the newly created post of General Officer Commanding-in-Chief, Middle East. While peace reigned he would have a watching brief, with only a small staff to help him; but should war break out, he would become supreme commander of the whole region.

Whatever weight he gave to the likelihood of war, on this occasion he showed none of the reluctance that he had expressed over Palestine. It was a great opportunity, and at the end of July he crossed the Mediterranean, bound once more for Egypt.

VII

BRICKS WITHOUT STRAW

On 24 July 1939 the Army Council set out the terms of Wavell's new appointment, in honour of which he had been knighted. His orders were framed in fifteen short paragraphs, and placed him in charge of an enormous region, of crucial value to the Empire, comprising Egypt, the Sudan, Palestine, Transjordan and Cyprus: 'Should war break out,' the brief continued, 'the area of your Command will be extended to include all military forces in British Somaliland, Aden, Iraq and the shores of the Persian Gulf.'

In effect, Wavell was to defend about three and a half million square miles of the British Empire, a patch of pink that – with the purely technical exception of Egypt itself – covered nine countries and lapped two continents.

In the event of war, the Middle East, a triangle linking the Mediterranean, the Black Sea and the Indian Ocean, was likely to become the most important strategic military area of all. Through it stretched the Suez Canal, the through-route to much of the Empire, in particular to India, and the shipping lanes from West to East – lines of communication vital in a major conflict that might draw in America, Russia and China, as well as the British Empire. It was the gateway to Europe through the Balkans, to Russia through the Caucasus, and to central Africa along the valley of the Nile. Besides the region's geographic importance, it was an economic treasure-trove, abundant in grain, fruit, cotton, chromium, oil and gold.

Britain first went to Egypt to safeguard the interest due on the £10 million debt owed to the original Suez Canal bond-holders; she was still there when the Royal Navy changed its power source from coal to oil, after which access to the oilfields was essential and the Canal took on an entirely new importance. Once other strategic coastal strongholds were established along the

Empire's trade routes, they also needed protection from foreign interference: the Canal was the vital link with the Persian oilfields and with India; Egypt was crucial for controlling the Canal; safeguarding the economic health of Egypt depended upon control of the Sudan, through which flowed the wealth-creating headwaters of the Nile; protection of the Sudan involved mastery of Uganda, and as it was necessary to link Uganda to the sea, a railway was built inland from the deep-water port at Mombasa, and the settlements along that route in time became Kenya Colony. Much of this domino territory was placed within Middle East Command.

By the time he reached Cairo, Wavell had little doubt that the prospects for peace were fading, as he told his former commanding officer:

> The news to me smells of high explosive and mustard gas and anti-septics and other unpleasant things, though all private persons I hear from at home seem convinced there will be no war. Why? What is now called 'wishful' thinking, I suppose. I should call it 'woolly'.[1]

Wavell's new appointment was one of the many official decisions that crowded upon each other as Britain belatedly prepared for war. By now many of those in positions of power in the Empire were Wavell's contemporaries and, even if they had not all been his schoolfellows, their educational and formative influences had been of a pattern. Yet, clever as many were, few appeared to have given much thought, at least in their professional output, to the basic question of whether the whole imperial structure, about to assume the huge expense of war, was financially worth preserving, or (that question's logical precursor) whether the money was actually there. The bald fact was that even after twenty years of peace Britain was no longer rich enough to fight a major war: 'By the Spring of 1939 the contrast between Britain's self-perpetuated role of first-class world and imperial power and her backward industrial economy had brought her within the zone of icy chill that spelt inevitable shipwreck.'[2] One consequence was the inability of the War Office to provide Wavell with the equipment he needed to carry out his new instructions.

This was partly because Middle East Command contained so much coast-line as well as inland territory that it was vulnerable to attack in a large number of widely separated places, which complicated Wavell's options for using the resources he had and those he hoped would soon arrive. He was directed to co-ordinate his plans with the General Staffs of Britain's potential allies in the fight, which initially meant the French, the Turks, the Greeks and the Rumanians. He was also required to 'maintain close touch with' the British Ambassadors in Egypt and in Iraq, and with the Governors, High Commissioners, Political Residents and other plumed personages dispensing power in the Sudan, Transjordan, Aden, Palestine, Cyprus, Somaliland and the Persian Gulf. In the defence of his huge command he had not only to act as a soldier, for which he was supremely well trained, but also enter the more uncertain world of politics and diplomacy.

He arrived in Cairo on 2 August 1939. Britain was still at peace, and the army authorities, modest in their estimate of what might be required of the new commander, offered him a staff of five. Making an early start with the proliferation that was soon to attract controversy to GHQ Middle East, his staff actually began life with seven people: the general, three majors, a lieutenant, a naval liaison officer and a young ADC from Wavell's regiment. As chief of staff he appointed an old friend, Major-General Sir Arthur Smith, a cheerful, fair-haired, religious man with a wooden leg. Although not without critics – who suggested that he ran his office inefficiently, gave Wavell bad advice and was partly responsible for allowing GHQ to turn into an 'unwieldy octopus' – Smith helped solve innumerable problems of staffwork for his chief, towards whom he felt an affection approaching hero-worship. These few people formed the seed that multiplied and eventually enabled the commander-in-chief to direct about a million men. 'A general,' Wavell aptly wrote, 'should never try to do his own staff work.'[3]

Two weeks after his arrival Wavell held a meeting with his fellow-commanders-in-chief: Admiral Sir Andrew Cunningham, the cheerful but pugnacious commander of the Mediterranean Fleet, and the senior airman in the Middle East, Air Chief Marshal Sir William Mitchell.[4] It was as clear to Wavell and Cunningham as it was to the War Cabinet that sea power was crucial. If Britain were to lose control of the Mediterranean, Egypt would also be lost, and without Egypt on the Empire's side, Turkey, Syria, Palestine, Iraq and Arabia would all be exposed to Axis expansion, including the looming threat from Japan in the east.

Without delay the three commanders instituted a Joint Planning Committee. Their basic assumptions were that the eastern Mediterranean would be the most important theatre of war; that Egypt would be the principal base for the Allied war effort; and that the prime objective was to eliminate Italy, unless she remained neutral, by fighting her as soon as possible, and thus prevent the enemy from gaining a foothold in the Balkans.

Wavell analysed the logical progression ahead of him. First, he could not engage an enemy unless he had established a firm base from which to operate. Second, he must give paramount consideration to the most important part of his command – Egypt. This would lead him directly into the minefield of Egyptian politics, and into close contact not only with the influential British Embassy in Cairo, but directly with the leading military and civil authorities in Egypt, including its King. Third, he had to importune his military and perhaps his political chiefs until he received the supplies and troops with which to go to war. After all that, he could devise strategies for major land operations both in defence of his command and beyond its borders.

The command was certainly varied: from polyglot, political Cairo to remote outstations with strange customs – such as Siwa, the most important oasis in North Africa, far away on the edge of the Libyan Sand Sea. In the 1930s it was a highlight of a Cook's Tour, and in ancient times the Army of Cambyses had been engulfed by a terrible sandstorm on their way there, and no trace was ever found of them. Until a few years before Wavell's arrival, marriages between male partners had been considered normal there and were registered in the town hall.

Wavell issued a general instruction to his subordinate commanders to assume that Italy would declare war, and to work out their requirements for the following six months on that basis. He ordered plans to be drawn up for offensive action in the far reaches of his command: for the capture of Bardia and the Jarabub Oasis in the Western Desert; for reinforcements for Iraq; for operations in Kenya and Sudan to 'destroy and disperse' Italian forces along the Ethiopian border; for supporting local uprisings in concert with a foray from French Somaliland; and for an attack on the Kufra Oasis in the Sahara, by joining up with French forces based in Chad for a drive north to attack the Italians in Libya.

Then he turned to logistics, to plan how Egypt could be transformed into a base to support operations in all the places in which he might have to fight. It all conformed to the higher commander's priorities as set out in the writings that had helped propel him to the top:

> the technicalities of his trade must come first, and a really sound know-
> ledge of administration, organisation, and transportation is the proper
> basis of technical military knowledge, rather than strategy and tactics.
> All the great commanders have had this understanding of the

principles and practice of movement and administration – the 'logistics' of war.[5]

He did not have long to reflect: one month after his arrival in Cairo, war was declared.

The dismal years of attempting to be reasonable to unreasonable men, of justifying the sacrifice of far-away countries, of exploring every dubious avenue in the desperate effort to maintain the veneer of peace had passed without success. Appeasement had failed:

> *Lord Halifax is ready*
> *To take off for Berlin,*
> *And if he gives them Danzig*
> *We just might save our skin.*
> *Why should we do the fighting*
> *The Jews will stand to gain,*
> *We are the ones who'll suffer*
> *If England fights again.*[6]

Wavell was playing golf when he received the news but, with an echo of Drake on Plymouth Hoe, he merely observed that there was nothing much that he could do about it, and finished his game.

The following months were to prove an anti-climax: the 'Phoney War' sedated the Western Front, and the British Government confined itself to putting economic pressure on Italy, issuing instructions that nothing should be done to provoke her to fight. For Wavell this was both frustrating and dangerous. He could do no aggressive forward planning either in the Balkans or in Africa itself, he could not build a network of spies in Italian territory or broadcast propaganda to encourage support for Britain, and the Suez Canal remained on a peacetime basis, so that Wavell had to allow the passage through it of ships bound for Italian East Africa, laden with explosives, ammunition and other war supplies, which would in due course be used against his own soldiers.

Despite their initial instinct to get to grips with the enemy, shortages in equipment and manpower constrained all three services. Without men and machines, their plans for offensives would be mere fanciful ideas: 'It was also clear to General Wavell that the land forces in the Middle East would sooner or later have to be appreciably strengthened if their contribution to the war was not to be confined to trying not to lose it.'[7] They also discovered in Egypt an entrenched reluctance to prepare for war. So they concluded that a period of Italian neutrality might suit them after all.

Wavell lost no time in taking the first logical steps for developing his command: planning the construction of a great military base in Egypt for fifteen divisions, in practice nearly 350,000 troops. This was a tall order, considering that when Wavell arrived in Egypt the country contained barely one-tenth of that. There was one mobile division; the 4th Indian Division, under strength; a New Zealand Division, also partially manned; two artillery regiments and fourteen British infantry battalions. However stalwart the men themselves were, what they had in common was incomplete training, too few guns, limited ammunition, insufficient transport and a lack of fighting vehicles.

With his other forces, in Palestine, Kenya, the Sudan, Aden, Cyprus and on the border of Italian East Africa, Wavell had an overall strength of about 86,000. In addition there was the Egyptian Army, an unknown quantity in a major battle, but one that might prove invaluable for sparing fighting troops from duties in rear areas. Although he did not know it, the forces he could count on when he started to make his plans were wholly insignificant in number compared with the Italian Army, which at the start of hostilities would easily exceed half a million men, supposedly burning to fight for the new Roman Empire in Africa.

The task of forming a base for the huge army that he had to create involved an enormous amount of ancillary planning and the design of a comprehensive infrastructure. A railway linked Cairo and the deep-water ports of the Delta, but along the Suez Canal wharves had to be built or refurbished, tracks laid and cranes and docking equipment installed. A few miles away, where the Pyramids of Giza had been quarried thousands of years earlier, caves designated as stores for bombs and ammunition would have to be prepared. Petrol and water had to be transported and stored, pumps fitted and pipelines laid. Building materials were needed for roads, railways and runways, and steel, gelignite, cranes, workshops, stores and a myriad items of equipment, large and small, were also required. Mobile and armoured forces might have to march and fight over long distances, on different types of ground and in all weather, and be equipped accordingly. Alexandria and the Canal had to be linked with the forward army base at Mersa Matruh, so that the troops, once equipped, could be sent into battle. And there was little time to spare.

A small peacetime staff could not begin to cope with such plans, which were in any case only the first stage. The staff at GHQ soon began to grow and then to mushroom. This was hardly surprising, and while in many ways they would do a superb job, they would become the butt of soldiers in the fighting line, as many of the staff, through no fault of their own, never went near the front. Because of the cloth of their formal service dress they became known as 'the Gaberdine Swine'. In Cairo GHQ established itself in two blocks of flats, surrounded with barbed wire. Known as 'Grey Pillars', it was a grim place with long corridors and cheerless, airless rooms, described by one general as 'a great, frowning fortress, full of robots, ruled by the old school tie principle, all trained to believe that not to think alike is an affront both to taste and to discipline'.[8]

High above the robots, Wavell installed himself in an office next door to his chief of staff, and contemplated the many aspects of his task. It was not the role of the commander-in-chief himself to follow the progress of his plans in detail, but to appoint a staff that he could inspire with his vision and with the logic of his approach, while keeping sufficiently well informed to detect delay or error and to order its rectification. Wavell had long had a knack of finding good officers to work for him, although inevitably, having to select so many during his career, he did make some bad choices.

Meanwhile, he took the next step in the development of his command – liaison with Britain's allies, actual and potential, in the Middle East theatre. In effect, that meant France and Turkey. Britain had come to regard Turkey, her bitter enemy in the previous war, as the linchpin of the Balkan states. She was thought to be worth courting because she supposedly had a strong army, manned by determined fighters. The Allies had already agreed a Treaty of Mutual Assistance with Turkey, and Wavell was ordered to go to the Turkish capital to sign the pact and pave the way for a military mission. Accompanied by Sir Arthur Smith, he arrived in Ankara for four days of talks with Marshal Fevzi Cakmak, the Turkish chief of staff, and with the French leader General Weygand. Wavell fully supported the mission as he believed that Germany might soon move into the Balkans, writing to the CIGS, on his return from Ankara:

Personally, I still do not believe that the Germans will make their big effort in the West, and I think that they will turn south east next Spring or earlier. The sooner we can get the Turk well provided and confident; have a much stronger Air Force out here; and give me a good Central Reserve here or in Palestine, the better.[9]

The meetings were inspired and led by Weygand, who, as Allied commander-in-chief in the Middle East, was senior to Wavell, and fully conscious of the importance of his position. Not yet having much military weight to pull, Wavell said little. So, apparently, did the Turkish representatives, who, as Wavell put it, concentrated on trying to find out what England and France would do, without disclosing their own intentions.

There was no let-up in Wavell's schedule of meeting the leaders in all the Allied power points in the Middle East. In December he flew to Baghdad to meet the British Ambassador, Sir Basil Newton, whom he balefully regarded as an appeaser; he also met the Chief of the Iraqi General Staff and the Regent, Abdulillah. This journey unnervingly – except for Wavell, who displayed no emotion in the matter – exemplified the dire effect he seemed to have on aircraft, and as many as five machines were required to complete the journey: two broke down, one crashed, a fourth turned back as it could not see in the dark, and he got home to Cairo in the fifth. It was perhaps rather strange that he was always so 'air-minded' and travelled by air wherever possible – a trait found in his offspring, with two of his daughters achieving a pilot's licence.

A few weeks later Wavell met General Nogués, commander-in-chief in French North Africa, in Tunis, to the east of which lay the Italian colony of Libya, which itself bordered Egypt. The French, in line with their Maginot mentality, had constructed a system of defences which they called the 'Mareth Line', along a natural barrier of hills in Tunisia. Wavell was most impressed by this, and by the number of troops in position, noting with rueful pleasure that the 'French count in Divisions, while we count in battalions'. He shared some of their optimism, telling Sir John Dill, although without any very obvious grounds for doing so, 'I don't think the Boche is really anything like as good as he makes out, or we apparently believe . . . [he is nothing] like the soldier he was in 1914, and I believe the machine might easily break down under a real strain.'[10]

He had visited the important stations of his command, met their commanders and given them instructions; he had made overtures to his French counterparts, and had taken negotiations with the Turks as far as they could go for the time being. Next, having set in hand a survey and plans for a major development of military bases, he turned his attention to the politics in Egypt, where Britain's long-predominant role and her military might gave the incumbent commander-in-chief a place of considerable importance.

As he examined the problems in Cairo itself, his overall duties were enlarged even further, by the Army Council extending his command to include British land forces in Turkey, the Balkans, East Africa and the Persian Gulf.

All this extra responsibility piled on his shoulders carried a nominal promotion, and he was made 'Commander-in-Chief, Middle East', while, informally, he began to be known as 'The Chief'. With the outbreak of war, the British Cabinet had decreed that its priorities were the defence of the United Kingdom, of Singapore and of the Middle East, in that order. Wavell was now one of the three most powerful people in one of the three most important places in the whole British Empire.

At the declaration of war Egypt had complied with its treaty obligations and broken off diplomatic relations with Germany, while turning a blind eye to a network of intrigue centred on the Italian Embassy, which had strong links to the palace in Cairo. Although, *in extremis*, imperial interests would override those of Egypt, it was incumbent on Wavell to help win Egypt's support without disturbing its neutrality. His main co-protagonist in this enterprise was the British Ambassador, Sir Miles Lampson.

The attitude of the young King Farouk was of crucial importance, partly because he had the power to dismiss the Government and to appoint the Prime Minister. He was only nineteen when Wavell arrived in Cairo, and required careful handling. He had lately been tutored by an Englishman, Edward Ford,[11] who, when he could engage the royal attention, had tried to advise the King on how to mix with his subjects and make the most of his position:

> Until he came of age he ruled through a Regency Council of three, with an uncle predominant, and spent valuable hours driving fast cars around the palace grounds, and going to nightclubs in barely effective disguises. When he drove into Cairo he had a cavalcade, with outriders and so on. Heady stuff. When I arrived I asked Lampson what I was to tutor him in, and he replied 'Oh, just teach him not to lose his temper when you beat him at tennis.' I tried to teach him history – we used H.G. Wells' *History of the World* and books like that, and I told him that he would have to make speeches, and should probably prac-tise; so I taught him what was needed – giving him passages to recite

from the *Oxford Book of English Prose*. He was rather good. The Comptroller of his Household was Hassanein Pasha, a cultivated man, Balliol and so forth; he was a Bedouin, really, and had explored in the Sahara, with Rosita Forbes, and down in the south east, on the Sudan border . . . But he wanted to control Farouk himself, and not the British.[12]

There was a real threat that Egypt might make difficulties in the event of Italy declaring war. Anti-British feeling ran high in the Egyptian Parliament and press, and the greater part of Cairo's native quarter had consequently been placed out of bounds to troops. Wavell believed that the internal situation in Egypt was more pressing than any external threat, explaining his view to the CIGS:

The Egyptians are not a warlike nor a stable race, and view the possibility of being involved in war, especially a totalitarian war, with an apprehension that would require very little to turn to panic . . . it would be folly not to recognise the serious possibilities of the internal situation in Egypt, with its excitable mob, irresponsible politicians, vulnerable communications and large European population to be protected.[13]

There was also evidence that the King and some of his courtiers were as pro-Italian as they were anti-British, although neither sentiment counted for much when set against their desire for a proper respect for their independence. Farouk had inherited from his father in Italy several million pounds,[14] one of a number of reasons why he was disinclined to rock Mussolini's boat. Behind the closed doors of the Abdin Palace there were other influences at work, softer, but not necessarily less persuasive. Each day Pulli, the King's Italian barber, whispered into his ear the Italian Legation view, and Mussolini had succeeded in introducing a number of beauties into the palace, primed to gather information about British forces. These silken strands helped to bind together the occupants of high places in Rome and Cairo.

Lampson was in the slightly embarrassing position of having a half-Italian wife,[15] which made it difficult for him to urge Farouk to divorce himself from his Italian cronies. In fact, most Egyptians appeared – at least in front of the British – more circumspect than the King. Mussolini's invasion of Ethiopia in 1935 had given the Egyptians a considerable jolt, and they had reluctantly come to accept that, with the Italians in Libya and Ethiopia, they would need Britain's support to remain independent. Despite its propaganda, which was absorbed with relish in the cafés and bars of Cairo, the Axis held little appeal for the large majority of Egyptians:

> War is feared, but in no panicky way, as there seems to be real faith in Great Britain's power to defend Egypt and a philosophic attitude towards the potentialities of the future . . . Italians are generally disliked, and it is remarkable how widespread is the story of the execution in Tripoli of some Arab leaders by throwing them out of aeroplanes.[16]

Yet the British Army wanted a more positive demonstration of loyalty, and Wavell continued to urge Lampson to press the Egyptian Prime Minister into a declaration of war. In the meantime it seemed likely that the Egyptian authorities would continue to co-operate with the British, even if without enthusiasm.

He now began to consider how he might meet an Italian attack, which he considered more than likely. That involved, first, a detailed assessment of the size of the forces on each side. During the early months of 1940, planning was based on the assumption that the French would deploy their Mediterranean Fleet and large land forces, and fight side by side with the British. It appeared that, even so, the Italians would have preponderance over the Allies. To gain time, Wavell had to deceive the enemy into thinking that he had considerably greater forces at his disposal than was in fact the case. This was a tactic that appealed to him.

His burdens had been made easier to bear by the arrival of his wife and daughters, in November 1939. Lady Wavell[17] had soon taken up good works for servicemen, establishing canteens and other forms of relief, where – by now an ample, rather motherly figure disdaining make-up – she would chat to the troops, smiling with her bright blue eyes, which she frequently closed while talking. Pamela had joined the VAD[18] and was working at the Scottish General Hospital outside Cairo; Felicity was employed at GHQ, and Joan, only sixteen, had been enrolled at the French school in the city. An apartment was found for the two girls and Miss Daisy Ribbands, a Lowestoft girl who had helped to bring up all four children, now serving as Lady Wavell's personal maid. Archie John, having recovered from his foot injury, was at home with the Black Watch.

Wavell and his wife moved in with General Maitland Wilson, who had offered to share his house with them. This 'modest villa', as the MP Chips

Channon called it, was a large white house belonging to the copper magnate Chester Beatty, and had an Arab courtyard and fountain, and a garden full of palms, hibiscus and bougainvillaea. It was situated on Gezira, an attractive island on the Nile, opposite the riverside Kasr-el-Nil army barracks and half a mile north of Garden City and GHQ. Nearby were several royal summer palaces; Cairo's botanical gardens, with its palms and eucalyptus; a racecourse; the opera house; and wide, tree-lined streets like the Sharia Amir Fuad, with elegant villas and apartments temporarily crammed with British service personnel. The river itself was a tonic to those at work in the city, flowing bright blue in spring, lined by Flame of the Forest trees covered with scarlet flowers, and with swift feluccas with white sails skimming past slow, heavy cotton barges creeping silently on their way.

Before breakfast, and the drive to Grey Pillars in the back of a sleek black Packard, Wavell would set out, striding quickly with his lithe, springy walk, over the short distance from his house to the Gezira Sporting Club and the racecourse where, before the Egyptian sun began to scorch, he would ride, followed by a swim in the club's pool, afterwards chatting, in his slightly grating voice, with senior officers. When riding he would often wear a pair of shiny black-leather Mexican chaps, unusual in Cairo, of the type made for cowboys to ride through undergrowth without their legs being spiked by thorns or bitten by snakes. He would be accompanied by an ADC and sometimes by one of his daughters, as the going was easy and no bravado was needed to match the general's fearlessness when on a horse. Although not so restrictive as accompanying his former commander, Sir Philip Chetwode, who forbade talking while in the saddle, riding with Wavell was a test of conversation as well as of equitation; as one of his ADCs[19] put it: 'Communication with Wavell was like a game of golf – you hit the ball down the fairway and it didn't come back. But every now and then some spark of reciprocity was ignited, and then it became a game of tennis, fast and furious . . .' Wavell enjoyed golf, at which he had a single-figure handicap, and frequently played it with young men on his staff, partly for a change from his ponderous contemporaries and partly to keep himself informed of opinion among the junior officers.

Meanwhile in London he received a boost to his reputation as a writer when the spring lists of new books – rather short, in the wartime conditions – included the first volume of his life of Allenby.[20] It was soon acclaimed by the public, even if it also drew somewhat caustic comments from would-be literary lions: George Orwell, reviewing the book in the magazine *Horizon*,[21] noted similarities between biographer and subject – Allenby had read widely, could translate from Greek texts and wrote good English – and concluded that 'he remains totally uninteresting – a fact which also tells one a good deal about General Wavell'. As it happened, Orwell's review, although written when the book was first released, was not published until December, when it coincided with news of the general's famous victory at Sidi Barrani, in the campaign that was to make him a household name. This resulted in a certain amount of egg on Orwell's face, and indignation in the columns of *The Spectator* and the *Daily Telegraph*.

Horizon's editor defended himself on the grounds that 'the review was written in the early summer, at a time when the title of general was unreassuring, and when Orwell had no inkling that the biographer of Allenby was to prove greater than his subject'. Orwell himself had the grace to apologise and to acknowledge that the laugh was on him: 'Mr Orwell states that he was mistaken about General Wavell, and is glad he was mistaken, sorry to have made the mistake.'[22] He also expressed his doubts as to whether anything he had said would seriously affect the general. That was certainly perceptive, as Wavell – like Allenby – would have been wholly unmoved by the eddies of hot air gusting around Bloomsbury.

Now, installed in Cairo, and with great works to be accomplished, he no longer had much opportunity to write, but some of his spare time was taken up with reading – sometimes books that were serious, at other times those that were less so, such as novels by Peter Cheyney or, for bedtime reading, James Hadley Chase's *No Orchids for Miss Blandish*, a tale of kidnap, sadism, rape and torture, much enjoyed by British troops at the time.[23] For further relaxation he would often carry with him *Le Morte d'Arthur*, by Sir Thomas Malory.[24]

Wavell now took on a new ADC in succession to Captain Michael Baker-Baker of the Black Watch: tall and good-looking, Peter Coats was a thirty-year-old officer in the Middlesex Yeomanry, part of the 1st Cavalry Division that had formed in Palestine. He had been recommended to Wavell by Sir George Clark, the divisional commander, who was acquainted with Coats' family. In one respect he was an excellent choice as ADC, for he turned out to have great talent as an organiser and general 'fixer', and the ability to erase minor irritations from the general's busy schedule. Like his boss he was a writer, and enjoyed quoting authors and reciting verse. He was a good linguist, and artistic, with excellent taste and an interest in people – the fact that his interest increased in proportion to their birth, wealth or other forms of glamour also suited the job, as Cairo had a rich and cosmo-politan society, which acted as a bridge between leading Egyptian politi-cians, the British Embassy and senior officers of the three services. It was also of general benefit that Wavell should be at his ease as much as his work permitted, and should be able to refresh himself for his arduous duties; and the bohemian, artist and man of letters in his blood yearned for an outlet beyond the constant demands of soldiering. To a high degree Cairo had something no longer on offer anywhere else in Europe or the Middle East: a vivacious round of dances, dinners, garden-parties, swimming, tennis, golf, riding and nightclubs, attended by the Egyptian royal family, high officials and servicemen, as well as by playboys and a fashionable international set. In this milieu Wavell made friends beyond his army comrades and their families.

He was, for example, intrigued by the diminutive and rotund Freya Stark, who worked as a propagandist for Britain's cause. Before long he gave his blessing to the 'Brotherhood of Freedom', the clandestine network of Arab sympathisers with Britain, through whom Miss Stark planned to counter Fascist propaganda and spread the gospel of the British Empire to Egyptian society and the wider Arab community beyond. She recorded her first impres-sions of Wavell: 'An officer with many ribbons, active, not tall, with grizzled hair and a steadfastness, as of friendly granite, about him; and in his genial expression, a look of gaiety and youth.'[25] Freya Stark was spellbound by Wavell, loving the 'informality and youthful high spirits' of the family's household in Cairo, besides being attracted to the glamour of his position and the circles in which he moved.[26] Lady Wavell, however, did not share her husband's liking for the vibrant and ubiquitous lady, coldly referring to her, if she had to at all, as 'that Miss Stark'.

Wavell also became better acquainted with the all-important 'Sampson and Delilah', as Sir Miles Lampson and his youthful wife were known. They introduced the general to a wide cross-section of people, and despite his habitual shyness he did from time to time become loquacious – at Cairo parties and nightclubs, for example, especially when in the company of attrac-tive women, or finding that he was with people who shared his knowledge and love of verse or literature. Even in such unmartial surroundings Wavell was an imposing presence, described by observers as sturdy and with a rasping voice, a direct eye and an attractive smile.

It was largely his new ADC who was the catalyst for exposing Wavell to this starlit society, and although it might seem strange that even in the social sphere a mere ADC should have much effect on a commander-in-chief, to some people in Cairo it seemed that Coats did so:

> Wavell, indeed, was a man of wide culture as well as natural talent, but he had spent his life in a rather narrow circle and had never been encouraged to talk. Peter Coats, who belonged to the sophisticated world of 'Chips' Channon and Lady Cunard, now became, as it were, his impresario. He stimulated Wavell's interest or sense of fun; fed him the gossip of Cairo and brought people to his house whom he would never otherwise have seen, but whose talk influenced opinion.[27]

Prior to Coats' arrival, uncharitable guests had commented on the rather dull atmosphere of the Wavells' dining-room: with the roost ruled by Lady Wavell, scant attention was paid to food, drink or creature comforts. Coats managed to change all that: haute cuisine took the place of roast meat and apple pie, while beer and whisky bottles made way for decanters of good wine. Meals for important visitors became enlivened by the presence of others chosen for their wit or good looks.

However, in the formal sphere that Coats had entered, the fact that he was homosexual could be described as slightly unfortunate. At that time in many circles, not least in the military, unorthodox predilections were frowned upon. There was also the risk that they might attract the attention of the police and lead to the customary sentence of two years' penal servitude, with solitary confinement in cells without mattresses, or worse discomforts. In a way, therefore, it was unwise for Wavell to have engaged Coats as an ADC: it suggested a certain innocence, especially as Cairo – home to every venal vice and taste – was a sink of gossip. Tongues began to wag, and all the faster some months later when Henry Channon, Parliamentary Private Secretary to the Foreign Office Minister R.A. Butler, passed through Cairo on his way to Yugoslavia in the course of official business and sought out the company of Coats, who had for some time been more than just a good friend.

Wavell either did not notice this defect in his new ADC; or, like Queen Victoria, did not understand – although the chance of that, for someone who had attended a Victorian public school, was less than slender – or he may just have been unconcerned. Likewise with Lady Wavell, who had vetted Coats before her husband agreed to take him on. 'Lady Wavell must have been quick to give her OK,' wrote Coats, after his interview with the commander-in-chief, 'because the c-in-c, who was very much under her influence, came back into the garden after quite a short time, and said could I report for duty the next day?'[28] The new ADC soon proved himself to be an excellent choice, and from the start of their association, which was to last for several years, Wavell greatly appreciated Coats' wit, culture, wide-ranging knowledge and general ability.

Meanwhile the presence of Wavell's family in Cairo had added zest to what the British Ambassador called an *Opera Bouffe* that was giving rise, in a very English way, to all sorts of resentment and general wasting of official time. This concerned what became known as 'illicit wives'. The settled policy of the War Office was that, except under very restricted circumstances concerned with war work, wives should not be allowed to stay in Cairo. However, many women could not endure being away from their husbands, with war injecting doubt into the long-term future of their marriages. In other cases wives were not only keen themselves to escape the dangers and drabness of England, but also wished to be helpful to their husbands by being on hand to protect them from the temptations of Cairo.

In this lively matter the British Ambassador took up the cudgels with Brigadier Shearer, Wavell's intelligence chief and the War Office Liaison Officer, who had spent much time vainly trying to clear the area of illicit wives. Lampson asked him how he explained the fact that he had himself exempted various ladies:

> I next asked, even more innocuously, how it came that Lady Wavell and her three daughters were apparently staying here? Wasn't that rather odd in view of the general embargo? [Shearer said it was because of special decisions at home in order to help Wavell entertain.] . . . This, though I naturally did not say so, is exceedingly rich seeing that the Wavells since they have been here have descended on Jumbo Wilson's house where they have remained firmly put, and have done practically no entertaining of any sort or kind since they have been here.[29]

Wavell remained serenely above such matters. Although a number of tenacious wives found sanctuary in the Interpreter Corps, or at GHQ as secretaries or other helpmates to high-ranking officers, he himself was sparing with their use. Not for him the dictation of an Eden or a Churchill, pacing the room as a clattering typewriter caught the measured cadences: he was a comparatively slow worker and would spend hours on his own, producing clear, succinct orders for his subordinates, or writing handwritten reports, dipping his wooden pen into an inkwell.

Beyond the lights of Egypt the situation in Europe was beginning to deteriorate, as the *Wehrmacht* drilled a series of deep holes into a disintegrating French Army, and as the British Expeditionary Force, shedding vital equipment all along the way, retreated into the pocket of Dunkirk. Wavell set out a blueprint for action should the battle for France be lost – something that, when war broke out, would have seemed to most people impossible, but which was not at all inconsistent with Wavell's pre-war opinion of the French High Command. His speculations, in his note entitled 'The Worst Possible Case', were remarkably accurate:

Germans obtain temporary air superiority in France. French collapse.
UK in state of siege and subject to heavy bombing attacks.
ME cut off and attacked by Italy, supported perhaps by German air or troops . . .[30]

In that calamity he also envisaged both an anti-British rising in Iraq and the evacuation of British Somaliland. All of the above, in one form or another, were actually to happen.

In what Wavell called the 'Mongoose Scheme', he examined the necessary General Staff work for a withdrawal.[31] He then considered an outlook even more dire, which he called 'Worse Case Still', in which he visualised the United Kingdom succumbing to invasion, leaving the Empire to provide a final great service to the mother country by carrying on the fight 'on the line Canada–S. Africa–India–Malaya–Australia–NZ'.

However, at the end of May 1940, even as the perimeter shrank around Dunkirk, Wavell took a more positive view and sent the CIGS a synopsis of his outlook on the war: it centred on oil, which, together with shipping, air and sea power, was in his view the key to ultimate victory. He concluded with lucid confidence that the Empire had access to practically all the world's supplies of oil, had most of the shipping and potentially the greatest air power, and 'therefore', he wrote, 'we are bound to win the war'.

Perhaps what happened next was set in stone from the moment Germany signed an Armistice, on a bleak November day in a railway carriage at Compiègne. France, bled white at Verdun, beat its swords into ploughshares and its spears into pruning-hooks and turned to the pleasures of peace, while the Germans, of a different mettle, settled for vengeance. After twenty years, disordered and corrupted each in their separate ways, the two nations fought once more, when one kick of the jackboot shattered the ancient, decorated door of France into a thousand splinters.

Italy watched these events with growing delight. Since the start of the war she had remained firmly on the sidelines, not wishing to risk her armies, or her hold on Ethiopia or her African colonies. Following the invasion of the Low Countries and the apparent collapse of the French Army, Mussolini became convinced that Germany would be victorious. He decided to join in before it was too late, so as to be able to claim a share of the spoils. Withdrawing all but the most formal contact with the Allies, and in touch, apparently, with a Higher Authority, Mussolini took his stance: 'The King Emperor and the Duce,' he proclaimed, 'have been charged by the Almighty to rouse the people to anger in the name of Justice.'

The fight was on. Italy declared war from midnight on 10 June 1940. Wavell was free to unleash his forces on an enemy that all along he had expected to face.

VIII

AIMING THE GUN

WITH a firm base established, and the co-operation of the Egyptians apparently secured, Wavell could turn to developing a strategy for attack.

Mussolini's grand design was to consolidate a new Roman Empire in Africa. To achieve that, he had to link his North and his East African colonies, an outcome that required the prior expulsion of the British from Egypt. For his purpose Mussolini had to be able to supply his colonies from the Italian homeland, and that depended upon control of the sea lanes through the Mediterranean and the Red Sea, and freedom of the air above Egypt. Italy already had bases along the coast of Eritrea, potentially enabling her forces to dominate the Red Sea, while Ethiopia, conquered by Italy in 1935 and bordering the Anglo-Egyptian Sudan, offered a launch-pad for attacking the British in East Africa. Italy's main need was to secure the Mediterranean, a major undertaking that would necessitate an invasion of Egypt from Libya.

Wavell's prime duty was to safeguard Egypt and the Suez Canal. His intuition told him that despite Il Duce's imperial dream, the Italians would not be ready to attack from Libya for many months, so he decided to clear them out of East Africa first, and then move his forces up to help defend Egypt. But he could not attack in East Africa until the heat of summer had lessened, so he would be running the risk that the Italians might attack in the Western Desert while he still had troops tied down in East Africa. He assessed the Italian mentality and decided that the risk was acceptable.

Skilful juggling was required, as the British force was still greatly below strength – only about 50,000 poorly equipped front-line troops were available, and they were faced on two fronts by an Italian army ten times larger. Further, as the Chiefs of Staff had agreed that Singapore and the United

Kingdom itself must take priority over the Middle East, Wavell had not yet received reinforcements of any significance. He had argued that Italy would soon turn hostile, when reinforcements would be vital. His pleas had been ignored – stonewalled, it seemed, by a lingering desire to appease the Italians. Many of the troops he did have were not fully trained, and certainly not equipped for modern war. The cavalry regiments in Palestine, for example, were still horsed; reports of Polish lancers charging German tanks and troop trains may have filled British cavalrymen with pride, but not with confidence.

The onset of war had ostensibly strengthened imperial ties: before long Australia had almost 200,000 men under arms, and New Zealand 80,000. India had offered to reserve a division to protect the oilfields in the Persian Gulf, and to send reinforcements to Egypt and the Sudan. Other parts of the Empire had also offered to help the mother country. In South Africa, for example, the United Party had been elected on a wave of Empire loyalty, and Jan Smuts was now Prime Minister of a coalition government, although not broad enough to embrace the Afrikaners, who were neutral in sentiment, if not pro-German. South Africa had agreed to place a brigade at the disposal of Middle East Command.

Wavell was grateful for all this badly needed support, even if the Egyptians – particularly parents and publicans with memories of the First World War – were wary at the prospect of another influx of Australian soldiers returning to Cairo. Wavell may have had that in mind in his address of welcome to one newly arrived batch, delivered with a touch of the Winchester school-master that volunteer citizen soldiers might not wholly have relished. He told them:

> I look to you to show them [the Egyptians] that their notions of Australians as rough, wild, undisciplined people given to strong drink are incorrect. The Egyptians, generally speaking, are a kindly and peaceable people, very easy to get on with. They have good manners themselves and very much appreciate good manners.[1]

Six battalions in Palestine constituted a mobile reserve, ready to quell trouble in Egypt or Iraq. Troops were also needed for Palestine itself, to guard the oil installations at Haifa or in case the country slipped back into its recent state of rebellious disorder. If the Italians blocked the Red Sea, the Suez Canal would become superfluous, yet Wavell had hardly any troops available to defend its entry point at Aden. He had a larger number – 17,500 – in Kenya and the Sudan, but even that was not many, considering that they had 2,000 miles of frontier to patrol.

Yet as the German armies rolled irresistibly towards the French coast in May and June 1940, Wavell was urged to send some of his slender force to England. When he declined to comply, Churchill complained of 'catalepsy' in the Middle East: 'It is quite natural,' he said on 6 June, 'that General Wavell should look at the situation only from his own viewpoint. Here we have to think of building up a good army . . . We are indeed the victims of a feeble and weary departmentalism.'[2] On the same day Wavell put his case to his old friend Sir John Dill, now CIGS and his champion against an ardent and insistent Prime Minister entering rapidly into the full flower of his greatness. The danger that Wavell sensed within Egypt itself, as well as the threat on its borders, seemed less intense to the Government far away in England. He cabled the CIGS:

> You, of course, can see the whole picture but I do feel I ought to put before you the psychological aspect.
>
> The Egyptians are frankly scared stiff at the idea of war, and the Prime Minister is always asking for more troops. Removal of troops would have a bad effect on their nerves and might give them an excuse for trying to keep out of their obligations . . .[3]

Loss of nerve was also a problem nearer to home, as the battle in France moved to a climax, and the matter was dropped. But a cloud no larger than a man's hand had appeared on the horizon – and in Churchill's capacious and retentive mind there lodged the memory of the general's plaintive response, as he saw it, to his call for help.

Successfully conserving such forces as there were in the Middle East, Wavell turned to the most effective ways of using them. The enemy, he believed, had fourteen divisions in Tripolitania and six in Cyrenaica, on Egypt's border. Of an estimated 215,000 men, some 40,000 were Blackshirts, their tails high with the joys of being in uniform and in a conquered land, but the morale of the rest, consisting of Italian regulars and about 30,000 Libyans, was questionable: they were poorly trained, weak in artillery and had plenty of good food – perhaps the wrong combination for martial ardour.

The Italian Air Force did, however, present a serious problem. Large numbers of fighters and bombers were based in Libya and the Aegean, but

Wavell, having been forbidden by the Government to fly over and look, had to guess at his enemy's strength; from his patchy intelligence he overestimated the figures by about 40 per cent. He also knew how close Libya was to Italy, and that, for the enemy, reinforcements would not be a major obstacle. He was advised that Italian aircraft were in theory slightly better performers than the RAF's Gladiators and Blenheims, but machinery depends on men, and the RAF commanders were confident that the Italian pilots were no match for their own, despite having recently had live target practice in the Spanish Civil War.

In the more distant part of the new Roman Empire, comprising Eritrea, Italian Somaliland and Ethiopia, the Italians had an army of occupation of nearly 300,000 men, a formidable number on paper, although two-thirds of them were not Italian and lacked some of the fervour of the Blackshirt battalions in their midst. The troops were certainly needed. The Italians were not popular with their native subjects, and had continual difficulty in keeping them down. Asmara, the capital of Eritrea, had for long been in a state of revolt, and the country's garrison of sixty-five battalions were forced to live in armed camps. Nevertheless, with this force opposing him, Wavell regarded the Sudan as practically defenceless for the time being, guarded by only three British battalions, a few thousand Sudanese troops, an assortment of mainly elderly bombers and no artillery. Although he could also call on British troops in Kenya and British Somaliland, and 5,000 Free French, it appeared that overall the Italians had a huge preponderance of forces. On the other hand, Ethiopia was surrounded by the British Empire on three sides – by Kenya, the Sudan and British Somaliland; and if the navy and air force, sustained by the British base at Aden, could dominate the coast, the Italian hinterland might effectively be blockaded, thereby cutting off fuel supplies and stranding the 200 or so aeroplanes that Wavell believed the Italians had ready.

The morale of most of the British troops was high. This had, in some indefinable way, trickled down from the commander-in-chief himself, even though the vast majority of the army (not excepting the already large numbers that worked at GHQ) hardly ever saw Wavell. Even the knowledge of his presence seemed to inspire optimism and determination. In his first month in the Middle East he had encouraged his officers by ordering a study to be made for an attack on Libya from Egypt, and also on Ethiopia from the Sudan. His attention to the troops' well-being also boosted spirits: he pressed the War Office to speed up mail delivery, and he wrote to the King's Private

Secretary suggesting the production of a gramophone recording of royal words of encouragement: 'Reference,' he suggested, 'might possibly be made to physical conditions of life in hot and dusty camps, and to the necessity for patience and the service rendered by waiting and watching, even if not actively engaged.'[4]

Although Wavell worked at a remote level, and when in public was largely undemonstrative, the affection in which the troops began to hold 'Old Archie' grew, and stories about him began to circulate. One of these became a favourite in the ranks of the Aussies – not a group of men instinctively well disposed to British generals. It seemed that one day the commander-in-chief was inspecting some newly arrived Australian troops and wearing his customary monocle, an item the boys from the Outback had never seen before. Nothing was of course said at the time, but when he inspected another Australian battalion the next day, every man in the ranks had some kind of eyeglass or penny in his eye. Wavell appeared not to notice, but marching to the front, having finished the inspection, he took out his own eyeglass, flipped it into the air, caught it in his eye and said, 'I bet none of you bastards can do that!' It is of no consequence that, on several counts, the story was hardly credible; the fact that such tales circulated increased in their small way the loyalty he inspired in his soldiers.[5]

Another encouragement for the men was Wavell's flair, at this point in the war, for picking out good subordinate commanders, in particular two spirited generals, Major-General William Platt, given command in the Sudan, and General Richard O'Connor, sent to the Western Desert Force. With Churchill replacing Chamberlain as Prime Minister,[6] and Italy abandoning neutrality, Wavell ordered his forces to begin offensive patrolling and to plan for action along the eastern border of Cyrenaica. General Platt, far to the south in the Sudan, was told to establish forward positions along the Ethiopian frontier and, conscious of the importance of instilling confidence into troops opposed by such large numbers, Wavell also called for plans to invade Eritrea.

Meanwhile he concerted his actions with the navy and the air force, both led by men as ready as he to fight the enemy from the very first day. He had created a firm base, had placed his few pieces on the board's vital squares and had begun to spread the will to win.

One week after Italy's declaration of war the French gave in. This dramatic change in the balance of the power radically increased the already severe pressure on Britain. In the Mediterranean the navy would face many more enemy ships, while the thousands of miles of imperial possessions bordering those of the French suddenly required an even greater defence commitment. The Germans would gain control of France's bases, and French industry itself would be harnessed to the needs of the Axis.

So it seemed that Wavell's brave show of defiance was reduced to not much more than that, as the forces ranged against the Italian legions were suddenly and enormously depleted in numbers. Now, with the French no longer on Libya's western border, Italy could concentrate her ground and air forces on the frontier of Egypt, while the defection of Syria, a French Mandated Territory, meant that Palestine no longer had a friendly country on its northern flank.

The Italians had not yet shown their form – whether they had a grand design of surging across the desert and joining in triumph the two halves of their empire; or whether they preferred, for the time being, to watch and wait. Faced with this uncertainty, Wavell unveiled another weapon: whereas he himself knew the size and state of his forces, the enemy did not, or so he hoped. He would therefore mislead them into believing that he was far stronger than was actually the case; he would use every practical form of deception that his imagination, and that of his intelligence teams, could devise. Until he could find reinforcements there was little else he could do. Anyway it was a line of attack that had been close to his heart for many years, since the day in Palestine when he had seen the devastating effects of a well-planned trick.

In 1940 Wavell had written a pioneering memorandum on deception for the War Office, and its contents had helped establish the 'London Controlling Section', and contributed to the institutionalising, as a significant factor in the British war effort, of subterfuge as a weapon of war. 'Practically all the ruses and stratagems of war,' he said, 'are variations or developments of a few simple tricks that have been practised by man on man since man was hunted by man.'[7] Deception, he suggested, should be an integral part of staff planning, and in the Middle East early in the war it was 'about the only effective weapon we had'.

'The father of the particular kind of deception employed in World War II was none other than General Sir Archibald Wavell. The heir he selected was Brigadier Dudley Clarke,' wrote the official historian.[8] Wavell himself was to write about Clarke: 'If he is ever able to tell the story of his work in the last five years of war the book will be, as Kipling once said of another story, "well worth buying but even more worth suppressing".'[9]

Wavell now set about creating his own deception force and inspiring it to confuse the enemy; in this he not only directed broad policy from the high level of a commander-in-chief, using his power to open doors, but also enthusiastically suggested ideas in detail.

Of the various intelligence groups in Cairo that Wavell championed and nurtured early in the war, probably the most celebrated initiatives came from 'A' Force, Mission 101 and the Long Range Desert Group.

The LRDG was largely the brainchild of Major Ralph Bagnold, a well-known explorer who had organised several expeditions into the interior of the North African desert before the war. However, it was Wavell who, with a quick grasp of the possibilities and by his determination to act against the enemy in secret and unorthodox ways, ensured that the force was equipped, supplied and encouraged into battle.

In 1939 Bagnold had been a reservist travelling in a convoy to take up a post in East Africa, when the captain of a nearby ship had got into a muddle with port and starboard; after the ensuing collision the troops were disembarked at Port Said and Bagnold caught a train to Cairo to enjoy some unexpected leave. Having been well known before the war, his arrival at the station was noted by an alert reporter for the *Egyptian Gazette*, a copy of which soon caught Wavell's eye. Without delay GHQ despatched an officer, who found Bagnold and told him: 'Just the man; Wavell wants to see you at once.' Bagnold wrote:

> I found a rather stocky man, with a grim, weatherbeaten face, with one very bright eye. He evidently knew all about me and asked whether I would not rather serve in Egypt. I said that I most certainly would, and that was that. Within two days the War Office had changed my posting.[10]

Bagnold was convinced that in order to take the enemy in Libya by surprise, self-sufficient columns, like the Light Car Patrols that had been so successful in the desert in the First World War, could reach them by crossing great tracts of the Qattara Depression, a 'bottomless salt marsh' in north-western Egypt that was held to be impassable for vehicles.

Having seen Wavell, Bagnold duly prepared proposals, only to have them summarily rejected by the various staff officers to whom he had to show them. Determined to persevere, he persuaded a friendly staff officer in GHQ to place the only remaining copy of his ideas in a prominent position on Wavell's desk. 'I was sent for within an hour,' recalled Bagnold. 'Wavell was alone. He waved me to an armchair and, picking up my memo, said quietly "Tell me more about this."[11]

Bagnold then spoke of the Light Car Patrols – small, self-contained, specially trained parties giving warning of attack from the west by penetrating the uninhabited interior of Libya and studying tracks to discover enemy offensives in preparation:

> He seemed a bit sceptical and asked, 'What would you do if you found no such preparations?' I said, 'How about piracy on the high desert?' At the word 'piracy' his rather grim face suddenly broke into a broad grin. Without a moment's reflection he said 'Can you be ready in six weeks?'[12]

Wavell then called in his chief of staff and dictated a 'talisman' ordering immediate and unquestioning compliance with any of Bagnold's requests for supplies. Having heard Bagnold's ideas, Wavell asked a few questions but, as was often his way, gave out no detailed orders. 'When you are ready,' he said, 'write out your operation orders and bring them to me personally. I'll countersign them . . .'

'I came away astounded,' recorded Bagnold. 'What a man! In an instant decision he had given me absolute carte blanche to do anything I thought best.'

On more than one occasion during the force's early development Wavell arrived, with his cortège of outriders, followers, pilots, pennants and ADCs, to see how preparations were progressing, and made a point of inspecting the first two columns before their opening patrol: 'The old boy looks as if he's dying to come with us,' one soldier was heard to say, and having read the reports of their early exploits Wavell ordered their numbers to be doubled; yet the LRDG was never more than 200 strong. Wavell called it his 'Mosquito Army'.[13]

Having ordered preparations to meet any Italian advance eastwards, and for offensive patrolling along the Libyan border until such time as he received enough reinforcements for a major attack, Wavell turned his thoughts once more to Italian East Africa. He concluded that its central strength was Ethiopia: if the Italians could be dislodged from its rugged citadels, then her coastal colonies, more vulnerable to the Royal Navy and the RAF, might succumb. Ethiopia therefore offered the best target for aggression.

The fact that even after five years of occupation the Italians had failed to pacify Ethiopia had presented Wavell with an opportunity that he had seized some months before Italy declared war. In this he showed uncharacteristic defiance of official policy, which was to adhere to the 'Bon Voisinage Agreement' of 1938, whereby the various colonial powers in East Africa agreed not to stir up restlessness among the natives in each other's domains. Wavell disagreed with the Foreign Office's policy of appeasing Italy and largely disregarded it in relation to Ethiopia. He began to consider how to foster discontent there, against the day when he could inspire a rebellion, to coincide with a British attack.

He knew exactly who could help him, and shortly after his arrival in Cairo he sent for Daniel Sandford, a former artillery colonel. Some years earlier Sandford had been farming north of Addis Ababa when he had come to the notice of Haile Selassie, the Emperor of Ethiopia, who had become perturbed by Italy's mounting pressure on his country. Sandford soon became a trusted friend, and when the Italians invaded Ethiopia he had been forced to escape from the country, along with the Emperor himself.

In due course, ignoring the fact that he had been told by the Government not to arrange contact with rebels in Ethiopia or to send agents into Italian territory, Wavell summoned Sandford and instructed him to prepare the ground for a rebellion in Ethiopia, should war break out between Britain and Italy: 'You are my expert on Ethiopia,' the general told him, 'I will leave you to get on with it until it comes my way.'[14] Sandford therefore came to plan, form and command 'Mission 101', which it was hoped would spark revolt in Ethiopia. Having examined Sandford's plans, Wavell endorsed them and at once exerted his influence to overcome Foreign Office reluctance and get them accepted by the Government.

Despite shortage of men and equipment Wavell himself had now, after eleven months in command, instigated, encouraged and put in place imaginative and unorthodox but practical ideas that were about to discomfit the enemy. He had shown exceptional skill in juggling the forces at his disposal and had instilled such confidence into his commanders that, by the time Italy did declare war, Britain had an army in the Middle East ready, willing and able to fight.

Wavell had also to secure Kenya and the Sudan against attack. To do that, he had to gather enough troops, and then train them to fight in particularly difficult and varied local conditions. He had in mind the transfer of Indian troops to East Africa, and General Smuts, having already sent a brigade of South Africans, was promising squadrons of fighters as soon as they could be assembled. When all these were ready they would converge, from Sudan in the north and Kenya in the south, on Ethiopia itself; there the natives would rise up and join them. Italy would be ousted from the country.

That was the plan. But Wavell realised that it would take many months to prepare an offensive: men and equipment were lacking, and heavy rains would hamper both movement and training. Unfortunately, reasons for delay seemed less cogent in London than to the people on the ground, and taken with other factors that were also hard to understand from afar, they began to concern the Chiefs of Staff and the Prime Minister, who started volubly to express impatience. In Churchill's mind there arose a faint doubt as to whether Wavell was actually making full use of the resources that the Chiefs of Staff were putting at his disposal, at great risk to the home country, and he wrote:

> Where is the South African Brigade of 10,000 men, why is it playing no part in the Middle East? We have agreed to-day to send further reinforcements of Hurricanes and other modern aircraft to the South African Air Force. What is happening to the concert of the campaign in the Middle East? What has been done by the Committee of Ministers I recently set up?[15]

Wavell had answers to all these points. Nevertheless, some of the responses that he gave, such as his explanation that the South Africans needed to 'become acclimatised and learn anti-malaria precautions etc.', failed to assuage the Prime Minister's impatience. And it was perhaps wise of him to reply to Sir John Dill rather than directly to Churchill himself, when commenting, 'I am sure you will keep considerations of geography, climate, deserts, distances etc., constantly in the minds of the Middle East Committee. It all looks so simple to them and others on a small-scale map.'[16]

Meanwhile the Duke of Aosta, commander-in-chief of the Italian forces in East Africa, also moved finally onto the offensive and ordered an attack on British Somaliland. This colony, sandwiched between Eritrea and French Somaliland, had little to justify its place in the British Empire – apart from having access to the sea through the rather shallow port of Berbera – except the pleasure of denying it to rival powers. Wavell, though, had said that it must be defended. He was unwilling to contemplate what would be the first ever retraction in the Empire's frontiers – apart from a patch of desert on the edge of the Sudan, which in 1931 had been ceded by the Foreign Office to Italy following a map-reading dispute.

British Somaliland was vulnerable to invasion from three sides, and early in August there appeared from the east, in heavy rain, a three-pronged force of medium tanks, armoured cars, artillery and twenty-six battalions, the air above them pulsating with fifty-seven Italian aircraft. Wavell had told the Chiefs of Staff that he would defend the territory, but that it would need five battalions. These he quickly scraped together from African and Indian regiments and the local Camel Corps, placing them under the command of a colonel of Marines, whom he promoted to brigadier.

It soon became clear that the Italians were mounting a major attack, against which Wavell could muster only a relatively small force, drawn from four different races and supported by a mere four howitzers. Quickly resorting to the juggling at which he was so expert, he ordered in the Black Watch from Aden, a convoy of troops from India and some guns from the forces in the Western Desert. An Australian navy vessel waiting off Berbera in case of the need for an evacuation made the kind offer of a three-pounder saluting gun with thirty rounds of ammunition. He also hurriedly found a major-general[17] to take overall command. The fact that there was no senior officer already there made the new commander's task all the harder. Even with a natural barrier of mountains inland from the coast at Berbera, the discrepancy in numbers made the result inevitable. The British troops manned the passes as best they could – one hill was defended by a petty officer and two ratings, manning the saluting gun mounted on an oil drum – but they were overwhelmed by the size of the enemy force rolling forward towards the sea.

In due course, while the civilians were ferried to safety, units from the British and Australian navies moved in to fire on the Italians as they drew near to the port, and to pick up the retreating British troops. Those taking part returned with accounts of the confusion that often attends a retreating army, including a premature destruction of an important bridge along the escape route. But the rescue force was determined not to leave anyone behind. The officer in charge of the evacuation was Commander Maurice Vernon, who told one of the surviving Black Watch officers of meeting the GOC, General Godwin-Austen, in the harbour:

> Vernon: 'We haven't got the Black Watch down yet. Three or four wounded came along, and then no more.'
> Godwin-Austen: 'I'm afraid the Black Watch are a write-off. You won't see them again, Vernon. The last I heard of them they were doing

a bayonet charge of one battalion against a Division of Italians. The odds are pretty high.'

Vernon: 'You can't write off a whole battalion just like that, General. The Black Watch can't be exterminated.'

Godwin-Austen: 'No, but another tragedy is that the only bridge at La Peron was blown up by mistake by the Sappers. We did of course have it mined, but I didn't send the signal. How they got it, I don't know, but the bridge was blown, so they can't get back.'[18]

'What a general,' Vernon said later. 'No wonder Churchill was angry.'

After a time a small group of soldiers from the Black Watch reached the port, singing and marching in good order, and not at all pleased to learn that they had been written off by their general.[19]

Including the civilians, a total of about 7,000 people were evacuated from Berbera. The British casualties were only 260, but all the stores had to be abandoned. The Italians, on the other hand, lost more than 2,000 men. Nevertheless it was a defeat; the unthinkable had happened, and a British colony had been conquered. The British public was shocked and, as the news spread, the damage to British prestige began to undermine support from the natives in the adjoining territories, in particular Kenya.

The war with Italy was now two months old, but for a year Wavell had been training and deploying his sparse forces with great ingenuity, although all his juggling could not conjure up non-existent equipment. Morale was high, and the army managed to contain potentially overwhelming opposition in an enormous area of land, by vigorous patrolling and through bluff. The Italians seemed for the time being to have been persuaded to stay their hand in Libya, while the damage they had inflicted in East Africa was very slight.

However, other pressures were at work. While Wavell had been building up his bases and his forces, preparing them for battle, he had – as is a commander-in-chief's job – also been pressing the Chiefs of Staff to reduce his deficit in men and equipment. His deployment in the Middle East had been calculated on the basis of the alliance with the French. When that collapsed in North Africa, Syria and Somaliland, he was left facing on his own an enemy that outnumbered him by a huge margin. The War Office had not yet had time to find and send him reinforcements, to fill the gaps or to replace his many items of antiquated and worn-out peacetime equipment.

The War Cabinet had other grave concerns besides the Middle East. Even in February 1940, before the Blitzkrieg erupted, senior generals had resisted the sending of reinforcements to the Middle East. Since then the German attack in the west had destroyed a large part of Britain's army, all its equipment in France and a great number of aeroplanes. And England was faced with the threat of imminent invasion.

Against this background the loss of British Somaliland, although accepted as being of little strategic significance, loomed large as the latest in a number of small actions in Africa in which Empire troops had fought with distinction, but which were nevertheless reverses, coming at a time when bad news, however slight, was hard to bear. Consequently the Prime Minister had become perturbed by the fact that there seemed to him to be a large number of troops who were on the ration strength, but who were not in the fighting line, an opinion that the Chiefs of Staff did not vigorously refute, although they did at the same time greatly respect the way in which Wavell was preparing his widespread command for battle.

It was the shortage of equipment that bedevilled Wavell most of all. In June he had told the CIGS that the internal situation in Egypt headed his list of problems. There was a real possibility that anti-British rioting might require all his reserves for keeping open the Suez Canal and his lines of communication to Palestine and the Sudan, and for the protection of Europeans. But Wavell had also highlighted the lack of defences at the naval base at Alexandria, and the fact that he had hardly any anti-tank or anti-aircraft guns. At the same time the RAF was repeatedly calling for more fighter squadrons with which to face the much larger Italian air force. In London the response remained that the threat of the invasion of England entirely precluded sending any equipment overseas.

Having moved onto the attack in East Africa, the Italians now began to show signs of life on the Libyan frontier. Wavell's strategy for defending Egypt's western border until he had full reinforcements in place was to deploy light armoured forces to dominate the frontier by aggressive patrolling and raiding. A small force of one armoured brigade, some artillery and a few units of mechanised infantry would harass an enemy that Wavell estimated at two or even three complete divisions – some five or six times the size of his own force, and formed up on Egypt's western frontier. If the enemy did begin a major eastward move, Wavell planned to fall right back to his base on the coast at Mersa Matruh, 130 miles from the Libyan frontier, across fifty miles of desert and a further eighty miles of road. He would tempt the enemy to follow on behind, while keeping armoured forces on his southern flank. By the time the Italians reached Mersa Matruh they would, he calculated, have a long and vulnerable line trailing back to their start point. Then he could fall on them with both a frontal and a flank attack, in effect severing the extended neck of the tortoise.

As an additional weapon Wavell had also sanctioned the opening of a camouflage school at a base at Helwan, where craftsmen produced large numbers of dummy tanks, to be placed in appropriate positions in the forward area, thus helping to plant in the enemy's mind a false idea of the size of the British forces. Wavell had taken an early interest in this form of bluff, and had himself suggested the idea of 'sunshields' – superstructures drawn over tanks to make them look like thin-skinned vehicles, which were then placed among lorries and other less important vehicles.

Meanwhile, the Italians were becoming more confident. The collapse of the French had released almost all the Italian troops on the Tunisian frontier, and they were now in position in Cyrenaica, bolstered by increasing amounts of supplies coming through the ports of Benghazi and Tobruk. Emboldened by their increase in strength, the Italians soon surged out of their camps, captured the border strongpoint of Fort Capuzzo and invested Sollum. On 31 July Wavell told London that he would have to evacuate it: 'Sad,' wrote Anthony Eden, the War Minister, 'but not unexpected.'[20]

Wavell knew that sooner or later a major attack would be launched, and his tune remained the same: he was desperately short of equipment. 'We cannot,' he told the CIGS, 'continue indefinitely to fight this war without proper equipment and I hope the Middle East requirements will be delayed no longer.'

England herself was in danger. Invasion was imminent. Beaches bristled with barbed wire; signposts were dismantled; armed with pikes and hammers, old men scanned the horizon, where German aircraft sprawled like bees over their newly conquered airfields. At that grave moment, with one enemy visible at Calais and another about to roll east to Suez, Wavell was summoned to London, to explain the dangers confronting him and to present his case in person to the War Cabinet, and to a Prime Minister whom he had never met.

He arrived in England on Thursday, 8 August, and met Anthony Eden, the War Minister. Eden had just sent a memorandum to Churchill, starkly stating England's danger: there was no anti-tank weapon of any kind, no anti-tank guns and no tanks: 'That,' as Eden later recalled, 'was in the area where, if the Germans were going to land, they might very well be expected to land. That was the state of the cupboard: *it was bare.*'[21]

Wavell's bleak report shook Eden even more: 'Wavell was in good heart,' Eden wrote, 'but the deficiencies are shocking. We shall have to make him up a parcel of what we can scrape together and send it out soon.'[22] As it happened, at this extraordinary and exhilarating hour, when the threat of invasion was acute, there were plenty of spare troops at home, kicking their heels in England or Scotland far from any likely battleground. But the unavoidable fact was that there was too little shipping either to send them out to Wavell, who vitally needed them, or to supply them if they did go.

Having had an initial talk with Wavell, Eden took him to a meeting with the Middle East and the Chiefs of Staff Committees, where the general was confronted not only by the most senior officers of all three services, but also by members of the Cabinet, including Churchill. To this formidable gathering he gave a comprehensive survey of his situation, reviewing the prospects in Egypt and the Western Desert, and ranging over his wide command, from Crete to Syria and from Cyprus to East Africa.[23] Eden commented:

> I thought then that Wavell's account was masterly, and it is even more so in retrospect. He admitted that if the Italians were to bring up a large force some withdrawal would be necessary for a while. The real danger would not arise until German armour and motorised units appeared. The outcome of this meeting was a strong recommendation of our committee and the COS that the despatch of convoys taking reinforcements to the Middle East should be hastened.[24]

There was tension in the air. A few days earlier Churchill had argued heatedly both with his War Minister and the CIGS about Wavell's merits, and the equivocal level of the general's support in the meeting reflected the fact that, masterfully as Wavell was managing the enemy threats, he had as yet delivered no victories: 'I'm sorry, Anthony, that all your generals seem to be such bad generals,' Chamberlain had said to Eden; although, coming from such a famous man of peace, that assessment may not have hurt too much. The country was still reeling from the shock of Dunkirk, and, as has happened down the ages, in the absence of victories politicians blame the generals.

Wavell stood higher than his peers in very many respects, and when he surveyed the Middle East before the assembled servicemen and politicians his mastery of soldiering was clear. Nevertheless, his reticence prevented him from reaching the hearts and minds of his audience, some of whom shared Churchill's feelings about the number of troops in the Middle East who were nowhere near the front line. As Shearer recorded:

> Knowing my Chief as well as I did, I could feel the temperature rising between him and the PM, whose interrogation seemed to me to become increasingly curt.
>
> Finally after Mr Amery[25] asked General Wavell to repeat his appreciation of Marshal Graziani's probable intentions in the Desert, I was aware that the electricity had really built up.
>
> My C in C rather impatiently repeated his previous statement. Now the PM interjected, 'But, Commander-in-Chief, you said . . .' In a flash, General Wavell replied, 'I did not'. And the relations between these two magnificent men were, at that moment, irretrievably damaged.[26]

A few days later there was another difficult meeting, at which the Premier questioned Wavell incessantly, like a terrier, his irritation being increased by Wavell's unwillingness to react. As Eden recorded:

> August 13th. Found Wavell waiting for me at 9 a.m. He was clearly upset at last night's proceedings and said that he thought he should have made it plain that if the Prime Minister could not approve his dispositions and had no confidence in him he should appoint someone else.[27]

The truth was, as Eden put it, that Churchill never understood Wavell, and Wavell never seemed to encourage Churchill to do so.

Yet the general won his way: his quiet determination and inner confidence, sustained by the brainpower that enabled him to master his case, eventually convinced his hearers. Despite the daily threat of invasion, and the desperate air battle over southern England, the War Cabinet agreed to send without delay a convoy to the Middle East; it would be laden with tanks, anti-aircraft guns, field guns, Bren guns, Bofors guns, anti-tank rifles and ammunition. Even so, compared with his enemy's strength, Wavell's manpower remained extremely weak, as the Italians had far more fighters and bombers. Yet now he would be able match their fire-power on the ground. Altogether it was a bold decision: with 104 tanks now to be sent to Alexandria, there would be only about 250 left in the whole of Britain.

That evening Wavell joined Churchill at Chequers, with Eden and Dill, the CIGS, in whose London flat he was staying. Perhaps, in the atmosphere of an attractive house in a lovely country setting, the tension might ease and enable relations between Premier and commander-in-chief to settle into proper harmony. Both men remained wary, but a little progress was made; as Eden noted, 'Wavell was not a man who could be drawn out, or one to make a special effort to please, but there was agreement as to what should be done.'[28]

However, after their return to London there was further discord over the question of whether the convoy should take its chance in crossing the Mediterranean or go by the longer, but safer route around the Cape. With an estimated date of arrival of 26 September via the longer route, Wavell opted for caution, believing that the Italians were unlikely to attack in force in the near future; but he postponed final judgement for his return to Cairo. Admiral Cunningham also preferred the Cape route. Churchill did not, and was scornful of their view. He was sure that if the Germans were frustrated in their invasion attempts, they would go to Italy's assistance with an attack on Egypt, and that September would be the critical month. Sending the armoured division around the Cape would mean that it could play no part in defending either England or Egypt, and that the services were wasting precious resources. It was a subject to which he was to return when the convoy finally did reach Egypt. Meanwhile he sent a note to Eden:

As to the other matters which we discussed last night I have a clear view, and I am favourably impressed by General Wavell in many ways, but I do not feel in him that sense of mental vigour and resolve to overcome obstacles which is indispensable to successful war. I find instead a tame acceptance of a variety of local circumstances in different theatres, which is leading to a lamentable loss of concentration upon the decisive point.[29]

Eden disagreed, replying a few hours later:

Dill and I were much perturbed at your judgment of Wavell. Neither of us know of any senior officer in the army better qualified to fill this very difficult post at this critical time . . . I still hope that our conversation tomorrow will enable you to recover any lack of confidence you may have felt in Wavell.[30]

Wavell was generous enough to agree wholeheartedly that at this time Churchill was an Atlas with the world on his back and that, despite the discontent caused to his ministers and commanders by the goads he applied to them, he was the cornerstone of the Empire, exasperating a few, inspiring millions; and that without him blocking their path, the enemy would very probably prevail.

During Wavell's short stay in England Churchill met him for another matter of major significance: he briefed him fully on 'Ultra', and how the teams of boffins at Bletchley Park were – in the strictest secrecy – beginning to crack the enemy's codes, offering to Britain the hope of countering the armed strength of the Axis to such a degree that final victory might after all be assured. Wavell was one of three men whom Churchill briefed personally on this great secret, and from then on he was to receive all relevant decrypts affecting his theatre of operations. Knowledge of the enemy's plans did not of course mean that they could thereby be thwarted, as would soon become apparent, but it placed a new and immensely valuable weapon in Wavell's hands.

Back in Cairo, he may have wondered whether his turbulent stay in England had not modified his future prospects; perhaps as an insurance policy, he wrote to the University Registrar at Oxford, reviving his interest in the Chichele Professorship and enclosing his CV 'in case the question of Swinton's succession crops up'.

He could now proceed with his plans for defending his command and giving battle to the Italians. As he did so, the revelation of casualty figures in British Somaliland sparked a further sharp exchange with Churchill. Initial news of the evacuation had been received in London without great concern, and the feeling was that at least the evacuated troops could be profitably used elsewhere. However, when Churchill later turned his mind to the casualty rate of just 260, of which the number of killed was thirty-eight, he was, as he described it, 'far from satisfied with the tactical handling of the affair'. The general in command had appeared to have 'precipitately discontinued' the action, and to have held back the Black Watch from the midst of the fray; his description of 'heavy losses' did not, in the view from London, tie up with the actual number of killed and wounded. Churchill went considerably further and sent a venomous cable to Wavell ordering him, 'in the absence of fuller explanation', to suspend Godwin-Austen and convene a court of inquiry. He expressed his displeasure to the War Secretary: 'If this is the sort of resistance that is to be expected and pass muster in the Middle East we must expect further tame and timely withdrawals.'[31]

Although Wavell agreed that the Italians had won Somaliland too easily, he declined to approve a court of inquiry because it would be bad for morale, and he emphatically rejected the notion that the troops had displayed a lack of martial ardour. It seemed hardly applicable, at any rate, to the Black Watch battalion pointing their bayonets at an oncoming Italian division, or to the three young sailors, under artillery fire and confronted by thousands of well-armed infantry, firing their few three-pounder shells from a saluting gun.

He stated his reasons in a cable that ended with the words 'a big butcher's bill is not necessarily evidence of good tactics', nor, as he elaborated to the War Office, of skilful fighting or good leadership, 'rather the reverse'. As a politician, military historian and former soldier, even though the tools of his trade included the frequent use of invective as well as charm, Churchill could hardly fail to bridle at this incautious remark, with its inference of military ignorance; Sir John Dill later told Wavell that his telegram, and especially its last sentence, roused Churchill to greater anger than he had ever before seen in him. Placed before a Prime Minister and Minister of Defence, it was strong meat and the taste lingered. Yet it was entirely within the rules, as Churchill knew.

For a while it seemed as though Wavell was battling on the home front as well as against the Axis. Sadly, the tension that had grown during his meetings with Churchill was to persist: it would slacken intermittently, but it would never be entirely relieved. To the CIGS he expressed his relief at getting away from the tension in London, and his gratitude for Dill's support:

> It was good to see you again, Jack, and to know that you were there in the right place, with your cool head and determination and sound judgment. Don't let the PM overwork you or bully you . . . Keep fit, for you are the only man for the job.[32]

Soon, and for a time, the arguments would be brushed to one side, as the flame of battle was reflected in the rubicund glow of Churchill's pleasure. But even as he took the next steps in promoting the strategies he had put in place, Wavell was given a further reminder of the difficult discussions that had occurred in London. On 23 August 1940 he received from Churchill a lengthy telegram, entitled 'General Directive for Commander-in-Chief, Middle East'. It set out detailed proposals for troop movements of divisions, brigades and even battalions, including ports of embarkation, for the 'tactical employment of the army in Egypt'. It also referred in detail to Kenya, an area at the core of Churchill's impatience with Wavell's use of the troops 'on the ration strength'. Churchill was the first Minister of Defence to be appointed, so there were no precedents for the prerogatives of his office, but this was a remarkably detailed directive, covering numerous matters properly the concern of staff officers way below general officer rank, let alone members of the Defence Committee. The document concluded, 'In this posture then, the Army of the Delta will finally defeat the Italian invasion.'

Churchill's telegram was followed a few weeks later by the War Minister proposing first to set out a programme of the forces and equipment that would be sent to the Middle East month by month, and second that Wavell should be asked for a related plan of campaign: 'until Wavell knew definitely and for months ahead what he was to receive, he had no chance to plan in advance'.[33] Generous as this sentiment was, as a supposedly independent commander Wavell had reason to feel as though he were being reined in and called more stringently to account, despite the intelligent and successful planning that he had implemented so far. As he said, 'It showed clearly that Winston did not trust me to run my own show and was set on his ideas.'

Understandably these men were living under tension and strain. Although accustomed to bearing the burden of the Empire's fight for survival, their lives were in constant danger; there was an enormous volume of daily work, argument and long meetings – often requiring fateful decisions. There was little rest or sleep, and not much humour. Men reacted accordingly.

Wavell shrugged his shoulders, responded to such parts of Churchill's directive as he considered it might be impolitic to ignore and turned to the pressing matter of defeating the enemy in Africa.

HIS FINEST HOUR

WAVELL'S original intention had been to await the invaders at Mersa Matruh.[1] In case the enemy bypassed Mersa and tried to push on towards the Nile Delta there were further defences prepared to cover the main water supplies; they would be guarded by troops in fixed positions, while the Armoured Division gradually withdrew east, but keeping outside the defended areas. The advancing enemy would find an armoured division on their right, and on their left a series of defended positions. Their lines of communication would become ever more extended, and their shortages, particularly of water and petrol, more acute by the hour. If, however, the Italians did manage to reach the Delta, they would face yet more troops in prepared positions covering Cairo and Alexandria. That was the plan: simple, powerful and the best that could be done with the limited resources available.

When Mussolini finally declared war, Wavell decided to initiate offensives along the frontier. But he was limited not only by the shortage of men and equipment, but also by a lack of intelligence, which prevented him from arriving at anything more than an estimate of enemy strength. Even so, he managed to despatch exactly the right troops, with the right training and with high morale, to seek out the enemy in the desert.

The pick of the troops, and anyway the only available reconnaissance unit, was the 11th Hussars. The front that they had to patrol was a triple line of mines and coiled barbed wire, laid down by the Italians and stretching over the Libyan sands until it reached the Mediterranean, its last few yards cemented onto a slab of rock above a deep pool. It was a black smudge across miles of gritty, fly-blown, barren, grey-brown scrub, scorched by the *khamseen* wind, easy to drive over, easy to get lost in. It was a bleak place to live and die. 'There was little water,' as one soldier put it, 'no restaurants, no bars, no cinema, no comfort, no sex. Instead there were flies, fleas, scorpions, and a few snakes.'²

The frontier was a world away from Cairo and its gymkhanas, where the Hussars would ride in desert boots and light cords, silk scarves around their necks, and where, they feared, the 'Gaberdine Swine', while not sitting in offices, were making their names with the illicit wives and other adventurous ladies enlivening Cairo life. Now they spent their time in vigil or on patrol, their only company the crew of their armoured cars, their sustenance bully beef and eggs fried on the vehicle bonnets, their luxury a few cigarettes.

Through the Hussars, Wavell took the war to the Italians in the desert. On the opening night of hostilities their patrols drove up to the wire, the foremost troops wearing rubber boots in case it was electrified. Removing the cement support-posts, they drove their armoured cars slowly backwards and forwards until the wire was cut and flattened. Then they advanced, and waited by a track. Before long four Italian lorries approached, lights blazing, their occupants wholly unaware that there were any enemy within miles. Suddenly rifles and machine-guns opened fire, an Italian bugle sounded the alarm, lorries swerved and halted, and men tumbled out in a din of roaring engines and a babble of shouting. A few hectic moments later sharp Italian commands rang out, their officers concluding that enough was as good as a feast and laying down their arms.

Constant vigilance was vital for both sides. The worst menace for the British was the *Regia Aeronautica*, flying low without warning over the horizon. Against it they had no protection, and the only hope of escape was to scatter. A Rifle Brigade officer, Patrick Hore-Ruthven, described those patrols as 'like the best pheasant shoot, only the birds spit back'.³ Their days in the desert, patrolling the wire until it dipped into the Mediterranean, were a heady mix of thrill and hazard, with the occasional moment of contemplation at the desert's silent majesty:

What a world of chance it is, but what fun getting up in the morning with no idea what the day will bring, a dawn attack and an air-raid, or the smell of thyme and the underlying presence of the sea . . .

This afternoon as I lay by the sea there was a light surf running and kicking up the sand, which made the water shine like shot silk, pink and green. The lap of the waves harmonised perfectly with the base of distant gunfire . . .[4]

To this strange, contrasting arena of war and peace Wavell, in his crumpled desert kit, made the occasional visit, to get a sense of his dispositions and to hearten his men by his presence: 'Looks like a terrier,' said one officer, 'who's been down after every badger in the county.'[5]

In the desert, the army was ready, waiting for the columns of dust to rise above Sidi Barrani, and the start of the enemy's great advance. The Italian commander, Marshal Graziani, had five divisions and a tank group poised to attack, and two further divisions in reserve on the coast near Tobruk. He also had 240 aeroplanes, a force far larger than the British, even if not as formidable as the 700 reported by Wavell's intelligence service. But Graziani and many of his generals had their doubts. Looking east, they did not see the beckoning streets of Cairo, the flowing Nile and the gateway to Italian East Africa, but instead 350 miles of desert with temperatures of up to 130 degrees. But Mussolini's impatience was mounting, and reluctantly Graziani gave the order for his 10th Army to advance. On 13 September 1940 the Italian army finally crossed into Egypt. 'Never,' commented the Italian Foreign Minister, 'has a military operation been launched with such opposition from its commanders.' Once it became apparent that an offensive move had begun, the British carried out a ruse, based on one that Wavell had learnt at Megiddo. They gathered together numerous camels and horses, some of them pulling brushes and harrows, and told their Arab owners to drive them forward, stirring up the dust of the desert like a column of tanks on the move. This gave the forward patrols, screened by the dust, just time to make ready for an attack, as the Italians wondered what could be afoot.

To Wavell, anxiously waiting in Cairo, it was clear that however tentative the Italian advance, it did involve a very large force. In its path lay only three infantry battalions and a relatively small assortment of tanks, artillery and armoured cars. They could perhaps delay the approaching tide, but at each stand they made they would use up valuable stocks of ammunition, and they ran the risk of being overrun before they could withdraw to their next line of defence.

Lack of intelligence remained the paramount difficulty. Wavell could estimate the approximate strength of the enemy in Libya – fifteen divisions – but he had no clear idea of their whereabouts or intentions. Aggressive patrolling on the border had provided a certain amount of information to augment Sigint (signals intelligence) and decrypt intelligence, besides an accurate picture of the enemy's Order of Battle pieced together from letters for home taken from prisoners, but there was little photo reconnaissance as almost all the aeroplanes that could do the job were in England, ready to meet the threatened invasion; and now that the airfields around Sidi Barrani were behind Italian lines, reconnaissance became even more difficult. Meanwhile, Wavell awaited the arrival of a convoy proceeding up the coast of East Africa with two new armoured regiments and a consignment of vital equipment.

The commander-in-chief knew exactly what he wanted to achieve, and had a good idea of what was possible. He considered every relevant point that his officers would need to work on, and set them out in simple, lucid terms. He directed them to consider road and railway building; the type of attack needed for each target; methods of advance; air support; and topography. Nothing was overlooked: 'Let us avoid,' Wavell had concluded, 'as far as we can the slow ponderosity which is apt to characterise British operations . . . What preparations can we make now? At any rate the sooner we can make an outline plan, calculate our requirements and submit them to the War Office, the more likely we are to have what we want when the time comes.'[6]

A week later, reports from Sidi Barrani began to come in:

Italian advance was carried out with some resolution but little skill. They moved in . . . 'hedgehogs', columns of several hundred vehicles, with tanks, anti-tank guns and artillery in front and on flanks and infantry in lorries in centre . . . our artillery got on to these massed vehicles at effective range and claim to have destroyed at least 150 vehicles, some of them full of troops . . . Our casualties about 40 including one officer killed . . .[7]

Then an extraordinary thing happened: instead of moving eastwards into the open desert where the small British covering force was withdrawing, the Italians halted, and after a short interval set about construction work. Soon there began to emerge a road, a pipeline and a series of perimeter camps in a wide arc across the escarpment from the coast. The Italians appeared to have gone onto the defensive while, far to the east, the British awaited an attack. Between the two lay the silent miles of desert.

A series of crosswinds now began to blow. While Mussolini and Graziani pressed upon each other reasons why their forces must or must not advance, and as the equinox approached – and, with it, the first faint hope that Hitler might miss the calm weather needed for an invasion – Churchill and the Chiefs of Staff turned their attention to the apparent immobility in North Africa.

The armoured contingents being carried in the convoy that was due shortly at Suez would be ready for battle by the middle of October. That provided one spur to Churchill's renascent impatience; a second was the number of troops apparently standing idle in Kenya, when instead they were desperately needed elsewhere, especially in Malta.

Despite these apparent inconsistencies, Wavell's strategy was slowly but surely taking its course. In planning an offensive, his mind had been drawn to the possibility of a German incursion into Africa, which, on the evidence of their fighting in Europe, would present him with an entirely different class of opposition. He therefore cabled the Government on 7 October, asking for more reinforcements of aeroplanes, anti-aircraft equipment and armour, in view of a possible attack by the Germans. This alarming possibility, spelt out by the commander in the field, increased the unease that Churchill felt at the lack of aggression from the main British forces in Africa. The Government therefore decided to send one of its own to assess the situation, and despatched to Cairo Anthony Eden, the Secretary of State for War.

As the sluggish and tentative advance of the Italian army appeared to have ground to a complete halt, Wavell formed a new idea for an attack:

About the middle of October, when the enemy had been stationary for a month and there seemed no probability of his further advance, I began to consider the possibility of an early offensive action. The enemy's defensive arrangements, which I studied daily on a map fixed to the wall facing my desk, seemed to me thoroughly faulty. He was spread over a wide front in a series of fortified camps, which were not mutually supporting and separated by wide distances.[8]

On 20 October, a day after the Italians had bombed the suburbs of Cairo, he gave an order to General Wilson:

I want you to examine the possibility of making an attack as soon as possible on the Italian positions in the Sofafi–Sidi Barrani–Buqbuq area. I believe that such an attack would have a very great chance of securing a decisive success, and it is unnecessary to point out the very great effect that such a success would have, not only locally but on the general war situation . . . The operation I have in mind is a short and swift one, lasting four or five days at the most . . .[9]

A good 'effect' was sorely needed. For the people of Britain, the shock of the defeat in France had been followed, after brief elation at the army's escape from Dunkirk, by the fear of imminent invasion. After a summer of strain had come the new tensions and hardships of the Blitz. By the time Wavell ordered the preparation of plans for an attack, London had been bombed for more than forty nights on end.

Wavell's plan was christened 'Operation Compass'. The intention was to attack and breach both ends of the enemy's new front line, and to exploit success westwards and north towards the coast – but then to withdraw, even if the battles were successful. The attack would be restricted to a 'short and swift one' of four or five days, the longest time for which Wavell felt confident that he could provide the attacking force with supplies. He did not set out an overall objective, although he did suggest various tactical possibilities. The plan did not satisfy General O'Connor, the desert commander, nor was it well received by Churchill.

Meanwhile the War Minister had arrived in Cairo, bent on his Cabinet mission of discovering what Wavell was up to – whether he had put in place a definite plan of attack, and how he evaluated the threat of a German intervention: 'Examine in detail,' Eden had been instructed, 'the field state of the Middle East Army so as to ensure the largest proportion of fighting men and fighting units for the great numbers on our ration strength . . . Not only the best but the second and third best must be made to play their part.' 'Please do not be content,' Churchill added, 'with the stock answers.'[10]

The situation in East Africa also remained a bone of contention. Wavell, Longmore and Eden flew to the Sudan for a conference with General Platt and his commanders to decide its future strategy. In Khartoum, where the town's streets were beautifully laid out in the design of a Union Jack, Wavell gave the order for a series of offensives. Cunningham was to advance from Kenya, invading Italian Somaliland as a first step to liberating Ethiopia from the south. In the north, Platt and the Sudan Defence Force were to retake the frontier posts previously captured by the enemy, and invade Eritrea. From within Ethiopia itself, Patriot rebels were to begin a guerrilla campaign.

The fact that the Italians now had 250,000 troops in East Africa, while in the Sudan the British could muster only 28,000, was shrugged off by the generals; it was decided that Platt would attack Gallabat in November and Kassala in January, and cross into Italian territory.

Eden and Wavell also had a meeting with Emperor Haile Selassie. They agreed to second to him two military advisers to co-ordinate the offensive, and that one of them should be Colonel Orde Wingate, the strange but enterprising man Wavell had kept tucked away in his memory as 'a notable character', who might one day be valuable as a leader of an unorthodox enterprise.[11]

On his return he asked for Wingate to be sent out from England, to work with the regular forces. He was to lead the Emperor towards Addis Ababa in a series of advances until they had penetrated the interior and established a stronghold on the Gojjam escarpment. However, Wingate's prickly persona was soon to antagonise Platt and his staff who, partly from a simple but intense dislike of the man, put a series of obstacles in his way. The commander-in-chief was unruffled by the icy breezes far below him. He later recorded how, at the end of the campaign, Wingate sent in a memorandum that would almost have justified his being arrested for insubordination: 'My staff,' said Wavell, 'were, to put it mildly, pained at its tone. I sent for Wingate and had out with him as man to man the grievances he had voiced.'[12] Wavell's willingness to get to the heart of matters 'man to man', even if it meant crossing a gulf of seniority, was a factor in his success both in keeping on top of the detail and in inspiring loyalty and affection in his troops.

Dramatic events were afoot further north. At 2 a.m. on 28 October the Greek Premier, General Metaxas, was awoken by the Italian Ambassador and informed that within hours Italian troops would cross the frontier from Albania. Metaxas' wife later described how her husband, still in his pyjamas, at once summoned the British Ambassador, Sir Michael Palairet, and told him: 'We are at war; help us, for we are ready to fight for our country's honour.' 'Then,' she added, 'he returned to our room and told me, "God is our help", and that he may not be back home until late at night. But as it turned out he was back for lunch.'[13]

Back in North Africa, Wavell was almost ready for his own offensive. He had prepared a stable base, gathered troops from many parts of the Empire, appointed good officers to command them, trained them to fight in unaccustomed conditions, equipped them as efficiently as possible from scarce supplies, and meticulously planned for simultaneous battles in several far-off territories. Across the desert from the ring of Italian camps – their rigours a little relieved by the skills of a motorised brothel – his forces prepared to march.

Wavell had insisted that his plans should be shrouded in secrecy – a rare commodity in Cairo, where the bars and nightclubs teemed with painted ladies and with hostile agents misusing their diplomatic immunity. Almost nothing had been committed to paper, save certain details recorded in the notebooks of a select few. Wavell reinforced secrecy by a judicious use of disinformation: 'I attempted,' he said, 'through certain channels known to my Intelligence, to convey to the enemy the impression that my forces in the Western Desert had been seriously weakened by the sending of reinforcements to Greece, and that further withdrawals were contemplated.'[14] These channels, which proved highly successful in misleading the Italian High Command, included dummy wireless traffic, rumour-mongers and false information planted on a highly gullible Japanese Consul in Aden.

Paradoxically, this was an unfortunate example of lies being best guarded by a bodyguard of truth, as Wavell now came under most unwelcome pressure to transfer some of his forces to Greece. Eden, still with Wavell in Cairo, quickly embraced the idea of rushing to the aid of the Greeks, now that the Italians were massing against them. However, all the reinforcements he proposed sending were earmarked for the forthcoming attack in the desert, and Wavell had to stop the War Minister in his tracks before he committed himself too deeply. He wrote:

The invasion of Greece by Italy brought a demand for support from Greece and instructions from the War Cabinet to send certain troops from the Middle East to occupy Crete and to assist Greece. These orders looked at one time like wrecking the plan, to which the code name Compass had been given, since it meant seriously weakening the fighter aircraft available, and also removed from the Western Desert some anti-aircraft guns, engineers, transport, and certain other personnel which we required in the operation.[15]

To forestall a haemorrhage, Wavell was now forced much against his will to disclose the great plan he had conceived, to prevent his being skinned, as he put it, to an extent that would make an offensive impossible. He declared his hand, and told Eden that he was devising not merely defensive measures but a full-scale attack, and that plans were in train for beginning the operation within the next month.

The impact of this disclosure was immediate – so much so that, among other things, it stopped Eden from questioning Wavell as to exactly why he had adopted the unusual stance of concealing his intentions from his superiors. In fact, secrecy had been paramount not only to thwart the Mata Haris in Cairo, but also to avoid his plans being held up to scrutiny or taken over in London, a likely consequence of 'Winston's sanguine temperament and desire to have at least one finger in any military pie'.[16] Whether in principle it was correct or wise to withhold such significant information from the Secretary of State for War and from the Minister of Defence – both ultimately responsible to Parliament for their actions – could be argued both ways. It certainly showed independence of spirit.

The potential confrontation was resolved as soon as Eden returned to London and described Wavell's plans. The effect was electric. General Ismay described the reactions in the Defence Committee:

> Every one of us could have jumped for joy, but Churchill could have jumped twice as high as the rest. He has said that he 'purred like six cats'. That is putting it mildly. He was rapturously happy. 'At long last we are going to throw off the intolerable shackles of the defensive,' he declared. 'Wars are won by superior willpower. Now we will wrest the initiative from the enemy and impose our will on him.'[17]

In the meantime Wavell pressed on, relying on Eden to interpret his opinions to the Prime Minister.

His elevated view did not match the outlook lower down. While they enthusiastically relished the instructions to go over to the attack, neither Wilson nor O'Connor liked their general's plans for doing so; first, because they would require tanks to cover ground to the south of the enemy positions, which was unsuitable for heavy armour, and second because they felt that attacking both ends of the Italian line would comprise two separate battlefields, where there would be insufficient air cover and between which there would be ample scope for confusion among the signallers.

So O'Connor submitted an alternative proposal, which envisaged a sharp thrust by two divisions through the gap between the Italian camp at Nibeiwa, and that at Rabia, fifteen miles to the south-west. Wavell agreed to this, but the overall strategy remained unchanged: a five-day raid to clear the Italians out of Egypt, followed by a withdrawal back to base at Mersa Matruh.

On 2 November 1940, in a rousing message to his desert commanders, Wavell gave his final approval:

I consider that the advantages of the operation entirely justify the risks run. Nor do I consider the risks excessive. In everything but numbers we are superior to the enemy. We are more highly trained, we have better equipment. We know the ground and are better accustomed to desert conditions. Above all we have stouter hearts and greater traditions, and are fighting in a worthier cause.[18]

Even as the preparations were finalised, the secret was kept from all but a few senior commanders and the Chiefs of Staff in London. Wavell now ordered a full-scale preparatory exercise, to give the troops last-minute practice in the skills they would need for the operation. 'Training Exercise No. 1', scheduled for 26 November, purported to train troops in a long approach march, a night move and a dawn attack on a camp in co-operation with artillery; it was lifted straight from the manual and based on the most recent available lessons – from the Great War. The battlefield was laid out as a replica of the Italian camp at Nibeiwa, south of Sidi Barrani, which was to be the focus of the first attack. Live tank and artillery fire would sharpen up the troops, many of whom had never seen action before. A further exercise was scheduled for the second week in December. In fact, though few knew it, 'Training Exercise No. 2' was to include the Italians.

Wavell went to O'Connor's headquarters to observe the exercise, taking with him Brigadier Dorman-Smith, whom he trusted and respected rather more than did many other senior officers. The brigadier then wrote an appreciation, entitled, 'A Method of Attack on an Entrenched Camp in the Desert', a masterly blueprint that was immediately accepted by Wavell as the basis for the actual operational orders.

In the meantime the Hussar squadrons embarked on a series of aggressive patrols to prevent the enemy filling the gap in their line, which O'Connor had realised offered the path to victory. Ammunition and petrol dumps were placed on the approach route through the desert, camouflaged as far as possible by the teams from Helwan. To allay careless talk, the dumps were variously described as being for use on a forthcoming exercise or to cover a withdrawal if the Italians renewed their advance.

While his commanders were ironing out the details for the land battle, Wavell convened a conference in Cairo to arrange the co-operation of the other two services. The navy agreed to form an Inshore Squadron, whose sole order from Cunningham was 'to help the Army in every possible way', an example of the confidence he had in the army commander. 'If Wavell thought that it was a good plan,' he had told his officers, 'that was good enough for me.' Plans went ahead for bombarding shore targets and for providing escorts for small ships to land ammunition and supplies and to embark prisoners and the wounded.

Wavell also had to resolve differences between the RAF and the navy over air support, strategic control of which Tedder, the RAF commander, was wholly unwilling to relinquish. The air force was the weakest link, and its senior commanders had repeatedly warned that an offensive by Italian squadrons, in each one of which were more aeroplanes than all the RAF's forward squadrons put together, would overwhelm them, especially if supported by the Germans – and it was known that many of the Italian pilots had been trained in dive-bombing by the Luftwaffe. Wavell maintained that without air cover the operation could not take place at all. Eden had also cabled a request for help, but Sir Cyril Newall, Chief of the Air Staff, being fully occupied with the Blitz, had offered only to replace obsolete aircraft and to try and increase the size of each squadron.

Yet the grand design was taking final shape – the political finesse, with the Egyptians, with India and with the Dominion Governments, and most of all with the Chiefs of Staff and the Defence Committee in London; the joint endeavours with the navy and the RAF; the countless hours of detailed staff planning; the equipping and the training; the measures of deception; and the containment of the enemy along hundreds of miles of frontier had now prepared the army to face an array of hostile forces some five or six times its size.

Wavell could not be sure where all the Italian divisions were, but he believed that his first clash would be with the five, or possibly as many as seven, forward divisions of Berti's 10th Army, close behind which were thought to be a further two divisions in reserve. So far Wavell had a low opinion of Italian soldiers, but the fact remained that stationed in North Africa were more than a quarter of a million well-armed men, stiffened by divisions of Blackshirts, ready, possibly, to die for the glory of Rome. At the front, 31,000 imperial troops would collide with 80,000 Italians: more than two and a half times their number.

Ready to pound his small army, and perhaps bomb Cairo and Alexandria, were at least 250 aircraft: fighters that could, by a small margin, outmatch the RAF's Gloster Gladiators, and bombers that carried a heavier load than their Blenheims. Many of the enemy pilots had performed with credit in Ethiopia and in the Spanish Civil War.

In fact at that moment Middle East Command did have, together with 1,000 pilots supported by 16,000 air personnel, nearly 1,000 aircraft in more than thirty squadrons, but many were obsolete or non-operational; only about 300 were ready for battle, and the chance of making an impact, in any one place in the huge area that they had to defend, was slight.

Waiting off the coast was the Royal Navy, but they were not the only ships at sea. Italian submarines were on patrol, and above them was a modern navy, a major threat even after the Fleet Air Arm had inflicted great loss on the Italian fleet in Taranto harbour, on the night of 11 November.

Support from the navy and RAF was essential, but it was for the army – 7th Armoured and the infantry and tanks of the 4th Indian – to show that with 'stouter hearts, greater traditions and a worthier cause' two divisions could prevail against five, or seven, or perhaps fifteen.

The British believed that their 275 tanks were more than double the enemy's number. On the other hand, the Italian artillerymen, who so far had proved determined and skilful fighters, were thought to have twice as many guns as Wavell had managed to collect. British armoured cars were not proof against aircraft shells or armour-piercing bullets and were only lightly armed, while the 'Matilda' infantry tanks (of which 150 had arrived with the reinforcement convoy) had been designed before the war for co-operation with infantry, and not for use in an armoured division. They could at times move at 15 mph, but in the desert or in battle conditions they could manage just half that speed. On the other hand, they were impervious to everything but anti-tank mines or a direct hit. There were as yet no tank transporters, but if the Matildas could be moved to the battle areas in good order, they might prove their worth. The enemy tanks were heavier, but they had thin armour and their turrets did not swivel. The reinforcements of faster 'Cruiser' tanks, with two-pounder guns, had now reached the desert, but their trials had been in England, and on arrival they were found to have unsuitable tracks. Providing supplies of food, water, ammunition and vehicle replacements would also be a strictly limiting factor.

On balance, Wavell believed that a five-day raid was the only course to follow.

However, on 28 November he gave General Wilson a directive stating that, despite the administrative and tactical difficulties of a deep penetration, an opportunity might arise for turning a local defeat into an outstanding victory:

> I know that you have in mind and are planning the fullest possible exploitation of any initial success of the Compass operation ... You and all commanders in the Western Desert may rest assured that the boldest action, whatever its results, will have the support not only of myself but of the CIGS and the War Cabinet at home ... I do wish to make certain that if a big opportunity occurs we are prepared morally, mentally and administratively to use it to its fullest.[19]

This was a remarkable directive. In effect it seemed to contemplate events that would call for a fundamental change in the basic concept that Wavell had outlined to Wilson on 20 October – an operation lasting four or five days at the most, with the assault to be followed by a withdrawal – on which all the logistic arrangements were based. It may have been in response to a signal from Churchill two days earlier, expressing growing fears that the Germans might begin a drive through Bulgaria into Greece while Wavell was still developing his offensive in Libya. The Prime Minister was anxious that Wavell should finish the job in Africa before that happened.

This was a very different proposition to a five-day raid, and it rendered the original instructions even more indefinite. At no point was General O'Connor ever given any ultimate objectives, such as where the offensive was to halt, and no mention was made of targets further west, such as Tobruk or Benghazi. When giving out his orders on 5 December, Wilson would tell O'Connor that 'the GOC-in-C wishes you to know that you have complete liberty of action as the operation develops'.[20] 'Do your best,' Wavell said, 'and exploit local successes to the full.'

That suited the fiery little general, who was to interpret 'local successes' in the widest possible sense.

The possibility of capturing the ultimate prize of Tripoli was not canvassed, and in the minds of each of those most closely involved – Churchill, Wilson, O'Connor and Wavell himself – the uncertainty of the operation's status rendered the Western Desert Force vulnerable to becoming a feeder for other operations, whether in Greece or Italian East Africa. For O'Connor, this added greatly to the difficulty of making plans in advance. He could not be sure exactly what resources would be available, and felt that it would have been better to have been given clear objectives.

By the beginning of December there remained not much more to do than to fix a date for the attack. Yet Wavell had to keep his eye on the operations in East Africa, and on 2 December he held another conference with Platt and Cunningham. He laid out the importance of beginning an offensive, commencing with the capture of Kassala. Believing that besides providing sufficient numbers he must attack with the best troops he could find, he made the dramatic disclosure that in mid-December he proposed to transfer 4th Indian Division from the Western Desert and send it down to East Africa.

Secrecy for this move was vital. It would be extremely risky to extract the troops from the midst of battle and replace them with a division now waiting in Egypt. But Wavell was thinking of the longer term, and that revolt in Ethiopia might be the catalyst for a comprehensive defeat of the Italians in East Africa, thereby releasing forces for the more important theatre in the north.

The most junior officer present at the conference was Orde Wingate. He was given ten minutes to speak, and sat down after thirty. He apparently impressed the generals: while Platt advanced in the north, he pronounced, and Cunningham sealed the border in the south, he would fight ahead of them, dispelling the suspicion in which white men were held, and urging the natives forward with the promise that after victory there would be no new imperialism. It was a dangerous picture to paint, releasing an entirely new concept that might prove very hard to restrict to Ethiopia. It was perhaps the first intimation that after the war, even if the British Empire defeated the Axis Powers, its subjects might wish to assume authority themselves.

On 4 December Wavell issued his final instructions, and the next day gave the order for attack. From far-away London the Defence Committee pressed him to give them a date for the start of the operation. This he was most reluctant to do, not wanting to be tied down to specific dates. He replied briefly that it would start when the weather conditions were right. Then, fearing that this might be considered an inadequate response, he quickly followed up with a cable to Sir John Dill, giving Monday, 9 December for the opening of the attack. Alarmed by Churchill's new idea that he should aim to expel the Italians altogether, and not just roll them back into Libya, he added:

Feel undue hopes being placed on this operation which was designed as raid only. We are greatly outnumbered on ground and in air, having to move over 75 miles of desert and attack enemy who has fortified himself for three months. Please do not encourage optimism.[21]

The Prime Minister insisted on Dill showing him this message, but the absence of vigour in its tone shocked him. It confirmed his growing prejudice that Wavell lacked the spark that Churchill considered essential for leading troops against the Axis. He told Dill:

If, with the situation as it is, General Wavell is only playing small, and is not hurling on his whole available force with furious energy, he will have failed to rise to the height of the circumstances. I never worry about action, but only about inaction.[22]

The last sentence was unreasonable, considering all that had gone into bringing 'Compass' to readiness, yet the difficulty in imagining Churchill writing the telegram that Wavell had sent, or vice versa, demonstrates how far apart were the emotions of the two men.

As the force moved up to the assembly points fifteen miles from the gap in the Italian line, the weather was a vital factor. The two columns had to remain concealed while crossing some sixty miles of desert, yet a bright moon was essential to illuminate the way. When they had penetrated the gap, part of the Armoured Division was to turn south towards the forces at Sofafi, on the edge of the escarpment, while the other brigades would drive north-west towards the coast, to cut the road and prevent the occupants of Nibeiwa from escaping westwards.

Meanwhile the infantry division would cross the gap and stealthily make its way round to the west of the camp, where air reconnaissance had revealed a track apparently used by the Italian transport for entering the camp. The infantry were then to dismount from their lorries and advance to the perimeter wire. In the early-morning silence, carrying heavy weapons, they had to make the distance within five minutes, reaching the wire at the very moment when the tanks were due to burst through the gates to unleash a storm of shell-fire. Surprise, it was hoped, would be complete, as it was the eastern side of the camp, where the enemy had sown their minefields, that they thought might be vulnerable to attack.

The commanders took up their battle stations. O'Connor, with a naval officer and signallers, went forward to be close to his divisions. Collishaw, who commanded the air support, set up a command post in Maaten Bagush, where he was joined by Wilson. Wavell held the reins at Grey Pillars. Secrecy had been preserved. Wilson remained in Cairo until the day the battle started, declining a dinner invitation for the next evening on the grounds that he had a 'previous engagement'. On the same day Wavell, appearing quite relaxed, took his wife and family to the races, and later gave a dinner-party at the Turf Club.

Far to the west the army had embarked on 'Training Exercise No. 2', and the troops were told that it was in fact an operation of war. A message from Wavell was read out, and the news was received with great enthusiasm, not least by the warriors of 4th Indian Division, who had tired of their defensive role and were 'bursting to get at the enemy'.[23] Throughout the daylight hours the two divisions had been stationary, spread over more than forty square miles, unable to advance for fear of disclosing their presence. Then, in the brief twilight, they moved forward once more. At midnight the fifteen-inch guns of the *Terror*, and two smaller gunboats, opened fire offshore, to drown the roar of the Matildas as they slowly approached the enemy. For a time the Italians in Nibeiwa seemed restive, flares went up, shots and a few explosions were heard, then silence fell once more.

Dawn broke. A desert haze gave cover to the waiting troops while the artillery positioned its guns and fixed lines on the camp ahead. At 5 a.m. a battalion of the 4/7th Rajputs, which had moved to the east of the camp, launched an attack to distract attention from the west where the main group was drawing close to its final position. Soon the Indians ceased firing, and the Italians stood down and returned to the business of preparing breakfast and getting ready for another day.

At 6.15 the Indians began their final advance towards the north-west entrance to the camp. One hour later a series of shattering explosions drenched the Italian army with smoke and high explosive as the artillery opened fire from the east. The armour then accelerated into its final charge, crashing through twenty enemy tanks innocently warming their engines outside the gates. All were destroyed. The 7th Royal Tank Regiment roared and rumbled through the camp's north-western gates, the infantry at its heels fanning out on either side. The enemy rushed to deploy its light and medium tanks, but was overwhelmed by the iron mass bearing down upon them. The Italian gunners put up a brave and 'extremely hot resistance', but they had been taken unawares. As they saw their shells bouncing harmlessly off the Matildas' hulls they rapidly lost heart:

Grenadiers were seen to rise from their trenches, hurl grenades at tanks, and become amazed, horrified and petrified when they observed that the tanks were impervious to such action. The tanks shot down those who did not surrender.[24]

The Italian commander, General Maletti, rushed from his dugout at the first sound of shooting, firing a machine-gun and still in his pyjamas. He was killed instantly.

By mid-morning all was over: 2,000 'demoralised and amazed' Italians, and thirty-five tanks, were in British hands. It had been achieved with the loss of only eight officers and fewer than fifty men. The troops rounding up the enemy were astonished to find beds with clean sheets, dress uniforms, hair-brushes, scent and other precious articles of war, in defence of which the fight had not been very long.

The next day, 10 December, the British advance was resumed. There were no landmarks by which they could steer their course. In the bitter cold of the Libyan winter, intermittent dust storms clogged their clothes and weapons, and icy wind and driving rain hampered movement and the ability to sight the enemy. Yet they carried on undaunted, and at four in the afternoon launched their attack on Sidi Barrani. In the swirling dust the fighting was confused, and low cloud grounded the RAF, but by nightfall the town had fallen, yielding as prisoners what were described as 'acres' of officers and three generals. As the defence collapsed, some of the enemy garrison rushed eastwards along the coast as fast as they could, unaware that they were on a collision course with others retreating in the opposite direction.

There was further havoc when the dust storm cleared. RAF fighters swooped down on a milling throng – tired and frightened, unclear of purpose and wholly confused. The fighters then flew on to attack the troops struggling westwards as they evacuated the Sofafi camps to the south.

The diary of an officer captured at Sidi Barrani disclosed that the Italians were apprehensive of parachute landings behind their lines. Wavell had no airborne troops, or much prospect of receiving any, but ever alert to the value of fooling the enemy, he saw at once that he might make the enemy think that he had. He ordered his intelligence department[25] to devise a way of introducing fictitious airborne troops into his Order of Battle. Accordingly, a plan was elaborated, involving 'Airborne' staff armbands, soldiers in the uniform of parachutists supposedly convalescing, dummy gliders, magazine photographs of 'parachutists in training' and similar red herrings. The plan was to persuade the Italians that the '1st Special Air Service Brigade', of one parachute and two glider battalions, had arrived by sea and were training secretly in the Transjordan Desert.

On the third day 4th Armoured Brigade confronted the reserve division that had gathered between the coast road and the sea. After only a brief battle they were astonished to be offered the surrender of a further 14,000 Italians. Suddenly they had become captors, faced with the hitherto unimagined problem of what to do with a teeming mass of enemy soldiers, in need of food, water, shelter and somewhere to go.

Further west, at Sollum, another force set off for Bardia, along the coast. But Bardia was in Libya. After three days of a 'five-day raid', the only Italian soldiers left in Egypt, apart from a few units still around Sollum, were either captive or dead. For the loss of 133 men killed, 387 wounded and eight missing, the British had captured fifty tanks, 400 guns and 38,000 prisoners. Tactical surprise was complete, and on the strategic level the Italians had had no inkling that a large-scale offensive was afoot. The scene of desert victory was far beyond expectation. Trudging eastwards were long, straggling lines and clusters of exhausted, unshaven, dirty, demoralised Italians, wondering whether their boots would hold out, where their next meal would come from and whether they would die of thirst in the desert. Il Duce was given the news of the disintegration of the proud army that had dreamt of Suez and Sudan, and of the death of one Italian general and the capture of another five. He replied, 'This is the ratio of Italians who have military qualities to those who have none.'[26] General Berti was sacked.

Wavell's triumphant men were like people who had booked tickets for a five-day Test Match and had travelled far, with rugs and picnics and keen anticipation, only to find that the match might be over with two days to spare.

The Prime Minister did not at first react to the unfolding picture of glory, but complained instead that Wavell was not dealing vigorously with his prey. Eden noted on 12 December:

Winston rang up early in the morning, and complained that we were not pursuing the enemy and had much to say about missed opportunities. After an angry riposte from me, it emerged that he had not seen the telegram that appeared during the night giving details of further plans. But this is all symptomatic of his distrust of local leaders which to my disappointment is not abated at all.[27]

A further report from the battlefield produced an entirely different reaction. Churchill sent a heartening telegram to Wavell, describing Parliament's delight at his victory and saying that he would be receiving a telegram from the King.

The cheering reports were a welcome lift for Churchill's continuing efforts to persuade Roosevelt to take America into the war: 'I am sure,' he wrote, 'that you will be pleased about our victory in Libya. This, coupled with the Albanian reverses, may go hard with Mussolini if we make good use of our success.'[28] In his enthusiasm Churchill continued to press his ideas on Wavell. Naturally, he suggested, pursuit would hold first place in the general's thoughts:

> The Army of the Nile has rendered glorious service to the Empire and to our cause, and rewards are already being reaped by us in every quarter . . . Your first objective now must be to maul the Italian Army . . . and rip them off the African shore to the utmost possible extent.[29]

The Prime Minister now told the Chiefs of Staff that neither East Africa nor the Balkans must detract from the surge in North Africa. As the glowing reports flowed across the desks at GHQ, Wavell had to make a crucial decision: whether to maintain the chase or hold to his original strategy.

O'Connor was impatient to move on: he had received reports of fresh Italian troops landing at Tripoli, and he had found at least a partial solution to his logistic problem – scores of captured Italian lorries, stores and petrol, which were now his for the taking. It was only two weeks since Wavell had urged his commanders to be prepared 'morally, mentally and administratively' to use a big opportunity, and the Prime Minister himself had spoken of plans for moving troops and reserves in long hops along the coast, to exploit success. It would be hard to conceive of a greater opportunity than had now appeared.

A halt could certainly be called, but the weight of argument was that a new situation had emerged, and that a good general should shape his design to meet it. Wavell's flow of telegrams to the CIGS reflected his exhilaration at the prospect rising before him, but he diluted his pleasure with caution, a defence perhaps against pressure from the great leader at home:

> *11th December*: Beaters now moving to position for afternoon drive after luncheon interval . . .

Impossible at present to judge extent of success but if all goes well we may, repeat may, carry pursuit to Egyptian frontier. Do not think even if enemy demoralised we can carry pursuit much farther. Supply difficulties are great and Bardia is strongly defended . . .

12th December: If Bardia falls, though I think this is unlikely, I have instructed O'Connor he can push on towards Tobruk to the limit of endurance of vehicles and men . . . 4th Indian Division will be withdrawn for Sudan . . .'[30]

That referred to the decision with which he was now faced, and which he had intimated to Platt and Cunningham ten days earlier. The day before the attack Wavell had told the CIGS of his intention to withdraw the Indian Division and send it to the Sudan to assist in retaking Kassala, one group to sail up the Nile and the remainder by sea. 'I presume,' he cabled, 'these will not affect strategy you have in mind for Middle East. I attach considerable importance to recapture of Kassala for moral effect on progress of rebellion and since freeing of railway will greatly ease administrative difficulties in Sudan.'[31] If he did not withdraw the Indian Division at once, it would miss its only chance of transport, a convoy shortly to pass through Suez, in which case his East African campaign would have to be restructured.

On the morning of 11 December, just as he was setting out to visit his commanders, O'Connor received a signal that brought him up short: 4th Indian Division was to leave for the Delta and be replaced by 6th Australian, which had just 'completed its equipment'. Within forty-eight hours of the fall of Sidi Barrani the long journey back began. It was a huge disappointment. 'I had received no warning of this whatsoever,' O'Connor wrote later, 'and consequently had made no plans to meet such a contingency. Its withdrawal at this juncture would produce a difficult situation . . .'[32]

Nor did it please the Indians themselves: they reacted with bewilderment and anger. Yet it was Wavell who perceived the overall strategy, and although the Indian Division was sixty miles further west than had been expected, and arranging its withdrawal would be complicated by the straggling mass of Italian prisoners in need of transport, guards and sustenance, he decided to proceed with the move.

The next day Wavell held a conference with Wilson and O'Connor. They decided to raise the game above its administrative difficulties and press on into the mass of Italians coagulating in the west. An Australian force was to occupy Jarabub Oasis, and the Armoured Division was to get astride the road to Tobruk and cut off Bardia, now full to the brim with Italian soldiers. If Bardia were to fall, O'Connor was to be ready to make for Tobruk.

Having sent O'Connor back to the battlefield, 'burning to go', Wavell contemplated the support that he would need. 'Maintenance difficulties,' he told the Chiefs of Staff, 'and the problem of air support were likely to become more formidable the nearer we approach established enemy bases.' For the Italian army and air force, on the other hand, each westerly step would take them closer to home and help. Yet he decided to go on. The five-day raid was forgotten, and the Western Desert Force was rechristened 'XIII Corps'.

Now, for the first time, the enemy put up solid resistance. Wavell's intelligence reports put the garrison at Bardia at 20,000. They were fresh troops, and reconnaissance showed that the small, whitewashed town and its harbour were protected by steep ravines and cliffs, honeycombed with caves, and surrounded by seventeen miles of strongly constructed wire and anti-tank ditches. He suggested to O'Connor that he leave an opening to tempt the Italians to escape towards Tobruk, the next haven along the coast, and he would encourage them to do so by laying on air and naval bombardment.

On the ground, the Australians were to make a frontal attack. Preparations took two weeks, but by 3 January 1941 they were ready. At dawn a deafening roar erupted as the 'Imperial Army of the Nile' advanced, the tanks' silencers removed to make the enemy think the force was far larger than it was. Three battleships, including Cunningham's *Warspite*, stood offshore, their shells cascading into the Italians' midst. The Australians emerged from the desert and advanced towards the wire. Weighed down with heavy greatcoats and implements for breaking through wire and anti-tank obstacles, balaclavas under their tin hats, they looked like ghosts from the trenches, the eerie picture completed by their First World War artillery.

With the Italian guns putting up a strong bombardment, the battle lasted two days. Repeating the pattern of the previous clashes, the enemy made a fierce attempt to repel the wave of tanks and infantry, before suddenly giving up the fight. Bardia was taken almost intact, with its invaluable supply of water. A further 40,000 men laid down their arms – a pleasant surprise, in view of the intelligence estimates – and the bag was filled with 430 guns, 700 trucks, nearly 120 assorted tanks and large quantities of ammunition. In Rome, a sombre Mussolini received the news: 'This is a washing,' he said, 'and it will take at least a week to dry.'[33] Even before the port had fallen,

O'Connor sent 7th Armoured the secret codeword that would speed them on towards Tobruk.

The air was sweet with victory, and the pace was now so fast that the troops began to joke about racing in the 'Benghazi Stakes'. The number of surrendered prisoners, guns, tanks, transport and supplies was beyond all expectation, achieved in an exceptionally short time and for minimal loss. Wavell might now question whether the Italians could any longer find the will to win or have a hope of forcing him back into Egypt. Yet he remained gravely aware, as did the Chiefs of Staff, that sooner or later the Germans might arrive.

From his lofty perch, the commander-in-chief, armed with his Joint Planning Staff's ideas and detailed responses to his requests, weighed his options. On the political and strategic level he had to blend his present course with his paramount objective – the defence of Egypt – and to decide whether he had already contained the danger from the enemy in Libya. If that were so, he should abort 'Operation Compass', withdraw from Libya, close the border and deploy his forces to protect Egypt, Suez and the Red Sea from the enemy in East Africa.

All along Wavell's idea had been that a raid would be enough to drive the Italians back across the frontier. However, he had been proved correct to such a degree that a new vision had appeared. He might now drive the enemy far back into Libya, and even out of North Africa entirely. He had to judge whether the attempt would be worth the risk; and if not, where he should halt his forces. If he were after all to abandon the idea of a five-day raid and send his army on into Cyrenaica and even Tripolitania, he had to help his commanders make tactical judgements about which of the obstacles ahead should be stormed and which bypassed. To do that he had to consider the flow of requests and directives that he was receiving from London, reflecting the wider implications of the war, and evaluate for the Defence Committee the merits of fighting for the various prizes that lay to the west.

One of the most valuable would be Tobruk, the best natural harbour for hundreds of miles, and he now decided to attack it. So, at dawn on 21 January, the Australians advanced towards it. Their plan of attack was substantially the same as that for the capture of Bardia; the fighting continued all day, and the Italians held on, but after dark, explosions were heard as they began to demolish installations. At daybreak the attack was renewed, and shortly afterwards the collapse began, the fortress fell and another cornucopia spilled its contents into the desert.

Wavell had now defeated eight divisions, captured a major coastal fortress and taken 70,000 prisoners. The way lay open for the navy to bring in supplies, radically reducing the problem of replacing the diminishing number of tanks and other vital components.

Beyond Tobruk lay Bomba and Gazala, and then, after the coast turned north, the small port of Derna, whose defences commanded the single metalled road, the width of two camels, that led to the cultivated land of the Jebel Akhbar. Beyond lay Benghazi, a vital harbour, but nearly 300 miles from Tobruk. If that were reached, it would not be unthinkable to look towards the ultimate prize of Tripoli: a major port and the nerve centre of the Italian administration of its colonies. That highlighted Wavell's dilemma: although it was only 200 miles from Malta, Tripoli was within reach of Sicily and Italy and was the obvious point of entry for Italian – or German – supplies and reinforcements, should Italy hold to its boast of driving the British right out of Africa. However, even from Benghazi it was more than 500 miles to Tripoli, an immense distance for armoured troops to travel in enemy country. Moreover, intelligence reports suggested that there were still 80,000 fresh Italian troops and 900 guns in Cyrenaica, with a further 90,000 men and 500 guns in Tripolitania.

If he went a step too far, he might lose all that he had gained. Yet the temptation to finish the job was almost irresistible. From Wavell's rudimentary maps it looked as though there might be a shortcut inland, from Derna to Mechili, and on to Msus and then Agedabia. Even that was 150 miles from where the coast turned north, and neither his intelligence nor the Long Range Desert Group – nor his commanders in the field – had any idea whether there were passable tracks for the tanks to follow.

As Wavell pondered his decisions, wider dimensions of imperial strategy began to affect the picture, in particular the increasingly strong currents drawing Britain towards a vulnerable Greece. Even more insistent were the enthusiasm and persuasiveness of O'Connor, who was thoroughly roused, like his troops, by the scale of the victories that had so swiftly been achieved.

Wavell let the momentum roll on. During the operation he had paid a series of visits to the various tactical headquarters, and his decision was partly influenced by the strength of his working relationship with O'Connor, who later wrote:

> It would be impossible to say what great pleasure and assistance these visits gave me, and also to all the other commanders and units which

he visited. He listened patiently to all our difficulties and made notes of everything; and I always received a wire from him on his return to Cairo, regarding which of my many demands he was able to supply. I felt the greatest confidence in him and knew that he would support me to the full in any bold action . . . all my instructions emanated from him, and it seemed to me that a further link in the chain of command was unnecessary.[34]

O'Connor called these times 'the most effective and happiest of my command'. Inevitably, however, the strain of battle caused tensions between the commanders. Maitland Wilson's position in the hierarchy was not easy, and had already seemed at times slightly redundant. He and Wavell did not see eye to eye on every point, yet 'Jumbo' had proved pivotal in devising the practical arrangements for the defence of Egypt. Unfortunately, at the height of the campaign, Wilson's staff issued a number of policy directions that conflicted with O'Connor's wishes, a conflict that came to a head with O'Connor dramatically expressing his intention to resign.

Once Wavell was apprised of the problem, he was quick to solve it. Wilson was made Military Governor of Cyrenaica, leaving O'Connor to establish a direct link with Wavell.

Growing reservations about letting the army chase the fleeing Italians further and further west had emerged in a memorandum from the Prime Minister to the Chiefs of Staff nearly three weeks earlier. This had begun encouragingly for Wavell and O'Connor: 'The speedy destruction of the Italian armed forces in N.E. Africa must be our prime overseas objective in the opening months of 1941.' Churchill had continued, 'Once the Italian army in Cyrenaica has been destroyed, the Army of the Nile becomes free for other tasks. It could not as yet be told what these would be.' He had ended with the comment that, 'With the capture of Benghazi this phase of the Libyan campaign would be ended.'[35]

It was clear to Wavell that he had not only to consider the weakening of his army through the wear and tear the armour and transport had already suffered, and its growing exposure as it went ever deeper into the enemy's heartland, but also that both he and the RAF might be asked to send some of their forces to Greece. In the coming weeks this pressure was to mount; in the meantime he directed O'Connor to pursue the retreating Italians without let-up.

Shortly before the attack on Tobruk the Greeks had declined a British offer of an immediate transfer of forces from Africa, so the Chiefs of Staff had given Wavell the firm instruction to take Benghazi. Wavell had flown up to O'Connor's headquarters, known as Piccadilly Circus, to decide on how a success at Tobruk might be followed up. He gave O'Connor an appreciation that he had drawn up for a 'raid' on the town, followed by a withdrawal, but now he had been instructed to go on to Benghazi. That was what O'Connor wanted. He would rob the Italians of the time and opportunity to regroup and stand fast; and clearing the Jebel Akhdar, in the 'bulge' of Cyrenaica, would give the RAF new bases. They would then be well placed to deter the enemy from attacking Malta or the Allied convoys that were now at grave risk as they passed through the Mediterranean Sea. Converting Benghazi into a British base would enable troops to be returned to the Delta ready to go to Greece's aid, should that – as seemed likely – be finally required.

Yet Benghazi was 700 miles from Mersa Matruh, where the whole operation had started, and Wavell was now threatened with an enemy behind him as well as in front. The Luftwaffe, using Rhodes as a refuelling base, had begun dropping magnetic and acoustic mines in the Suez Canal, causing it to be closed repeatedly. Wavell's whole plan and its logistics had originally been based on a five-day raid, and by now, although the troops themselves were at a peak of morale and resolve, and a wealth of serviceable Italian vehicles had been captured, tank numbers had fallen to danger levels and their condition was parlous. A second armoured division had arrived at Suez but, even if Tobruk fell, it would take a considerable amount of time to prepare a further advance and to deliver to the port the newly arrived regiments and the fuel, ammunition and spares now desperately needed by 7th Armoured. Although their morale had been severely damaged, the Italians were entering familiar territory and might finally regain the spirit to resist.

However, hopes for further success suddenly rose. The Italian forces to the west appeared to split into two main groups, one around Derna and one inland at Mechili. Derna fell on 30 January, but just as O'Connor had estimated that it would take two weeks' preparation before he was ready to move again, air reconnaissance revealed that the enemy had already abandoned Mechili and was fast withdrawing even further west. O'Connor decided to move at once, and sent the faithful Dorman-Smith back to Wavell's headquarters to request permission.

Shown into the commander-in-chief's office he found Wavell at his most inscrutable. Sparse hair combed neatly back, stocky figure giving nothing away, he arranged and rearranged unsharpened pencils in parade ground drill as he listened, prompting him with 'Yes, Chink, I see' at intervals. At the end he met Chink's gaze: 'Tell Dick he can go on, and wish him luck from me. He has done well.'[36]

Even so, Wavell warned O'Connor that an advance to Benghazi would be in the nature of an experiment: he was to improvise, but in the face of strong resistance was to pull back.

Wavell had concluded that if he were finally to cut off the enemy's retreat, he could not afford to wait. It was doubtful if the armoured division had enough petrol to get to Benghazi along the northern road and then fight a battle, but the administrative staff thought that via the 150-mile shortcut inland they could reach the coast road leading south from Benghazi into Tripolitania. He therefore ordered a pincer movement: 6th Australian Division was to chase the northern Italian group along the road towards Benghazi, while the 7th Armoured Division and an infantry brigade group raced southwest across the desert, pursuing the enemy towards the coast. It was an ambitious plan; if it worked, either the enemy forces to the north and south would each be overtaken and defeated, or they would collide and be crushed by the claws closing around Benghazi.

On the other hand, there might be a disaster. Reinforcements had not yet arrived at Tobruk, nor were the supply arrangements complete. The cold was intense and visibility was blurred by driving rain and a tearing southeast wind. The route had not been reconnoitred, and the spectre arose of columns foundering on impassable tracks, bombed by Italian aircraft, the few remaining tanks surrounded by fresh enemy divisions.

But the enemy might repeat the form it had shown ever since its first surprise at Nibeiwa, and replace initial resistance with rapid retreat. It was becoming clear that Italian determination had been battered by successive reverses, as the rumours of each new British success spread through their armies. The appearance of British forces so far into Cyrenaica might cause a final collapse.

Besides the caution reflected in his calm exterior, Wavell had a gambler's streak. He believed that the Italians would regard the shortcut across the desert as impossible for his army, and intercepted Italian messages confirmed his intuition. But speed was of the essence: he had only fifty modern tanks left, and they had to get to the coast road before the Italians appeared on it; if they did reach it, they might succeed in trapping the enemy once and for all.

At dawn on 4 February the column, led by the armoured cars of the 11th Hussars, set off into a desert strewn with rocks and scarred by gullies, praying that their petrol would last and wondering whether they had embarked on a wild goose chase. At noon the next day the vanguard poured out of the wilderness and saw the prize it had sought: the main road from Benghazi, empty of traffic. Thirty minutes later the Italians roared down the road from the north; they were too late and came to a halt, astonished to find their path blocked by British soldiers. Then the road rapidly became clogged with vehicles; long columns of Italians poured out of Benghazi, heading south; but collision and confusion awaited them.

Thursday, 6 February dawned bleak and grey. In the torrential rain that scudded across the coastal plain, the tank battle raged all day. In their desperate attempts to break south through the British line, the Italians lost four-fifths of their armour. At nightfall the fighting ceased, the sky bright with burning tanks, lorries, armoured cars and spilled petrol. Then came the news that Benghazi had surrendered.

The following morning the enemy tried one last time to punch a hole through the encircling forces in their path. In a final gesture the remaining thirty tanks of the famed 10th Army advanced; they faltered, failed and were battered to a standstill. The last Italian tank to be knocked out had reached the ropes of the Rifle Brigade's officers' mess tent.

Surrender was sudden and complete. Italian soldiers in their dark-green uniforms began to lay down their rifles. Suddenly a bus emerged from the midst of the column and stopped at the line of British armoured cars; inside were a group of ladies, powdering their noses and attended by a priest. It somehow characterised the enemy that the British had been fighting.

At 9 a.m. on Friday, 7 February 1941, O'Connor heard that the fighting was over. It was just sixty-one days after the campaign had begun. He took a message pad and told Dorman-Smith, who had accompanied him as he bumped across the desert with the advancing force, that they should send a message to Wavell. Knowing that he was a keen hunting man, it began, 'Fox killed in the open', and was sent 'in clear' so that there should be no doubt or delay about its contents reaching Rome.

Glowing articles filled the press, and banner headlines proclaimed the victory, in America and throughout the Empire:

Thus in successive stages the flower of the Italian army in Libya was destroyed or captured – at Sidi Barrani, at Bardia, at Tobruk, Derna and finally Benghazi. An army which was planning to capture Alexandria and Suez has ceased to exist, and the country stretching 500 miles behind it has fallen completely into British hands.[37]

Far away in Oxford the Summer Fields School Magazine included a brief entry in its 'News of Old Boys' column; it read: 'Wavell has done well in Africa.' The illustrious pupil may have liked that most of all.

Wavell's despatches have been variously described as 'very scholarly' and 'as laconic as Julius Caesar's'. His own account of his finest hour needs no embroidery:

During the two months from 7th December to 7th February the Army of the Nile had advanced 500 miles. They had beaten and destroyed an Italian army of four corps comprising nine divisions and part of a tenth, and had captured 130,000 prisoners, 400 tanks and 1290 guns, besides vast quantities of other war materiel.

In these operations we never enjoyed a larger force than two divisions, of which one was armoured . . . The 7th Armoured Division took part in the operations throughout, at the end of which it was practically reduced to a skeleton.

Our casualties were extremely light, and amounted to 500 killed, 1371 wounded, and 55 missing only.[38]

To win one campaign with sparse resources is hard enough. He would soon be directing five others.

X

THE GRECIAN URN

IN the months that followed 'Operation Compass' Wavell's contribution to the war in the Middle East had a profound effect on the Empire's fortunes. Almost as soon as the Italians had been ejected from Cyrenaica, controversy arose over the decision not to let O'Connor continue on to the vital port of Tripoli after the victory at Beda Fomm, and over the despatch of an expeditionary force to Greece.

The two were interlinked and raised the question of whether Wavell had applied the optimum amount of resources to the campaign in East Africa. Controversy also surrounded the withdrawal of 4th Indian Division from the Western Desert and its despatch to the Sudan – a manoeuvre that so delayed the British advance that the enemy still held Tripoli and western Libya when the decision to send an army to Greece was taken.

The questions are significant because the Middle East campaigns that followed the victories in Cyrenaica were largely disastrous for the Empire, whose forces were first expelled from Greece, then from Crete and then, recoiling through North Africa, lost all the ground that had been gloriously won in Wavell's opening battles. So much so that at length the army had retreated almost back to its start-point at Mersa Matruh. These stark reversals involved great loss of life, and thousands captured and left to eke out long years as prisoners-of-war.

From its earliest stages Wavell's strategy had centred on ensuring the safety of Egypt, and concentrating there reserves for the future needs of war. To achieve that objective he had to bring the Italians to battle and extinguish their power both in Libya and in East Africa. To compensate for his forces' numerical inferiority his tactic was to puzzle and confuse, and to keep the enemy guessing as to where or when they might be attacked. And so for the Duke of Aosta he sharpened a fork with many prongs: one to thrust from the Sudan into northern Ethiopia, and from there to Eritrea and the Red Sea port of Massawa; another, further south, to penetrate the Ethiopian interior where Sandford and Wingate were coaxing the tribes towards the threshold of rebellion. From Kenya a dual advance was ordered: one column to cross into southern Ethiopia and the other to march through Italian Somaliland and conquer its capital, Mogadishu, before wheeling north to Harar and Addis Ababa and so to the heart of the Italian Empire. To the east Wavell planned to send a force from Aden, crossing the sea to Berbera and restoring to the Empire British Somaliland, its missing piece.

That was Wavell's grand design. It was the setting for his withdrawal of the 4th Indian Division from 'Compass' after the fall of Sidi Barrani and its transfer to join Platt's forces in the south. Wavell knew that only for a short time would he be able to support more than one armoured division and one motorised brigade in the Western Desert. Even so the move was courageous: when he ordered it he had not foreseen the collapse at Sidi Barrani or the ensuing rout, and had accepted the risk of sending into battle replacement troops with no fighting experience. Churchill called it a wise and daring decision, yet it delayed his advance through Libya for three crucial weeks.

Without that delay General O'Connor would probably have reached Benghazi that much sooner. From there he would have found the road to Tripoli wide open, giving him time to reach it before the Italians had regrouped and London had called a halt in Libya and switched the spot-light onto Greece. By then, Rommel was on his way to Africa and about to gain a foothold there that would lead to a further two years' desert fighting and enormous numbers of imperial casualties.

At the time, of course, Wavell could not have foreseen the dramatic conse-quences that would flow from his failing to advance to Tripoli. Yet he did not need second sight to realise almost from the start of 'Compass' that the Italians had insufficient good equipment or fighting skill suggesting that they were never going to mount a strong attack in East Africa, either. Wavell could therefore have concluded that the threat to the Sudan was less than he had originally feared, and that he could reasonably transfer troops from East Africa to the Western Desert. Nevertheless, despite the dust clouds raised by the Italian warriors fleeing across Libya, he stuck to his plan to move the Indian Division to the Sudan, and it was not long before questions arose as to why he had not instead sent into battle either in East Africa or in Cyrenaica some of the 75,000 troops in Kenya that he had so far hardly used at all.

The answer lay in the importance of matching troops to the theatres for which they were best trained, which Wavell understood probably better than Whitehall. He had good tactical reasons for his plan: 4th Indian was a mechanised division, something that he needed in East Africa, and it was complete in transport, so that it could move to Suez under its own steam. Wavell believed that it would fight well in harness with 5th Indian Division, which was already in Eritrea, both divisions being mountain troops and naturally suited to East African conditions. Also, he was restricted by the scarcity of shipping; he had been informed that a convoy, the last for some time, was due to leave Suez in December, and he seized the opportunity of using it to carry his Indians to East Africa. All this he considered worth the risks that the delicately timed move might cause.

So Wavell switched 4th Indian to the Sudan, his advance through Cyrenaica was delayed and the chance of reaching Tripoli was lost. In January 1941 he was confronted with a further threat, when the Luftwaffe descended upon Sicily and from there began to operate in the central Mediterranean against both the RAF and the Royal Navy. This new development might have meant that the British could hardly have held Tripoli even if they had managed to reach it, because once the German Air Force had started operating from Sicily, it would have prevented the RAF and the navy from providing the support without which the army would have been stranded.

As it later turned out, if the British actually had forestalled Rommel by capturing Tripoli, it might have tipped the scales, in Hitler's mind, against sending an expedition to North Africa at all, or at least at that time, as the impending attack on Russia was already absorbing the full attention of the German High Command

However, Wavell had no knowledge of Hitler's plans for Russia; instead he believed that Germany would go to the defence of the Italians if she saw them embattled in Tripolitania – something that the presence of German officers, reported at the end of January by Bedouins, already suggested.

Yet neither in respect of an advance to Tripoli nor of help to Greece did Wavell's stance seem clear-cut. His advice to the War Office was guarded and lacked the force of a full-blooded optimist such as General Patton, or even his own subordinate, O'Connor. Instead, caution tempered robustness, perhaps also diluted by an innate inclination to comply with higher authority.

Like many intellectuals, Wavell saw each side of a question, as was illustrated by the signal he sent to the CIGS on the fall of Benghazi:

Extent of Italian defeat at Benghazi makes it seem possible that Tripoli might yield to a small force if despatched without undue delay. Am working out commitment involved but hesitate to advance further in view of Balkan situation unless you think capture of Tripoli might have favourable effect on attitude of French North Africa.

Further advance will also involve naval and air commitments and we are already far stretched. Navy would hate having to feed us at Tripoli and Air Force to protect us. On other hand possession of this coast might be useful to both.[1]

This was not a telegram blazing with conviction and confidence – either that there should be a further advance or that there should not. As General Ismay[2] later told O'Connor: 'Wavell never put forward even the vaguest hint that you should go on to Tripoli. Had he done so, I am pretty sure that the Prime Minister would have jumped at it.'[3] Ever since his days as a young officer in the Boer War, Wavell had understood the importance of administrative support for the front-line troops, and he knew that his startling advance across the desert had taken the planners by surprise. A further 500-mile trek into enemy territory, in the state to which his army had been reduced, might indeed seal his success in North Africa; on the other hand, it might cause the whole campaign to unravel: it would be an enormous gamble.

A Bonaparte – or a Rommel – might have burnt the blueprint and chanced all. Indeed Rommel, a mere seven weeks later, when the British were in full flight from the Afrika Korps, took the opposite view to Wavell and brushed aside misgivings about the state of his vehicles: 'One cannot,' he said, 'permit unique opportunities to slip by for the sake of trifles.'[4] For a long time afterwards O'Connor himself believed that an incalculable opportunity had been lost, and that the victory at Beda Fomm had altered the strategic situation in an afternoon. He knew that 6th Australian Division had a brigade ready to advance in captured Italian lorries and calculated that they could have reached Tripoli in thirty-six hours, maintaining themselves there by raiding the Italian depots in Sirte and in Tripoli itself.

In fact, immediately after Beda Fomm the 11th Hussars did almost reach Sirte, which was halfway to Tripoli, having ranged forty or fifty miles along the coast without opposition. They could have refuelled and continued their advance – the RAF had sighted the remnants of the Italian 10th Army retreating as fast as they could along the vaunted Via Balbia, four vehicles abreast. Had the navy, and the RAF from Malta or from their newly captured airfields in Cyrenaica, then been deployed in force, they might have prevented either the Italians or the Germans from reinforcing Tripoli. The troops themselves, ignorant of these questions of strategy, were longing to advance: 'The first question I was always asked at the time,' O'Connor recorded, 'was "Aren't we going on?"'[5]

Wavell was not persuaded. He concluded that not only would the army become dangerously extended, but a considerable air effort would be required to cover an advance and that Benghazi could not be relied on as a supply port. He later wrote:

> About the advance to Tripoli, I did naturally consider this but I am quite clear that it was not on, and that if we had attempted to do it we should have landed ourselves in a worse mess in the end. The ruling factor was the air; we simply had not got enough planes to support the advance, or to enable the navy to operate in the Western Mediterranean.[6]

Without Wavell calling for the capture of Tripoli, as a glittering prize for the taking, the War Office stuck to its view that the Libyan campaign had become a strain on the navy, was expensive in aircraft and tanks and an impediment to other plans.

The moment passed, and the chance was gone: far from the Benghazi battlegrounds the Cabinet had decided to send help to Greece. The strategic map was redrawn, putting an end to the matter and removing it from Wavell's hands. When, on 12 February, O'Connor sent word to his commander for permission to race on west, it was too late. By the time that Dorman-Smith, the emissary, arrived at Wavell's office, the desert charts had been stripped from the walls and in their place were maps of the Balkans. 'You find me,' he told Dorman-Smith, 'busy with my Spring campaign.' That same day, 1,000 miles to the west, Rommel landed in Tripoli.

Meanwhile in East Africa the Italian Empire was about to be invaded from many sides. After its long preparation the British Army was finally ready to turn upon its enemy, in whose heartland native Patriot rebels, armed and primed by Wingate's gun-runners, were poised to revolt. It was to be a carefully timed and inexorable pincer movement.

Wavell thought that in Eritrea, which supplied the Italians with the best of its native troops, a British victory might be conclusive and topple Mussolini's empire. He saw that the linchpin of the enemy's domination of the country was Asmara, the most important town. Described as being as Italian as Gibraltar was English, Asmara was the administrative centre of the Italian Army, housing its main workshops and most of its reserves of equipment. There, if anywhere, the Italians felt secure, happy to forget the war and spend hours of relaxation in the arms of native 'hostesses' in the town's famous nightclub 'La Croce del Sud'.

But first the British had to reach Asmara. It was linked with the Sudan by rail and road, but the route lay through the Keren Heights, a sheer, rock-strewn wall of hills rising 2,000 feet above a valley, a huge natural obstacle blocking the way east. If the Italians, faced with a British offensive, decided to cut and run to Keren, they could turn and close off the way to Asmara, and to the Red Sea beyond.

From Cairo to Khartoum the plans gestated, the layers of detail thickening as orders passed down the chain of command. Wavell, at the top, could not resist descending from on high and entering the tactical arena, full of ideas for subterfuge. With some 250,000 Italian troops at large in East Africa, he needed every trick he could think of, so he had created a department to dream up ruses and put them into effect. It was run by Colonel Dudley Clarke, answering directly to the commander-in-chief himself, and became known as 'A' Force.

One of its early operations was conceived and christened by Wavell himself. 'Operation Camilla' was planned as a cover for the 4th Indian's move to the Sudan, and was aimed at convincing the Duke of Aosta that the British intended to transfer Indian troops from Egypt and South Africans from Kenya to recapture British Somaliland. If the Italians believed the story, it was hoped, they would move their forces east towards the Red Sea, leaving the interior open to conquest.

Wavell wrote a supposedly secret memorandum to his intelligence department with the order that it was to be deliberately leaked:

The loss of British Somaliland has always rankled bitterly both with my Government and myself. I got a rocket from the Government and nearly lost my job at the time of the loss of Somaliland. I have orders to recapture it as soon as resources are available, and am most anxious to remove this blot on my reputation . . .

My plans depend entirely on surprise and I am therefore taking elaborate precautions to keep my intention secret, and especially to simulate an offensive both in the Sudan and in East Africa in order to draw the Italian forces towards these points . . .

As part of this plan of deception I am sending two brigades of Indians to the Sudan, hoping that their presence will become known to the enemy and will make them think an offensive in the Sudan is intended . . .'[7]

He then asked the War Office to send him a telegram that began: 'Following from Chiefs of Staff to Commander-in-Chief: You should at once prepare plans for an operation to recapture British Somaliland.' 'The advantage of it seems to me,' said Wavell, 'to be that most of it is true; the enemy will see for himself that the greater part of it is actually being done. What we want is for him to place the wrong interpretation on what he sees.'[8] Sherlock Holmes himself might have admired the cunning.

The first move in the main campaign came on 6 November: an attack on the fortress at Gallabat, one of the 'gateways' into Ethiopia. Leading the imperial troops was a Brigadier Slim, soon to win fame and a field-marshal's baton.[9] The opening attack achieved complete surprise, and Gallabat was stormed by two Indian battalions. A third, British battalion was less fortunate: some of its tanks blew up on mines and the tracks of others were broken on the rocks; much of the RAF cover was destroyed by Italian fighters, leaving the skies above the battlefield clear for Caproni bombers to pulverise the British troops struggling towards a force three times their size. This initial reverse delayed the whole campaign, and for the time being the boost to Patriot morale failed to materialise. But it was only a delay. Early in the new year Wavell's long and complex dealings with the War Cabinet, the Chiefs of Staff and his fellow commanders-in-chief began to bear fruit, threatening the Italians with the loss of their entire East African empire just as, further north, their soldiers fled headlong across the Western Desert.

Yet in London it still seemed as though very little was being achieved. 'I continued,' wrote Churchill, 'to gird at the numbers and inaction of troops in Kenya.' His girding intensified when Smuts offered to place a second South African Division at Britain's disposal, only to have Wavell decline the offer: it was transport and supplies that he needed, not more men in Kenya.

When reports of the catastrophe at Sidi Barrani and the loss of the fortress of Bardia reached the Duke of Aosta and his men, the effect on morale was palpable. The news sped along the enemy lines and their confidence cracked. On 18 January word reached Platt that the garrisons at Kassala and Gallabat had melted away; he realised that he had to move at once, even though most of the 4th Indian Division was still in transit, some in the Suez convoy and others sailing up the Nile.

Now the campaign began to accelerate. Prodded by Churchill and the Chiefs of Staff to insist on more activity from the large numbers of troops in East Africa, Wavell issued a warning to his staff that unless a victory could be speedily achieved, the East African campaign must be subordinated both to Libya and to the Balkans, with the consequent transfer of troops. So Platt opened his offensive at once and the Italians retreated eastwards into the mountains. The chase was on.

The key to Eritrea was the Asmara Plateau, and the key to that was Keren. The door that opened to Keren was Agordat, which units of the 4th Indian Division attacked at the end of February. After two days the town fell, and the enemy fled east towards Keren. There they turned and stood, aiming their guns from the almost impregnable heights into the gorge below. The rest of the 4th Indian Division had joined Platt by the beginning of February and had now almost caught up with the enemy. But just as they drew near the rocky escarpment, huge explosions rocked it, hurtling thousands of tons of rocks into the valley, blocking the only way through. Platt and his officers gazed up at their enemy, wondering what to do next.

At the same time one part of Cunningham's force was marching north from Kenya, battling with hostile tribesmen, the harsh climate and rugged terrain, while a second column crossed into Italian Somaliland and began to move up the coast towards Mogadishu. In Ethiopia's dark interior Wingate and the Emperor unleashed their Patriot rebels and advanced on Addis Ababa, the country's capital. From four different directions Wavell's complex, crablike advance threatened a mesmerised enemy of greatly superior size.

Meanwhile, as Aosta's forces retreated through the rocky slopes and jungles of East Africa,[10] and Bergonzoli's Blackshirts fled across the desert to the green hills of the coast, another cloud of war appeared: the gaze of Britain's leaders had turned to the north, across the Aegean Sea.

There now followed a series of events that entirely changed the course of the war in the Mediterranean and jolted Wavell's career into a radically new direction. They formed a cautionary tale of the staples of war and politics – honour, folly, courage, naivety – ending, true to an ancient setting, in hubris pursued by Nemesis. It took a mere three months for the fortunes of Britain in general, and Wavell in particular, to slide from the realms of hope and glory into a tangle of doubt and difficulty, a descent studded with the capture, injury or death of many men, the loss of huge quantities of valuable equipment and the forfeit of much of the reputation that attended success. For the Empire, although it was hardly realised at the time, the hopes of future predominance in the Middle East sailed even further out of reach – further than the expense of war was already putting them. These deep misfortunes flowed from a fatal confusion of strategy and politics.

The War Cabinet and the commanders-in-chief seem to have allowed politics and an admiration for an ancient democracy to take the place of a cool appreciation of military dangers, embroiling the Empire's forces in a hopeless campaign that would change the balance of war throughout the Middle East. The judgement of the leading actors in the drama – Churchill, Eden and Wavell – seems, even if subconsciously, to have been affected by the fact that the new victim of Axis venom was Greece. The prevalence of a classical education in Britain, which influenced much of the governing class, induced it to believe that Greece was the cradle of civilisation and democracy. It is hard to believe that the hearts and minds of British policy-makers would have been similarly touched by the plight of less familiar nations such as Rumania or Bulgaria. The bravery of the Greek Army in the face of the Italian invaders – perhaps not in this case matching the standards of Ancient Rome – also stirred British emotions, possibly fortified by schoolday memories and Byron's sunlit inspiration:

> The isles of Greece, the isles of Greece,
> Where burning Sappho loved and sung,
> Where grew the arts of war and peace
> Where Delos rose, and Phoebus sprung.

However, love and song now fell into abeyance, and the arts of war and peace became rapidly disordered.

The first ten months of war had not much affected the Balkan states, which had happily carried on their main economic preoccupation of supplying Germany with grain and oil. The collapse of France, however, had put new heat under the simmering politics of south-east Europe, melting the veneer of peace. Russia was the first to make demands on its neighbours. Two days after the Armistice was signed she handed Rumania an ultimatum demanding the cession of Bessarabia and northern Bukovina, claiming them as her spheres of interest under the Nazi-Soviet Pact. Hungary and Bulgaria then asserted their own claims against Rumania; Russia and Yugoslavia resumed diplomatic relations; and Italy asked Germany for help in planning an attack against both Greece and Yugoslavia. England approved Russia's annexations and also Hungary's claims. France's views no longer counted.

Pre-occupied with the invasion of England, Germany wished to keep the Balkans quiet. She therefore swallowed Russia's belligerence and in the meantime forced the squabbling Balkan states to settle their disputes. In the resulting agreements Rumania ceded 35,000 square miles and six million of her inhabitants, and shortly afterwards invited Germany to send her a military mission. The request was granted: the SS arrived in September, followed by tanks and a motorised division.

These events enraged Mussolini. He determined to reinflate his prestige, and on 28 October, the anniversary of the Fascists' March on Rome, he sent his own army across the Albanian frontier into Greece. The direct reason for Britain being drawn into the growing turmoil was that in April 1939 she had guaranteed to support Greece if she decided to resist a threat to her independence. Determination to honour that obligation was hardened by the Government's lingering disquiet about the extinction of Czechoslovakia following the Munich Settlement and by unease about the fate of Poland, on whose behalf war had originally been declared, but to whom no help had yet been sent. This time, the Empire would not stand by: 'We will give you,' Churchill told the Greeks, 'all the help in our power. We will fight a common foe and we will share a united victory.'[11]

The Greeks had made a request for air support in their campaign against the Italians, who had occupied Albania in May 1939 and were now using the country as a base for operations against Greece. They had not had much success, and quite soon after crossing into Greece they had been pushed back into the Albanian mountains. The Greeks also asked Britain to reinforce Crete, which Greece owned, and to assume responsibility for the island's defence. Britain acceded to these requests, fearing that without British aid the Greeks might make peace with the Italians, as Germany was pressing them to do. These events occurred as the winter of 1940 drew near, coinciding with a reduced likelihood of an invasion of Britain, so that the War Cabinet no longer felt that the defence of the homeland precluded an adventure elsewhere.

At first the merits of joining in a Balkan melee wholly escaped the Middle East commanders, and Wavell certainly dissented from the proposal. He pointed out the threat from the enemy air force in Libya, and the fact that the anti-aircraft and anti-tank equipment for which the Greeks were asking was what he himself most needed in the Western Desert. Eden consequently concluded that a brigade of infantry was the maximum that could be spared, although that could hardly affect the issue and would strip Wavell of his only reserve. Eden also reminded Churchill and Dill that the Greeks had been warned only a month or so earlier that no assistance could be given until the Axis threat to Egypt was finally liquidated, and that the security of Egypt was as vital to the future of Greece as to that of Britain.[12]

As sound strategy, nothing could be clearer than that. Of course, with his feeling for diplomacy, Eden might have asked himself how his advice squared with Britain's guarantee to Greece. Nevertheless, reflecting the collective military opinion in Cairo, he explained his conclusions:

> These are my frank first comments. Your plan involves complete reversal of previous policy and I fear may have disastrous consequences. Risks are being taken at the expense of Egypt, which is a vital theatre, for Greece, which is not. You are taking away a third of our fighter aircraft from the Western Desert where we are already woefully weak. It is this which is the staggering blow . . . One object of enemy invasion of Greece may well be to cause us to withdraw our forces from here. In this they are succeeding.[13]

Those frank comments accurately summarised the situation. Yet somewhere along the Damascus Road the War Minister and the three commanders seem to have been converted, by what blinding light remains unclear. It seems likely that Eden's preconceptions about the Axis threat to the Balkans were only momentarily disturbed. For some time he had feared growing German influence in Bulgaria and Rumania, and he was worried that Greece might come to terms with both Italy and Germany and adopt complete neutrality. If that happened, the Turks and the Yugoslavs might be tempted to do likewise or even join the Axis; all along, Eden seemed to harbour an optimistic view both of the value of having Turkey 'on-side', and the chances of her becoming so.

In any event Eden changed his mind and cancelled his cable, instead sending to Churchill and Dill on the same day a new one in exactly the opposite sense:

C-in-C ME, AOC-in-C and I agree that although reinforcements ordered in the Chiefs of Staff telegram involve additional risks in the Western Desert and probably increased casualties, these risks must be faced in view of political commitments to aid Greece.[14]

As the rapid successes of 'Operation Compass' began to raise the possibility of expelling the Italians from North Africa altogether, Balkan strategy was driven briefly from the forefront of War Office priorities. It was not dislodged for long. As secret intelligence of German interest in the region began to accumulate, the Chiefs of Staff elaborated their view for Wavell:

... The extent and effectiveness of aid to the Greeks will be determining factor in the attitude of Turkey and will influence the United States and Russia. This decision means that assistance to Greece must now take priority over all operations in the Middle East once Tobruk is taken, because help for the Greeks must, in the first instance, come almost entirely from you. This need not prevent an advance to Benghazi if the going is good, nor need the Kassala operation be abandoned.[15]

This was most unwelcome to Wavell. The Italians were in full retreat and he knew the folly of 'whipping hounds off a hunted fox'. His opinion veered back to its starting-point:

Our appreciation here is that German concentration is a move in war of nerves designed with object of helping Italy by upsetting Greek nerves, inducing us to disperse our forces in the Middle East and to stop our advance in Libya. Nothing repeat nothing we can do from here is likely to be in time to stop German advance if really intended. It will lead to most dangerous dispersion of force and is playing enemy's game. Most sincerely trust COS will consider most earnestly whether enemy's move is not bluff to cause dispersion of force and loss of Greek morale. I am desperately anxious lest we play enemy's game and expose ourselves to defeat in detail.[16]

That ball was speedily returned; nor was the Prime Minister impressed by Wavell's suggestion that Hitler's iron legions were conducting a war of nerves. Churchill had seen Enigma decrypts about German troop movements, and they did not look like bluff. The fact that he had also seen a Joint

Planning Staff report, delivered a mere three days earlier and asserting that 'To intervene in the Balkans is to invite a second and even more disastrous Dunkirk', did not divert him from his course. He wrote:

> You must therefore conform your plans to larger interests at stake. Nothing must hamper the capture of Tobruk, but thereafter all operations in Libya are subordinated to aiding Greece . . . We expect and require prompt and active compliance with our decision for which we bear full responsibility.[17]

Debate was not invited, as was underlined by the coded invitation to Wavell to resign his command if he could not agree to the Committee's requests.

A number of imperatives now began to coalesce in the minds of the British leaders, propelling them towards the idea of a landing in Greece. The principal objective was to establish a Balkan front, disrupt the enemy's timetable and compel him to dissipate his forces. For Churchill, the overriding issue was the need to engage the enemy, discommode him and disturb his plans – a principle also highly valued by Wavell. Helping the Greeks fight the Italians in Albania would have the effect both of preventing the Italians from sending reinforcements to North Africa and of barring them from access to Greece's harbours, which were of great use to the Royal Navy.

There was also Turkey to be considered; besides having an army of 750,000 men, she was the only country around which there was any chance of forming a Balkan bloc. Turkey also provided depth for the defence of the Suez Canal, the Persian and Iraqi oilfields, the Abadan oil refineries and the pipelines running west to the Mediterranean. If the Axis broke into the Middle East, it could gain control of all of these, besides securing the grain and oil of the Ukraine and the Caucasus. Having severed Britain's imperial links, Germany could join hands with Japan and decisively alter the world order – not least at the expense of the British Empire. It was vital that she should be prevented from doing so.

The Government believed that refusing to help Greece would not only be a source of eternal shame, but would destroy Turkey's fragile confidence that Britain would honour her understandings. Wavell, however, as experienced in dealing with the Turks as any senior British soldier, believed that the country was too weak to be of any help as an ally. The Turks seemed to share his view themselves, remaining obdurate in their refusal to adopt the role in which Churchill had optimistically cast them. They had seen the

Germans drive the British out of France the previous year, and had their own view as to who might win a fight in the Balkans.

A fourth objective for Britain was to court US opinion. Churchill was determined to draw America into the war. It was of no matter that in terms of moral obligation alone, America had just as great a duty as Britain; nor was the fact that America had failed to give a guarantee to the Greeks, or to any other country in need, so that she could hardly reproach Britain for not sending an army to help them. Churchill believed that riding to the rescue of the Greeks would inspire influential Americans, and that standing back as she was subjugated would have the opposite effect.[18]

Wavell was therefore ordered to go to Athens, where on 13 January he arrived incognito for discussions with General Ioannis Metaxas, the Prime Minister, and General Alexander Papagos, the commander-in-chief. Wavell's instructions were to offer to withdraw two or three divisions and a small number of aircraft from Egypt for use in Greece. He had also been ordered to urge the Greeks to accept the immediate despatch of a token force of two regiments and about sixty tanks. These were for deployment in eastern Greece and around the port of Salonika, notwithstanding the fact that any such troops could be of use only against Germans invading from the north or east and that it was hardly relevant to the Greeks' war against the Italians in Albania. The offer was also a lure to the Yugoslavs, who would be of little value to the Allied cause unless Salonika was protected, as it was the only port that could handle the military supplies that might give Yugoslavia at least the chance of resisting a German attack. Churchill, who agreed with many elements of the Zionist cause, may also have noted that a significant, and successful, portion of Salonika's population was Jewish.[19]

Metaxas announced that he could spare only four divisions for an eastern front, whereas nine divisions with corresponding air support, would be the bare minimum needed; Britain, he said, would have to make up the difference. This at once exposed a grave misconception on the part of the Greeks: Wavell explained that Marshal Graziani had a large army, and his own was small; that he simply did not have the spare divisions and could provide only two or three at the most. This news greatly discouraged the Greeks, especially as at that moment British intelligence reports, passed on to the Greeks, suggested that Germany had available in the region as many as thirty-five well-trained and equipped divisions, several of them armoured, and 500 aircraft: a preponderance of about five to one.

So Metaxas thanked Wavell for the offer, but declined it as inadequate.

No troops, he said, should be sent until the British could offer 200,000. The meetings closed.

But the British Government would not let up. Wavell was ordered to go back to Athens once again and insist that the Greeks accept his offer. This time he told a sceptical Metaxas that his government believed that an attack on Salonika was imminent, and that it could not understand the Greek refusal of help; it was now, he said, or possibly never. He tried to encourage the Greeks with his own, rather optimistic view that Germany would hesitate to enter Bulgaria, violating Bulgarian neutrality and exposing the Rumanian oilfields to air attack from the south.

Once more Metaxas dutifully examined the matter, but to him it remained as clear as day. The Germans were greatly superior in numbers and equipment, and they held the initiative. If the British intervened, it would only hasten a German intervention while offering little scope for repelling it; moreover, if the Turks and Yugoslavs realised how weak was the force the British were offering, they would be confirmed in their inclination to neutrality. General Papagos also made the obvious point that if Wavell continued his advance into Libya while Greece was being attacked, he would hardly be able to provide any serious or timely assistance, and that splitting the British forces would be a grave error:

At all events, the abandonment in one theatre of the war of operations which gave every promise of ultimate success, and which would produce substantial results for the whole allied struggle, in order to embark on another operation in a quite different theatre, with means and under conditions which doomed it to certain failure, would be to commit a strategic error in contradiction to the principles of sound strategy. [20]

Not only was that the opinion of the Greeks, but it was exactly the argument that Wavell and Eden had so recently pressed upon the British Government.

There was now yet another change of course. The Defence Committee, with second thoughts, welcomed the Greeks' refusal of help. Now that the offer had been declined, it felt that honour had been satisfied and duty done. 'Quite right,' said Churchill, 'never force little dogs to eat good mutton.'[21] In the fluid context of war, flexibility of mind is essential and changes of plan are inevitable, but the speed with which they were now occurring seemed bewildering.

Wavell was relieved. He had done the Government's bidding and, even though he disagreed with the policy, had tried to cajole the Greeks. Displeased with the difficult negotiations, tired by the noisy flights, with their ever-present danger of engine failure or the sudden appearance of enemy fighters, he returned to Cairo.

He had now been commander-in-chief for well over twelve months, in a time of continuous danger, during which he had directed campaigns in two theatres, constructed a Middle East base and reserve, negotiated the tortuous paths of Egyptian (and now Balkan) politics, while subject to almost contin-uous political pressure from London. He seemed to be one solid, reliable pillar of strength, doing the job of many. But it was taking its toll, and the heavier jowl, thinning hair and deepening lines on his rather puckered face betrayed the stress that he bore. Yet in Cairo, Wavell could find at least some comfort, shed his shyness and talk freely in his rather thick voice. Among a few close friends and his happy family he emerged from his shell.

He liked to escape the army atmosphere when he could, and often made the surprising remark that soldiering bored him. He seemed to yearn for people who preferred art and culture. He would dine, for example, with Freya Stark, whose admiration for him now bordered on hero-worship:

A quiet dinner party, only six of us and we had a quiet and frivolous evening and talked of Samarkand, and he quoted a lovely poem by Oscar Wilde about those remote places . . . He is the most modest man in this world, and no one would think he had just brought off one of the biggest victories of the war.[22]

It is unlikely that Wavell was bewitched by the epicene nature of long-haired poets, but he did share their aesthetic sense. More in line with expectations, he admired men in a more heroic mould such as Cromwell, whom he thought 'a common-sense country gentleman with a gift of simple direct speech, who had great faith, who saw things were wrong and set himself to put them right'.[23]

Yet even in bohemian company Wavell rarely lost his air of serene detach-ment. He sometimes needed it even in his family circle. Lady Wavell's habitual lack of punctuality, especially in the morning, which had caused a certain inconvenience since the time when Wavell was a major, was slightly more noticeable now that they were living in the limelight.

A typical incident in the city's hothouse atmosphere arose over the Red Cross and Red Crescent Balls, organised jointly by Lady Lampson, Queen

Farida and the Egyptian Prime Minister's wife. Lady Wavell was much admired for running a series of 'Lonely Hearts' dances, popular with wives and girlfriends in Cairo suffering from the pangs of separation from their desert warriors, but her good works did not extend to taking the slightest interest in Queen Farida's Ball, and even less in the 100 tickets that the ambassador sent to her in the hope that she would sell them to the army. An exasperated Lampson pressed into service Peter Coats, who managed finally to achieve a sale of four tickets. The Ball was a pet project of the foremost Cairo wives, and Lady Wavell's lack of enthusiasm ruffled diplomatic feathers; as the ambassador said: 'The thing therefore has a considerable political importance and it is really rather monstrous that the British army should wash their hands of it simply because they are bored, or rather because Lady Wavell is.'[24] The problem was solved only by the MP Henry Channon[25] delving into his pockets and buying up the remaining tickets.

Channon, assistant to the Foreign Office minister Rab Butler, was staying at the Embassy en route to Belgrade, on a mission to Prince Paul, the Regent of Yugoslavia. Since university days the two men had been close friends – Channon once described Prince Paul as 'the person I have loved most and longest'[26] – and it was hoped that he might be able to attract Prince Paul to the Allied cause, or at least discover whether he was likely to resist German pressure to join the Axis.

Coats was thrilled by Channon's arrival,[27] while wondering how a very rich, *mondaine* American, who had embraced the glittering world of political high society, would be viewed by the rather less exuberant Wavell. He need not have worried: it was the beginning of a surprising friendship of opposites, and when Wavell took Channon to one side at a party and talked to him at length, he seemed to the MP to be 'one of the most rare, gentle, detached, good people I have ever met. His charm is insidious.'[28]

Another vivid bird of passage then in Cairo was Colonel William Donovan. Round and rubicund, a charming and persuasive American, he was reputedly the most decorated American soldier of the First World War. His mission, reporting directly both to Roosevelt and to Churchill, was to encourage the Balkan states to join the Allies by convincing them that America would never allow Germany to win the war, and by easing their fear of Communism, which was somewhat greater than their dislike of Germany. His object was also to size up how the British were handling their war effort and to report to those who, to a significant extent, had become the Empire's paymasters.

Donovan, displaying searching intelligence, seems to have had a significant influence on Wavell as he made his circuitous intellectual voyage towards recommending an expedition to Greece. It was when dining alone with the ebullient American that Wavell seems finally to have concluded that there was no alternative to sending help. As Lampson recorded:

> Donovan put over very well his idea of looking at the Mediterranean not as an east–west corridor but as a No-Man's-Land between two opposing fronts. The North–South conception seemed to strike Wavell very forcibly, and he was clearly impressed by Donovan's insistence on the need for keeping a foothold in the Balkans.[29]

Weather forecasts suggested that a German move into the Balkans would be unlikely before March, and so, concluding that there was still time to prepare a defence, the Cabinet changed its stance yet again. General Metaxas had suddenly died, to be replaced by General Papagos, who now accepted the idea, in principle, of military aid, even if he did not apparently accept the need for British forces to be in place before any resistance could be offered to the Germans. Abandoning its position that the Greeks had killed the offer of help, the Cabinet ordered Wavell to make another attempt to win them over. Wavell's cable of 10 February, suggesting that Tripoli might yield to a small force if despatched at once, was therefore dismissed, and prompted instead the directive that the major effort must now be to help Greece:

> . . . This rules out any serious effort against Tripoli, although minor demonstrations thitherwards would be a useful feint. You should therefore make yourself secure at Benghazi and concentrate all available forces in the Delta in preparation for movement to Europe.[30]

A new theatre of war was opening up, and Wavell was told to create a mobile reserve of four divisions and an armoured division for use in Greece or Turkey within two months.

The CIGS, Sir John Dill, had at first told the Cabinet that he was wholly opposed to sending help to Greece, on the grounds that there were insufficient forces for the purpose; however, Churchill's sharp rebuff of that suggestion caused Dill at once to see the error of his ways. His rapid change of mind seems to have infected the three commanders-in-chief in Cairo, so that they also changed their tune, with Wavell pronouncing that from the military point of view the project had, after all, a reasonable chance of success.

Eden – also impressed by Donovan's references to US opinion – and Dill, once more in Cairo, cabled the Prime Minister:

While no one can guarantee success, all in the Middle East hold the same conviction as those in London, namely, that we were prepared to run the risk of failure, thinking it better to suffer with the Greeks than to make no attempt to help them. Though the campaign would be a daring adventure they were not without hope that it might succeed to the extent of halting the Germans before they overrun all Greece.[31]

The idea of a daring adventure was hardly a substitute for a sober appreciation on which the Cabinet could reasonably make a decision. It is not clear on what military grounds the commanders had made their volte-face – although they may have been influenced by the outlook following the fall of Benghazi on 7 February – partly because it seems that the Cabinet neither requested nor received any purely military assessment of the situation; instead it appears to have adopted Dill's attitude, summarised by his reply when reproached by an admiral who could not understand the reasoning: 'Oh, but we *must*!' The fact that Dill, a chronic pessimist, had espoused the cause of Greece made a strong impression on the Chiefs of Staff.

Confusion of purpose increased when Eden's cable setting out the commanders' warlike conclusions crossed with one in the opposite sense from Churchill, which expressed the Defence Committee's renewed doubts:

Do not consider yourselves obligated to a Greek enterprise if in your hearts you feel it will only be another Norwegian fiasco. If no good plan can be made, please say so. But of course, you know how valuable success would be.[32]

There were other warning voices: when Wavell, 'obviously with a heavy heart', told General Marshall-Cornwall, heading the mission to the Turks, that he had decided to send an expedition to Greece, he received the horrified reply that it was a gamble and could only lead to disaster. 'Possibly,' Wavell replied, 'but strategy is only the handmaid of policy, and here political considerations must come first. The policy of our Government is to build up a Balkan front.'[33]

Accepting the risk of another Norwegian fiasco, Eden and the service chiefs in Cairo determined to proceed. They now started to devise a plan.

One crucial factor would be the strength of the force that Wavell proposed to leave in Africa to guard Egypt's frontier; a second would be the state both of the Greek Army and of those of the other potential allies.

Wavell's view of Greece was cloudy, but he received from his staff a clearer picture of the threat to Libya. For some time Cairo intelligence had discounted a German invasion of Greece, believing that the enemy would prefer to make for the Suez Canal via North Africa. Yet just before Wavell left for Athens, Brigadier Shearer gave him an appreciation of probable German intentions, warning not only that at least twenty divisions had arrived in Bulgaria, but that the eventual total might reach forty. The possibility that the Balkan roads might be unable to cope with anything near such numbers seems not to have weighed much with the intelligence staffs – nor, presumably, with their German counterparts. Shearer made another telling point:

> The question . . . is whether it is worth taking serious risks on the prob-lematical chance of securing a precarious foothold in Macedonia from which, if we are finally ejected, the security of our whole position in the Middle East will be badly shaken . . .
>
> If, in Macedonia, the spectacles of another Norway followed by Dunkirk were to be repeated, our strength to resist a renewed attack from Tripoli would be seriously impaired.[34]

It all cut little ice with Wavell. Quoting General Wolfe's dictum that 'war is an option of difficulties', he said that he would be more likely to be 'playing the enemy's game' by remaining inactive:

> If we do not act we lose almost as much prestige and influence as if we suffered a defeat, for the enemy will say that we were afraid or unable to go to the assistance of our Greek allies; we shall lose any chance of Yugoslav assistance, and we shall risk losing that of Turkey . . .[35]

'Provided', he concluded, 'that conversations with the Greeks show that there is a good chance of establishing a front against the Germans with our assistance, I think we should take it.' It was a crucial proviso. Meanwhile he continued to assemble an expeditionary force, and to prepare 'Operation Lustre', its transport across the sea.

On 22 February a meeting to untie these tangled knots was held at Tatoi, the royal palace near Athens. It was mainly a diplomatic agenda, into which

Eden pressed the military opinions. While once more offering troops to the Greeks, he stressed that the offer depended partly on whether the generals now thought an expedition held a reasonable prospect of success. As the latest intelligence suggested that the Germans were ready to unleash approximately six times as many divisions as Wavell could find, and more than five times the number of aeroplanes, hopes of success would seem to have called for a generous helping of blind optimism.

From the start the emphasis seems to have been on defence rather than attack. It may have appeared to be the only option, but it could not have been encouraging for the commanders in the field, and therefore for their men. Equally, it would have been difficult for Wavell to see how he could nourish and sustain a force once it had reached its various objectives. The facts before both him and the War Cabinet suggested that the navy would have great difficulty in supplying the expeditionary force to the extent needed to halt, let alone drive back, German invaders. Since early in his career Wavell had been impressed by the need to put in place the back-up necessary to sustain forces in battle; yet in this case he was prepared to run the considerable risk of being unable to do so, with the imperial force consequently being stranded.

Nevertheless, the British commanders began to study the country's topography. There appeared to be a choice of four natural defensive lines, marked by mountains and rivers. The most feasible barrier was the natural obstruction formed by the Aliakmon river, the basis of an 'Aliakmon Line' spanning Greece from Mount Olympus to the Albanian border. A proposal to stand on the Aliakmon would be contentious because, among other things, it would mean abandoning Salonika. But Wavell maintained that 'unless we could be sure of the Yugoslavs joining in, it was not possible to contemplate holding a line covering Salonika: in view of the doubtful attitude of Yugoslavia, the only sound plan from the military point of view was to stand on the Aliakmon Line'. In practice this meant abandoning the hope that the Yugoslavs would join in, and likewise any serious hope of forming a Balkan bloc. Nor might the Aliakmon prove a sound defensive position: although the Greek Army had proved its skill in mountain fighting, that would be of little use if the Germans bypassed the mountains by forging through the roads and valleys.

After much wrangling, and obviously pained at the idea of abandoning a square yard of Greece, Papagos appeared to agree to defending the Aliakmon position. From then on, the discussions descended into confusion and contradiction, and the whole foundation of the plan began to crack. It had been the British understanding that the Greeks would order the immediate withdrawal of most of their troops on the Bulgarian frontier and move them to the Aliakmon Line, but instead of leaving the discussion at that point, Eden intervened, qualifying the conclusions by proposing that 'preparations should be made and put into execution to withdraw the Greek troops . . . to the line we should be obliged to hold if the Yugoslavians did not come in'.[36]

This confusion of preparations with execution was to prove deadly. It let the Greeks off the hook. Their soldiers in Albania were upholding national honour by successfully resisting the Italians. Those in Macedonia were not only in strong defensive positions, but almost all came from that region and were defending their own homes and families. Those troops would hardly countenance abandoning their kin to the Bulgarians or Germans. The last-minute reference to preparations – unwitting as far as Eden was concerned – confirmed General Papagos in the belief that discovering Yugoslav intentions was a necessary preliminary to the actual movement of troops; at the same time, withdrawing to a line chosen on the assumption that the Yugoslavs would stay out negated Wavell's fundamental premise that success depended on Yugoslavia, and probably Turkey, coming in.[37]

For the Greek leaders to order a withdrawal would require a large measure of political will, yet neither Wavell nor anyone else on the British side appears to have questioned whether the Greeks had it, or to have asked them if they really were prepared to face the unpopularity of ceding territory to the Bulgarians without a battle. It was an obvious question, given the Greeks' ambivalence towards Germany and their loathing of Bulgaria, especially as senior Greek officers had warned the British Military Mission that many of their generals were willing to fight the Bulgarians, but not the Germans.

'Alas regardless of their doom, the little victims play . . .' Eden, Dill and Wavell set off for more talks with the Turks, confident that the Greeks would at once start to move their troops south to the Aliakmon. Back in London, the Chiefs of Staff thought the proposals lacked logic or consistency, but felt that they must defer to the combined wisdom of the Foreign Secretary, the CIGS and Wavell, who perhaps could see something that was not apparent in London.

The talks in Ankara proved fruitless; then, returning empty-handed to Athens on 2 March, Wavell was appalled to find that a now obviously defeatist Papagos had taken no steps at all to withdraw to the Aliakmon Line, on the grounds that he was still awaiting a response from Yugoslavia.

The situation was critical. New intelligence disclosed that the Germans, doubtless overcoming any fear that the RAF might retaliate against the Rumanian oilfields, had begun crossing the Danube into Bulgaria, which meant that they would be able to reach Greece before any withdrawal to the Aliakmon was complete, even if it began at once. In fact the opportunity had been lost, and the bottom had fallen out of the plan even before Wavell's forces set foot in Greece. But by now the advance British parties had left Alexandria and embarkation orders had been issued to the main force; reversing the process risked administrative chaos. So the British declined to withdraw their offer, and accepted, with misgivings, Papagos' offer to transfer to the Aliakmon a lesser number of troops – untested in battle and without artillery.

Churchill himself now began to alter his stance: 'Situation has indeed changed for worse . . .' he said. 'We have done our best to promote Balkan combination against Germany . . . We are advised from many quarters that our ignominious ejection from Greece would do us more harm . . . than the fact of submission of the Balkans which with our scanty forces we have never been expected to prevent.'[38] This directly contradicted the argument that a show must be made in order to please the Americans, and the failure of the Greeks to move their troops had altered the position entirely.

Once more the Foreign Secretary and the three commanders met in Cairo, to agree on a final recommendation. They were joined by General Smuts, the Cambridge-educated Anglophile Prime Minister of South Africa whose advice the British leaders valued so highly, and whom Wavell described as 'one of the greatest and wisest men living'. Smuts' sense of honour and imperial vision soared above Papagos' failure to move his troops. The Empire would be held up to ignominy, he declared, if it did not stand by the Greeks. Wavell agreed; he stuck to his story that, provided he could get his forces into Greece, there was 'a good prospect of a successful encounter with the Germans'. In fact he had taken matters into his own hands even before the CIGS and the Foreign Secretary reached Egypt, as Eden recorded:

Dill and I were sent out, after Wavell's victories, to Cairo, to look into this business; well, when we got there Wavell said, 'now I hope you won't mind what I'm going to say: I didn't think I ought to waste time, and I've begun the movement of troops and the concentration to enable us to go to Greece.'[39]

Wavell had not waited to be convinced: 'The results of success,' he said 'would be incalculable and might alter the whole aspect of the war.' It was a statement that illustrated his innate capacity to believe that all would somehow be well in the end. His gambler's streak often produced brilliant results, sometimes less so. Yet perhaps Wavell was at heart less sanguine than he sounded, as later recorded by the American Ambassador in London:

> After reaching this decision Dill boarded his plane for England. As he stepped aboard Wavell turned to him and said, half laughing and half sadly, 'Jack, I hope, when this action is reviewed, you will be elected to sit on my court martial.'[40]

There was one other fundamental precondition without which the Government could hardly approve an expedition, and that was an assurance from Wavell that he could leave a screen of forces in Cyrenaica sufficient to protect Egypt from attack. This he duly gave: on 2 March, on the basis of his latest intelligence appreciations, he advised the War Office that Cyrenaica was secure. That, for a time, removed North Africa from the equation, and on 7 March the War Cabinet ordered that the expedition proceed.

In order to dovetail his troops into the Greek lines Wavell needed a clear view both of the state of their army and of the territory to be occupied, but it was proving hard to attain. Even now, for fear of provoking the Germans, the Greeks refused to allow any reconnaissance in the north of the country. Although the Aliakmon Line was therefore in forbidden territory, Wavell did eventually manage to take a reconnaissance flight along it. He was appalled by what he saw. The roads running along the line were mostly tracks, impassable to British vehicles, and possibly even to Greek pack-animals, whereas the passes that cut through it offered to German armour a clear way into Greece.

It was intended that the preparations should be kept secret from the Germans. That was optimistic, especially as the fact that Germany and Greece were still at peace allowed German diplomats to move around more or less at will – which they did, alert for information. Their military attaché, Prince Erbach, spoke excellent English and dressed like an English gentleman. He made sure that he was on the quay at Piraeus as the first British contingents began to arrive. He strolled up to an officer supervising his men:

'Fancy seeing the well-known cap-badge of the Northumberland Hussars,' he exclaimed; 'many a good day's hunting have I had in the past with the Percy Hounds. What have you done with your horses?'

'Oh, we had to leave them behind,' replied the officer; 'we now have anti-tank guns instead, but they're quite useless, and in any case we have no ammunition with us because the ships were wrongly loaded in Alexandria.'[41]

It was a matter of hours before this helpful information was being analysed in Berlin.

Because much of the force available consisted of Australians and New Zealanders, it was essential for the Government to gain the wholehearted support of the Dominions. They seemed at once to have grasped a crucial point, and stated that their main requirement was an assurance that the decision to proceed was based on military advice rather than political convenience: in effect, as Churchill said, 'because Dill, Wavell and other Commanders-in-Chief are convinced that there is a reasonable fighting chance':

Please remember in your stresses that, so far, you have given us few facts or reasons on their authority which can be presented to these Dominions as justifying the operation on any grounds but *noblesse oblige*. A precise military appreciation is indispensable.[42]

Noblesse oblige not being a concept that much preoccupied Antipodeans in their daily lives, the lack of a precise military appreciation was regrettable.

It seemed that the Australian Prime Minister had conferred with Wavell in Cairo and had readily agreed to allow some latitude over the use of Australian troops; even so, his government agreed to their use only with reservations, one being that plans were completed beforehand 'to ensure that evacuation, if necessitated, will be successfully undertaken . . .'[43]

That thoughts of evacuation had arisen even before the expedition left Egypt suggests that a hint of pessimism might have entered the whole project. There were already voices suggesting the result was a foregone conclusion, although whether that was really felt at the top of the tree of command is not recorded. Wavell himself had fought shy of promoting evacuation plans – for which he was later rather unjustly criticised – but he now received a cable from Dill with even more pessimistic implications, asking if his 'Worst

Possible Case' scheme, for abandoning Egypt itself, still held. There remained a great gulf between Churchill and anyone so defeatist as even to contemplate, let alone plan for, a major retreat. When, at Chequers the following weekend, the Prime Minister learnt that Wavell had prepared just such a scheme the previous year, he responded with a violent flux of rage, warning of firing-parties for the generals, as Alanbrooke and others around the table maintained a bleak and anxious silence.

In Cairo, Wavell's staff had nevertheless begun to consider the logistics of a forced evacuation, not a usual preliminary to plans for a successful campaign. Unfortunately, little was done with the logistics beyond considering them. The result was to contribute to the ill feeling that grew in the aftermath of the campaign, especially in view of the chaotic conditions that developed on some of the bullet-swept evacuation beaches.

It was also vital that Wavell should inspire the imperial generals. In command of 2 New Zealand Division was General Bernard Freyberg, VC. On 17 February Wavell ordered Freyberg to make his division ready to go to Greece, and the next day he outlined his plans to the Australian commander Thomas Blamey. He told them both that London had already been in touch with their governments. As commander-in-chief, however, he did not seek their advice: 'My opinion was never asked,' Freyberg said, 'I was told the bare facts – to get ready to go.' And he added, 'I never expected to be asked my opinion by the commander-in-chief. He was far from co-operative. He had secrecy mania.'[44] Nor were Blamey's views sought: as he put it, 'I felt that I was receiving instructions.'[45]

Yet Wavell was, after all, the commander-in-chief, to whom the Dominion generals were subordinate, and it was Britain that was leading the struggle. There was no requirement for him to enter into a debate. His paramount duty was to take forward a military operation of great hazard. The Dominion leaders were not so sure. The patriotic fervour of previous generations, when the bonds of Empire were cherished and Britain ruled the wave, was fading. As the Prime Minister of Australia, who was at the time in Cairo, was informed by his own government:

My colleagues and I feel resentment that while some discussions appear to have taken place with the High Command, Blamey's views as GOC of the force which apparently is to take the major part in the operations should not have been sought and that he was not asked to express an opinion. This . . . deeply affects the question of Empire relationship . . .[46]

It was a step along the path that within a few years was to lead the Dominions, for all their prominence in the imperial galaxy, to turn to America as their principal partner in world affairs.

The resentment was increased by the tone of the generals' subsequent comments: 'I'm satisfied this expedition to Greece is hopeless', Blamey observed, after a conference with Wavell, and followed it up by asserting that 'the Greek expedition hadn't a dog's chance from the start'.[47] Yet they could have said so clearly at the time: at their first briefings by Wavell, both Blamey and Freyberg were restrained in their comments, and certainly did not express themselves strongly enough for the commander-in-chief to feel that he had to warn the War Office.

On 5 March the army was ready to sail, and the convoys plied the placid sea from Egypt to Piraeus, bearing 'W Force' on its journey to the assembly areas at Larissa, and on to the thyme-scented rocks of Mount Olympus where the Greeks awaited them. The snows had melted in the mountains, fruit trees blossomed and the fields were full of flowers. It was a heady contrast to the harsh light of Egypt, and a brief respite for the troops before they had to face the German armour.

As early as 13 December Hitler had issued orders for an attack on Greece through Bulgaria. At dawn on 6 April the onslaught began, without any diplomatic notice to Greece, although on the same day Germany declared war on Yugoslavia. The campaign is well documented and needs little retelling. For the Allies it was a tale of courage and confusion, of old equipment and little air support. For the Germans it was one more glorious, intoxicating descent onto other people's property, with superbly co-ordinated armour, infantry and artillery abetted by the paralysing effect of dive-bombers. Their furious three-pronged attack cut simultaneously through the frontiers of Greece and Yugoslavia. Like rolling surf it swept through the valleys and mountain passes, obliterating British aircraft on the ground and isolating the Greek armies from Thrace to Albania. Then, like a 'grey caterpillar on a carpet of green', it debouched onto the plains. There it collided with the Greek Army – a straggling, creaking column of mules and carts retreating at one mile an hour.

The Greeks' determination to fight the hated Italians had not extended to challenging the might of Germany. Morale faltered, commanders lost control and soldiers began to slip back to Athens. Jumbo Wilson, the British Commander in Greece, and Blamey soon realised that they would have to withdraw even further south, to a line where they were not dependent on the Greeks. They chose the Pass of Thermopylae, of which Wilson, with some foresight, had ordered a study when he first arrived in Athens. It was the scene, as Wavell knew, of a battle in ancient days, when Leonidas and his 300 Spartans faced similar problems: 'The German Air Force will take the place of the Persian arrows, darkening the sun, and British tenacity and Greek devotion will fight in the shade.'[48]

As in the battle for France, the Luftwaffe had mastered the skies. There was only one road back to Athens, narrow, cratered and difficult, with bridges so flimsy they were vulnerable even to a near-miss. The retreating columns were easy targets. The German pilots proved surprisingly inaccurate, but the threat they posed was sufficient to demoralise their enemy. Movement by day became impossible; exhaustion set in, and drivers fell asleep at the wheel, blocking the roads and immobilising troops, who found themselves helpless when the dawn skies filled with Stukas. After a difficult interview with his king, the Greek Prime Minister shot himself. Confidence waned.

The appearance of any aircraft or the sound of an aircraft was sufficient to bring movement to a standstill. One Australian battalion in MT movement left their vehicles and scattered from the roadside at the appearance of an eagle. It took a long time to get them back.[49]

Having set the strategy and appointed the commanders, there was little that Wavell could add, and during the three-week campaign he went to Greece only twice. He had too much else on his hands to spare the time. He could not be everywhere, although he was needed everywhere. His calming presence might have spurred Wilson's staff to a more effective performance, and to organise the campaign without it being bedevilled by a series of misunderstandings with senior Dominion officers.

On 18 April Wavell did fly to Athens, holding a conference there at which it was agreed that the only option was evacuation. The proposal was not discouraged by the Greek Government, who thought it might save their country from devastation. Wavell questioned whether reinforcements could be summoned or the army maintained, but bravely stated that the British Army would fight for as long as the Greeks.

Besides the emotional burden of an evacuation there were enormous physical obstacles. On the night of 6 April an air raid had badly damaged Piraeus, the only large and serviceable port in the country, and the obvious point of exit. During the raid the *Clan Fraser*, laden with 200 tons of TNT, was in the harbour. Poignantly, the steamer was due to be unloaded that day, but the British authorities refused to pay the extra wages the stevedores requested for working on a Sunday, so its cargo was left on board. The ship was hit, caught fire and exploded, sinking seven merchant ships, twenty-five caiques, sixty lighters and an ammunition barge. The entire Free Zone dock was demolished and strewn with red-hot wreckage, some of which landed on an ammunition train that also blew up, causing further devastation to quays, offices and shops. The sound of the explosions echoed for twenty miles and the port was closed completely. It was the opening day of the campaign.

That left the beaches. Wavell instructed General Wilson to fix the dates for evacuation, and to ensure that he consulted Blamey and Freyberg. This his staff failed to do, which was to add to the bitterness that grew in the wake of the campaign. He also told Wilson to liaise with the navy, an essential but difficult task as there was no naval commander ashore, or a direct representative of the naval commander-in-chief.

Events began to accelerate: on 21 April, without warning to the British, the Greek forces in the west surrendered, and two days later the Luftwaffe destroyed on their airfield the RAF's twelve remaining Hurricanes, putting paid to the only available air cover. On 24 April the remaining Greek divisions capitulated.

Nevertheless, nearly 50,000 of the 63,500 who fought in the campaign were saved, after five nights of evacuation amid scenes of outstanding bravery by soldiers and sailors alike.

The imperial troops had fought with distinction, and the number killed in the campaign was approximately the same for both sides. But it was the overwhelming power of the German Air Force that sealed the result, rendering the retreating troops dazed and exhausted by serial bombing and cannon-fire. Besides the men left in Greece, dead or alive, about 8,000 vehicles, all guns except personal firearms and all other equipment were left behind. Abandoning so many vehicles was extremely serious for Wavell. His overall Middle East strategy had assumed the delivery of about 3,000 vehicles per month, mostly from America, but only an exiguous proportion of these were actually arriving. The shortfall after the losses in Greece would darken further an outlook that was already becoming murky in the extreme.

'It was not really,' he later said, 'such a forlorn hope from the military point of view as it may seem from its results.' Originally there may have been grounds for hope, if nothing more, but events did not bear them out. 'Thus,' he said in his official despatch, 'while the whole expedition was something in the nature of a gamble, the dice were loaded against it from the start.'[50] Later he accepted that it was probably not a glittering military prize that drew the British in:

> I think it may have been psychological and political considerations that tilted the balance in the end over the military dangers. To have withdrawn at this stage, on grounds which could not have been made public, would have been disastrous to our reputation in the USA, and with other neutrals, would have ended all hopes of Yugoslavia joining the Allies and would have shaken our ally Turkey . . .[51]

Eden later reflected on the failure:

> One has to admit that we didn't obtain the objectives we'd hoped for. We weren't able to conduct, with the help of the Yugoslavs, any effective campaign in the Balkans. Turkey, it is true, remained a defensive player, but we lost Greece and we lost many men, brave men, and more were captured. So in that sense the balance sheet was much against us; and it was a depressing time, no question of that.[52]

The campaign became known as one of the most splendid failures in British military history. However, the decision to fight (if not its result) was welcomed in America. Britain was saluted as a country gallantly keeping her promise in a world where that seemed all too scarce. American headlines told of 'heroes' fighting in Greece, and cash flowed in to fund-raisers calling on Roosevelt to declare war. Wavell had been convinced of the need to impress the Americans and justified his confidence that the expedition would 'play in Peoria'.

Since then, there has been much discussion about whether it was worthwhile because it may have delayed the German invasion of Russia which eventually began on 22 June, 1941. However, the paramount cause of the crucial delay that changed the course of the war is still not certain. Wavell thought it was the battle for Greece, on the grounds that the armoured divisions that reached the Peloponnese had been earmarked for the invasion of Russia, and had to be refitted after their long journey through Greece and then back to the north.[53] An alternative theory points to events in June 1940 when Russia handed Rumania an ultimatum demanding the cession of Bessarabia and northern Bukovina. Thereafter the Germans feared that the oilfields at Ploesti[54] – their main source of oil – were dangerously close to the Russian Army, a threat that they had to remove.

Whatever the main reason for 'Barbarossa' – the codename for Hitler's invasion of Russia – the fact remains that a German attack on Russia was not a factor for any of the British planners concerned with the Greek expedition.[55]

As the battered imperial soldiers retreated forlornly through the villages of Greece, their inhabitants cheered and saluted them with flowers, although they could sense that the battle was over. The editor of a famous Athenian newspaper published an open letter expressing his people's emotions:

> We turned . . . to the English. And to those whose own homeland was in flames, those who were keeping anxious watch and ward on the Channel, those who, they said it themselves, had not sufficient material for their own defence. They came and they came immediately.[56]

The sound of gunfire faded. Silent, stoical Greeks stood among the bright stones of the Parthenon, the air fragrant with camomile. Soon they would be dying of starvation at the rate of 400 a day. Meanwhile they wondered what was in store for them, and hoped that Hitler would spare their ancient citadel.

For Wavell and his army, honour served and duty done had their own rewards. But the price was high, and it was now to be paid on several different fronts.

XI

SANDSTORM

WAVELL was now faced with conducting five campaigns, at all points of the compass, four of them simultaneously, and with resources that he bluntly described as completely inadequate.

Apart from the operations in East Africa, successful in almost all their stages and moving towards a victorious conclusion, danger now emerged to his west, east and north – from the Western Desert, Greece, Crete, Iraq and Syria. All pointed ultimately to Egypt and the Suez Canal. He therefore had to repatriate as many troops as he could to Egypt, to re-equip them and prepare them once more for battle. His obvious course was to transport the survivors of the Greek expedition direct to Alexandria or Suez. However, at once he ran up against one of the problems that had dogged his efforts for so long: the scarcity of shipping. The crossing from Greece to Alexandria took twenty-four hours even in calm waters, and for much of the journey risked exposure to aerial attack. It was therefore hurriedly arranged that most of the troops lifted from the beaches should be taken first to Crete, which was only about fifty miles from the Peloponnese and an obvious staging-post between Greece and Egypt. Some units could continue straight on to Alexandria, but it was hoped that disembarking the majority in Crete would enable a quicker turnaround of rescue ships, and save more of the expeditionary force from the clutches of the Germans.

No sooner had the evacuation started than Wavell was forced to revise his objectives. Secret messages intercepted by Bletchley Park revealed that the Germans intended to transfer their attack to Crete as soon as they had completed mopping up operations around Athens. At first Wavell thought their preparations would take the enemy at least four weeks, but their efficiency was such that on 27 April 1941 the Joint Intelligence Committee was forced to a bleaker conclusion. Estimating that the Germans already had nearly 900 aircraft in the Balkans, besides troops and shipping for a seaborne operation, they realised that a combined sea and air attack was imminent, with waves of troops ready to land in their thousands, by ship, glider and parachute. The Prime Minister confirmed the matter the next day, in a cable to Wavell, who also received the JIC report:[1]

> It seems clear from our information that a heavy air-borne attack by German troops and bombers will soon be made on Crete. Let me know what forces you have in the island and what your plans are. It ought to be a fine opportunity for killing the parachute troops. The island must be stubbornly defended.[2]

Wavell's own intelligence did not match the War Office appreciation, and suggested a lower figure – approximately half – for the number of aircraft available to the enemy. Nor did he think that the Germans had enough shipping available for an invasion on the scale envisaged in London. Ever suspicious of German trickery, he suggested that the threat to Crete might be another bluff, perhaps cover for an attack on Cyprus, Syria or Iraq. Disclosing the real plan only at the last moment, he told Churchill, 'would be consistent with German practice'.[3] However, a further swift and furious offensive against a weakly defended target – also consistent with German practice – soon seemed the likely development.

On 30 April Wavell flew to Crete, to assess the situation for himself. Even without decrypt information, it was obvious that the island was vulnerable. It was only 700 miles from the Rumanian oilfields, which the Germans still thought might be a British target, and a mere 250 miles from North Africa, and so a valuable base from which to attack British convoys and Egypt itself. Furthermore, the closing operation of the mainland campaign had been a parachute attack on the Corinth Canal, and its results could be expected to have reinforced German confidence in such assaults.

To the Chiefs of Staff – still unaware of Hitler's intention to invade Russia – there was another reason why the island was a likely target. Crete is 500 miles from Malta but is far nearer to Alexandria, which had become the navy's main base after Italy had entered the war. Yet Malta remained a crucial bastion and had to be protected. If Crete were held, it could be used by the navy as an advanced refuelling base, or even developed into a major harbour, thereby making the defence of Malta considerably less hazardous.

Defending the island should therefore have been high on GHQ's list of commitments, and the previous October the Greeks had in fact asked the British to take over Crete's protection. With foresight, GHQ would then have set in hand plans for proper fortifications, in case the enemy attempted to occupy it. But at that stage Wavell had more pressing concerns. 'An attack on Crete,' he signalled, 'while the navy is operating or unless Greece is completely overrun seems most unlikely.'[4]

As early as 13 December Hitler had issued orders for an attack on Greece through Bulgaria. At dawn on 6 April the onslaught began, without any diplomatic notice to Greece even though Germany declared war on Yugoslavia on the same day. The campaign is well-documented and needs little retelling. For the Allies it was a tale of courage, confusion and old equipment, and exhausted troops desperate for air support. For the Germans it was another glorious, intoxicating descent upon other people's property, with superbly co-ordinated armour, infantry and artillery surging through an enemy paralysed by waves of dive-bombers. Their furious three-pronged attack cut simultaneously through the frontiers of Greece and Yugoslavia. Like rolling surf it swept through valleys and mountain passes, obliterating British aircraft on the ground and isolating the Greek armies from Thrace to Albania. Then, like a 'grey caterpillar on a carpet of green', it debouched onto the plains, and a thousand young, strong, fit, trigger-happy fanatics, hearts racing, pennants flying, steel glinting, collided with the Greek army – a straggling, struggling, creaking column of men and mules, retreating at one mile an hour.

Yet Crete's defences did need a considerable amount of development. Its only airfields and its one road suitable for military transport were on the north side, as was Suda Bay, a natural harbour whose facilities would have to be enlarged to be of any use to the navy. The whole area was vulnerable to Axis air attack, the more so after Greece had fallen and allowed the Germans to establish a semi-circle of airfields nearby from which to launch offensives.

For six months the island had been within Wavell's command, and the fact that in that time little of the necessary work had been done led to further friction with Churchill, who as early as November 1940 had announced that bases had been established in Crete that would allow an extension of the activities and the radius both of the navy and the RAF. He had also on several occasions called for Suda Bay to be made into 'a second Scapa'. Crete's strategic value was not disputed, but the staff in Cairo seemed not to have taken in the need for a plan for the defence of the island as a whole – in any event they had not produced one. Yet, as perhaps seemed more obvious in Cairo than in Whitehall, the call for something to be done could not well be answered if the resources to do it did not exist.

As soon as the expeditionary force had been pushed back to the coast of Greece, the navy started ferrying it to Crete, and among those disembarked at Suda Bay on 29 April were the battered remnants of the 6th New Zealand Brigade, together with General Freyberg himself. The next day he was called to a conference at a large brick villa on the island's northern shores, where he found a group of senior officers from each service, including General Wilson, now the highest-ranking officer on Crete. Wavell had already instructed that the island be held at all costs, and Wilson had made a rapid appreciation of the situation, concluding that the Germans would probably make an imminent attack by both air and sea.

Shortly before midday on 30 April a staff car drew up and out stepped Wavell, looking, Freyberg noted, 'drawn and haggard and even more tired than any of us'. As the conference resumed he was handed a message from Sir John Dill recommending that Freyberg be placed in command of all the troops on the island and made responsible for its 'stubborn defence'. The appointment had been proposed by Churchill, who greatly admired Freyberg's courage in action; he had long been fascinated by the general's twenty-seven wound scars, and by the romance that surrounded his career. Like Churchill himself, Freyberg had been a friend of Rupert Brooke, and he had helped to dig the poet's grave on the island of Skyros – not far across the sapphire sea from where, twenty-five years on, he now contemplated another battle.

After a private discussion with Wilson, Wavell took Freyberg aside and ordered him to take command. The commission was ill received by Freyberg; it immediately brought to the surface past difficulties between the two men, when Wavell had hived off some of the Dominion forces for service with the British Army. Now, a considerable portion of the New Zealand Division had been ferried back to Egypt, with the remainder offloaded in Crete; it was a situation that, said Freyberg, would not be acceptable to his govern-ment. Also, GHQ in Cairo had unwisely let Freyberg's signals and Headquarters Group proceed to Alexandria, leaving the general bereft of administrative support. However, Wavell was the chief, and he told Freyberg that it was his duty to take command, offering him promotion into the bargain. Freyberg spurned the offer of promotion, considering it to be out of place, but he had a strong sense of duty and his course was clear to him.

'In the circumstances,' recorded Freyberg, 'I felt I could do nothing other than accept.'[5]

Wavell warned the general to expect a combined sea and air attack, but said that no further air protection could be provided by the RAF – which was in fact shortly to remove its few remaining aeroplanes from Crete to preserve them from destruction. He then told Freyberg that from time to time he would be supplied with secret information from an unimpeachable source, that it would be directed to him by the senior air officer[6] and that all such messages were to be burnt after being read. It is not clear whether Wavell then explained what Ultra was, or whether he disguised the source as a spy in the German High Command in Athens;[7] certainly the head of British Intelligence[8] baulked at making Ultra directly available in Crete, where there was a risk of British Headquarters being overrun. But Wavell did tell Freyberg that the source was described as 'Orange Leonard' (OL)[9] and, whether or not he said more, he assured Freyberg that such intelligence should be treated as wholly reliable. Crucially, he told Freyberg to take no action that could be ascribed to such information alone, in case it aroused the enemy's suspicion that its codes were being read.

The picture painted for Freyberg was uninviting. Nearly 30,000 imperial troops had arrived from Greece, many without weapons, some without boots, and most without blankets or eating utensils. Despite his brave and pugnacious nature, the general protested that there were not enough troops to meet the forecast scale of attack, and urged that unless naval forces and more fighters were made available, the decision to defend the island should be reviewed. Wavell, not entirely convinced by the JIC report, replied that the scale of attack might have been exaggerated. It would certainly be serious, he said, but added that he was confident the troops would be equal to the task.

Having returned to Cairo, Wavell sent Freyberg detailed confirmation of the War Office's estimation of the scale of the threat: 'I could scarcely believe my eyes,' Freyberg wrote. 'I realised how great were our difficulties if the appreciation proved correct and I felt that the sooner I introduced a little reality into the calculations for the defence of Crete the better.'[10] He warned Wavell that he would have to brief the New Zealand Government on the position, as there were nearly 8,000 New Zealanders on the island with only their personal weapons, hardly any entrenching tools, no evidence of naval forces to repel a seaborne invasion, and a total air strength on the island of six Hurricanes and seventeen 'obsolete aircraft'.[11] Feeling that, with this array, the chances of repelling an invasion were somewhat slender, Freyberg suggested both to his government and again to Wavell that the decision to defend Crete should be reconsidered – an academic request as there were not in any case the ships available to evacuate the troops. They had to stand and fight.

With the apparent inconsistency between his own expectations and those of the War Office unresolved, Wavell left Freyberg to conduct the defence of the island as he thought best. Beneath the surface tension between the two men lay mutual admiration. Although Freyberg was popularly thought of as a 'red-necked thug who ate two Germans for breakfast, and who looked like a big Boy Scout', he was an intelligent man, although sometimes obstinate. His initial despair gave way to the hope that the appreciations would not prove correct. He had concluded – and he would stick to his story – that a large part of the attack would after all be a seaborne invasion, which the navy would help defeat. He expected an air attack as well, but not as heavy as the intelligence indicated or as the War Office believed.

Wavell had very few tanks and they were badly needed elsewhere, but having returned to Egypt he ordered that twenty-one be sent to the island. However, the rocky terrain was to prove unsuitable for tanks; field artillery, readily available in Egypt, and radio sets would have been more valuable. Landing supplies of any kind was to prove an almost insuperable problem. Wavell remained sanguine: 'German blitzes,' he said, 'usually take some stopping. But we have stout-hearted troops, keen and ready to fight under a stout-hearted commander . . .' [12]

It was accepted in London, Cairo and Crete that there was the possibility of attack both by sea and by air, but Freyberg, Wavell and the War Office each formed differing conclusions about the priority to be given to defence against airborne invasion. Freyberg's appreciation, made partly from his reading of the 'secret source' information, led him to deploy troops to counter a major attack both from the sea, where it lapped a fourteen-mile strip of beach on the north-west coast, and from a landing by gliders and paratroops hoping to capture the three serviceable airfields on the island: at Retimo, Maleme and Heraklion, although only the last-named had concrete runways. The Ultra information suggested that Freyberg's emphasis was misconceived, and that much the heaviest attack would come from the air. But, charged with the defence of the whole island, Freyberg could hardly have deployed all his troops inland and relied largely on the navy – hard-pressed and short of ships as he knew it to be – to deal with an assault from the sea. In that case, if the navy did not sink the enemy, the defenders would be done for. It would have required great imagination to adopt that policy. Freyberg believed that he had a dual task: to defend the airfields and the beaches, and so he set aside troops for both.

Freyberg's astonishingly detailed forewarning of when and where the Germans were intending to land was confirmed on 11 May, when Wavell sent Brigadier Dorman-Smith to Crete with information gleaned from intercepted German messages, now orally elaborated by Dorman-Smith.[13] However, Freyberg was constrained from using this information because Wavell had ordered him not to take any action based solely on the 'secret source', reminding him in a personal letter sent via Dorman-Smith, 'Be very careful of SECURITY, Crete is certain to have many enemy agents. Especially keep all knowledge of OL to yourself.' Freyberg's reply to Wavell, dated 11 May, concluded with the handwritten message, 'P.S. I will be very discreet over OL', which confirms that Wavell had told Freyberg about the source of that name, even if not in what detail.[14] Freyberg subsequently claimed that Wavell had gone one step further and told Dorman-Smith to order him not to use Ultra intelligence, even if he did have corroborative information from another source. The commander-in-chief apparently feared that Freyberg might inadvertently expose the existence of Ultra, with which he was unwilling to take the smallest risk. The authorities, he told Freyberg, would prefer to lose Crete than risk jeopardising Ultra.

Once Freyberg had digested the intelligence that Dorman-Smith had brought him, he realised that although there would undoubtedly be attempted landings from the sea, it was likely that by far the heaviest attack would be from the air: his dispositions were therefore dangerously skewed. Even though it was secret-source intelligence that prompted him, Freyburg decided that he must redeploy his force and consequently proposed to transfer New Zealand troops from the seafront to ground to the west of the airfield at Maleme, whose defences now seemed insufficient to withstand fierce attack. In fact, Freyberg had already ordered a Greek regiment to move to Maleme from a camp at the far west of the island; now, armed with the information brought by Dorman-Smith, and conscious of Wavell's instructions about the use of 'OL' information, he asked Wavell for permission to proceed with the transfers. Wavell refused. He himself was bound by the Ultra rules and could not accede to Freyberg's request without dispensation from the authorities in London, which he had not received.

In retrospect it seems excessively cautious to think that such troop movements would have made the Germans suspicious. It would have been entirely reasonable for the British to fear a determined attack from the air, and for the Germans to expect their enemy to prepare defences accordingly – doing so would have been evidence of good military sense rather than an indication of codebreaking.

Furthermore, by an extraordinary chance, as a result of a discovery made by his acting Intelligence Officer, Geoffrey Cox,[15] Freyberg was presented with a cover story with which to disguise his use of secret information, if he wished to. In the hours before the attack Cox had been working in the Divisional Intelligence dugout and had seen a photograph on which there was a red circle around the house in which he was billeted, which was also used as the officers' mess. Deciding that in the circumstances he would prefer to sleep elsewhere, Cox moved his sleeping-bag to the back of the dugout, but before going to bed he looked through two sandbags full of captured documents due to be sent off to GHQ in Cairo. Having been a newspaper correspondent in Vienna before the war, he spoke German and had with him a pocket German dictionary. As he examined the documents he realised that one of them was the airborne commander's operational order for the attack on Crete. Cox recalled:

I told John White,[16] the general's personal assistant, and he took me along to the general's dugout, where Freyberg was sitting at a trestle table with a hand grenade on it in case there were any intruders. I translated the document for him, and – I of course didn't realise this – it freed him from the Ultra restraint: here was a document containing the entire German plan of attack.[17]

The information confirmed the Ultra intelligence, although, logically, it would be safe to use it only if the Germans realised that their plans had fallen into enemy hands. The discovery made no difference to Freyberg, who, according to John White, was so impressed by the importance attached to Ultra that even though he had corroborative information right in front of his eyes, he did not dare risk using it. Cox continued:

He was not prepared to use the other source. The entire operation order was there, and he could have cited it. But my view was that he thought 'Look, Ultra means trouble.' This was the old soldier in him, and he thought 'I'm not going to buy trouble, by taking the least risk with anything to do with Ultra.'[18]

So the troops were not moved; the Germans arrived; Maleme was captured; and the island was lost: 'All for the want of a nail . . .'

There were of course many other factors that contributed to the fall of Crete, including a premature withdrawal from Maleme, an under-strength counter-attack at that airfield and the failure to plough or crater the runways, a measure prohibited by GHQ Cairo. But the paramount cause of the loss of Maleme, and therefore of the loss of the overall battle, seems to have been the restriction that Wavell placed on Freyberg's use of his secret information. However, Wavell cannot fairly be blamed for that, if he was under orders to enforce the Ultra rules. In fact, the problem could well have been the result of confusion between Churchill and Sir Stewart Menzies – Churchill for his part seemed to expect that Freyberg should use the Ultra intelligence to help him defeat the German attack. He later complained to the Chiefs of Staff about Wavell and Freyberg being slow to act on the intelligence they were receiving.[19] The lay observer might also wonder why Freyberg was supplied with so much Ultra information if he was not to be allowed to act on it.

The onslaught that came in due course was described as worse than any bombardment at Passchendaele or on the Somme, and it engendered acts of magnificent endurance and bravery. The confusion of battle was described by a naval officer who had been drafted in to fight with an infantry unit:

> We were a motley collection about 200 strong. We didn't know where our people were; we didn't know where the enemy were; many people had no rifles; many people had rifles and no ammunition. Everyone was desperately tired, thirsty and hungry. We had no food and no water; we had no objective to make for. If anyone fired at you, he might be [a] an enemy, [b] a friend who thought you were an enemy, [c] a friend or an enemy who didn't know who the hell you were, [d] someone not firing at you at all.[20]

Within a week the battle was over, although the subsequent withdrawal to the south coast was hard-fought, at least by the best troops. On 26 May Freyberg signalled that his men had reached the limit of their endurance and that the position was hopeless, whatever the commanders-in-chief might decide. Wavell drew the inevitable conclusion. From London came exhortations to keep the flag flying: 'Victory in Crete essential at this turning-point of the war,' said Churchill. 'Keep hurling in all aid you can.'[21] It was something that Wavell had already strained every nerve to do. He signalled:

Fear we must recognise that Crete is no longer tenable and that troops must be withdrawn as far as possible. It has been impossible to withstand weight of air attack which has been on unprecedented scale and has been through force of circumstances practically unopposed.[22]

In the end 40,000 men were embroiled in the battle, a quarter of them having no fighting capability; more than 17,000 were killed, wounded or captured. The island's loss rendered the Suez Canal otiose as a link with the East – although it continued to be considered a vital defence against German land attack in the Middle East. The east end of the Mediterranean would now be closed even to the fast convoys previously used in vital cases – dangerous as they were to protect. Although most supplies and reinforcements for the Middle East were already routed around the Cape and up through the Red Sea, protecting which had been the paramount reason for Wavell's East African campaign, the loss of the faster alternative through Suez was a severe blow.

The battle for Crete had been a painful burden for Wavell, who had encouraged the gallant defenders in every way he could. Lady Wavell recalled how her husband always managed to sleep during the progress of earlier battles, but during the last few nights of the Crete campaign he had paced the floor, unable to rest.

More than 40 per cent of those involved in one way or another became casualties of war: it was bound to lead to questions, especially after the losses sustained in Greece. Defeat on Crete exposed once more a picture of brave men being sent out to face an enemy that had overwhelming air power. Although Wavell understood the value of trying to concert the operations of the three services, the RAF – through lack of pilots and aeroplanes – appeared so rarely above the convoys and the battlefields that anger was widespread, with airmen in the bars of Alexandria being booed by soldiers and sailors.

Almost immediately an official enquiry was convened, and it fairly set the cat among the Cairo pigeons, partly because of the youth of those on its committee and partly because of their conclusions. In London the loss of Crete was a sensation, and the House of Commons was deeply upset. Almost immediately Wavell received a list of questions from the CIGS: why were his tanks ineffective in protecting the airfields; why could artillery not have been used to prevent the landings; were the airfields mined; what happened to the mobile detachments detailed to fall upon the paratroops? Patiently but speedily Wavell supplied his answers: enemy air supremacy made the movement of tanks by day impossible; the Germans discovered the artillery range and landed beyond it; the airfields were not mined, as GHQ had hoped that the British would use them later on; the paratroops were in fact effectively dealt with, until they started landing out of range. But his clear responses were engulfed by political emotions running high, and people, as Churchill's Private Secretary noted, remembered only his complaints that 'he could not spare even a dozen tanks, that they were all having their tracks mended, their engines greased, or something, in the Delta'.

The committee's damning report was issued with a psalmist's lilt: 'The campaigns in Norway, France and Greece had produced a wealth of lessons; they had been ill-digested. Committees have sat, but their labours appear to have been in vain.'[23]

Wavell initialled his copy of the report and returned it to London before he had read it through. When, on his way to India some months later, he did examine it in detail, there was a rare display of emotion: 'he nearly hit the roof,' his ADC recalled. To Wavell's relief the report was later suppressed, partly because some of its contents might have raised unwanted questions about secret sources of information.

Once more 'the Chief' had been forced to make bricks without straw, but the defence of Crete was so valiant, and the casualties to the invaders so great, that the Germans never again used airborne forces for a major assault. The paratroops proved helpless while slowly floating down to the defenders below them, and many were dead or wounded before they landed. Others plummeted to earth with 'Roman candles', which inspired Wavell's 'A' Force agents to spread the story that the parachutes were made of Japanese silk. So from disaster came some good, and a particular consequence of the Germans' disillusionment with airborne assaults was that Malta, crucial to the Middle East campaign, was saved from subjugation.

Wavell had scoured his command for resources to send to Crete, but had found few to spare, distracted as he was by threats of increasing gravity from the east and from the west. Turbulence was now swirling along both those horizons and had taken GHQ by surprise.

On his eastern flank Wavell was suddenly faced with a critical situation in Iraq, a land that for centuries had lain tranquil under Turkish rule, but which had responded to its replacement by the British mandate after the First World War by sliding into a state of chronic resentment, disorder and violence.

Containing some of the richest ground in the world, Iraq was a leading source of both cotton and dates, but its traditional produce was overshadowed by the country's rapidly growing significance for the international petroleum industry. For centuries oil had seeped, disregarded, to the surface of Iraq's deserts, its occasional spontaneous combustion generating the myth of Nebuchadnezzar's fiery furnace. It was the enormous increase in industrial demand early in the twentieth century that transformed Iraq's political and economic significance, greatly enhanced in 1927 by the discovery of a vast oilfield at Kirkuk.

Even before the war broke out, many Iraqis had become admirers of Hitler, believing that he shared their views on the Jewish question and that Germany had no territorial ambitions in Arab lands. They began to view Hitler as a potential champion of the pan-Arab movement, of which they regarded themselves as standard-bearers, little realising, as they anticipated the end of British dominance that Hitler might bring about, that in the Nazi galaxy the black hole destined for Arab independence was only marginally less engulfing than the one destined for the Jews.

By the spring of 1941 it seemed to the power-brokers in Baghdad that the moment to rebel against the British had arrived. Iraq now had 46,000 troops, 12,000 police and large numbers of civilians trained to arms, and its government had asked Hitler for all kinds of armaments and the equipment for a full division.[24] Although the Germans had the will and the materiel, they had a delivery problem: the only practical route to Iraq was through Turkey. While Turkey was already allowing Allied armaments trains to travel through her territory to Iran and Afghanistan, it was thought unlikely that she would give the Germans permission for the passage of arms to Iraq. If they wanted to use trains for that purpose, they would have to try and conceal their contents.

The stakes were certainly high. If Hitler were to overrun the oilfields of the Middle East, he would also capture those of the Caucasus, and the German share of world oil production would jump from 1 to 17 per cent. Not only would it cripple Britain's ability to continue the war, but the Empire would be split in two, the western half separated from its source of raw materials and the eastern half starved of supplies. There also remained the danger that further British defeats might ignite a pan-Arab revolt across the entire region and engulf Egypt itself, which Britain feared more with each demonstration of apparent German invincibility.

To the British, it seemed an obvious move for Hitler to advance on Egypt. Although decrypts from Bletchley Park were indicating new developments along the Russian frontier, neither the intelligence analysts in London nor Wavell's advisers in Cairo appreciated their significance. The fact remained that Germany had well over a hundred divisions in eastern Europe – well trained, well equipped and unemployed.

In Baghdad violence erupted at the end of April, when a coup d'état was staged by a clique of ambitious colonels known as the 'Golden Square', together with their figurehead, Prime Minister Rashid Ali el Gailani, who formally declared war on Great Britain. The aim of the Golden Square was to overthrow the pro-British Regent of Iraq[25] and install a puppet government, under Rashid Ali. They hoped to promote Arab nationalism and to consolidate the independence that Iraq had gained in 1932. Since the departure of the Ottomans after the First World War the Iraqis had begun to regard themselves as the standard-bearers of Arab nationalism and were now determined to eject France and Britain from the entire Middle East. For this, the Golden Square believed that once they had seized power, they would receive active support from Germany, which had for some time been supplying Rashid Ali and his followers with gold. The Iraqi air force and a large proportion of the army were supporters of the Golden Square, having long resented the British presence and influence in their country.

Just in time the Regent heard, from his cook, of the plot to arrest him. He slipped into the dark of the night a few minutes before the doors of his palace were forced open by the Golden Square, accompanied by doctors equipped with a poisoned syringe and a signed death certificate which already stated that the Regent had died of coronary thrombosis.

In the preceding months siren voices in the Foreign Office and other British Government circles had whispered that Iraq should be appeased, partly on the basis that, as there were no troops to spare for a new commitment, it seemed wise to avoid an open breach until diplomacy could be backed by force. Wavell agreed. He was always ready to take a calculated risk, but that was balanced by an innate caution, and a reluctance – to which the Greek foray was a notable exception – to be distracted from the main objective, or to make new enemies unnecessarily. He was therefore strongly opposed to committing troops to Iraq, and disagreed with the Chiefs of Staff, who quickly urged armed intervention. He warned the Foreign Office that Britain's military presence in Iraq was exiguous – two small contingents of the RAF – and that the time was past when a comparatively small force might restore British prestige and influence.

Wavell was particularly distracted by a danger that now loomed on another front. As it became clear that the Germans had finally landed at Tripoli, he welcomed the suggestion of General Auchinleck, commander-in-chief in India, that Iraq was properly a matter for the Government of India and not for Middle East Command. When, on 2 May, the Defence Committee asked Wavell if he would object to the Army Command in Iraq reverting to the Middle East, on the basis that only troops in Palestine would be able to get to Iraq in time, he replied that he most certainly would object. As a palliative he did agree to try and create the impression of assembling a large force in Palestine. But he was far from enthusiastic, perhaps conscious of the fact that the cavalry in Palestine was the only force he had that was not already fully committed, but that a large proportion of it still went to war in the saddle.

It seemed to Wavell that the Germans arriving in North Africa were a far more serious threat than their plots among the Arabs, and he was adamant that he was stretched to the limit and could not afford to take on Rashid Ali. He therefore advised the Government that it would be better to open talks, especially as the Turks had offered to mediate. He expressed this opinion to Lampson in Cairo. It met a bleak response. Not only did the ambassador object in principle to a British climb-down, but he felt it would have a disastrous effect on Middle East opinion:

> Wavell told me this morning quite casually that he saw no alternative but to offer to treat with the Iraqis! I was horrified, but he said there was no alternative . . . he had no troops to do it with and the best thing was therefore to parley with them. I repeat I was horrified.[26]

Wavell was unyielding, telling Lampson that unless Britain negotiated, he foresaw the most tragic results. He bluntly warned the Chiefs of Staff that they were taking 'little account of realities'. 'You must face facts,' he said:

> I feel it my duty to warn you in the gravest possible terms that I consider the prolongation of fighting in Iraq will seriously endanger the defence of Palestine and Egypt. The political repercussions will be incalculable, and may result in what I have spent nearly two years trying to avoid, namely, serious internal trouble in our bases.[27]

He was treading on thin ice; his advice was unwelcome, particularly to the Prime Minister, who deplored Wavell's attitude. It was still not the complex campaign in East Africa, or the danger in Crete, in Cyrenaica, in Syria or Iraq that caught Churchill's attention, so much as the ration strength of Wavell's command and thoughts of the convoys battling through the seas to bring him more supplies. Once again the Defence Committee stated that it would accept responsibility for the action that the commander-in-chief seemed reluctant to order, and once again a gulf opened up between Churchill and his general. Already fighting on two fronts, beset by a lack of resources and perhaps understandably irritated by the readiness of the Defence Committee to heap new commitments on his shoulders, Wavell was not repelled by the idea of parley with the likes of Rashid Ali. For all his vision and mastery of detail, he lacked the iron obstinacy of those whom, many years later, Mrs Thatcher would describe as 'one of us'.

Yet duty called, and once the decision had been taken, Wavell accepted it. On 5 May he shouldered the commitment to Iraq: 'Nice baby you have handed me on my fifty-eighth birthday,' he told Sir John Dill, 'I have always hated babies and Iraqis but will do my best for the little blighter.'[28] He began to organise a scratch force and aim it at Iraq. In command he placed General Maitland Wilson, his order resounding with an imperial echo: 'Jumbo, I want you to go to Jerusalem and relieve Baghdad.'

How faint the echo was would not have impinged upon two generals fighting in desperate times, but the fact that so many Middle Eastern countries required constant armed vigil was evidence of the disintegration of the imperial order that was accelerating around them. For good public servants such as the Wykehamist Wavell and the Etonian Wilson, the stage still seemed set just as they had been brought up to expect. But their code of duty and service would be redundant in the world that was soon to emerge from the shambles of war. Within a few short years, far from simply going to Jerusalem and relieving Baghdad, they would have to queue up and have their passports duly stamped by the local – native – authorities.

Meanwhile the fighting had already started: at dawn on 2 May the ancient RAF aeroplanes at Habbaniya – a mixed circus of biplanes, and Gordons normally used for towing targets – took to the air, many with trainees at the joystick, and with improvised bomb holders wired to their sides. Having attacked the ranks of Iraqis on the escarpment above the camp, they flew on to Mosul, in the north of the country; there they found an assortment of aircraft – some in Iraqi colours, others disguised as Vichy French, some without markings at all. Nor was there any mistaking the presence of the Luftwaffe: the swastikas on Messerschmitts and Heinkels shone bright in the desert sun. Meanwhile in Baghdad 350 men, women and children, British and American, sought refuge in the British Embassy and its two-acre garden on the banks of the Tigris.

With only four days' notice, General Wilson cobbled together a flying column of yeomanry, mechanised cavalry and artillery. It was christened 'Habforce', and set forth in a cavalcade of vehicles requisitioned in Palestine, with almost no extra tyres or spare parts, and driven by civilian drivers bordering on the rebellious. The force was bolstered by assorted irregular units, including Glubb Pasha's Arab Legion, known, for their flowing locks, as 'Glubb's Girls'. This strange amalgam, soon reduced when a number of Arabs mutinied at the frontier, crossed into Iraq and headed east on the 400-mile trek to Habbaniya.

Despite their numbers, a defensive mentality soon settled on the enemy, while the scratch British force drove forward, short of weapons, short of water, shelled by the Luftwaffe and ambushed by rebels – but with brio and brave hearts, the officers shooting sandgrouse along the way.

Ten days into the advance Wavell flew to Basra to see General Auchinleck. The Indian troops he found there were raring for a fight, and he ordered an immediate advance up the railway line to Baghdad. The days passed, and the slender ranks of imperial soldiers drew near the doubting Iraqi divisions; then, having despaired of the arrival of any reinforcements, and not having sighted a single German, Iraqi resolve faltered. Dismay spread; the martial music and Nazi propaganda that had blared across Baghdad's public radio system and roused the mob ceased as suddenly as it had started, as the city filled with rumours of a hundred British tanks just over the horizon – a far cry from the reality of 1,400 men and no tanks at all. The clouds of revolt began to dissolve, and despite the presence of an Iraqi division in Baghdad, and another force in rear of the British columns, Rashid Ali and his gang fled to Teheran. At dawn on 31 May the Mayor of Baghdad raised the white flag.

For the present, the day had been won; but the seeds of dissent had been sown, some of which were carried to fertile soil in Egypt, where young nationalist officers had been secretly willing the Iraqis to success. They included two of the country's future leaders: Gamal Abdel Nasser and Anwar Sadat. 'It was the first sign of the liberation of the Arab world,' recorded Sadat, 'and we followed the course of the revolt with admiration.'[29] Far below the surface, the props of Empire had shifted.

In the immediate aftermath of the revolt it was clear that Wavell, despite his fears, had scored a swift victory, at little cost. However, there was no time to celebrate: yet another threat had already emerged. In Syria, the enemy bridgehead established so close to Iraq had exposed the flanks of Wavell's command:

Syria, therefore, which had been an uncertain and somewhat sinister neighbour ever since the fall of France, now began to present a definite threat to our position in the Middle East. Thus the crisis in Iraq was no sooner over than matters came to a head in Syria.[30]

Methods of dealing with an uncertain and somewhat sinister neighbour included appeasing it, containing it by masking its borders, and eliminating it. Wavell was in favour of the first, and strongly opposed to the last.

Yet he was granted no pause or respite; nor, ultimately, was he left with much choice in the matter. Across his desk the signals flashed, as High Authority fixed its gaze along the Damascus road. No sooner was he rid of the turbulent Iraqis than Wavell was pressed to intervene in a country that he had long determined not to provoke.

When Wavell took command in the Middle East, politics and diplomacy had added exciting new dimensions to his military life. For someone whose mind was able to absorb and retain a mass of complicated detail, if not always the nuance, these extensions to his work increased its interest and attractions. By the spring of 1941, however, custom had staled their infinite variety: he had borne the heaviest of burdens for nearly two years and the gravity of his position had greatly increased with the course the war had taken. The politics of Syria therefore no longer appealed to him as formerly they might; quite the reverse, to say nothing of the military difficulties that he foresaw arising from a disturbance of the status quo.

Besides having to blend his approach with the wishes of the embassy in Cairo and his superiors in London, Wavell had also to take account of the French. Syria and the Lebanon had long been mandated to France, and after the armistice in 1940 their governments became an outpost of Marshal Pétain's Vichy regime, enjoying the strange form of independence allowed to overseas French territories. However, the Vichy variety of Frenchmen loathed the Free French led by General de Gaulle even more than they detested the English and disliked the Germans. Wavell was therefore sceptical of the hopes of General Catroux, the Free French High Commissioner for the Middle East, that if an imperial and Free French force entered Syria it would be welcomed by the inhabitants, thereby removing the threat of Syria becoming a launch-pad for a German attack on Egypt and the Suez Canal.

Wavell believed that it would be wiser to leave Syria be; having had no spare troops to send to Iraq, he could afford none for a new front. At the very least he needed to play for time, until he had regrouped from the Greek and Cretan adventures, withdrawn troops from East Africa and stabilised Cyrenaica. Although Lampson urged him to accept that Vichy neutrality was a false refuge, wholly vulnerable to German pressure, Wavell would not be moved. Obvious signs of German infiltration – their use of Syrian airfields to help Iraq – did not greatly perturb him or distract him from the drama unfolding in the west; nor did intelligence reports that Vichy had ordered the Syrians not only to allow German aircraft free passage, but to shoot down the RAF.

Instead, Wavell advocated keeping the Arab leaders quiet with diplomacy and bribes, and letting the Syrian authorities know that Britain wished to help them keep order. However, agreement on what policy to adopt proved elusive, with the Foreign Office, the Free French and the War Office all adding their voices. The lines of communication were further disturbed by the role of General Louis Spears, liaison officer between Wavell and de Gaulle, who regarded the military authorities in Cairo as a vast tangle of tentacles, each hardly knowing what the others were doing. Spears shared Lampson's view that GHQ meddled dangerously in politics, and he blamed John Shearer, Wavell's intelligence chief, for fostering the belief that if nothing were done in Syria all would be well. His view was perhaps tainted by his personal dislike of Shearer, known at the Embassy as 'Norma', whom he called 'a shiny brute who always makes me feel he is trying to sell me scent'.

Like Lampson, Wavell was upset by the fact that Spears had direct access to the Prime Minister, bypassing both the Foreign Office and the War Office. He was also reluctant to have de Gaulle in Cairo, although on one level there was common ground: a meeting in Wavell's office between the two generals began in prolonged silence, until Arthur Smith saved the situation by suggesting to Wavell that he show de Gaulle his map; the two men studied it in silence for some minutes before the Frenchman took his leave. A few moments later Smith took in some papers and Wavell looked up from his writing to say, 'I like that man: he doesn't talk.' Yet he was under no misapprehensions, for he told Spears, 'I understand that I can't do anything right as far as the Free French are concerned; they don't like me. I am pretty tired of them myself.'[31] However, his hands were tied by government policy, which had decreed that the Syrian problem should be solved with the help of the Free French.

The ideal solution would have been for de Gaulle's men to dislodge the Vichy regime in Syria and bar it to the Germans. Unfortunately the Free French were too weak to manage such an operation by themselves, and unless large numbers of French and Arabs changed sides once Syria was invaded, the Free French would have to be reinforced by Wavell.

Meanwhile Wavell tried to delay, if not arrest, the whole project. But the pressure from London was too great; as he had said of the Greek expedition, strategy is the handmaiden of government policy, and, unless he resigned his command, ultimately he had to comply with it. 'A supreme effort,' said the Prime Minister, 'must be made to prevent the Germans getting a footing in Syria as a jumping-off ground for air domination of Iraq and Persia. It is no use General Wavell being vexed at this disturbance on his flanks.'[32]

The fact that his vexation was obvious did not help Wavell's cause. When the Syrian threat arose, he was engaged in suppressing the Arab revolt in Iraq, fighting desperately in Crete and facing great new dangers in the Western Desert. Yet he was also being asked to enter a well-armed country that might prove vigorously hostile: 'I realise the importance of trying to forestall the Germans in Syria,' he told Dill, 'but these political adventures and Jameson Raids are dangerous.'[33] Overcoming his reluctance, he began to assemble an imperial force for 'Operation Exporter', drawn from Indians, Australians and the 5th Cavalry Brigade, many of them with their horses. They would all accompany the Free French into Syria.

Once more a gulf yawned between general and Prime Minister, but this time it was overt, and more dangerous to Wavell than its forerunners. He signalled the CIGS:

Am making preparations for combined British and French operation if the situation is favourable but you must trust my judgment in this matter or relieve me of my Command. I am not willing to accept that Catroux, de Gaulle or Spears should dictate action that is bound seriously to affect the military situation in the Middle East.[34]

That signal soon reached Churchill. He was stung by the suggestion that Spears or the French were making the running. Dill was distinctly uncomfortable at a repeat of hostilities between Defence Minister and general, but made no vigorous intervention. The Chiefs of Staff were instructed to make the position clear:

Our view is that if the Germans can pick up Syria and Iraq with petty air forces, tourists and local revolts we must not shrink from running equal small-scale military risks and facing the possible aggravation of political dangers from failure.[35]

Talk of tourists and small-scale risks hardly chimed with the assumption that the Germans were working towards conquering Egypt and the Suez Canal, dealing the British Empire a blow that would prove terminal to its war effort. The scale seemed to have shrunk.

Now, far from the commotion in Cairo, a radical idea about how to deal with Wavell – stirring private thoughts and secret counsels – finally broke surface in London. The CIGS responded to his signal on a personal note, prompted by Wavell's reluctant attitude, and with an unmistakeable implication: 'For this decision we of course take full responsibility, and should you find yourself unwilling to give effect to it arrangements will be made to meet any wish you may express to be relieved of your Command.'[36]

This time Dill did offer his thoughts to the Prime Minister:

> It is my opinion that we have now come to the point where we must either allow Wavell to carry out the policy which he believes to be sound or relieve him of his command.
>
> My own feeling is that at this juncture we should trust Wavell. It is no time to make a change.[37]

It was an endorsement, if hardly a clarion call.

Privately, Dill tried to solace his old friend, while making several uncomfortable references to Churchill losing confidence in him:

> My dear Archie,
>
> What a time you are having. How I wish that I could be of more help to you. I do not know whether or not you will pack up on receiving the telegram from the Defence Committee – or rather from the PM . . . From your personal point of view you will be sorely tempted to hand in your portfolio – you could hardly go on a better wicket – but from a national point of view it would I feel be a disaster. And yet I feel that the PM has only two alternatives – to trust or to replace. But even if he does not trust, it would, I feel, be disastrous for you to go <u>at this moment</u> when you are handling so many difficult, if not critical situations.[38]

Wavell was not a natural quitter, and he found himself able to brush off these telegraphic barbs. He had no desire to go.

Generals Wilson and Catroux polished their plans, the various staffs having recourse to 'Colonel Wavell's Monograph', still the standard text on operations in the former Mesopotamia. Ever alert to the value of surprise, Wavell ordered the spreading of stories of disagreement between him and de Gaulle, and of his refusal to enter Syria. He sanctioned a commando landing on the Lebanese shore, while the navy would bombard coastal defences, and three squadrons of RAF would range above the biblical plains. Fighting was to be avoided as far as possible, in the hope of encouraging widespread defections among the Vichy troops. Propaganda and leaflets were to be used instead, together with a show of readiness for action. French-speaking officers, with megaphones and white flags, would call upon the occupants of French posts to 'make way so that we can get at the Germans'. The Australians' response, on hearing of these arrangements, was concise and rather direct.

At dawn on 8 June 'Operation Exporter' was unleashed. After ebb and flow, as column met column, the Allies prevailed and within two weeks entered Damascus. At the same time troops released after Rashid Ali's fall entered Syria from the east, two brigades making for Aleppo while 'Habforce' marched on Palmyra, with French Dewotine fighters swooping low from over the horizon and picking off the ancient lorries. Yet the three-pronged attack, the naval bombardment and, as in Iraq, the absence of Germans riding to the rescue, extinguished the enemy's resolve, and on 11 July they sued for peace.

Meanwhile in East Africa, at least, Wavell had been rewarded for his patient strategy. He had urged Platt and Cunningham to speed up events wherever they had a chance, and Platt had entered Eritrea on 19 January. Having finally won Keren at the end of March, he captured the vital link of Asmara on 4 April, and four days later expelled the Italians from the Red Sea port of Massawa. Cunningham had entered Italian Somaliland and taken Kismayu on 14 February, and Mogadishu two weeks later. By early March he had crossed into Ethiopia from the south. Berbera had fallen three weeks earlier, to a part of his force marching north-east and meeting up with units shipped from Aden. Before long Cunningham had conquered 360,000 square miles of territory and taken 50,000 prisoners, all for the loss of 150 men killed.

When Massawa fell, the news flashed across the world, and on 11 April President Roosevelt declared that the Red Sea was no longer a combat zone. US merchantmen could begin supplying the Middle East direct, without the requirement to trans-ship and unload in England; it was a valuable reward.

In early May the pincers began to close. As Haile Selassie entered his capital, the South Africans moved north and Platt's Indian Division marched south; in the middle were 5,000 Fascist soldiers, all that remained of Aosta's mighty force. The collision occurred at the rocky stronghold of Amba Alagi, and there, on 16 May, the Union Jack was raised. A month later Barclays Bank opened a branch in Asmara. In one small part of the world the worst was over.

The results were later described by the Italians in their own newspaper, *Il Tempo*:

> Wavell's strategic plan consisted in starting several columns from different points of the compass, with the object of keeping the enemy perplexed and taking advantage of his indecision. The Italian High Command, faced with the threat of several columns moving at the same time towards the centre, would have felt deeply embarrassed not knowing which to oppose . . . The Duke of Aosta was baffled by the enemy's game. His own resources were so vastly superior that, operating through interior lines, he ought to have been able to meet and disperse each column separately. The Italian commander-in-chief was not the kind of man to lose his head, but he made the fatal miscalculation of fighting a retreating action.[39]

Wavell could feel relieved that Iraq and Syria had been subdued at such small cost, and although the Germans had mysteriously failed to appear on what ought for them to have been an open road to the Empire's vital artery, his forces remained stretched to danger-point, and he had lost great quantities of materiel, for which he was almost starved of replacements. Now, having all but finished with East Africa, he was at long last able to increase his reserves and turn his full attention to the west. It was not before time, as the Empire's ramparts were shaking there under a new onslaught.

The Germans had not thrust south into the Middle East, yet it was still believed both in Cairo and in London that they planned to do so. Hitler in fact wanted to keep Syria and the Balkans quiet, and had scant interest in Iraq, but that was quite unsuspected. The purpose of a huge aerial armada and nearly 150 divisions massing on the borders of Russia had remained an extremely well-kept secret. Even though Wavell, like Churchill, believed that battle should be taken to the enemy wherever there was an opening, it turned out that their fears of a drive to Suez were without foundation. Yet the butter, as Wavell put it, was spread dangerously thin, and the fears that had made

him so reluctant to take on new adventures were beginning to prove justified, in full measure and at alarming speed.

On Thursday 27 March the British Ambassador entered in his diary the
cheering news that the Italians had suddenly 'packed up', and that the British
were on their way to Asmara. He also added 'the jarring note' (little realising
how ominous it was) that the enemy were back in Agheila on the western
confines of Cyrenaica; 'but,' he added brightly, 'I gather that our soldiers are
not in the least fussed by this'. Their insouciance was seriously misplaced: this
was not so much a jarring note as a tolling bell. Within a few days Dill and
Eden had arrived in Cairo with a marked air of pessimism. Far away across
the desert an armoured unit had for some reason cracked and been overrun
by a German force, with considerable loss of men and materiel – now extremely
scarce as the Greek expedition had absorbed so much. At first the commander-
in-chief exuded his customary reassurance: 'Wavell explained with his usual
lucidity what the position is now in the west, and certainly it is alarming, but
Wavell is completely unruffled and as usual inspires confidence.'[40]

The next day the ambassador's tone changed:

I looked in upon Anthony Eden and found an atmosphere of abysmal
gloom. Apparently Wavell had come round just before dinner with
extremely alarming news, to the effect that our people had cracked still
more, that news of a reliable character is practically non-existent, and
that Neame, the GOC in the field, has sent a most alarmist telegram
admitting that he had lost touch with his forward elements and feared
the worst. I found Eden for the first time really showing signs of considerable emotion and agitation.[41]

It would be hard to exaggerate the effect in Cairo and London of the
news that the desert flank had been breached. With the arrival of spring,
invasion was once more expected, the Germans were masters of Europe,
Britain was stretched to the limit and the rain of bombs on her cities was
continuing without let-up. As the *Wehrmacht* massed in the Balkans, news
came that the one great theatre of war that was thought to have been done
with, so recently the scene of martial triumph, had exploded into battle again,
with imperial forces retreating in disorder. Wavell was deeply affected. As
Eden put it 'he aged ten years in the night'.

On Wednesday, 2 April, a few hours before rebellion broke out in Baghdad,
Wavell held a lunch-party for de Gaulle. In the course of it he received the

report that the Germans had arrived in Tripoli and were forcing their way west. Although at first apparently unruffled, his demeanour belied his mood, as described by the popular novelist, Evelyn Waugh:

> The Commander-in-Chief was despondent as he had good reason to be. Everything was out of his control and everything was going wrong. He ate in silence. At length he said: 'I'll tell you the best poem ever written in Alexandria.'
> 'Recitation,' said Mrs Stitch.
> 'They told me. Heraclitus, they told me you were dead . . .'

He abandoned the party to fly to the Western Desert. In a cramped and draughty bomber he read and memorised Greta Briggs' poem 'London Under Bombardment', seeking a little relief from the knowledge that he had been caught with insufficient strength to meet a heavy counter-attack.[42]

After Wavell had departed, the table talk at his party turned to the fact that in Cairo the leading soldiers had always insisted that the Germans could be held if they tried to attack in the west. This prompted Lampson to remind Sir John Dill that the whole scheme of sending assistance to Greece had been based on a definite and positive assurance from the soldiers that they could easily hold the west. It was not a welcome comment.

British strategy had indeed been based on the assurance from Middle East Command that an effective screen had been erected in Cyrenaica. However, on 12 February, as Cunningham continued his victorious advance through Italian Somaliland, a new element had entered the African scene. At Castel Benito, just south of Tripoli, an unknown German general set foot in Africa for the first time: Rommel. A day later the first armoured units of what would be christened the Deutsches Afrika Korps were unloaded in Tripoli harbour.

Clever as he was, Wavell's powers of evaluation were affected by a streak of optimism and by a touch of cynicism about his foes, bred of his interest in deception. He was soon aware that the Germans had entered the equation, but he did not believe their arrival would make an immediate difference. Although he had no first-hand evidence for the opinion, Wavell was convinced that the new generation of Germans were not the men their fathers were; as Sir John Dill said of him, it was a pity that he was not present at the Battle of France, to see for himself Blitzkrieg in action and how good the new German army was at armoured warfare.

In any event, Wavell discounted the importance of early reports that

Germans had landed in Africa, and when he did turn his full attention to the situation, his staff applied British standards in assessing how long it would take the enemy to present a practical threat.

Wavell later explained the view he formed when, early in the spring of 1941, the military outlook lost its bright glint:

> I estimated that it would be at least two months after the landing of German forces at Tripoli before they could undertake a serious offensive . . . I accordingly considered that a garrison of one armoured brigade and one division would be sufficient . . . and that it would be safe to have comparatively unequipped and untrained troops there . . .[43]

In fact, he did not have a free hand in the matter. As the 7th Armoured had to be allowed to rest and recuperate in Egypt after its hard campaign, and men had to be found for the expedition to Greece, risks had to be taken somewhere. Yet Wavell believed that there was time enough, and that by May he would be able to reinforce Cyrenaica, not with troops from Greece – presumably he expected that the expeditionary force would be staying there and holding the line – but from East Africa, where he expected the fighting to be over by May.

In reply to his staff's first appreciations Wavell had written, on 17 February:

> I do not view the risk of a German / Italian counter attack in Cyrenaica very seriously at present. The enemy has not sufficient command of the sea . . . The Germans have as yet no experience of desert warfare and we know it takes considerable time to acquire it . . . Prisoners' evidence does not show any considerable number of Germans in Libya studying desert conditions . . . Any advance from Tripoli . . . would require large quantities of transport which the enemy certainly does not possess in Libya at present.[44]

However, unconfirmed reports that had reached Cairo included decrypted Fliegerkorps messages confirming Rommel's arrival in Tripoli and dates for the arrival of the Afrika Korps. Two weeks later the benign impression was changing, and Wavell's Director of Intelligence, Brigadier Shearer, produced an impressive appreciation, as if written by the enemy, suggesting that the German Armoured Corps that had arrived so quickly could retake Cyrenaica after a few weeks' training in desert warfare, unless the imperial forces in Libya were substantially reinforced. Wavell was not persuaded, telling Shearer that he was being unduly pessimistic: 'Your evidence,' he said, 'is far from conclusive.' However, it was unlike Shearer to be pessimistic; in fact he was subsequently dismissed largely because his appreciations proved consistently over-optimistic, which made things difficult for Wavell and, through him, for the Chiefs of Staff. In the meantime Wavell stood by his man – loyalty to those he had appointed being one of his enduring, if sometimes misplaced, qualities.

The Germans lost no time in assembling their forces. They unloaded troops and equipment as soon as they docked, working through the night, heedless of the threat that the harbour lights might attract an air raid. They also began quickly to reinvigorate the Italians, whose morale had been crushed by the divergence between what Mussolini had led them to expect and what Wavell had actually done to them. Rommel took a leaf out of Wavell's book by ordering his workshops to produce large numbers of dummy tanks. Remarkably, the Germans had no idea that British attention had turned to Greece: with a mirror image of Wavell's view, they feared that the British would move on Tripoli before there were enough troops in place to defend it. Rommel therefore determined to establish a defensive line at the salt marshes at Agheila, an almost insuperable twenty-mile barrier. When he reached it, he found to his great surprise that no one tried to bar his way. In what seemed an extraordinary development, it began to appear that, rather than preparing to renew their western advance, the British were thinning out the whole area.

On the other side of the hill, Wavell did not have a wide choice as commander in Cyrenaica. O'Connor, the obvious choice, was ill and needed to recuperate from his arduous victories, so instead Wavell appointed Lieutenant General Sir Philip Neame, VC, who had replaced Jumbo Wilson as Military Governor of Cyrenaica. Neame was not well known to the commander-in-chief, but as the author of a book on strategy and a former instructor at the Staff College, his intellectual credentials were in order. Wavell usually made excellent appointments, but this was not one of them. He also came to regret placing Major-General Gambier-Parry in command of 2nd Armoured Division, which was about to bear the brunt of battle. But the field of choice was limited and Gambier-Parry had been recommended by a number of senior officers.

Neame's orders were couched in dispiriting terms. He was told that 'The enemy, if he attacks, will have local superiority both on the ground and in the air, until it is possible to send you reinforcements at a later date', and that his most important job was to safeguard his forces from a serious reverse.[45] It was a sharp contrast with East Africa, where Berbera and Mogadishu had just fallen and Wavell's forces were everywhere in the ascendant. Even more discouraging, it was just forty days since the victory at Beda Fomm, when a jumbled mass of demoralised Italians had fled west along the desert road; now, in the opposite direction, came an impressive array of armour, infantry and artillery – an Axis force whose spearheads were fanatical Germans, well armed, blooded in battle and superbly led.

On 7 March the War Cabinet agreed to send an army to Greece, and in America the Lend-Lease Bill was passed by the Senate. The same day Wavell met Smuts and Cunningham in Cairo and planned the recapture of Berbera, which was to fall nine days later. In Cyrenaica British troops were moving east, leaving Neame's command for the adventure in Greece; much of the remaining transport was sent back to Tobruk to collect supplies for his forward troops. The confusing cross-flows of men and armour continued as the March weeks passed, and a weak, poorly equipped, largely immobile garrison settled uncertainly in the desert.

In mid-March Wavell and Dill went up to inspect the ground, and soon began to realise that an attack was imminent. Dill gave General Neame a few words of encouragement, inspiring him with some of his customary fire: 'You are going to get a bloody nose here, Philip,' he said, 'and it is not the only place where we shall get bloody noses.'[46] Wavell saw that he would have to conjure up reinforcements without delay; he had none to hand, and he could hardly halt the movement to Greece, but he did accelerate the recall of troops from East Africa. In London the Chiefs of Staff became uneasy at the enemy advance: 'It is their habit,' Churchill said, 'to push on whenever they are not resisted. I presume you are only waiting for the tortoise to stick his head out far enough before chopping it off.'[47] At this point Wavell made the unwelcome admission that, in order to find a force for Greece, he had taken a considerable risk in Cyrenaica. It was a thunderbolt, and although the Greek liability had been accepted before it was known that the Germans had arrived in Tripoli, the disclosure was received with consternation.

At the end of March, just as their ally was collapsing at Keren, the Germans opened a concerted counter-offensive. It had not originally been intended as a serious attack, but when Rommel saw how weak his opponents were, he exploited the opening. On 2 April, the day of Rashid Ali's putsch and a day after the Italian collapse at Asmara, Agedabia was captured; it was just 150 miles from Benghazi, which was abandoned by the British the following day.

Wavell had told Neame that if he were attacked, he must delay the enemy's advance from Agheila to Benghazi for two months, by which time reinforcements would have arrived. With the Germans covering the spring course of the Benghazi Stakes in four days, that timetable became somewhat redundant. Although his orders allowed Neame to cede ground, even including Benghazi itself, he was instructed to hold the escarpment above the port, and Wavell, who had not seen the ground, believed that it was a natural barrier that would give strength to the whole British screen in Cyrenaica. This erroneous belief stemmed from a report on the area's topography that he had received some time earlier from General Wilson. It led Wavell to think that there were very few ways up the escarpment, and that a mobile reserve driving quickly along the top could block any attempt to surmount it. In fact, the escarpment was not at all like that: its broad slope could be ascended almost anywhere. Had Wavell been able to organise the defence himself, instead of being kept in Cairo discussing the Balkans and broad strategy, he might have made it more effective. Indeed, he claimed that despite the supply problems he would certainly have caused the Agheila salt marshes to be fortified, had he been able to inspect them. But he had not inspected the ground, and Neame was left to his own devices.

Rapidly the worst began to happen. When Wavell reached the front, he realised that his commander had lost control:

I found that he was proposing to place an infantry brigade in one long thin line from the sea to the escarpment south of Benghazi. It would have been completely sacrificed, as it had no transport. I ordered him to move it to the escarpment, just above Benghazi, and thereby at least saved it from annihilation, and for the eventual defence of Tobruk.[48]

Even a few days earlier a threat to Tobruk would have been fanciful, but no sooner had Agedabia fallen than orders were given to abandon Benghazi. A hurried retreat began, descending rapidly into confusion. It was not helped by uncertainty in the command tent. On 2 April Wavell arrived at the forward HQ, to find Neame on the point of letting the 2nd Armoured abandon the road to Benghazi and move inland. The commander-in-chief immediately intervened, insisting that the Benghazi road must be covered, even though that meant losing the chance of blocking the desert route towards Mechili and Tobruk – the shortcut along which O'Connor had raced so famously, what seemed an age ago.

A change of command seemed essential. Wavell sent for O'Connor, but when he arrived and had grasped the situation, he begged to be excused, considering it unwise to make a change in the middle of a battle. Under pressure, O'Connor agreed to stay and advise Neame. This placed both men in an awkward position: Neame had to continue with the battle, yet clearly lacked the confidence of his commander-in-chief who, although a generous superior, had correctly concluded that he had lost control.

This was a moment for the touch of ruthlessness that every commander needs. For all his brilliance, this was arguably a quality that Wavell lacked. He was reluctant to be rid of incompetents if he felt an obligation towards them. It was a generous side of his nature, but best suppressed on the battlefield. Even Lady Wavell said in retrospect that he kept some people around him for too long; occasionally it was for spurious reasons – for instance, if they amused him. Neame's case arose in altogether graver circumstances and, as Wavell was later to say, it might have been wiser to take Neame back with him to Cairo. Instead Wavell left him in charge, with O'Connor looking over his shoulder. In vain: on 3 April the Germans entered Benghazi and a week later had reached the gates of Tobruk. Insult was added to injury when Neame and O'Connor, together with John Combe, the flamboyant commander of the 11th Hussars, were taken prisoner by a German patrol. They had been making their way across the desert and the dogmatic Neame was at the wheel, clearly lost but insistent (despite O'Connor's freely expressed doubts) that he knew where he was going; the fact that they were in a white Cadillac did not help to conceal them from the enemy.[49]

Bletchley Park now intercepted a message from the German General Staff to Rommel, making clear to him that as he was short of vital supplies, with exhausted men and long lines of communication, he was not to continue his advance. Churchill felt that nothing was now more important than defeating Rommel, and this message convinced him that the opportunity to do so had arisen:

All our hearts at home had throughout been set on beating Rommel in the Western Desert . . . The tragedy of the evacuation of Greece, the distractions in Iraq and Syria, the dire struggle in Crete, all paled before the gleam of hope which we attached, and rightly, to victory in the Western Desert.[50]

On 21 April 1941 the Cabinet Defence Committee assembled. The atmosphere was sombre as the service chiefs considered a telegram from Wavell, saying that the Axis forces in Africa were now stronger in armour than anything he could raise, and that he had received intelligence of a new and fresh Panzer division that was ready to roll towards him.

The Defence Committee knew how great was Wavell's need, and so despite the CIGS remaining adamant that tanks should not be removed from an England still threatened by invasion, they agreed to send a special convoy of 238 tanks and their crews, and forty-three Hurricanes. It almost stripped England bare, but Churchill was determined that it would seal Rommel's coffin. 'If this consignment gets through . . .' he signalled to Wavell, 'no German should remain in Cyrenaica by the end of the month of June.'[51]

The convoy was codenamed 'Tiger'. Churchill insisted that to reach the desert army in time, it must risk all and cross the Mediterranean – infested as it was with submarines, its harbours mined and, out in the middle, the Italian Navy. 'If Wavell does not get his armour,' said Churchill, 'the Germans will take Egypt and the Suez Canal, and with them the British Empire and all that we are fighting for.' In deepest secrecy, so that even its commander did not know his destination, the 'Tiger' convoy left England. The order came in mid-voyage: steer east, past the Rock of Gibraltar, into the Mediterranean Sea.

On 4 May the weather was fierce and the seas were rough. The ships were cloaked in mist and fog, beset by wind and squalls. 'Tiger' and its western escort, Force H, sailed on. At dusk on 8 May they reached the entrance to the Skerki Channel. They were ninety miles west of Malta. Far to the south-east Admiral Cunningham and the Alexandria fleet were steaming to meet and protect them. Somewhere between the two lay the submarines and battle-ships of the enemy.

Cunningham was on the bridge of his flagship *Warspite*. Cloud and storm had prevented them from taking a star-setting for two days and they could not be sure of their position. Ahead, they prayed, they would find the four vital ships laden with tanks, perhaps all that lay between Wavell and defeat.

Dead ahead, through the mist and rain, they saw the outline of a ship. From below came the throb and beat of the engines. Above, on the bridge, not a word was said. A signal flashed out, and everybody tensed. An officer scribbled on a piece of paper. He turned to Cunningham: 'Sir,' he said, 'it reads . . . *Dr Livingstone, I presume.*' A broad smile spread across the admiral's face: 'Reply,' he said, '*On, Stanley, On!*'

The convoy reached Egypt on 12 May, but Wavell ordered his army to attack even before it was unloaded. He had seen what he called a fleeting opportunity to overwhelm the Germans. In part he was reacting to the secret decrypt to Rommel, forwarded to him by Churchill, but he was also determined to attack before the Germans were reinforced to overpowering strength. Having read what he called 'disquieting' intelligence that part of the 15th Panzer Regiment had landed at Tripoli, he now believed that a complete armoured division would soon be ranged against him. If that were so, he had cabled, 'it will take a lot of stopping', and he knew he had to drive the Germans back from Tobruk before it arrived. It was the urgency of that situation that had prompted the despatch of 'Tiger' through the Mediterranean.

On 15 May Wavell sent fifty-five tanks into the enemy lines near the Sollum and Halfaya Passes, both of which were of enormous strategic importance. His aim was an operation, codenamed 'Brevity', to occupy the Halfaya Pass and force the enemy back beyond Tobruk, before unleashing a major offensive – 'Operation Battleaxe' – when the convoy tanks were ready. The first attack started well: by forgoing a preliminary bombardment, surprise was achieved and a large number of Italians were captured while having breakfast. The British had then been forced back by a Panzer counter-attack, but managed to retain the pass and leave a garrison there to await Wavell's second attack. Meanwhile the 15th Panzer reinforcements had also arrived, enabling the Germans to retake the pass.

On arrival at Alexandria, the tanks had to be made ready for desert warfare, involving time-consuming adjustment to engines, systems and camouflage. Churchill had come to cherish his 'Tiger cubs', and was disconcerted by the fact that they did not drive straight off the ships into battle. Within a week of them reaching Egypt he pressed Wavell strongly on the matter: 'Tremendous risks were run to give you this aid and I wish to be assured that not an hour will be lost in its becoming effective . . . Are they yet in the hands of the troops? Why does it take a fortnight to bring them into action? What work has to be done on them? How are they to be moved to the front?'

Wavell was fully alive to the need to fight before the Germans became too powerful, but had to ensure that the tanks were ready for battle. Unforeseen delays had occurred – parts needed changing, guns had to be tested and tactics practised: 'It would be folly,' he told the War Office, 'to take the formation into battle against expert German formations without a short period to shake down. W/T practice is needed: the tank battle depends on it.'[52] Although Wavell believed that a few days for the division to 'find itself' would double its chance of success, he was urged forward by London; consequently the tank crews had only five days' training. It was not enough: when the brigade was finally sent into battle, it was unready, both technically and tactically.

There could be no certainty of the outcome to this vital contest, and 'Operation Brevity' was hardly an auspicious introduction to the more ambitious 'Battleaxe'; Wavell himself was beset by misgivings, bluntly telling the Chiefs of Staff: 'I think it right to inform you that the measure of success which will attend this operation is in my opinion doubtful.'[53]

On 15 June 'Operation Battleaxe' – what the Germans called the Battle of Sollum – opened along the plateau and coastal plain just inside the Egyptian frontier. The British commander, General Beresford-Peirse, was an orthodox tactician who had not previously commanded armour in battle. To such a man Rommel would be a dangerous opponent. From the start the British were at a disadvantage after a calamitous failure in wireless security gave the enemy nine hours' notice of the impending attack and an accurate picture of the British dispositions. Beresford-Peirse also faced the fundamental difficulty of working with tanks of two quite different types. The heavily armoured Matilda 'infantry tank' and the faster but more lightly gunned 'Cruiser' were wholly different horses, now yoked in the same harness – a legacy of the fruitless and acrimonious attempts at modernisation in the inter-war years. And no tactics had been devised that could combine the tanks effectively against the Afrika Korps.[54]

The battle rapidly turned into a violent clash of tanks. The Germans unveiled what proved to be a dramatically successful surprise: carefully sited and concealed ground positions from which 88mm and 105mm anti-tank guns fired into the advancing British armour, with devastating effect – as Wavell later put it, 'Rommel was sufficiently unsporting to produce an elephant gun against me.'[55] There were simply not enough tanks for Wavell to sustain losses for long, and at the very moment when only twenty Cruiser and fewer than twenty 'I' tanks were left in action, the British were appalled to see, shimmering on the desert horizon, 200 enemy tanks supported by 'numerous artillery'.[56]

The situation was made graver by enemy interception of signals disclosing not only Wavell's shortages of armour and ammunition, but also a picture of confusion in the higher command. The crisis came on the second day. The German 5th Light Division overwhelmed the 7th Armoured when Rommel unexpectedly shifted the weight and direction of his thrust and, anticipating a strong British attack early the following morning, took his enemy by surprise with an even earlier flank attack of his own.

On the third day Wavell called off the battle. He had lost 220 tanks to the Afrika Korps' twenty-five. Flame and black smoke rose above the sand. He cabled the War Office, 'I regret to report failure of Battleaxe. After initial success troops have been driven back by counter attack practically to starting positions with heavy loss of tanks.' A few days later he followed up with a contrite signal to Churchill:

> Am very sorry for failure of Battleaxe and loss of so many Tigercubs . . .
> I was over optimistic and should have advised you that 7th Armoured
> Division required more training before going into battle. Feel I should
> also have deferred Exporter till we could have put in larger force, but
> in both places I was impressed by need for immediate action.[57]

In fact, nearly three weeks earlier he had given the War Office precisely that advice, yet it had been discounted and he had been urged to press on regardless. Now Churchill was aghast: why, he wondered, with reason, had the garrison in Tobruk not joined in, instead of hanging back idle, as the battle raged. As it happened, Beresford-Peirse had initially proposed a wide sweep by 7th Armoured towards Tobruk, but Wavell had rejected the plan. The reports and explanations did not convince, and revived Churchill's lingering feeling that Benghazi had been abandoned too easily: 'There are always excellent reasons in favour of retirements,' he wrote, 'victory rewards those whose will-power overcomes these reasons.'[58]

For all Wavell's careful planning, the slow speed of the 'I' tanks prevented him from matching the moves of his opponent's faster armour. Yet the victor paid tribute to his opponent: 'What distinguished him from other British army commanders,' said Rommel, 'was his great and well-balanced strategic courage.'[59]

As with the Greek expedition, there had been a blur between policy and strategy. Wavell had ordered the attack to go ahead, even though he was not convinced that militarily it was the right thing to do. The War Cabinet itself had not ordered the start of 'Battleaxe', but it is clear that it had exerted heavy pressure on the commander in the field, by its telegrams and by rushing the tanks through an area of great danger so as to reach him as soon as possible. Whether the result would have been any different had Wavell delayed until the Tiger cubs had been properly fitted and tested can only be surmised. As he noted, the Germans were also bringing up armoured reinforcements, and that contributed to his decision to advance at once. But one way or the other, his time was up. As Sir Henry Pownall wrote: 'He [Wavell] didn't take a rosy view of our chances in Crete, nor of the recent attack in Libya; and he made a good prophecy about Syria. Taking a gloomy view, but an accurate one, he came under suspicion of being a commander without self-confidence.'[60]

Churchill had already sent a message to Lord Linlithgow, the Viceroy of India:

> I have come to the conclusion that a change is needed in the command of the Middle East. Wavell has a glorious record, having completely destroyed the Italian Army and conquered the Italian Empire in Africa. He has also borne up well against the German attacks and has conducted war and policy in three or four directions simultaneously since the beginning of the struggle. I must regard him as our most distinguished general. Nevertheless I feel that he is tired and that a fresh eye and an unstrained hand is needed.[61]

It was decided on high that Wavell should swap places with General Auchinleck, commander-in-chief in India. The CIGS and the Chiefs of Staff might now have raised their hands for Wavell but, weighed in the balance, they were found wanting: they shared the view that he was tired.

The Cabinet appointed a Minister Resident in Cairo and an Intendant General for the army's administration – as previously recommended by Wavell himself; it seemed that three men were now thought necessary for bearing the burden that one had carried alone.

Early on the morning that Hitler invaded Russia, Sir Arthur Smith took in the Prime Minister's fateful message. Wavell's reaction was wholly graceful: he was shaving, he paused, glanced at it and murmured: 'The Prime Minister is quite right – a new eye and a new hand are required for the job.'

A few days later General Auchinleck arrived in Cairo, and Wavell introduced him to the US envoy Averell Harriman; the commander-in-chief dispelled his American guest's embarrassment:

> His [Wavell's] first words were: 'I am sure you will want to see General Auchinleck. He is waiting in the library to talk to you'. I then expressed to Wavell, in the name of the American people, our respect and gratitude for the masterful way in which he had destroyed the Italian armies

in the Western Desert and in Eritrea against heavy odds. Tears came to his eyes and he said quietly: 'It was the men I led.'[62]

Wavell was not permitted to return to England, much as he wanted and needed a rest. The Viceroy and Secretary of State for India both felt that he should 'get into the saddle' at once. Churchill agreed, adding that he would rather not have Wavell 'hanging around London, and living in a room at his club'. There were bound to be dark thoughts that he was being made the scapegoat for the difficulties that had beset the Government throughout 1941, and when word spread through Cairo that he was to leave, there was an effusion of the affectionate loyalty that his rugged persona seemed to inspire. De Gaulle was among the few who were unmoved: when he heard that three senior French officers had been to bid Wavell goodbye, he placed them under close arrest for a month.

Wavell handed over his house to Auchinleck, complete with Lady Wavell and a mumps-stricken daughter who could not travel. Early on the morning of 7 July 1941 he went to the aerodrome. 'Only Senior Officers present,' recorded Lieutenant General Sir Arthur Smith, 'mostly from GHQ. We hated it.'

XII

THE POISONED CHALICE

CHURCHILL observed that Wavell should enjoy 'shaking the pagoda tree' in India, like some nabob of the East India Company counting out his money. By doing so he gave the impression that he was despatching his erstwhile commander to lush pastures far from the noise of battle. The public's reaction to its hero's transfer in July 1941 seemed to be one of surprise, and a belief that it was in some way a promotion to enable him to offer his skills to the Empire in the East. Those near the centre of events thought him in need of a rest. The Viceroy, the Secretary of State for India and their senior staffs knew that an arduous and immediate task awaited the incoming commander-in-chief, tired or not. India needed someone of Wavell's stamp to maintain order within the country and to prepare its defences against the spread of war.

His victories in the desert had brought him formal honours. In March he had been made a GCB[1] in recognition of the success of the operations leading to the capture of Benghazi; and for his 'outstanding services' he was appointed ADC General to the King. Formality also attended his new job in India. He was now His Excellency, second in rank only to the Viceroy, in a country two-thirds the size of Europe and containing nearly 400 million people. Wavell was soon struck by the rather stately atmosphere that prevailed, with India on far less of a war footing than the Middle East. He was now fifty-eight, but as often occurs with people who are at heart young and vigorous, many of his contemporaries seemed to him to be older and slower. The members of the Viceroy's Executive Council, he confided to his ADC, were in his opinion a 'pretty hoary-headed crowd', and he asked who all the old gentlemen were whom he saw lined up in plain clothes to greet him on

Scholarship boy.

Lieutenant Wavell, back from India
and shortly before taking up duties
at the War Office.

'Wavell of the Middle East'.
October 1940.

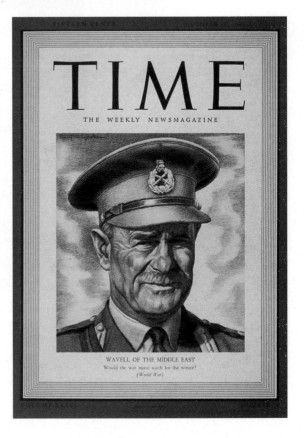

WAVELL OF THE MIDDLE EAST
Would the war move south for the winter?
(World War)

Joan Bright Astley at her desk.

At Home, Cairo 1940.

Wavell, with Sir Thomas Rutherford, Governor of Bihar, inspects famine conditions in Calcutta, November 1943.

'The Comptroller', Peter Coats.

Chips Channon at home.

Lady Mary Herbert.

Wavell inspects the mortar section of a Dogra regiment, Singapore, January 1942.

Wavell and Montgomery: London, June 1943.

Wavell Rides Out. Cairo, 1940.

'WE DO OUR DUTY'

May 1945: A cartoon in the *Hindustan Times* reflects news that the Viceroy was denied entry to the India Office when the policeman on duty failed to recognise him.

'Godfather to the New India', as described by *Illustrated*, October 1945.

Wavell, his daughter Felicity, and Lady Wavell embark for India, October 11, 1943.

Jinnah and the Magi: A.V. Alexander, Stafford Cripps and Frederick Pethick-Lawrence.

Old friends: Cripps and Gandhi.

Wavell greets Chakravarthi Rajagopalachari at
the Simla Conference, June 1945.

Wavell and Vinegar Joe Stilwell,
December 1942.

Churchill, Sir Sikandar Hayat Khan
and Wavell in Egypt, 1941.

'Go and find the General, Peters, and tell him that if he doesn't come in to lunch instantly he shan't have any.'

The Vicereine.

Archie John Wavell.

Wavell's three daughters: Joan, Felicity, Pamela.

Golf at Viceregal Lodge, Simla.

Cecil Beaton, Captain Bruce Fortune (one of Wavell's ADCs), the Viceroy, 1944.

Another day in the office. Wavell at his desk.

New brooms: Mountbatten and his wife on their way to take over as Viceroy and Vicereine.

Man of letters.

'Twilight and evening bell'.

his arrival at New Delhi station. They were in fact senior officers from GHQ. He was not pleased, and his first order was that officers should wear uniform at all times, except when taking exercise.

The Government's base for the summer months was at Simla, where Wavell settled into the official residency, Snowdon, with its vista of towering Himalayan peaks. He formed an immediate liking for the Viceroy, Lord Linlithgow, whose nature was kindly, if formal, his superficially forbidding demeanour being caused, as with Lord Curzon, partly by a steel corset that he had to wear to support his back. The presence of Linlithgow's three daughters – who, because of the family name of Hope, were known to young officers as 'Some Hope', 'Little Hope' and 'No Hope' – warmed the viceregal atmosphere. The Wavell family, due to arrive in August with their factotum Peter Coats, was to add further wisps of friendly informality.

Meanwhile, starting each day with his customary ride, attended by an ADC and any close friends who cared to join him, Wavell eased himself into his new work, as recorded by an ADC soon after they reached Simla:

> The Chief is in wonderful form and averages one first class story every walk or ride, and never shows signs of boredom at having no one of his own age to talk to. He works very hard but is naturally nothing like as worried as he was in the ME. He is very modest and never lays claim to have done anything unless it is to bring out some story's point.[2]

As commander-in-chief of Indian forces both within the country and overseas, Wavell answered to the Viceroy, to the Secretary of State for India and to the Chiefs of Staff in London. He was responsible for the navy and RAF in India, as well as for the army. One of his first duties was to embark on a tour of service establishments around the country, to each of which he gave an off-the-cuff and well-received pep-talk, usually standing in the middle of a circle of soldiers. Returning to Simla and a degree of state slightly alien to his Wykehamist spirit, Wavell prepared his official despatch on the war in the Middle East, forgoing his customary pen and instead pacing around his room with his hands behind his back, dictating without notes the outline of the strategy, politics and details of four months' fighting in five different campaigns.

He had also to grapple with political duties. As Defence and Military Member of the Viceroy's Council, a body recently resuscitated to help stabilise a deteriorating political situation, he was a member of India's Legislative

Assembly. This required the occasional speech – not, for Wavell, the ideal medium, but the contents of which he assembled with ease. However, he soon began to realise that such obligations might consume a large amount of time, which would more profitably be directed to the war. As his chief of staff he appointed Lieutenant General Thomas Hutton: tall, thin, grey and a very good staff officer, Hutton was carrying forward the transformation of the Indian Army from a small force of horsed cavalry and unmechanised infantry into a modern army that would eventually swell to two and a half million men. As in the Middle East, the demands on Wavell's attention were diverse from the start, so it was a pity that his deputy was not an 'old India hand' with a good presence – as General Auchinleck observed, 'I think the personal touch of the c–in–c means a lot in India, and Tom Hutton hasn't got a personality anyway.'[3]

Wavell's attention was directed to grand strategy within a week of his arrival, as the smouldering embers of the Iraq revolt glowed red once more, in neighbouring Iran. Even before he left Cairo he had been warned by his new master, Leopold Amery,[4] that trouble might be brewing in Iran. The German advance into Russia had heightened fears that they would thrust through the Caucasus into the Middle East. That would deprive the Empire of its main oil supplies, threaten India and abort the Allies' intention to establish a route – as a supplement to the hazardous Arctic shipping lanes – along which to supply Russia with the equipment it needed to stay in the war. That was the paramount purpose of the Americans' request for a great base at Basra, in the Persian Gulf, which fell within Wavell's command.

The situation in Iran now aggravated the danger. Rashid Ali, the Grand Mufti and their discomfited associates had fled Baghdad and had found in Teheran fertile soil in which to sow anew their anti-British seeds. Their presence was tolerated by a Shah whose regime the British profoundly distrusted. But it seemed to Wavell that the distrust was rather tepid, especially in view of Iranian troops reportedly gathered near the oilfields and on the Russian and Iraqi frontiers. The country contained an effective fifth column of approximately 3,000 Germans, masquerading as diplomatists, engineers, archaeologists and tourists, ready to play their part in loosening Britain's hold on the oilfields. Curiously, Wavell's reaction was almost the mirror-image of his approach to the revolt in Iraq, albeit that he had in that case been under intense pressure from the Germans on his western flank. This time it was he who took the initiative, telling the CIGS that he thought the attitude of the War Office was complacent, and urging that the Germans be cleared out of Iran at once. Then

British forces could join hands with the Soviets, giving added protection to India; '. . . if the present Government is not willing to facilitate this,' he said, 'it must be made to give way to one which will'.[5] Wavell's own suggestions to the COS included infiltrating agents into the Caucasus to encourage resistance and sabotage should the Germans look like overwhelming the Russians, and to get Turkey to persuade Mohammedans in the region to maintain their support for the Soviets – a suggestion that was spurned in London.

The contrast with his previous attitude, to Syria and Iraq, was in the circumstances entirely valid. The war situation had changed, with Germany's attack on Russia placing the Middle East much nearer Germany's grasp. On his initial tour as commander-in-chief, Wavell had found the defences of the North-West Frontier – the traditional entry point for invaders – to be relatively sound, but the small and unmodernised Indian Army lacked the transport, munitions and aircraft for the country to be successfully defended. Yet the policy of sending aid to Russia, and Rommel's alarming successes in Libya, meant that nothing could be spared for the frontier.

On 16 August 1941 Britain and Russia delivered formal protests to Iran about German infiltration, but diplomacy proved futile and on 25 August it was superseded by an Anglo-Russian invasion. The Iranian Army was reputed to have a million men, but if that was the case, it seemed that only a small proportion chanced to find themselves available for the campaign. Expecting to meet well-defended road-blocks, the British advanced with concentric movements, ready to take their enemy in the rear. Fighting only the occasional skirmish with Iranian troops commanded by officers in immaculate high-heeled field boots and well-brushed kepis, the British were greeted without animosity and with great relief that they were not the Russians. After four days the Iranian King, Reza Shah, concluded that perhaps discussion was after all a preferable option, and the campaign was over.

Meanwhile Lady Wavell and her daughters had arrived at Simla. Wavell himself had arranged a visit to England, with short stays en route in Iraq and Cairo, and arrived in London on 8 September. He had not been home since his first, difficult meetings with the Prime Minister a year earlier, but even now he was initially rebuked for thinking of returning while India needed his guidance. He assured Churchill that all was in hand and that he was not coming on holiday – much as it was reasonable that he should have one, if not at that moment – but to discuss important matters of strategy. Fortunately Churchill's pique soon dissolved in his pleasure at the successful outcome in Teheran, which had resulted in the installation of a more complaisant government.[6]

The change of scene and the cool air of Simla had worked quickly on Wavell's constitution. Even so, after more than a year of stress, a brief return to England was an attractive prospect, welcome and long overdue after, as he was to describe it, 'dry years of sun and dust and Eastern skies . . .'[7] Ten days after leaving Simla he reached London and was reunited with his son, who had travelled from his regiment's base in Scotland to be with his father. Settling into Sir John Dill's flat in Victoria, Wavell began a round of meetings to discuss the situation in Iran and the development of trans-Iranian railway and road routes with which to supply Russia. Sir Alan Brooke, commander-in-chief of Home Forces, who in December would take over from Dill as CIGS, dined with Wavell, finding him 'silent as usual'. Wavell also had an audience with the King, who liked and admired him, although he was mildly disconcerted by his shyness – he later christened him 'the oyster'. Wavell told the King that he liked India, but hoped 'to be able to wake things up a bit there'.[8]

He hoped to be able to wake things up a bit in Whitehall as well. On the same day as he saw the King, Wavell presented a paper to the War Cabinet. In his short time as commander-in-chief in India he had mastered its defence brief. Now he spelt out the country's needs. They were urgent, and his request for 60,000 British troops and large amounts of replacement transport resonated when he pointed out that there was not one modern tank or armoured car in the subcontinent, or a single aircraft capable of taking the air against modern German or Japanese machines.

In the meantime, Dill noted, Wavell was anxious that Japan be kept quiet by any means whatsoever. In drawing attention to Japan he was ahead of the War Office, as the minds of the planners in London had not yet accepted the gravity of the threat in the East. Wavell already foresaw trouble on the horizon and urged that both Burma and Ceylon be brought within India Command, pointing out that if the Japanese occupied Siam (now Thailand), it would place their bombers within reach of the industrial belt around Calcutta; India's munitions works would be vulnerable and there were no anti-aircraft guns or fighter aeroplanes to repel them. However, with the first hint of the political complications that were soon to absorb much of his time, Wavell was told that he could not take Burma into his command because of China's sensibilities about the Burma Road, the lifeline that carried its vital supplies from America.

Meanwhile Wavell heard that Churchill had established a 'Special Information Centre' in the War Cabinet Offices, and there he went in search of figures for aeroplane and tank production. The centre was under the aegis of General Ismay[9] and was run by a young woman called Joan Bright. Its purpose was to provide visiting commanders-in-chief and other high officers with maps, statistics and all kinds of war information, so that they could keep abreast of war theatres other than their own. Following his first visit, Wavell was often to repair to the centre when he was in London. Now Miss Bright escorted him around her offices:

> I went down to the Map Room and said 'I'm going to bring General Wavell down to you.' They fell off their chairs with pleasure. They all admired him tremendously. Having put those flags all over the Western Desert, you can imagine. So I took him down there, where they adored having him . . . then he invited me out to lunch at the Senior, the old Naval & Military. Perfectly ordinary, really. And we went across St James's Park in silence, and I remember so well him suddenly saying in his grating voice 'Joan, why does the Prime Minister dislike me?' Well, it was something right out of my ken, really. I thought, what can I say? 'You don't talk enough. You don't express enough. He wanted to hear from you what the situation was like, in Greece, in the Middle East, but you sit there silent. He can't get anything out of you, and he gets impatient.' I asked him at lunch why he found it so hard to express himself. 'Well', he replied, 'I date it from my childhood when I was brought down to the drawing-room and made to sit there and they all questioned me and I became shy then and I've never got over that. I find it very difficult.' And he did, you see. All Winston wanted from him was a dissertation on where his army would be, where he expected to go, what he expected to do. But, of course, he sat in silence. It didn't help. The Prime Minister was fighting the battle pretty well single-handed at that time, one must remember that. I thought it was a very poor excuse, because in those days everyone was brought up in that way, weren't they. It's just that he was a shy man; he wasn't taciturn, he was very pleasant, he was just tongue-tied.[10]

Miss Bright soon joined a small group of women, which included Freya Stark and Lady Mary Herbert, with whom Wavell maintained a lively correspondence, encouraged in Joan Bright's case by her ability, because of her job, to understand the problems of his war.

Wavell greatly enjoyed writing to his friends; it enabled him to express what was often hidden beneath his martial exterior: modesty, a poetic nature and the suggestion at times of an inner loneliness. His letters often illustrated that he was not at heart a conventional man – his inclination and his intellect were both against that – and to an extent they demonstrated also that he valued an outlet for his emotions, which were muted by his shyness and by army custom. On his return to the East he glanced wistfully back, writing to Joan Bright:

> I've thought of you a great deal, and the very pleasant and rather improbable circumstance that you took as immediate liking to me as I to you. I wish we had more time together, but you will be something to look forward to. I wonder when we shall next meet.[11]

His journey back to India had its fair share of wartime uncertainty, and although his flying-boat did not encounter the Luftwaffe, he had a lucky escape when it was damaged on landing at Gibraltar and began to fill with water – another flying mishap that left him quite unperturbed. A few hours later he was warm and dry and dining off roast partridge with the Governor.

Soon after returning to Simla, Wavell had once more to leave India on a mission. Anxious to proceed with supplying the Russians, Churchill had concluded that Wavell, having completed his campaign in Iran, was an obvious choice to promote contact with the Soviets, not least because he was almost the only senior officer with a command of their language – until his death, the Army List described him as qualified in Russian at interpreter level, which carried the bonus of extra pay. So in mid-October he was despatched to Tiflis, to discuss, as Churchill put it, 'the right hand we shall give to the Russians in and about the Caspian basin in the forthcoming campaign'. In the ensuing meetings Wavell suggested staff talks, exchanges of information and a British loan of transport and equipment, and tried to persuade the Russians to withdraw from the Iranian territory they had occupied. Asking the Russians to do any such thing was to place hope high above any reasonable expectation, but Wavell proved adept at keeping the stubborn and suspicious Russians to the points at issue without treading on their toes.

While doing so he had to find the stamina required to consume, at the strangest times of day, large amounts of the obligatory alcohol and caviare and yet speak coherently in Russian. He manfully put duty before pleasure while being force-fed with vodka, resulting one evening in his having to be carried bodily back to his hotel in a state of collapse, insensible, but with the Russians admiring him all the more. The conferences cemented a certain amount of goodwill, but little of substance emerged, the Russians being happy with the concept of receiving – whether information or supplies – but less so with that of giving, and not anxious to have British personnel stationed in their midst.

So Wavell returned to India and on 23 October arrived in Delhi, where GHQ had moved for the winter. Despite the lack of urgency, or at least time, that the Government seemed to attach to the subject, Wavell turned to the growing belligerence of Japan as she developed her plans for what she euphemistically called the 'Greater East Asia Co-Prosperity Sphere'. To him it was clear that if Japan were to continue her diplomacy by other means, and resort to war, his command would soon be in the front line. Knowing how weak India was, he therefore responded at once to an invitation from Air Chief Marshal Brooke-Popham, commander-in-chief in the Far East, to visit his eastern neighbours Burma, Malaya and Singapore.[12]

Burma had been a separate military command since 1937, when the country had received its independence from India,[13] partly on the theory that the Burmese were a reasonable and docile people and that if self-government succeeded there, it might be useful as a model for India. It produced oil, teak and other valuable commodities, and now provided vital access to the Chinese armies in Yunnan as well as, in theory, forming a barrier to protect the industrial areas on India's east coast. In Wavell's view, however, separating Burma from India Command was 'a cardinal mistake'.

In practice Burma would be able to put up little in the way of defence against attack by Japan: the only two Indian brigades there were supported by eight battalions of the Burma Rifles and the Burma Frontier Force, both of which were of doubtful fighting quality. There were few tanks, exiguous stocks of ammunition, and the artillery contingent boasted four mountain batteries and some old field guns. Staffwork, even though not a major complication for a force of that size, left much to be desired. In pleading for reinforcements, Brooke-Popham had done everything short of resigning, but he was too weak a character to command attention at a time when so much was at stake in the Middle East.

The air situation was thought to be even worse. A huge swathe of imperial territory, from Hong Kong to the borders of India (Malaya alone was considerably larger than Eire), lay without adequate air cover. For the defence of this immense area Brooke-Popham commanded a mixed bag of fewer than 200 aircraft, none of which were long-range fighters. Japanese air strength was not known, owing to the paucity of intelligence, but in fact comprised about 700 fighters and bombers, many with detachable long-range fuel tanks. At the end of 1940 the Chiefs of Staff had calculated that the defence of Far East Command required 336 aeroplanes, but little action had been taken: 'What can you do for us?' Brooke-Popham had pleaded; the answer was next to nothing.

Being new to the Far East, Wavell sensed at once the drift and sloth that were no longer noticeable to those who lived and worked there. In Singapore he found a wholly unwarlike atmosphere, and quite inadequate defence arrangements in Malaya, which he described as a completely lotus-eating land. Few around him seemed much concerned that a threat might be growing to their east – the government of Malaya (in fact the British community in general) was apathetic, most having come to Malaya for what they could get out of it. Yet Wavell felt that the Japanese were much too close for comfort. Their entry into French Indo-China had led to the severance of China's rail supplies from the south, and the neighbouring Siamese Government was reported to be sympathetic to Japanese overtures. If Burma were overrun, India and Australia would lose valuable supplies of oil, while defeat in Malaya would mean the loss of one of the world's economic prizes, producing the rubber and tin that were vital to the British war machine.[14] Wavell's brief tour of these areas convinced him that Far East Command would not be able to handle an attack on Burma, so he applied once more to the CIGS for its transfer to his own command, enabling him to take a hand in shaping plans for its defence.

Paradoxically, while he detected a fatal complacency among Malaya's authorities, who appeared not to believe that the Japanese could invade the country,[15] his innate optimism seemed for a time to survive his tour. Writing to Brooke-Popham, he concluded:

I am left with the impression that you ought easily to be able to deal with any Japanese attack on Malaya provided that you get the necessary air reinforcements when required. Personally I should be most doubtful if the Japs ever tried to make an attack on Malaya, and I am sure they will get it in the neck if they do.[16]

There was little evidence for that view, or for supposing that the necessary air reinforcements would actually materialise. Unfortunately Wavell had no experience of the Far East – it had not been his job to gain it – but the War Office itself seemed little better informed. Because of the crisis in the West, few senior officers had been able to pay much attention to developments in the East. It was many years since Wavell's friend Everard Calthrop[17] had been killed; in his time at the War Office he had been almost the only man with a good knowledge of Japan. It seemed that little had changed.

'Imagination,' wrote Churchill, 'without deep and full knowledge is a snare, and very few among our experts could form any true impression of the Japanese mind. It was indeed inscrutable.'[18]

As it happened, the momentum towards war in the East reached its climax in the small hours of 8 December, local time, when – without warning or ultimatum – the Japanese landed on the east coast of Malaya, and, far to the east, launched attacks on the Clark Air Base in the Philippines and the Pearl Harbor naval base in Hawaii, all but destroying, with shattering speed, the twin supports of the American empire in Asia.

Since the war had begun the Chiefs of Staff had been fully occupied with the war in the West and had not had the time or resources to consider in detail contingency plans for defending Britain's interests in the Far East. Nevertheless, one idea that had been conceived by Far East Command was codenamed 'Operation Matador', intended for just such an emergency as a surprise Japanese attack. On 7 December Matador's moment came – or should have come – when Japanese convoys were sighted sailing towards Malaya. However, the plan involved sending troops into Siam to forestall a Japanese landing on the Kra Isthmus, and as it was British policy to avoid offending the Siamese unless it were really necessary, the Malayan authorities were forbidden to implement 'Matador' unless Japan had actually violated Siamese neutrality or was clearly intent on attacking Malaya. A fleet of Japanese warships heading straight for the Malayan coast apparently did not count.

This pusillanimity was a product of policies that were greatly to restrict Wavell's own strategy. One of these was that, as long as war had not actually broken out in the Far East, priority for war resources had to be given to the Middle East and Russia. Further, although Lieutenant General Arthur Percival, GOC Malaya, did command nearly 90,000 troops, their training and equipment were inadequate, and the Indian units – half his total – had been 'milked' of their best officers and NCOs, who were needed in the Middle East. The situation was made worse by the widespread belief that

Malaya was safe from attack because the jungle was impenetrable, certainly for tanks – which perhaps explained why thousands of War Office pamphlets on how to fight tanks lay undistributed at GHQ Singapore.

On 5 December the Cabinet at last gave Brooke-Popham a guarded discretion to implement 'Operation Matador'. To no effect. When news of the convoys arrived, he and the Governor of Singapore, Sir Shenton Thomas, clung to the belief that the ships might in fact have been heading for Indo-China. Then they came to the supine conclusion that if they were hostile, they could not be prevented from reaching Singapore, so it would be too late to launch 'Matador', which was designed to forestall an invasion. Finally they persuaded themselves that the whole circumstance might be a Japanese feint. Such tortuous havering was to be disastrous, even if in hindsight it is accepted that British military weakness at the time made it unlikely that a more robust reaction would have made any real difference.

The Japanese attack achieved almost instant results. They overcame the Siamese after just six hours and met with only light defences on the Malayan beaches, where they were at their most vulnerable. Sixty British aircraft were lost on the first day of battle, the Japanese neutralising an already weak RAF by attacking its airfields. The initial landings of more than 26,000 Japanese soldiers were therefore largely unopposed. Further south the news was dramatically bad. As a political gesture, and in the hope that the vague potential menace of capital ships at large would upset Japanese naval strategy, the British Government had despatched the battle-cruiser *Repulse* and the battleship *Prince of Wales* to Singapore, where they arrived on 2 December. Accompanied by four destroyers but no aircraft carriers, the combination was too small to form an effective fighting unit. 'Today,' wrote the Resident Minister's wife, 'a little fleet arrived to help, camouflaged to kill; a lovely sight but on the petty side.'[19]

On 8 December Admiral Sir Thomas Phillips led the flotilla out to sea, determined to prevent further Japanese landings. With the Nelson touch he sent a farewell signal: 'We are going out to look for trouble, and no doubt we shall find it.' He did so two days later, when eighty Japanese aircraft swept down upon his ships. Despite being discovered he failed to call for fighter help, a remarkable oversight, and by 1.30 both capital ships had capsized and disappeared beneath the South China Sea. 'So ended,' in the words of the Official History, 'almost before it had begun, the career of the Far Eastern fleet.'[20] After three days of the Far East war, the prestige and sea-power of both Britain and America lay on the ocean bed. From the coast of Africa to the far Pacific, control of the seas was lost and, for Britain, the illusion that a two-hemisphere empire could be defended by a one-hemisphere navy had been shattered.

Yet for all his frustrations the previous year, the Prime Minister still had a solid, reliable master of the military trade ready to face the threat from the East. Accordingly on 10 December a signal arrived for Wavell in New Delhi: 'You must now look East. Burma is placed under your command. You must resist the Japanese advance towards Burma and India and try to cut their communications down the Malay peninsula.'[21]

Wavell was already well aware that Burma would be crucial: it formed the eastern bastion of India itself, and although the mighty Singapore fortress would supposedly protect Burma from naval attack, the opening of the Japanese land offensive was a real threat, not least because Burma's defence was a matter of great importance to the Empire's new ally, China. With his respect for the lessons of history Wavell turned to the past for inspiration: 'How did we get to Burma the first time?' he enquired, and his staff scuttled off to find documents about the events of 1824. At once, as he had when he had first arrived in Egypt, he began to grip the diffuse strands of an unprepared command, and assess the ways of halting the enemy and retaking what might be lost.

By the time he assumed command of Burma, the battle joined in Malaya had already reflected the earlier failures of will and preparation that stemmed from the concept that the mainstay of imperial interests in East Asia was the naval base at Singapore that had been designed to enable the navy to protect Britain's colonies in the Far East. However, as there was no navy to use the base, the decision had been taken to concentrate on air defence instead, with aircraft stationed as far forward as possible. Airfields had been constructed in the north of Malaya, but they, in turn, had to be defended by the army, which as a result was widely dispersed across the country, too weak to withstand invasion from the north and in the wrong place to meet landings from the east.

Further, when the Japanese did strike, the air force proved inadequate. Reinforcements had begun to arrive, but the total was still far short of the 336 aircraft deemed necessary. Nor were the aircraft types suitable for modern warfare, being obsolete machines, many of which were generally accepted as being more of a menace to their pilots than to an enemy.

The day following the Japanese landings an entire squadron of Blenheims was destroyed on the ground, and within a short time aircraft numbers began to dwindle rapidly. Replacements were vital: 'When may we expect

Blenheims?' Wavell cabled the Chiefs of Staff, 'Unless they arrive very soon it may be too late . . .'[22]

The speed of the enemy advance threatened to make everything too late. The Chiefs of Staff diverted four fighter squadrons, but events in North Africa precluded the despatch of any more. Rommel was far from defeated, although in the current phase of the 'Benghazi Stakes' he had just been pushed back from Tobruk and was about to lose Benghazi itself. Wavell would have to wait upon the outcome in the desert before he received any significant help. The British defence plan had depended on air superiority, but that seemed to have gone already, and the emphasis now switched to the battle on the ground. On 11 December the Japanese won a fierce battle at Jitra, just inside Malaya's northern border, where two full brigades with artillery support were bounced by a single Japanese battlegroup of about 1,500 men and a mere twenty tanks. The next day the sky above Penang filled with dive-bombers, civilians were massacred in their thousands and the commander of the Indian III Corps evacuated his position. The first duty of an imperial power, to be able to defend its subjects, was left unfulfilled.

The evacuation was conducted in unseemly haste. Retreating commanders clung to the hope that somehow or other relief would get through, and civilian officials had forbidden the destruction of any Chinese-owned facilities. Troops therefore abandoned their positions without taking action to deny to the advancing enemy vital stores and equipment: tin stocks, rubber plantations, dredging machinery and large amounts of military supplies consequently fell undamaged into Japanese hands. With the fiasco at Jitra and its immediate aftermath, the defenders took an uncomfortably large step along the road to disaster.

On 16 December, Penang was abandoned to its fate, and two days later Wavell flew to Calcutta to meet General Pownall,[23] the newly arrived commander-in-chief, Far East, with whom it seemed he would have to work to stave off defeat. Then he flew on to Rangoon. To the people he saw – afraid and disoriented – he brought invaluable qualities: an ability quickly to perceive the needs of the hour, to assess plans for defence or attack and to determine what dispositions, units and equipment were required to make them effective. Perhaps most of all he cheered people with his air of imperturbable confidence; however misplaced it would prove, it was a fine encouragement to his troops. He could not of course produce reinforcements where none were available, and even were he to wring from the War

Office agreement to despatch men or equipment, the transit time could be up to three months. In the context of the fast-moving battle in Malaya there was little practical help that Wavell could offer. But, for a time, his air of calm understanding inspired the belief that he would conjure up what was required, and provided a vital boost to morale at a moment when the heavens were falling. As the future looked bleaker by the day, his presence was like that of an eminent doctor or learned counsel, imparting quiet assurance that the problem is not intractable, that the answers will be found and that in time, when all is in place, the difficulties will be overcome.

The Japanese attacks on 7 and 8 December had been directed both at the Americans and the British, threatening the Dutch East Indies, while opening China's eyes to the chance of increasing her presence on the world stage. Japan had greatly internationalised the conflict, and Wavell was now to work with new men in a new theatre of war, more complicated because it would require him to deal with Chinese and Americans, neither of whom had any great admiration for Britain or her soldiers.

It was now essential that the new Atlantic partners agree on their strategic objectives. Roosevelt's determination that China should be treated as a world power became a matter of importance for Britain as soon as the United States declared war. It was in Britain's interest to pay heed to the President's aims for China, not only to satisfy the Americans, but because if she was defeated or made peace, large numbers of Japanese troops would be freed to attack the British Empire. Meanwhile China herself wished to be free of the Japanese. These various interests converged in Burma, through which lay the only land route by which China could obtain the equipment to keep her in the war.

Chiang Kai-shek, China's leader, now called for an international conference in his capital, Chungking, on the River Yangtze in remote country to the north of the border between Burma and Indo-China. He invited representatives from the Soviet Union, the Netherlands, the US and Britain to co-ordinate war strategy, and it was Wavell whom the Chiefs of Staff asked to attend. He now crossed once more the uncertain boundary between top-level soldiering and international politics.

On 20 December he flew to Rangoon, on the first stage of his journey to the Chinese province of Yunnan, where he discussed with the Governor the state of Burma's defences. His fears were confirmed: little had been done to protect the port, the country's essential supply point, while the quality both of the administration and the available fighting forces gave cause for serious misgivings. The plan of defence seemed to rest on the hope that bombing would prevent the arrival of the Japanese: 'This is contrary to all experience of this war,' Wavell told the CIGS, 'and anyway,' he added bleakly, 'we have now no bombers.'

Other than sending to London a list of requirements, there was little he could do. He set out on the next leg of the hazardous journey to Chungking, there to meet the all-powerful and enigmatic Chiang Kai-shek, 'Generalissimo' of the Chinese Army. Chiang spoke no English – substituting, according to Wavell, 'clucking noises like a friendly hen' – and omnipresent at his elbow was Madame, almost as well informed and as influential as her husband. In effect, their meeting was the first inter-Allied conference in the East, and it was of great importance that it should be a success. Unfortunately it exposed instead the ragged edge of British-American ideas on the importance of China, and of what role she should play in the Japanese war. The talks turned primarily on the participation of Chinese troops in the defence of Burma, and Chiang offered Wavell his 5th and 6th Armies, albeit with circumspection because in the brief interval since the attack on Pearl Harbor he had seen with growing dismay the reports of British setbacks in Malaya. The Chinese were beginning to wonder whether the British Empire was a paper tiger.

It was the Chinese offer of troops that caused military and political issues to become rapidly confused. Both the quantity and quality of the Chinese Army were, in Wavell's opinion, doubtful, and so, balancing his needs against what he believed the Chinese could actually supply, he told the Generalissimo that he would accept one division of the 6th Army, with another division kept in reserve. This was a far from full-blooded response brimming with gratitude, and it was tinged not only by Wavell's scepticism about the effectiveness of the Chinese offer, but also by the fact that the British did not really want the Chinese to enter Burma at all. Unless disaster struck, Wavell believed that reinforcements of British and Indian troops should be adequate for the task of defending Burma, and, as he put it, 'a country of the British Empire should be defended by Imperial troops rather than foreign'. It would not do for the Chinese to think that the British needed help in protecting their Empire.

Nor was there any certainty that the Chinese, once in Burma, would leave it when asked to do so. There was also the likelihood that, given the chance, they would stir up trouble with the Burmese, who had no love for their northern neighbours, partly because the Chinese were adept at making money out of the Burmese, investing it in banks and shipping and other British institutions, and thereby helping to cement colonial rule. At the same time Chinese antagonism to Western empires, which had made fortunes out of special privileges in China for almost a century, remained deeply felt, even in the unfolding war.

Wavell felt that on a strictly military basis he was wholly justified in not accepting the Chinese offer in full. He did not believe that the Japanese would try to invade Burma while their hands were full in the Philippines and Malaya, and he thought that the promised British reinforcements would reach Rangoon in time to deploy and shore up the country's defences. Furthermore, ever alert to administrative problems, he saw that there was not enough food or transport in Burma to cope with an influx of soldiers from the north. He therefore added the proviso that if they did come, they must be supplied from China.

This all made sound military sense, but it was not the best approach politically. Wavell had entered a wider arena, its atmosphere swirling with eddies that he either did not perceive or chose to ignore. The Americans present were aghast, briefed as they were that their President wanted to please China and draw her into the war. They feared that the Chinese, if disgruntled, might make a separate peace with Japan, thereby releasing large numbers of troops to fight the Allies. They also suspected that the Chinese knew more of Japanese intentions than the British did.

Wavell had received no prior knowledge of the American attitude to China, which had not yet become clear even to Churchill or the Foreign Office, although at this moment politics, diplomacy and even psychology were as important as hard military fact. Nor had he picked up along the way how much importance the Chinese attached to 'face', and so, at their first meeting, he unwittingly exposed the Chinese leader to its loss.

Reports of the dialogue reached Churchill in Washington, where he had gone to discuss with the President and American service chiefs the future of the war, and the news that Chiang Kai-shek was 'somewhat displeased' by the unenthusiastic response to his offer – a rather mild description for the emotion that the Generalissimo actually displayed – momentarily weakened Roosevelt's already considerable regard for Wavell.

In Chungking the cool atmosphere also affected discussion of Lend–Lease supplies that had reached Rangoon. Although they were destined for China, Wavell considered that he had immediate need of them, especially munitions vital for the defence of southern Burma. His view was that it was in China's own interests to help keep the enemy out of Burma, and that the American supplies would be worthless if his forces could not now press them into service. The Generalissimo failed to see the logic of that argument, not being confident, on the evidence he had heard so far, that the British would have much success with the materiel even if it was handed to them. So, when the British authorities in Rangoon finally felt compelled to appropriate some of the stocks, in advance of American or Chinese authorisation, the atmosphere in Chungking cooled even further.

Wavell's response to all this discussion was that of the plain, upright British soldier: his partial acceptance of the Chinese offer was justified, he said, by the military situation at the time, and he had no reason to know that great political importance was attached to the offer. While the Generalissimo, whom Wavell thought was unpractical and visionary, wanted to discuss global strategy, Wavell was himself interested only in the defence of Burma.

On Christmas Eve he returned to Rangoon, tired by the two days of difficult talks. After an eventful flight – in which his aeroplane was lost over Siam for most of a night, with all the passengers, with the apparent exception of Wavell and an easy-going pilot, becoming progressively more alarmed – they reached their destination marginally ahead of fifty Japanese bombers. Fortunately, the RAF and the American Volunteer Group[24] scrambled their fighters and put up a superlative performance, shooting down thirty raiders for the loss of only four.

After their aircraft had managed to land at Rangoon they tumbled out and ran for cover. It was Christmas Day 1941, the Japanese were entering Hong Kong, and peace and goodwill had clearly not settled upon Rangoon, either. Lying in a storm of exploding metal beneath a fierce air battle did not make for happiness. Wavell was unscathed, but even though seventeen bombs had landed around his slit-trench and he had been within feet of being blown to smithereens, he arrived at Government House quite unperturbed and accepted a cocktail, as though, in the Governor's description, he had just come in from a pleasant game of golf.[25] He then turned his attentions to Miss Gibbs, 'a most attractive person, as pretty as a picture and inclined at times to be a bit of a flirt'.[26]

Wavell then had the less pleasant duty of replacing the officer commanding in Burma, General McLeod, whom he described as a nice old gentleman, but who according to the Governor had fallen prey to a 'lack of energy'. He decided to replace him with General Thomas Hutton, whose administrative skill and intimate knowledge of what India Command could provide for Burma seemed ideal,[27] However, Hutton had never shown aptitude for command in battle, and Wavell's choice suggests that he had not yet wholly accepted the idea that the country was about to become a battlefield rather than merely an administrative area.

On Boxing Day Wavell returned to Calcutta, and spent a long day writing an appreciation of Burma's prospects for Sir Alan Brooke, the new Chief of the Imperial General Staff.[28] With fighter strength threatening to fall to zero, the situation was rather discouraging and matched the wider outlook that Christmas, expressed by Clementine Churchill to her husband: 'It's a horrible world,' she wrote, 'Europe overrun by the Nazi hogs and the Far East by yellow Japanese lice.'[29] At the end of a long and difficult day, having finished his reports, Wavell sought congenial company and a few hours' respite, and went out to the nightclubs with Lady Mary Herbert,[30] with whom, as his ADC observed, 'Master rather fancies himself'.

Meanwhile, an unexpected development had occurred in Washington. The British and the Americans were agreed that it was imperative to defend the Malay Barrier, the long chain of islands stretching south-east from Malaya to northern Australia, with the focal point at Singapore. But the chief concern of the Americans, who were losing hope of retaining their position in the Philippines, was to hold Australia and from there maintain a line of communication with the United States. Burma and Australia were now the essential support positions for this huge area, between the east and west of which communications had all but been extinguished. The Americans had concluded that the best chance of halting the disintegration was to impose unity of command in each war theatre, calling for one 'Supreme Commander' for the entire South-West Pacific battle-zone, and proposing a single command for the naval, land and air forces of the Allies – British, Americans, Dutch and Australians, with the New Zealanders and the Chinese forming southern and northern appendices respectively. Chiang Kai-shek, whom the Americans recognised had been considerably upset by events in Burma and the trouble over Lend-Lease supplies, would as an inducement to co-operate be offered the post of Supreme Allied Commander of the Chinese theatre. Burma would be included in the new command, which would be known as ABDACOM.[31]

The force behind this grand design was the single-minded and determined American Chief of Staff, General George Marshall, who had assigned to a rising star, Brigadier General Eisenhower, the job of preparing papers to convince the President of the merits of the plan. Marshall's particular friend among the British military establishment was Sir John Dill, who had on several occasions spoken up for Wavell, whose African triumphs had already excited the admiration of both Marshall and the President. For that and for various political reasons, Marshall had concluded that Wavell was the man to fill the post he had in mind, and he had little difficulty in persuading the President to agree.

What may have struck the Americans, and what occurred to the British, was that the proposed ABDACOM area would almost certainly be a lost cause, with little chance of stemming the Japanese onrush or of regaining the initiative in the foreseeable future. Whoever was placed in command would therefore be likely to find himself the 'fall-guy', as the Americans put it, and 'it was almost certain that he would have to bear a load of defeat in a scene of confusion'.[32] Churchill and the British Ambassador, Lord Halifax, were as sceptical as the Chiefs of Staff when they heard of the idea, and in the ensuing discussions there emerged the faint suspicion that the American proposal might have stemmed from a preference that the consequences of any disaster should sit upon British shoulders rather than upon their own. Whether for that or more reputable reasons, Roosevelt insisted that the commander should be British, and that Wavell was the man: there was no suitable American available, he claimed, except General Douglas MacArthur, and it was out of the question to move him from his current command in the Philippines. Meanwhile the new CIGS noted in his diary that the whole scheme was 'wild and half baked'.

The plain fact was that the Americans had become the paymasters of the British Empire, and were beginning to take the paramount position in what had finally become a world war. So now Roosevelt persuaded Churchill, and he in turn convinced the Chiefs of Staff. Dill had also doubted the idea of one commander, 'but when,' he told Wavell, 'the President and Marshall asked for you by name there was nothing more to be done about it'.[33] With ABDACOM they would brook no argument.

It was only six months since Wavell had become commander-in-chief in India and, having begun to instil some order into its defences, he had taken on Burma too. Yet now he was to move to an entirely different project. He could hardly expect any personal glory from it, and it was a complete surprise, as he told Hutton, to come back from a day's pig-sticking in the Kadir to find a telegram from the Prime Minister telling him to take over the command.

It would be an arduous, wide-ranging, thankless task, but duty called and he answered without demur or delay. Wavell was to defend an area of twelve million square miles, 2,500 miles from north to south, and stretching 5,000 miles around a crescent from Burma to New Guinea, a line three times as long as the Russian front. Over that whole area the Japanese were advancing like a spring tide, submerging a huge tract of scattered islands and peninsulas, far apart and hardly defended, and threatening to expose both India and Australia to overwhelming attack. Opposing them were the meagre forces at Wavell's disposal: 'a confusion of races, religions, and national interests, violently assaulted by a tidal wave of fanatics of one race, one religion, one allegiance and one common purpose'.[34]

Effectively ABDACOM fell into three divisions: the mainland of Burma and Malaya; the archipelago that formed the Dutch East Indies; and the south-eastern islands that stretched down to Australasia. The challenge on the mainland was to prevent the Japanese invading before the troops already there were driven so far back that reinforcements would be useless. The chain of islands could not, Wavell believed, be long defended, and the only possible strategy was to try and gain time for reinforcements to arrive before the enemy reached the main bases of Java and Sumatra in the west, or Australia in the south. It was a bleak outlook, but at least in the Philippines resistance was proving successful, as General MacArthur held fast on the Bataan peninsula.

Before leaving India for this great new adventure, Wavell broadcast a magisterial New Year's message, lamenting the 'red, stormy dawn' and castigating those who had plunged the world into a war more widespread than any in mankind's history:

> We can name the nations who started the fire, Germany and Japan, stupid ill-bred children who have never been properly brought up or learnt good international manners. Their silly little girl friend Italy joined them in hopes of some cheap fun, and now finds herself being taken for a ride with two really bad boys, and that is not going to be cheap for her or much fun. The older and wiser nations who are now putting out this great conflagration ought never to have allowed any of them to play with matches. We had plenty of warning that they meant mischief.[35]

War is hateful and horrible, he concluded, but sometimes brings understanding and progress: 'If we can only keep alive after victory the spirit and energy that war brings to a virile nation, and can direct it to the ends of peace and prosperity, we can do great things.'[36]

Wavell left Delhi on 5 January 1942, reaching Singapore two days later.

There he was starkly confronted with the weakness of the British position, in a situation transformed since his visit at the end of October. The commanding officer, General Arthur Percival, had orders to hold Singapore until the arrival of the navy, and for that purpose he had to prevent the enemy from conquering Malaya before Singapore was reinforced; he had said that he would need five divisions and air cover – but he had neither.

Three weeks earlier Duff Cooper, a former member of Neville Chamberlain's Cabinet, had arrived in Singapore as Resident Minister, but Wavell's appointment made the position redundant and Cooper had already been recalled. He had, however, submitted to London a report on the dangers to Singapore caused by its tangle of conflicting authorities. There seemed to be a reckless attitude to the island's situation: no measures of conscription for war work had been introduced, and there was a complete lack of the speed, efficiency or even warnings to the public that the inexorable approach of the Japanese demanded. The civil authorities' view was that any disturbance of normality would cause public morale to collapse – a pernicious view unfortunately shared by General Percival. Having concluded that neither the Governor, Sir Shenton Thomas, nor the Colonial Secretary, Stanley Jones, had the will or the intelligence to take emergency measures, Cooper urged Wavell to appoint a military governor and impose martial law. With so much at stake, it was vital that the civil authorities should be galvanised into action, as it was they who would have to organise a labour force and measures of civil defence. But although Wavell was persuaded that both Thomas and Jones were inadequate, he believed that if they were both sacked the confidence of civilians and troops would fall to a dangerous degree. He settled for removing Jones.

The occasion demanded much more than preserving a bureaucratic façade, since Britain was clearly failing the needs of the island's million civilians to whom the Empire owed the duty of protection. As Supreme Commander, Wavell was vested with the overriding authority to impose his will, and with one sweep of his sword he could have cut through the tape and imposed martial law. Yet he demurred, and the authorities continued with their normal lives and duties, closing their minds to the battle raging a few hundred miles to the north and drawing nearer each day. Reality began to dawn in the offices of Singapore only with the arrival of reports that white captives of the Japanese, to whom it had been assumed the Geneva Convention would apply, were being bound and used for bayonet practice and treated no differently from the natives.

On 8 January Wavell flew up to Kuala Lumpur and went to the Indian corps HQ. There he met the commander, Sir Lewis Heath, who was taut and grey with fatigue as he tried to sort out the havoc following the disaster that had befallen his troops the previous day, when Japanese medium tanks had swarmed through the 11th Indian Division at the Slim River and almost annihilated it. Then Wavell visited one of the divisional headquarters, before driving further north to visit some brigades. All around him there were alarming developments. The imperial forces, confused by the enemy's tactics, had been driven back continuously for a month and now seemed to be on a course that would finish in Singapore itself. Almost all the men were tired, depressed and lethargic, disorientated by the sprawling jungle, frightened by indiscriminate bombing and attacked from front, flanks and rear.

They also lacked essential equipment. In one division, of the complement of 1,400 anti-tank mines, only twenty-four had been issued to meet a tank attack. However, while retreating before the Japanese they had made a series of stands, setting up road-blocks in the hope of delaying the enemy who was fast pursuing them. The Japanese, pouring down the open roads in tanks and buses, would for a brief moment be brought up short. Then the din of battle would erupt – tanks head to tail, engines roaring, crews shouting, grenades flying, machine-guns spitting, mines exploding, mortars pumping, cannon firing. The enemy would either punch their way through or recoil, vanish into the trees and move down the flanks. They had soon learnt how to advance through jungle and had proved it by crossing Malaya's mountain spine, which the British had thought impassable. The scent of success was quickening their thrust, spurred on by their commander, General Tomoyuki Yamashita, a superb commander but a man who, although taking more care than most of his colleagues to keep the troops under control, was neverthe-less a barbarous thug.

The enemy had already disembarked a large number of tanks, while the imperial forces had very few. Equipped with light automatic weapons and mortars, and using no artillery except that which they captured, the invaders moved swiftly through the jungle on foot or on bicycles.[37] Lightly clad, and living off sparse rations of rice and dried fish, they were masters of the terrain, able to manoeuvre their tanks deftly through the well-spaced rubber trees. The imperial forces, on the other hand, weighed down with heavy 'corner-shop' food and unsuitable kit, were short of maps and compasses, had few radios and moved mainly in motor transport, as they could be controlled by their officers only if they stayed on the roads. It did not take the enemy long to see what was happening, and they began to bomb the roads, which were increasingly clogged with retreating vehicles, or simply to advance through the jungle on either side.

The flanking movement was something of which the Japanese now revealed their mastery. By professional and imaginative training they had learnt the technique of moving part of an attacking force rapidly and secretly through the jungle and appearing behind their enemy, closing in from both front and rear, and often from the flank as well, and causing the ponderous British troops the utmost alarm and despondency. On their advance down the Malayan peninsula the Japanese were able to speed up this process by carrying troops along the coast in an array of fishing boats and other coastal craft that they pressed into service, repeatedly landing behind the retreating front line. The process became known as the 'hook', and both in Malaya and in due course in Burma numerous units of the imperial forces found themselves well and truly hooked.

Apprised of the situation, Wavell issued orders for the soldiers' kit to be lightened and for unnecessary transport to be moved out of the battle areas, but there was little more that he could do immediately. Many of the newly arrived troops were equipped for other theatres of war; they were also unfit, having had a three-month voyage before being immediately sent up to forward camps concealed in the jungle, where their general dejection was increased by the lack of sunlight. Of the men who had served in Malaya for a number of years, many now discovered that their erstwhile fighting abilities had succumbed to the enervating Malayan climate.

The Japanese had gained the paramount advantage of air supremacy by destroying the meagre RAF forces both in the air and on their airfields. Since the opening days of the campaign they had commanded the skies, and had relentlessly pushed south, sailing down the coast, capturing airfields, crossing rivers, securing bridges, taking towns, ransacking villages, burning, killing and destroying as they went, and maintaining momentum partly by leapfrogging units so that fresh troops were always on hand to replace those that had become tired or reduced by casualties. Many of the defending troops fought well, and sometimes heroically, but as casualties mounted they began to lose faith both in the higher command and in themselves. The continuous lack of air cover had a cumulatively depressing effect on the imperial forces, whose difficulties were compounded by GHQ's inability to find naval support to prevent the enemy moving down the coast and landing behind them. Nor could they deploy sufficient armour and artillery to halt the advancing tanks;

so the retreat gathered pace – towards Johore, Malaya's southernmost state, beyond which lay Singapore. The years of peace had been squandered, and as those of the country's helpless inhabitants who were not killed or maimed watched the imperial armies retreat, jeering 'Orang Puteh Hari'[38] as they did so, they were witnessing also the incipient recession of the British Empire itself.

The Supreme Commander now intervened in the tactics of the operations. His immediate problem was the near-annihilation of 11th Division on the Slim River. Once he had seen the situation for himself, Wavell sketched out his intentions for a series of unit movements designed to remove weak troops from the point of impact with the enemy, establish a line further back and man it with troops who he hoped would be sufficiently fresh and experienced to halt the Japanese advance while the defences of Singapore were made good. Central Malaya, he accepted, was probably no longer tenable. Ordering an accelerated withdrawal of III Corps to Johore, he hoped that the pursuing enemy would expose his extended lines of communication to what remained of the RAF.

Having flown back to Singapore, Wavell sent his impressions to the Chiefs of Staff in London. The crisis required a swift response, but speed had to be matched with sound decisions – and ruthlessness. It would be crucial to stop the Japanese in Johore, so he constructed a new plan for its defence, establishing a front that ran from the west coast at Muar to the east coast at Mersing. He went into considerable detail, setting out directions for control and movement not only for the corps HQ, but also for divisions and even brigades. He then took the apparently impulsive decision to entrust field command to the Australian general, Gordon Bennett: it was to prove a lamentable choice.

Wavell's overall plan was more or less the opposite of that concocted by GHQ Malaya Command. Nevertheless he summoned Percival, handed over the plan and ordered him to implement it. Wavell's actions hardly suggested that he had confidence in the general, and it was clear that a strong hand was needed. But if he did not approve of what he found, the appropriate course might have been to relieve Percival – and in General Pownall he had on hand a tried and trusted alternative. Yet Wavell held back from those stern actions. At least his presence, his swift appreciation of the situation and his direct response put some energy into his subordinates and gave the boost to morale and confidence that comes with clear instructions. In the face of Japanese supremacy, however, the effect was to be short-lived.

Yet the fact that the Supreme Commander of the whole of ABDACOM, with a headquarters – still incomplete – thousands of miles away in Java, was issuing orders down to brigade level recalled the detailed directives that Wavell had himself received in Cairo, to his displeasure, from Churchill in London. With a general officer commanding in Malaya, a corps commander, three divisional commanders and sundry brigade commanders all on the same pitch, it was arguably an unwise procedure. Interference with the established chain of command risked confusion, besides disorientating the various commanders. But confusion was already widespread, and perhaps an incisive set of instructions from the highest authority seemed the quickest way of dispersing it.

Although his was the only viable scheme, Wavell's directive meant abandoning a large tract of Malaya in the hope of gaining time to establish a defendable line. Unfortunately, it left wide open to the Japanese the relatively good road system that led through the southern states of Malaya, enabling them to advance with two divisions instead of one. Within a few days they were barely 200 miles from Singapore.

Wavell now turned to the urgent problem of the island's landward defences. A decade and a half earlier he had himself been on the committee charged with planning Singapore's development, but now he found that little effective work had been done since. The great naval base had been constructed, but there was no navy for it to shelter, and the harbour was undefended on its landward side. Mighty guns had been installed, but they were designed to repel attack from the sea, and were quite useless for repelling a land attack: although they could traverse to points inland, their flat trajectory and armour-piercing ammunition would hardly delay an infantry advance. Nor did the general in command dispel doubt or fear. Whatever his merits – he was a clever man and had made a name in the savage war against Sinn Fein during the 'Troubles' in Ireland – the chinless Percival had neither the character nor the appearance to inspire in times of crisis. 'One could almost shoot snipe off him,' observed Wavell's ADC, in an apt, if threadbare, expression.

On 9 January Wavell took this white-kneed general to inspect the island's northern defences. They were pitiable. Singapore's Chief Engineer, Brigadier Ivan Simson, was an able, determined man, full of fierce ideas for the island's defence; his brain bubbled with trenches, tank traps, fire trips, sky-lights, pillboxes, sunken traps, floating wire, lines of fire and many a colourful, nasty jar for the odious Jap. Yet Percival had forbidden him to put any of them in place, holding that the morale of both the army and civilians would wilt if they knew that defences were being built on the island itself. When Wavell heard of this he was shaken, and for a moment his habitual calm gave way to anger. He dismissed the morale argument out of hand, pointedly suggesting to Percival that it would be very much worse for morale if thousands of Japanese swarmed across the causeway onto the island itself. He ordered that defences be constructed at once.

Even now Wavell could have gone one step further and sacked the general. He must have doubted Percival's ability to rise to the occasion, even if supplied with clear instructions. He had the knowledge, Wavell told General Pownall, but not the personality to carry through a tough fight. Yet there was no one to replace him. Having already overruled Percival's plan, Wavell himself had to give orders for the island's defence. Sir Lewis Heath, commanding Indian III Corps to the north-west, could not be spared from delaying the enemy's advance. Nor could the fiery Australian, Gordon Bennett: although Wavell was impressed by his insistence that his troops were skilled and fit and raring to fight, his 8th Australian Division was now in its reserve position in Johore and could not sensibly be moved.

The dangers of making a change at such a moment seemed to Wavell too great to risk, and they reinforced his habitual reluctance to demote commanders, even if apparently incompetent. So Sir Shenton Thomas and General Percival each retained their posts. To sack or support was a hard decision for Wavell, but for a Supreme Commander it was vital to make the correct choice of subordinate generals. Now that the battlefront was likely to be widened by an enemy thrust into Burma, it is a wonder that he left Hutton in charge in Rangoon, when General Pownall, his chief of staff at ABDACOM, was clearly better suited for that post too. Hutton was not a naturally vigorous leader, and his state of mind had been numbed by the shock he had just suffered in an aeroplane crash, in which he had very bravely beat out a fire with his greatcoat and dragged to apparent safety a pilot so badly burnt that he died soon afterwards.

Meanwhile, far to the east of the battered brigades in Malaya, 30,000 Americans were beleaguered in the Philippines, but bravely supported by a Filipino army fired equally by ghastly tales of Japanese atrocities and by the promise of independence from America. By now this army was down to only fifty rounds per rifle, yet an orderly withdrawal was in process, towards well-placed defence positions on the island bastion of Corregidor, at the entrance to Manila Bay, and on the Bataan peninsula. The US commander, General

Douglas MacArthur, had carefully chosen these sites as offering the one chance of repelling the Japanese, even with their superior numbers. If he met with success he might yet preserve the vital link with Australia.

These various armies, thousands of miles apart, and the forces in between, were all under Wavell's direction, and it was time for him to complete his headquarters. He would still have a major disadvantage: the immense size of his command was to mean that he could pay only short, sporadic visits to its various parts, and, as happened, none at all to the far Philippines. This drawback was compounded by his lack of intelligence about enemy intentions, and by an as yet inadequate understanding of Japanese strength and skills.

Wavell flew down to Java, where ABDACOM was to be established, initially in the Hotel des Indes, Batavia. Remote as were his surroundings, at least he had the pleasure of one familiar face – that of his daughter Felicity, who, leaving her mother and sisters in India, had followed the drum and taken a post in the cipher office. Archie John meanwhile was also in India, training with his regiment.

In the Dutch East Indies, Java itself was the ultimate enemy goal, with its fertile farmland and abundant minerals, its seat of government and the only naval base within a great distance. Yet Wavell found there, to defend this nerve-centre of his command, a motley force of one American field-gun regiment, twenty-five light tanks and three anti-tank regiments whose equipment had all been sunk. The Dutch, in defence of the jewel of their imperial crown, offered seventeen battalions and a few warplanes apparently dating from the dawn of flying history. In all, out of a population of forty million, they had raised the princely total of 50,000 men.

Against this featherweight assortment, the enemy, it was estimated, could muster 1,300 aircraft, almost unlimited naval resources and the pick of an army of seventy-two divisions, twenty-six of which were already in the south-west Pacific.

Wavell considered the position. Supported by the leaders of the Allied forces, he established a routine of two conferences a day, at which broad strategy could be reviewed in the light of daily reports from the various fronts, intermittent and confusing as they were to prove. Thereafter a staff conference would implement the Supreme Commander's directions. He had notionally divided his command into three sectors, to make some sense of its size and to reflect the apparent strategy of his adversaries. In the north, the complaisance of Siam and the occupation of Indo-China had given the enemy a firm base, which solved for them the difficulty of long sea communications with Japan itself. In the east, the enemy were battering the American and Filipino armies with greatly superior numbers, but as yet unsuccessfully. And further south, they had already landed in Borneo and the Celebes.

He pondered the possible enemy strategies: to contain the Chinese, who were attacking towards Canton and threatening to move south from Yunnan; to overrun Malaya and Singapore, and assault Burma from the south; and to capture the Philippine Islands and the chain of British and Dutch islands that stretched away to Australia. As he looked at his maps Wavell discerned a pattern of four separate advances, with the enemy attacking airfields in southern Borneo and Celebes; Timor, the refuelling base for air reinforcements from Australia to Java; and Amboina, within reach of New Guinea.

Hong Kong had fallen, Singapore was threatened, the northern islands were in enemy hands, the Philippines besieged. Yet Wavell's inner spirit seemed untroubled. 'Bless you,' he said to General Pownall, 'we will see this thing through, or do our best, or something.' Meanwhile he had to assess what reinforcements were needed, persuade the War Cabinet to provide them, decide where each component was required, arrange the details of its delivery and give directions to the commanders in the field, ensuring that they kept abreast of changing circumstances. Most importantly, he must establish a communications system through which his headquarters could receive timely information on which to act. Meanwhile, to make the whole enterprise possible, he had to select points at which to concentrate his force, defend airfields on which his aircraft could land, guard his sources of oil and food, and protect the sea lanes through which his supplies and forces could move.

To achieve all or even any of that, Wavell would have to delay the Japanese advance. He was in a race against time. The paramount difficulty was shipping; the Americans were grappling with the dire problem of how to achieve the necessary steep reductions in loading and transit time from the US to the Pacific. 'It's a difficult and complicated show to run,' he told Hutton, 'at the moment there is nothing one can do except sit and wait for reinforcements, and wonder whether they will be in time.'[39]

Having ordered the army in Malaya to disengage and regroup in the south of the peninsula, Wavell now decided to concentrate attacks on enemy airfields and shipping. Although he planned to fight forward in the northern islands – the Moluccas, Celebes, Dutch Borneo and northern Sumatra – he decided, contrary to the wishes of the Dutch and the Americans, not to reinforce them. Instead he called for a line of defence further south, to stretch from Port Darwin in Australia, via Timor and Java to southern Sumatra, and including Singapore, the focal point of the whole Malay Barrier. If that vital fortress fell, the enemy could seize control both of the Indian and the Pacific Oceans and move west to attack India's eastern seaboard and Ceylon. That would raise the spectre that Wavell had long feared, of the Axis powers linking hands in the Middle East, to form an iron chain stretching unbroken from New Zealand to the Channel Islands.

On 15 January 1942, some two weeks after he had received his great commission, ABDACOM was formally established. After days of delay while telephone lines were laid, he moved its headquarters from the sticky heat of Batavia and raised his standard at the Grand Hotel, Lembang, some ten miles into the hills. There at least conditions were conducive to planning and discussion. In the afternoons he would go for a peaceful walk with his ADC, preserving his serenity in matters great and small despite the incessant and growing problems of command:

He even figures out for quite an appreciable time whether he will take his hat with him on a trip, but the decision once made he will not change, and it does not take him much longer to decide to do something really important, like the move of a division.[40]

From the start Wavell commanded respect and admiration, but he had to sterilise international infections. The Dutch were hurt at not being consulted about ABDACOM; the American naval commander, Admiral Hart, with his 'anti-Limey' instincts, did not relish the US Navy coming under the direction of a British general; and the Australian Government was rapidly becoming strongly anti-British, dismayed that their forces were far from their homeland, invasion of which was moving from the unthinkable via the possible to the probable.

Singapore was the linchpin in Wavell's strategy for defending the whole Malay Barrier, and his plans were predicated on the island being able to hold out for three months. Yet as the Japanese continued to forge southward, there arose a dreadful doubt about Singapore itself. On 20 January Wavell flew up once more to order a reluctant Percival to plan for a retreat to the island if the Johore front could not be held. Having already found it necessary to issue a series of instructions to Percival, it might have been wise to ascertain whether they were being properly executed, but Wavell carried out no personal inspection of what improvements (if any) had actually been made to the island's landward defences. Instead he turned at once to considering the alternative directions from which an attack might develop. As there were not enough troops to defend the whole of the seventy-mile front across the north of the island, a major risk had to be taken in deciding where to establish strongholds. Wavell believed that the north-west, although swampy land broken by rivers and creeks, would be the enemy's likely direction of approach. Percival disagreed, proposing instead to deploy his freshest troops, including part of the newly arrived British 18th Division, in the north-east sector.

Although he had previously overruled Percival several times, Wavell now deferred to the decision of the man on the spot. It is hard to see why, or to avoid imagining how swiftly General Montgomery, for example, might have sent Percival packing. Moreover, on this occasion Wavell's insight was to prove absolutely correct, and Percival's calamitously wrong. Had he enforced his view, as he had with Neame in the desert, Wavell's forces would have been in position directly on the line taken by the Japanese, and it is just possible that in that case the enemy would have been delayed long enough for the island to be defended until more reinforcements and, eventually, the Royal Navy arrived. Yet Wavell did not feel sure enough to deny to the commander on the spot the freedom to decide his own tactics.

He had already fixed upon the causes of the unhappy way that the campaign had developed: lack of vigour in peacetime training, cumbrous tactics and equipment, and the difficulty of matching Japanese skill in jungle fighting. Under no illusions, he now sent a warning to the Prime Minister: 'I am anxious,' he wrote, 'that you should not have false impression of defences of Singapore Island. I did not realise myself until lately how entirely defences were planned against seaward attack only.'[41] He knew that Percival must now be prepared for a breach of the defences that he had ordered for the north of the island, which might lead to the loss of Singapore's vital reservoirs. That thought had also occurred to the Chiefs of Staff in London, which had already warned Wavell that a lack of water had forced Hong Kong's surrender, and had pointedly asked whether Singapore might face a similar danger.

However, urgent and crucial as this was, Singapore was only one of several imminent threats that Wavell had now to meet. All across his command, except where MacArthur was holding his ground in the Philippines, the enemy was advancing unchecked. Japanese aircraft were attacking along an immense front all the way from New Britain, off Papua New Guinea in the furthermost south-east, to Burma in the north-west. Even MacArthur had to appeal urgently to Washington for help, and he warned Wavell that his ammunition was dwindling. The Australian Government – and press – already incensed by talk of evacuating Singapore, were further dismayed by news that their soldiers had been driven from their positions in the north of New Britain, uncomfortably close to Australia itself.

Now the enemy attack began to widen on yet another front, as reports started belatedly to confirm rumours that Japanese troops had crossed the Siamese border, were pouring into Burma and had already taken airfields within range of the all-important port of Rangoon, lifeline of the Chinese armies. A succession of signals began to arrive from General Hutton, pleading for reinforcements. Wavell, trying to control his several fronts from far-off Java, had little to offer. While he sympathised with Hutton's plight, he questioned why the Japanese seemed to be winning what he considered to be cheap victories, amid a series of hasty British withdrawals. Resolute himself, he expected his commanders and troops to be likewise. His reaction to news of setbacks was incredulity, followed by a demand for immediate improvement. This stance epitomised the opinion he had held for some time, and could not yet bring himself to amend, that the Japanese were, if not a rabble, then an enemy that imperial forces, stoutly led and properly organised, should have no difficulty in repelling. Events were soon to persuade him otherwise: that he was faced with greater skills than he had anticipated, compounded by a malaise among his own forces that he had not previously experienced. Meanwhile, he puzzled over the unexplained movements of the flags on his map.

The reports from Burma certainly began to paint an alarming picture, and it was clear that Wavell would have to see for himself what was going wrong. On 23 January he flew the 2,000 miles up to Rangoon. Several weeks previously he had given General Hutton a clear directive that his forces were to be deployed as far forward as possible, in order to cover a wide front – in fact several hundred miles – blocking all the possible approaches. On arrival he found that Hutton had failed to do that, and had instead allowed the bulk of his forces to withdraw from their forward positions around Moulmein and Martapan. They were now in the area of the Salween River, the first of three rivers between Moulmein and Rangoon, two of which offered formidable lines of defence, even in the dry season. Once more he urged Hutton to fight forward and to exhort his forces to stand their ground.

Ominous as were the developments in Burma, the pressure further south was becoming critical. By 25 January a hundred Japanese aircraft a day were taking off from captured RAF airfields and attacking Singapore, and after repeated damage to its aeroplanes on the ground, the very existence of the air force there was now in question. Wavell therefore ordered the remaining bombers and their base units to withdraw to Sumatra and Java, and from there to attack the Malayan airfields from which the air raids were being launched.

On 30 January, the day Johore Bahru was abandoned, and when a general air of resignation among the British was replaced by the more excitable sounds of widespread looting, Wavell flew once more to meet Percival. He was shocked to find that although there now seemed no alternative to withdrawing the army to the island itself, there had still been almost no progress in constructing the landward defences. Then he went up to confer with the two generals in the field, and agreed that all remaining troops should retreat onto Singapore Island, after which the causeway would be breached. The fight for the mainland could no longer be sustained, and twenty-four hours later the Japanese were in control of the whole of Malaya.

The enemy had nearly 70,000 combat troops at the ready, and outmatched the defenders by a proportion of four to one in the air. Now they faced Singapore itself. Wavell had somehow to inspire his troops to stand firm and defend the island, without knowing from which direction it might be attacked – although he himself believed that they were being deployed in the wrong sector. If they could regain a proper fighting spirit, it might conceivably be possible to encourage the million or so civilians on the island to contribute to its defence.[42] It was an uphill task: civil morale had collapsed, affecting the spirits of the soldiers; nor could police orders have inspired a fight to the last: 'In the event of the fall of this Fortress, HE instructs that the civil population could best be served by placing our organisation at the disposal of the Japanese commander, should he wish to make use of it.'[43]

It was far from the spirit of 1940, when Churchill urged his Cabinet Ministers to die 'choking in their own blood' rather than surrender.

The Chinese element had the will to resist, born of a venomous dislike of the Japanese, and some had gone to fight as guerrillas in the north; but they had not been formally trained or armed, and that was now too late to rectify. The loyalties of the rest of the population were uncertain: the Indian elements remained essentially non-belligerent, in conformity with the ethos of their Hindu teachers, while the native population of Malaya had so far proved completely uninterested in the war, or in the fate of their imperial masters. The outlook was also complicated by the presence of sullen, armed deserters skulking in the city, looting and hiding in bomb-proof buildings, while parties of newly arrived, untrained troops, their morale non-existent, had forced their way onto ships or seized small boats in which to flee.

Wavell also faced the hard question of whether reinforcements drawing near should now be diverted, and whether any of the existing garrison should be sent away. Until now he had assumed that a vigorous stand would enable the island to hold out until rescue arrived – at some point, from somewhere – and day by day further units, including Australians and the balance of the British 18th Division, had continued to arrive at the port. Now the first faint doubt arose as to whether they should have come after all. On the other hand, he believed that diverting forces finally approaching Singapore would be a death-knell for those already there and a terrible signal to a watching world. It was also clear that troopships attempting to slip out through the narrow approaches would be vulnerable to heavy air and naval attack. Further, he had already withdrawn the bombers from Singapore, and a considerable number of fighters, including some modern Hurricanes, were now on nearby Sumatra: there was at least a chance of a valiant air defence.

Wavell was also being pressed by the Prime Minister. Informed by the CIGS that with 100,000 men in Singapore, Percival had a much larger army than his enemy, Churchill was determined that the battle should be fought to the bitter end: '. . . the whole reputation of our country and our race is involved. It is expected that every unit will be brought into close contact with the enemy and fight it out.'[44]

Wavell agreed: there could be no question of ceding further ground. He told Percival:

> I look upon you and your men to fight to the end and prove that the fighting spirit that won our Empire still exists to enable us to defend it. There must be no thought of sparing the troops or the civilian popu-lation and no mercy must be shown to any weakness. Commanders and senior officers must lead their troops and, if necessary, die with them. Every unit must fight it out to the end and in close contact with the enemy.[45]

While both Wavell and the War Cabinet were insisting on an unflinching defence, Percival received a message from General Yamashita 'based on the spirit of Japanese chivalry', advising him to surrender the whole of his forces in Malaya. It was not yet a tempting suggestion, and neither the basis nor the advice was considered deserving of a reply. Yet the increasingly fraught outlook was beginning to cause dissension even among the soldiers at the top: when Heath and Bennett both suggested that their forces could no longer fight, Percival responded that it was a matter of honour that they continue to do so, to which General Heath observed, 'You need not bother about your honour. You lost that a long time ago, up in the north.'[46]

Wavell now had to make a fundamental personal decision: whether to take command in Singapore himself, and if necessary die fighting with his men. Both his inclination and his sense of obligation pointed that way, but he was forced to conclude that his great responsibilities – for many thousands of men of different nations, spread over millions of square miles – ruled out that option. He would not be doing his duty if he allowed himself to be killed or captured. So he set off once more for his headquarters, but in the black of the night he suffered a painful accident: his car stopped on the quay where he was to board a seaplane for Java and, walking a few yards from the car, he fell off the edge and heavily onto barbed wire and concrete below. Reid Scott, his ADC, who like his chief had lost an eye in battle, was not with him, and later reproached himself that had he been there, he would have had the instinct to ensure that Wavell did not get out of a car on his blind side. In considerable pain, the Supreme Commander reached Java the next morning and was confined to bed for four days; he then discharged himself from hospital and returned to his headquarters – to the 'scandal', as he put it, of his anxious doctors.

Shortly afterwards the Japanese vanguard crossed the Singapore straits and battle for the island itself was joined. Almost continuously, formations of thirty Japanese aeroplanes dropped bombs and anti-personnel mines on soldiers and civilians alike, while heavy shelling started a series of fires on the embarkation quays – a further source of discouragement; the will to resist began to fray. Anticipating a desperate climax, Wavell had issued Percival with an Order of the Day, leaving him to decide whether to publish it, but to ensure that its message reached his commanders:

It is certain that our troops in Singapore Island greatly outnumber any Japanese who have crossed the Straits. We must destroy them. Our fighting reputation is at stake, and the honour of the British Empire. The Americans have held out in the Bataan Peninsula against far heavier odds, the Russians are turning back the picked strength of the Germans, the Chinese with an almost complete lack of modern equipment have held the Japanese for 4½ years. It would be disgraceful if we yield our boasted fortress of Singapore to inferior forces.[47]

It was a pointed and stirring message, issued in extreme circumstances; its inspiration was betrayed by its Churchillian language, and whether it flowed easily from the pen of the quiet Wykehamist may be questioned. Nor was it universally appreciated by his forces: the Australians were infuriated, and a number of commanders declined to issue it to officers and men whom they knew had already fought bravely against superior odds. Wavell might have recalled his own dictum that a general should only address his troops if he has a gift of saying the right thing: 'An unfortunate remark or tone, or even appearance, may lower his stock and do more harm than good.'[48] But he knew that he had to dispel all thoughts of surrender; even when Percival signalled that his troops could no longer either counter-attack or withstand a strong attack from the enemy, and that they were in danger of being cut off without food and water, Wavell ordered them to persevere, from house to house if necessary – where there was enough water, they must fight on.

On 14 February Churchill finally relented and gave Wavell the discretion to decide – if he thought that further fighting would achieve no results – to allow Percival to ask for an armistice. Even so, Wavell still urged resistance, saying that the gallant stand was serving its purpose and must be continued to the limits of endurance. But later that day Percival signalled that enemy action had, as the Chiefs of Staff had feared, practically exhausted all stocks of water, petrol, food and ammunition, and that resistance could no longer be maintained. As the loss of the fortress became inevitable, Wavell gave Percival discretion to cease firing if he felt that nothing more could be achieved.

On 15 February 1942, at 8.30 p.m., London time, Singapore was surrendered. The gates of the fortress drew back, revealing to an incredulous Japanese soldiery nearly 100,000 able-bodied men. It was exactly one month since the birth of ABDACOM.

In a situation that from the start had looked doubtful at the very least, it is fair to say that by his visits to the front Wavell's calm and rugged presence did project a degree of confidence and determination among many of the troops. There were exceptions, however: it would be strange to conclude, for example, that his repeated interference with Percival did anything other than sap whatever confidence that unfortunate commander still retained.

On the other hand, it is just possible that, as Supreme Commander, Wavell might have defended both Malaya and Singapore for longer. Had he not underestimated how effective Japanese combat groups could be, especially in close country; had he replaced commanders in whom he did not have confidence; had he issued a broad plan offering the best chance of withstanding the enemy advance, and then held to the conventional policy of a commander-in-chief not interfering in the tactics of the campaign, he might just have held out. It seems unlikely. He simply did not have forces strong enough to repel such a determined enemy, and probably nothing that he could have done would have kept the Japanese out. Besides, the fundamental premise of Singapore's existence was to guard a fleet and, as it turned out, there was none to guard.

In fact ABDACOM was a poisoned chalice, and Singapore its most bitter ingredient. Considering that its fall – more than anything else – tolled the knell of the British Empire, any imperial servant associated with it, especially in high places, must have fervently wished it had all been a dream. 'In all professions,' Wavell had written of Allenby, 'and especially in the military, character is of greater importance than brains or experience.'[49] Neither Wavell's brains nor his experience were sufficient to avert disaster in the Far East; but his character at least allowed him to withstand the shock.

Across the rest of Wavell's wide command events were increasing in speed and intensity. Barely one week later the last rites were administered to ABDACOM itself, and Wavell resumed his post as commander-in-chief in India. The triumphant Japanese swept on, in the Pacific almost to the shores of Australia, and, to the north, deep into the heart of Burma.

XIII

NIL DESPERANDUM

WAVELL had conceived a fourfold strategy for ABDACOM: to erect a barrier along the 5,000-mile front, to stabilise it, to retard Japanese momentum until reinforcements arrived and then to plan a counter-offensive. However, the loss of Singapore forced him to review the position, and brought into sharp focus the broad image of the battlefront. Japanese tactics were proving highly successful, with their rolling pattern of selecting a target, winning the ground, landing reinforcements, establishing airfields, launching air cover and advancing to the next target. Wavell had attempted to erect a barrier, but now it was down: breached in Malaya, submerged in Singapore, battered in the Philippines and being bent in Burma. From Singapore it was a short step to Sumatra and another to Java, and from there the enemy was effectively within reach of Australia.

The loss of the rubber from Malaya and the East Indies was a body blow to the Empire's ability to maintain its forces – in Britain rubber was now more tightly controlled than petrol – and the question of oil supplies had also become urgent. If the enemy took Java and Sumatra, the two largest islands in the chain, the Allied forces would have no reserves of oil between America and the Persian Gulf save those in Burma. If that fell, Australia and New Zealand would have no oil at all, except such as could be transported to them by sea, which Japanese naval supremacy rendered a precarious prospect. So if Wavell could not save all of his command, he must at least turn to its most vital points – Burma and Australia.

Burma was vital to the defence of India, not only for its precious natural resources, but also because through it ran part of the 715-mile Burma Road, which stretched from Kunming in China to Lashio in northern Burma, where it linked up with the route winding south to Mandalay and thence down the gigantic River Irrawaddy to Rangoon. The Burma Road was crucial to Allied strategy; it was the only route by which Chiang Kai-shek could be supplied with the equipment he needed for his three vital objectives: containing the fifteen to twenty Japanese divisions already in China; disrupting from the north an invasion of Burma from the east; and allowing the establishment of a base from which, eventually, to attack the Japanese homeland itself.[1]

The loss of Sumatra and Java was now a probability, jeopardising the whole chain of Pacific islands and raising the question of where Wavell should direct the reinforcements that were now slowly sailing towards him. He had already diverted the battle-hardy 7th Armoured Brigade to Burma, but the 6th and 7th Australian Divisions and the British 70th Division were still on their way from the Middle East. One Australian division had been ordered to Sumatra, on which the Japanese had already landed, and the other was destined for Java. Now he feared that it would arrive too late. He calculated that his air strength was down to fewer than 140 aircraft, against which the enemy could muster nearly 900. The gulf between the Allied and Japanese naval and land forces was similarly unbridgeable, even allowing for the unpredictable fortunes of war. Drawing the inevitable, unpalatable conclusion that his centre must give, Wavell advised the Chiefs of Staff that it was for America to sustain MacArthur in the Philippines and keep open the supply link to Australia, and that the approaching Australian reinforcements should be diverted to Burma. Once there, they might in due course advance into Indo-China and attack the Japanese, thereby giving vital encouragement both to China and to India.

The more ABDACOM's power waned, the more the momentum of the enemy increased. In brisk succession the Japanese invaded Bali, landed in Timor and even launched a devastating air raid on the mainland of Australia, at Port Darwin. With their mastery of the skies, the enemy were now able to marginalise the Allies' navies and provide air cover for their seemingly unstoppable ground forces. Although Wavell believed that he had lost the race against time by only four to six weeks, he had finally, for now at least, to accept defeat. On 21 February 1942 he wrote to the Prime Minister:

I am afraid that the defence of ABDA area has broken down and that defence of Java cannot now last long. It always hinged on the air battle.[1]

Although he was determined not to give up entirely, and urged that the naval and air reinforcements destined for the Java Sea should continue on their way, to harass Japanese convoys, Wavell saw that he could add little more, and that Java would soon be overrun. So, rather than move his headquarters, as the Chiefs of Staff recommended, he suggested that ABDACOM be dissolved and urged that all resources should be concentrated on saving Burma. Australia would have to rely on American help.

The War Cabinet accepted his bleak assessment and returned Burma to India Command. ABDACOM was finished. With characteristic modesty Wavell took it all on himself: 'I feel I ought to have pulled it off,' he wrote, 'but the dice were rather heavily loaded and the little yellow man threw them with considerable cunning. I hate making excuses. I was given a job and have fallen down on it . . . I think it wanted a bigger man than I have ever pretended to be. So that's that.'[2] To Churchill, he also offered an apology: 'I have failed you and the President here,' he said, 'where a better man might perhaps have succeeded.'[3]

Others thought more highly of Wavell than he appeared to do himself: on 23 February he received a cable from the Prime Minister: 'When you cease to command the ABDA area you should proceed yourself to India, where we require you to resume your position as Commander-in-Chief to carry on the war against Japan from this main base.'[4]

His eminence as a general was not questioned but, perhaps for that reason, he was once more being asked to take charge of a position where the odds were stacked against him, and which might be saved only by the provision of ample force in good time. Even the greatest soldiers risk losing their touch of brilliance if they are too often handed responsibility for conditions that only a miracle could restore. Although Wavell was too good-natured to fret about such matters, if he had to oversee yet another retreat, it would probably impact on his personal prestige.

On 25 February he handed over command of Java to the Dutch and embarked for India. It was two days before the Japanese inflicted a comprehensive defeat on the Allied navies in the Battle of the Java Sea. Even now Wavell's burdens did not disturb his calm: after some hours' flying, his Liberator aircraft caught fire, but when the crew woke him to apprise him of this possible adjustment to his long-term future, he merely enquired if there was anything he could do to put the fire out; when the distraught pilot replied that there was nothing, Wavell responded, 'Well, wake me up if there's anything I can do. I am going to have a little sleep.'[5] Such quiet courage matched Wavell's quintessentially English appearance, yet it was perhaps fortified by a streak of oriental fatalism.

Having seen how the rapid collapse in Malaya had deprived him of the time to deploy reinforcements and defend the south-west Pacific, Wavell was determined to prevent a repeat of the process in Burma. Even before he left Java he had become disturbed by the apparent lack of resistance being shown by Hutton and his forces, and knew well the danger of a defensive, if not a defeatist, mentality spreading through an army. From his distant headquarters the omens did not seem good.

The Japanese had launched their attack on Burma in the middle of January, far earlier than had been expected. Their commander, General Iida, had been directed to capture Rangoon and then move north to Mandalay and the oilfields at Yenangyaung.

The limited intelligence at Wavell's disposal had not picked this up, and had indicated instead that any invasion of Burma would be via the Shan States in the central part of the country. Wavell had consequently established a line of defence to meet that threat, but, believing that the wooded hills along the border with Siam were themselves a natural barrier, he had directed Hutton to fight forward, defending a wide front and closing off all possible approaches from the east. Unfortunately, when the attack did come it was from the south, the surprise being more effective because Wavell, coping with his other heavy responsibilities and with the enemy's rapid advance down Malaya and into Singapore, had not had the opportunity to assess the fighting value of the British and Indian troops in Burma, or of the Burmese division on their northern flank. In the opening operations these troops did not fight quite as well as he had hoped, and the line of defence, too long and thin, was decisively pierced. It was partly for this reason, and being disturbed by reports of troops in full retreat, that on 5 February Wavell had flown to Rangoon. He soon realised that a major offensive was developing, and diverted the 7th Armoured Brigade, the most reliable force within reach, from Singapore.

The British force in the south of Burma consisted of 7,000 men of the 17th Division, under Major-General Sir John Smyth,[6] VC, lately joined by an Indian brigade; it was a raw and unreliable formation, with one part trained and equipped for desert fighting, and the other not trained or equipped for any sort of fighting. The enemy had already captured Moulmein, but from there the approach to Rangoon was barred by three rivers, on each of which Wavell believed his forces ought to be able to make a stand. Yet, incomprehensibly, that did not seem to be happening. In a bewilderingly rapid advance, some 18,000 seasoned Japanese troops had crossed the River Salween and driven the British from Martaban, to the west of that river. Smyth had then withdrawn to the River Bilin, which on the map looked like a defendable line, but which at that time of year was at low water and easily fordable. Wavell had severely berated Hutton for allowing Smyth to retreat even that far; yet now it seemed that his division had abandoned the Bilin too, and Hutton was bleakly signalling not only that his best hope was to hold the line of the Sittang River, even further west (and the last defensive position before Rangoon) but that he feared resistance might collapse there also, in which case the loss of Rangoon itself must be faced.

Wavell read these signals with consternation, as did the CIGS, who confided to his diary: 'Cannot work out why troops are not fighting better. If the army cannot fight better than it is doing at present we shall deserve to lose our Empire.'[7] To Wavell it seemed clear that the men had lost their vigour and determination, and that he must rapidly inspire them. He had already warned the Prime Minister that he was disturbed at the apparent lack of toughness of mind and body, and of fighting spirit, shown by his troops in Malaya, and so far in Burma: it was alien to his whole outlook and to his own personal performance. Yet he knew that he should encourage as well as chastise, and must raise morale by instilling confidence that support and reinforcements were on their way.

Like the commanders under him, Wavell had still not really acknowledged that he was up against a skilful, ferocious enemy. His view was that the Japanese must be faced, and could be halted. He would tolerate no further withdrawal. He signalled to Churchill: 'we have got to fight repeat fight these Japs some time somewhere. Burma is not ideal geographically but represents almost our last chance to show the Japs and the world that we do mean to fight.'[8]

Wavell was determined not to repeat his mistake of failing to spy out the land in Cyrenaica when Rommel first attacked, so now he flew to Burma, a map-reader's hell of high mountains, rain forests, paddy fields, swamps, scrub, desert and vast rivers.[9] On 1 March he reached the headquarters of 17th Division, some fifty miles from Rangoon. Just as at Bellewaarde, twenty-seven years earlier, his decisive and confident presence quickly put heart into his officers in the field, as he sized up the situation and issued clear instructions. Determined to call a halt to repeated withdrawals, he insisted that the present position should be held, not least to win precious time for the 7th

Armoured to disembark at Rangoon and make its way to the battlefield – a process hindered by the fact that all the dockworkers had fled the city.

With the enemy advancing so furiously from the east, Wavell was clear that India's endemic leisurely tempo was no longer acceptable. Once back in Delhi, he called a conference to review the situation within India Command. There were dangers for almost all the areas for which he had become responsible, but it was clear that the most imperative problem was Burma. It seemed that the enemy's immediate purpose in making for Rangoon was to capture airfields from which to protect its lines of supply and reinforcement. Wavell had an equally pressing need for those airfields, to help him push the Japanese back from southern Burma until he was reinforced by land and air from the west, and by Chinese armies from the north. So, only a day after completing a lengthy and arduous journey from the south seas to India and being briefly reunited with his family, he set off once more for Burma, to confer on the spot with the Governor and the officers in command.

Hutton had told Wavell that if no further reinforcements were to be sent to Rangoon, he would begin to demolish its vital installations – stores, pumps, oil, plant and transport. On arrival in Burma, Wavell gave Hutton a severe dressing-down and, with an instinctive dislike of pessimism, directed that the installations must not be destroyed unless they seemed about to fall into enemy hands. Instead, he ordered that Rangoon must be fought for, especially as the imminent arrival of the 7th Armoured might save the day. Wavell's determination and optimism put heart into those remaining in the city. Sir Reginald Dorman-Smith, the Governor of Burma, later described Wavell's arrival as a 'miracle' and said that in those days of doubt, turmoil and the threat of imminent disaster, his air of calm confidence encouraged all who saw him:

> We saw a lot of Wavell, who was always a most welcome guest. He seemed to make a habit of dropping in on Burma whenever things were getting particularly sticky . . . He was a great comfort to us all. He was the personification of confidence and sanity, having that priceless knack of putting everything in its right perspective in the minimum of time and with economy of words . . . His power to detach himself from his immediate surroundings and to concentrate was a wonder to behold. The best appreciation of the situation which I saw him produce was written just before dinner in our drawing-room where some twenty people were chattering away over their gins and sherries.[10]

General Hutton – who, as Auchinleck had predicted, had proved an uninspiring commander – was now removed and replaced by General Sir Harold Alexander. Although many of the troops and commanders were in a state of agitated disarray, there were no two men more unruffled or imperturbable than Wavell and Alexander; the latter's arrival had been preceded by stories of his sangfroid on the beaches at Dunkirk, not least the legend of his commenting approvingly on the quality of his breakfast marmalade as shells and bombs fell all around him.

Wavell's directive to General Alexander was brief: he was not to give up Rangoon without as aggressive a battle as resources permitted; but if it could not be held, he was to extricate his army in order to fight further north. Not an attractive type of order for any commander to receive, and similar in its lack of specific instructions to the all-encompassing briefs issued by War Ministers. Alexander might have preferred a clear instruction that there must be a fight for Rangoon, with reasons given, but that the ultimate requirement was for the army to be preserved. As it happened, Wavell's bold instruction very nearly led to the capture of the entire British force: when Alexander arrived on the scene, he could not see any immediate threat to Rangoon, and so cancelled Hutton's evacuation order. Then, in keeping with the spirit of his instructions, he put in a counter-attack with the armoured brigade and an Indian infantry brigade. It failed, leaving Alexander to realise to his dismay that if he did not immediately abandon Rangoon he would be surrounded. So he hurriedly reinstated Hutton's original order – ignoring the army maxim of 'order, counter-order, disorder' – only to find that in the meantime the Japanese had erected a road-block across his army's only escape route, the road leading north to Prome.

The situation rapidly grew desperate, as tanks repeatedly hurled themselves against the apparently indestructible road-block, in front of which a vast column of transport and troops began to congest, soon stretching along the forty miles of road that led back to the port. The Japanese columns were drawing nearer by the hour, and catastrophe seemed inevitable. There then occurred the most unexpected stroke of luck for the beleaguered army. During the night the enemy commander, unaware that he had caught an immensely valuable fish, and (in the Japanese way) rigidly obedient to the letter of his orders to enter the city from the west, lifted the road-block once his division had passed across the road and proceeded on his way. By dawn the road lay open, allowing the armoured brigade and 17th Division to escape to the north. Had that chance not occurred, Alexander, having only just arrived in

Burma, might have been killed or become a guest of the Japanese, the blame for which would have attached to Wavell.

On 7 March the installations were destroyed, the sky above Rangoon bright from the inferno. The news jolted Wavell, and he cabled Alexander at once for an explanation of 'this very grave step', and for assurance that there had in fact been a battle for the city. Alexander sent back the simple reply that he had been directed to ensure his force was not cut off and destroyed, which in the event he had accomplished, although, as he admitted, 'by a very narrow margin'.[11] One part of the campaign was now over.

With his limited stock of transport aircraft, Wavell did arrange for an airlift of stores from India, and some 9,000 people were evacuated on the return flights. But with Rangoon occupied by the enemy, the RAF had to operate from airfields that had no air-raid warning systems, and as an effective force it was soon destroyed. So for the ground forces there was no air cover as they began a long and perilous march to the north, constantly harassed by an enemy breathing the sweet air of success, whose officers (as they had in Malaya) encouraged their men by allowing them to tie up captured British soldiers, hang them upside down and use them for bayonet practice.

Helplessly attacked from the air, ambushed by an enemy moving swiftly through the enveloping jungle, short of guns and ammunition, confused by Burmese fifth columns, beset by tigers, ticks, hornets, leeches, centipedes, snakes and other noxious inhabitants of the forest, the columns rapidly became depleted. Blackwater fever proved a scourge, and above all mosquitoes, against which British and Indian Army uniforms gave little protection, while stocks of mepacrin, which was essential for combating malaria and as valuable as ammunition itself, were soon exhausted. Slowly the retreating army wound up the Irrawaddy valley and made for Mandalay.

It was a mere three months since the start of the war in the East. Not only had Malaya and Singapore been overrun, but also, on successive days, Rangoon and Java. Nor was there any immediate action that Wavell could take. He could not succour Alexander's army, even had he been able to find worthwhile air or land reinforcements. The loss of Rangoon in the south and the lack of a serviceable road in the north meant that the retreating columns were isolated.

However, before he could turn his full attention to plans for the future, he was ordered to send the Prime Minister a review of the events of the immediate past. On 29 January 1942 – a day which brought news that the Germans had entered Benghazi and that the Japanese were less than twenty miles from Singapore – Churchill had faced a vote of confidence in Parliament. The subsequent fall of Singapore had led to renewed hostility in the Commons, with MPs attributing it to 'the worst strategy since Ethelred the Unready'; Churchill was striving to avoid an official inquiry into the debacle. 'We have so many men in Singapore,' he said, 'so many men – they should have done better.'[12]

'Generally speaking,' Wavell conceded, 'the conduct of operations in Malaya lacked drive, energy and foresight, and in some instances troops did not fight with the skill or determination expected, especially in Singapore. The same applies to the civil administration.'[13]

Wavell confirmed what he had already suggested as the causes of the disasters, and at last revised his opinion of Japanese soldiers, now describing them as an enemy fully armed, trained and disciplined on the continental model, but using the mobility, independence of communications and unorthodox tactics of the savage in thick jungle. It was, he said, 'a well-prepared, enterprising, almost fanatical enemy who had planned operations in detail and was emboldened by success'.[14]

Yet Wavell's confidence remained undimmed, and he reported to Churchill that 'our tails are well up, but not wagging very much as yet'. Back in India, he made a shrewd appointment, summoning General William Slim from a divisional command in Iraq to take on a corps shortly to be formed with its headquarters in Calcutta. He also took the only action that might quickly help the army still in Burma, ordering improvements to the fair-weather jungle track that ran from the Indian frontier across 200 miles of overgrown mountain to the River Chindwin and into central Burma. He could only hope that it might prove a lifeline for Alexander, who was struggling towards him through the jungle.

Meanwhile there had erupted a political threat to India itself. Internal calm in the country was a necessary precondition for erecting a barrier to keep out the Japanese, and a disturbance of the political situation was as dangerous as it was inconvenient. That disturbance arrived on 22 March, in the person of Sir Stafford Cripps: in his way as clever as Wavell, vegetarian, teetotal and a fellow-Wykehamist. At one time England's highest-paid barrister and now Lord Privy Seal, Cripps descended upon Delhi on a momentous mission from the British Government, to present to the Indian political leaders a blueprint for the country's constitutional future. It was also hoped that his mission would be approved in the United States. The British Government, in desperate need of American support, knew that

President Roosevelt was anxious for Britain to make a political gesture to India, and it was with one eye on the Americans that the mission was sent at all.

Even though the Indian Army was now fully arrayed against the Japanese, the battles raging on either side of the subcontinent seemed to be of little interest to the mass of people within it, of whom only about two or three million out of nearly 400 million were actively co-operating with the war effort. For Wavell, this was wholly undesirable: not only could he ill spare troops to deal with internal unrest, but he needed the wholehearted effort of Indians to produce materiel for the army and to provide labour to work on the roads, railways and airfields necessary for preparing an offensive. Now he was compelled to turn from those vital tasks and spend a considerable amount of time closeted with Cripps and the Viceroy, trying to ensure the success of the mission.

Concerting a plan was made more difficult by Cripps himself, who seems to have gone beyond his brief and dealt with matters that were properly the province of the Viceroy, whom he failed to keep fully informed. 'I think he is baiting the trap with my cheese,' Lord Linlithgow complained to Churchill. The Prime Minister then invited the Viceroy to communicate directly with him, the result of which was that Cripps was persuaded to retract his offer of establishing in Delhi a government consisting of Indians. That disillusioned Cripps' close friends in the Congress Party, particularly Jawaharlal Nehru:[15] their friend at court had gone back on his word, and from that moment on Congress attitudes to Britain were to harden.

Although the currents running deep below the surface could probably no longer have been diverted by fine words from any of the Empire's rulers, it was, paradoxically, Wavell's own eminence, and the degree of confidence that he inspired, that was partly the cause of the mission's failure. Cripps had arrived with an offer for India's political leaders, which clearly set out the steps that the British Government proposed to take for the earliest possible realisation of self-government. It stated that in due course an Indian Union would be created, with the status of a dominion within the British Empire. In a series of broadcasts, press conferences and meetings with the leaders of the Congress, the Muslim League and outstanding individual leaders, Cripps painstakingly explained how this structure might be assembled.

Yet the talks foundered. The problem, a running sore throughout independence negotiations, was that the prospect of an effective transfer of power confronted Indian political leaders with the seemingly insoluble question of who would wield the power once transferred. There was scant evidence of any co-ordinated approach: in fact the leaders did not meet Cripps together, but separately, and appeared not to have discussed the matter with each other at all, even in private. Nor was there any united body, representative of Indian opinion, with whom the British could negotiate. At that moment it might not have mattered: underlying the stalemate was the fact that to those representing the most prominent body of opinion – Gandhi and the Congress Party – it looked very much as though the Japanese were going to win the war in the East, and that the British were negotiating from weakness. It did not escape their notice that their offer, famously described as 'a post-dated cheque on a crashing bank', was made just after the fall of Rangoon.

Gandhi, the mentor of the Congress Party, had himself submitted a resolution to the Congress stating that Britain was incapable of defending India, and that if the country were freed, her first step would probably be to negotiate with Japan. The Congress was therefore reluctant to make a fundamental commitment to the future, especially as Cripps had no immediate constitutional changes to offer. Instead, the argument eventually turned on who should manage the country's defences, with the Congress maintaining that only the leaders of a free and independent India could organise a defence on a national basis or create a mass psychology of resistance. By contrast the Cabinet, the Viceroy and a very large number of other people, fearful of a Japanese attack, inclined to the view not only that it was to General Wavell that they looked for the security of India, but that if there had to be an alternative to the British commander-in-chief, it should not be a caucus of Indian politicians without any discernible mandate.

Wavell himself had several objections to any change in his role. He maintained that he could not separate his civil functions from those as Defence Member without completely dislocating the administration of defence, and he also feared that Cripps' Declaration might unsettle the Indian Army, on which so much depended.

Nevertheless, at an early stage of the discussions agreement was almost achieved, thanks partly to President Roosevelt's personal representative, Colonel Louis Johnson,[16] whose efforts, sometimes opaque and mysterious, overcame a natural feeling among the British that matters of Empire were not America's business. The President's view, from far-away Washington, was that India's war effort would be more successful if the whole country was behind it. The British were doubtful, foreseeing grave problems in governing efficiently if too many Indians were involved. However, they knew that they must be wary of American opinion, not least because Delhi contained several American journalists of what the British Minister of Information described as the most poisonous type, eager to vilify Britain. Roosevelt himself was warning that the American public resented Britain's reluctance to concede self-government, despite the Indians' willingness – or so at first it seemed – to leave matters of defence to Britain. Should negotiations collapse, the President said, and a Japanese invasion lead to military defeat, it would have a serious effect on American opinion.[17]

The Congress also raised strong objections to the British offering to individual provinces a right of opt-out from the proposed Union. The Hindus feared the 'balkanisation' of India and insisted that it was politically indivisible, a stance directly opposed to the one that was to become the cardinal policy of the Muslims, who were becoming convinced that the Congress' attitude would mean permanent domination of Muslims by Hindus. Although to Cripps the partition of India made no sense, economically or in any other way, his offer (if it meant anything at all) had the seeds of partition in it, with the opt-out provision in fact opening the door to a Dominion of Pakistan.[18] Despite this, the Muslim League rejected it, mainly on the grounds that it did not concede outright the principle of partition.

The discussions were further complicated when the Congress radically altered its stance, demanding that the Viceroy's Executive Council should itself be transformed into a Cabinet Government 'with full power'. Despite his zealous inclination to satisfy the Congress at any cost, that was too much even for Cripps to concede. The British knew that India lacked the resolve to take charge of its own defence, and insisted that for the present Britain must retain full responsibility for the country's security. Accepting that in this particular caucus-race there could be no winners, Cripps decided to return to England at once, announcing that 'we revert to the position as it was before I came out here – though not quite to that position'. It was left it to the Indians, if they wished, to unravel exactly what that meant.

For Churchill, at least it was a good propaganda exercise. He had doubted all along that the mission would succeed, and at a moment of great political difficulty for him the fact that the failed mission had been led by Cripps, temporarily seeming rather too powerful, may not have been wholly unwelcome. However, in India the rejection of the offer was to have fundamental and far-reaching consequences along the route to independence: it was to lead to the 'Quit India' movement and to open the way for the Muslims to press for the creation of Pakistan.

Wavell's daily life was now running along concentric lines. On the outside were his military duties, to defend India and to plan a strategy, remote as might seem its ultimate aim, for regaining the lands that had been so swiftly and ignominiously overrun. Alongside soldiering lay his political role, to ensure that India was garrisoned both for external defence and for the maintenance of order within the country. And at the centre was his domestic life, loyally supported by Lady Wavell, who had for many years now helped him carry the growing burdens with which he had been saddled. In the stress and difficulties that he had endured almost without cease since August 1939, his family were of the greatest importance to him and he found them a continuing solace. He was also sustained by the physical comfort of his home surroundings. In the various dwellings of the commander-in-chief he was attended by large numbers of willing and efficient servants, and his personal needs were met almost before they arose by his smoothly efficient major-domo, Peter Coats, and by a succession of keen young ADCs. Lady Wavell meanwhile busied herself with her 'Wavell Canteens', Red Cross events and other good works in Delhi.

Private and family life, with its familiar faces and themes, wove a comfortable pattern through Wavell's working day. His eldest daughter Pamela, working in Cairo, had married Francis Humphrys, son of a former High Commissioner and Ambassador in Iraq, and in January 1942 Joan had married one of Wavell's ADCs.[19] The wedding had taken place in New Delhi and, as a guest noted, it revived a pre-war atmosphere, with 400 people crowding the church and reception, 'all able to wear their best for once'. Sandy Reid Scott was the best man, but it seemed – with good reason, as it turned out – that Wavell himself would have preferred it if he had been the groom. Reid Scott himself may have felt the same way, having become greatly attached to 'Joanie', but he was too good-natured to say so. 'Poor Sandy Reid Scott,' wrote one of his friends, 'the rejected lover, has asked to go back to his regiment in the Middle East – quite the right traditional behaviour under the circumstances.' Wavell was sad to part with Reid Scott, describing him as 'one in a million', an opinion that seems to have been widely shared.

Joan and Felicity were both now working at GHQ in Delhi, and Archie John had arrived in India, his regiment having been ordered to General Slim's jungle training course at Ranchi. The feeling that most of his family were, in their various ways, somewhere near helped the hard-pressed commander-in-chief maintain a sense of proportion at his laden desk.

There, his gentle touch of irreverence would enable him to push aside for a few moments the piles of documents that seemed never to subside. His secretary described how a sheaf of important cables included, for some reason, one describing how the luggage of a certain Mrs Foster had gone missing on a train journey from Bombay. This caught Wavell's attention, and before he got on with other work he became deeply engaged in writing a lament about the unfortunate lady:

> Poor Mrs Foster
> I fear she has lost her
> Dresses and frocks
> And undies and socks
> And everything frilly
> And is feeling quite chilly
> With nothing to wear –
> Is she really all bare?
> Fun for the chaps?
> And for Mrs F – perhaps
> But rotten for Foster.[20]

Wavell also kept as physically active as possible. He had taken up pig-sticking – at a relatively advanced age for the sport – and took advantage of the exceptional shooting that India had to offer, although his outings were more formal than when he was a young subaltern. Early in January, for example, he set off with his entourage, including Peter Fleming and the Auchinlecks, to Bharatpur, where the sky was black with duck; at the end of the day the party had shot 2,400, and the waterways boiled with collie dogs fetching their masters' kill.

When 'off-duty', at least formally, he could enjoy the splendour of his surroundings. His day started at 6.15 in the morning, when he would emerge into the bright Indian sun. Sometimes he would play golf – he was a consistent player, although clubhouse gossip had it that he used 'woods' only, until he had reached the green. More frequently he would ride, accompanied by one or more ADCs and occasionally a daughter or guests. He had a particularly comfortable hunter, called Royalty, and a dog aptly named Rommel. After riding he would bathe in the garden pool. In the evening there would often be a film show, usually with a short introductory item not too confusing for the military mind – Wavell's favourites included *Mickey Mouse* and *Canine*

Caddie. He had a succession of guests who formed a halfway house between pleasure and duty, often Indian governors or senior military figures, and also journalists, including Americans, to whom it was considered important to present a favourable impression of the Empire's struggle.

Wavell went frequently to Calcutta, to see Sir John Herbert, Governor of Bengal, who was responsible for an area where sound administration was particularly vital for India's defence arrangements. This involved both business and pleasure as Wavell was slightly enamoured of Sir John's wife Mary, who, despite founding the alarmingly named 'Bengal Women's War Committee', had a full set of feminine allures. Whilst in Calcuttta, Wavell would sometimes elude the constant attentions of his ADCs and go off with this tall, attractive and vivacious lady, with whom he would have midnight swims and appreciate the beauty and quiet of the Indian night.

Meanwhile the magnitude of the Field-Marshal's job, the shock of the way the war in Asia had developed since Pearl Harbor, and the injury to his back were becoming cumulatively oppressive. Wavell rarely allowed this to show, but he did draw back the veil in his letters to friends: 'I'm rather weary,' he told Joan Bright, 'this will be my fourth summer in the East, and I've hardly had a day off since the war started; so at all costs I shall try to get home for a few weeks' rest this summer.' His heart may not have been in the highlands, a-chasing the deer, but having been away for so long he did, like so many soldiers separated by war from old and familiar surroundings, feel the occasional pang for England, Home and Beauty:

> . . . *Large white peonies in big glass bowls,*
> *Asparagus 'au beurre', whitebait in shoals,*
> *A sunny breakfast-room, a library with books*
> *Close cropped grass, huge trees and cawing rooks*
> *Clean white housemaids in new print frocks,*
> *Coachmen turned chauffeurs, footmen on the box;*
> *Dinner parties all in evening dress;*
> *Glamorous women drenched in 'Mary Chess';*
> *Charades and paper games; hot houses with the heat on;*
> *Superficiality and Cecil Beaton;*
> *Shrimps from Morecambe Bay, port that is tawny,*
> *Claret and Beaujolais, soles that are 'Morny';*
> *Hot scones for tea, thick cream, the smell of logs,*

Long country walks, thick shoes and spaniel dogs,
Ducks in the evening, swishing swans in flight,
Fires in bedrooms, flickering at night . . .[21]

Learning from experience, Wavell did now try to keep the Prime Minister informed of how he saw the war progressing, while avoiding, he hoped, the dual pitfalls of providing too little detail or too much. He wrote to a friend:

Well now, the personal to PM telegrams. I do send him quite a lot but perhaps they aren't the right sort as I don't always get an answer. But I think I've kept him fairly well in the picture how the war goes, and what is in my mind. Lately I have sent him some rather petulant ones, perhaps, but I think they were justified and they seem to have produced some results . . . I'm still convinced that once I can get a strong long-range air striking force here, and really set about their aerodromes, bases and shipping it will be the first nail in their coffin . . .

We shall win the war all right, but shall we go back to our old ways again, or shall we regenerate ourselves . . . I do realise ever more how near we were to becoming completely decadent. A few more years' peace and we should have given up, like the French.[22]

Wavell kept a Commonplace Book – unusual for a general – and one of the quotations he put in it summarised his rather reproachful feelings about the loss of Britain's previously pre-eminent position in the world:

In the last resort it was not compromise which made our diplomacy impotent, it was our collective persistence in living in a world of unrealities, the deliberate nourishing of the illusion that we could continue to be great without sacrifice, that seated upon a heap of riches, and trusting to a minimum of weapons and a maximum of bluff and good fortune, we possessed a mysterious title to survive unscathed amidst a ring of ravenous and powerful rivals.[23]

He wrote a short pamphlet to help senior officers, analysing the defects and causes of his armies' defeats, and suggesting remedies:

We have experienced, in the five months of the war against Japan, a series of humiliating defeats which may tend to destroy the morale and confidence of the Army in India, unless we realise what is wrong and take steps to put it right . . . It can be done by training, but only by real hard, intensive training, such as we have not yet undertaken.

Echoing Marshal Zukhov, he concluded with the words 'Live Hard, Fight Hard, and, if necessary, Die Hard'.[24]

Through the weeks of April 1942 he had to find cover for the last stages of the withdrawal of the army from Burma. Slowly and painfully General Alexander was winding his way towards India with 8,000 British and 25,000 Indian troops; alongside him were 10,000 Chinese, for whom bases, equipment and training would have to be provided, and whose enforced stay might bristle with political difficulties with the Indians, as well as with the Americans and with the Generalissimo. After a final battle on the banks of the Chindwin, into which they drove the last of their tanks, the rearguard made its celebrated Kalewa crossing and struggled over the mountain range, 200 miles wide, but leading finally to India. So ended the longest retreat in British military history.

The defeat in Burma spawned the most serious consequences. Apart from the huge damage to the prestige of the British Empire, for the foreseeable future the Burma Road was lost, as was the ability to supply the American bomber bases in Yunnan. A wedge had been driven deep between China and India, threatening the air link between the two, and placing still more obstacles in the way of developing an effective alliance with Chiang Kai-shek. Meanwhile the Royal Navy withdrew towards Africa, leaving the Japanese fleet in a position to isolate both India and Australasia. Its air force was within range of India, no doubt unaware of the fact that in the entire subcontinent there were only eight anti-aircraft guns. Trouble loomed in every direction.

Disaster also finally befell the Americans in the Bataan peninsula, in the Philippines, where nearly 25,000 troops surrendered on 9 April and were forced onto the infamous Bataan death march. The American force in Corregidor would surrender early in May.

Yet Wavell was not downhearted; one of his staff recalled him standing in front of his wall map saying how stretched the enemy must be. 'They've pushed on much quicker than we thought they could,' he mused, 'they've taken all this enormous area from us and from the Dutch; they've been right down through Singapore, and they've come right up through Burma. They must be stretched absolutely to the limit. If I had anything,' he continued, rock-like before his map, 'I'd go for them now. But I haven't. I haven't got one division fit to fight.'[25]

Perhaps even in this grim time he recalled Rudyard Kipling's haunting lines: 'Come you back, you British soldier; come you back to Mandalay.' Wavell often produced imaginative verses, and the poem he wrote in the rhythm of *Mandalay* was poignantly apt:

> *By the old Moulmein Pagoda, at the corner of my map*
> *There's no Burma girl awaiting, but a nasty little Jap.*
> *Yet the cipher wires are humming, and the chiefs of staff they say*
> *Get you back, you British soldier; get you back to Mandalay.*
> *Get you back to Mandalay*
> *Where mosquitoes fall in May:*
> *And the Jap comes up through jungle like a tiger after prey.*
>
> *The anopheles is buzzing, and his bite is swift and keen,*
> *The rain falls down in torrents, and the jungle's thick and green;*
> *And the way back into Burma is a long and weary way,*
> *And there ain't no buses running from Assam to Mandalay.*
> *On the road to Mandalay,*
> *Where the flying Zeros play,*
> *And the Jap comes up through jungle like a tiger after prey.*[26]

On 16 April Wavell issued a directive to his planning staff to consider an offensive to reoccupy Burma. It struck an inspiring note, and news of the commander-in-chief's defiance created a pulse of hope through an army heavily oppressed by withdrawal and defeat.[27] Before an offensive could take shape, however, a vast amount of detail had to be mastered, even at the lofty level of commander-in-chief. Large-scale building works would be necessary to transport a force even only as far as its forward bases. To move men and equipment by rail from Calcutta to Assam would involve railways of two different gauges and a barge crossing of the River Brahmaputra, a bottle-neck between Bengal and Assam, especially as most of the steamers that formerly acted as ferries had been sent away to the Tigris to help establish a supply-route for the Russians through Iraq. Roads and railways on either side of the river would have to be laid or improved for access to the north-east borderland, and a road across the Assam mountains was needed. Meanwhile the Eastern Army had to defend 800 miles of coast and frontier with just one brigade, brought down from the North-West Frontier, and two incomplete divisions.

Wavell firmly believed that any action was preferable to none at all. In other parts of the world the battle was continuing: Malta was defending itself against all-out attack by the Germans, while the Americans had staged the first air raid on the Japanese mainland, with sixteen American B-25 bombers. Wavell was determined to keep his troops fighting if he could, but the monsoon season ruled out any further action until at least October. Meanwhile he established a corps at Imphal, near the Burmese frontier, and began the move to forward bases in Assam. He also turned to the defence of the rest of India, planning a Central Command, at Agra, to be responsible for internal security and for the training of new armies: a Southern Army, to protect the south from invasion from the sea; and a Northern Army, in case the Germans broke through the Russian defences and crossed the Khyber Pass. There were plenty of Indian recruits, with 60,000 volunteers per month, and, just as he had called for the creation of a great base in Egypt soon after his arrival there, he now ordered plans to be laid for the comprehensive organisation and development of air, sea and land forces in India, and for the infrastructure to support them.

From his desk the succession of directives went forth, to create the pistons that would drive the Japanese back to their lairs – armoured forces, paratroops, medical services, officer training, barrage defences, air-raid warning systems, telegraph systems, bridges, railways, ferries and roads. Provided he won the co-operation of the Indian workforce, Wavell was confident that he could accomplish it all in time to halt the Japanese at India's frontier. Then he could begin his own offensive.

A full-scale invasion of Burma was a long-term undertaking. In the meantime Wavell could only consider lesser operations to take the war back to the enemy. For those, he would have to co-ordinate his strategy with Chiang Kai-shek, in far-off Chungking. The point of contact between Delhi and Chungking was the American Major-General Joseph Stilwell,[28] Roosevelt's personal representative, who had been appointed chief of staff and chief military adviser to the Generalissimo. Stilwell had shown outstanding courage when, although almost sixty, he had placed himself at the head of the Chinese columns stranded in Burma and cajoled and guided them on the great retreat to India. He carried no candle for the British, however, whom he habitually described as 'mother fuckers who always want to cut our throats'. Like many senior American officers, he was convinced that there had been enough troops in India to save Burma, had the British meant business, but that Alexander had been under orders to put up only a token resistance and then withdraw.

Stilwell thought of Burma as the vital link to China, where he believed the campaign against Japan itself should begin. The main plank of his strategy was to reopen the Burma Road and, until that could be done, to develop the airlift from India to China: a perilous supply-route, requiring unarmed transport aircraft to fly 700 miles over the 'Hump', above 15,000-foot Himalayan peaks stretching south from Tibet, through turbulence that could tear the wings off heavily laden aeroplanes.

Chiang Kai-shek's objectives matched those of Stilwell, but Wavell had his doubts. In his view, without a single strategy the Chinese Alliance would be as much a hindrance as a help, and he suspected that the Americans had a different set of priorities from the British. At the same time, on his other flank, Churchill himself was now considering that Burma might be bypassed altogether in favour of operations to recapture Singapore, the only prize that in his view would restore Britain's prestige in the region.

Wavell's relations with Stilwell were of great importance, as together they had to assimilate the divergent British and American objectives of the war in Asia. Fortunately, Stilwell's churlish ways – he declined to stand up for the British national anthem, for example – his sour view of 'Limeys' and his inability to perceive the British Empire's extensive force for good in the world were not sharp enough darts to prick the sturdy commander-in-chief. He claimed to like Stilwell and to get on well with him, thinking him rather a 'character' who looked like an old tortoise, saying very little and thinking quite a lot. If at first Wavell's benevolence towards Stilwell was surprising, it became less so when Wavell had heard of the American's outstanding courage and drive on the retreat through Burma. At least they shared a derogatory opinion of the Japanese. 'When I think,' Stilwell wrote, 'how those bowlegged cockroaches have ruined our calm lives it makes me want to wrap Jap guts around every lamp-post in Asia.'[29]

Most Americans did not condone imperialism – in order to salve her conscience, America had promised that she would grant independence to the Philippines by 1946 – and did not consider the contrast between the peaceful and ordered lives of the Empire's subjects in Asia and what would befall them if the British did not return. Indifferent to the customs of the East, Roosevelt considered that the British Empire was all but finished and should make way for a bright new alternative in the form of local democracy. Consequently he thought that helping to restore colonial rule and white supremacy would not only jar with American public opinion, but would hamper his country's future relations in Asia. Such feelings cut little ice with the British, who considered the American attitude to be self-interest dressed in sentimentality, and who intended to emerge from the war with the Empire intact once more.

The British Government, and GHQ India, were not convinced that diverting resources to China would pay an adequate dividend, military or political, and remained suspicious that if the Chinese did enter Burma, they might find spurious oriental reasons for remaining there, perhaps renewing ancient claims to parts of the country that now rightfully belonged to Britain. Wavell shared these doubts, which greatly complicated his ideas for what he called 'the return match' in Burma, while accepting that a role for the Chinese was a political (if not a military) necessity.

Meanwhile, without long-range aircraft, or airfields in Upper Burma, there was little Wavell could do to engage the enemy. As an initial move he ordered plans to be drawn up for small columns to cross the Assam mountains after the monsoons had ended, in order to reoccupy the country north of Mandalay, which he hoped might be accomplished by the following spring. He then convened an inter-Allied conference at GHQ in New Delhi, to discuss the prospects before the United Nations,[30] which he thought would be helpful after the 'somewhat disheartening experiences' of the army in Burma. He could not attend himself as he had fallen off his horse while pig-sticking, and was confined to bed while his back mended. He was therefore unable to witness the ebullient performance of the Director of Military Intelligence at the War Office, General Davidson, who had come out to brief the conference. Davidson confidently announced:

Germany's defeat in 1942 is probable, not possible. Probable. Germany's defeat by the end of 1943 is inevitable. That is what we think. Why do we think it? Because all the facts, all our information, permit of no other deduction being made . . . I will make another bet: If Japan is still at war in 1944 she will have German forces in the field against her before the end of that year.[31]

Hopefully the general's bet was a small one; his brisk optimism must have come as rather a surprise to his audience, particularly to Stilwell and the Chinese War Minister, General Lo Tso-Yin, who had until then expressed marked scepticism about the prospects of British reinforcements for the Far East.

Churchill now pressed Wavell for information about his plans: 'Tell me what you can do, and when. I had hoped that you would try for Rangoon by the end of September . . .'[32] He was not satisfied by the limited scale of Wavell's initial proposals: it was 'very nice and useful nibbling', the Prime Minister replied, but he thought it was nothing like enough. Taking Rangoon in the autumn, however, was an unrealistic prospect, and Wavell tried to explain that he had neither the aircraft nor the airfields that would enable him even to reach southern Burma. The exchanges echoed the crossfire that had interrupted Wavell's work in his first year in Cairo.

Early in June 1942 the pressure intensified when the War Cabinet heard the momentous news of the victory of Midway Island, in which the Americans sank four of the enemy's six aircraft carriers and in three days of battle extinguished Japanese dominance of both the south-west Pacific and the Indian Ocean. For Churchill, this presented an intoxicating prospect. He at once suggested an amphibious operation: an advance from Chittagong down the Arakan peninsula, on the west coast of Burma, to be followed up by the launch of 40,000 or 50,000 men across the Bay of Bengal: 'This would be seizing the initiative,' he wrote to Wavell, 'and making the enemy conform, instead of being, through no fault of your own, like clay in the hands of the potter.'[33] While the full consequences of the Midway triumph could not be assessed immediately, Wavell concluded that the chance of an invasion of Ceylon or of southern or western India had been radically reduced, and he decided to raise his game: 'We can now begin,' he told Churchill, 'definitely to plan the recapture of Burma, which has been in my mind ever since it became obvious that I was likely to lose it.'[34] He ordered his staff to draw up plans for an offensive to retake Rangoon; it was given the codename 'Anakim'.

The stage was set for Wavell to move onto the offensive, but the players were not agreed on their parts. Churchill urged a major operation in three phases: to bear down on the enemy in the north; to seize Akyab island, at the foot of the Arakan peninsula, which the Japanese were using as a forward refuelling base for air raids on Calcutta and on shipping in the Bay of Bengal; and finally to launch an attack on the coast around Rangoon and Moulmein. Wavell, on the other hand, was for the time being confining himself to less ambitious practicalities, with a plan to send small columns into Upper Burma.

He also had to assure the defence of Assam. In view of the Japanese capacity for surprise, it could not be taken for granted that they would halt their advance just because of the rains. Unfortunately, as the summer months passed, administrative difficulties began to mount even for the first phase of Wavell's plans. Torrential rains all but halted the flow of supplies to the start-line on the Imphal plain, while reports of the enemy advancing up the peninsula from Akyab had meant hurriedly despatching a division to Chittagong, to block their path.

The chief agent in Wavell's immediate designs was a former Kenya farmer, Lieutenant-General Noel Irwin, commander of IV Corps, of the Eastern Army. He was a reserved, unsmiling man, and even the broad-minded General Slim had complained of his rudeness.[35] At the end of July, Irwin was appointed army commander, only to find that although on paper there were six divisions in his new command, only two were organised and available for operations; and his plans to make good the deficit were suddenly upset by disruption from an unexpected quarter.

Anti-British agitation in India had increased since the departure of Sir Stafford Cripps. It came to a head on 8 August 1942, when the Congress passed a resolution demanding the immediate cessation of British rule in India. It became known as the 'Quit India' resolution – a slogan that usually drew from British squaddies the response 'I only wish I could'. As Gandhi, the engine as well as the figurehead of the independence movement, urged 'Leave India to God or anarchy', he issued a call for a campaign of *satyagraha*, or 'sit-down-strike', of non-violent civil disobedience to the British authorities. There was no room for negotiation, he decreed: 'either they recognise independence, or they don't'. The British did not, and within twenty-four hours Gandhi and the Congress Party leaders were safely behind bars where, for a time, they could do no further damage to the country. At the same time the British accepted that these were the men with whom they might one day have to negotiate independence, so they were treated generously throughout their stay in prison.

Nevertheless, the resolution and its attendant instructions inspired a wave of strikes, absenteeism, subversion of soldiers and government officials, bomb outrages, burnings alive of policemen, and mob violence – much of it by students. British officers were chased by angry crowds in Delhi, and several of their sauntering grounds had to be placed off-limits, although the leaders of the campaign were careful not to seriously harm British personnel – none were killed, and warnings were always given in advance of, for example, sabotage to railway lines. Mass detentions were carried out, and soon more than 30,000 Congress activists had been imprisoned. That in turn sparked more terrorist activity, particularly attacks against the troop-trains that ran through the bandit country of central Bihar along the line to Assam and the Burmese frontier.

On the British side, both at home and in India it was felt that by responding to Cripps' offer with the 'Quit India' movement, most of India's political leaders had confirmed that they were implacably anti-British. The movement was an insult to add to the injury of the extant boycott of British goods, inspired by Gandhi and the cause of widespread hardship and many cases of ruin in the previous few years.

It was shortly before the start of the campaign that Wavell became aware that the Congress was preparing to cause disruption. Although he had quickly deployed troops to the likely troublespots, it was to little avail. The main disturbances were in the coal- and iron-producing areas, in the north-east, where great dislocation to transport and industry soon developed. With the Japanese threat looming, the protests began to assume alarming implications, as disruption hit airfield construction, training and the production of munitions for the army, and held up the Eastern Army's movement programme. The vital lines of communication to the Burma frontier were cut by political activists, often waving the Congress flag, and to contain the trouble Wavell was forced to deploy fifty-seven infantry battalions.

Other obstacles now emerged: when Churchill had first expressed his hopes for a two-pronged offensive, he had warned that priorities for the use of men and equipment would be dictated by the situation on the Russian front and in the Middle East. Now Wavell found essential men and equipment hived off from his command. By August[36] the news from Libya was grave, as the Afrika Korps drew near the Nile Delta itself, and it seemed as if Wavell's Worst Possible Case might after all come to pass. Reinforcements for operations in Burma would clearly have to wait.

Wavell was summoned to a conference in Cairo, where Churchill himself had gone in order to see what was amiss with the desert army. Wavell's presence was not entirely welcome to Auchinleck, the Middle East commander. Relations between the two men had become strained when Wavell had sent a cable offering the Auk his 'help' in his current difficulties, a well intentioned suggestion that was not well received. Auchinleck had been further annoyed – as had Churchill – when Field-Marshal Smuts, also in Cairo, had extolled Wavell's virtues and had referred to his presence as 'a note of hope from the East'.

Even as the talks were in progress, the threat of a German breakthrough in southern Russia became so serious that the War Office ordered Wavell to send troops to Iraq, to reinforce the barrier across the path to the oilfields of the Middle East and to India. He thereby lost another valuable part of the armoury he was trying to construct for his offensive. He could not, however, yet return to India to direct the rebuilding of the army – partly because of his ability to speak Russian, he was ordered to accompany Churchill and Brooke on their onward journey from Cairo to Moscow, where they hoped to persuade the hard-pressed Russians to drop their demands for a second front in Europe. It was only after that difficult expedition was concluded, with a second front having to wait until it stood some chance of success, that Wavell returned to Delhi.

Before doing so, he despatched a rather unusual letter:

Dear Prime Minister,

I have never before asked you for anything for myself, but I am going to ask you now for promotion to the rank of Field-Marshal . . .[37]

In his letter Wavell referred to his responsibilities and campaigns, and drew the Prime Minister's attention to the important nature of his commands, both past and present. He pointed out that he now had more than a million men under his command, and that promotion to the army's top rank would increase his influence and prestige with the Indian Army, and would be taken as a compliment by them. He accepted that there already were supernumerary field-marshals in the army list, and he knew that a proposal for another one might snag on the question of precedent, but he said that apart from Lord Gort he was the senior general in the army, and, quite unabashed, stated that he thought he had fair claims to the rank.

Whether or not this request originated at the suggestion of his family has not been publicly disclosed, but being a master of his profession and at its very peak, Wavell perhaps felt that in his case there was little reason for the restraints of custom to apply. As set out in his letter, his great victories in Africa at a time when the country badly needed uplift, his former office as Supreme Commander, his present wide command and his esteem in the eyes of the public were arguments of strong merit.

Nevertheless the request could only be described as unusual, displaying a rather engaging innocence, unperturbed by the possibility of an indignant rejection. It probably would not have occurred to Wavell that some people might have considered him naive to make the request, and it is unlikely that he would have been embarrassed about asking for the honour. In any event,

Churchill's well of magnanimity was deep, and instead of responding as lesser men might have done, he at once told the Secretary of State for War, P.J. Grigg, that he was strongly in favour of accepting the suggestion, as was the CIGS.

Grigg himself was a lesser man, at least in this context, and he responded by suggesting that any special appointments as field-marshal might more properly wait until such time as the army had some resounding success to its credit; that Wavell's name should not be put up to the King unless Gort's was also; and that, as Gort was Governor of the hard-pressed but vital island of Malta, the matter should wait upon the outcome of the defence of that island, and a possible victory in North Africa. For good measure Grigg threw in his personal view of Wavell's abilities, saying that he was shocked that the general could have brought himself to ask for promotion. Churchill was unimpressed by this rejoinder, telling Grigg that his views about Wavell would astonish most people who had served under him, as they did the CIGS. Nor, added the Prime Minister, did he see any reason for the announcement being 'carefully synchronised with a victory'.

There was also support at the highest level of all. On 13 October the King agreed to make the appointment in the New Year's Honours, provided that Lord Gort was also appointed. Wavell had received an accolade befitting his stature, and a just reward for the unceasing work he had carried out, without a break, since the war had started.

BANZAI

As a consequence of his journeys to Cairo and Moscow, Wavell was away from India for three crucial weeks during the planning for 'Anakim'; by the time he returned it had become clear that the combination of the grave threat in the Middle East and the administrative, political and climatic difficulties in India meant that the operation would not be ready for launching before the next monsoon season. In effect it would have to be postponed for a year, a conclusion reinforced as the fortunes of war began to change in North Africa and plans went forward for 'Operation Torch', a landing on the North African coast in November 1942.

Wavell was all the more determined that General Irwin should start his operations as soon as possible. But it soon became apparent that even these limited plans had been fatally compromised, partly by the Quit India campaign, partly by the disruptions caused by the monsoon, and partly by malaria among the troops. General Irwin concluded that his offensive could not begin before March 1943.

That was not to Wavell's taste. The commander-in-chief would not accept passivity. He responded by encouraging a number of imaginative new initiatives, unconventional and otherwise. Ever attracted to unorthodox tactics, he had accepted the War Office's offer of the services of Colonel Orde Wingate, whose tough style in Palestine Wavell had admired as much as his role in the campaign in Ethiopia. Wavell saw that Wingate might do good work in Burma. Wingate had arrived in India in early March 1942, with strange new ideas on penetration behind the Japanese lines. He was convinced that small units fighting deep within enemy-occupied territory were as valuable as much larger formations at the front, and that they could be trained to operate without the need for lines of communication, being supplied by air instead. The enemy would be confused by action far behind their lines: it could inflict disproportionate damage to roads, railways and other communications, while agents and specialist soldiers gathered the intelligence that so far in the Far East campaigns had been almost entirely lacking.

Wavell was instinctively opposed to special units, such as commandos, which he thought drew good men away from their regiments. Instead he preferred units to be specially trained as a whole. But he now accepted the need to compromise on this principle, as Wingate's proposals seemed to offer a way of getting back at the enemy, in a part of Burma on which the Japanese hold ought not to be strong, and in a manner that might catch them off-guard. He saw that the immediate campaign was already lost, but there was still time to study the enemy's tactics in jungle warfare. Perhaps, for the first time, his forces might gain the initiative: 'I have a hunch,' he told General Irwin, 'that the Jap is pulling out and that the appearance of Wingate may just turn the doubt into the reality.' His hunch could not have survived long, as the Japanese continued to race far above what Wavell believed was their form, and yet, true to his indomitable nature, he looked through apparent defeat to the victory he was sure would eventually be won.

With no available avenues for immediate action, Wavell responded to Wingate's compelling and enthusiastic approach. It was after his own heart, and represented Bagnold's 'piracy on the high desert' once again. His opinion of Wingate was not widely shared; in fact, Wavell was almost alone in his support for the eccentric colonel, who arrived at GHQ with a distinct redolence of Lawrence of Arabia and immediately enraged almost every officer with whom he came into contact.

Wingate buried himself in papers on Japanese military tactics (not widely read, at GHQ), long reports on the plants and animals of Burma (likewise) and tracts of oriental philosophy (even less so).[1] Wavell then despatched Wingate on a reconnaissance of Upper Burma; it resulted in the now-famous *Memorandum on Long Range Penetration and the Conquest of Burma*. The paper was greeted with disdain by almost everyone but Wavell, who authorised the establishment of a long-range penetration group, to be known as 77th Indian Infantry Brigade, the name of which, as with the Special Air Service, was itself designed to deceive. The unit formed in July, and at once began an intensive jungle training programme.

In the black days of April 1942, when it seemed as though the enemy might finally surge into India itself, Wavell had also called for the formation

of 'stay-behind' parties, to operate along the Assam border. V-Force, as it
became known, was officered by reliable men with local knowledge, many of
them policemen, and soon expanded to include Burmese villagers. They
formed the eyes and ears of the army in remote parts of the country, developing an intelligence network and reporting on enemy troop movements.
Wavell had received advice on this concept from Captain Peter Fleming, a
Grenadier officer who originally had the idea for its use in England, should
a German invasion succeed. Wavell was attracted by Fleming's daring ideas
and had taken him onto his staff.[2]

At the end of April Wavell sent Fleming into Burma to put his theories
into practice. It proved more difficult than trying to fool the Italians or
Germans, in that the Japanese were not particularly interested in what the
British were up to:

> Deceiving the Germans had been very different; they wanted to know
> our plans and expected us to try and deceive them. That had been like
> playing chess with someone not quite so good as oneself; with the
> Japanese, it was like setting up the chess-board against an adversary
> whose one idea is to punch you on the nose.[3]

Fleming's first adventure was 'Operation Error', almost a carbon copy of
the Meinertzhagen haversack trick that had been so successful against the
Turks in Mesopotamia in 1917. He set off for Alexander's headquarters and,
having received the distracted general's approval, was directed to the Ava
Bridge, over the Irrawaddy,[4] where it seemed that there was a suitable place
for his subterfuge. There he abandoned a car containing a briefcase with
papers, 80 per cent of which were genuine and the rest false, in the hope
that the enemy would find them and be led astray. Besides sundry personal
items, Fleming had (at Wavell's suggestion) included a document that
contained a reference to his biography of Allenby. Whether that particular
operation did any good is unclear, but overall Wavell's encouragement of
men like Fleming, Clarke, Bagnold and Wingate paid considerable dividends
as the war unfolded.

By September 1942 the monsoon season was nearly over, and six months'
campaigning weather lay in prospect. Wavell had never lost his conviction
that the Japanese could be taught a lesson if only his forces could rediscover
their zeal, and he was determined that the 'dry' season should be used to
the full for that purpose. He was in no doubt of ultimate victory, and his

confidence and optimism remained undimmed by the many setbacks to his plans. On 17 September he handed his chief of staff a document headed 'Operation Fantastical': 'I have a "hunch",' it began, 'which may be quite unjustified, that we may find Japanese opposition very much lower than we expect in Burma if we can only act with boldness and determination . . .'

In view of events in Burma since the Japanese had crossed its frontiers, it is not wholly clear on what evidence Wavell based his hunch. But he followed it up with a clarion-call: 'The first thing I want is to create a spirit everywhere from GHQ downwards of determination to get as far into Burma this winter as possible, to recapture the whole of Burma without a day's delay that can be avoided; to be profoundly dissatisfied with our present programme and to be determined to exceed it . . .'5

With his hunch and his optimism – and determined, as he had put it, 'to fight repeat fight these Japs some time somewhere' – Wavell began to review his objectives. Although he was commander-in-chief, he did not have a free hand. He was constrained by shortages of men and equipment, and particularly of aircraft, as well as by poor communications into and through Burma.

He had also to marry British objectives with those of the Chinese and the Americans. Britain's aim was to recapture the whole of Burma and reinstate imperial rule as a stepping-stone to regaining her other lost Far Eastern possessions; for those purposes the co-operation of China was not a military necessity. The Chinese, however, whose aims were endorsed by the Americans, were unwilling to fight for the restoration of the British Empire unless it was unavoidable in order to defeat the Japanese. With the enemy occupying China's coast, the Burma Road was the country's only land outlet to the world. Chiang Kai-shek's paramount objective was therefore to beat the Japanese back from the Burma Road, so that the British and Americans could supply him with equipment that would both maintain him in power (his first priority) and save China from what Stilwell, in particular, feared was imminent political, economic and military collapse. Opening the Burma Road, or developing alternative channels of supply from India to China – either over the 'Hump' or by new road construction – was thus as important to Chiang Kai-shek as the recapture of Burma was to the British. Wavell had to frame his plans so as somehow to please all the guests at the party.

His options, however, soon began to narrow even further. By reason of the priorities of operations in other theatres, particularly 'Torch' in North Africa, 'Anakim' was effectively ruled out for the 'dry' winter season of 1942–43. Also, by September it was clear that Irwin's Eastern army was still not in a fit state to fight, so Wavell told the Chiefs of Staff that he was for the time being confining himself to improving communications by building three roads into Burma. Meanwhile, recognising the need for some action at least, if only to impart experience and confidence to the troops, he set his planners to work on an Arakan campaign on its own. 'Operation Cannibal' was to be an amphibious attack on Akyab Island, preceded by an advance down the Arakan peninsula. Wavell therefore directed Irwin to establish, by the beginning of December 1942, brigades at two points about fifty miles north of Akyab. He decided to send Wingate's columns into northern Burma at the same time, and enemy attention would also be diverted, he hoped, by Chinese advances from Yunnan and Ramgarh.

Pressure to blend his aims with those of his allies was increased when he received a visit from Stilwell, armed with a Chinese plan for driving the Japanese out of Burma. On 14 October the Generalissimo had agreed to undertake an offensive, but on the condition that there would also be an amphibious attack on Rangoon, and that before the start of operations the British must regain air and sea control in the Bay of Bengal, without which 'Anakim' was unlikely to succeed. Having got the promise, at least, of action from the Chinese, which had proved a long and uphill task, Stilwell arrived in Delhi, determined to get Wavell to follow suit.

It was to be one of many meetings between Chinese, Americans and British in which all three tried to draw agreement on strategy and tactics from a well brim full of suspicion and dislike, even if it also contained mutual respect. Stilwell's new proposal was that American aircraft should land three divisions in northern Burma, as a preliminary to a southerly advance. Wavell thought this impracticable: the Chinese would be outnumbered by six to one, and they would have to be supplied from India, for which purpose some 200 airfields would have to be built to provide air cover. Besides, between British supply depots and the Chinese lay the huge and largely untracked Assam mountains. Wavell put the idea to his Joint Planning Staff for an appreciation; not surprisingly, they concluded that the plan was unworkable. Stilwell was not pleased. Wavell asked him if he accepted the conclusions:

'Are you satisfied that your plan will not work?'
'I am.'
'Are you satisfied on purely military grounds?'
'I am.'

'And what shall you say to Chiang Kai-shek?'

'I shall tell him the bloody British wouldn't fight.'

There was then a stunned silence, broken by Wavell saying 'I see', and closing the meeting. It was a curious reaction, but whereas many people might have become vociferous, repaying Stilwell in his own coin, Wavell's silence gave the impression, at least to some of those at the meeting, of 'controlling immense reserves of inner strength'. 'We were left wondering,' said one, 'what he *would* do . . .'[6]

Yet at least an army was beginning to take shape. General Slim had moved his corps headquarters to Ranchi, in central Bihar, to be near the Ramgarh camp, where he had established an invigorating jungle training programme for four divisions and an armoured brigade. Slim's direction was starting to impart to the troops a new confidence and the beginnings of a belief that they might be a match for the Japanese. Morale was rising at last.

Wavell's overall strategy, against the day when the wider war situation and his own strength permitted, was to launch a three-pronged attack on Burma. It would consist of an advance by IV Corps from Assam across the Chindwin River into Upper Burma, supported by the Chinese armies moving south ('Operation Ravenous'); an advance down the Arakan peninsula by land and sea from Chittagong, to attack the air base on Akyab Island ('Operation Cannibal'); and eventually also an amphibious attack on Rangoon and Moulmein ('Operation Anakim').

On 17 October 'Vinegar Joe' Stilwell arrived in Delhi to confer with Wavell and to plan a combined attack. By now he was confident that he was beginning to master the art of keeping the Chinese and the British actively in the ring, while advancing his own government's 'Support China' policy. He disclosed his intentions in a letter home:

Hell, I'm nothing but an errand boy, I drum up to Chungking and jerk the Gimo's [Generalissimo's] sleeve. I tell him he better get ready to move into Burma from the south . . . and the Chinese are going to lose a lot of face if the British do it alone. Then I fly down to India and jerk Archie's sleeve, and tell him, 'the Gimo is going to move down the Salween and you better get going too. You Limeys are going to have a hell of a time with the White Man's Burden if the Chinese have nerve enough to fight and you haven't.'[7]

Despite this sort of brash quirkiness Wavell still felt that his relations with Stilwell were good. 'I like him and think him co-operative and genuine,' he said, attributes that could just about co-exist with Stilwell's consuming distaste for British officers. However, the path was rarely free of thorns, and at this conference Wavell, under pressure from the Viceroy, expressed reservations about the arrival of two more Chinese divisions for training at the Ramgarh centre.

Wavell accepted the purpose of this camp, but without enthusiasm. Its military value already seemed slight, and a further two divisions would congest the railways and drain resources from the Indian Army. Stilwell, however, had with great difficulty persuaded Chiang Kai-shek to increase the force at Ramgarh, which was being trained by Americans with American equipment, and he was aghast at the unexpected discouragement:

> Wavell, a lot of bull and crying about this and that. He made it plain the Ramgarh Training Centre is not welcome. All sorts of difficulties – railroads, roads, water, food, transport. Will hinder Indian Army development . . . Well, to hell with the old fool. We have just smoked them out. They don't want Chinese troops participating in the retaking of Burma. That's all. (It's OK for US troops to be in England though) . . . Limeys getting nasty about Ramgarh. Wavell must have a formal request – for the Viceroy. How many troops to come and what for? WHAT FOR? My God! I told them, to help our allies retake Burma.[8]

He might as well have read the minutes of the Chiefs of Staff report in London at their meeting a few weeks earlier: 'Burma is a British sphere and any operation for its recapture and for reopening the Burma Road must be undertaken almost exclusively by British forces.'[9]

But the main plans – Operations 'Ravenous', 'Cannibal' and 'Anakim' – seemed for a brief time to satisfy all parties: 'We have now got both the Limeys and the Chinese committed and working on it,' reported Stilwell. 'If we can keep a fire lit under Wavell and horn in our command and training on this side, the job is in a fair way to get done.'[10]

Yet almost at once difficulties arose, partly over who should control the Chinese troops once they had entered Burma – the Chiefs of Staff insisting that it should be Wavell – but more immediately because Wavell was not yet in a position to take any of the three operations forward. 'Ravenous' was compromised by the damage to communications caused by the monsoon, and by the ravages that the troops had suffered from malaria. 'Anakim' was likely to be starved of its essential naval support for some considerable time; and the necessary air superiority for 'Cannibal' had not been achieved, so that landings down the coast of the Arakan peninsula would be exposed to severe attack by Japanese air forces from Akyab long before Wavell's army could get there to help.

For a few weeks Wavell waited in the hope that the situation would improve, and that the assault craft he needed would be released from other operations in the Indian Ocean and would arrive in time for his offensive. By mid-October it was clear that the essential preconditions had not been achieved, and on 17 November he cancelled the operation.

Unwilling to let go, he remained intent on launching an attack of some sort, somewhere, even one without great strategic or even tactical value – provided of course that the troops did not perceive it as that – in order to give his divisions confidence and restore their morale. Also, as had been in part his aim in sending the army to Greece, he was determined to bring the enemy to battle and force it to use up resources.

The only option now was to move by land only, and so, two days later, he ordered an advance down the length of the peninsula, from there to attack Akyab Island, a short distance across the water. The campaign was to become known as 'First Arakan', but even at its inception Wavell was doubtful about what it might achieve: 'This plan had the disadvantage that it made surprise most unlikely, and Arakan was a most unfavourable theatre, into which I should certainly have not made a deep land advance on any scale had sea transport been available . . .' [11]

GHQ could not spare any steamers to transport the army down the coast, so it was faced with the unappealing prospect of a slow advance through steep and barely penetrable jungle. As a priority, therefore, the planners had to weigh the advantages that success might bring against the likelihood of it being achieved at all – and about that there developed a lively variety of opinions among the various commanders involved, and no doubt also amongst their men.

Wavell has sometimes been accused of lacking a full quotient of ruthless-ness, but the Arakan campaign certainly belies that suggestion. As shown by his determination not to yield in Malaya or Singapore, his attitude had hard-ened since his days in North Africa, and it is possible that he had come to feel chastened by having let the last of the Italians escape his net, and by failing to stand firm in Cyrenaica when Rommel first appeared in Africa.

During the five months of fighting his opinions about the quality of Japanese soldiers were to an extent revised, in the face of the bloodstained evidence of their skill and determination, although he still maintained his conviction that they could be overborne by fortitude on his own side.

The Arakan is a long finger of land resembling a narrow inverted triangle starting from the Assam border and stretching down the north-east coast of Burma for about 400 miles. Its northern part is a peninsula, with a mountain range forming its spine. The plan was for the army to split, moving south on either side of the mountains – not an easy task in an area accurately described as 'some of the worst country in the world, a mixture of mountains, malaria and mud'.[12] Surprise would be essential, necessitating the deployment of well-trained troops and moving them quickly to their objectives. Those requirements were not met. The troops were insufficiently trained, and without sea transport – of which there was none – they had no chance of reaching the enemy before it had time to reinforce. Instead they were faced with a land advance down the peninsula, which meant negotiating nearly ninety miles of steep, uneven terrain, mostly covered in thick jungle. In General Slim's description, it would be like walking along the teeth of a saw.

Yet, at least in the early stages of planning, the chance of success seemed reasonably high, as the original concept was to have co-ordinated the operation (or at least part of it) with a Chinese offensive, which Stilwell had assured Wavell would begin on 1 March. However, it was well into February when the news came that Chiang Kai-shek had changed his mind.

Wavell had planned to send Wingate into Burma at the same time as a Chinese advance, because he thought of the type of operation that Wingate proposed, away from the front line, as an old-style cavalry raid designed to draw the enemy's attention from the main attack. But the raid's chances of success would be radically altered if the Chinese did not after all move into northern Burma, as the Japanese, once they discovered what was happening, would be able to turn their full attention to flushing out Wingate's men. Further, they would have been alerted to a new method of attack and might implement steps to impede future operations. The military solution seemed to be to stand Wingate down. However, Wavell's instinct told him that the force, tuned to a fine pitch and filled with martial ardour, might nevertheless do considerable damage. Above all it would gain invaluable experience of living and fighting in the jungle, knowledge of which was perhaps his army's greatest lack.

Early in February 1943 Wavell met Wingate at his camp at Imphal. He brought with him the grave news that the British were not ready to advance from Imphal, that in Ledo the Americans were still unprepared and that the Chinese would not move from Yunnan. Yet despite learning that the whole premise of his operation had fallen away, Wingate, after two hours of intense talks, succeeded in persuading Wavell that the 'Chindits'[13] should march. At a peak of readiness and full of fire, they set off into the jungle on their own, their ears ringing with Wingate's famous Order of the Day. They included among their number Wavell's son, Archie John, who fought with them with distinction, was wounded and decorated for gallantry.

Meanwhile preparations continued for the Arakan offensive. Enthusiasm for it was not widespread. Among the officers concerned, support for the project seems to have been in proportion to seniority, particularly as the campaign unfolded; it was not helped by a top-heavy command structure, with Irwin, as Army Commander, dealing directly with the divisional commander instead of using the services of a corps headquarters, while at the same time having Wavell at his elbow, prodding the advance forward.

Speed was vital: even if at first the Japanese had few troops in the peninsula, they would rush in reinforcements as soon as they realised that a full-scale advance had begun. In fact, as had applied to the British adventure up the mainland of Greece the previous year, the planners ought to have wondered how Akyab Island could have been defended and maintained even if it were actually taken.

Wavell decided to use the 14th Indian Division for the advance, partly as it needed training and experience, and partly because it was conveniently based at Chittagong, at the top of the peninsula. Its commander, General Lloyd, suggested to Irwin that early in December he make a swift advance to Maungdaw, about three-quarters of the way down the peninsula, as he believed it to be lightly held. However, Irwin demurred, on the grounds that the left flank would be exposed. Unwilling to take chances with inexperienced troops, he ordered Lloyd to assemble a larger force before he moved.

This caused a delay, so that when Lloyd did reach Maungdaw he found that the enemy were fast retreating to the tip of the peninsula, where they believed that they could hold their line, protected by wide waterways on their right and the sea on their left. This start to their campaign disconcerted the British who felt, as Irwin expressed it, rather cheated of a fight. Wavell felt the same:

I was disappointed in Arakan; I thought the Jap would fight . . . and I think we could have given him a knock. Now he has withdrawn into Akyab, which is a much harder proposition. Still, it is something to have the Jap going backwards and I think we are beginning to hit him fairly hard in the air.[14]

Perhaps at that early stage they might have given the enemy 'a knock', but as it happened it was the British who received the knock, even before they had drawn their swords, partly through malaria and partly through the attrition caused by the appalling terrain and conditions. As the Indian division inched wearily south through almost impassable country, it seemed, to use Churchill's metaphor, as though the tortoise was stretching out his neck – always an unwise procedure and one that did not go unnoticed by the enemy.

Previously, and despite a lack of evidence to support the theory, Wavell had expressed the belief that the Japanese were not as good in defence as in attack, but he was now to see an enemy building and occupying defences that were as impregnable as some of the best trench positions of the First World War. They constructed a series of strongpoints, well dug in and with clear fields of observation, protected by mutually supporting lines of machine-gun fire. Their defenders looked out from deep-set bunkers, made of wood and in some cases concrete, and so well disguised and sited in the sides of the hills that they were to prove largely impervious to tanks and field guns, let alone to mortars and rifle-fire. Lines of infantry advancing over open ground were pinned down by grenades, machine-guns and sniper fire, leaving them only the smallest chance of success or even survival.

However, Wavell urged Irwin on; he sent down some notes entitled 'How to Fight the Japs' – appending the comment that 'We quite obviously don't yet know how to' – and seeing no reason why his superior force should have difficulty in disposing of the apparently small number of enemy troops. He was convinced that he would eventually succeed by weight of numbers, and so through January and February attack followed attack, until in time the troops had to pick their way over ground littered with their dead companions, whom the Japanese showed no interest in burying. It was to no avail, and Wavell did not seem pleased.

Eventually it began to dawn upon General Irwin that no purpose was being served by these tactics, and that the weather would soon make a landing on Akyab impracticable. More particularly, he noted that the campaign was not, among other things, achieving the hoped-for lift in the division's morale: 'Shall we agree,' he asked Wavell on 6 February 1943, 'that Akyab is too remote for this Spring season?' The answer was no. Wavell himself was being pressed, by the War Cabinet, to keep up the offensive: 'Very great forces have been gathered in India,' he was told, 'and it would be a disaster if they were to stand idle at a time when the whole Empire must be in closest contact with the enemy.'[15] Irwin then sent Wavell a detailed warning about the state of the troops, arguing that the balance of risk and advantage was against continuing; instead, he suggested, he should consolidate the ground already won.

Wavell did not agree with that, either. He still considered that, with superior numbers, he should be able to repel any flank attack, reach Akyab Island and restore the morale and prestige of his troops. It was not happening: by 18 February Lloyd had made four frontal assaults on Donbaik, a defended position on the coast about seven miles from the tip of the peninsula, with no result other than Allied carnage. The troops were greatly unsettled by the seeming invisibility of the well-armed Japanese: nerves were frayed and morale had failed. One night a battle broke out and the clearings in front of the Indian line were illuminated by flashes, tracer bullets and explosions as the jungle hills reverberated to the sounds of excited shouts, orders, mortars and machine-gun fire. Unfortunately, when morning came it was seen that two companies of an Indian battalion, alerted by what they thought was an imminent attack, had held a prolonged firefight with each other. There were a number of casualties, and a rather bleak inquiry was held on the spot. At its conclusion the divisional chief staff officer slapped his papers down on the trestle and said, 'Well, at least we won *that* battle.'

On 26 February Wavell renewed the pressure on Irwin, directing him to order Lloyd to take Donbaik 'by sheer weight of numbers'. V-Force agents now reported the arrival of fresh Japanese troops, and the risks increased. However, to the planners at GHQ in Delhi it seemed to be a containable threat, and Wavell remained sure that perseverance would pay: 'I should like,' he signalled, 'to finish up this campaigning season with a real success which will show both our troops and the Japs that we can and mean to be top dog.'[16]

Yet now Irwin seemed to have lost confidence in Lloyd, while Wavell considered the frontal attacks to have displayed a complete lack of imagination. He offered his own suggestions – bringing up field guns to point-blank range, distraction by the noise of low-flying aircraft, night advances.

'The only way to upset the Japanese,' he said, 'and wrest the initiative, is to take Mayu, control the river mouth and threaten Akyab – make him move his troops . . .'[17] But no one seemed to have an adequate plan: 'I see no good alternative to your proposals,' Wavell told Irwin, 'but I do not like them. We have let the Jap get the initiative, and I don't see how we can regain it.'[18] In Malaya, along the Pacific island chain and now in Burma, the infiltration and outflanking tactics of the Japanese had, like the German Blitzkrieg, wholly confused the Allies. The lessons of Sandhurst and the Staff College, however well memorised, were of little use: creativity and improvisation were required.

Once it had seized the initiative, the enemy began to roll the Indian division back towards Chittagong. Wavell was determined not to yield, sure that his force could still turn the tables: 'the object of future operations,' he told Irwin at the beginning of April, 'is to regain the initiative and inflict a severe defeat on the enemy'.[19] With losses mounting, malaria rife and morale all but dissolved, inflicting a severe defeat did not seem to be an immediate option, but Wavell was now planning for the monsoons; if he could only cajole his troops into a dominating position, they could perhaps hold fast until the next dry season, when the situation might have changed.

At length, in mid-April, Wavell did rationalise the structure of the Eastern Army, by inserting General Slim's XV Corps headquarters between Eastern Army Command and the division in the field. But the consequent increase in efficiency was too late to alter the thrust of the campaign. It did, though, remove the need for tactical intervention from on high – such as the occasion when Wavell, from his office in Delhi, instructed Irwin, in his office in Calcutta, to order Lloyd, in the Arakan, to use a particular brigade, the 6th, for one aspect of the operation. Such kinks in the chain of command jeopardise success in the field, not least where detailed tactics are decided by senior commanders who have other, broader matters to settle. Wavell wrote:

My troops have not been doing very well in Arakan; they simply don't know how to fight like the Jap, although I think they try hard enough. My fault, I should have taught them better, I suppose, but I really get very little time for honest soldiering. I seem to spend most of my time being War Minister: nearly three hours I spent the other day at the Viceroy's Council discussing statutes for Delhi University, measures against speculators in cotton, and the Hindu Marriage Bill.[20]

The campaign ended with a rout, when six Japanese battalions comprehensively vanquished seventeen British. Although Wavell said that his troops tried hard enough, they lacked resolve, skill and fitness not least because of the heavy toll caused by malaria. This might perhaps have been mitigated by a policy of consolidating ground gained, thereby avoiding the need for repetitive attacks against strongly held positions. In retrospect General Irwin calculated that the Japanese had started with a 30 per cent advantage in quality over his own troops, who were inadequately trained before being committed to battle, unfit for jungle fighting and greatly depleted by malaria. In those circumstances, it may not have been the best decision for GHQ to order them to advance again and again against a well-defended enemy, and to make decisions that could have been made lower down the chain of command. By mid-May the Arakan force was back on the line from which it had brightly set off in December.

Yet with the gleam of hope that would flash out from Wingate's first expedition, and with the inspiration that Slim was giving the troops who were training for the jungle at Ranchi, Wavell was right to be confident for the future. On 14 April he summed up the operation to the National Defence Council: 'There is nothing to be depressed about. We have gained very valuable experience, our troops have fought well, and man for man are quite as good as the Japanese.'[21]

Yet privately he considered the Arakan result to be unsatisfactory. He did not think that the strategy was wrong, but that the tactics were misconceived and not what he had called for. Meanwhile, his mind had been ranging over other possibilities. He switched his gaze to the south Pacific where, building on the seminal naval success at Midway in June 1942, General MacArthur's forces had held off the Japanese through the autumn months of the Guadalcanal campaign – in increasingly bitter fighting, so much so that an order had to be issued to US troops that 'no part of the enemy's body may be used as a souvenir'. The Americans' tenacious actions at the eastern end of the barrier had raised a glimmer of hope that the Japanese tide might be on the turn. Wavell conceived a new objective: to seize control of the straits between Java and Sumatra: 'This would threaten Singapore,' he told his planning staff, 'and the whole Japanese position in the Netherlands East Indies.'

But by then there had been a development on the highest plane of the war's direction, at a conference between Roosevelt and Churchill in Casablanca. The service chiefs who accompanied them, particularly the Americans, led by Marshall, King and Arnold, were determined that the recapture of Burma – its main purpose, in American eyes, being to help

China – should not be delayed by campaigns elsewhere. Wavell was instructed to frame a plan that would achieve the capture of Burma in one season, and to state what his requirements would be.

By the middle of January 1943, when the Casablanca Conference convened, the Arakan offensive had made little progress, but it was agreed that 'Cannibal' should be attempted, and Akyab captured by May. It was also accepted that 'Anakim' must retain pride of place, the consensus being that it could be launched and completed in the coming campaigning season. For this purpose it would be essential to gain the support of Chiang Kai-shek. The leading Americans, together with Sir John Dill, set off for Chungking to present their case, while also having to explain to Chiang why he had not been invited to the conference, despite the fact that the Americans regarded China as one of the four main props of the post-war free world.

The seals of agreement were affixed at New Delhi, where Wavell met the Americans, both on their way to see Chiang and then for final meetings on their way back. There, he gave them his plan for occupying western Burma and gaining a foothold for the eventual conquest of the whole country. However, it did not match the comprehensive framework drawn up in Casablanca, highlighting instead the obstacles that faced such a wide-ranging operation. It seemed to both Arnold and Dill that the 'plan' was not a plan at all, but 'several pages of well written paragraphs, telling why the mission could not be accomplished'.[22] As Wavell admitted to Leopold Amery, he never liked the 'Anakim' plan, but it was the best that he could work out under the terms of reference he had been given at Casablanca, which confined him to the reconquest of Burma.[23]

Wavell agreed that retaking Burma and opening the Burma Road was the only way to hasten the defeat of Japan, but he feared that the forces necessary for 'Anakim' might simply not be found. Air cover in the Bay of Bengal could not be provided without a fleet of aircraft carriers, and a large naval force would also be needed in case the Japanese Navy arrived in the Indian Ocean. He was also clear that he could not prepare the operation unless he received some 183,000 tons of stores and equipment for each of the following six months, a period during which it looked as though there would not be enough ships to meet his requirements.

It was not entirely clear that Chiang Kai-shek would participate in the operation. He had already made a further demand on the seemingly pliant Americans, for 10,000 tons per month of airlifted supplies, and Wavell was now asked to co-operate on a major airfield building programme in Assam, as the only way of meeting the Chinese request. He saw at once that this would involve shipping huge amounts of construction material, as well as aviation fuel and the supplies for China, and was compelled to conclude that he did not have the facilities for establishing the communications necessary for maintaining a force large enough to invade Burma, as well as for providing enough airfields to support China. Despite that, Wavell decided to give priority to airfield construction. At least, if the British did have to accommodate America's policy of helping China, giving priority to airlifts over the 'Hump' was the lesser of two evils, as it would delay – perhaps permanently – the opening of land links between China, Burma and India, which would pose problems of their own for future imperial dominion.

That decision would, however, compromise preparations for 'Anakim', raising the awful prospect that the recapture of Burma might be delayed for yet another year, in which case it would not be completed, even if all went well, until the spring of 1945. With such a radical shift in the timetable that had been agreed at the highest level in Casablanca, it was clear that Wavell must meet the War Cabinet face to face, to hold 'Anakim' up to the light and to discuss the wider aspects of the Far East war. On 1 April he suggested to the Prime Minister that he return to England in June.

At least he could draw solace from good news in North Africa, where Montgomery had driven the Germans back from Egypt, with the so-called 'Benghazi Stakes' being rerun, this time in the Allies' favour. Wavell expressed his feelings in verse:

> *Herr Flieger, are you making for Berlin?*
> *Go tell them what a nasty mess we're in.*
> *Say I, Bosch Rommel, take for my device*
> *A party-coloured Neapolitan ice,*
> *Outspread on plate before a greedy boy,*
> *Say I am melting fast, say 'Strength Through Joy'*
> *Has ceased to be my motto; instant speed*
> *Through weakness is just now my pressing need.*
> *Say many a faint and disillusioned wop*
> *Abandoned to our foes is crying 'Stop'*
> *In vain to Rommel. He not stopping here*
> *But much, much further west.*
> *Go say this, Flieger dear.*[24]

In view of the proposed major changes to the plans, Wavell received a summons for immediate consultation in London, along with the naval and air commanders of the Indian region. He arrived in England on 22 April, and the following week dined with Churchill, Eden and Admiral Somerville:

Prodigious quantities of Champagne and brandy disappeared, and the talk flashed from one segment of the spinning globe to another. By this time the London Directors of Plans and the London Chiefs of Staff had accepted our argument that really decisive operations against Burma could not take place till a year later than had been supposed at Casablanca. By the end of the dinner the Prime Minister had accepted it too and about two in the morning he had suddenly decided that he must go to Washington to discuss this and other things with President Roosevelt.[25]

Wavell's comment on this jamboree was characteristically muted:

PM quite pleasant but not much business talked, except that I said I thought we ought to go to Washington since Stilwell and Chennault were there, and PM said he did not think he could trust me to discuss plans alone with the Americans; he or Chiefs of Staff or both should go also. I said I was sure someone ought to go, now that it had been decided that the plan agreed with the Americans in India in February for Burma could not be carried out in full.[26]

Faced with Churchill's disarming frankness, there was little that Wavell could say, and so, with a hundred or so others, on his sixtieth birthday he boarded the RMS *Queen Mary*, at that time used for ferrying prisoners-of-war, but for the prime ministerial voyage displaying notices in Dutch to confuse a gullible public, or equally gullible German spies, and with its peacetime fittings restored to part of the 'sun deck'.

The Washington conference, between Churchill and Roosevelt and their top military advisers, was christened 'Trident'. A great deal of preliminary planning had been done even before the ship reached America. Some of the work concerned operations in the Far East, which had been the original stimulus for holding the conference, and great importance was attached to preparing a good case for the postponement of 'Anakim', as the proposal was sure to upset the Americans. Wavell attended a number of conferences with the Chiefs of Staff and other experts, particularly on the availability of shipping, on which the proposed Burma operations depended so much, and as a central figure in the Far East discussions he came once more into close contact with the Prime Minister.

Wavell's relations with Churchill had been distant but cordial since his transfer to the East, during which time they had been together only for the meetings in Cairo and Moscow the previous summer. However, it seemed that they could not long be in close proximity without a cooling of the atmosphere, and on board the *Queen Mary* it took barely an instant for Wavell's affection for Churchill to be all but smothered, leaving in its place only the respect and admiration for the great man's abilities that, despite provocation, it was not in Wavell's nature to lose.

It is probable that when Wavell arrived from India he carried with him an unmistakeable air of fatigue, and of being finally worn down by his gruelling work. He was as robust as his fabled mountain-gun, but there had barely been more than a week or so in two long years for him to rest and recuperate. However invigorating the prolific duck-shoots in Egypt or the pig-sticking in India, and however much he was attended by personal servants and by staff to deal with administrative chores, his short visit to England the previous August was about the only change of air that he had been allowed since the outbreak of war. 'I wish I could get a good rest,' he had said, a week or so earlier, 'I feel stale, flat and unprofitable', and it was noticeable around the conference tables on the *Queen Mary* and then in Washington: 'Winston thinks Wavell is tired out,' Leopold Amery noted, 'and means to supersede him for Anakim.'[27] At varying levels in the minds of the military chiefs, particularly those who had been at Casablanca, Wavell's aspect reinforced the opinion that the whole Burma theatre needed some kind of invigoration.

Churchill's dissatisfaction with the progress of the Arakan offensive – which he had characteristically described as munching a porcupine quill by quill – was expressed in a lengthy paper that he wrote on board ship, on the whole position in the Indian and Far Eastern spheres. He did not give to the paramount problem of shipping the weight that arguably it deserved, being the chief cause of Wavell's difficulties in mounting a strong offensive, but instead disparaged the efforts made so far and cast around for alternatives:

Going into swampy jungles to fight the Japanese is like going into the water to fight a shark. It is better to entice him into a trap or catch

him on a hook and then demolish him with axes after hauling him out
on to dry land. How then to deceive and entrap the shark?[28]

Besides illustrating his ideas with vivid analogies, Churchill made various
unflattering references to the Arakan operations, including expressions such
as 'complete failure' and 'deep disgrace'. Wavell took these to heart, partly
feeling insulted on behalf of his soldiers, and partly because of the difficulty
in which he was placed by the circulation of such comments to a wide circle
of officers. He recorded:

> This made me furious, and I wrote a letter to him to the effect that,
> if he considered the operations such a failure and disgraceful, he could
> remove me from my command, but as long as he continued to entrust
> it to me I would not have such remarks circulated to junior officers,
> some of whom were on my staff. It was rather a good letter; but I then
> decided to sleep on it and consult Alan Brooke (CIGS) in the morning.[29]

Brooke had the highest opinion of Wavell, and the next morning his icy
clarity persuaded Wavell to think better of resigning: 'If I were to take
offence,' Alan Brooke said, 'when abused by Winston and given to understand that he had no confidence in me, I should have to resign at least once
every day.'[30] Amends were made when the Prime Minister expressed complete
confidence in his commander-in-chief, but with Wavell afterwards
commenting, in a rather Pooterish way, 'Later, he called in all copies of his
note, and amended the offending paragraph, thereby really calling more
attention to it.'[31]

So Wavell arrived in Washington, charged with the unappealing task of
explaining to the Americans why 'Anakim', as planned, could not be carried
out. At the time there had been little intermingling between the two peoples,
and each country's distinct national characteristics were more marked than
they are now. The corridors were filled with confident, brash, America-first
officers, and the British delegation was the centre of lively interest – Churchill,
naturally, but also Brooke, the CIGS, who was reputed to dislike Americans;
and Wavell himself, a proper old-fashioned British field-marshal, their man
in the Far East, where the Empire was – if not everywhere collapsing – at
least retreating fast, and where the US was ready to take its place for a new
dawn. Other exotica had arrived in America, notably Madame Chiang Kai-
shek who, to Roosevelt's vexation,[32] was to put up in the White House; and

the old tortoise Stilwell, together with General Chennault, with whom he was locked in battle as to who should win the President's ear, and largesse.

The British contingent entered the conference certain that events since Casablanca had ruled out the feasibility of 'Anakim' in the 1943–44 campaigning season, and it fell to Wavell, as military commander in the theatre, to explain to the Combined Chiefs of Staff why this was so. It was an uphill task, not least because the cards had been marked against him by those on his own side who, he maintained, had misunderstood and mis-represented the Arakan operations; and, just as effectively, by Stilwell and other senior Americans in India who had consistently 'briefed against' him, partly to stop the politicians in Washington from focusing on Stilwell's failure to get the Chinese to move into Burma.

Even without that handicap, it was a difficult brief – but one of great import-ance as the decisions taken at the conference would be vital for the whole Allied strategy over the coming year. Wavell's mastery of the military facts, his understanding of the variations that affected them and his certainty that the British had arrived at the only possible conclusions were second to none. But as he presented a Job-like catalogue of the monsoons, floods and mosqui-toes that would beset an invading force, his arguments slithered away from his audience, who found themselves listening to what seemed to be a counsel of despair. When General Somervell, the American Quartermaster General, acidly enquired, 'And do you suppose we don't have mosquitoes in the Pacific?', Wavell had lost the hall. 'Thus,' reported an observer, 'was a very gallant gentleman ignominiously silenced, and I am sure that even some of the American hearts bled for him.'[33] 'With Wavell in command,' observed Stilwell – himself tongue-tied in front of the President – 'failure was inevitable; he had nothing to offer at any meeting except protestations that the thing was impossible, hopeless, impracticable.' In effect it was impossible, but this was not what the bright, confident Americans wanted to hear. The atmosphere cooled.

When the President had explained his objectives in China, he asked Wavell to express his views on Burma and the 'Anakim' operation. It was a circular discussion, as Brooke recorded: 'Then Wavell was called upon, followed by Somervell who contradicted him. Then Stilwell who disagreed with both, and with himself as far as I could see. He is a small man with no concep-tion of strategy.'[34] Wavell presented the salient facts and concluded that 'If success was assured, it would be worth hazarding the losses . . . however, an unsuccessful expedition would be much worse than none at all.' No doubt it was unreasonable to expect a less equivocal assessment.

However unjust, in Washington it had begun to seem that, despite his strong constitution, Wavell had become palpably subdued. When Henry Stimson, the Secretary of the Interior, spoke to Churchill of Wavell's lethargy and defeatism in the India Command, and that it needed attention, Churchill did not disagree. Stilwell also had a private interview with the Prime Minister and ploughed the same furrow, noting with surprise that he was not contradicted. The Americans, with all their forceful optimism, did not like hearing Wavell's unswerving presentation of the realities: that until greatly increased resources had been poured into India, it could not serve as a major base for future operations. They had hoped to hear positive arguments; but without a generous application of gloss, which it was not in Wavell's nature to apply, it was hard to conclude that the situation actually was positive.

As Churchill recorded, 'There was profound dissatisfaction in Washington, which we all shared, at the lack of vim in the recent operations in Burma. I considered re-modelling the commands by making Wavell C-in-C India, with Auchinleck as his deputy, and one of the best younger Corps Commanders as C-in-C of the East Asian front.'[35] He began to air his thoughts with some of his colleagues, as the CIGS recalled:

> After the meeting the Prime Minister called us all in and started discussing whether Archie Wavell still had enough drive and energy to carry on with his job, and to discuss his proposed plans for changes. He wishes to restrict the commander-in-chief in India to the pure command of India alone, and to divorce him from the operations outside India. The problem is complicated by the desirability of appointing a Supreme Commander to co-ordinate the activities of Americans and British in this theatre . . .[36]

Brooke recorded his impression:

> It was growing very evident at this stage that Winston had again lost confidence in Wavell. He had never been able to appreciate his sterling qualities or his strategic ability. His quiet manner and his long silences Winston considered an indication of lack of drive and energy.[37]

When Wavell suggested that he return to India after the conference, Brooke replied that Churchill wanted him to stay in England until he could discuss the set-up of command in India with him. Wavell was surprised: 'I could

not quite understand why we did not raise and discuss the Joint Anglo-
American command in Washington; but I sensed that there was something
working in the PM's mind which he was not prepared to discuss or mention
to me at present . . .'[38]

So the conference ended. Churchill, Marshall, Brooke and their high
entourage set off for important business in Africa. Wavell returned to London,
to wait upon events.

FIELDS FRESH

On 29 April 1943, the day after dining with Churchill, Eden and Admiral Somerville, Wavell went down to Northwick Park in Gloucestershire, to see Captain George Spencer-Churchill, the son of Lady Wavell's godmother. Over the rolling Cotswold hills, silent streams and green fields chequered by old grey walls lay an atmosphere of deep peace that brought long-sought solace to the field-marshal, worn down by arduous battles in the swampy jungles, tired by his voyage and agitated by his effervescent dinner in Downing Street. The tranquil old house contained a fine collection of pictures, by Holbein, Cuyp, Reynolds and Leonardo da Vinci, among others. One in particular, the 'Madonna of the Cherries', Wavell contemplated with especial pleasure, its colours, form and serenity stirring the sensitive spirit beneath the martial crust. Moved by its grace, he wrote a sonnet:

> *. . . Long years of battle, bitterness and waste,*
> *Dry years of sun and dust and Eastern skies,*
> *Hard years of ceaseless struggle, endless haste,*
> *Fighting 'gainst greed for power and hate and lies.*
>
> *Your red-gold hair, your slowly smiling face*
> *For pride in your dear son, your King of Kings,*
> *Fruits of the kindly earth, and truth and grace,*
> *Colour and light, and all warm lovely things –*
>
> *For all that loveliness, that warmth, that light,*
> *Blessed Madonna, I go back to fight.*

Those lines were to mark the closing page of a book on which Wavell had been working for many months, in brief intervals snatched from the demands of his campaigns, his conferences, his planning and his politics, over all of which loomed the threat of the Japanese, swarming just over the horizon. 'A blessing to you, my Lady,' he had written, 'and to all beautiful things that help us to forget the dreariness of war.'

The idea of composing an anthology of the poetry that he knew by heart had been suggested by Archie John, who loved to hear his father recite his favourite lines. Wavell himself took little persuading that it would bring happiness to his family if his treasures were collected in a volume – and not such a slim one, considering the enormous amount of verse that at one time or another he had committed to memory. Further encouragement came from Peter Coats who, as the project took shape, suggested the title 'Other Men's Flowers', culled from the French essayist Michel Montaigne, who wrote of one of his own works, 'And one might therefore say of me that in this book I have only made up a bunch of other men's flowers, and of my own I have only provided the string that ties them together.' It was an apt choice: 'I have borrowed his title,' Wavell wrote, 'my memory being the binding thread.' As he included more than 250 poems, many of them lengthy in their full version, the thread was remarkably robust.

His own contribution was offered with retiring delicacy: 'At the end of my garden of other men's flowers, outside the gate, I have put this little wayside dandelion of my own. It has no business here, even outside the garden, but the owner of the lady for whom it was written is anxious for it to be included. She is a beautiful lady, designed though not actually painted by Leonardo da Vinci, and I have loved her ever since I saw her.'[1]

The concept was raised to a higher plane by Peter Fleming, who was on Wavell's staff when the project took wings and was soon convinced that the anthology deserved to be placed before a wider audience. Fleming had written a number of books before the war, and he was able to take the matter forward, even from India, through his relationship with his own publisher, Jonathan Cape, and because he was a friend of Rupert Hart-Davis, who was on Cape's board of directors.

'I cannot claim,' Wavell wrote, 'that I can now repeat by heart all the poems in this anthology. I think I can safely claim that I once could; and I can still repeat to myself – for repeating verse to others is seldom popular – nearly all that is printed here.' His generous qualification of the original premise, that he knew by heart everything in the book, resulted from inconsistencies in the submissions observed by its editor, and from the tensions that inevitably arise when a project takes on a commercial aspect.

However, as preparations continued, the atmosphere became slightly querulous, mainly because of the attitude to the project initially adopted by Cape's colleague, Daniel George Bunting, who was handed the job of honing the work for publication:

> It was a large collection, and many of the poems, though familiar, were imperfectly remembered. Daniel George's sardonic report on the manuscript betrayed his realisation of the unwelcome job that someone, and doubtless he, would have in editing it for publication . . .[2]

Bunting appeared not to take in the unique aspect of the collection – that Wavell knew, or had at some point known, its entire contents by heart. Without the impulse of that astonishing factor, the anthology did not seem to him to justify publication, albeit that it was an eclectic, intelligent and attractive selection, compiled by a famous soldier:

> I found a large number of the pieces where I expected to find them and where, I suspect, the anthologist himself found them, in the Oxford Book of English Verse . . . When I pointed out the number taken from the OBEV Jonathan said, 'I suppose we must make some acknowledgment!'[3]

The temperature rose when Wavell received from Jonathan Cape an unabridged copy of his colleague's opinions, together with a bill for £50 to account rendered, a package that unsurprisingly upset the field-marshal. Hart-Davis took up the cudgels on his behalf:

> He was clearly dying to be told that his book was excellent and that his publishers thought so . . . Further, to a man who is probably a bit shy about knowing and liking poetry at all, to describe his poetic treasures as 'familiar school recitations advancing in close formation' is tantamount to a sock on the jaw . . . You see, he looks on the book as a lifelong treasure, which doesn't require much work on it. We know there's a lot to be done, but really that's quite a minor point. The important thing, surely, is that we have the complete bones of a tremendously saleable book.'[4]

Feeling slightly bruised by the publisher's response, Wavell was not pleased when the book's existence became known in Washington. On board the *Queen Mary*, Lord Cherwell[5] had accosted Peter Coats with the suggestion that Wavell was rather a dull dog, whereupon the loyal ADC had unwisely attempted to defend his master by referring to the anthology, leading Churchill, at an inopportune moment, to perplex Roosevelt and other senior Americans with the tidings that the field-marshal was employing his spare time in compiling a book of verse.

The publishers milled and turned, and the volume began to take its final shape. *Other Men's Flowers* was eventually published in 1944, when it proved an instant success, cheering a public wearied by nearly five years of war, raising their spirits above the shambles of bombed cities, the shortages in shops and the sorrow of bereavement. Wavell's reputation, and the respect and affection that he inspired, boosted sales, and perhaps the fact of a soldier putting his name to a book of verse made poetry more acceptable to stiff-lipped Englishmen reluctant to admit a desire to read any, but happy to be reminded of lines they had learnt in their schooldays, as they explored the lush pastures presented by the cultured field-marshal.

The variety in the anthology was remarkable, ranging from poems that the public would have expected from a square-jawed soldier, with chapters entitled 'Good Fighting' and 'The Call of the Wild' – parading martial verse such as 'The Red Thread of Honour',[6] 'The Battle Hymn of the Republic', John Bunyan's 'Pilgrim' and 'England's Standard' ('Ho! strike the flagstaff deep, sir Knight: ho! scatter flowers, fair maids . . .') – to a section demurely headed 'Love and All That', introduced by the amiably perceptive comment that 'Love is almost as universal an experience as death, with the advantage from a poet's point of view that it is possible to write of it from personal experience.' The opening section was entitled 'Music, Mystery and Magic', the last two having more importance for Wavell, who was almost tone deaf and no lover of music.

It is not only the sheer amount of the verse that Wavell had by heart which is so impressive – and presumably he knew considerably more that was not included – but also its diversity. 'On the whole,' he wrote of his selection, 'I think it is a reasonable choice from the almost inexhaustible treasure of English poetry, for a workaday man who prefers plain gold, silver or metal work to elaborate jewellery.' It was a characteristically modest description: besides the well-loved verses that many of Wavell's generation had learnt at school, the selection included difficult, unusual and imaginative poems. The opening entry, for example, is from 'The Hound of Heaven', by Francis Thompson, an opium-addict famous for discovering, while 'pausing in reverie' a minute, a white-soled child sitting within an arum lily. Wavell first read the poem while on a golfing holiday in the prosaic setting of St Andrews, and while ordinary mortals might have to concentrate hard in order to understand it at all, Wavell had it by heart 'in a very few readings'; in the book he extolled the magic of the imagery of what he called 'this greatest of all lyrics':

> On the wilful face of skies,
> I knew how the clouds arise
> Spumèd of the wild sea-snortings;
> All that's born or dies
> Rose and drooped with; made them shapers
> Of mine own moods, or wailful or divine;
> With them joyed or was bereaven.[7]

Browning and his disciple Kipling hold pride of place in the anthology, accounting for about one-fifth of its contents: 'they have courage and humanity,' Wavell wrote approvingly, 'and their feet are usually on the ground'. The selections were explained by pithy and often amusing notes, which, Wavell diffidently recorded, were not altogether his fault: 'the publisher asked for them'.

In one note he expresses his workaday man's opinion of modern poetry: 'To my poor ear and old-fashioned understanding most modern poetry lacks dignity and has neither beauty nor tune; magic is replaced by unintelligibility; and the only mystery to me is that anyone reads much of it.' The mystery did not excite avant-garde literary circles: 'It is impossible to pretend that this volume has great merit as an anthology,' wrote Stephen Spender, in Cyril Connolly's magazine *Horizon*, despite observing that it had been treated with reverence by several famous reviewers in the daily papers and chosen by the Book Society. 'I must pay tribute,' the critic continued, with faint praise, 'not only to his memory, but also to his conscience, which has prevented him from printing anything that he does not remember. This limits the quality of his selection, though not its impressive quantity.'[8] And the reviewer was affronted by the anthologist's rejection of the poetry of Wordsworth and Tennyson as both 'earthy' and 'star-gazing'.

Another characteristic of the Anthology is that Lord Wavell is not ashamed of his old friends. He puts in poems that are hackneyed and out of fashion and might be said by the highbrows to appeal only to a childish taste. It is perhaps this that specially contributed to the success of the Anthology, since it contained so many childhood favourites.[9]

Wavell is unlikely to have been disturbed by the prejudice of the modernists, instead describing Tennyson's poetry as rather like eating an egg without salt, while Wordsworth's was like eating an egg with sugar instead of salt: 'I go back,' he wrote, 'and warm my aging memory at the embers of the older, braver poets whom I know.'

George Orwell, then working for the BBC, reviewed the book for *The Observer*;[10] he commented that 'to review an anthology is inevitably to find fault', but wryly concluded his strictures by admitting that 'such complaints add up in the end to the statement that the only perfect anthology is the one you have compiled for yourself'. The radical former Eton master took pleasure in Wavell's dry humour: 'It was a neat touch to reprint the passage from "Henry IV" in which Hotspur complains of the "popinjay" who came to claim the prisoners and head it "The Staff Officer".' Orwell ended his piece with a characteristic tribute: 'This is not a perfect anthology, but it is quite good enough to make one feel a certain regret that the man who compiled it should be wasting his talents on the most thankless job in the world.'[11]

The publisher's doubts, and the critics' certainties, were confounded by the demand from the public. The first edition sold more than 23,000 copies, and the hardcover version ran to a further five impressions besides a Memorial Edition. The book is still in print, in paperback, more than sixty years on – a result that might have surprised Wavell, who had at first maintained that 'it wouldn't interest anyone but myself'. Nevertheless many of his friends happily received a copy, some bearing his bookplate of a William Orpen drawing of a private in the Black Watch. He dedicated the book to his son 'who shares my love for poetry but thinks his father's taste a little old-fashioned'. He himself was sure of his taste, and that good English verse should bridge the generation gap: 'For my god-daughter Mary,' he wrote in a copy he gave to the child, 'who will like poetry, I hope, when she grows up, and not be too new-fashioned to like old-fashioned poetry.'

Wavell was to remain in London from April to October 1943, for much of that time being away from his wife and daughters, who had stayed in India, and from his son, who would be in the Far East for a large part 1943 and 1944. For the first six weeks or so he was left wondering what the Cabinet had in mind for him.

Although the 'Trident' discussions were principally about the war in Europe, and how best to keep Chiang Kai-shek in the fight, both the Americans and the British had agreed that it was necessary to change the shape of the Far East Command in order to improve Allied co-operation and revitalise the war against Japan. For that purpose a new broom was needed. There followed the question of what to do with the old broom, who had played so great a part in the war so far, and whose feats in North Africa still cheered American leaders and the British public. Churchill sent a minute to the Deputy Prime Minister and to the Dominions Secretary:

> In the opinion of Alan Brooke and Ismay, Wavell has aged consider-
> ably under the strains he has borne during this war, and I am sure that
> he would not be the best man to command the East Asia front, which
> it is urgent to establish. On the other hand, Auchinleck would seem
> far better qualified to deal with the much magnified Indian Army.
>
> I should be very sorry to leave Wavell unemployed, as he has justly
> acquired a high reputation.
>
> It would be best for all interests if Wavell could succeed Gowrie as
> Governor-General of Australia. He would discharge this work admirably
> and would probably establish good relations with MacArthur . . .[12]

To the Australian Government, however, this proposal did not have an overwhelming appeal. In their minds the fame of Wavell's desert victories was tarnished by stories of Greece and Crete, and latterly of Singapore. A week later, therefore, Churchill altered his sights and wrote to the Prime Minister of South Africa, Field-Marshal Smuts, reflecting his colleagues' views:

> I am not satisfied with the way things have gone in Burma and at
> Washington I found a strong undercurrent that we were not really
> trying there. I therefore propose to divide the Command . . .
>
> This leaves Wavell spare. He seems to have aged somewhat under
> the strain of the last three years and is certainly tired. Otherwise he is
> as good as ever and I should not want to leave him unemployed. I
> wonder whether you would consider him . . . he would make a most
> dignified and attractive Governor-General . . .[13]

Smuts greatly admired Wavell, and in his reply to Churchill praised his military expertise and his skill at the sort of diplomacy that would be required of a Governor General. But the politics of South Africa were complicated by the attitude of the Boers, who were strongly represented both in the country and in Parliament, and Smuts, in rejecting the proposal, may have had the insight to see that Wavell's liberal outlook – which was soon to come to wider notice – might fix upon the controversial status of Indians in South Africa, and would not easily gel with the Afrikaner creed.

The matter of where Wavell could next serve the Empire blended with a larger problem that had existed for some time, but was now becoming urgent. It was at the meeting that Churchill convened after the White House talks on 21 May that Brooke had gained an idea of what might be going through Churchill's mind:

> He was anxious to replace him [Wavell] in the command of operations in Burma, and, as far as I can remember, it was this same day when he began to consider Wavell as a possible candidate for the Indian Viceroyalty which he was having serious difficulties in filling.[14]

The position of Viceroy of India was the most illustrious and important of all imperial offices. Its holder was the King-Emperor's representative, responsible for relations with all the provinces of British India, as well as with the many princely states, large and small, that made up the rest of the country. Besides carrying out ceremonial functions beneath a halo of regal splendour, the Viceroy also had political power, exercised through the Governor General's Executive Council: he could veto legislation passed by the legislature, established in India in 1919, and was responsible for matters of defence and foreign affairs, ultimately to the British Government, but directly to the Secretary of State for India.

Since 1858, and the review of India's administration that had followed the Mutiny, the Viceroyalty had been held by many fine and noble men, most colourfully exemplified by the pomp and circumstance of Lord Curzon. Technically the appointment was held at the King's pleasure, although conventionally it was for a term of five years. The current Viceroy was the Marquess of Linlithgow, who had been appointed in August 1935, but whose term had twice been extended. Now he was tired; he had run his course, and was eager to hand over to a new man.

The Government acknowledged Linlithgow's claim on retirement, and had for some time been seeking a successor. The new Viceroy would be called upon to deal with Americans and Chinese as 'Operation Anakim' developed, and probably the governments of countries such as Siam, from which it was expected that the Japanese would before too long be expelled. The ideal candidate should therefore have diplomatic skills, and would need the experience and ability to control both the military and the political situation in India, as the two were interdependent at a time when the country's mood – difficult since the failure of the Cripps mission – was becoming unsettled. He must also have the presence and personality that were so important in dealing with Indians; and he should be young enough to remain in his post for two terms, as his time in office would almost certainly span the transition from war to peace: that was likely to be a period of great difficulty, and how India was then managed would be of paramount importance for the whole British Empire. Most importantly, he would need to retain the confidence of the Cabinet and perhaps, above all, of Churchill. No one with these sundry and manifold qualities had yet been found, and the position was till vacant.

By the spring of 1943 the shortlist, the repository of which was principally the Prime Minister's mind, had expanded and contracted frequently, at the impulse either of those from time to time on the list or of the Cabinet ministers most closely involved. It contained just under twenty names, including Oliver Lyttelton, Samuel Hoare, Roger Lumley, James Stuart, Richard Law, Archibald Sinclair, Cyril Asquith, John Anderson, Rab Butler, Wilfred Greene, Lord Knollys, Lord Harlech, Clement Attlee, Leopold Amery, Lord Cranborne, Sir Miles Lampson and Anthony Eden. That list now began to shrink, as those on it were drawn closer to the spotlight, revealing in the process flaws that barred some of them from final selection. In some cases they were personal – one or two were found to have unsuitable wives, and the Vicereine had an important part to play – or they were political: Churchill was reluctant to appoint a member of the War Cabinet, which in its current shape was working well. By the time of the Washington conference the front runners had been reduced to Cranborne, Lampson and Eden, of which the last-named was the clear favourite. There were drawbacks to the choice of any of those three, and it was at this point that Churchill began seriously to consider the field-marshal, partly as a way of finding him a suitable position, but also because he believed that Wavell would bring to the Viceroyalty the qualities required.

Lord Cranborne then ruled himself out on medical grounds while, after much agonising, it was decided, not least at the urging of the King, that Eden could not be spared from the Government; he retained Churchill's full confidence and had shown that he also had the respect both of the Americans and of the Russians: it might be a great disadvantage were he not at the centre of events when the war ended. A lively interest in the matter now also developed in India, with the press, which was largely in the hands of anti-British Congress politicians, claiming that the delay in announcing a new Viceroy was explained by the reluctance of good men to take it on.

Although it did not distract from the search for a Viceroy, the pressure to reach a decision now exposed some fundamental contradictions in the theoretical basis for India's future. An elastic approach seemed essential: as the Secretary of State for India put it, the new Viceroy must have a determination to keep India within the Empire while being genuinely sympathetic to Indian nationalism, and must have the personality to put both those ideas across in public and in private – and presumably the genius required to perform the mental acrobatics that marrying these concepts would require.

Side by side with a desire to preserve the fabric of government, a new idea was coming to fruition. Many leading British administrators had begun to welcome the concept of a British Commonwealth of Nations, first referred to in the Statute of Westminster in 1931, in which a family of fully self-governing countries might, through allegiance to a common figurehead, generate prosperity in peacetime and provide stability when it was threatened. It was a lofty, altruistic idea that appealed to the paternalistic but liberal men brought up on a diet of classical imagery and late-Victorian ideals, who had now reached the high passes of government offices and the Indian Civil Service. But Britain herself would draw little strength from such an arrangement, and anyway it could not come about without putting it in the place of the Empire, therefore fundamentally altering Britain's political status in the world, and in all probability her financial strength as well.

Whatever appeal the notion might have for British administrators with liberal hearts, it would be unlikely to cut much ice with proponents of the new strands of nationalism that had emerged since the Great War, that had caused periodic trouble in Egypt, were now seething below the surface of the Middle East and of which India was beginning to display virulent symptoms.

Few in the Cabinet warmed to ideas of demoting the Empire, and regarded Indian politicians as tricky, venal, anti-British, in the pay of self-interested industrialists and anyway unrepresentative of the Indian people. India, it was felt, was not ready for democracy in the British mould. As one Cabinet member[15] put it:

> Government by parliamentary majority for India is indeed a ridiculous idea . . . Government by parliamentary majority can only work in a country where periodic elections may shift the majority from side to side, and where the minority feels confident that its day will come, and that in the meantime, it will be treated decently by the majority.[16]

The Indian minority, especially Muslim politicians, had no such confidence, and were being encouraged by their leaders to believe that they would acquire it only over the corpse of the Congress Party, the creature of the Hindus.

Leopold Amery,[17] the Secretary of State for India, to whom the Viceroy was constitutionally responsible, faced both ways. He had been coached in the imperial school of Lord Milner,[18] whose 'Kindergarten' of young assistants when he was High Commissioner for South Africa at the turn of the century had been the paramount proving-ground for future administrators of the Empire. Amery considered himself a proud servant of Empire. He was strongly opposed to the Conservative Party associating itself with the internationalist ideas that were beginning to gain currency, and maintained that he was interested above all in a 'healthy and constructive Empire policy';[19] yet he believed, as he told Parliament, that 'Britain has never regarded her contribution to India as a claim to permanent domination . . . The policy to which we are committed is not one of reluctant retreat but of willing advance . . .'[20]

Men like Amery, with their brains, background and positions of power, had grown up with the concept of the Empire as an eternal verity. They did not seem to accept that if they removed India from its imperial pedestal, the rest of the Empire might follow soon after; that India, even if it somehow became an equal partner in a British Commonwealth, would still be unable to defend itself against a major attack without the help of British forces; and, further, that if India seceded from the Empire in order to govern itself, it would be unlikely to continue to identify primarily with British objectives. The term 'Commonwealth', which was increasingly substituted for 'Empire', added little but confusion.

The Prime Minister was quite aware of the political pressure for a radical change in India's constitutional position, but was determined to withstand it.

As he said to the King, it would be a 'dismal conclusion to all the glories which this war may bring to our country if India were finally separated from Your Majesty's Dominions, and all that great story came to an inglorious end. Such a melancholy episode would dim our fame in this age to future generations.'[21] Here was a circle that it would be the prime task of a new Viceroy to square.

By early June the choice had narrowed to Wavell or Sir Miles Lampson, whom Churchill had sounded out, receiving an enthusiastic response. The Prime Minister then decided to seek the opinion of the incumbent Viceroy, who was quite clear in his view: 'It seems,' Churchill wrote, 'after reading your various messages that Wavell would be far the better man. We want younger men in the field but he has a great name, knows the situation on your Council, and has a much broader outlook than most soldiers . . .'[22] Lord Linlithgow's advice had been that Lampson was unsuitable: the Viceroy would need long political experience, he considered, in order to provide vigorous and inspiring leadership during the war, and then to deal with demobilisation and post-war reconstruction. He did not consider that Lampson had quite the speed and resource for that great task, and also suggested that Lady Lampson, while 'pleasant and decorative', might not at her tender age – she was twenty-three – have had time sufficiently to master the arts of protocol and diplomacy, or to bring to the post of Vicereine the gravitas and concentration required.

The weekend of 12 June included a Bank Holiday, and Amery invited Wavell to stay at his house near Chichester for part of the weekend. By then Amery knew that Churchill had decided upon Wavell for Viceroy, but he had been told not to sound him out on the subject. Conversation on the journey must have seemed slightly surreal, and the image is evoked of two amiable, elderly men proceeding side by side at mental cross-purposes as they motored along the quiet English roads:

Amery asked me to motor him down on Saturday evening. The whole way down he talked Indian politics. I took a languid, even somnolent interest. I do not much like talking in a car, Amery is a little deaf and so am I, and I had made up my mind that whatever happened to me I should not be bothered with Indian politics much more.[23]

Amery recorded his own thoughts: 'Wavell is shrewd and not illiberal, and the experiment should work. But who except Wavell can fill the bill of a Supreme Commander for South East Asia?'[24] That question was also absorbing Wavell, to whom the answer seemed fairly obvious: no one. His own suitability for the highest military posts in a new phase of the war could surely not be in doubt. Notwithstanding the whole tenor of the Far East discussions in Washington, Wavell retained the opinion that he was admirably fitted to the proposed East Asia Command, and even to other momentous roles:

> I considered, rather vaguely, the possibility that the PM might intend to bring me home to take charge of the Forces for the invasion of the Continent, but thought this improbable as it would be a waste of my Eastern experience; in fact I did not quite see how the PM could avoid the conclusion that a Joint Command and a Supreme Commander was the right solution for the East Asian theatre; or that I was the obvious choice as a Supreme Commander . . .[25]

At first blush it might seem surprising if Wavell, with his knowledge of military history, did not recall that generals in the early stages of wars are often replaced as campaigns develop, especially after setbacks. By now there were a number of younger generals, newly seasoned in battle, thrusting their way into the limelight, and for Wavell to suppose that he was still the 'obvious choice as a Supreme Commander', or that he might be given charge of the forces for the invasion of the Continent, needed a generous dose of optimism, and did not reflect developments in the Allied High Command. On the other hand, it would be reasonable for him to have observed that so far during the war he had indeed been entrusted with a series of supreme commands – in the Middle East, the south-west Pacific and Burma, and that he was well accustomed to the role.

Wavell's family was still in India while these decisions were gestating, and Wavell had been left to his own devices in London. On Whit Monday, 14 June, he was bidden to dine alone with Churchill. Almost as soon as dinner started the Prime Minister announced that he had decided that Wavell would have to give up as commander-in-chief of India and instead become Viceroy. Wavell was dumbfounded. His first reaction was to say that he would have preferred to remain in a military appointment. For a man who had been a soldier for more than forty years, becoming Viceroy would be an entirely new departure and a change of the utmost significance. It was not an offer that could reasonably be dealt with in the course of a single conversation.

Churchill, however, had not contemplated a demurrer and had already secured the King's approval. Over dinner the conversation wound in and out of the topic, but by the end of the evening a telegram had been despatched to Lady Wavell:

Have been offered by Prime Minister, with approval of His Majesty, appointment of Viceroy for duration of war or possibly longer period. Have accepted subject to your consent . . . Shall want all your help if we are to take on this great responsibility . . .[26]

'You will do your part,' he assured Lady Wavell, with his customary modesty, 'better than I mine', that good opinion being endorsed by Amery: 'Queenie will do very well,' he noted. As it happened, it was unfortunate that she also was not in London: to seek his wife's agreement before accepting the offer of the Prime Minister and the command of his King was, to Wavell, the natural and gallant course, although it would be uncomfortable to imagine the reaction if Lady Wavell declined. Yet that a delay should be caused while messages had to be encoded and telegrams sent off to distant parts of India was not very well received, and in the Private Office caused a certain amount of stupefaction, especially when two days passed without a reply. Coats was 'getting anxious', recorded Henry Channon, 'as he says she is so unreliable'. At length the comptroller's anxiety, and impatience in somewhat higher reaches, was relieved. 'I have now heard from my wife,' Wavell informed the Prime Minister, 'that she is prepared to share the heavy responsibilities of the Viceroyalty with me, so I send you my formal acceptance.'[27] A welcome response, but a faint breeze had chilled the air even as the project was launched on its steep and rugged pathway.

Henry Channon, MP[28] known to his wide circle of friends and acquaintances as 'Chips', was a rich, amusing and gregarious member of political and high society; an intelligent observer of his fellow-men and their surroundings, he noted their strengths, and weaknesses, in a diary some of which was later published to wide acclaim. He had developed a keen interest in Wavell's activities, partly as the field-marshal had been staying in his house for the past six weeks; during the months that Wavell spent in England before taking up his post as Viceroy, Channon and he were to form a firm friendship.

To many people it appeared strange that the two men should spend much time together. Superficially they seemed poles apart – Channon's heartfelt description of one colonial city as 'a hell of a place; too Kipling to be true' would have applied to much of the atmosphere in which Wavell spent his days. Channon had no interest in soldiering or outposts of Empire. He preferred the talk and work of the House of Commons; he had held junior office in the Government, and his friends were from the world of politics, riches and high society, a far cry from the cantoonment. However, he and Wavell shared considerable artistic and literary interests, and both were published authors.[29] Channon liked to be associated with the famous and influential people of the day, and at this time in London Wavell's name was a household word. For his part, Wavell had just emerged from a long period of exhausting, difficult and dangerous work that had almost eclipsed the opportunity for refreshment at the well of culture. He knew from Peter Coats that Channon liked and admired him, and that in his company he might meet a new, amusing and interesting set of people. It would, for a time, be a welcome change from soldiers and serious politicians.

Accordingly, once Wavell had suggested to the Government that he should return to England, he sent word to Channon, who on 2 April received 'a long, fascinating letter from Wavell, which flattered and surprised me'.[30] The day after his arrival in London the commander-in-chief had gone to Channon's house, and the cocktail party that his host arranged for him that evening was the first item in what was, over the next two months, to be an almost hectic round of socialising. Channon introduced the field-marshal to a large array of artists, authors, playwrights, diplomats, politicians, servicemen and socialites. 'The old warrior,' noted a fellow-guest when Wavell dined with Cecil Beaton, 'evidently responded to the novel charm of these surroundings, and appreciated the clever people he encountered there, and the lively, uninhibited talk he heard.'[31] Many of them lionised Wavell in their turn.

28 April. A Wavell day. I had the Field-Marshal here for several hours, six in all, and my axis and friendship with him have already caused considerable comment. The day began when he proposed himself to luncheon, and I hurriedly collected not only food, but some guests as well, and we had a distinguished and successful little party. Lady Wilson, wife of General Sir Jumbo, self, Lady Willingdon, the Field-Marshal, Diana Cooper, Rab, Virginia Cowles and Peter. Lady Willingdon was abrupt and direct but almost comically pleased to meet Wavell, whom she had never met, while Diana made him talk, and Virginia Cowles fascinated him. As he left, he rather shyly and affectionately asked me

if he could have a cocktail party here in the afternoon as he had so many people to see, and in due course nearly 30 people came. My additions were the Kemsleys, Oscar Solbert and Lady Colefax, who were all enchanted, and the party went on till 8.30, when Wavell left to dine with Winston at Number Ten.[32]

Among the guests were Wavell's two sisters, Nancy and Molly, regarded by their friends as a wonderful old couple; now, rather incongruous among the fashionable London crowd, they reflected the straightforward good nature of the host:

These two placid, natural, unassuming, well-bred, middle-aged English ladies seemed to have no affinity with their smart surroundings, and yet their good breeding kept them from looking out of place. On the contrary, their modest demeanour and appearance made everything else in that glittering room seem a little extravagant, a little tawdry, a little overdone. Quietly they moved about together, keeping to the wall, and the less conspicuous corners of the room.[33]

Learning that their brother was about to publish the second volume of his biography of Allenby, they asked Wavell how he had found the time, before observing, 'Of course, it is always possible to find time for anything important.'[34]

Wavell was certainly billeted in unusual comfort: however agreeable the houses of the commander-in-chief in Cairo or Delhi, they were nothing compared to the Channon abode at no. 5 Belgrave Square, filled as it was with fine furniture and pictures and containing probably the most superbly decorated dining-room in London. There Wavell could drink good wine, supplement wartime rations with well-cooked food fresh from Channon's country estate, and listen to sparkling talk from an almost endless stream of guests. It was a far cry from the drab, grey, hungry people queuing for exiguous amounts of unappetising fare elsewhere in the city.

While staying with Channon, Wavell was often out during the day, but he had few official engagements. His mental refreshment and physical rest during these weeks were enhanced mainly by being among a set of people entirely new to him. His son was in India with his regiment, and his wife and daughters were still in Delhi. He was alone, his spirit free, in fields fresh and pastures new. He was wined, dined and fawned upon. But sometimes he did not respond on cue, even if he appeared to be delighted. Channon described taking his new friend to a dinner-party thrown by Lady Cunard:

> Wavell was in high spirits, and as he was treated like royalty, soon domi-
> nated the dinner and made it hilarious. Afterwards we were joined by
> Francis Queensberry, and before long Wavell was quoting from Keats
> and Kipling, and it became a duel between him and Queensberry.[35]

On this, slightly precious, occasion – windows shut, blinds down – not all the guests beamed as broadly as Channon, and another observer of the same events was clearly in less benign mood:

> I sat next to Jamesey[36] and Chips, who is bear-leading Wavell, and
> indeed treating him as a considerate owner would a performing bear
> before an audience, sitting in the background with a proud expression
> on his face and flipping the whip gently from time to time. Wavell is
> stocky, with a smiling rugged face and a wall-eye. He is slow, distracted
> and shy . . . Lord Queensberry came in at 10.30 and recited Shakespeare
> sonnets in a torrent of venom. Wavell was coaxed by Chips into reciting
> Browning and Ernest Dowson, which he did in a muffled, inarticulate
> voice, incredibly badly. Much too much applause from Emerald and
> his prompter. It seems extraordinary that a man in his position should
> be staying with a flibbertigibbet like Chips. I found him cosy and culti-
> vated. The other guests were disappointed with him.[37]

It would be an exaggeration to say that Wavell bubbled in this efferves-
cent milieu – his aspect remained largely 'still life' – but he could with reason have felt pleased and flattered at being presented to a lively array of people whom he might otherwise never have encountered. Dining with the likes of Siegfried Sassoon, Desmond McCarthy and Ronald Storrs, photographed by Cecil Beaton, he shed the aura of command and placed himself in Chips' hands:

> Tonight was the Kemsleys' banquet in honour of the new Viceroy, and
> though it was hurriedly arranged, it was a huge success . . . As he had
> no clothes, I lent him an old dinner jacket and helped to dress him,
> putting in his links (mine) and tying his tie . . . The banquet was a
> stupendous send-off for the Viceroy designate. He was both charmed

and charming, and Peter was blissful; the dinner will perhaps rank with
the farewell one for Lord Curzon . . .[38]

Keen as Channon was on his new friend, he expressed some reservations
about Wavell's selection as Viceroy:

I am almost over-emotioné by this dazzling appointment, I rejoice at
it but which secretly I rather deplore. Wavell, though a great man, is
really not quite up to it: he is too deaf and too bourgeois in many
ways . . .

Still, for me personally it is a triumph.[39]

Chips was in his element: 'My great new friend, Field-Marshal Sir
Archibald Wavell, gay, debonair and affectionate, returns about 5 o'clock.
The man is both an inspiration and a saint.'[40]

To others, unaware that the famous soldier also had an artistic side, Wavell
seemed to be ploughing a rather strange furrow. It was not only the indefatigable diarist James Lees-Milne who had noted the incongruity between
the Viceroy-designate and his new companions. The subject had cropped up
at a lunch-party attended by the King's Private Secretary, who noted, 'Bet
Asquith and Eny Strutt told hair-raising tales of the mischief that Wavell's
entourage, Channon and Coats, are doing him'.[41] Senior and old-fashioned
members of society had only lately recovered from the trauma of the
Abdication, and, detecting the presence of some distinctly louche elements
in the rather fast London set in which Wavell was making at least nodding
acquaintances, they did not deem the situation wholly becoming.

Further suspicion fixed upon Channon's own predilections, and in some
quarters disapprobation strengthened when the talk strayed to the status of
Major Peter Coats. The two men's friendship remained as private as possible,
but the nature of the society in which they – and, for a short time, Wavell
– moved, did not encourage discretion. In June, for example, Wavell, Channon
and Coats went to stay with Lord and Lady Dudley at Himley Hall, where
it was noticed that two men had occupied only one four-poster bed. When
Archie Coats, Peter's brother, stayed at Belgrave Square for a weekend he
departed prematurely, shocked by the comings and goings of young soldiers
at the house, later angrily telling his friends that his brother ought to be
cashiered.

For Wavell, it was a happy interlude in a smooth landscape of comfort and protection: it was a well-deserved, intellectually stimulating and exhilarating change from his hard war experiences, and no doubt all too short:

> From being silent, he became talkative. From being – or seeming grim – he became gay. The brilliant and fascinating women of London made much of him. Though Lady Cunard found him 'riddled with idealism', she expected him to dine with her twice a week. The redoubtable Lady Oxford reclaimed him as 'the Empire's Hero'. Diana Cooper felt she 'might fall in love with him'. The fabulous French Daisy Fellowes flattered him and reported his social progress to the Prime Minister, who was her close friend. Nancy Mitford exchanged books with him.[42]

Wavell enjoyed spending time among such exotica, but was also happy when relaxing quietly, often with Channon, Coats and Joan Bright, who, during this short escape from his professional life, formed a small coterie of special friends. With them he liked to cast off his public mantle and be entirely informal. When Coats spoke of his culinary skills, Wavell responded rather wistfully in verse:

> A Ballad of Kedgeree
> (For Peter Coats, who boasted he could cook one)

> *Let's take a little cottage by the sea*
> *(If we can find one at a modest price)*
> *Just Peter, Peter's mother, Chips and Me*
> *And Joan of course, to give the thing a spice.*
> *If all went well, it might be rather nice*
> *(Provided that our temperaments agree);*
> *Joan will keep cats to scare away the mice,*
> *And Peter Coats shall cook a Kedgeree.*

He occasionally sounded as if he yearned to get far away from his official life.

He was therefore unreceptive to suggestions emanating from the highest circles that a move away from Belgrave Square society might not be a bad idea. On one level, of course, there was little reason why a literary and clever man like Wavell should not be free to spend time with like-minded people, but work of great importance lay ahead of him and it was felt that he should do nothing to compromise his future influence with the many serious and significant figures with whom he would soon have to deal. The King's disapproval of some of the people Wavell had been meeting, which was no secret, was not likely to be good for the future Viceroy's image, or his influence. Advice along those lines was passed through Alan Lascelles[43] to Downing Street: 'Pug Ismay making the mischief,' recorded Channon, 'one of Winston's favourites and buddies.'[44] General Ismay was, however, unwilling to approach Wavell himself, as an officer to a Viceroy-designate, so he passed the parcel to Joan Bright, who worked for him, and asked her to undertake the task; she also was loath to be the bearer of disagreeable news, pleading that there was nothing she would be able to do. At length she gave way:

> So I went, and Wavell was sitting at a desk in the India Office, and really I had to laugh, because he closed one eye and then in that grating voice said he was very comfortable staying with Chips, and he met a lot of very attractive people, and that was that. Oh well, I thought, all right; nothing more to be said, really. So nothing was done, of course. I think he moved out, eventually.[45]

As it happened, the Vicereine-designate was soon to arrive in London: 'Lady Wavell is enchanting, voluminous and untidy,' wrote Channon, 'but she has a gay, girlish giggle and a seductive smile. She quite rules her "Archie" . . .'[46] Anticipating her arrival, Wavell decided to move to a suite in the Dorchester Hotel.

Somewhat heavy weather has been made of Wavell's brief excursion into the haut monde, with the suggestion that his inclinations, like those of some of its members, burnt with a hard, gem-like flame. There seem to be no grounds for this. Whereas his soul may have warmed to the society of writers, artists and fashionable hostesses, it did not, like that of Lord Alfred Douglas, walk between passion and poetry; in mind and body he remained the red-blooded soldier, usually with his feet on the ground – like Browning and Kipling.

As the representative of the King-Emperor, Wavell was now to take off his khaki for good, donning instead the bright raiment worn at the pinnacle of the Government and society of India. He was also to receive a peerage, the first in the family's 700-year history in England, and it was as Viscount Wavell of Cyrenaica that he would set off to a country with many aspects of which he was very familiar. For the three months that remained until his departure his days would be filled with engagements, but the emphasis began to switch from social life to politics, and to the pressing matters in India for which he was to become responsible.

Beyond the eastern gates of the subcontinent were gathered men, ships and aircraft intended, it was feared, to support a final move westward by the Japanese Imperial Army. Preparations to meet them, along the Calcutta seaboard and around the camps of Assam, were gathering pace: soldiers trained, mules and vehicles were assembled, and trains hauling troops and munitions were heaved along the ageing railway tracks. Allied commanders were marshalling their forces – first to repel an invader, and in due course, it was hoped, to roll forward to the reconquest of Burma.

Within India itself there was relative calm: bullocks turned the mill wheels and drew rumbling carts along the dusty paths; farmers tended their fields; smallholders harvested their crops; and industrialists amassed the riches of a wartime economy, as the government of 400 million people followed its daily placid routine, directed by provincial assemblies and the Viceroy in his Executive Council. The apparent peace was partly a consequence of the containment behind bars of the majority of the Indian political leaders who might otherwise object to such an acquiescent state of affairs. Beneath the shallow crust, however, currents of dissent continued to flow around the prison walls and to disturb the various forums where politicians, especially Muslim leaders, who had not been incarcerated, proclaimed their views of the present and the future.

Meanwhile it was the mandate of the Viceroy, in concert with his Secretary of State, to maintain the country's peace and harness its contribution to the war effort until victory was won. Only when the war had ended, the Cabinet asserted, should the question of the country's constitutional status be properly addressed.

In Britain, with so much other business to be dealt with for the daily prosecution of the war, the large majority of politicians, economists, administrators and servicemen paid little attention to the constitutional future of India. But the subject was part of the daily diet for the Secretary of State, who placed it from time to time before the Cabinet's India Committee, which in turn advised the Government – men responsible to a Parliament containing left-wing socialists eager for the demise of the British Empire, right-wing Conservatives determined upon the opposite, and a central swathe without a pressing interest in the matter. Now there was also Wavell.

It might have been supposed that the process of selecting a new Viceroy would have included a searching inquiry into the candidates' political bent and their opinions about India's future relation to the British Empire. But when he had dined with the Prime Minister on Whit Monday, the conversation had in that context been back to front, with offer made and acceptance anticipated even before preliminary discussions had taken place.

In fact, in the context of the long-term future of the British Empire the problem of India had already become insoluble, despite the quantity of intel- lectual energy being applied to the subject by the finest administrative minds. Over the previous quarter-century the wide question of India's place within the Empire had been so narrowed by constitutional change that the predilec- tions of a Viceroy could affect only the timing, and no longer the direction, of developments. By a series of proclamations, declarations and Acts of Parliament between 1908 and 1940 the British Government had given a raft of pledges that India would in time be granted self-government. From that commitment there was now no relief.

In an even earlier period, when Indian policy was developed by liberal and high-minded Victorian paternalists, the concept of the British Raj had been based on the assumption that the country was held by Britain in trust for the Indians, against the day when they could become responsible for their own future. That seed had been planted in the minds of Indians themselves early in the nineteenth century, after Lord Macaulay had induced the Government of India to establish Western, rather than oriental, Classics as the basis of higher education in the country. Thereafter, the Empire's administrators instilled, as best they could, the ethos of the clas- sical empires that they themselves had been taught to admire, and, 1,500 years after winning their own Home Rule, determined to plant it in the alien soil of India. A process was set in motion that led inexorably to only one conclusion:

> The problems of extending representative institutions in India will have to be faced in a not very distant future. That such privileges should be claimed is nothing more than the logical consequence of our reso- lution to govern India by English rather than Asiatic methods. The nation which has set the rest of the world the standard example of constitutional government cannot consistently decline to apply its own doctrines to its Asiatic subjects as soon as they have shown themselves fit to make a proper use of them.[47]

This long evolution had culminated in statements made by the Viceroy in 1940, when he pledged to India dominion status and the promise of full and equal partnership within the British Commonwealth. Since then, the Cripps whirlwind had arrived and subsided, but with the Government subsequently stating that although the draft Declaration must be considered withdrawn, the intention that it represented still held good. That was confirmed by Churchill, when he told the House of Commons that the broad principles of the Cripps Declaration 'must be taken as representing the settled policy of the British Crown and Parliament. These principles stand in their full scope and integrity. No one can add anything to them, and no one can take anything away.'[48]

However, statements in Parliament and formal documents have a habit of inviting more than one interpretation, and in this case cross-purposes seem to have arisen within a short time of Wavell's appointment.

At first, Churchill and his Cabinet seemed relieved to have solved the problem of finding a new Viceroy, and hoped there might now follow a further period of quiescence in India, so as to permit the undisturbed use of the country as a base for fighting the war against Japan. Wavell, it might be supposed, had been put in as a military Viceroy to clamp down on India for the duration of hostilities.[49]

Meanwhile, politically minded Indians had anticipated another extension of Lord Linlithgow's term of office. They had not reckoned on the promotion of the commander-in-chief, and its announcement on 19 July 1943 was something of a bombshell. The Hindu politicians, having a chronic dislike of soldiers, were upset and unconvinced by the Government's reasons for promoting one. But the decision was well received by the Muslim martial classes of north-west India – which supplied half of India's army – and by the Indian princes.

At first, in thoughtful Indian circles, doubts were expressed about Wavell's experience of civil administration and political life, but before long, finding nothing against him personally, they softened their opinions, on the basis that the change of clothes gave him a more pleasing appearance. They hoped that when Wavell returned to India in October he might, as a soldier, find some way of breaking the political deadlock by a bold and original stroke. 'It would be foolish to rule out the possibility,' wrote the nationalist *Tribune*, 'of a new Viceroy bringing a fresh mind to bear on Indian problems.' Leading officials noted approvingly that Wavell's talks to the National Defence Council had been the one thing that had made it work, and that his manner, although taciturn, was easy and informal.

Despite his fame he was rarely recognised by the public in London. They caught the occasional glimpse of a monocled figure with many rows of ribbons being driven past in a long black Packard car, but even at the cinema – when, for example, he watched *The Life and Death of Colonel Blimp* – his presence went unnoticed. Now, in order to be introduced to a wider public, his diary was filled with a round of press conferences, lunches and dinners, and despite the hesitancy of his delivery he generally made a good impression.

It was not at first apparent how he intended to shape his role, it being generally assumed that he was what he appeared to be: solid, conservative and a 'safe pair of hands', which was why he had been chosen. Soon, however, he began to unveil his own opinions, which were far from sympathetic to the right wing of the Conservative Party, and the colours in which he proposed to paint his great project started to emerge. They appeared to contain more pink than blue: 'Wavell,' noted Amery, very early on, 'has already suggested having an Indian as Assistant Private Secretary, a more dubious prospect than Indianising his Council. How far Winston and India, or Winston and Wavell, are really of the same mind is another question.'[50]

Some of his new friends were quick to express their views on the matter, but although at first only a few clever souls perceived that beneath the rugged exterior there beat a tender, liberal heart, indications of his stance were soon to become available to a wider audience through the second volume of his biography of Lord Allenby,[51] which was nearing publication. The first volume had already received critical acclaim, and success was expected also to attend the second, in which Wavell considered, among other things, the constitutional development of Egypt after the First World War. The parallels with India some twenty years later were remarkable: political impasse between the British and Egyptian Cabinets; bitterness, mistrust and the paralysis of government in Egypt; government being carried out by British Under-Secretaries of State; a promise of independence to Egypt, but hedged with conditions; and a charismatic populist leader inciting the people to resentment and demanding a reward for loyalty during the war.

Wavell noted how Allenby, as High Commissioner in Egypt, had developed his own initiatives, and had all but offered a commitment to part with sovereignty over Egypt before Britain had in return received a formal guarantee that its interests would be preserved, particularly rights over the Suez Canal area. In the view of the British Government, Allenby had exceeded both expectations and his mandate. Wavell had written of Allenby:

Can there be any doubt now that his solution was the right one? The only alternative amounted to virtual annexation and military rule, which, quite apart from questions of morality and justice, was unthinkable in view of the temper of the British nation at the time and the inconstancy of their rulers. How long would British opinion have tolerated military rule in Egypt, and how long would the Government have supported their representatives in such a rule?[52]

There could indeed be doubt, and it was entertained by, among others, members of the British Government. Wavell had also alluded to 'unrepentant imperialists' in an obviously disapproving manner, seeming to distinguish his own sentiments from those who accused Allenby of 'selling the pass' and giving away Britain's position in Egypt. 'Actually, there was no pass to sell,' he wrote, 'since there was none that could have been held . . . There was a last ditch that some foolish people might have died in, from which Allenby's common sense preserved us.'[53]

Whether or not Wavell was yet conscious of the ominous parallel between Egypt after the First World War and India during the Second, his sympathies seemed to lie with the Egyptians rather than the British; one way or another, his words did not express the sentiments of a Conservative imperialist. The point was noted by George Orwell, reviewing the book in the *Manchester Evening News*:[54] 'He is not, of course, using Allenby as a mouthpiece for his own opinions, but from his comments on the Egyptian situation and the final settlement that was made we can probably get some idea of the policy that he himself would like to put into operation in India.'[55] Orwell perceived how Wavell endorsed Allenby's stance: 'Lord Wavell makes it clear that Allenby saw from the start the necessity of declaring Egypt independent, and that if he had had his way he would have done it promptly and made the Nationalist politicians into friends instead of enemies.'[56] It was not yet clear that the Viceroy-designate had embarked upon a collision course, but the possibility was not lost on Amery, who recorded:

Wavell's *Allenby in Egypt*. Short and extremely well-written. It will give Winston fits if he ever reads it, both because of its views on Allenby's handling of Egyptian nationalism, and the implications for India . . .

I am not sure whether Winston would have been so keen about Wavell as Viceroy if he had read how thoroughly Wavell backs up

Allenby's policy of sympathy with Egyptian nationalism. I should not be at all surprised if Wavell went a long way in trying to find a solution to the Indian problem . . .[57]

That problem, essentially, was that Britain had determined on the transfer of political power from British to Indian hands, but had yet to discover which Indian hands could accept it without bringing about civil war or general anarchy. Progress on framing a new constitution for India remained in the deadlock that resulted from the failure of the Cripps mission. The Government had declared that India should attain practical independence as soon as possible after the war, under a constitution devised by Indians, and their intent was subsequently reflected in the principles of the Atlantic Charter, which proclaimed that in the bright, new, post-war world people should be free to choose their own form of government. In the case of India, the paramount difficulty was to identify the people who should be free to make that choice: the subcontinent contained two great communities, disparate in religion, culture and outlook, and mutually as antagonistic as any of the countries now fighting each other in Europe. Beyond them were many other substantial minorities, besides the princely states that were not included in 'British India' at all, but which covered an enormous amount of territory.

The banner of a free India had been appropriated by the Congress Party unmoved by the political existence of Muslims, Sikhs, Christians or other minorities, and with an ingrained conviction that it was the natural heir to the Raj. It had already betrayed the way it would handle the reins of power by the actions of its ministries in the provinces in which it had gained power: their disregard of opposition opinion, and the close control kept by Congress' central politburo at its base in Wardha, had dismayed the Muslims. In response they accelerated their demand for an independent future for the provinces in which Muslims formed a majority. The campaign for a separate Muslim state – 'Pakistan' – had begun.

The attitude of Congress was anathema to the authorities in London, both because of the English sense of fair play and because of political calculations that a Congress government of all India would spell deep trouble. The very large population of India, which had grown by 30 per cent in the previous thirty years and was now rising by nearly five million a year, lent urgency to the problem. Besides the Hindus, there were in British India ninety million Muslims, and sixty million Untouchables, so called because their Hindu co-religionists considered themselves defiled if in their very presence, or even in that of their shadow. There were also ninety-five million inhabitants of the princely states, from whom the Congress had no mandate. More than 60 per cent of the population, therefore, had little connection or sympathy with the Congress; nor did that party represent even the Hindu masses, being instead a self-serving political organisation run by a party machine and sustained by outside financial and manufacturing interests. The British authorities felt that those who thought it worth negotiating with Nehru and the Congress leaders, in order to arrange the transfer of power, were listening to sirens singing on the rocks. There was also Gandhi, who enjoyed widespread popular support and whose advice was followed by the Congress even though he claimed to be at arm's length from it.

It was now time for Wavell to form a view as to what must be done (and with whom) to preserve India's polity, and when. Having suggested appointing an Indian as his Assistant Private Secretary, he embarked on a more fundamental step, doing so after receiving nocturnal inspiration and the sanction of his wife, as recorded in his journal:

> August 20. Woke up about 3 a.m., with some ideas about possible procedure in India, and feeling wakeful wrote them out. Q approved them next morning but I doubt whether official opinion will or whether my ideas are really practicable.[58]

For a preliminary reaction he submitted his note to his Private Secretary, Evan Jenkins,[59] an outstanding member of the Indian Civil Service. Jenkins suggested that the chances of success for his new master's proposals were five to one against, but thought them worth pursuing nevertheless.

Wavell's fundamental request was to be allowed to try and convince the Indians that Britain was sympathetically disposed towards the country's independent future. He subscribed to the belief that the history of the past twenty or thirty years ruled out the retention of India by force; he accepted that the clever use of even small forces might succeed for a time, but realised that most British soldiers would not want to stay in India after the war, and that neither British nor overseas public opinion would be likely to support the idea. Although, he was advised, India could not reach Western standards of efficiency for the foreseeable future, Britain must accept a degree of inefficiency along the road to independence: inefficiency could not, in the brave new world, be grounds for resisting independence.

Meanwhile it seemed that the present Government of India could not continue in office for long, and Britain was nearing the uncomfortable position of having responsibility without power – the converse of Stanley Baldwin's harlot. The long-fabled efficiency of British administration in India was under severe strain; the recruitment of British officials was already moribund; post-war recruitment would be extremely problematic; and current civil servants were tired and disheartened. On the surface, India seemed tranquil; below, it was an ominous murk.

In Wavell's view, to retain India in the Empire called for an imaginative and constructive move almost at once; certainly well before the war ended. In this he was to be proved correct, as victory over Japan was to bring the release of political prisoners who would foment discontent, with food shortages and with the rise in unemployment that would follow the closure of war industries and the ending of temporary administrative jobs. Yet it remained unclear to whom an approach should be made. There were excellent reasons for distrusting Gandhi and Jinnah,[60] but they were the ones who led the dominant parties, and the Congress controlled the press, the electoral machine and the political money-bags. Even if Gandhi and Jinnah were to leave the scene – and Wavell noted that the emaciated Gandhi was not what insurance companies would call 'a good life' – he saw no prospect of any reasonable replacements. In the end, he believed, Britain must negotiate, as it had with de Valera in Ireland, and with Zaghlul in Egypt: if she were not to rule by force, she would have to use persuasion. A sincere and friendly move must be planned at once.

Wavell therefore began to develop ideas for convincing India that Britain was sympathetic towards her aspirations, and he wrote out some proposals that made their way, via the Secretary of State and the Cabinet's India Committee, to the Cabinet itself. He made four basic points: first, that the ultimate aim of policy remained as defined by the Cripps proposals, but Britain's immediate intentions remained unclear. Second, the choice lay between continued inaction and a revival of some sort of Cripps offer. Third, inaction implied the retention of the present administration, in effect unofficial government by the Viceroy's Executive Council; that might be safe in the short term, but risked a bitter and uncontrolled situation at the end of the war. Lastly, there could be a revival of the Cripps offer, with a positive attempt to carry out the 'immediate' portion of that offer and to bring the Indian political leaders into the Executive Council; this would be dangerous in the short term, but the only course that might make a post-war solution possible.[61]

Wavell recommended building on his fourth point – a revival of the Cripps offer – in some form or other. He proposed to the Cabinet that he should invite a comparatively small number of the different party leaders to a private discussion among themselves, with a view to establishing a coalition government to replace the existing Executive Council. He would give them a pledge that Britain was prepared to give self-government to India, and that such was also the earnest wish of the people of Great Britain and of the British Empire – although whether the people did in fact have that earnest wish was hardly more than conjecture and did not appear on the agenda.

The leaders with whom Wavell proposed to confer would include Nehru, leading light of the Congress Party; Jinnah, for the Muslim League; Mudaliar, a moderate on the Viceroy's Executive Council; Congress politician Rajagopalachariar;[62] and, modestly claiming to think and speak only for himself, but in fact the inspiration of most of the influential members of the Congress Party, Mahatma Gandhi. When, however, Wavell put up his proposals, which included the release of Nehru and Gandhi from gaol, they caused immediate consternation, even though he qualified them by saying that he would ask for the War Cabinet's permission to call in the party leaders only after deciding both that there was a reasonable prospect of success and that there would be no detrimental effect upon the war effort. That was not considered much of a safeguard: to many in the Cabinet and in Parliament, Wavell's whole approach was unacceptable. In their view, Gandhi and most of India's political leaders were implacably anti-British, which they had proved by responding to Cripps' offer with the 'Quit India' movement, which they still refused to halt. The Congress element was in prison, but the Muslim League, which claimed to speak for all Muslims – but to Britain's democratic mind did not do so – was also anti-British; and it was intransigent in its attitude to the Congress, with which it was not prepared to co-operate in any way.

Nor could the Cabinet overlook the fact that neither of the two major Indian communities had made any attempt to help the Empire's war effort or to protect their country from the Japanese. India had been constitutionally obliged to follow Britain's entry into the war, but the fact that the Viceroy had declared war without first consulting the Congress, which had raised few complaints at the time, was later worked up into a grievance. In due course Gandhi had pulled the Congress Ministries out of office in the provinces in which they held power, thereby creating deadlock in the government of the country, and placing an enormous weight on the Viceroy and the provincial governors as the Japanese raced towards the country's borders.

To the Prime Minister, the Lord Chancellor, the War Minister and those in the Cabinet, Parliament and the Empire who shared their views, bringing into the government such people, who could make no valid claim to represent 60 per cent of the population, let alone a large proportion of the Hindu masses, was not a rosy option. It would be an affront to fair play, and to all those in India who looked to Britain to uphold their future freedom. In the Cabinet, therefore, the submission of this carefully considered initiative from the Viceroy-designate even before he reached India was treated as both premature and unwelcome. The Secretary of State for War expressed those views:

In the discussions which took place in London before Lord Wavell actually took up his office, some of us were perturbed to discover that he had already acquired a firm conviction that he was ordained of Heaven to bring about a lasting settlement of the Indian problem, and in spite of all we could say or do, this Messianic belief remained with him. Another thing which I noticed – and confirmed from some of my friends who had thirty or forty years of public service in India – was that he seemed to have insufficient appreciation of the fact that the ninety million Muslims were becoming as highly organised as the Hindus under Gandhi's Congress, and further, that our policy towards these Indian Muslims would affect the attitude towards us of that chain of Islamic peoples from Cabul to Cairo and Constantinople.[63]

By August 1943 the tide of war was perceptibly turning. Churchill and Roosevelt had met in Quebec[64] to discuss plans for the invasion of Europe, and had agreed to establish a unified 'South East Asia Command' (SEAC) under Admiral Mountbatten. Sicily had been successfully invaded and the Allies had landed in southern Italy, leading to Mussolini losing the support of the Fascist Grand Council and being imprisoned. In northern Europe 1,000-bomber raids had devastated Hamburg and bombed German rocket sites at Peenemünde, while in the far Pacific, American forces had successfully started the 'Bougainville Offensive'. But there was no certainty that Japan would recoil for long, and in Burma she still reigned supreme. In these circumstances it was vital that no new difficulties disturbed what was at least surface peace in India.

Wavell was fully conscious of the need for Indians to support the war effort wholeheartedly, and his proposals for a conference with the political leaders included the requirement that they give that promise, together with a disavowal of any intention to renew the campaign for civil disobedience and acceptance of the main principles of Cripps' offer. Although to expect agreement to those conditions would be a triumph of hope over experience, Wavell, even though still in London – he was not due to leave for India until October – was so impressed by the perils of the situation that he was determined to devote every ounce of his patience and resolve to finding a solution.

The War Cabinet's muted response to the proposals did leave it open to Wavell to recommend a further step when he felt the moment was right. Meanwhile he was forbidden to pursue any precise course of action until he had reached India and studied the problems on the spot. The idea of negotiating with Gandhi was ruled firmly out of court, certainly not before the Congress leaders had disavowed their support for the 'Quit India' resolution.

Even the King was taken aback:

Wavell has had an extraordinary idea of starting his Viceroyalty of India by asking Gandhi and Nehru to be members of his Council. The War Cabinet has told him forcibly to do no such thing. Gandhi is now discredited in the USA and in India by his behaviour, and to let him out of confinement now is a suicidal policy. I was very annoyed when I heard of it some days ago.[65]

The result was that instead of securing agreement to his proposals, Wavell received a directive from the Cabinet – something to which he was by now sadly accustomed – this time couched rather in motherhood-and-white-bread terms and restricting him by its generality rather than the reverse. He was directed to defend India; to protect the material and cultural conditions of the people; to induce Hindus and Muslims to work together; and to declare that self-government within the Empire was an inflexible aim. He was free to make proposals towards those ends, but he was not to give undue concentration to political issues while the enemy was 'at the gate'.[66] Wavell relished neither the issue nor the contents of the directive, but he accepted Amery's practical advice that 'he had better regard it as a gentle breeze to waft him on his way and accept it from Winston without cavil, and presently interpret it in his own way'.[67] Even his draft of the statement that he planned to make on his arrival was edited and abridged by the Cabinet. In fact the gentle breeze was, as Amery subsequently commented, a wave of hot air, although perhaps blowing from more than one point of the compass.

Wavell was already clear about the principles he wished to observe, determined that a way to independence must be found as soon as possible. Not only did he regard it as the sole safe way forward, but it matched the feelings of his heart. However, as in his distant days in the Middle East, when he had had to assert the right to make decisions as the 'man on the spot', it once more seemed as though he was not to be trusted without firm guidance.

The succession of meetings, speeches, conferences and dinners continued as the day of his departure drew near. On 24 September he was sworn of the Privy Council and had lunch with the King and Queen, both he and Lady Wavell receiving medals and royal portraits to mark the occasion. Two weeks later a farewell dinner was held in his honour at Claridge's Hotel. Churchill and others in the Cabinet were still bridling at the new Viceroy's apparent attitude towards India, and there was the occasional edge to the bonhomie. In his speech, Churchill was gracious about Wavell, but emphasised his own attitude to India, pointing out that there had been no war there for three generations, unlike almost everywhere else:

> America torn by civil war, Europe ravaged again and again, Africa torn, China in anarchy and civil war and then subjected to invasion – here in India, under the British flag and under the shield of the King-Emperor, this great calm area, this teeming people, have not suffered the evils which have been almost the common and universal lot of man . . .[68]

'I am in a state of subdued resentment,' he added, 'about the way in which the world has failed to recognise the great achievements of Britain in India . . . and I pray that we should never cast down our responsibilities there.' Amery sought to have that part of Churchill's speech cut from the version earmarked for the press. Wavell's own address was also warmly applauded, but its hopeful and conciliatory tone challenged Churchill's whole position. The Prime Minister was angry, but thought it was all at Amery's instigation. That was not in fact the case. The new Viceroy was determined to be his own man: 'Rather it is Wavell who has insisted on pushing forward his view and getting definite Cabinet direction on it now,' Amery noted, adding that while he was anxious they should work together, he was only doubtfully persuaded of the wisdom of action in the near future, and that he felt like a man tied to horses galloping in different directions.[69] In the end it was agreed that neither speech should be published.

On Monday, 18 October 1943 Lord and Lady Wavell arrived at the Viceroy's House in New Delhi. Lord Linlithgow was waiting for them; after seven years in office he was exhausted, and his relief and pleasure at the prospect of departure were palpable; they shook hands on the long flight of steps in front of Sir Edwin Lutyens' magnificent building: 'I am glad to see you,' said the outgoing Viceroy, 'I've never been so glad to see anyone in the whole of my life.'[70]

Lord Linlithgow was handing on the plumes and feathers, and placing in Wavell's hands the future of nearly 400 million people and the Empire's brightest jewel. Hardly rested from his unrelenting years of battle, Wavell was now to take arms against a new sea of troubles, of the gravest political complexity. He turned and entered the great house, with its marble, mosaics, columns, fountains and 500 servants.

XVI

INDIAN SUMMER

I⊤ would be hard to devise a more wide-ranging task than the one that the Cabinet had given to Wavell. He was to defend India, to see to the welfare of its people and to induce them to live and work in harmony. It would be essential that he did not succumb to overwork. To help him he had a Private Secretary, a Deputy Private Secretary and an Assistant Private Secretary, all men of skill and experience bred in the Indian Civil Service;[1] he had also a Military Secretary, with a deputy. Wavell liked to involve members of his family in his daily routine: Pamela's husband, Francis Humphrys, was his Military Secretary for six months, and Simon Astley, another son-in-law, was one of his five ADCs. Peter Coats became Comptroller of the Viceregal Household, smoothly effective in ensuring that the Viceroy suffered minimal personal inconvenience; and there were enough servants to perform any imaginable chore. Military planning was now the province of SEAC, under its Supreme Commander, Lord Mountbatten, and his deputy 'Vinegar Joe' Stilwell, while army administration was the task of GHQ Delhi, led by Sir Claude Auchinleck, sacked from his post in North Africa and instead appointed commander-in-chief in India.

Wavell worked standing at a lectern in his air-conditioned office, and from the start his days were filled with strain and effort. He described himself as a reasonably quick worker who did not concern himself unduly with details, but in the solemn hush of the Viceroy's House he was appalled by the reams of paper that flowed into his room. Almost at once he found that he was kept busy for six or seven hours of steady work a day just to keep the wheels turning on what he called the 'huge, ponderous machine', even before he addressed the exceptional problems before him. But no one, he comforted himself, had yet succeeded in working him beyond a certain limit: 'after that, I do crossword puzzles or play golf'. He was too modest: although it was observed that he was slightly restive under his burden, he soon impressed his exacting civil servants by the steadfast way in which he tackled it. He described himself as having three jobs: Prime Minister and Foreign Secretary of a country about the size of Europe; Head of State for constitutional functions and social duties; and Crown Representative for dealing with the Indian states and their rulers. He was also the equivalent of a Minister of State for dealing with the new South East Asia Command (SEAC).

The military situation lay in the balance. Stilwell's Chinese forces had finally descended into northern Burma, closely followed by armour-plated bulldozers and army road-builders, determined to link the 'Ledo Road' with the 'Burma Road' and so forge a route to China. Meanwhile pilots battled each day with the dangers of flying their precious loads over the 'Hump'. Further south, deep in the Burmese jungle, Wingate was attacking enemy communications, while the Japanese themselves had poured west across the Assam hills, capturing Manipur State, bypassing Imphal and drawing near Kohima, from where they threatened to strangle the Allies' plans of attack. There were battlefronts in Upper Burma, in the Arakan and on the Assam–Burma frontier, and India itself faced continuing naval threat. Yet although the dangers remained acute, the belief was growing that – however long it might take – victory was ultimately certain.

In his first days in office Wavell set out on a whirlwind tour, setting himself the target of visiting every province in British India before the cold season ended. This ambitious programme – he was to travel 30,000 miles during his first year in office – was soon greatly admired by those of moderate Indian opinion and was to pay an early dividend to his Viceroyalty. On official tours the exigencies of war were oddly matched with stately customs and rigid hierarchy, where, 'up-country', for example, an elephant was provided to accommodate the viceregal 'thunder-box' while the staff made do with holes in the ground. In one area of scarcity, near the Burmese frontier, ADCs had managed to collect 300 eggs to sustain the official visitors, all that there were in the district: after the first viceregal meal they had all gone. 'Three hundred eggs don't go far,' remarked an ADC ruefully, 'not in a Government House soufflé.' At least Wavell was now provided with appropriate transport: Lord Linlithgow, like previous Viceroys, had made his stately journeys around the country in a long white train shimmering in the sunlight; his successor, more Roundhead than Cavalier, left the train in its shed and chose instead to use a fast and comfortable Lodestar aircraft.

On 20 October 1943, before an audience of 500, Wavell was sworn in as Viceroy and Governor General, Lady Wavell at his side decked in ivory satin. But hardly had the process run its stately course when he was confronted by three rapidly worsening crises: sharply rising inflation, a fuel shortage and a potentially disastrous breakdown in the food chain – famine had struck.

As he peered at the voluminous piles of documents in front of him, Wavell began to see what he was up against. India was a country of subsistence farmers, feeding not only themselves but, by a disorganised flow of grain from innumerable smallholdings, the 10 per cent of the population that lived in the large towns. The country as a whole was nearly (but not quite) self-sufficient in food, with the deficit just small enough to provide for the people, in their seemingly permanent and accepted state of under-nourishment, if everyone was honest and efficient. Unfortunately there was an endemic absence of both those qualities, leaving the whole system precarious and vulnerable to dislocation from a severe shock. When Wavell arrived, the country was reeling from just such a shock: the Japanese had slammed the door on the entire supply of the Burma rice crop and prevented the westerly shipment of food from anywhere in south-east Asia.

However, imports from Burma accounted for just 6 per cent of the total: to explain the shortages, other forces must be at work. Besides the fact that the Japanese had adopted an unhelpful attitude to allowing the passage of food to India, the winter harvest in the north (the main growing area), which was already below normal, had been severely disrupted by a cyclone and floods that washed away vital railway links. With fears of a Japanese landing in the Bay of Bengal, the British had adopted a scorched-earth policy over a wide area along India's eastern borders. The combination of these events led to a grave loss of confidence and resulted in widespread hoarding.

Attempts by the central government to encourage the distribution of food had also run up against obstruction and lack of co-operation by provinces that were in surplus, which, for a variety of not wholly uplifting reasons, paid little heed to those in famine. Surplus provinces, such as the Punjab, and even districts within provinces, appeared to think only of themselves, happy to drive a hard bargain with any supplicant that approached them. This state of affairs was aggravated by the fact that the government's policy of 'Indianisation' had resulted in the replacement of efficient revenue officers who might have obtained information about rural areas where crops were failing, and then arranged appropriate transfers from surplus areas. In Bengal, pilfering and corruption in the administration had become so widespread that relief measures were largely ineffective. 'I fear the present harvest,' Wavell wrote to Amery, 'will go underground or get into unscrupulous dealers' hands like the last. There is much graft and knavery.' As he contemplated the pathos and devastation on his doorstep, he might have recalled the words of his favourite poet:

> *Take up the White Man's burden –*
> *The savage wars of peace –*
> *Fill full the mouth of Famine*
> *And bid the sickness cease;*
> *And when your goal is nearest*
> *The end for others sought,*
> *Watch sloth and heathen Folly*
> *Bring all your hopes to nought.*[2]

As a consequence of these various man-made clogs on the processes of nature the price of food had risen sharply, at a time when a boom in employment in the war industries had caused large numbers of able-bodied men to desert their villages and families and set out in search of work in the cities. Great numbers of people, mainly abandoned women, children and old men, had followed thereafter, in search of food – 150,000 making their way to Calcutta alone. The death toll from the famine and its consequences rose rapidly, and would in due course reach three million.

Within a week of becoming Viceroy, Wavell, together with his wife, set out to see the situation for himself. This was the sort of initiative for which many Indians had hoped, and it was well received by Indian public opinion, which wrote him down as active and sympathetic. In Calcutta the viceregal couple were deeply shocked as they investigated scenes that would have made many people physically sick. Hordes of destitutes filled the streets, swarming around dole kitchens and sleeping rough, without any attempt at sanitation. Hundreds lay dead on the pavements, while alleys and doorways were littered with corpses: some 'wet', in the Indian parlance, and some 'dry', and many half-consumed by pi-dogs. The new Viceroy and Vicereine insisted on inspecting the ghastly situation by night as well, a dangerous and unpleasant process for which they were further admired: 'one has to walk warily and use an electric torch in the black-out,' they ruefully remarked.[3]

Wavell paid two early visits to Bengal, to which, as he told the Indian Parliament, 'nature has vouchsafed so generous a crop'. At first the harvest had indeed seemed abundant, the valleys standing 'so thick with corn that they shall laugh and sing', but then it was discovered that the crops were blighted. Taken by surprise, the administration was at a loss as to what to do; consequently it had done very little. Nor, on the other hand, had the Government of India. Wavell discerned a grave lack of public spirit. Provincial autonomy, he concluded, had broken the spring of the civil services: the old spirit and power of action of the Indian Civil Service had gone. In the worst districts of Bengal 10 per cent of the population had died, having sold their tools to buy food, and when their money had run out they had taken to the roads, with cholera, dysentery and malaria hot on the heels of hunger. Wavell realised that not only was the Government not up to the job of procuring and distributing food, but it did not really understand what was happening. The pace was also forced by the press. Graphic pictures in the *Statesman* were distributed across the world, one result being that Leopold Amery had to go down to the House of Commons and try to explain why the situation had been allowed to arise.

Wavell requested that Bengal should be administered by its governor, under emergency legislation. 'I admit,' he told Amery, 'the importance of supporting Provincial autonomy if we can possibly do so but there must be a limit to the price we are prepared to pay . . . we cannot permit malad-ministration to result in widespread misery and starvation, whatever the constitutional technicalities.'[4]

His request was denied. This stand-off was the first of what were to be a litany of differences between Wavell and the home government, but the Viceroy was sure of his ground. 'I am afraid,' he reported to the King, 'that the present state of Bengal is at once a very serious blot on our record of rule in India, since we still hold the guiding reins, and there is evidence of the inability of an Indian administration to cope with an emergency.'[5] Britain's long record of sound administration in India was tarnished. The damage to imperial prestige was not as obvious as at Singapore, but it was insidious nonetheless.

Wavell had no deep grasp of economics, but he had sound instincts and abundant common sense, which he could supplement with advice from the best minds in the Indian Civil Service. He soon concluded that the key to restoring the situation in the famine-stricken areas was to re-establish confidence, which could best be achieved by imposing a visible system of rationing and price controls. He was blunt and firm and, applying a clear military approach, reinforced by the persuasive power of a Viceroy newly in office, he cajoled the Bengal Ministry into accepting the army's help in distributing food, much of which was being trundled to market in carts or even on the heads of its growers. In respect of Calcutta, where the problem was greatest, he extracted from the Governor an agreement in principle to impose rationing, price controls and the wholesale removal of destitutes to camps outside the city, where, in theory, it ought to be less difficult to minister to them. Whether agreement in principle would lead to action in practice remained a matter of conjecture.

By directing the army to take over the main work of transporting food to where it was needed, by rationing consumption in the cities – where more food than normal was being eaten by workers prospering in the war economy – and by legislating to control the price of food, Wavell hoped to spread the belief that stocks of food grains were after all sufficient to meet demand. If he was successful, it might tempt onto the market food hoarded by the suppliers, and by unscrupulous dealers and profiteers, who could see the profits of a seller's market glittering before their eyes. That in turn might cause prices to fall, and so draw out further quantities of stored food. That would drive down inflation, of which food costs were the paramount ingredient, and which was becoming a grave danger to the whole economy of India. There was a touch of the Indian rope trick in the strategy, but the public were reassured by the announcements of controls and by the sight of army lorries bringing food to the hungry. Wavell's action also impressed the Secretary of State: 'I do feel,' said Amery, 'that you are really taking hold and that your initiative, both through the Army and through the Governors, will get things into ship-shape condition before it is too late.'

Over the country as a whole there remained huge difficulties: besides the indigenous requirement for food, there were the needs of the troops amassed for the country's defence, their numbers now swollen to more than 2.4 million.[6] Wavell therefore turned to the Government in London, and asked it to arrange for imports to cover the deficit caused both by the famine and by the supplies needed for the army.

His plan was to work towards a nationwide food economy on a more or less uniform basis. In order to seek guidance on achieving it, he summoned a conference of the governors of all eleven of the provinces in British India, the first to be held since 1930. To the governors he explained that India could not provide a vital base for large-scale military operations while its people were in acute hunger and distress. Surplus provinces must make good their neighbours' deficits, rather than leaving the Viceroy to appeal to London. The eyes of the rest of the Empire and of America, he warned, were upon them. Sympathy in Whitehall, he suggested, was diluted by suspicions of a lack of determination and efficiency in India.

With his confidence in ultimate victory Wavell also used his first Governor's Conference to encourage ideas for post-war planning. He had already been struck by the dangerous situation created by what was in practice the suspension of recruitment to the Indian Civil Service. The country had always been administered, hitherto very successfully, by a handful of the brightest and most industrious men from the public schools, happy to seek the cachet of what had traditionally promised to be a fulfilling lifetime career. Now the very future of the civil service was in grave doubt: it was stretched to breaking-point, and experienced men – as the situation in Bengal had revealed – were badly needed. Recruitment from Britain had been suspended in 1939, the new policy being that as many places as possible should be filled by Indians; but Wavell feared that chaos would ensue unless a core of English officials were left in the country after the war; unfortunately both Britain's pledges of independence and the rising tide of nationalism in the East argued against that happening.

Wavell wanted Indians to feel that British officials were there by request, not by compulsion. However, with doubts overhanging India's constitutional future, it was hard to know where British recruits could be found. He therefore felt that the only effective way forward was to entrust more power to Indians in the actual administration of the country. That would apply particularly to senior government portfolios, and most of all to that of Finance Member of the Viceroy's Council. However, despite Wavell's pleas, the British Government would not countenance an Indian Finance Member, especially as the country's sterling balances in London were upsetting the Cabinet, which took the line that the Indian Government could perfectly well put its house in order if it set its mind to it. Wavell maintained that if HMG thought it important that India should be efficiently administered, men would simply have to be found: 'Our troubles will not be cured by lectures on economy from clever young men at the Treasury, nor by criticism of alleged slowness and inefficiency of the Indian machine.'

He also grasped that it was important to dissipate the belief, widely held, particularly in the United States, that Britain had failed to develop India's natural resources or improve its people's standard of living. Britain, he told the provinces' governors, must recapture the sympathy of the Empire's subjects:

> British opinion was, I believe, shaken by the apparent apathy of the people of Malaya and Burma to the Japanese invasion. British administrators had, it seemed, failed to inspire affection for the British connection, or even contentment, in those countries. The journalistic spotlight was rapidly shifted to India, where it was easy to discover poverty, ignorance, disease and dirt on a gigantic scale . . .

That, he maintained, was a great distortion of the true picture, in which irrigation, railways, public works and district administration had changed the face of the country.

Wavell's dialogue with the Cabinet and the India Office, although reasonably cordial on the surface, soon began to sound a faint note of discord, and to expose how his own attitude to India differed from that of many members of the Cabinet. He began to feel the need to press for more support from London: 'If India is expected to carry a substantial war burden indefinitely,' he told the India Office, 'we do need substantial sympathy and help.'

Hovering between New Delhi and Downing Street was Leopold Amery, the Secretary of State. While his sympathies lay with Wavell, in Cabinet meetings he was often unable to put across a persuasive case. It was in the matter of the Bengal famine that Wavell now needed him to do so. The rice crop in Bengal had been adequate, despite the provincial ministries getting in a muddle with their sums and having to make a series of revised forecasts. In its appeals to London, however, the central government concentrated on the shortage of wheat. This met with a dusty response: 'Are we to conclude,' the Cabinet asked, 'that starving Indians will not eat rice?' Churchill's closest advisers were sceptical:

> Yet we are told that the failure to provide half a million tons of cereals will result in a reduction of national output, a refusal to export food, famine conditions, civil disturbance, and subversive activity among troops in the Indian Army. Obviously an extra 1% would not make the difference between famine and plenty. Actually, it appears that the shipment is required not to make good a deficit in grain but in order to deter the Indian profiteers from hoarding, by the fear that imports will

cause prices to drop. This seems a roundabout way of tackling the problem. In any event, it is a little hard that the United Kingdom, which has already suffered a greater drop in the standard of life than India, should be mulcted because the Government of India cannot arrange its affairs in an orderly manner.[7]

Besides believing that his proposals would solve the problem of hoarding, Wavell feared that publicity about famine conditions was playing into the hands both of Japanese propagandists and of Congress politicians. So he pressed the Cabinet to send to India one and a half million tons of food grains, one-third being for a reserve to meet local emergencies and to break the speculative market.

To Wavell that seemed a simple request, and he was indignant at the Government's reluctance to comply with it. The Cabinet suggested instead that the Government of India should set its house in order, by imposing more effective rationing on urban consumers, raising taxes and controlling commodity prices. Most of all, it fixed upon the fact that shipping extra grain to India would require about fifty ships and would mean a loss of two million tons of imports into England. Churchill was not prepared to place Indian import needs above British ones and declined to authorise the necessary shipping. Amery was forced to tell Wavell that strategic requirements, including Britain's obligations to America and Russia, meant that his request was denied.

These prickly particles were kept swirling in the air partly by Cabinet resentment at the financial arrangements prevailing between Britain and India. This was a saga that long predated Wavell's appointment, but as far as the Cabinet was concerned, he became tarred with its brush once he had settled in as Viceroy. It had been discovered that Britain had managed to run up a debt to India of £800 million,[8] a figure that by mid-1943 was rising by about £1 million per day. The discovery of gross overcharging of Britain for India's petrol intensified suspicions that Indian accounts were not being scrupulously managed, as did the placement of government contracts at inflated prices, which the Indian Treasury was happy to recoup in Excess Profits Tax. As so often, expert economic advice was both persuasive and contradictory, but one way or another the problem was expected to add to the financial difficulties with which Britain would be saddled at the end of a war that she felt she was fighting partly to defend India's freedom. It all contributed to difficult relations between the two governments at a time when Wavell needed the support and encouragement of his colleagues in London, if he was to carry India forward in the way that he wished to do.

From the very beginning of Wavell's viceroyalty a certain tension arose between him and the Cabinet. There grew the feeling that the Viceroy was proving slightly awkward, and not doing exactly what had been envisaged or was wanted in London – which, essentially, was to accept that until the war was over, politics and constitutional matters should be left undisturbed.

It may after all have been unwise of Wavell to submit his radical Indianisation proposals before he had even left for his new kingdom, as the friction created had already made difficulties for him in his requests for famine relief. Many years previously he had proposed amending the army's Field Service Regulations to assert that 'time spent in reconnaissance was almost always wasted', but now he was hoist with his own petard. Had he waited until he had been in India for a year or so, as instructed by his directive, his proposals, both on Indianisation and on the Bengal famine, might have had a better hearing. Instead, the result was that his plaintive requests began to cause resentment.

Nor, at the other end of the field, did his positive actions for India's welfare cut any ice with the militants in the Congress Party, their bodies incarcerated at His Majesty's Pleasure, their minds imprisoned by their dogmatic political agenda. Nor, for their part, was the Muslim League seduced into co-operating with the Government, although at least it was not hindering the war-effort. Yet among the apolitical public, the new viceroyalty had got off to a good start. For his swift and determined action to deal with famine, which had probably saved the lives of hundreds of thousands of Indians, Wavell earned respect and admiration. Here, it was said, is a down-to-earth soldier grasping the reins of power, but with a heart that cares for Mother India. For Wavell, with his liberal tendencies, pleasure at that sentiment may have counted for more than the doubts of the Government in London, or the intransigence of the political factions.

He had certainly assumed a heavy burden, soon to become considerably heavier; but, as with his previous appointments, the authorities had chosen a man with solid strength.

. . . This is the hardest work I've ever done, and I'm not naturally a worker, as you know. When I'm not on tour I just spend eight hours or more in the office, and the tours are almost more strenuous than the office. I have to meet so many dull people and do so many ten minute talks. It usually takes me ten minutes to start talking at all to anyone new. And it is irksome always to be on the red carpet and on my best behaviour, such as it is. Some of it is interesting but very much of it is dull, and a great deal is very discouraging. I'm afraid I'm making an infernal nuisance of myself to HMG over food imports but I think I'm saving them from serious errors, and mean to go on.[9]

He drew the line at press conferences, and when some foreign correspondents suggested that he hold them, he modestly replied, 'No, I should be no good at that, my brain does not work fast enough.'[10] After six months he had visited all eleven provinces in British India, including three tours in Bengal, and had stayed a week in each one, usually accompanied by Lady Wavell. He loved the majesty of the Indian countryside, which stirred the poet in him, and made him wistful. Staying at the Residency in Sikkim, he looked out over Mount Kanchenjunga, describing it as a finer mountain than Everest, and that it was apparently quite unclimbable 'as such a mountain should be'. 'I suppose', he said, 'that some day this will become a hydro-electric, hydropathic, engineer-ridden, tourist-haunted week-end appendix to the Great World. But not yet.'[11]

Away from the famine-struck areas, he found, India was more prosperous than it had been for many years, as able businessmen employed cheap labour to develop the country's abundant natural resources. Crop prices were high, there was little for farmers to spend money on, and instead they were reducing their debts. The prestige of the Government was greater than it had been for a considerable time, partly as a result of lingering respect for the Raj's firm reaction to the 'Quit India' movement, and partly because of Wavell's measures to relieve famine.

When not on tour, he held court in the imposing surroundings of his house in New Delhi, the magnificent dark-pink sandstone palace designed by Sir Edwin Lutyens. It was so full of activity that it was in effect a business of its own, run by the Viceroy's staff and employing enormous numbers of uniformed servants, more than a hundred of them tending the ornate gardens – on the face of it extravagant, but in fact employing many who might otherwise go hungry. Wavell viewed it all with pleasure, but a certain detachment. On one occasion, returning in his aeroplane from a tour, he looked down on the vast house and its many gardens: 'Be it never so humble,' he quietly observed, 'there's no place like home.'

His administrative staff was led by his Private Secretary, Evan Jenkins,[12] who brought to the job detailed knowledge and exceptional clarity of mind, and who was supported by the equally outstanding George Abell. His Foreign Secretary was Sir Olaf Caroe, a very experienced member of the ICS, whose 'Brains Trust' regularly studied problems likely to confront India in the post-war world. His public relations were managed by Brigadier Ivor Jehu.[13] Although many people considered Wavell to be a simple soldier who had to rely on his civil servants, that was not a fair assessment. The help of his civil servants was invaluable, but he was far too much his own man simply to 'sign off' proposals put to him. 'I don't think there is even a moment when there is not a file or files about,' the Viceroy observed. 'Now, my Private Secretary reads files for recreation and poetry from a sense of duty, I think. I'm the other way round.'[14]

Wavell liked to dine with his staff from time to time, even when they were off-duty; on such occasions the atmosphere would be comparatively relaxed, sometimes to the point of silence:

> They sat there at the table,
> And Wavell looked at Abell,
> Abell looked at Wavell's navel,
> Not a word was said.[15]

The private household was run by Coats, as Comptroller, and by the ADCs, of whom there were usually four in number: one to look after the Viceroy, one for the Vicereine, one for the guests and one spare. Almost invariably they included a member of the Black Watch, and often from Wavell's family. Their retreat was the Tiger Room, where they would entertain their friends and girlfriends, although the tolerant streak in some of the ADCs led the previous Vicereine to dub it 'the pansies' parlour'.

The days of gilt and plumes were now few and far between, and the ADCs made do with blue armbands on khaki uniforms. Although less ceremonious than formerly, under Coats' influence the atmosphere was warmer, with good food, a gramophone, new books and 'a welter of wonderful flowers', reminding one guest of fashionable pre-war parties.[16] Because he was the representative of the King-Emperor, Wavell inevitably had to maintain a degree of pomp, but wartime conditions and his own preference played it down. He was a relatively informal dresser, wearing open-necked shirts when not on show, but he knew that standards had to be maintained, and on one occasion administered a severe reprimand to an ADC for untidiness when ushering an Indian VIP into the viceregal presence. The domestic arrangements were still very grand, with fifty guest rooms, yet they were restrained in comparison with previous regimes: Lord Curzon might even have considered the atmosphere unbecoming a Viceroy and a gentleman.

There was nevertheless a constant flow of people through the house, managed by fixed procedures. At receptions the ADCs had to take selected people up to the host and, when required, swiftly lead them away again. When Wavell considered that his conversation with a guest had reached saturation point, he would signify the fact by stroking his collar, at which point an alert ADC would immediately produce a replacement. Before dinner, the guests would be marshalled into a large anteroom, junior guests at each end, top people in the middle. It was all redolent of an eighteenth-century dance: the Viceroy and Vicereine would make their entrance and slowly walk down the line, an ADC calling out the name of each person to be introduced – a valuable service for Wavell, who was chronically unable to remember faces. After dinner there would be 'talkies'; the Viceroy happily making the transition from minuet to *Mickey Mouse*. He liked the occasional cartoon, but was largely unmoved by films; on the whole he preferred reading. One film, *Casablanca*, which had received wide popular acclaim, he described as 'a typical film story of the sentimental-thriller type', but said that he himself was neither touched nor thrilled.[17]

Actors, writers or entertainers whose war work had brought them to India would often be invited to the Viceroy's House. In January 1944 Cecil Beaton came to stay, on a mission to prepare a book of photographs 'to defend the record of Empire'. He took a number of photographs of Wavell, who rather liked him, although he mildly objected to what he called a somewhat pansy voice and manner. Other guests included John Gielgud, due to act the part of 'Hamlet' for soldiers in Leave Camps; the BBC's 'Gert and Daisy', whom Wavell described as two very nice, plump, comfortable sisters from Lancashire; Joyce Grenfell; the writer Beverley Nichols; and the fashionable portraitist Simon Elwes, who painted the Viceroy, as well as various luminaries of the Indian Army. Noël Coward also stayed and sang for his supper, but caused eyebrows to rise when, upon leaving, he called out to Coats, standing near various dignitaries, 'Goodbye, Comptroller *Dahling*.'

Wavell and his wife encouraged the arts, and the Wavell Theatre was established with their patronage, its debut being Edith Evans' performance of *The Late Christopher Bean* before 1,400 troops. The Viceroy also arranged the acquisition of premises so that one of his ADCs could set up an art school.

Despite his lack of small-talk, the Viceroy was a kindly man, and outbursts of displeasure were rare; he was occasionally cantankerous, and if something irritated him – such as his horse failing to stand still when asked to do so, or his groom not holding it properly – he could become terse. When an ADC, riding on the Viceroy's blind side, cannoned into his mount, it caused five minutes of fury; but such episodes were soon forgotten. With those whom he knew Wavell demonstrated a sense of humour, but he would chuckle, rather than laugh: he did not engender hilarity. There were exceptions, when his feelings would break through his restraint. At one formal lunch-party, for example, held in one of the gardens, Wavell presided at the centre of the table with an extremely nervous Indian on his left, and on his right a very grand English lady, the wife of a colonel. As Wavell was deaf in his right ear and blind in his left eye, luncheon conversations were often handicapped from the start, even without the field-marshal's habitual reticence. On this occasion the proceedings were distinctly sluggish until the guests were startled by a loud and unaccustomed explosion of laughter from the Viceroy, as tears started from his eye. His laughter continued, with some vigour, more or less without interruption for the rest of the meal. After lunch one of the guests asked him what the lady had said to him that he had found so funny:

'Oh,' said Wavell, 'didn't you hear?'

'No,' replied the guest, 'of course I didn't, from the far end of the table.'

'Well,' said the Viceroy, 'I asked her whether she had any children, and her reply was, "No. I've *tried* and *tried*, but I've only ever had *dachshunds*".'

In the private apartments the family liked to keep rather to themselves, and the atmosphere was relatively quiet, although they were often lively together. During 1943 and 1944 Archie John was training in central India and then fighting in Burma and liked to spend leave at the Viceroy's House. In the private apartments he and his sisters often played draughts or backgammon, while their father read. Wavell sometimes turned to poetry before going to bed, as a contrast to official papers, 'which', he said, 'are prose, or meant to be'. He liked to chat to old friends and intelligent senior officers, such as Sir Arthur Smith, for whom he often sent, while silent servants would bear silver trays of gin and lime – the Viceroy disapproved of champagne being offered in wartime. He often sat silently doing crossword puzzles, and could usually do the one in *The Times* in about twenty minutes. At one point the fashion for 'Pelmanism' reached the household. As a good memory brings success in the game, Wavell decided to learn it, and hired a tutor, a Miss Tuck. After half an hour he turned to her and said, 'I think I've done enough now, thank you, Mrs Hunt.'

Pamela and Felicity often stayed in the house, Pamela with Francis, the Viceroy's first grandson; Felicity was working at Naval Headquarters and Pamela for the Red Cross. Wavell's youngest daughter, Joan, was at the Foreign Office in London while her husband, Simon Astley, was on a course at Camberley. Archie John sometimes brought brother officers of the Black Watch, on leave from jungle training in the Central Provinces; later in the year he would be presented at Buckingham Palace, his father being alarmed that he would attend with 'his long, wild hair'.

The Viceroy's day would start at 6.30 a.m., with an hour and a half's ride, accompanied by an ADC, and by guests and family if they chose: there was usually quite a large procession. Occasionally he played nine holes of golf instead. He would sometimes go off to shoot tigers, and he was a friend of Jim Corbett, the famous Big Game Hunter. When his party shot six tigers in the Central Provinces, Wavell noted that he was very near the scenes of Kipling's *Jungle Books*. Shooting birds was also a relief from work, and although he was not an outstanding shot, like some of the maharajahs, he was able to hold his own. Bags were high, as at the famous Bikaner imperial sand-grouse shoot, when the party's twelve guns shot 1,550 birds in under three hours. Such distractions, and his domestic life, were invaluable in helping Wavell shoulder his burden, one that would become heavier as the world of Indian politics began to stir from its temporary quiescence.

On the surface it seemed, for a time, that political life and thought were in suspense, so that the Viceroy might reasonably have been tempted to adopt a conservative approach and let the conveniently sleeping dogs lie. Partly because of his nature, that was not to be the case. By the spring of 1944, when war conditions had brought an improvement in the economic lot of a large number of Indians, Wavell noted that only a small percentage of the population was taking even a passive interest in politics. The politically conscious minority comprised, on the Hindu side, educated men and women such as lawyers, doctors, businessmen and students. The new generation of educated Indians supported the Indian National Congress, which was sustained also by big business and the press, and they had almost all grown up with an instinctive feeling that the British must go. In fact the chance of bridging the divide between that class of Indian and the Raj had probably been extinguished nearly a generation earlier, by the fatal bullets fired at some 400 people protesting in a cul-de-sac at Jallianwalla Bagh.[18]

In vain Wavell sought for a method of harnessing others to the political process: the princes, landowners, capitalists and the men who had come forward for the Viceroy's Executive Council, for example. But they all seemed to be either apathetic or overawed by the nationalist leaders. As he was to find with both civil servants and soldiers, once people became convinced that the British were going, they would begin to look to new masters.

The Hindu politicians seemed to have no ideas beyond calling for the release of their leaders and returning to factious politics. The leaders themselves, in so far as they were able to say anything much from their prison cells, showed no signs of changing their policy or of wishing to co-operate with the British. Meanwhile Gandhi, in his Congress shrine, maintained 'his attitude of injured innocence and righteous self-approval'.[19]

The educated Muslim classes were less politically minded than the Hindus, but they were being encouraged by their leaders to put some grit into their opinions and to support the All India Muslim League. This organisation was becoming rapidly more militant, largely because of the activities of its single-minded president, Muhammad Ali Jinnah – reserved and dignified, whose own forebears were Hindus. His success with the Muslim League had, rather to his surprise, led the British authorities to acknowledge that he had become some sort of power in the land, and he was one of the leaders consulted by the Viceroy on the day after India joined the war: '. . . up to the time of the declaration of war,' he said, 'the Viceroy never thought of me but of Gandhi and Gandhi alone . . . I wondered within myself why I was so suddenly promoted.' He then realised that the Muslim League had established itself as the leading alternative to the Congress and a power to be reckoned with.[20]

The Congress Party's ill-advised policy of withdrawing from government had left the field clear for Jinnah. His party was now in the ascendant, and in no mood to compromise with the Hindus. The Muslims were determined to go their own way, even if it meant splitting India in two. Jinnah's view, although few on the British side would accept it as realistic, was that India could not be both democratic and united: at various times the subcontinent had been brought into a temporary unity, but that had been by force, whether Muslim, Hindu or British despotism, benevolent or otherwise. There never was, Jinnah argued, nor ever could be, unity of the people: the divergence was too great, too deep, with endemic, overriding economic or social differences. Muslims, he maintained, were quite different from Hindus, not ethnically, but certainly culturally and spiritually. 'India,' he would say, 'is a sub-continent, not a nation. She can never be a nation.'[21] Determined to develop mass support, Jinnah had fixed upon the talisman of 'Pakistan' with which to entice his following, and to encourage it to militancy; he drew considerable encouragement from the Viceroy's statement of August 1940, approved by the War Cabinet, that Britain would not contemplate transferring power to any system of government whose authority was denied by large and powerful elements in India's national life – in effect a promise of 'Pakistan', should the Muslims insist upon it. That one concept was to prove enough to sweep away the tangled webs woven by Congress politicians, and to break the thin red line of the Raj.

Wavell's first principle for his Viceroyalty was that it was essential for the Empire, and in fact for the world, that India should be united, stable and friendly towards Britain. He was determined to promote that stability and friendliness, and somehow to square a circle in which the stability depended on British control that was itself precluding the friendliness. Having soon established in his own mind that there was no one in the country ready to step forward as a moderate leader, he felt that he had to try and bring together the leaders of the Congress and the Muslim League. Always ready to look to the future, he was well aware that with a population of ninety million – more than the combined populations of all the Arabs in the Middle East – the Muslims were a force that it would be in the Empire's interests to conciliate. But he did not have a free hand, for while the War Cabinet had not forbidden political initiatives if and when it seemed to the Viceroy that the moment was right, it firmly discouraged parley with the Congress Party leaders until they disavowed their 'Quit India' resolution, and, on the subject of dividing India, with the Muslim League at all.

The Viceroy now occupied a pivotal position in a complex and in some ways makeshift constitutional framework. In five of the eleven provinces parliamentary government had been suspended. Their ministries, creatures of the Indian National Congress, had abandoned their duties as a mark of the Congress' displeasure at India declaring war in 1939; each of those provinces was being administered by its governor. Parliament had provided for a federation to include both the provinces and the princely states, but the federal part of that Act was in temporary abeyance as the states had yet to steel themselves to join in the arrangements. To that extent, an earlier Act, of 1919, remained in force, providing for a central government in the form of a legislative assembly and a council of state that wielded powers not devolved to the provincial governments. The executive arm was the Viceroy's Council, not responsible to the legislature, but as far as possible working in harmony with it and functioning much like a Cabinet. The net effect was that major decisions relating to the government of India were largely in the hands of Wavell and his council, of whom ten members were prominent and experienced Indian administrators or politicians and four were British, including two top civil servants and the commander-in-chief of the army.

This intricate structure was a weir designed to control the stream of power emanating from the British Parliament until such time as the sluice could be raised and that power transferred to India. Wavell could not – and certainly did not want to – halt the fundamental impulse towards the transfer of power, and his influence was the stronger for the lack of real understanding, in Britain, of the Indian situation. Even at the India Office there were few officials who had spent much time in the country. Therefore, provided that he managed to avoid being halted in his tracks by the Cabinet, Wavell, who knew a great deal about India, could to some extent accelerate or retard the movement towards independence.

Had he wished to do so, he could have adopted a strong line and have attempted to restrain hostile political activity. In the opinion of leading members of the Government, particularly the Prime Minister, that would have been the best policy. However, Wavell was at heart a liberal man, and almost as soon as he had accepted his appointment he adopted a progressive view of India's future. Less rigid than previous Viceroys, he intended to put out feelers wherever he could, diverging from the spirit, if not the letter, of his brief, in order to encourage leaders of all sections of the Indian community to co-operate with the Government, and thus perhaps remove the political deadlock.

His predecessor's Private Secretary had observed that in one way Wavell was fortunate in there being an acute food crisis for him to grapple with at the start of his term, as it was a distraction from politics and gave him a good excuse for keeping it on the shelf until experience put him in a stronger position to address it.[22] He had now reached that position, and the descent of politics from the shelf, at least as far as Wavell was concerned, was marked by the opening of dialogue with Mohandas K. Gandhi.

On 17 February 1944, Gandhi, detained in the Aga Khan's Palace at Poona, sent a letter to Wavell. The Viceroy, eager to foster friendly relations with Indians, may have been struck by its wording: 'Dear Friend,' it began,

'Although I have not had the pleasure of meeting you, I address you on purpose as "Dear Friend"', with the explanation that Gandhi regarded himself as a friend and servant of humanity – a category in which he generously placed the British.

In other circumstances the Representative of the King-Emperor of India might have deemed it inappropriate to enter into correspondence with a man imprisoned for sedition, but Wavell felt that he must at least consider an approach from such an important figure in the landscape. The Hindus were by far the largest community in the country, and Gandhi, although claiming to answer to no one but himself, was their mentor. Partly because his compassionate nature was stirred by the recent death of Gandhi's wife, and partly because he did not want to stamp on the approach, Wavell decided to reply to Gandhi's letter, which included the puzzling assertion that 'Quit India' was 'an expression charged with the friendliest feeling for Britain in terms of the whole of humanity'. Wavell did not solve that puzzle, but the two men continued to correspond over the following months, keeping alive Wavell's hope that cordial and constructive relations could be resumed, if only the Congress would adopt a constitutional approach.

Yet there was no meeting of minds, and in due course Wavell, reporting to the King, was forced to conclude that Gandhi was '70% extremely astute politician with a fixed dislike of the British and determination to rid India of them; 15% saint and 15% charlatan. I am always pretty clear,' he added, 'about the first of these percentages, but my estimate of the second and third proportions changes frequently.'[23] Later experience confirmed him in his view and led him to describe Gandhi as 'an exceedingly shrewd, obstinate, domineering, double-tongued, single-minded politician',[24] and to discount the attribute of saintliness, although accepting that he may have been a saint by Hindu standards.

Wavell's letters to the palace were very well received, and he learned that the King had described his first one as 'the most informative document that he had ever received from any of his Representatives overseas and that there could not be a more lucid analysis of the whole complicated Indian picture'.[25]

It was not only the Cabinet, but also senior civil servants in India who advised that it would be dangerous to accelerate the process of constitutional change while the war was on. It would mean diverting labour from the war-effort; and the Cripps proposals – which is where the matter of Indian independence had been left – would, if revived, involve as a first step an all-India general election on a grand scale. Even if such a huge undertaking could be arranged it would bring to a head, in acute form, all the controversies and rivalries that most of the authorities felt must be kept dormant in wartime. Troublemakers would thrive, and minorities other than the main political parties would lose confidence that Britain would take account of their interests.

A major constitutional initiative might also sap the morale of the fighting services; arguably, they had as much right as any to share in shaping India's future, but they were away at the war, and it would not be fair to the soldiers if a political initiative was made at least partly in order to satisfy civilian politicians who had not helped the war-effort at all – and, in the case of the Congress, had endeavoured to hinder it. With the mass of the population uninterested in politics, and without a countrywide demand for immediate change, Wavell was advised that it might be better to fight one war at a time.

He was not convinced. However, it was not long before Gandhi himself interrupted the peace, this time inadvertently. Wavell was on tour in Sikkim when he received a telegram in the small hours of the morning saying that the Mahatma's health had entered a rapid decline and that he might die at any minute. An array of governors and officials at once urged the Viceroy to order his immediate release. In particular Wavell was advised that Gandhi was never likely to be an active factor in politics again. Wavell gave the order, believing that although the Government would gain little credit in the matter, it had nothing to lose, and that the sooner Gandhi was released, the better. 'We had to let the old man out sometime,' he told Amery, 'and I think that the opportunity of his illness has not been a bad one.'[26] If Gandhi had in fact remained too frail to re-enter politics, that might have a fair comment; instead, he managed a remarkable recovery and was soon back in the fray. Amery was reminded of Lord Byron's remark in a similar circumstance: 'My mother-in-law has been dangerously ill; she is now dangerously well.'

With his habitual circumlocution, Gandhi now signalled that he wanted to meet the Viceroy. He was stirring, Wavell informed the King, with 'cunning and casuistry', his object being to obtain the release of the Congress Working Committee without giving much in return; his two-year-old attitude of 'stand and deliver' was unabated. Wavell declined the invitation for a meeting, but left the door slightly open by saying that he would be glad to consider any definite and constructive proposal for India's welfare. On 26 July 1944 Gandhi offered to instruct the Congress that mass civil disobedience 'cannot be offered' – presumably meaning that it should cease – and to agree to full co-operation in the war-effort if a declaration of immediate Indian independence were made and a national government formed.

The stakes were increasing, and the fears of the Cabinet were aroused. The need for courtesy and friendliness did not travel well, and the very fact that Wavell had been corresponding with Gandhi at all, let alone courteously, was not popular. The Cabinet insisted on amending the draft to Wavell's letter. The Prime Minister said:

I hope the Cabinet will stand firm and not be disturbed by the attitude of the Viceroy. He thinks that because Gandhi wrote a letter to him he is entitled to reply in terms which do not commend themselves to the War Cabinet. As a matter of fact he has no right to negotiate with Gandhi at all, considering he was responsible for passing to us the medical opinion on which we were told he would never be able to take a part in politics again.[27]

With some asperity Wavell replied that he was not negotiating, only reminding Gandhi of the British Government's position, and that anyway he could not have ignored the medical opinions, although he admitted that 'they have proved mistaken, as medical opinions sometimes are'. He was adamant that he was complying with his original directive, but that he had constantly to bear in mind the need to compose the differences between the Hindus and the Muslims. 'I think it is wrong from every point of view,' he added, 'for HMG to adopt an entirely negative attitude.'

The Cabinet took a different view. They considered that the correspondence wore the aspect of a great parley between the Viceroy and the newly released invalid, and felt that there was a strong risk it would look as though negotiations had restarted; something that would be misunderstood by other minorities, particularly the Muslim League. Wavell's reply was reworded in London, leaving it unchanged in substance, but with the friendly tone expunged. He was not at all pleased, writing:

Indians are most sensitive to the tone of communications, and HMG's revised draft will undoubtedly be considered as hostile and provocative, and will increase bitterness in the feeling of all political Indians. It will also, I think, be bad in its effect on opinion in the USA and elsewhere . . .

I am assuming that HMG are sincere in their wishes to make progress towards a political settlement. I can assure them that it is my considered opinion that their proposed reply will do more harm than good.[28]

Politeness would cost nothing, he said, and would pay a dividend both in India and England, and also in America: 'You must,' he concluded, 'accept the advice of the man on the spot . . .'

They did not do so, and the London version prevailed. As Wavell had warned, it received a bad press, with the Congress and the liberals describing it as 'worse than Cripps'. Wavell expressed his annoyance: the Cabinet had now turned down his recommendations for an Indian Finance Minister, for an alteration to India's diplomatic status in Washington, for direct rule in Bengal and for his own reply to Gandhi. 'I feel very sore about this,' he wrote, 'some day we have got to negotiate with these people, not necessarily Gandhi perhaps, and this letter has destroyed at one blow a reputation that had been accorded me in the Congress press of being at least straightforward and courteous in my correspondence with the Congress.'[29]

The controversy laid bare the difference between those who felt that it was neither safe nor profitable for the Empire, or for the Indian people, to disturb the status quo until the war was over, and those, like Wavell, who had an urge to seize the moment, if not to create it, and proceed with the transfer of power to the Indians – if only it could be discovered which among them had the stature and impartiality to receive it.

The Viceroy now seemed to be as much at odds with the Cabinet in London as with the Congress Party in India. He accepted that his instructions were not to enter into negotiations, but he could not, he complained, shut himself up and refuse to see Indian politicians or try to find out what they were thinking. It was not as easy to be frosty in India as it might be in far-away London. Although it would not become apparent until a little later, Wavell's correspondence with Gandhi and the fact of his release, even if on medical grounds, had already set in motion a new process. It marked a shift in British thinking from a determination to extend fair play equally to all communities and minorities, towards accepting that it would have to be mainly with the Congress Party that the transfer of power should be managed, if terms to suit both countries were to be achieved.

At this point all eyes switched to talks arranged, against all the odds, between Gandhi and Jinnah, who had invited Gandhi to his grand new mansion in Mount Pleasant Road, Bombay, with its spreading lawns and terraces of Italian marble. The press arrived in swarms, hanging from the branches of trees to get photographs, and police cordoned off the area. For the first time since Indian politics had so dangerously polarised, the two great protagonists, seeking to sway the fortunes of 400 million people, were to meet face to face: Jinnah with his Savile Row suits, silk shirts, co-respondent shoes and expensive cigarettes; Gandhi in his loincloth. Wavell did not entertain high hopes of any agreement between what he described as 'two obstinate, intransigent crafty old men'.[30]

For three weeks the two leaders sparred, never really negotiating, but talking and writing to each other along parallel lines – their correspondence amounted to some 30,000 words. The real purpose of each had in fact been to strengthen his position for bargaining with the British, and unsurprisingly there was no resolution to the impasse. The two men had no dislike for each other, but Jinnah did not accept Gandhi's saintliness: 'Why,' he asked, 'does the Viceroy allow himself to be led by the nose by that mountebank?' For his part, Gandhi had set his face against partition, and that also hindered progress. The talks ended, as Wavell put it, 'on a note of complete futility'.

The stalemate was largely caused by Jinnah. He stuck doggedly to his 'Two-Nation' theory: that 'geographically contiguous areas in which the Muslims are numerically in a majority should be grouped so as to constitute independent states, autonomous and sovereign'. These areas were in the north-west and the north-east of the country. The Muslims wanted no connection with 'Hindustan' except by treaty arrangements. It was the clarion-call of 'Pakistan', and before long it would be answered with mayhem and massacre.

Wavell had now been Viceroy for nearly a year. He could be satisfied with many aspects of his work, but there had been no significant constitutional developments. Yet he was as convinced as ever that progress must be made before the war ended, in view of the complications that post-war reconstruction would bring. There was now a new factor: the prospects of an end to the fighting had radically altered. The renewed Japanese offensive, begun in March 1944, had failed. The enemy had actually crossed the Burmese frontier into India, but had beached themselves on the plain of Imphal, in Manipur, and there followed a swift, deep and dramatic recoil. Their commander, General Mutaguchi, had counted on capturing bases at Imphal and Kohima before the monsoon struck, but the Allies had held him off. The enemy were on the retreat, and far from home; the tables seemed finally to have turned. Starved, felled by dysentery and malaria, spewing an iron trail of smashed equipment, pursued by the 14th Army, which had finally found strength and soul, they were driven back over the mountains to the line at Sittaung from which they had first advanced six months earlier.

Believing that the retreat of the Japanese intensified the need to solve the political deadlock, Wavell reverted to the proposal that he had submitted before he left England: that he should convene a conference of political leaders, with the aim of forming a provisional central government, within the existing constitution and representative of the main parties. Having regretfully concluded that there were no political leaders worth the name except those associated with either the Congress or with the Muslim League, it would be those two with whom he would have to treat. On the agenda, he suggested, would be an attempt to reach agreement on a new constitution under which self-government could be granted when the fighting finally stopped.

The Secretary of State's initial reactions to his proposals were exactly what Wavell had feared – fatuous and wholly unfavourable – as he recommended that a future constitution should be a matter for the National Defence Council, a body that included neither Gandhi nor Jinnah, whom Wavell was adamant could not possibly be bypassed.

Wavell now sent a report to the Prime Minister, candidly reviewing his twelve months in office: 'I have served you now for over five years and we should know one another reasonably well. I know you have often found me a difficult and troublesome subordinate. I have not always found you an easy master to serve . . .'[31] Although he emphasised the importance of India to the Empire, Wavell did suggest that its position on the imperial map was actually the result of a wrong turn that Britain had taken two or three decades earlier, 'in a mistaken view of Indian conditions and in an entirely misplaced sentimental liberalism'. It was a remarkable admission, the sentimental liberalism in question being exactly the spirit with which he and so many like-minded men in the Foreign Office and the colonial services had, to at least some extent, been imbued. Wavell wrote:

To my mind, our strategic security, our name in the world for statesmanship and fair dealing and much of our economic well-being will depend on the settlement we make in India. Our prestige and prospects in Burma, Malaya, China and the Far East generally are entirely subject to what happens in India. If we can secure India as a friendly partner

in the British Commonwealth our predominant influence in these countries will, I think, be assured; with a lost and hostile India, we are likely
to be reduced in the east to the position of commercial bagmen.[32]

In those few sentences Wavell described the alternatives that seemed to
face the Empire. Whether or not he was properly aware of them, new economic
and political currents were already rising to the surface in the Far East,
particularly in the colonies, almost all of which were being ravaged by conflict.
The war was altering the financial relationship between India and the mother
country, with India becoming a far less attractive economic prospect. The
Americans, with their chronic resentment of the British Empire, had for
some time been signalling their desire for change in India – it was one of
the reasons for the Cripps mission, in 1942 – and their influence was growing
stronger in inverse proportion to Britain's.

As it was to turn out, the Japanese conquest of Britain's Far East colonies,
especially Singapore, had dealt a terminal blow to British prestige, and
although it could not then be predicted for certain, the chance of Britain
being reduced, in Wavell's phrase, to commercial bagmen was uncomfortably high. The hope that a happy settlement with India would assure a revival
of predominant British influence in the East had probably gone with the
wind.

'I have, as you know,' Wavell's report to Churchill concluded, 'no axe to
grind. I did not seek this appointment or wish it.' The Cabinet remained
unmoved by this apparent selflessness: the damage was done. By resusci-
tating his original proposal to arrange a conference between the leading
Indian politicians, Wavell had stirred up a hornets' nest. The Cabinet's
complaints highlighted the contrast in attitude between it and the Viceroy.
Wavell was criticised for not accepting that the breakdown of talks between
Gandhi and Jinnah merely served to confirm that Indian politicians could
not agree with each other, while the Viceroy maintained that his patient,
dogged approach would make them keep trying, and that with his encouragement they would sooner or later succeed.

Into this mesh he had also to weave the Indian princes and their states,
of which there were nearly 600, connected by constitution directly to the
British rather than to the Indian Government. Thirteen were huge princi-
palities – Hyderabad and Kashmir were each the size of England and Scotland
combined – while about 550 others varied in size from an English county
to a small farm. Some of the rulers were barely solvent, others immensely

rich and colourful, with aeroplanes and Western ways – one maharajah, for example, filled his swimming-pool with champagne on the birth of a long-hoped-for son and heir. The princes' relations with Britain were based on the concept of 'paramountcy', by which Britain retained ultimate control, but with the tacit acceptance that it would not be exercised except to prevent gross injustice or misrule – if detected – or to ensure a reasonable standard of administration.

However, the princes were becoming distinctly unsettled. The two main political parties were determined that in the long run the princes should be stripped of their power, which they coveted for themselves. In the meantime, the Indian Government objected to the fact that large numbers of businesses had left British India and established themselves in the princely states, where there were no trade unions, and where they could avoid tax, red tape and other pernicious imposts of a central government.

The states had loyally contributed to the British war effort, and felt that in return they deserved entrenchment of their constitutional position. Most of the princes were as yet unconscious that in the post-war world their long-term future might be in question, or that a reforming Viceroy at the helm made it advisable, at the least, to participate in discussions about India's future. Wavell had somehow to draw them in, while not allowing questions of their status to impede agreement with the politicians who wanted to abolish the states altogether.

Meanwhile, upset by the tepid water that the Government had thrown over his revived proposals, Wavell insisted on returning to England to put his case in person. On 19 March 1945 he left India for what was to be almost three months. Essentially his purpose was to get the Cabinet's permission to substitute for his existing Executive Council appointees from a new list submitted by leading Indians for his approval. He wanted to convene a great conference to discuss the matter, and to inspire all the leaders to settle their differences. He was sure that if he were given a free hand, he could form a government suited to the needs of the hour.

These notions did not appeal to the Cabinet. They conceded that it was important to find a constructive outlet for the energies of educated Indians, but felt that an initiative at that moment might prejudice a proper settlement at the end of the war; that communal rivalry would be aggravated; and that the Viceroy's powers might be compromised. Further, if the delegates to Wavell's conference did not accept his proposals, a point of principle would have been surrendered without any dividend.

In any event, ministers appeared to be in no hurry to see the importunate Viceroy, and after an initial and inconclusive meeting with the India Committee, he was left kicking his heels in his suite at the Dorchester Hotel. He filled in time by sitting to Jacob Epstein for a bust, flying to Germany to see Field-Marshal Montgomery and going to the theatre, being impressed by Laurence Olivier's *Richard III* and Gielgud's *Hamlet*. He also had lunch with the royal family. There the talk was somewhat slow, slightly displeasing the Queen who felt that Wavell should perhaps have made an effort to 'come half way'.[33] But she was Colonel-in-Chief of the Black Watch, so at least regimental affairs provided common ground. A line of enquiry with the young Princess Margaret was less productive: Wavell asked her kindly what she thought of *Alice in Wonderland,* one of his favourite books, only to receive the reply that she did not think about it, much; after that, the conversation lapsed.

Wavell now became frustrated by what he called the deep inertia and silence of the India Committee: 'I am getting tired,' he wrote, 'of being treated as an Untouchable in the presence of Brahmins.'[34] Despite his fatigue, the India Committee continued to function: sometimes he attended its meetings, sometimes not. As he recorded in his diary: '. . . they find my presence troublesome, apparently, and prefer to come to decisions without me. Then they get annoyed if I raise objections to their work later on . . .'[35] A further delay came with the German surrender, on 8 May, and the subsequent resignation of the Government in preparation for a general election. By 24 May he had heard nothing from them for four weeks, nor from the Prime Minister for seven. Fortunately Wavell's humour and his touch of oriental fatalism did not desert him:

> May 26th. No word from PM or Eden or anyone. Went and stood in a queue outside a News Theatre with Pam and Francis, and the feeling was quite familiar after all these weeks of waiting on Ministers. But we did get into the theatre in the end; while I am still in the queue for a decision on India.[36]

The Viceroy had been kept waiting in London for about three months when Churchill suddenly decided to meet his requests. He had belatedly been warned that there was a significant chance Wavell would resign if the proposals were turned down, which Churchill's political advisers feared might be a considerable embarrassment during the imminent election campaign, enabling the Opposition to portray him as obstructionist. The Cabinet, in which only Cripps and Amery shared Wavell's views, may also have believed that there was scant chance of the politicians in India coming to any agreement, so that there would be few results to worry about even if a conference went ahead. At the end of May the proposals were approved. The Viceroy felt it was a personal triumph. He could now return to India, summon a great conference of the governors of the provinces and the most influential Indians in the land, and plan a new Executive Council, representative of organised political opinion and including caste Hindus and Muslims in equal numbers. It would establish an interim government until a full-scale administration could be set up under a new constitution. British membership would consist only of the Viceroy and the commander-in-chief. A great leap forward was in prospect.

By early June 1945 Wavell was back in India, having broken his journey by staying with King Ibn Saud in Saudi Arabia, where he was persuaded to wear Arab dress, eat with his fingers and sit cross-legged on a rug by the side of the King. Once back in New Delhi, he gave a nationwide broadcast, setting out his plans. It breathed a spirit of magnanimity and was well received across the country, especially by business interests, already involved in trade discussions in Britain and America and anxious to see political conditions stabilised. 'The Wavell Plan' seemed a realistic compromise between Hindu and Muslim claims and to offer a solution to the deadlock.

Announcing the immediate release of the members of the Congress' Working Committee still in gaol, the Viceroy sent out his invitations. He ran into difficulties at the outset, as Gandhi and Jinnah began to prevaricate, behaving, as Wavell put it, 'like very temperamental prima donnas'; they would not give a simple reply to his invitation, and cajoling them to attend was clearly going to require considerable patience: as his Private Secretary remarked, it would be like trying to get mules into a railway truck. Yet applying his special mix of tact and firmness, he eventually managed to get the mules aboard.

The day before the conference was due to start Wavell at last came face to face with Gandhi, who arrived at the Viceroy's House at the appointed hour – he was always punctual to the minute, with the aid of a cheap Ingersoll watch that hung from a piece of string below his loincloth – and finally gave his blessing to the conference. 'A little later,' wrote Wavell, 'I had 1½ hours with Jinnah, who is much more direct than Gandhi, but whose manners are far worse.' The Viceroy considered both men tricky in the extreme, but said that, even so, comparing Jinnah with Gandhi was like comparing a ramrod to a corkscrew.

The Muslim leader was a curious blend of East and West: determinedly independent, he was at one time India's most highly paid lawyer; fond of good clothes, good food and good living, he spent lavishly. Lady Wavell found him, even in his late sixties, one of the handsomest men she had ever seen, combining, as she put it, the clear-cut, almost Grecian features of the West with oriental grace and movement.

Jinnah had spent part of his life in England and had acquired a taste for Western ways and comforts: on one occasion, wearing his customary well-tailored suit and two-tone shoes, he was being interviewed by a journalist when, in the middle of a long discussion on high politics, he looked down and abruptly stopped talking; turning ashen-white, he hurriedly left the room, muttering that he must excuse himself. It seemed clear that he had been taken badly ill. Five minutes later he re-entered the room, beaming all over his face and saying, as he sat down, 'Do you know, that dam' fool bearer put the wrong cuff-links in my shirt?'[37]

Wavell's great conference – with the organisation of which he had persisted for many months, and which would not have been remotely practicable without his efforts – opened at Simla on 25 June. What happened next is quite a simple, hopeless tale. Wavell had few grounds on which to hope for a successful outcome, and although nothing was going to stop him from trying for it, tradition, ill-feeling and a habit of non co-operation were not easily overcome. Wrangling began almost at once and continued unabated for the following three weeks. In what seemed a hopeful start, all the British proposals were accepted, save the vital questions of the composition of the new central government and the procedure for submitting candidates' names to the Viceroy. In smoke-filled rooms behind closed doors the fruitless arguments continued, until, after numerous personal interviews and long hours of attempted persuasion, Wavell made one final effort. He proposed that he would himself try to form a government that would represent a fair balance of power, and would invite each party to submit names, with the Viceroy adding some of his own, if necessary.

He had expected that Jinnah would submit names for the Muslim seats and the Congress for the Hindus, but that idea turned out to be far too simple. Instead, the Congress put up names for all fifteen seats on the proposed council, including not only stooges from the smaller minorities, but also Muslim names: they even – one of them appeared to have a sense of humour – nominated Jinnah. If he were to accept that list, Wavell would find himself presiding over the nationalist government to which the British had objected all along. In any event, Jinnah naturally refused even to discuss a list unless it was accepted that all Muslim nominees would be selected from the League and that any council resolution to which the Muslims objected would not be passed without more than a simple majority, a process that clearly would have made efficient government almost unachievable. Finally Wavell spent ten hours closeted with Jinnah, trying to get him to co-operate, but in vain.

The conference failed. The root cause was Jinnah's obstinacy – Wavell later confessed that the talks would never have succeeded with him present: aside from ambitions for personal power, his stance reflected the Muslim fear that the British did not accept their dream of Pakistan and would insist on India remaining united, in which case the transfer of power from Britain to a united India would merely result in a 'Hindu Raj'. It had been only a hundred years or so since the Muslims' own empire was predominant: the conquerors of the Moguls were themselves going now, and the Muslims did not want them replaced with others, far less fair and benevolent than the British.

It was later alleged against Wavell that he should have proceeded to form a government without the Muslim League. However, with no early end to the Japanese war in sight, a Congress ministry was too great a risk to take. He would have had to consult the Cabinet; and as it had been most reluct-ant to sanction the conference at all, a proposal for a Congress Council, without any Muslim members, would have stood no chance of approval.

Despite the failure of Wavell's efforts, praise for him came from near and far. There he had stood, through weeks of tortuous and bitter argument, a rock-like referee, always on hand, without fear or favour, trying to solve the insoluble. Although he knew how devious the politicians could be, it was clear that his own integrity was beyond question and that he was wholly reli-able. Characteristically, he took responsibility for the failure upon himself, but prejudices wilted as the leaders departed. 'This time,' Gandhi told him, 'you have taken the blame on your shoulders. But the world will think other-wise. India certainly does.' A gallant effort, the King described it, sure that everyone thought so, and certainly the 'great majority of sensible people all over the world'.[38]

Very soon events were to take a new course: Roosevelt died, atomic bombs exploded over Japan, the war ended, and Churchill's ministry was obliter-ated by a landslide of socialism. A new era began, with a new Secretary of

State, and a new Government announcing that elections in India would be held over the winter.

The results of the British general election[39] were awaited as keenly in India as they were at home. The Wavell family listened to the wireless as the details came in, Archie John and his sisters hoping as fervently for a Labour victory as their parents were for the opposite. Soon after the stunningly unexpected Labour landslide the Viceroy was summoned home once more, to meet his new masters and to portray for them the situation in India, and, in particular, to agree to announce that elections to the central and provincial assemblies would be held in the autumn. For him, it was the beginning of eighteen months in which he would have to deal with a government of which few members, with the notable exception of the Foreign Secretary, Ernest Bevin,[40] lost much sleep over the Empire, being instead predisposed to an early transfer of power to the Congress Party, among whom some had personal friends. Most of the new ministers knew little about India and were not inclined to learn, being more interested in their own departments. As a consequence the Government's India policy was shaped largely by the new Prime Minister, Clement Attlee,[41] and by Stafford Cripps, both of whom were convinced that the time for prolonged deliberations had passed.

Wavell arrived in London at the end of August 1945, by which time the Japanese had surrendered.[42] He was at once propelled into a series of meetings with the new Secretary of State, Frederick Pethick-Lawrence, the Prime Minister and others on the India Committee. It was only a week before he had reached what he described as 'rather a crisis with HMG'. The deep and growing problems of India, while prominent in Wavell's focus, were just one of many items on the incoming government's wide-ranging and reforming agenda, and by no means the most important. Nor did Wavell feel that the Cabinet's priorities were correct. He came away from one meeting with the Prime Minister, on 4 September, quite clear that the new government was more concerned with placating opinion in the Labour Party and in the US than with the good of India. He concluded that politicians in London, whether Labour or Conservative, were poor judges of the difficulties with which he was faced, or of their appropriate solutions. It began to feel like a repeat of the arduous process that he had endured during his visit home six months earlier. Consequently, he considered refusing to be a party to the India Committee's 'plans to quit India'. However, he soon overcame any such thoughts: his habitual deference to His Master's Voice prevailed, and he publicly associated himself with the Government's policy.

For their part, Labour ministers did not like Wavell reminding them that a constitutional settlement ought to please not just the Congress politicians and the Muslims but also the many other minorities, in particular the princely states, that had been considerably shaken by the socialists' election victory. Wavell also put to them a major problem that he said had to be brought into the open and properly addressed – that of Pakistan, which the Cabinet, because of its inclination to the Hindu view, were reluctant to regard as a serious proposition. However, whether as the bright star seen by the Muslims or as the black hole feared by the Congress, the problem of Pakistan was growing by the day.

Wavell returned to Delhi, where he published the results of his addresses to the Cabinet: confirmation of elections to the Central and Provincial Legislatures; the convening of a constitution-making body, a new consideration of Cripps' 1942 offer; a treaty between Britain and India, once independence was proclaimed; and a new broadly based Executive Council, to administer the country while all these weighty matters were gestating.

Back in India, his unremitting viceregal duties and tours were resumed. At least they offered an invigorating contrast between ceremony and relaxation, and the stern, thankless and seemingly unending political days. He inspected Gurkha battalions back from prisoner-of-war camps in Malaya – bitter, it appeared, about the Indian National Army, 'from whose hands they had worse treatment than from the Japs'. Wavell wrote to a friend:

Her Ex and I are up at Dehra Dun for a few days, and being very hard worked, looking at camps and hospitals and institutes and soldiers and schools and canteens and all the other things that Their Excellencies are supposed to like looking at, or which like looking at Their Excellencies . . .'43

Meanwhile anti-British communal agitation had begun to increase, fomented by a number of political leaders. Nehru, in particular, wanted to use the forthcoming courts martial of Indian National Army officers to stir up dissent, not least because, in Wavell's opinion, he intended to use returned army officers as a spearhead of a violent mass movement to intimidate the police and divide the army, thereby depriving the British of their traditional weapons, recently used so successfully to suppress the 'Quit India' movement.44

The elections, at the end of March 1946, demonstrated only too plainly the stand-off between the Hindu Congress and the Muslim League, and the Prime Minister therefore came to the conclusion that the problems could not now be resolved by the Viceroy and the Secretary of State alone, 'however able they might be'.

The Cabinet therefore went a step further: not satisfied with the Viceroy's ideas, they resolved to send their own delegation to India, to discover at first hand its problems and possibilities, confident that a new eye and a new hand might steer the country towards independence more smoothly and swiftly than seemed to them to have happened so far. Their three-man mission, Cripps, Pethick-Lawrence and the First Lord of the Admiralty, A.V. Alexander[45] – the latter very much on what would today be called 'a learning curve' – arrived at the end of March 1946, attended by 'unofficial excrescences', as Wavell described them, in particular two Quaker pacifists who had joined Gandhi's entourage and who soon ingratiated themselves both with the mission and with the Congress camp.[46]

The delegation was to stay for three months; it proved to be an inauspicious period as, in Wavell's description, their progress took place against a background of continuous and unbridled abuse, in the Assembly, in speeches and in the press, of the Government, of officials and of the police; with serious rioting in Bombay and Calcutta; mutiny in the Royal Indian Navy;[47] indiscipline in the air force; unrest in the army; threatened strikes on the railways; drought; famine; and a general atmosphere of lawlessness.

It was inauspicious for Wavell also. Shortly before the delegation arrived from London his son-in-law and ADC, Simon Astley, was killed in a road accident in Quetta. Astley's occasional high spirits and fast friendships had caused one or two problems during his time in the family, but it was still an appalling shock, particularly for his young wife Joan, with her infant child. Wavell could perhaps console himself to a small degree with having just been appointed Colonel of the Black Watch, which gave him pride and pleasure.

The task of the trio of Cabinet ministers, dubbed by Wavell 'The Three Magi', was twofold: to help the Viceroy achieve agreement on the method of framing a constitution, and to assist him in forming a new, representative Executive Council, which could carry on government while the constitution was hammered out.[48]

Come what may, the Three Magi were determined to get some sort of agreement: 'we can't leave this country without a settlement of some kind,' noted Cripps,[49] 'if we did, there would be bloodshed and chaos within a few weeks.' Blood might also have been shed in London, he may have felt, were he unable to present the Cabinet with some success. Unfortunately negotiations seemed likely to break down right from the start, as the Cabinet delegation arrived with an obvious bias in favour of the Congress, and neither they nor their lengthy retinue seemed anxious to be even-handed in their contacts. 'We *must*,' wrote Cripps, 'at all costs come to an accommodation with Congress. We can get through I believe without the League if we have Congress with us but not without Congress even if we have the League.'[50]

In fact the Congress already had warm relations with the Labour Party, particularly with Pethick-Lawrence and with Cripps himself, who had become a good friend of Nehru, whereas Labour politicians' contacts with Muslims were virtually non-existent. Wavell did not at first take this in, but as the weeks passed, and the mutual understanding between Nehru and Cripps increased, it began to hinder his attempts to broker a deal and allowed suspicion, if not antipathy, to arise between him and Cripps and, later, with other members of the Government. In the meantime, Congress politicians subverted the Viceroy's position behind his back, whispering in Cripps' ear that it was a reactionary Viceroy and his advisers who represented the obstacles to progress. Cripps, clever though he was, and used to the wiles of politicians, failed to see the malice in such tales, and relations between the two men gradually became soured, until on his eventual departure to London, Cripps did not even bother to say goodbye to the Viceroy.

On the other hand, the initial conversations between the Indian politicians and the British ministers, with Wavell ever at hand but rarely leading the talks, were mostly cordial; even so, they failed to lead to agreement. After a fruitless series of meetings Wavell and the delegation decided to draw up themselves a scheme for a new form of administration, and to hope that each side would accept it. This resulted in what became known as the May 16 Statement. It proposed a three-tiered structure of government, described as 'ABC': a Union Government at the top, dealing with nationwide topics such as defence and foreign affairs, trade and communications; two groups of provinces below it, one mainly Hindu, the other mainly Muslim, to deal with matters suitable for group administration; and, below them, individual provinces dealing with everything else. The groups, to be established with the consent of the provinces, broadly reflected today's Republic of India, on the one hand, and today's Pakistan and Bangladesh on the other.

Although the May 16 Statement was written by Cripps, a clear-minded lawyer, its terms proved a recipe for confusion. Crucial descriptions of complex voting procedures in the proposed Constituent Assembly – whose vital purpose was to frame the various constitutions – were interpreted in one way by the Congress and in an entirely different way by the Muslim League. The statement also rejected the concept of an independent, sovereign Pakistan, not least because if India were partitioned, forty million Muslims would remain in India, while Pakistan would include areas containing large minorities of Hindus. The alternative of radical partitions of Bengal and the Punjab would result in a smaller Pakistan, dismissed by Jinnah as 'maimed, mutilated and moth-eaten'. Nevertheless, the arrangements grouped the Muslim homelands together and seemed to give them electoral protection against the Hindus, besides providing for an opt-out from the structure after ten years. Congress agonised on whether or not to agree to the proposals, but on 6 June the Muslim League accepted them.

The Congress, and Nehru in particular, felt that the plan would create too loose a federation. They wanted a strong, centralised government – its power exercised by themselves – disliking the idea of Muslims achieving prominence in the north of the country. Muslim culture, they felt, was inimical to their vision of a modern, industrial India filling the gap that the British would leave. Indian businessmen were already touring the United States in search of economic support.

Meanwhile, in accordance with the May 16 Statement, Wavell tried to form an interim government acceptable to all parties. He soon hit a rock in the form of Muslim League demands for parity with the Hindus and for the exclusive right to nominate Muslims to the government. Realising that he would probably fail to secure agreement to this, he produced an alternative policy of a radical nature. It was now presented to the Government as a blueprint, but without result. Later in the year he was to elaborate on it and present it again, but then it was to prove a significant factor in his downfall.

In the end, we are really faced with the same alternatives – repression or withdrawal. If it is decided that repression is not a practical proposition, we are left with the various alternatives of withdrawal: a complete and immediate withdrawal from all India, which is unthinkable; withdrawal by a certain date, which I think is equally impracticable; and a partial withdrawal, to northern India.[51]

Wavell's suggestion for a partial withdrawal was for the British to evacuate southern and central India and move to the Muslim-majority provinces of north-west and north-east India – in fact to what Jinnah hoped would become Pakistan – where support for the British was greater, before finally sailing away. He also pointed out that those areas were nearest to regions susceptible to Russian or Chinese influence, and where a continued British presence might, therefore, be valuable. Selected members of his staff had toured the country making secret preparations for an evacuation, disguising their work as that of the 'Honours Committee'. It would not be a good course, Wavell admitted, and one to be avoided if possible, but it would be the only practicable one. Others were to consider it beyond all reason.

Wavell christened it the 'Breakdown Plan'. It was his solution to final political deadlock, as a way forward should the Cabinet delegation's proposals fail:

> . . . if we are forced into an extreme position, we should hand over the Hindu provinces, by agreement and as peaceably as possible, to Hindu rule, withdrawing our troops, officials and nationals in an orderly manner; and should at the same time support the Muslim Provinces of India against Hindu domination . . .[52]

A later improved version suggested that Britain retain control of some Hindu provinces, partly to prevent it appearing as though Britain was planning to remain in the Muslim areas to facilitate the creation of Pakistan. Included in the plan was a proposal to withdraw from the whole of India by 31 March 1948.

From the moment it first surfaced, the 'Breakdown Plan' irked Attlee and his colleagues. Its pessimistic name gave them an impression of failure and retreat, and of sending an unfortunate signal to the rest of the world, as though it were the first step in the liquidation of the British Empire, rather than the logical conclusion of the trend of many years. Attlee felt that it smacked of abandoning the search for a solution before all avenues had been explored.

In India the tortuous, unending arguments continued, and would have driven to distraction a man less stolid than Wavell. Exceptionally, the Viceroy did go 'completely off the deep end' as Cripps put it, when, shortly after the mission had announced the May 16 Statement, it received a letter from Gandhi filled to the brim with misrepresentations of what the British had told him. However, the Viceroy rarely allowed his emotions to surface, although he had cause enough to do so. He was far from impressed by the way in which the delegation handled their meetings: Cripps was blatantly one-sided, and Alexander, although quickly grasping the realities of the situation, was a little 'at sea', as Wavell put it, and not up to making any real mark upon them; for the elderly and frail Pethick-Lawrence, whom Wavell described as a sentimental pacifist, the heat of India was clearly too much; he frequently gave a passable impression of being asleep during discussions, but when he did come to life he was apt to be infuriatingly woolly and verbose, causing Wavell at times to yearn wistfully for 'a large piece of green baize, a knobkerrie or some other extinguisher'.[53] It was evidence of the peaceful decline of a man who, in his youth, had achieved both a criminal record and more than one prison sentence for violent behaviour. It was Alexander who seemed to Wavell to be the most congenial, as the two played golf at Simla and dined together in the air-conditioned luxury of the Viceroy's Lodge.

The mission had no basic plan, which meant that it 'negotiated as suppli-cants asking for favours, rather than as masters granting them'. The Viceroy was appalled at the deference shown to Gandhi: 'We are still masters of India,' he noted, 'even if a little precariously. We showed ourselves much too eager to make a bargain, almost at the price of honour and peace . . .'[54] It may have stirred unpleasant memories of Munich and appeasement, yet it was not out of line with the basic principle that underlay the whole of Wavell's Viceroyalty: that of striving for friendliness with India. With one crucial difference that separated Wavell from Gandhi and the Congress – Wavell's belief that India's independence should be preceded by its democratisation – the Cabinet delegates were closer to the Congress than to the Viceroy.

Having accepted the mission's statement, Jinnah was emboldened to think of the possibility of a government being formed with Muslims in a domi-nant position. But his hopes were soon dashed: within a fortnight Wavell, perhaps finally succumbing to a desire to leave no stone unturned in drawing the Congress into government, or perhaps fearful of the Cabinet's reaction to an interim government that included the Muslim League but not the Congress, decided to bring matters to a head and announced that he was aborting negotiations. Instead, he would issue invitations to fourteen men to form a coalition government. Crucially, he added that even if either party, as represented on his list, declined to join the coalition, he would go ahead and form it anyway, making it 'as representative as possible of those willing to accept the statement of May 16th'.

Suddenly it seemed that Wavell's new move might prompt Congress as well as the Muslims finally to accept the statement:

All the labours of the past twelve weeks – the endless discussions in the sweltering heat, the skilful and patient elaboration of a plan to suit all parties, the drafting and redrafting of statements and formulas – seemed on the point of being richly rewarded.[55]

They were not so rewarded. At the last moment Gandhi entered the fray. 'I smell trouble,' recorded Pethick-Lawrence's Private Secretary,[56] 'the nasty old man has grasped that he can get what he asks for and so goes on asking for more and more.' Now Gandhi insisted that as the Congress claimed to be a national movement for all India, it must be able to nominate Muslims as well as Hindus to the Constituent Assembly. This strangled the hope of agreement more or less as it emerged from the womb. Wavell was later to reflect that it was the intervention of Gandhi – the old humbug, as he called him, whom he wholly mistrusted – that wrecked a plan that might have secured a united India and avoided all the massacres that were soon to take place. It seemed to confirm the Viceroy's experience that Gandhi was a purely negative force, incapable of imposing or inventing a positive solution.[57] Meanwhile he lapsed into parody:

> *And as he mused with pointed phrase,*
> *The Gandhiji, on wrecking bent,*
> *Came tripling down the bangi ways,*
> *And waffled as he went.*[58]

Tangling the web even more tightly, the Congress decided after all to stay out of the proposed coalition government, while at last accepting the long-term proposals for devising a constitution. Even then, their acceptance was qualified and ambiguous, as was soon to become apparent. Having heard the news, Jinnah hurriedly accepted the invitation for the Muslims to join the coalition, and thereafter, with impeccable logic, called upon Wavell to implement his pledge to form a coalition. It would have been an unexpected outcome for the Muslims to be brought into government with a majority, and it was not to be: ignoring Jinnah's challenge, Wavell backed away, saying that he would allow time for 'reflection and reconsideration', and form a 'Caretaker' Executive Council instead.

Meanwhile the Cabinet delegation was determined to patch up some sort of agreement, however specious, so as to avoid returning to London empty-handed after more than 400 meetings. Stretching the Congress' words to breaking-point, they decided that their acceptance of the plan for the long-term process extinguished the obligation to proceed with a coalition government containing Muslims but no Congress. The Muslim League was outraged; Jinnah felt comprehensively let down, his faith in British honesty and integrity shaken to the core. The last straw was hearing of Nehru's contemptuous references to grouping, at a press conference on 10 July. He now withdrew his acceptance of the long-term proposals, and within a week had ordered what was to be a cataclysmic programme of 'Direct Action to Achieve Pakistan'.

Wavell, however, remained adamantly opposed to the formation of Pakistan. Apart from the heartfelt British desire to leave India undivided – the unification of the country being long considered the finest achievement of the Raj – he believed that Pakistan would be quite unsustainable, and greatly damaging to India's economy. It would also cause insurmountable defence problems, not least because Pakistan would, as Wavell foresaw, almost certainly have to be created as two distinct regions, separated from each other by part of India. There would be the high cost of troops on internal order duties, and garrisons would be needed to deter the unruly North-West Frontier tribes, as well as the Hindus over the borders with India. Even those commitments would pale beside the country's inability to defend herself against Russia in the west or China in the east, which would expose India herself to aggression. These considerations also carried particular weight with the Prime Minister.

While Wavell maintained that Jinnah's call for Pakistan could not be conceded, the Cabinet took the view that the Muslim League's lack of co-operation could not be allowed to hold up the process of administration. Believing that it was after all out of the question to continue with the newly born caretaker government, they welcomed Wavell's further attempt to form a coalition government. With a singleness of purpose, the Viceroy once more took upon his own shoulders the heavy burden of leading protracted negotiations, involving long, rambling meetings almost daily, upon which hung the prospects of interim government and Constituent Assembly alike. Early in August he finally succeeded, when Nehru accepted the invitation to form an interim government to include the Congress, Muslims and other minority members. Yet it now seemed that it would after all be the Congress Party, so long regarded as unrepresentative, bad for India and unworthy of receiving the Empire's mantle, that would inherit power. Attlee had in effect pushed the Viceroy into giving the Congress the major say, and they, having been given an inch, reached out for an ell.

Yet Wavell would not relax his determination to bring both the parties into government. Convinced that the mutual antipathy between them would be lessened by a spell of working together, he continued to put pressure on Jinnah. At last, it bore results: at the end of October the Muslims agreed to join the coalition. Unfortunately, it soon transpired that they had done so not in a spirit of goodwill and co-operation, but more in order to stake out claims on the governmental machine, and to demonstrate beyond a doubt that Hindus and Muslims could not co-operate.

Meanwhile the Muslims' 'Direct Action' campaign had begun. On 16 August 1946, rioting in Calcutta marked the start of what became known as 'The Great Calcutta Killing'. The day's programme began early in the morning, with sporadic rioting, murder, arson and looting, later spreading to parts of the city where Hindu and Muslim quarters adjoined. The following day the taxi-drivers of the city, all Sikhs, parked their cabs and joined in the affray. The lid blew off a cauldron of primeval fury. A British officer recorded:

> February's killings had shocked us all, but this was different: it was unbridled savagery with homicidal maniacs let loose to kill and to maim and burn . . .
> . . . in one particular place a man had been tied by his ankles to a tramway electric junction box, his hands were bound behind his back and a hole had been made in his forehead so that he bled to death through the brain. [59]

Contrary to the convictions of the country's politicians, it seemed as though it was one another that Indians hated, and not the British.

The Bengal premier – described by Wavell as 'one of the most inefficient, conceited and crooked politicians in India, which is saying a good deal' – showed how far from even-handed was his control of events, as the police stood by, claiming to have been ordered not to intervene. Three days later, with nine army battalions patrolling the city, 5,000 Indians lying dead and 15,000 wounded, a semblance of peace returned.

The unrest spread rapidly into the country, and by early September the whole of Bengal was on the verge of civil war. It now became starkly apparent how thin had become the veneer of British rule, and how much it had depended on prestige and on the co-operation of the natives, on whose own system of local justice it was superimposed. Once disorder began to spread, there was little that could be done to quell it, short of deploying the army in strength. And as fears of a chain reaction grew, murder and brutality spread – from the United Provinces to Bihar, where Jinnah estimated the total killed to be 30,000, and then to the Punjab, the traditional home of five million Sikhs, containing their holy cities and hemmed in on either side by Muslim territory.

From Muslim areas came an increasing flow of reports of organised hooliganism, arson, looting, murder, mutilation of women and forcible conversion to Islam. Hindu trade was boycotted, and Muslims were urged to join the National Guard. Murderous thugs cut roads and cordoned off villages, their inhabitants robbed and killed. Men, women and children, dead or alive, were thrown down wells, poisoning the water supplies of a huge area. Hundreds of houses were burnt, and thousands of villagers were left homeless and wandering, some finding shelter in hastily prepared relief camps. The police were outnumbered, their loyalties divided: 'Unless military help is rendered,' ran one plea, 'the entire Hindu population will be extinct.' But the British administration was fast running down, its remaining servants exhausted and depressed. Early retirement for policemen was about to be introduced, and it was feared that it would lead to an exodus from the force. Soldiers, also uncertain about their future, could no longer be relied upon to obey orders. The situation, said Wavell, was 'far beyond anything that I think has yet happened in India since British rule began'.[60] Nehru himself, touring in the north, was aghast, and wrote to Wavell in despair:

> A vast area of Bengal has ceased to have any Government functioning, any security, and has just become the happy hunting ground of the worst elements in the community. Mass slaughter, arson, burning of human beings, rape, abduction on a large scale, forcible conversions and all manner of other horrible things are happening . . . India is sinking into barbarism, or something much worse . . . Bengal is rapidly becoming a shambles and a ruin . . .
>
> What is the good of forming the Interim Government at all if all we can do is watch helplessly and do nothing when thousands of people are being butchered and subjected to infinitely worse treatment?[61]

With the Congress holding out for a united India, and the Muslim League insisting on an independent Pakistan, 'All the characters in this charade were frozen into their habitual postures, at a time when decisive action was more necessary than ever.'[62] Now at last Nehru and the Congress began to feel that perhaps it might after all be best to allow the Muslims to form their own country. It was becoming clear that even a loose federation would not be sustainable, whereas a new state of Pakistan might consist of territories that, if retained, would make little contribution to the modern Indian state on which Nehru, his colleagues and their business backers had set their hearts. The prevalent feeling among leading Hindus was that they had by now been in the wilderness for a long time, they were no longer young and it might be better to accept what was possible, and be masters in their own home, rather than continue to strive for the perfect solution.

Soon even Wavell began to lose heart, and to feel that there was little more he could do to produce a solution. He was also dismayed by the attitude of the politicians in London: 'I do not believe,' he complained, 'that these men face their fences honestly.' He himself was not a political animal, and while his straightforward integrity gained him respect from the Indians, he found it hard to discern political nuances, or to analyse in detail the motivations even of his own side. One of his staff recalled accompanying him on an early morning ride and the Viceroy saying wearily, 'Next month I finish three years in this job.' 'How does it compare,' asked his companion, 'with your three years in the Middle East?' 'There is no comparison,' Wavell replied, 'I knew something about that job.'[63] The paramount fact remained that all along he was completely tied down by the Cabinet and its India Committee: he could scarcely arrange even an interview without prior reference to London. He simply did not have the freedom to mark his Viceroyalty with much of what he would have liked to achieve.

He still had to attend to his other duties, and they gave him some respite from the growing disorder in the country. He had lost the services of his long-standing Comptroller, Peter Coats, but the household's comfort and efficiency were undiminished. As it happened, although the glamour and interest of the work appealed to Coats, his attention had been drawn to a rather different and pressing matter. Earlier in the year one of Wavell's other ADCs, the artistic and homosexual Captain Billy Henderson, had been ill and had consequently returned to London, where he had stayed with Henry Channon in Belgrave Square. A few months earlier Channon had met the budding playwright Terence Rattigan at a dinner-party and started an affair with him. Convalescing in Channon's sumptuous house, Henderson had noticed that Rattigan seemed to be rather a frequent guest, and when he had recovered and returned to New Delhi he lost no time in warning Coats, 'If you think that you're making your career out of Chips Channon you had better get back to London quickly, as someone else is there and dining every night.' This unwelcome intelligence electrified Coats, increasing his desire to move on from being the Viceroy's Comptroller. Wavell reluctantly agreed to let him go, with the proviso that he produce a substitute, adding, 'It had better be someone good.' So Coats persuaded Henderson to take on the job.

Keen as Coats was to return, Channon was in two minds, and in fact was slightly grateful for various impediments that delayed Coats' arrival in England: 'Peter's return,' he wrote, 'is delayed and although I want him back I am grateful for the delay, for I want this Terentian interlude to continue, for a time at least.' [64]

Wavell was also soon to return to London. The pressure to bring to life the Constituent Assembly was increasing in proportion to the deterioration in the state of the country, and its first session had consequently been set for 9 December. In the hope of making a last appeal to reason, the Government invited the parties to a conference in London at the beginning of December. The realisation that Britain really did intend to leave India had finally begun to sink in, and it had become essential to consider in detail what might be the practical effects – particularly on the British in India – of a transfer of power. After consulting his military and constitutional advisers, Wavell sent his conclusions to London, highlighting three main areas: strategic, economic and the effects on British prestige.

The principal effect of transferring power, he advised, would be strategic. The fundamental strategy for the Empire was to maintain the ability to move troops and material across the world without hostile interference. To achieve that, Britain had established naval bases to protect and sustain its merchant shipping, in order to preserve its lines of communication with the Far East and Australasia, and to provide for the safe passage of oil from the Persian Gulf. An essential ingredient in all that was a friendly India, which would ensure that the Indian Ocean would remain free of enemy bases. Further, India's greatest asset was its manpower: without the contribution of two million soldiers from India, strengthening the Far East at its weakest point, the war in the east might have been lost. For the future, a defensive alliance with India would be necessary, both to fill the gaps in British armed strength and to establish a base from which Britain could fight if the need arose.

In the economic field, India had enormous sterling balances – Britain now owed her nearly £1,400 million;[65] she was one of Britain's main trading partners, and her markets would increase with the expected post-war economic regeneration. Wavell asserted that Britain would gain in prestige and in economic power if the granting of independence was orderly and if a satisfactory defensive alliance could be established. On the other hand, 'If India lapses into chaos, Britain will lose trade, strategic advantages and prestige, and a danger to world peace will be created.' However, he warned, 'Any advantages to Britain that can be anticipated as a result of handing over political power are conditional on there being a stable successor Government that can rule the country'[66] – preferably one friendly to Britain, as Russia might well try to extend its influence into the subcontinent, whether by India's choice or after a communist revolution, or in the wake of a collapse of responsible government.

Attlee and his colleagues had only to look to the chaos already engulfing both Greece and Palestine to realise the risk of anarchy in India. Communists and monarchists in Greece, Jews and Arabs in Palestine, were threatening to tear their countries apart, and by late 1946 Britain was on the verge of being drawn into civil war in both those countries. While in the middle of these warring factions stood the hapless British soldier, Labour ministers, in a government that had after all been elected to usher in a bright new age in Britain, attached greater priorities to conditions at home than in the Empire. Besides, Britain was almost bankrupt, and the Government needed all the dollars it could find for establishing the welfare state, rather than maintaining the Raj, or British forces in Greece and Palestine. For that purpose it was essential to retain the goodwill of American politicians, most of whom preferred to see Britain take its troops out of these trouble-spots and leave them to their independence.[67]

Unpalatable as it may have been to Wavell, one obvious interpretation of his appreciation was that it might after all be better for Britain to delay handing over power for many years. He maintained that a small force, ruthlessly applied, could still enforce an entrenchment of power while recruits were hurriedly drawn back into the administrative services, and that the loyalty of the Indian regiments would soon be assured if they knew Britain intended after all to remain to protect their interests for a further substantial period.[68] Yet time to embrace such a policy was fast running out: throughout the period of British rule the co-operation of Indian officials had been indispensable, but they were now beginning to look towards new masters.

The British administration was at the end of its tether. As long ago as 1919 the Indian Civil Service had come under stress, and as the imperative for Indianisation gathered force, it brought a concomitant increase in the difficulty of recruiting Europeans. Recruiting had ceased in 1939 and by 1946 the Indian Civil Service could boast a mere 500 British officials; there were only 500 British policemen and the Indian Political Service, which dealt with the princely states and the North-West Frontier, was down to 126 political officers. In India's fast-changing conditions 1,200 men, however wise and just, were no longer enough for the administration of a country of more than 1.5 million square miles, containing 400 million people of 300 different ethnic groups.

In any case, the possibility of staying on had been firmly expelled from the minds of the liberal men who now held the levers of power in the Empire, and by the down-to-earth and practical Prime Minister, who was soon to set out the prospects for the dominion leaders:

> We do not consider that a reversal of our policy and pledges to India and a reassertion of United Kingdom authority by force would, even if it is practicable, be likely to lead to any solution of the Indian problem or be desirable from the point of view of our international reputation. In the long run it would result in the spread of revolutionary extremism, probably in a communist form. We do not think opinion in this country would support the measures necessary, or be prepared to shoulder the costly burdens of responsibility in India under such conditions for another fifteen years. Apart from this, the necessary troops are not available.[69]

British troops were certainly thinly spread. In fact there were now fewer than there were in Palestine, the size of a large Indian District. A significant force was required for garrisoning Germany and other territories surrendered by the Axis; nor would the Government entertain the idea of sending out to fight in India troops that had at long last come home from the war. Memories of the massacre at Amritsar[70] made the authorities risk-averse to using troops in aid of the civil power. For Labour, it was a case of butter before guns. Whether or not, as Jinnah's deputy Liaqat Ali Khan had suggested, the best solution would be for Britain to stay, for years if necessary, to provide the stability and good administration that the masses needed, she no longer wished to do so:

> ... the Labour Party had for a long while taken a special interest in India's emancipation, and some of its leaders were on terms of warm friendship with Congress leaders. British intellectuals had for years preached the moral wickedness and economic unsoundness of imperialism. They were now reinforced by the inferences drawn by the public from the collapse during the war in Malaya and Burma and the indifference of the people of these countries to British disaster.[71]

At the beginning of December 1946, with the tortuous search for a solution becoming increasingly urgent, Wavell, Jinnah and Nehru arrived in Downing Street. In a private meeting with the Cabinet's India Committee the Viceroy set out the stark realities. The Congress believed that the Cabinet dared not break with them unless they did something outrageous; their aim was to extinguish Britain's power and influence as soon as possible, leaving them to fill the vacuum, after which they could deal with both the Muslims and the princes, 'the former by bribery, blackmail, propaganda, and if necessary force; the latter by stirring up their people against them, as well as the other methods above'.[72] The Sikhs, who had for so long been loyal to the Empire, had now switched their allegiance to the Congress, convinced that the British would no longer oppose it. For their part, the Muslims felt they were not getting a fair deal from Britain; many of their leaders were becoming desperate, while their followers had become so inflamed with the idea of Pakistan that it would be hard to satisfy them with anything less.

Ignoring political niceties, Wavell opposed the Government's policies.[73] He introduced his appreciation by saying that unless the Cabinet cleared the air and explained what they had meant in their May 16 Statement, asserting their own interpretation of the voting procedures for the Constituent Assembly, they would be unable to persuade the Muslim League to join; the Cabinet delegation's plan would then be dead. If that happened, he said, there were four alternatives. First, to re-establish authority and stay in India, which it had been decided was politically impossible. Second, to negotiate a new settlement, which would inevitably involve the partition of the country; that was not practicable. Third, to abandon the attempt to be even-handed and let the Congress have its way; that would mean leaving the other minorities in the lurch, and would lead either to a British scuttle from the country or its expulsion by the Congress. In his view, that alternative would be both unwise and dishonourable. Fourth, for Britain to announce that it was going to withdraw, in its own way and in its own time.

He now put up his 'Breakdown Plan' once more. If it were adopted, he said, it would be essential for the Government to announce a date by which the withdrawal would be completed. That might force the Indians finally to reach agreement among themselves; but if it did not, it would at least mean that Britain had a plan ready and waiting before disorder became widespread; it would offer protection to her own people, even if the Indians fell to fighting among themselves.

To the military mind, it was a sound insurance policy; there had long existed plans to evacuate British civilians in the event of severe danger, and Wavell's plan was a complex development of those. It envisaged the Muslims in their own state, but without forcing non-Muslim populations into it; Bengal and the Punjab would have to be partitioned. Although the whole idea was painful to Wavell, who regarded the subcontinent as a natural unit, he admitted that he could think of nothing better.[74] In fact, Wavell had previously sent to London a map of his suggestions. It was a remarkably prescient document, and those who drew it up[75] for the Viceroy's approval later explained that it was the definition that was in fact used for partition when India at last became independent, in August 1947. Lord Mountbatten, Wavell's eventual successor, at first tried to draw up his own partition arrangements, but had to concede that he could not improve upon those of Wavell, who was therefore in effect the creator of Pakistan. 'I think,' Wavell had earlier told the India Office, 'the award would be recognised by world opinion as a just one, and that it would be realised that we had done our best.'[76]

That was not the Cabinet's view. They did not like the shape of the Breakdown Plan. They felt its military stamp was out of place in the new, post-war atmosphere. 'Your proposals,' the Secretary of State told the Viceroy, 'have raised a great many doubts in our minds.' The Prime Minister described the plan as 'extraordinary'. He felt that it was defeatist and bore the assumption of antagonism, and that the Indians would assume that the Raj was on the run. He also failed to see the merit in taking eighteen months for Britain to leave India, and felt that Wavell had made no allowance for the legislative process required at home. He fixed upon the fact that the plan would involve the early abandonment of Madras and Bombay, which were the two best places from which to embark Europeans, while the British remained in the most difficult parts of the country until last. He concluded that the Viceroy did not realise the problem was political and not military, and he began to doubt that Wavell had the finesse to negotiate the next step.

The chorus of dissent grew: Cripps believed that it would invite major unrest – it was axiomatic with both him and other Labour leaders that Britain should no longer be drawn into far-away civil wars – while others felt that even if it were practicable as a military operation, politically it was not realistic, tempting fragmentation and administrative breakdown. If they were not careful, Attlee suggested, Britain might find herself leaving India not simply to civil war, but to political movements of a totalitarian character – and they had seen quite enough of those. The Prime Minister was determined to hand over the government of India as a going concern.

For all the care that had gone into his proposals, the Viceroy had lost his audience. Fatal doubts had pierced the Cabinet's mind, about Wavell's military image and about his whole approach to India. His plan, Wavell told them, 'must be treated largely as if it were a military plan made in time of war'.[77] But they were civilians, in time of peace. Their unfavourable impressions deepened. The Viceroy, they felt, kept bringing them the problems, but not the solution. In deference to the Cabinet, Wavell explained that he recognised the parliamentary difficulties, and the reluctance to announce a date for withdrawal without first having handed power to a functioning Indian government. Yet he maintained that it was unfair to let Parliament continue in the belief that the present situation could go on indefinitely; it was also unfair to the British in India. The Prime Minister agreed that the Indian leaders still did not seem to realise how serious the situation was – although Nehru had certainly made Wavell aware of his fears – and that, perhaps subconsciously, they believed that in the end they would be able to turn to the army to keep the peace. That confidence, he said, was no longer justified: it was clear that the country might descend into civil war.

Although Wavell's resolute presentation caused disquiet in the Cabinet, it did at least, after all the delay and indecision, force a clear expression of what was meant by the May 16 Statement. It also brought to the surface an altogether different development. Although it had become a matter of urgency to settle the details of how and when Britain should leave India, actually doing so confronted Attlee and his colleagues with their doubts that Wavell was any longer the man for the hour. For long months the Viceroy had patiently tried to lead the parties into a positive and constructive union, but success had eluded him. He was not, in the Cabinet's opinion, a good negotiator: they thought he was a stick-in-the-mud; in fact they convinced themselves that there would be no breakthrough while he remained Viceroy. Although there was no place for defeatism in Wavell's nature, the Cabinet had formed a different impression. It reinforced the view, held in particular by Attlee, that it was no longer appropriate to have as Viceroy a man who was not only a soldier – although they accepted that Wavell was more than that – but was viewed as one by Indians.

In London the talks ended; in India the violence spread. The Cabinet's response was to turn to 'sacking the messenger'. Clutching at straws, it convinced itself that a change of Viceroy might be the way to achieve a breakthrough. The Foreign Secretary wrote:

I do not believe that the Indian Army is in the bad way that people suggest. I can quite understand that with a view like Wavell's the demoralisation of the whole of the Army and the Police must be inevitable, and I would strongly recommend that he be recalled and that you find somebody with courage who, even if he were the last man left there, would come out with dignity and uphold the British Empire and Commonwealth.[78]

In fact the Foreign Secretary's letter expressed concerns far beyond India: 'You cannot read the telegrams from Egypt and the Middle East nowadays', he wrote, 'without realising that not only is India going, but Malaya, Ceylon and the Middle East are going with it, with a tremendous repercussion on the African territories.' The Labour Government was beginning to perceive the results of giving practical expression to their theoretical dislike of Empire.

In reply, Attlee told Bevin that he agreed that Wavell had a defeatist mind and also that he was thinking of replacing him, but adding 'in fairness to him I must say that he has the support of the most experienced civil servants in India'. The India Committee needed little persuasion: civilians all, they 'considered that it was wrong to press too far the analogy of a military withdrawal'; instead they would pursue a political plan.[79]

Forceful as he remained, in his quiet way, Wavell had once more begun to display signs of weariness, although he was still determined to achieve a smooth transition of power, so closing the history of Britain in India on a proud and inspiring note. As he reported to the King:

The tragic part of the business is that I do not believe that the solution would be really difficult if tackled by sensible people in a spirit of compromise; and the prospects of advancing India a long step on the way to prosperity are so fair, given good administration for the next ten years or so. But I shall be very surprised if we get either compromise or really good administration.[80]

Wavell had already responded with some vigour to a condescending suggestion by Attlee that he take on a political adviser, who might make it easier for him to deal with politicians. 'I have no personal ambition,' he told the Prime Minister, who later tried to revive the idea, 'I have already reached a position far above my expectations or merits.'[81] But he insisted that he had had plenty of political experience and must be allowed to exercise his own judgement. His words made little impression.

A schism had developed. Wavell was advocating a policy that the Cabinet believed to be mistaken. In December, even while appearing to go along with Wavell's 'Breakdown Plan' and authorising a statement to Parliament to that effect, the Prime Minister had put out secret feelers to find a new Viceroy, and had been lured by the bright charisma of Lord Mountbatten. At first neither Mountbatten nor his wife seemed much attracted to the idea, with Lady Mountbatten expressing her opinion at a New Year's Eve party by announcing, 'If anyone wishes me a Happy New Year, I'll shoot them.'

However, Attlee believed that Mountbatten had the right personality; he had made a good impression at SEAC,[82] and had made friends with a number of the nationalist leaders in the Dutch and British Far East colonies. He had the added advantage of being a cousin of the King-Emperor, which would, it was thought, be an important factor in negotiating with the Indian princes.

Certainly the seemingly youthful sailor presented a bright and lively contrast to the weary soldier, who, while maintaining an outward air of confidence and solid reliability, had inwardly become ill at ease. In his journal Wavell described 1946 as the most gruelling and in some ways the most unhappy year he had ever had:

> While I have not had a day's real illness, I have never been really 100% fit. The main trouble has been that I have been sleeping badly, waking up too early, to be assailed by doubts, fears and problems, official and private. It is a great strain on a small man to do a job which is too big for him, if he feels it too big. Health and vitality suffer.[83]

Early in the new year Wavell received from the Prime Minister a letter he described as 'cold, ungracious and indefinite. It summoned him home for yet more discussions. He thought the proposal rather pointless, and replied that there would be no advantage in his coming back in the near future. This further irritated the Cabinet. Attlee did not agree, and the wheel turned another notch. At the beginning of February 1947 a special messenger from Downing Street brought a letter for Wavell. It called attention to 'a wide divergence of view' as to the course which should be followed. 'I think you may agree,' the Prime Minister said, 'that the time has come to make a change in the Viceroyalty.'[84] Wavell did not agree – but to no avail: he had been given a month's notice.

'Not very courteously done', he observed, with more than a little justification. So summary a dismissal was hardly in keeping with the dignity of his high office – 'shorter notice,' as Lady Wavell put it, 'than you are compelled to give a housemaid.' Insult followed injury. For its announcement of Britain's final withdrawal from India and for the change of Viceroy, the Government had chosen 19 February: it was the day before Felicity Wavell's wedding,[85] following which 1,400 people were due to attend a reception in the Mogul Gardens at the Viceroy's House. Wavell was most upset and remonstrated with the Prime Minister, who agreed to postpone the announcement by a day; nevertheless the news leaked out and caused embarrassment: 'Really,' said one of the guests, 'they might have waited.'

On 20 February the Prime Minister rose in the House of Commons to explain to Parliament not only that the Government had decided that, come what may, Britain would quit India by the end of the following June, but also that Wavell was to be replaced by Mountbatten. The statement caused uproar. As Attlee had feared, both sides of the House were incensed at the idea of the Cabinet deciding to quit India and going so far as to name a date, without finding a successor government to which to hand power. Angry MPs asserted that the proposal amounted to a reversal of all previous statements, and without any safeguards for minorities; as Opposition peers said in the House of Lords, it would be an abandonment of India 'under conditions which, to many of us, can give no hope of a peaceful and prosperous future for her people'.

The reason Attlee gave for the appointment of a new Viceroy was that it had originally been agreed that Wavell's was to be a 'wartime appointment', and that it seemed appropriate to terminate it at 'the opening of this new and final phase in India'. On this point the Conservatives were particularly vociferous: Churchill led the attack claiming that the government was 'making use of brilliant war figures' to cover up a melancholy and disastrous transaction. He pressed an intransigent Prime Minister for an explanation, claiming that if the appointment had been only for wartime, it would have come to an end eighteen months previously. He was sure that there had been a disagreement with the Viceroy, and that there was more to 'this momentous new departure' than was being disclosed, insisting:

There must be some reason. Surely, the rt. hon. Gentleman did not wake up one morning and say 'Oh, let us get another Viceroy' . . . some reason or explanation should be given for the extremely important executive action which the Government have taken, and which must have been animated by some motive accessible to human intelligence.[86]

Despite the clamours of 'Answer', Attlee declined to discuss matters of human intelligence any further, either in respect of Wavell or of the decision to cut and run. 'It is a fact,' he said, 'that despite all the declarations we have made, there are still people in India who think they can hang on and let things drift. We are against drift.'[87]

Years later, in a television interview, Attlee did record his reasons for replacing Wavell, explaining that in his view the situation had called for someone with a more flexible mind. 'Wavell,' he said, 'was a great man but a silent man. I don't think Indians appreciated silence much. It was quite clear to me that we wanted someone with more flexibility. I thought the one man was Mountbatten.'[88]

Although there is an element of truth in that rather glib summary – Wavell's lucid prose could not entirely make up for his failure with the spoken word – it does little justice to the Viceroy's proven skill as an administrator, his indefatigable negotiations with intransigent Hindus and Muslims, and his conviction that he had to create viable authorities that could accept the transfer of Britain's power. In fact there is reason to suppose that had Wavell remained in charge for the eighteen months that he believed remained to Britain in India, far less disorder would have resulted than ensued from his successor's take-it-or-leave-it policy of quitting India in August 1947.

Wounded by his dismissal, Wavell was sustained by a wry acceptance of 'outrageous fortune'. Letters of support arrived almost at once; among the first was one dated 20 February, from the Congress politician Rajagopalacharir:

> I am very sad. It is a misfortune in my opinion to us all that you are to leave us. You were firm – you were just and you were a gentleman. You have worked hard with no aim but to act conscientiously and discharge your duty. You hated violence and you wanted a settlement honourable to all. And you worked for it with great ability . . .[89]

At one of Wavell's farewell staff parties he told his guests that his fate reminded him of that of King Nebuchadnezzar, who was dismissed by an angel of the Lord – 'which I suppose,' he said, 'is similar to getting a cable from Whitehall' – and he quoted some lines about the great king:

> The exiled monarch, now put out to grass,
> With patient oxen, and the humble ass,

Said as he champed the unaccustomed food,
'It may be wholesome, but it is not good.'[90]

The decision to end the Raj willy-nilly within eighteen months was gravely unsettling for India, but the subsequent decision to compress the remaining period of British rule into just six months was a disaster. For some time Wavell had regarded the Sikhs as potentially the gravest threat to peace in Bengal, and his fears proved well grounded. Until near the end, most Sikhs had little idea that partition would actually be imposed, but early in 1947 – after the end of Wavell's time as Viceroy – they did realise it, and unleashed a form of 'terror'. In some states Sikhs were almost in a majority and a concerted effort, led by some of the princes, including the Hindu Maharajah of Kashmir, was made to regain Sikh predominance in what had been, less than a century earlier, the Sikh Empire of the Punjab, established by Ranjit Singh. At the same time the Muslims realised that 'Pakistan' was to be created after all, and they began killing Sikhs in large numbers, seeing the chance of acquiring their land. Chaos and massacre swiftly spread.

Tales of the ensuing violence have been told many times – how seemingly interminable columns of desperate families wound their way towards their respective homelands, many of them mutilated, branded, with broken bones, without food or water, stark naked – Muslims and Hindus alike determined at least to be buried in their own sacred soil. Much of the tragedy was never recorded, but while the people wrung their hands at Mother India's self-inflicted wounds, the politicians were determined that in the end it would be all for the best. The daughter of a judge in the Punjab has never forgotten the response of Pandit Nehru:

We were Sikhs, living in the Punjab. I was in Lahore, and had just finished college. I and other young girls were hurriedly recruited into nursing, as terrible violence had broken out all around us, you know, Sikhs were coming in, heavily wounded, as you know how the Muslim way of killing is slitting the stomach with a knife, and all these men, were coming in from the fields, and the agricultural parts of the Punjab, and they would walk from their villages to Lahore, holding their intestines together, to get medical attention. I was staying with my aunt then, as we knew that we were not going to get a fair deal, and we had been driven out of Lahore, even as Christians, and there were marauding gangs and rioters, and disorientated refugees. In August I was sitting

in my aunt's drawing-room, and Mr Nehru came – he was a great
friend of my aunt, and often visited – and I said to Nehru that I thought
it was a terrible shame what had happened, and we didn't know what had
hit us, because out in the country we were unaware of the politics. And
I said to him, 'Mr Nehru, did you not foresee these terrible things,
and what would happen?' He looked down at me and said, 'Young lady,
you should be proud that the Punjab has been sacrificed for the good
of India'. To say that to me, when I'd seen my home gone, my friends
killed, and looting and rioting . . . Sacrificed! I wanted to say that surely
sacrifice should be voluntary, that nobody asked us for a sacrifice; but
you know, we were a very Victorian household, and my aunt gave me
a look, that I should hush. So I hushed.[91]

For all their long associations with the British, kind and faithful Indians
became utterly confused as partition was imposed and new allegiances were
forced upon them. The results were often pitiable. One of Wavell's ADC's
described an event just after partition that could stand proxy for many:

A Muslim lady came to friends of mine and told of her Hindu cook,
who had been with her for 35 years and had served her well and truly
for all that time. One afternoon this lady heard an unruly band of hot-
headed Muslims, obviously out for blood, coming down the road. She
said to her cook, 'You go up on the roof with my children; you'll be
safe up there'. So up he went, and when the trouble-makers banged
on the door and asked if she had any Hindus in the house, she said no.
They took her word for it and went off. She called up to her cook and
told him he was safe and he thanked her. She advised him to go back
to his own village where he would be safe, and this he did. She then
went upstairs, and found that all her three children were dead, murdered
by the Hindu cook.
    'Have you ever', added the Muslim friend, 'heard of anything so
ghastly and cold-blooded?'[92]

Unfortunately there were very many such outrages, as up to two million
people were killed, countless more were wounded and seventeen million abandoned their ancient homelands. For both Indians and British, sanity seemed to
have fled the world. Against such a background, Wavell sent the King a telling
summary of the objectives that he had tried to achieve with his Viceroyalty.[93]

British power in India, he wrote, had always depended not on numbers, but on prestige; its decline began even during the First World War, and was hastened by the fall of Singapore and Burma, whose recapture did little to restore the vital esteem that had been lost. By then, in Wavell's view, the greater part of the Indian population wanted the British to leave, and from what he had seen of the psychology of the British people, both at the end of the First World War and during the Second, he believed that they were no longer prepared to endorse the effort necessary to retain control. 'The really fatal thing,' he said, 'would be to hang onto responsibility in India when we had lost the power to exercise it, and possibly to involve ourselves in a large-scale Palestine.'[94] He therefore tried to bring Indian politicians together, to devise a new constitution before the war's end lessened the unifying effect of the danger on India's frontier; so he had convened the Simla conference.

The effects of the conference's failure were exacerbated by the election of a Labour Government and by the collapse of Japan. Wavell had lost the chance of bringing Indians into government while the war still offered the Viceroy the excuse for a measure of direct guidance, and he had to deal with a Cabinet that knew little of India. Although he thought the three-tier plan was probably the best to have been constructed, it failed partly because the Cabinet mission did not promote it vigorously as an award, but tendered it hesitantly, even apologetically, as a basis of discussion. The Cabinet mission was, Wavell believed, the last chance of establishing an agreed government; it was essential, in case the chance was lost, to have ready an alternative policy, to protect British interests and personnel – of which 100,000 remained in the country, even excluding the army. Withdrawal in accordance with a plan, and at a date announced well in advance, would probably, he believed, forestall attacks on Europeans and would avoid the army being drawn into civil war.

Perhaps he expressed his true feelings when, dining one evening with brother officers of the Black Watch, he said, 'We could do this all right if we took fifty years, which is just a blink in the history of time, but not in less.'

It was to be very much less. Wavell had pressed for eighteen months to allow the British to leave, but after his replacement the whole operation was, at Mountbatten's insistence, compressed into six months. Although, as it turned out, British casualties were minimal, the widespread confusion and distress among Indians were perhaps exemplified by something that occurred on 16 August 1947, the very first day of independence. There were only two routes for Muslims to travel from Delhi to their new homeland: the grand trunk road and the railway. Both routes were beset by great danger, as they passed through Sikh tribal lands, where armed bands lay in wait, bent on massacring as many refugees as possible. On that morning a train crawled and clanked its way into Lahore station; most of the carriage doors hung open, and bodies were slumped on the steps. The walls and ceilings of the compartments and corridors were smeared with blood, the floors invisible beneath the dead and dying – victims of Hindu gangs that had swarmed onto the train when the engine stopped to take on water. On the platform at Lahore an Indian railway official, proud and smart in his uniform, had been chatting to a BBC reporter. As the train drew to a halt he fell into a stunned silence. At length he turned to the journalist; horrified by the collapse of long-accustomed order, in fact of his whole world, and with deep sorrow in his eyes, he said quietly: 'Sahib, it is hardly worth issuing tickets now.'[95]

The Raj had ended; a new order had settled upon a fifth of the human race.

On Saturday, 22 March the Viceroy gave a final lunch-party, on the terrace of the Mogul gardens, in the shadow of the vast imperial palace. For a moment he seemed to have shed his cares; he talked affably all through the meal, discussing wartime publishing, and a new book sensation, *The Last Days of Hitler*. The Nazis' story, said Wavell, was just another version of *Faust*. After lunch the Mountbattens arrived, with bow and curtsey, and Wavell formally welcomed the great-grandson of the Queen-Empress herself, who was to be India's twenty-ninth and last Viceroy.[96]

Having received such short notice of his recall, there was a great deal to do in very little time, but Wavell's good nature shone through even amongst the problems of packing up. One of his ADCs, Captain Beaumont, had a small daughter for whom some time earlier Wavell had agreed to write a fairy tale. On his last day the child met the Viceroy in a corridor, looked up at him and said, 'You've never written me your fairy story and now you're going and you promised you would.' Wavell paused for a moment and replied, 'Give me an hour'; he then shut himself away and wrote the story.

At 8.15 the next morning he and his family left the Viceroy's House. Their two-day journey took them to Karachi and Iraq and then on to Rome, where they inspected the Sistine Chapel. On arrival in London, Wavell went to Downing Street, to meet the India Committee. He was questioned for a time, in a rather perfunctory fashion, 'as if they knew all the answers already', until at length the Secretary of State asked, 'Is there any general advice you can give us on how to proceed?' Wavell looked at them and replied that he had already given them advice, and that they had not liked it.[97]

XVII

DISTANCE RUN

FEW people's careers had a future beyond the office of Viceroy of India. It was a richly encrusted pinnacle, but a professional cul-de-sac beyond which lay only honourable retirement. At sixty-four Wavell was ready to step back and take stock and, after years of unceasing endeavour, to rest. Having finally left India, his displeasure at not being allowed to finish the job, and the manner of its termination, faded slightly, both with time and with the change in his surroundings. A friend recalled going to see him one morning, very soon after his return, and finding him in the kitchen preparing scrambled eggs: 'I think I can still do this,' he said. A week or two earlier he had been master of more than 500 servants.

After a brief stay in Claridge's Hotel, and debriefing meetings with the Government, he and Lady Wavell moved to a club while considering where to live. Without fixed plans for the future it was hard to decide where to go, but eventually they settled on a flat in Knightsbridge. Neither of them liked it much, and that, combined with the sense of anti-climax that inevitably followed the return from India, seems to have induced a certain malaise 'in these drab days', as he described them, 'when I have pavement instead of grass under my feet, and can hunt no more'. He abandoned his journal for nearly six months, and its entries thereafter, at a much-reduced level, betray a loss of enthusiasm.

His spirits gradually lifted a little: he had plenty of time to spare for Scotland, where he spent many weeks shooting, stalking and playing golf, particularly at St Andrews. His calendar began to fill up again, with offers of the laurels due to him for his long and exceptional career. At Winchester he had chosen the Army Class in preference to university but, as it turned out, that had not been quite the desperate step his Head Master had feared, and now that lacuna was filled – he received honorary degrees from both Oxford and Cambridge, as well as from four other universities, including Aberdeen, of which he had become Chancellor in 1944.

Wavell seems to have retained a slight regret that he had not been appointed to the Chichele Professorship, but now the possibility arose of his becoming Master of Magdalene College, Cambridge. 'I should like my name to be considered,' he wrote to an intermediary in the matter, 'though it is difficult for me to say at present whether I could accept if selected, since I have other offers which I have to consider, including one from another Cambridge college.'[1] In the event, he ran up against the spirit of the new, rule-bound, specialist times, and the incumbent Master and his colleagues decided that his age presented a difficulty, besides his lack of experience in the educational field and, more telling of the post-war atmosphere, 'the importance of avoiding the implication that these posts are to be the perquisite of Field-Marshals, Admirals and Air Marshals'.[2]

Having been granted an earldom to mark the end of his Viceroyalty, Wavell took his seat in the House of Lords, and in October 1947 carried the Sword of State at the Opening of Parliament, alongside Cunningham and Portal, his old co-warriors in the North African campaign. At the wedding of Princess Elizabeth and Prince Philip he carried his baton as a field-marshal, musing that it would probably be the only time he would do so.

His sense of fair play led him to wage a long struggle with the Government, mainly in the form of Sir Stafford Cripps, to improve pension arrangements for British members of the Indian services, who had received a raw deal. He presented his case tirelessly to a stonewalling Government, which tried to shift the problem back to India, and he raised the matter on several occasions in the House of Lords. After eighteen months the Government ceded the point.

Wavell had been appointed Colonel of the Black Watch in March 1946, and regimental affairs now took up a good proportion of his time; he paid visits to affiliated regiments in Canada and South Africa, as well as on several occasions visiting the regiment where it was stationed in Germany, reminded by his sense of history that he was near the site of a famous defeat of the Roman legions that had halted for ever the spread of civilisation to eastern Europe. In the company of his regiment he did seem content and happy, although warning the junior officers that the Russians were not the threat to peace as much as the old foe, Germany, a leopard that he did not believe would change its spots. While discussing literature and poetry in the officers' mess with his former ADC, Bernard Fergusson, it was observed with pleasure how 'he almost reached a state of animation'.[3]

Fergusson was then commanding the regiment, but as he was a bachelor, Wavell stayed with the second-in-command and his wife. She recorded how, in the company of old friends, he could seem 'cosy'. She also recalled how Wavell, her husband and Colonel Fergusson had gone out to a formal dinner, leaving her behind with a soldier-servant whom her husband had detailed to look after the field-marshal. This man had wasted no time in becoming grossly inebriated, and had ranged around the house in a most alarming manner, at length passing out on a sofa in the hall. When, after midnight, Wavell and the others eventually returned, they saw a rather nervous lady of the house at the head of the stairs, and the comatose corporal on the sofa in the hallway. Fergusson at once called out, 'Oh! Look at that. There's loyalty for you. The poor man's absolutely exhausted.' From behind the colonel, Wavell looked up the stairs with a broad grin, and gave a tremendous wink.[4]

Back in England he felt rootless. In June 1947 he stayed at Henry Channon's house in Essex, but wrote:

I am rather lost at present, wondering what to do. I shall have to find some way to make some money, and somewhere to live. Meanwhile her-Ex and myself are wandering around to friends rather like egg-less cuckoos; with no house, no cabinet, no ADC, no secretary and no particular objective, and I am a little lost at present, and a little Micawber-like.[5]

In August of that year Wavell received an invitation to join the board of the mining giant De Beers, and in February 1948 he spent a month in South Africa as the guest of its chairman, Sir Ernest Oppenheimer, inspecting the great diamond workings at Kimberley. He also visited the battlefield and famous monument at Magersfontein, marking the war in which he had fought as a young soldier nearly fifty years earlier. In Cape Town he met Field-Marshal Smuts, and discussed the long-drawn-out dispute between South Africa and India that had caused him difficulties during his term as Viceroy, and which had now worsened, with India imposing sanctions.

He was in demand as a lecturer, and his increasing collection of honorific posts led to many speaking engagements, none of which he shirked. Despite a lifelong dislike of making speeches, and aware that his delivery was not compelling, Wavell was well used to giving talks, having made so many ten-minute speeches when touring as Viceroy. He was self-confident and his content was always good,[6] usually with liberal use of quotations from Greece, Rome, Shakespeare or the Bible. Some of his talks were to university audiences, where his subjects were often suitably abstruse. One such was a talk that he gave at St Andrews entitled 'The Triangle of Forces in Civil Leadership', in which he demonstrated how down the ages civil leaders had to take account of aristocrats, priests and the people, whatever their contemporary guise.

His greater interest, and skill, was in writing, and in discussing literature. Although he found that he could not settle to a major project, he wrote numerous articles for magazines, usually on military subjects, and introductions to several books, especially memoirs of or about unorthodox military figures, such as Wingate, or Spencer Chapman, for whom he introduced *The Jungle Is Neutral*. As befitted his love of the theatre, on one occasion he stood in as drama critic of *The Spectator* magazine, and he also wrote the occasional article on poetry. He had become president of the Poetry Society, and *Other Men's Flowers* continued to sell briskly, and to be much in demand from those who prefer borrowing to buying books. One article, for *The Geographical Magazine*, entitled 'Poetry of Place', was a small anthology of its own, describing places that Wavell knew or would like to have visited, and the sonorous poems that inspired him to think of them:

> So long as Tara Devi sees
> The lights of Simla Town
> So long as Pleasure calls us up
> Or Duty drives us down.[7]

'Those who have taken the road to Simla,' he wrote, 'as I did for Pleasure as a subaltern or for Duty as a Viceroy and will take it no more, may still feel a faint nostalgia at those lines.' Kipling's verse was never far from his heart, and he much enjoyed being president of the Kipling Society, an office he had assumed in 1946.

He had also been appointed president both of the Royal Society of Literature and of the Browning Society, and corresponded with the poet and playwright T.S. Eliot, who agreed to advise on Wavell's script for an address to the Virgil Society, yet another society of which he had become president. 'I am afraid it is very light metal,' Wavell characteristically described his speech, 'but the task was really beyond my range.' He congratulated Eliot on his award of the Nobel Prize, in a letter largely discussing education, which had long been an interest of Wavell's and about which Eliot seemed to have fixed opinions. Wavell wrote:

When I was in India I did my best to resist what seemed to me a fatal mistake, the introduction of primary universal education for all. I tried hard to persuade my Indian Councillors that what India wanted in her present stage was to spend all the money available for education in training leaders and technicians and doctors and skilled men in all professions, and that it was a sheer waste of time and money to give every villager and worker, man or woman, a smattering of education, for which neither the teachers nor the schools could possibly be available for many years. The sensible Indians saw the point but they one and all said the same thing: 'We must remove the reproach of illiteracy from our country.[8]

Archie John, now Viscount Keren, had although remaining in the army, also become greatly interested in education. He preferred teaching – the Middle Ages being his favourite period of history – to taking up a place at the Staff College, which his father regarded as 'tiresome of him'. He had been on an education course in India, subsequently touring camps and bases encouraging formations to start their own courses, and on his return to England he continued in a similar vein at an army education school in Cornwall. Wavell, however, felt that his son had spent enough time on education: schoolmasters, he said, are usually dull and tiresome people, and he wanted his son to associate more with the broad-minded.

A full diary did not prevent life in grey, rationed, war-torn London from continuing to weigh upon Wavell's spirits; nor, after being so long at the centre of great events, did the many honours and offices that came his way seem to reawaken his customary robust, good-natured approach to life. 'A thoroughly bad year' is how he described 1947, 'I came home, unable to settle down to anything or to make a plan; taking things as they come, accepting invitations to lecture, to dinners, and to functions of all kinds without really wanting to do any of them . . .'[9] 1948 did not appeal to him much more: 'I have had an aimless, purposeless, unprofitable year, and have settled down to nothing . . .'[10]

There was another reason for despondency. St Paul's and Big Ben had survived the Blitz, but they were symbols of an Empire that was now crumbling fast. The ethos of the upbringing and education of Wavell and his contemporaries emanated from the concept of a mighty British Empire that was a force for good and for justice in the world, and of the future of which there was little question. That Empire had been acquired over many generations by men of courage and determination, but those who taught the young Wavell and his contemporaries about the stirring deeds of the builders of the Empire seemed to have overlooked the importance of a vital ingredient: the grit required to resist not just enemy legions, but also the less visible but more insidious forces of socialism at home and nationalism abroad, both clearly perceptible even in Wavell's youth.

Pressure on the Empire had been building since the Boer War, but as they climbed the ladder of power, Wavell and his generation seemed neither to have heeded the danger nor to have formed the iron resolve by which alone the Empire could be maintained. Perhaps it was anyway too late: consciously or otherwise, they were already pulled along by an inexorable ebb-tide, with Britain 'a nation uneasy with its greatness, tired of empire and its responsibilities, wanting to turn inwards and concentrate on its social and economic ills'.[11]

With the rout of imperial forces in the Far East, the damage to the Empire became irreparable. Wavell had long objected to American encroachment on British spheres of influence, insisting that British possessions should be defended, and then recaptured, by British forces, and he did not question the notion that once the enemy were defeated, the status quo ante should be restored. Yet it turned out that neither he nor most of his contemporaries in British governing circles had inherited the imperial zeal of previous generations after all.

The collapse in Malaya and Burma, and most of all in Singapore, exposed the fallacy that Britain could remain an imperial power if its servants abandoned, perhaps subconsciously, but – in the cases of many of 'the great and the good' – deliberately, the will to rule. The plumes and pukka uniforms remained on parade, but their wearers were all dressed up with nowhere to go. Wavell had been born into an Empire of seeming permanence, but he had in fact entered an age of decadence, and by the time he became Viceroy, sixty years later, only the shell remained.

For all his experience of the chaos of war, and his deep feeling for history, Wavell was of a generation of imperial servants that seemed blind to the trouble that might follow if the Empire were allowed to disintegrate. Perhaps he did not sufficiently care, and subscribed after all to the high-minded theory that self-government is better than good government. Certainly, his approach to the future of India was at odds with the imperial tenets of men like Churchill, and in his way he himself hastened the demise of the Empire. However warm a feeling his liberal attitudes may have given him, cold reality presented a depressing picture of disorder and disintegration in many countries that had as colonies existed in peace and harmony, and his spirits were affected accordingly.

Yet his mood contrasted with the affection and admiration of his many friends. War memoirs were beginning to appear, and discussion of the great leaders was rife. The prevailing opinion of Wavell was fuelled by the veneration in which he seemed to have been held by his staff, many of whom were moved by his selflessness, and by the learning and vision that he had displayed in their presence, with his frequent relating of his difficulties to those of famous men in history. 'What would Belisarius have done?' he would ask, 'or Wellington?' He also had a special place in the public's heart, as the deliverer of triumph when the Blitz, the threat of invasion and the fear that the war might be lost had been an unremitting anxiety. That was quite in accord with Liddell Hart's analysis of military genius: 'In wartime the people tend to crave for a hero-leader, and as a natural consequence the leaders of the moment are invested with the properties of genius – until disillusionment strips them.'

It was at that time too soon to judge the performance of military leaders except perhaps with emotion rather than cool analysis. Now it is possible to see more clearly the threads that run through Wavell's discharge of the great works he was asked to undertake. Paramount, perhaps, is the combination of steadfastness of mind and body, allied to great intellectual power, that enabled him to create the means of a famous victory and deliver it when, in comparison with the enemy he faced, he was starved of resources. Only a man with great robustness, a quality he greatly admired, combined with a touch of the Elizabethan buccaneer could have so patiently and determinedly created and trained such a force, and matched it to a strategy that successfully gave battle on so many fronts at once.

That he was trusting of his subordinates – and of the advice that in many cases led him to appoint them – reflected his good nature, which his professionalism did not suppress. Yet where advice chimed with his own instincts he was sometimes too ready to accept it untested, and that led him to make some poor appointments and to embrace some bad ideas. He also managed to blend cautiousness with optimism, at times when neither was appropriate: he overestimated the Italians, for example, while consistently underestimating the Germans, even after they had demonstrated a ruthless ability to act and react with great force and speed. He also misjudged the Japanese; although in their case he had almost no intelligence on which to base firm opinions, he formed them nonetheless; however, they did not match the evidence of the fanatical power that drove his troops from the jungles of Burma and Malaya.

That aspect of his nature reflected what appeared to be an occasional rather surprising innocence. For example, on one occasion while he was Viceroy, Wavell was told of the immoral behaviour of someone in his inner household. He received the news quite blankly – as also in that case did his wife – unable to comprehend or accept what he was hearing. Nor did he seem to think that unorthodoxy should be a bar to the office of ADC, being happy to appoint at least three homosexuals to the post, regardless of, or at least unconcerned by, the resultant adverse comment in army and viceregal circles. Maybe he was well aware of such situations, but saw no reason not to be broad-minded, provided the men in question were in other respects suitable. Or perhaps he simply detached himself from the matter – let others mind, if they wish. He was a big enough man not to care.

One obstacle that consistently impeded Wavell, from the eve of war until his last days as Viceroy, was an inability or unwillingness to develop cordial relations with important politicians in the governments that he served. This could not have been only because he did not converse easily – that had not prevented him from rising to the top of the army. It may be that his attributes were those that soldiers value more highly than do politicians, who appreciate a certain deviousness in approaching problems, and who like to be flattered. Wavell was not a flatterer, nor was he in any way devious, while his obvious bravery and reliability appealed more to soldiers than to politicians. He seemed to lack an instinctive understanding of politics, and to have a prejudice against politicians, whether he knew them or not. He made little attempt to conciliate them when doing so might have smoothed his path towards the goals he wished to reach. He appeared to be more reluctant to communicate with his natural associates than with others with whom he had little in common: he seemed to have a greater desire to be polite to Gandhi and Nehru, for example, than to members of the Cabinet, whether Churchill's or Attlee's.

Yet in seeking an enduring solution for India, Wavell worked far harder and more doggedly than could have been expected of the most dedicated public servant, while inevitably making a number of mistakes along the way – such as the hasty dissolution of a tried and experienced Executive Council and its replacement by a nondescript 'caretaker' government of officials. For all that, a large part of the credit for breaking the deadlock between Britain and India was owed to him; by doing so he finally established Whitehall's bona fides, and thereafter Indian opinion never doubted his desire to press on towards the goal of the country's freedom. Nevertheless he failed to break the deadlock between the Hindu and Muslim politicians, a fundamental requirement as his plans were based on preserving the unity of the country, and consequently upon securing agreement between the two main parties. But he was pursuing a goal that was probably impossible to achieve: the Hindus and Muslims were never going to agree to a compromise framed within a united India. Nehru and his advisers, such as V.P. Menon, had convinced themselves that no compromise would work, and that a Muslim Raj would be a hopeless proposition for the new India in the post-war world. Jinnah, on the other hand, believed that by sticking to his position he would eventually receive sufficient concessions for his purposes and that all would be well in the end: he had, for instance, kept on his house in Bombay and had hoped to live there in retirement.

Wavell was also hindered by his ingrained deference to higher authority, on occasions when he might have stood firm for what he believed was the proper strategy. Whereas that might have been appropriate in some contexts – civil servants advise, ministers decide – amid the dangers days of war the Cabinet sought, and needed, dispassionate military opinions, not conformity with their own preferences. If on occasion Wavell believed that the War Cabinet's plans would be disastrous and would uselessly sacrifice men and materials, he could have said so, to the point of asking to be relieved of his command if his proposals were spurned. Instead he fell back on the doctrine that 'strategy is the handmaid of policy' and conformed with the wishes of his political masters. After the collapse in the desert, and the consequent change in command, the Chiefs of Staff – with hindsight – were determined that there should be no repetition of the confusion that had occurred and took steps to ensure that, in future, commanders in the field should make the reasons behind their recommendations clear to the Government. The CIGS wrote to Wavell's successor, General Auchinleck, in those terms:

. . . pressure often comes from very broad political considerations; these are sometimes so powerful as to make it necessary to take risks which, from the purely military point of view, may seem inadvisable. The main point is that *you* should make it quite clear what risks are involved if a course of action is forced upon you which, from the military point of view, is undesirable. You may even find it necessary, in the extreme case, to disassociate yourself from the consequences.[12]

Governments need logical military appreciations to help them formulate policy – as evidenced by the Cabinet recording that its decision to go to the aid of Greece was founded upon the military appreciations that they had received from Wavell and the other service chiefs in the Middle East – despite the fact that the arguments they supplied 'told against, rather than in favour of, their advice'.[13] In fact, in 1941 there seemed little more strategic imperatives for sending an army to Greece than for not pressing on to Tripoli. There were, however, political considerations, and in both cases Wavell seemed ready to accept political direction in the matter when the politicians were in fact looking for an assessment based on military advice. When sending a force to Greece was first mooted, Wavell firmly and successfully disabused the Foreign Secretary of his initial support for the idea. There seems to be no clear reason why in that case he did not stick to his instinct, and to his own military appreciation.

It has been alleged against Wavell that he lacked the ruthlessness that might have prevented Rommel's early successes, but there seems to be no merit in that argument: it was not lack of ruthlessness that led to the failure to halt the Afrika Korps, but lack of men and resources. While it was not clear at the time that the main German thrust would not come through the Balkans to Suez, had Wavell marshalled his forces in North Africa, kept out of Greece and – having blockaded Ethiopia – left it to stew, his resources might have been sufficient to deny North Africa to the Germans. But he did not do so, apparently to conform with political directives. Even so, he displayed the greatest skill in his deployment of the relatively meagre forces at his disposal. As Liddell Hart told him, 'It seems to be your fate in this war to be always destined to tackle the most awkward problems, and under the most difficult conditions.'

Nor was it lack of ruthless leadership that led to the collapse in the Far East. Dismissing Percival in Singapore would not have saved the day; indeed, less erratic interference from above might have sustained what little confidence the general still had. Wavell did on occasion deal ruthlessly, for example with Sir John Smyth and General Irwin, but to little immediate effect – it is unlikely that at that stage of the war any divisional generals, however inspiring, could have stemmed the Japanese tide. It had to beach itself.

As Viceroy, Wavell blended deference to authority in London – something that had not troubled Viceroys in earlier days – with an attitude that did not encourage cordiality from the Cabinet. Yet his patience and determination to establish a government to which to transfer power, without appeasing ambitious Indian politicians, very nearly succeeded. He himself believed that it probably would have done so, had he taken a stronger line with the Cabinet mission, whose performance he regarded as near-disastrous. But in that case also he deferred, without sufficient objection, to authority, although he could with reason have been sure that his own ideas were wiser than those of the Cabinet.

Even had he adopted a less proactive and liberal approach towards India, and instead kept the political situation firmly on hold during the war, there is little reason to suppose that the Muslim League and the Congress Party would have dealt any more easily with each other thereafter. Also, the current was flowing too strongly towards independence to be diverted or much delayed unless Britain decided to reverse its policy of withdrawal, something that it no longer had the will or the means to do. It is hard to imagine anything that Wavell had not tried earlier that might have brought the opposing parties together in 1947 or 1948. As Jinnah maintained for so long, without autocratic rule to keep India unified, partition was inevitable. Yet Wavell did not adhere to the brief that he was originally assigned: very early on his liberal streak made him alter the course he had been set. Overall, perhaps it could be said that his difficulty in communicating with people, which often rendered him unable to sell his ideas, and which made Indians shy and uncertain, would have made him the right Viceroy had he – or, properly speaking, the Government – wished to keep the governance of India largely unchanged until the end of the war, but less so if, as was the case, he preferred to push the political process forward.

His knowledge of literature and history inclined Wavell towards the unorthodox and the bohemian, while at the same time preventing him from being single-minded or even always enthusiastic about soldiering, which he often said bored him. But he was clever enough for any lack of wholeheartedness not to matter, as he was so good at his job that outside interests did not impede his performance. It is just possible that he might have found more satisfaction out of uniform altogether: he would have made an excellent professor of military history, as he himself appeared, somewhat wistfully, to believe. Yet he was fulfilled as a soldier, perhaps most of all when he was a brigadier, with his first independent command, a happy home in the country and without so much responsibility that it interfered with other aspects of his life. It was at that moment in his career that he was most able to take pleasure in being with his family, and sharing with them the country pursuits that he loved.

His greatest exhilaration was probably derived from his brief excursion into the rich and cultured world of Henry Channon, when, after a long period of strain and discomfort, he suddenly found himself in easy circumstances. Then, for a time, he was the lion of the salons, able to bare his feelings to people who shared some of his interests and who were full of fun and laughter. However, although many of them were bohemian and unorthodox, and in their way attractive, Wavell was not naturally of their stamp and might not have warmed to their society for long. It was with his family, close-knit, good-natured and content, that he found enduring pleasure.

The admiration, and sometimes adulation, that people felt for Wavell contrasted with his modesty and detachment. Many soldiers who came to know him well – particularly those younger than he, for example his junior officers and his ADCs, seemed unable to find fault in him, and painted portraits that he would probably think gleamed rather too bright. Yet people from many other walks of life also described him as a great man. T.S. Eliot did not know him well, but wrote:

> What I do know from personal acquaintance with the man, is that he was a great man. This is not a term I use easily; there are very few men whom I have met in all my years in two continents, and amongst all the variety whom I have known, who seem to me great men. But about Wavell I feel not a doubt whatever.[14]

Even Churchill probably ultimately accepted that Wavell had done very great things for his country.

His own nature would probably have led Wavell to ignore such emotions, not really caring, one way or the other, what most people thought of him – or what they wrote. In that respect he was curiously like his mentor, Allenby, as Wavell described at the outset of his celebrated biography:

Allenby was the last man who would have cared what his biographer wrote of him, or, indeed, that his biography should be written at all. He never troubled to explain his successes or to justify any action he had taken; he bore no grudge against his critics or detractors. [15]

Although he may not have been greatly moved by the way most people regarded him or of his achievements, had he lived longer Wavell might have recorded his own story. He kept a chronicle of his engagements over many years, and he had prepared chapter headings for a memoir, with the title 'Reasons in Writing'; with such a powerful memory and associative mind, it would have been a valuable record of momentous times.

Perhaps when he returned from India he was subdued through unconscious ill health. Towards the end of 1949 he complained of not feeling well, but medical examinations disclosed no illness. However, his discomfort persisted, and early in the New Year the doctors decided that he had jaundice. They were wrong: he had in fact developed liver cancer. At that time there was neither the knowledge nor the remedy to reverse or halt the damage, and on 1 May 1950 he was admitted to a nursing home in west London. Four days later he had an operation, but to no avail, and on 24 May 1950, he died, three weeks after his sixty-seventh birthday.

The funeral arrangements were full of pomp and circumstance. The authorities offered a burial in Westminster Abbey near Allenby's tomb, but the family decided instead on interment at Winchester College. Even so, the field-marshal's coffin was taken by river from the Tower of London to Westminster Pier, the first state river cortège since Nelson's funeral in 1805. Great and solemn ceremony marked the hour, and people lined the streets as the coffin was drawn slowly to the abbey, accompanied by a Household Cavalry escort, and to the sound of the pipes and drums of the Black Watch. Wavell's courage and success in battling for England in her hour of need had earned him the dues which, on 7 June, the country visibly paid.

Many of the arrangements were made with the advice of Colonel Bernard Fergusson, who recorded his misgivings about how parts of the order of service would have displeased Wavell, a convinced agnostic. However, he knew that the great soldier would have approved of a formal occasion inspiring both those taking part and the silent crowds. Wavell had expressed his own opinion of himself more modestly – in answer to a young staff officer who had sent him a letter of fulsome praise, he had said:

Myself – quite small light table beer, I am afraid; a good journeyman soldier who knows his job reasonably well; not afraid of responsibility, but not seeking it; quite intelligent, for one of the Unintelligentsia; confident enough of his normal judgment of things military, but no divine fire for leadership of a people. So that's that.[16]

After the service, Wavell's body was taken to Winchester, of which he had been granted the freedom in 1943. His coffin was laid in the shadow of the college's chantry, where the pipers played 'The Flowers of the Forest'.

His tombstone might have borne witness to the symbols of his deeds and his valour: field-marshal, Viceroy, earl, privy councillor, GCB, GCSI, GCIE, CMG, MC, besides decorations from many other countries, including America, Russia, China and France. But that would not have been his way. Instead, except for the dates of his life, the plain stone bore the one word:

WAVELL

EPILOGUE
ARCHIBALD JOHN WAVELL

AFTER Lord Wavell's death his titles passed to his son, Archie John, who therefore became 2nd Earl Wavell, Viscount Wavell of Cyrenaica and of Winchester, and Viscount Keren of Eritrea and Winchester.

Like his father, the 2nd Earl Wavell was a gallant officer, and was awarded the Military Cross for courage and fortitude in an action in Burma on 12 June 1944. He was then commanding a company of the South Staffordshire Regiment, at that time part of 77th Infantry Brigade, as he had been too ill to accompany his battalion of the Black Watch when they had been sent into Burma. 77th Infantry Brigade had been ordered by General Stilwell to take Mogaung 'at all costs', as its position at the junction of the Ledo Road and the Burma Railway was vital. Captain Wavell had led his company in an attack on strongly held Japanese positions north of the River Mogaung, but had been driven back; however, he believed that during the firefight he had located all the Japanese positions and therefore asked his brigadier, the legendary Mad Mike Calvert, for permission to make another attack, in order to obviate the need for some of the brigade to be withdrawn, which would have been of considerable advantage to the Japanese.

Wavell led the ensuing assault, which turned into a hard hand-to-hand fight, in which about twenty-five Japanese were killed and forty more were driven off. Wavell was badly wounded, but stood his ground and consolidated the company's position, even though his wrist was hanging by only half an inch of bone and gristle: his hand had to be amputated that night. The citation for his Military Cross described him as an outstanding example to all ranks and 'worthy of the great name he bears'.

He remained in the army after the war and became greatly interested in teaching, playing an important part in the development of education for Other Ranks. On Christmas Eve 1953 he was tragically killed while serving in Kenya. That day, all the fighting officers and men in his detachment, except for him, were out on patrol when a Mau–Mau gang attacked their camp. Wavell, then a major in the Black Watch, had remained behind to look after the camp, which at the crucial time contained only men on administrative and catering duties. Impetuously, but with characteristic bravery, Wavell picked up a rifle and charged the gang, but was fatally wounded in the head by a single shot. He was thirty-seven.

ACKNOWLEDGEMENTS

I am most grateful to Ellah Allfrey and Will Sulkin, my publishers at Jonathan Cape, and to James Gill and Marcella Edwards, my literary agents at PFD, for the guidance they have provided in the preparation of this book. I am also most grateful to the trustees of the Society of Authors for their encouragement.

I am grateful to Lady McTaggart (Wavell's granddaughter) for her suggestions at the outset of this project, and I would also like to thank Owen Humphrys (Wavell's grandson) for giving me access to documents and photographs in Lord Wavell's archive, and for responding to my questions with courteous patience and with many useful suggestions and criticisms.

I would like to thank Lady Kelvedon and Hon. Henry Channon for allowing me to consult the diaries of Sir Henry Channon, and for the help of their assistant, Sophie Allan.

I am most grateful to the many archivists, librarians and scholars who have dealt with my numerous requests with unfailing patience. I should particularly like to thank Verity Andrews, at Reading University; Milissa Burkart, at the University of Tulsa; Patrick Cadell, at Hopetoun House; Pam Clark, Registrar of the Royal Archives; Sue Donnelly, at the London School of Economics; Jack Flavell; Ivana Frlan and Natalie Milne, of Birmingham University Library; Keith Haines, at Campbell College, Belfast; Andrew Hambling, at Haileybury; Colin Harris, at the Bodleian Library, Oxford; Caroline Herbert, at Churchill College, Cambridge; Simon Lawson, at the Indian Institute, Oxford; Lucy McCann, at Rhodes House, Oxford; the Trustees of the National Library of Scotland; Patrick Maclure, at Winchester; Tony Money, at Radley College; John Montgomery, at the Royal United

Services Institute; John and Virginia Murray, at the John Murray Archive; Kate O'Brien, at the Liddell Hart Centre for Military Archives; Andrew Orgill, at the Royal Military Academy, Sandhurst; Richard Ramage, at the Taylor Institution, Oxford; Will Richmond, of *House & Garden* magazine; Andrew Robinson and Charles Milne, at Eton College, and also Penny Hatfield, the College Archivist; Roger Sims, at the Manx National Heritage; Nicholas Smith, at the Oxford University Archives; Nicholas Smith, editor of the Royal Geographical Society magazine; Erica Somers, at the Faber Archive; Carl Spadoni and Amanda White, at McMaster University; William Spencer and Rachel Bell, at the National Archives; Professor Hew Strachan and Norma Aubertin-Potter at All Souls College, Oxford; Roderick Suddaby and Simon Robbins, at the Imperial War Museum; Mrs. T.S. Eliot, Debbie Usher, at St Antony's College, Oxford; Debbie Whitfield, at the T.S. Eliot Archive; and XaioWei Bond, at the India Office Library.

Those who knew Lord Wavell and who kindly agreed to discuss his career with me include Mrs Joan Bright Astley, Captain F.S. Burnaby-Atkins, Dame Frances Campbell-Preston, the Duke and Duchess of Grafton, Colonel David Rose and Major-General Andrew Watson.

I received many valuable suggestions about aspects of Wavell's career as a soldier, and other military matters, for which, and for permission to quote from their papers, I should like to thank the following in particular:

Andrew Ardington, at Spion Kop; General Sir Norman Arthur; Correlli Barnett; Dr Niall Barr and Chris Hobson, at the Defence Academy; Field Marshal Lord Bramall; Professor Brian Farrell; Dr Neil Faulkner; General Sir David Fraser; James Holland; Professor Sir Michael Howard; Tony Lavelle, of the Army Personnel Centre; Randall Nicol; Brigadier Andrew Parker-Bowles; Andrew Roberts; Viscount Slim; and Thomas Smyth, and the trustees of the Black Watch Museum.

My research into Wavell's work in India was made less difficult as a result of my discussions with, in particular, Youssuf Baig; Mrs Fay Campbell-Johnson; Christopher Carnaghan, of the Indian Police Association; the Reverend J.R. De Chazal; Patric Emerson, of the Indian Army Association; Baroness Flather; Ramachandra Guha; Hugh Hall, of the Indian Political Service Association; Professor Alastair Lamb; John McAleer, at the British Empire and Commonwealth Museum; Divya Mathur, at the Nehru Centre; Countess Mountbatten of Burma; Amit Roy; Professor Ian Talbot; and Jaya Thadani.

A great many people were kind enough to address my queries, or in various other ways ease my progress, including Nicholas Aldridge, Lady Allendale, the Marquess of Anglesey, Dugald Barr, Lady Bayliss, Mrs Alice Benson, Nigel Blackwell, Hon. Lady Bonsor, James Bristow, Anthony Brotherton-Ratcliffe, Lt Cdr Henry Bruce, Nony Buchanan, George Burnett-Stuart, Lord Charles Cecil, Anne Christie, Prue Coats, Camilla Coats-Carr, Artemis Cooper, Theresa Courtauld, Sir Geoffrey Cox, Sir Hew Dalrymple, Professor Alex Danchev, Professor David Dilks, Lord Egremont, George Fergusson, Elizabeth Floyd, Sir Edward Ford, Mrs Susan Fortune, Hon. Mrs Hugh Fraser, Edward Fremantle, Hon. Annabel Freyberg, Ivry Lady Freyberg, Leonie Frieda, Dr John Gayner, Sir David Gilmour, Irial Glynn, Jenny Hacker, Duff Hart-Davis, Susannah Herbert, Jackie Ingram, Jacqueline Lady Killearn, Lord Killearn, Victoria Legge-Bourke, Sir Patrick Leigh-Fermor, the Marquess of Linlithgow, Mrs David Lowe, Lady Anne Mackenzie, Philip Mackenzie, Piers Mackesy, Angela Moray, Jill Mure, Basil Postan, Sarah Powell, Simon Prior-Palmer, Lord Quirk, Gavin Rankin, David Reid Scott, Malise Reid Scott, Kenneth Rose, the Dowager Marchioness of Salisbury, John Saumarez Smith, William Seymour, Richard Shepherd, MP, Lady Caroline Simmonds, John Slater of the Kipling Society, Colonel David Smiley, Xan Smiley, John Stewart, Dr Frank Tait, Ian Thorne, Count Nikolai Tolstoy, Heather Tylor, Hugo Vickers, Laura Wallace, Gerald Ward, Hon. Sir John White and Philip Ziegler.

LIST OF ABBREVIATIONS

ABDACOM	American-British-Dutch-Australian Command
AMEL	Leopold Amery Papers, CAC
BGGS	Brigadier General, General Staff
BL	British Library
BWRA	Black Watch Regimental Archive [Perth]
CAB	Cabinet Papers
CAC	Churchill Archive Centre
CHAR	Chartwell Papers, CAC
CID	Committee of Imperial Defence
CIGS	Chief of the Imperial General Staff
COS	Chiefs of Staff
DMI	Director of Military Intelligence
HMSO	Her Majesty's Stationery Office
ICS	Indian Civil Service
IOR	India Office Records, British Library
LASL	Sir Alan Lascelles Papers, CAC
LH	Liddell Hart Archive, LHCMA
LHCMA	Liddell Hart Centre for Military Archives
MECA	Middle East Centre, St Anthony's College, Oxford
MO5	Intelligence Section, Military Operations Department, WO
OKW	Oberkommando der Wehrmacht
PREM	Premier Papers, PRO
PRO	Public Record Office
RA GVI	Royal Archives, King George VI Archive
RA PS	Royal Archive, [Private Secretary]

RUSI   Ronald United Services Institute
RLEW   Ronald Lewin Papers
WO   War Office

NOTES

Chapter 1: Shaping Up

1. Kipling was a winner of the Nobel Prize for Literature.
2. Rudyard Kipling, *Something of Myself*, Tauchnitz, London, 1938.
3. Almost always known as the Black Watch.
4. Memoir by Lady Burne-Jones, quoted in Nicholas Aldridge, *Time To Spare?*, Talboys, Oxford, 1989.
5. A.P. Wavell, *Other Men's Flowers*, Jonathan Cape, London, 1944.
6. Wavell writing to Freya Stark, 23 December 1949. John Murray Archive, London.
7. As stated by the famous, and later notorious, Eton master, William Johnson Cory, qualifying his otherwise tolerant view of the teaching of science.
8. Wavell to Stark, op. cit., 29 December 1943.
9. Raymond Asquith to H.T. Baker, 28 February 1897. Quoted in John Jolliffe, *Raymond Asquith: Life and Letters*, Collins, London, 1980.
10. Geoffrey Drage, MP. In an address to Etonians, 1890.
11. Basil Collier, *Leader of the Few*, Jarrolds, London 1957.

Chapter 2: First Blood

1. Cecil Rhodes, *Confession of Faith*. MSS. Afr.t.1, no.17, Rhodes House Archive, Oxford.
2. The reef soon became famous as the 'Witwatersrand' (white-water reef).
3. A message of solidarity sent by Germany to Paul Kruger, President of the Boer South African Republic on 3 January 1896, during the extraordinary

events in the Transvaal which led to the British incursion that gained worldwide notoriety as the Jameson Raid.

4. See, for example, note 1, supra. Rhodes, who wielded immense political and economic influence, was for a time Premier of Cape Colony, and had visions of extending British hegemony northwards from the Cape all the way to the Mediterranean.

5. John Connell, *Wavell: Scholar and Soldier*, Collins, London, 1964.

6. See Lisle March Phillipps, *With Rimington*, Edward Arnold, London, 1901.

7. Quoted in Connell, op. cit.

8. Phillipps, op. cit., p.202.

9. Rudyard Kipling, 'The Return', *The Complete Verse of Rudyard Kipling*, Kyle Cathie, London, Revised Edition, 2002.

Chapter 3: Outposts of Empire

1. Marquess Curzon of Kedleston, *The True Imperialism: The Nineteenth Century and After*, vol. 371.

2. The Diary of William Walker, 2nd Black Watch, India 1903–6, BWRA 0689, The Black Watch Regimental Archive, Perth.

3. Private John Gethins, *The Red Hackle*, The Black Watch, Perth, April 1969.

4. Quoted in *Plain Tales from the Raj*, ed. Charles Allen and Andre Deutsch, London, 1975.

5. Ibid.

6. R.J. Collins, *Lord Wavell*, Hodder & Stoughton, London, 1947.

7. Correlli Barnett, *The Collapse of British Power*, Pan, London, 2002, p.43.

8. A *canard* started by *Punch* magazine, who famously but erroneously suggested that Sir Charles Napier announced his conquest of Scinde with a one-word telegram that read '*Peccavi.*' In the note to the poem in his anthology of poetry, *Other Men's Flowers*, Wavell rightly seems to query whether that ever happened (in fact, the idea was first propagated by a schoolgirl, Catherine Winkworth. See *Army Quarterly*, vol. LIX, January 1950).

9. Rudyard Kipling to Margaret Burne-Jones, quoted in David Gilmour, *Recessional*, John Murray, London, 2002.

10. Rudyard Kipling, *The Complete Stalky & Co.*, Macmillan, London, 1929.

11. Meaning 'the language of the camp'.

12. In February 1904. It lasted for more than eighteen months and was marked by a series of Russian defeats which caused great embarrassment to the Tsar and his government and was a major factor in the revolution of 1905.

13. Sir Alfred Zimmern, *The Third British Empire* O.U.P., London, 1927.

14. Philip Mason, *The Men Who Ruled India*, Jonathan Cape, London, 1953–4.

15. *Round Table*, vol.1, Nov. 1910.

16. Ibid.

17. Parliamentary Debates, HC, vol.183, col.1373.

18. R.H. Kiernan, *Wavell*, Harrap, London, 1946.

19. A.P. Wavell, *The Palestine Campaigns*, Constable, London, 1928.

20. Rudyard Kipling, 'The Young British Soldier', *The Complete Verse of Rudyard Kipling*, Kyle Cathie, London, Revised Edition, 2002.

21. Quoted in Connell, *op. cit.*

22. Wavell to Dover Wilson, Wilson MSS, f. 32, National Library of Scotland.

23. Army Order 233: 12.9.1906

24. On 5 October 1930 the airship crashed near Beauvais, on its maiden voyage, killing all fifty-four people on board.

Chapter 4: A Proper War

1. Connell, op. cit., p.70.

2. In January 1912.

3. General Staff Officer, Third Grade.

4. Maj. Gen. Sir Ernest Swinton (1868–1951), later Assistant Secretary CID and War Cabinet; Swinton was the moving force behind the creation of the Royal Tank Corps. He was Oxford's Chichele Professor of Military History from 1925 to 1939. See Chapter 6, below.

5. Sir Henry Newbolt (1862–1938). Educated at Clifton College, the setting for the famous first verse of 'Vitaï Lampada'. Appointed Official Naval Historian, 1923. Made a Companion of Honour, an award described by Somerset Maugham, when he received his, as meaning 'Very well done, *but . . .*'

6. From 'Vitaï Lampada' by Henry Newbolt, *Collected Poems 1897–1907*, Echo, T. Nelson & Sons, London, 1918.

7. Connell, op. cit.

8. From A.E. Housman, *A Shropshire Lad*, quoted in Jeanne MacKenzie,

The Children of the Souls, Chatto & Windus, London, 1986.

9. See MO5 War Stage. PRO. WO 106/494.

10. Connell, op. cit., p.82.

11. Ibid., p.95.

12. Alastair Horne, *The Price of Glory*, Penguin, London, 1993.

13. Henri Barbusse, *Under Fire*, tr. Fitzwater Wray, J.M. Dent, London, 1917, quoted in Horne, op. cit. When eventually the trauma of the war began, very slightly, to fade from men's minds, a few writers steeled themselves to write of their experiences and impressions of trench warfare. The forerunner was *All Quiet on the Western Front*, but perhaps the most powerfully written, and the most graphically appalling, was Henry Williamson's *The Patriot's Progress*, published in 1930.

14. The marriage took place on 22 April 1915 at Holy Trinity, Sloane Street, in London.

15. A.P. Wavell, *Allenby: A Study in Greatness*, Harrap, London, 1940.

16. Usually – to much post-war criticism – far from the front line, heedless of the old army saying that 'no gentleman ever consents to serve in a head-quarters beyond the range of a medium gun'.

17. Connell, op. cit., p.101.

18. H.S. Clapham, *Mud and Khaki*, Hutchinson, London, 1930.

19. PRO. WO 95/1426, 9th Infantry Brigade War Diary, 16 June 1915.

20. Clapham, op. cit.

21. The award, for gallantry during active operations against the enemy, was established at the end of 1914 for officers of the rank of captain or below.

22. General Sir Aylmer Haldane diary. National Library of Scotland, MS 20254 f.107.

23. A.P. Wavell, 'Recollections', quoted in Harold Winton, *To Change an Army*, Brassey's, London, 1985.

24. Now known as Tbilisi, capital of Georgia.

25. Connell, op. cit., p.114. He also had vigorous opinions: when the baleful Rasputin was at the height of his powers, he sent a message to the Grand Duke saying that he was coming to inspect his army and would arrive by special train at 2.00 and expected to be met. Nikolai telegraphed a reply saying, 'Will meet you at 2.00 and hang you at 2.30.' Rasputin decided not to go.

26. ROB 8.1.62, LHCMA.

27. T.E. Lawrence ('of Arabia') also repaired to the animal kingdom for inspi-

ration, and used to describe Allenby as 'Our Lion, in whom we placed dreamlike confidence'.

28. His life of Allenby has been much admired since its publication in 1928.

29. A.P. Wavell, *Allenby in Egypt*, Harrap, London, 1943.

30. Allenby Papers, 7.1.5., LHCMA.

31. Ibid, 8.1.65.

32. See, for example, Sir Philip Chetwode to Wavell, 17 February 1939. Allenby Papers, 6.VIII.31, LHCMA.

33. Wavell, *Allenby: A Study in Greatness*.

34. Wavell to Capt. Basil Liddell Hart, 24 March 1934. LH 1/733, LHCMA.

35. 'Brigadier-General General Staff', in effect, the chief staff officer for operations.

36. Wavell to Liddell Hart, 18 May 1935. LH 1/733, Pt 2, LHCMA.

37. At least in the opinion of St John the Divine: see Revelation, ch.XVI, v.16.

38. A.P. Wavell, *The Palestine Campaigns*, Constable, London, 1928, pp.238, 239.

Chapter 5: Reputations

1. Archibald John Arthur was born on 11 May 1916 and Eugénie Pamela on 3 December 1918.

2. Quoted in Connell, op. cit., p.152.

3. A second daughter, Felicity Ann, was born on 21 July 1921, and a third, Joan Patricia Quirk, on 23 April 1923.

4. Lieut Col A.P. Wavell, CMG, MC, 'The Strategy of the Campaigns of the Egyptian Expeditionary Force (With Sketch Maps)', *Army Quarterly*, vol.3, October–January 1921–22, p.235 et seq. The article was based on a lecture that he gave at the Senior Officers' School, at Woking, when he was on a course there in August 1921.

5. All correspondence quoted between Wavell and Liddell Hart is in LHCMA, 1/733.

6. Colonel A.P. Wavell, CMG, MC, 'Night Attacks – Ancient and Modern (With Map)', *Army Quarterly*, vol.30, April–July 1930, p.325 et seq.

7. A.P. Wavell, *The Good Soldier*, Macmillan, London, 1948, p.20. On their occasional forays in search of sympathy from other nations, the Germans were not helped by their ponderous language: whereas, for example, in the First World War the British Army settled for describing its brave

new weapon as a 'Tank', the Germans had to make sure of the matter by calling it a *Schützengrabenvernichtigungsautomobil*.

8. Quoted in Connell, op. cit., p.156.

9. A.P. Wavell, *The Palestine Campaigns*, Constable, London, 1928.

10. Wavell to Liddell Hart, 1 December 1927. LH 1/733, LHCMA.

11. Wavell to T.E. Lawrence, 8 January 1928. Bodleian Library, Oxford, MS Eng. D. 3341.1543–7.

12. Quoted in B.H. Liddell Hart, *The Memoirs of Captain Liddell Hart*, Cassell, London, 1965.

13. Ibid.

14. From an article in *House & Garden*, published in October/November 1950.

15. Ibid.

16. Connell, op. cit., p.160.

17. Lavinia Graecen, *Chink*, Macmillan, London, 1989.

18. A system adopted, exceptionally, by the Rifle Brigade, and also dating from the Peninsular War.

19. Prime Minister addressing the House of Commons, 4 June 1940.

20. Graecen, op. cit.

21. Major Henry Cadell, Royal Engineers, diary, 22 September 1933. Private collection.

22. Mrs John Benson to author.

23. See, for example, the prologue to Evelyn Waugh's *Brideshead Revisited*.

24. Proceedings at RUSI, London, 15 February 1933.

25. Ibid.

26. Quoted in Graecen, op. cit.

27. A.P. Wavell, from 'T.E. Lawrence to T.E. Shaw', *The Listener*, 7 March 1934.

28. T.E. Lawrence, 'Evolution of a Revolt', *Army Quarterly*, vol.1, October–January 1920–21, quoted in Dr Neil Faulkner and Dr Nicholas Saunders, 'War Without Frontiers: the Archaeology of the Arab Revolt, 1916–1918', a paper presented at 'The Frontiers of the Ottoman World' conference, and published in 2008, Great Arab Revolt Project, Department of Archaeology and Anthropology, University of Bristol. Archaeological investigations begun in southern Jordan in November 2006, led by Dr Faulkner and Dr Saunders, suggest that the Arab Revolt and the guerrilla activities subsequently promoted by T.E. Lawrence had a considerably greater effect on Turkish conduct of the war than had

previously been believed, and that the campaign was far from being 'a sideshow of a sideshow'. It seems that Wavell was fully justified in his far-sighted opinions.

29. Ibid.
30. A.P. Wavell, *Soldiers and Soldiering*, Jonathan Cape, London, 1953.
31. Wavell in *T.E. Lawrence by his Friends*, ed. A.W. Lawrence, Jonathan Cape, London, 1937, pp.147–50. Lawrence had a fatal accident on his motor-bicycle in late May 1935.
32. A courageous warrior, with VC, DSO and Bar. See Chapter 11, below.
33. Wavell to Liddell Hart, 5 January 1935. LH 1/733, LHCMA.
34. Liddell Hart to Wavell, 20 March 1934. LH 1/733, LHCMA.
35. *House & Garden*, October/November 1950.
36. Lord Ballantrae, *Wavell: Portrait of a Soldier*, Collins, London, 1961.
37. Sir Brian Horrocks, *A Full Life*, Leo Cooper, London, 1974, p.72. Horrocks took part in the 'Golden Fleece' exercise.
38. Ballantrae, op. cit., p.18.
39. Quoted in Connell, op. cit., p.177.
40. See p.77, above.
41. See Field Marshal Earl Wavell, 'Mickey – A Cad', *Blackwood's Magazine*, June 1950.
42. PRO. WO 32/4157.

Chapter 6: Countdown

1. During the Second World War the Grand Mufti escaped first to Iraq, where he engineered a rebellion, and then to Berlin, where he closely advised both Himmler and one of his best friends, Adolf Eichmann, on their ideas for dealing with European Jewry. He died in 1974 without returning to Jerusalem, and his former place as leader of the Palestinian Arabs was taken by his nephew, Yasser Arafat.
2. Known as the Peel Report, after the commission's chairman, Lord Peel. It was a strong commission, and its report had been eagerly awaited by all sides in the dispute.
3. Lewis Andrews, an Australian reputedly friendly to the Jewish cause, and District Commissioner of Galilee, was murdered on his way to Evensong on Sunday, 26 September 1937.
4. Connell, op. cit., p.194.
5. Riots had broken out in Egypt as part of a revolt led by the nationalist

leader Sa'ad Zaghlul, who opposed continuation of Britain's Protectorate in Egypt.

6. About £11 billion today.
7. Wavell, *Soldiers and Soldiering*.
8. Connell, op. cit., p.183.
9. Captain B.H. Liddell Hart, *Memoirs*, vol.ii, Cassell, London, 1965, p.63.
10. Ibid., p.65.
11. R.J. Minney, ed., *The Private Papers of Hore-Belisha*, Collins, London, 1960.
12. Connell, op. cit., p.193.
13. Collins, op. cit.
14. Ibid., p.181.
15. Professor Frederick Lindemann, later Viscount Cherwell, was Churchill's closest friend for twenty-five years. He joined the Cabinet during the Second World War and advised the Premier on a large number of vital scientific and economic developments. Achieving early fame as a physicist of the first rank, he had been the first man to demonstrate, by an act of suicidal courage, how to recover from aeroplane spin.
16. *House & Garden*, October/November 1950.
17. Connell, op. cit., p.200.
18. Major-General Swinton also wrote stories under the pseudonym 'Ole-Luk-Oie', the name taken from Hans Christian Andersen's Dream-God.
19. Wavell to Liddell Hart, 28 September 1938.
20. The lectures were later published in Wavell, *Soldiers and Soldiering*.
21. General Wilhelm Keitel, Chief of the OKW, *Deutsche Wehr*, Karlsruhe, 1939. Although Keitel was later considered to be a 'prize booby' and little more than a Hitler lackey, his comments on Wavell were noted elsewhere in the German Army.
22. Connell, op. cit., p.204.

Chapter 7: Bricks Without Straw

1. Wavell to Sir Henry Jackson, 21 August 1939. BWRA 0335, the Black Watch regimental archive, Perth. Jackson wrote one of the glowing 'Confidential Reports' that helped Wavell reach high rank in the army.
2. Correlli Barnett, *The Audit of War*, Pan, London, 1996. See also his *The Collapse of British Power*, Pan, London, 2002.

3. A.P. Wavell, *Generals and Generalship*, Lees Knowles Lectures, 1939, Times Publishing Co., 1941.

4. In May 1940 Mitchell was replaced by Sir Arthur Longmore.

5. A.P. Wavell, 'The Higher Commander', a lecture given by Major-General A.P. Wavell at the Royal United Services Institute on 4 December 1935.

6. Alan Bennett, *Forty Years On*, Faber & Faber, London, 1969.

7. I.S.O. Playfair, *The Mediterranean and Middle East*, HMSO, 1954, p.60.

8. Gen. Sir Edward Spears, appointed by Churchill to head a mission to the Free French; his work took him frequently to Cairo in 1940–41.

9. Wavell to CIGS, 23 October 1939. PRO. WO 32/4157.

10. Wavell to Sir John Dill, 7 January 1940. Dill Papers 3/17, LHCMA.

11. Later Sir Edward Ford, Assistant Private Secretary to King George VI.

12. Sir Edward Ford to author.

13. Wavell to CIGS, Notes on the Middle East. PRO. WO 201/2119.

14. At least £100 million in current money.

15. Jacqueline Lampson was the daughter of Aldo Castellani, one of the world's leading experts on tropical diseases, who had been surgeon-general to the Italian forces during Italy's war against Ethiopia; he would later become medical adviser to the Italian High Command. He was subsequently to live in London's Harley Street.

16. A. de C. Hamilton, Assistant Oriental Secretary, Notes on a Visit to Upper Egypt, 1939. PRO. FO 371/23305.

17. Now so called, following her husband's knighthood.

18. Voluntary Aid Detachment, a nursing organisation.

19. Bernard Fergusson, later Lord Ballantrae and Governor General of New Zealand; referred to above.

20. Wavell, *Allenby: A Study in Greatness*.

21. A new and avant-garde magazine of art and literature, edited by Cyril Connolly.

22. *Horizon*, vol.iii, no.14, February 1941.

23. Orwell said that reading *No Orchids* was like taking a header into a cesspool; despite, or perhaps because of, that, it was a massive best-seller.

24. His soon-to-be adversary, Rommel, frequently carried with him Wavell's *Generals and Generalship*.

25. See Molly Izzard, *Freya Stark*, Hodder & Stoughton, London, 1993.

26. Ibid.

27. Julian Amery, *Approach March*, Hutchinson, London, 1973. Amery's father was at that time Secretary of State for India and Burma. Amery

himself subsequently became MP for Brighton Pavilion; like Wavell, he had been educated at Summer Fields, where he had been a memorably precocious youth: as a ten-year-old he had opened a speech to the school debating society with the words, 'Mr President, I am in favour of conscription; I have been so all my life.'

28. Peter Coats, *Of Generals and Gardens*, Weidenfeld & Nicolson, London, 1976.
29. Lampson diary, MECA, St Antony's College Archive, Oxford.
30. Quoted in Connell, op. cit.
31. Dill Papers 3/17, LHCMA.

Chapter 8: Aiming The Gun

1. Notes for a Talk with Australians, February 1940, A.P. Wavell, *Speaking Generally*, Macmillan, London, 1946.
2. Prime Minister to Secretary of State for War, 6 June 1940. Quoted in Winston S. Churchill, *Their Finest Hour*, Cassell, London, 1949.
3. Wavell to CIGS, 6 June 1940. PRO. WO 201/2481.
4. Wavell to Sir Alec Hardinge, 12 June 1940. Dill Papers, LHCMA.
5. Such an action would have been quite out of character for Wavell, and would anyway seem physically almost impossible. However, it was later widely credited in the Middle East, and in India, and, according to one Intelligence Officer in India, 'not just by those who frequented the bar of the New Delhi Club'.
6. On 10 May 1940, about twelve hours after the Germans invaded the Low Countries.
7. Quoted in Anthony Cave Brown, *Bodyguard of Lies*, W.H. Allen, London, 1976.
8. See below.
9. The official historian of deception in the Second World War asked Clarke if he would allow himself to be identified as the creator of strategic deception in the war, jointly with Wavell. See also David Mure, *Master of Deception*, William Kimber, London, 1980; Dudley Clarke, *Seven Assignments*, with an introduction by Earl Wavell, Jonathan Cape, London, 1948; and Charles Cruikshank, *Deception in World War II* (an account based on official records), OUP, Oxford, 1979.
10. Ralph A. Bagnold, *Sand, Wind, and War*, University of Arizona Press, Tucson, 1990.

11. Ibid.

12. Ibid.

13. Some years later Bagnold found among family papers a letter dated 14 January 1881, from Wavell's uncle to Bagnold's father, congratulating him on the success of the Royal Engineers' 'Telegraph Troop'.

14. Quoted in David Shirreff, *Bare Feet and Bandoliers*, Radcliffe Press, London, 1995.

15. Churchill to General Ismay, 23 July 1940. Ismay Papers, LHCMA. Sir Hastings (later Lord) Ismay was Chief of Staff to the Minister of Defence, 1940–45, and Deputy Secretary (Military) to the War Cabinet, 1940–45.

16. Ibid.

17. Major-General A.R. Godwin-Austen, who was en route to East Africa to take over the 2nd African Division.

18. Lt Col David Rose, DSO, the Black Watch, to author.

19. Ibid.

20. Anthony Eden, later Earl of Avon, became Secretary of State for the Dominions on the outbreak of war in September 1939, and Secretary of State for War, with a seat in the War Cabinet, in May 1940. In December 1940 he became Foreign Secretary.

21. Earl of Avon, interviewed for the Thames Television 1973 series *The World At War*.

22. Earl of Avon, *The Eden Memoirs: The Reckoning*, Cassell, London, 1965.

23. For details of his report, see COS (40) 255, 8 August 1940. PRO. WO 106/6108.

24. Avon, *The Reckoning*.

25. L. S. Amery, CH, PC, Secretary of State for India and Burma, 1940–45

26. Brigadier John Shearer, private memoir, quoted in Ronald Lewin, *The Chief*, Hutchinson, London, 1930, p.37.

27. Avon, *The Reckoning*, p.131.

28. Ibid.

29. PRO. PREM 3/284/10.

30. Ibid.

31. Churchill to Eden, 29 August 1940. Avon Papers, AP 20/8/123, University of Birmingham Library.

32. Wavell to Dill, 19 September 1940. Dill Papers 3/19, LHCMA.

33. Avon, *The Reckoning*, p.142.

Chapter 9: His Finest Hour

1. COS(40) 255. 8 August 1940. PRO. WO 106/6108.

2. Jake Wardrop, *Tanks Across the Desert*, William Kimber, London, 1981, quoted in Robert Clarkson-Leach, *Massacre at Alamein*, Square One, Upton-upon-Severn, 1996. There was also the welcome sight of light vans marked 'Come and Get It', which contained cigarettes and other sustenance, and which travelled to the forward troops, sometimes even driving beyond 'The Wire'. They were the result of an initiative of two ladies: Mrs Fielding and Mrs Marriot, the latter a well-known American hostess in Cairo.

3. Quoted in Pamela Cooper, *A Cloud of Forgetting*, Quartet, London, 1993. Hore-Ruthven transferred to the SAS and was killed in 1942. Pamela Cooper, whose first husband was Hore-Ruthven, was one of the wives who managed to reach Cairo to be near her husband. She worked for Intelligence in GHQ, and then helped Freya Stark with her 'Brotherhood of Freedom'.

4. Ibid.

5. Ibid.

6. A.P. Wavell, Notes on Genesis and Working Out of 'Compass' Plan, 15 December 1940. Dill Papers, LHCMA.

7. Wavell to CIGS, 19 September 1940. Dill Papers, LHCMA.

8. Wavell, Genesis Note.

9. Ibid.

10. Prime Minister to Secretary of State for War, 26 October 1940. Avon Papers, AP 20/8/165, Birmingham University Library.

11. See Chapter 6, supra. Wingate was brave but odd. In Ethiopia he would occasionally walk around naked save for a belt from which hung an alarm-clock in the position normally reserved for a sporran; it was apparently supposed to remind onlookers of man's mortality, the due process of which he later tried to pre-empt by attempting suicide. He recovered, after which Wavell was to employ him in Burma, where he showed outstanding courage and enterprise.

12. A.P. Wavell, Foreword to Charles Rolo, *Wingate's Raiders*, Harrap, London, 1944.

13. P.J. Vatikiotis, *Popular Autocracy in Greece, 1936–41*, Frank Cass, London, 1998.

14. Wavell, Genesis Note.

15. Ibid.

16. Ibid.

17. General Lord Ismay, *Memoirs*, Heinemann, London, 1960.

18. Wavell to Wilson, for senior commanders, 2 November 1940. Genesis Note.

19. PRO. WO 169/16.

20. Wilson to O'Connor, 5 December 1940. PRO. WO 189/16.

21. Wavell to CIGS, 6 December 1940. Quoted in Connell, op. cit., p.288.

22. Ibid., p.289.

23. 4th Indian Division War Diary. PRO. WO 169/602.

24. Ibid.

25. In this case 'A' Force; see Chapter 10, below.

26. Count Ciano, *Diaries, 1937–43*, 7 January 1941, Phoenix Press, London, 2002.

27. Avon, *The Reckoning*, op. cit., p.209.

28. Prime Minister to President Roosevelt, 13 December 1940, FDR Library, Hyde Park, New York. Quoted in Joseph P. Lash, *Roosevelt and Churchill, 1939–1941*, Andre Deutsch, London, 1977, p.267.

29. Churchill to Wavell, 17 December 1940. PRO. PREM 3/288/7.

30. Connell, op. cit., p.294.

31. Wavell to Dill, 8 December 1940. PRO. WO 169/16.

32. O'Connor Papers, 4/3/1, LHCMA.

33. Ciano, *Diaries*.

34. Gen. O'Connor note. Lewin Papers, RLEW 4/1, CAC.

35. Minutes of Chiefs of Staff meeting, COS (41)2(o). PRO. WO 106/6108.

36. Graecen, op. cit.

37. *The Spectator*, 14 February 1941, p.162.

38. A.P. Wavell Despatch. Western Desert, 7 December 1940–7 February 1941. PRO. WO 106/2133.

Chapter 10: The Grecian Urn

1. Wavell to CIGS, 10 February 1941. PRO. PREM 3/288/7.

2. General Lord Ismay, Secretary to the War Cabinet in 1941.

3. Ismay to O'Connor, 19 January 1949. Lewin Papers, RLEW 4/6, CAC.

4. *The Rommel Papers*, quoted in Connell, op. cit., p.396.

5. O'Connor Papers, 4/4/8, LHCMA.

6. Wavell to O'Connor, 27 June 1945. O'Connor Papers, 4/3/1, LHCMA. See also Brigadier George Mallaby, note on questions that might be

raised in debate on the despatch of British forces to Greece, Dill Papers, 3/23, LHCMA.

7. Note on 'Operation Camilla'. PRO. WO 106/5127.

8. Ibid.

9. Besides being a soldier of the highest distinction, Field-Marshal William Slim had a sense of humour. Writing of attacks such as Gallabat, he said, 'I have a theory that, while the battles the British fight may differ in the widest possible way, they have invariably two common characteristics – they are always fought uphill and always at the junction of two or more mapsheets.' He also recounted the occasion when a particularly pompous and prickly brigadier had read out, rapidly and largely incomprehensibly, an operational order, and then rhetorically asked the assembled officers if they wished him to read any parts again. His Australian brigade-major replied: 'I should like you to read it *all* again, Sir, taking the funny parts slowly.' Viscount Slim, *Unofficial History*, Cassell, London, 1959.

10. Their resistance finally ended at Gondar, on 28 November 1941.

11. Winston S. Churchill. *The Second World War*, vol.ii, *Their Finest Hour*, Cassell, London, 1949, p.472. On these and subsequent Balkan developments see Ernst Presseisen, Prelude to 'Barbarossa'. *Journal of Modern History*, 32, 1960, and *History of the Second World War*, HMSO, London, 1956–1976, vol.ii, J.R.M. Butler, *Grand Strategy, September 1939–June 1941*.

12. Foreign Office to Greek Government, 22 September 1940, and Eden to Churchill and Dill, 3 November 1940. Avon Papers, 8/210, Birmingham University Library.

13. Eden note to CIGS, 5 November 1940. Avon Papers, 20/8/219.

14. Eden to Churchill and Dill, 5 November 1940. Avon Papers, 8/360. For Eden's outlook see also David Carlton, *Anthony Eden*, Allen Lane, 1981.

15. War Office to Wavell, 10 January 1941. PRO. PREM 3 288/7.

16. Wavell to COS, 10 January 1941. Ibid.

17. Churchill to Wavell, 11 January 1940. PRO. PREM 3 288/7.

18. For the American viewpoint see, for instance, Herbert Agar, *Britain Alone*, The Bodley Head, London, 1972.

19. When the Germans did in due course arrive, all of Salonika's Jews, some 20 per cent of the population, were exterminated.

20. Alexandros Papagos, *The Battle of Greece, 1940–1941*, J.M. Scazikis 'Alpha Editions', Athens, 1949. See also General Alexander Papagos, *The German Attack on Greece*, Greek Office of Information, London, 1946.

21. Quoted by General Ismay, Deputy Secretary to the War Cabinet, to General Sir H. Jackson. Black Watch Archive, Perth.

22. Izzard, op. cit.

23. George Mallaby, *From My Level*, London, Hutchinson, 1965.

24. Lampson diary, 24 January 1941. St Antony's College, Oxford.

25. Henry Channon (1897–1958) was Member of Parliament for Southend from 1935 to 1950, and for Southend West from 1950 until his death. He was Parliamentary Private Secretary to the Under-Secretary of State for Foreign Affairs (R.A. Butler) from March 1938 until July 1941.

26. *Chips, The Diaries of Sir Henry Channon*, ed. Robert Rhodes James, Weidenfeld & Nicolson, London, 1967, p.20. At the end of December 1940 the Prime Minister had ordered Hugh Dalton's Special Operations Executive to undermine Belgrade's pro-Axis regime and to restrain the Yugoslavians from signing the Tripartite Pact and so co-operating fully with the Germans. Subsequently SOE was instructed to go further and use its influence to bring down the regime, but although that was brought about, who actually precipitated it is unclear. See D. Stafford on SOE and the Belgrade coup: *Slavic Review*, vol.36, no.3, September 1977, pp. 417–19.

27. Coats and Channon had fallen for each other at a famous ball held at Blenheim Palace during the last summer of peace.

28. Channon diary, 4 January 1941.

29. Lampson diary.

30. Churchill to Wavell, 12 February 1941. PRO. PREM 3/288/7.

31. Eden to Churchill, 21 February 1941. Ibid.

32. Churchill to Eden, 21 February 1941. Ibid.

33. General James Marshall-Cornwall, *Wars and Rumours of Wars*, Leo Cooper/Secker & Warburg, London, 1984.

34. Brigadier E.J. Shearer, Deputy Director of Military Intelligence, to Wavell, 17 February 1941: 'German intentions in South-East Europe and in North Africa'. PRO. WO 169/924.

35. Wavell to Shearer, 19 February 1941. Ibid.

36. See PRO. PREM 3/294/1.

37. Papagos, op. cit.

38. Prime Minister to Foreign Secretary, 6 March 1941. PRO. CAB 69/2 Annex 1.

39. Earl of Avon, interview for *The World at War*.

40. John Winant, *A Letter from Grosvenor Square*, Hodder & Stoughton, London, 1947.

41. See Charles Mott-Radclyffe, *Foreign Body in the Eye*, Leo Cooper, London, 1975.

42. Prime Minister to Eden, 7 March 1941. Churchill, *The Second World War*, vol.iii, *The Grand Alliance*, p.93.

43. Gavin Long, *Australia in the War of 1939–1945*, Australian War Memorial, Canberra, 1953, p.15.

44. David Horner, *Blamey*, Allen & Unwin, St Leonard's, Australia, 1998; see also PRO. PREM 3 288/5.

45. Long, op. cit., p.18.

46. Ibid., p.19.

47. Horner, op. cit.

48. John O. Latrides, *Ambassador MacVeagh Reports, Greece, 1933–47*, Princeton University Press, Princeton, 1980. MacVeagh was for a time US Ambassador to Greece, and was a keen observer of the Battle of Greece.

49. Commander-in-chief's Greece Report, PRO. WO 201 5/3.

50. A.P. Wavell, Despatches, *London Gazette*, 3 July 1946.

51. A.P. Wavell, 'The British Expedition to Greece, 1941', *Army Quarterly*, vol.59, January 1950, p.181 et seq.

52. Avon broadcast.

53. Wavell, 'The British Expedition to Greece, 1941'.

54. In Rumania; during the war they were a target for many long-range bombing expeditions by the RAF.

55. An exhaustive analysis of the possible causes of the delayed start to Germany's attack on Russia is in Martin van Crefeld, *Hitler's Strategy, 1940–1941: The Balkan Clue*, CUP, Cambridge, 1973, and in the *European Studies Review*, January 1972, pp.69–86, by the same author. Operation Barbarossa was named after Friedrich Barbarossa, the legendary king who was asleep deep within the mountain opposite Hitler's eyrie at Berchtesgaden.

56. Vlachos Kathimerini, quoted in Miles Reid, *Last on the List*, Leo Cooper, London, 1974.

Chapter 11: Sandstorm

1. War Office to C-in-C, Middle East, 28 April 1941. PRO. PREM 3/109.

2. Prime Minister to Wavell, 28 April 1941. Ibid.

3. Wavell to Prime Minister, 29 April 1941. See also Wavell to War Office, 1 May 1941. PRO. PREM 3/109.

4. Wavell to War Office, October 1940. Ibid.

5. Freyberg Papers, quoted in Paul Freyberg, *Bernard Freyberg, VC*, Hodder & Stoughton, London, 1991; Freyberg's report to NZ Minister of Defence, quoted in D.M. Davin's official *History of New Zealand in the Second World War 1939–45*, War History Branch, Department of Internal Affairs, Wellington, 1953.

6. Group Captain George Beamish, later Air Vice-Marshal G.R. Beamish, CB, CBE; in May 1941 he was commanding RAF Crete.

7. The latter is the official version. By contrast General Freyberg's son said that in 1962 his father took him to Hyde Park, where nobody could hear, and told him in the strictest confidence (because Ultra was at that time still classified as top secret) that Wavell had told him about Ultra, and that his hands had been tied by the knowledge.

8. Always known as 'C', but in this instance Sir Stewart Menzies.

9. Wavell Papers. OL was the name given to Ultra intelligence relating to Crete.

10. Freyberg, *Bernard Freyberg, VC*, p.271.

11. Ibid.

12. Wavell to Churchill, 15 May 1941. PRO. PREM 3/109.

13. Freyberg detested Dorman-Smith, but in the circumstances would have paid close attention to him.

14. Freyberg to Wavell, 11 May 1941, Wavell Papers. Wavell had written to Freyberg on 8 May, his letter being delivered by Dorman-Smith on 11 May.

15. Lt Geoffrey Cox, former journalist with the *Daily Express*. Later appointed Chief Intelligence Officer to the 2nd New Zealand Division. Subsequently Sir Geoffrey Cox, CNZM, CEO of ITN and creator of *News at Ten*.

16. Later His Honour Sir John White, MBE, and a judge of the High Court of New Zealand.

17. Sir Geoffey Cox to author.

18. Ibid.

19. Freyberg, op. cit., p.280. See also Ronald Lewin, *Ultra Goes to War*, Penguin, London, 2001; Antony Beevor, *Crete*, John Murray, London, 1991; Callum MacDonald, *Crete 1941: The Lost Battle*, Pan, London, 2002.

20. Evidence to the Inter-Services Committee on Crete, June 1941. PRO. WO 201/99.

21. Churchill to Wavell, 27 May 1941. Quoted in Churchill, *The Grand Alliance*, p.262.

22. C-in-C Middle East to War Office, 27 May 1941. PRO. PREM 3/109.

23. Inter-Services Committee on Crete op. cit., PRO. WO 201/99.

24. Memorandum submitted to von Ribbentrop, German Foreign Minister, Pol. VII 123 g. RS, 7 March 1941, quoted in *Documents on German Foreign Policy 1918–45*, vol.XI, HMSO, 1962.

25. Abdulillah, uncle of the four-year-old King Faisal II, whose father, the Old Harrovian playboy King Ghazi, had been killed in a car crash two years earlier. After the escape of the Regent, King Faisal was left in the charge of his English nanny.

26. Lampson diary, MECA, 3 May 1941.

27. Wavell to Chiefs of Staff, 5 May 1941, quoted in Winston S. Churchill, *The Second World War*, vol. iii, p.228.

28. Connell, op. cit., p.438.

29. Anwar El Sadat, *Revolt on the Nile*, A. Wingate, London, 1957.

30. I.S.O. Playfair, *The Official History of the War in the Middle East*, HMSO.

31. Wavell to Spears, 12 May 1941. Spears Papers, St Antony's College, Oxford.

32. Churchill to COS, 8 May 1941. PRO. PREM 3/422/6.

33. Wavell to Sir John Dill, 22 May 1941. Dill Papers, 3/17, LHCMA.

34. Wavell to Sir John Dill, 21 May 1941. PRO. PREM 3/422.

35. CIGS to Wavell, 21 May 1941. Ibid.

36. Ibid.

37. Dill to Churchill, 21 May 1941. Ibid.

38. Dill to Wavell, 21 May 1941. Dill Papers, 3/25, LHCMA.

39. Report in *Il Tempo*, Rome, quoted in 'A' Force Narrative War Diary. PRO. WO 169/24847. Ethiopia was the first country to be released from imperial rule, and almost at once complex questions arose about the future of imperialism, raised particularly by the Americans. See, for example, *Foreign Affairs*, vol.20 (1941–42), *The Future of Ethiopia*, p.535 et seq.

40. Lampson diary, 5 April 1941.

41. Ibid., 6 April 1941.

42. 'The Commander-in-Chief at lunch', taken from Evelyn Waugh, *Officers and Gentlemen*, Penguin, London, 1964. In the opinion of George Orwell Greta Briggs' poem was 'very bad' but one that could have been written only by a true lover of poetry. Wavell included it in *Other Men's Flowers*.

43. Wavell Despatches, supplement to *The London Gazette*, 3 July 1946.

44. Wavell to DMI, 19 February 1941. PRO. WO 169/924.

45. Orders to Lt.-Gen. P. Neame for the defence of Cyrenaica, 19 March 1941. Dill Papers, 3/25, App. XX, LHCMA.

46. Lt Gen. Sir Philip Neame, *Playing With Strife*, Harrap, London, 1947.

47. Prime Minister to Wavell, 26 March 1941. Churchill, op. cit., vol.iii, p.178.

48. Wavell to O'Connor. RLEW 4/6, CAC.

49. The large American car had been found by Peter Coats, at the behest of General Maitland Wilson's ADC who considered that his master needed a conveyance appropriate to his new position as Military Governor of Cyrenaica. The fortunes of war had delivered it into the charge of Neame, accompanied by O'Connor, as they retreated before the Germans.

50. Churchill, op. cit., p.298.

51. Ibid., p.220.

52. Wavell to War Office, 31 May 1941. PRO. WO 216/9.

53. Wavell to CIGS, 28 May 1941. Quoted in Churchill, op. cit., p.304.

54. See Chapter 6.

55. CHAR 20 9AB, CAC.

56. Wavell, Despatch, *The London Gazette*, 3 July 1946.

57. Wavell to War Office, 18 and 21 June 1941. PRO. WO 216/9.

58. PRO. PREM 3/291/1, quoted in Martin Gilbert, *Winston S. Churchill*, vol.vi, Heinemann, London, 1983, p.1149.

59. Liddell Hart, *The Rommel Papers*.

60. Sir Henry Pownall, *Pownall Diaries*, ed. Brian Bond, Leo Cooper, London, 1972–74.

61. Churchill to Viceroy of India, 20 June 1941. Prime Minister's Personal Telegram, T309, CHAR/20/40/14, CAC.

62. Averell Harriman, *Special Envoy to Churchill and Stalin, 1941–1946*, Hutchinson, London, 1976.

Chapter 12: The Poisoned Chalice

1. Knight Grand Cross of the Order of the Bath, a high order of chivalry.

2. Lt Alexander Reid Scott, MC, diary, July 1941. Private collection.

3. General Auchinleck to General Ismay, 12 October 1941. Ismay papers, CAC.

4. Rt Hon. L.S. Amery, MP, Secretary of State for India and Burma.

5. Churchill, op. cit., vol.iii, p.424.

6. The Shah abdicated in favour of his son, Mohammed Reza Pahlavi, who reigned until deposed in 1979, when he was replaced by the Ayatollah Khomeini.

7. In his 'Sonnet for the Madonna of the Cherries'.

8. RA GVI/PRIV/DIARY/1941:11 September.

9. Lt Gen. Sir Hastings (later Lord) Ismay; then Deputy-Secretary of the War Cabinet.

10. Mrs Joan Bright Astley to author; and see Joan Bright Astley, *The Inner Circle: A View of War at the Top*, Hutchinson, London, 1971, reprinted 2007.

11. Wavell to Joan Bright, 12 September 1941. Private collection.

12. Although Brooke-Popham, by now a lame duck, remained in charge until near the end of December, on 5 November 1941 he was officially relieved of command, as the War Office considered that the commander-in-chief should now be a soldier rather than an airman, and should be younger – Brooke-Popham was sixty-three. He was later given a baronetcy. The first choice to succeed him had been General Sir Bernard Paget, but changes following the planned replacement of Sir John Dill by Sir Alan Brooke as CIGS resulted in Lt Gen. Sir Henry Pownall, VCIGS, being chosen; he was nine years younger than Brooke-Popham. See note 23.

13. The novelist-turned-administrator John Buchan, Lord Tweedsmuir, was sounded out to be the first Governor General of Burma.

14. Probably also the most important colony for Britain's post-war economic health: it had to be controlled at all costs, hence the efforts made in the Malayan Emergency, which continued until 1960.

15. See Wavell's foreword to F. Spencer Chapman, DSO, *The Jungle Is Neutral*, Chatto & Windus, London, 1949. Like Orde Wingate, Spencer Chapman was a pioneer of stay-behind parties and deep penetration of the Japanese-occupied jungle; he received Wavell's strong encouragement.

16. Wavell to Brooke-Popham, 13 November 1941. Brooke-Popham Papers 6/5, LHCMA.

17. Captain Everard Calthrop had known Wavell when they were both at the War Office in 1914: see Chapter 4, above.

18. Churchill, op. cit., vol.iii, p.516.

19. Diana Cooper, *Autobiography*, M. Russell, London, 1979, quoted in

Christopher Bayly and Tim Harper, *Forgotten Armies*, Allen Lane, London, 2004.

20. Maj. Gen. S.W. Kirby et al., *The War Against Japan*, HMSO, 1957. With a rare touch of humanity the Japanese sent an aircraft out to drop memorial wreaths over the water above the *Repulse* and the *Prince of Wales*.

21. Churchill, op. cit., vol.iii, p.564.

22. Wavell to Chiefs of Staff, 17 December 1941, quoted in John Connell, edited and completed by Michael Roberts, *Wavell. Supreme Commander, 1941–1943*, Collins, London, 1969.

23. Sir Henry Pownall (1887–1961) was Chief of Staff of the British Expeditionary Force in 1940, VCIGS in 1941, C-in-C British Far East Command 1941–42; he acted as Wavell's Chief of Staff at ABDACOM until the fall of Singapore, and was subsequently appointed Chief of Staff to Lord Louis Mountbatten, 1943–44. See note 12.

24. The American Volunteer Group was a highly successful force of Tomahawk fighters, at that time being trained for the defence of Chungking. Commanded by Brigadier General Claire Chennault, their pilots were brave men, richly deserving the prize money they received for 'kills'; the group was known as the 'Flying Tigers'.

25. Dorman-Smith Papers, BL, EUR 215.

26. Ibid. Miss Gibbs was the Governor's tame gibbon, which Wavell wooed 'with soft, loving words, and bananas'.

27. Brooke-Popham Papers, LHCMA.

28. Brooke had taken over as CIGS from Sir John Dill on 1 December 1941.

29. Clementine Churchill to Winston Churchill, 19 December 1941. Quoted in Martin Gilbert, *The Churchill War Papers*, vol.iii, Heinemann, London, 1993.

30. Wife of Sir John Herbert, Governor of Bengal. See Chapter 13, below.

31. American-British-Dutch-Australian Command.

32. Churchill, *The Second World War*, vol.iii, p.600.

33. Dill to Wavell, 9 January 1942. Dill Papers, 3/26, LHCMA.

34. Churchill, quoted in Herbert P. Bix, *Hirohito and the Making of Modern Japan*, Duckworth, London, 2000.

35. A.P. Wavell, commander-in-chief's broadcast to India, New Year 1942. Quoted in Wavell, *Speaking Generally*.

36. Ibid.

37. 6,000 bicycles were issued to each Japanese division. Being the world's major rubber producer, Malaya was the last place in which it might have

been difficult to mend punctures or find new tyres. Also, the Japanese had no problem with spare parts, as the success of their pre-war export drives meant that there were spares in all but the most remote villages.

38. 'The white men are running.'

39. Wavell to Lt-Gen. Sir Thomas Hutton. Hutton Papers, 3/1, LHCMA.

40. Reid Scott diary.

41. Wavell to Churchill, 21 January 1942. Churchill, *The Second World War*, vol.iv, *The Hinge of Fate*, p.49.

42. Many units did retain their fighting spirit, particularly the Gurkhas and the Argylls, the only two that had received any jungle training. One battalion of the Argyll and Sutherland Highlanders, for example, fighting with great bravery, lost 700 out of 800 men on its retreat to Singapore. They were led by Lt Col I. Stewart, whose successful ideas on jungle fighting were dismissed by Percival and Brigadier Torrance as those of a crank, but who was much admired by Wavell, who later selected him to train troops in India. He also wrote the foreword to Stewart's history of the Malayan campaign.

43. Straits Police Orders, 11 February 1942. Rhodes House Archive, Oxford, MSS. Ind. Ocn.s.123.

44. Prime Minister to Wavell, 10 February 1942. PRO. WO 259/63.

45. Wavell to Percival. Percival Papers, Imperial War Museum.

46. Quoted in Bayly and Harper, op. cit.

47. Supreme Commander's Order of the Day, 10 February 1942.

48. From *Generals and Generalship*, Wavell's lectures delivered at Trinity College, Cambridge in 1939, discussed above.

49. Wavell, *Allenby: A Study in Greatness*, Harrap, London, 1940.

Chapter 13: Nil Desperandum

1. Churchill, *The Second World War*, vol.iv, p.127.

2. Wavell to Joan Bright, 20 February 1942. Private collection.

3. Wavell to Prime Minster, 21 February 1942. Churchill, *The Second World War*, vol.iv, p. 127.

4. Ibid., p.128.

5. *Per* Sir George Abell, writing in the *Aberdeen University Review*, vol.XXXIII, no.103, Autumn 1950.

6. Smyth was even more taciturn than Wavell. One young lady, placed next to him at dinner, turned to him as they sat down and announced brightly,

'My parents have bet me that I can't get more than seven words out of you at dinner.' Smyth replied, 'You've lost', and resumed his silence.

7. Sir Alan Brooke diary, 18 February 1942. Quoted in Field Marshal Lord Alanbrooke, *War Diaries*, ed. Alex Danchev and Daniel Todman, Weidenfeld & Nicolson, London, 2001.

8. Wavell to Churchill, 22 February 1942. Quoted in Connell, op. cit., p.192.

9. See, for example, Anthony Montague Browne, *Long Sunset*, Cassell, London, 1995.

10. Sir Reginald Dorman-Smith, *Memoirs*, February 1942. BL, MSS Eur., E. 215.

11. GOC Burma to Wavell, 10 March 1942. PRO. WO 259/62.

12. Harold Nicolson, *Diaries and Letters 1939–45*, Collins, London, 1967, p.211, Churchill won the vote by 464 to 1. In December 1941 General Auchinleck, Wavell's successor in the desert, had retaken Tobruk, Derna and Benghazi from Rommel, but on 21 January the Germans began a successful counter-offensive, capturing Agedabia and then Beda Fomm. See PRO. WO 259/63 for Churchill and an official inquiry into the fall of Singapore.

13. Wavell to Prime Minister, 10 March 1942. PRO. WO 259/62.

14. Ibid.

15. Jawaharlal Nehru, (1889–1964), first Prime Minister of independent India.

16. Also known as 'Sam'.

17. *The Transfer of Power in India*, ed. Nicholas Mansergh, HMSO, London, 1970–82. See vol.i, no.611.

18. 'Pakistan' as a term originated in the early 1930s, being derived from the word *Pak*, meaning pure or clean, and something that is sacred for a Muslim.

19. Hon. Simon Astley, son of Lord Hastings, and a captain in the 7th Hussars.

20. Quoted in Coats, *Of Kings and Cabbages*, Weidenfeld & Nicholson, 1984.

21. From 'Home Thoughts from a German Prison Camp', by Hon. Kenneth Davison, a successful fighter pilot (later Lord Broughshane), quoted in Coats, *Of Generals and Gardens: the autobiography of Peter Coats*, Weidenfeld & Nicholson, London, 1976.

22. Wavell to Joan Bright, 20 May 1942. Private collection.

23. A.P.W., Notes and Ideas, 1939–1946, quoting Lord Elton, *St George or the Dragon*, Collins, London, 1942.

24. A Note on Training for Commanding Officers, May 1942. IOR,

L/MIL/17/5/22/23, BL. Marshal Zukhov used to encourage his soldiers with the phrase 'Train Hard, Fight Easy'.

25. Philip Mason, Secretary of the Indian Chiefs of Staff Committee, recollections. Rhodes House Archive, MSS. Brit. Emp. S. 527 (3).

26. Rudyard Kipling, 'On The Road To Mandalay', *The Complete Verse of Rudyard Kipling*, Kyle Cathie, Revised Edition, 2002. Kipling's poem began: 'By the old Moulmein Pagoda, lookin lazy at the sea,/There's a Burma girl a-settin', and I know she thinks of me,/For the wind is in the palm-trees, and the temple-bells they say:/Come you back, you British soldier; come you back to Mandalay!'

27. See PRO. CAB 66/23 for diplomatic reports of Japanese views and expectations, including their great surprise at the ease with which they had defeated the British, and their desire for an end (provided it were successful) to the fighting in China.

28. Joseph Stilwell (1883–1946), known as 'Vinegar Joe', was chief of staff to the Generalissimo, with whom he had frequent arguments and to whom he referred as 'Peanut'.

29. See David Rooney, *Stilwell the Patriot*, Greenhill Books, London, 2005.

30. A term that came into use for describing the nations opposed to the Axis powers. The Arcadia Conference was held in Washington from 22 December 1941 to 14 January 1942, between US and UK delegates, headed by Roosevelt and Churchill. One result of the conference was formal agreement to establish the United Nations Organisation.

31. DMI to Delhi Conference, 30 May 1942. Peter Fleming Papers, Reading University archives.

32. See PRO. COS (42) 156 (o).

33. Quoted in Kirby, op. cit.

34. Quoted in Michael Howard, *Grand Strategy*, vol.iv, HMSO, 1956–76.

35. See H.H. Arnold, *Global Mission*, Hutchinson, London, 1951. Arnold was head of the US Army Air Forces. He tells of Irwin's treatment of Slim when he finally crossed from Burma into India at the head of his defiant army.

36. By the summer of 1942 the situation in North Africa had been deteriorating for some months: in Cairo, Wednesday, 1 July had become known as 'Ash Wednesday', the air black with the embers of secret papers piled on bonfires at GHQ and in the garden of the British Embassy, amid preparations for an evacuation. When Wavell was told that Auchinleck had decided to make his stand as far back as Alamein, not far from the

Nile Delta itself, he was almost disbelieving: 'Not till Alamein!' he repeated, 'not till there!'

37. PRO. WO 259/66.

Chapter 14: Banzai

1. See Antony Beauchamp, *Focus on Fame*, Odhams Press, London, 1958.

2. For treatment of this topic, see Peter Fleming, *Invasion 1940*, R. Hart-Davis, London, 1957, and Spencer Chapman, op. cit. Peter Fleming's younger brother was Ian, the creator of James Bond.

3. Philip Mason, *A Shaft of Sunlight*, Vikas Publishing House, New Delhi, 1978, p.169.

4. Soon to be the main thoroughfare for supplies and ammunition for Japanese armies in the north. See Anthony Montague Browne, *Long Sunset*, Indigo, London, 1996, p.20 et seq.

5. Quoted in Roberts and Connell, op. cit., p.240. General Montgomery, arriving the previous month to take over 8th Army in the Western Desert, had similarly addressed his officers, saying, 'Let us have a new atmosphere . . .' As his chief intelligence officer, Col Edgar Williams, reported, 'You could have heard a pin drop, were such a thing possible in the sand.' The story of Monty's address, and its effect on those who heard it, had already spread through the army, not least for Monty's gung-ho humour: 'Everyone must be determined to kill Germans,' he had said, 'yes, even the padres – one per day and two on Sundays.'

6. Mason, op. cit., p.168.

7. See Rooney, op. cit.

8. Ibid., p.101, and see *The Papers of George Catlett Marshall*, ed. Larry I. Bland, Johns Hopkins Press, New York, 1991, p.385.

9. PRO. COS (W) 269.1.9.42.

10. Quoted in Howard, op. cit., p.98.

11. A.P. Wavell, Despatch on Operations in Burma, Supplement to *The London Gazette*, 17 September 1946.

12. Lewin, op. cit.

13. Correctly, 77th Indian Infantry Brigade. The name 'Chindits', suggested by an officer of the Burma Army, was a corruption of *Chinthay*, a mythical beast that guards Buddhist temples. Four members of the force were awarded the Victoria Cross.

14. Wavell to Joan Bright, 23 December 1942. Private collection.

15. Churchill to Wavell, 2 February 1943. CHAR 20/161, CAC.

16. Wavell to Irwin, 7 March 1943. Irwin Papers, Imperial War Museum, London.

17. Irwin Papers, 2/7–9.

18. Ibid.

19. Quoted in Kirby et al., op. cit.

20. Wavell to Joan Bright, 8 April 1943.

21. Wavell, quoted in *Speaking Generally*, p.162.

22. Henry H. Arnold, *Global Mission*, Hutchinson, London, 1951, p.107. Arnold was commanding general of the US Army Air Forces and a member of the Joint Chiefs of Staff and the Combined Chiefs of Staff.

23. Wavell to Leopold Amery (then Secretary of State for India), 29 April 1943. Amery Papers, AMEL 7/37, CAC.

24. Wavell to Joan Bright, 8 April 1943. Private Collection.

25. Mason, op. cit., p.170.

26. *Wavell: The Viceroy's Journal*, ed. Penderel Moon, OUP, London, 1973, p.2.

27. Amery diary, 3 May 1943. Amery Papers, AMEL 7/37, CAC.

28. Churchill, *The Second World War*, vol. iv, pp.702–3.

29. *The Viceroy's Journal*, p.3.

30. Field Marshal Lord Alanbrooke, *War Diaries*, ed. Alex Danchev and Daniel Todman, Weidenfeld & Nicolson, London, 2001.

31. *The Viceroy's Journal*, p.3.

32. The Roosevelts were offended by Madame's insistence on using her own sheets while staying at the White House, and her general capriciousness did little to enhance Chinese stock.

33. Air Chief Marshal Sir William Elliot to General Sir Henry Jackson, 11 December 1961. Black Watch Archive, Perth.

34. Note on a meeting at the White House with the President and Prime Minister, 14 May 1943. Alanbrooke, *War Diaries*, p.403.

35. Churchill, *The Second World War*, vol. iv, pp.715–16.

36. Alanbrooke diary note, Washington, 21 May 1943, quoted in Arthur Bryant, *The Turn of the Tide, 1939–43*, Collins, London, 1957, p.623.

37. Ibid., p.624.

38. *The Viceroy's Journal*, p.4.

Chapter 15: Fields Fresh

1. The painting is by Joost van Cleves, one of an estimated twelve on the same theme by Flemish artists.
2. Michael Howard, *Jonathan Cape, Publisher*, Jonathan Cape, London, 1971.
3. Daniel George Bunting, 4 April 1943. Hart-Davis Papers, University of Tulsa.
4. Rupert Hart-Davis to Jonathan Cape, quoted in Howard, op. cit.
5. Formerly Professor Frederick Lindemann, Churchill's closest friend and adviser, who was now in the Cabinet as Paymaster General.
6. A story told by the imperial hero Sir Charles Napier; referred to in Chapter 3, above.
7. Francis Thompson, 'The Hound of Heaven', *The Oxford Book of Mystical Verse*, ed. DHS Nicholson & AHA Lee, Clarendon Press, Oxford, 1917.
8. *Horizon*, vol.x, no.57, September 1944.
9. Abell, op. cit.
10. 12 March 1944; see also *The Complete Works of George Orwell*, vol.xvi, 'I have Tried to Tell the Truth', pp.120–1, ed. Peter Davison, Secker & Warburg, London, 1998.
11. Ibid.
12. Prime Minister to Deputy Prime Minister and Dominions Secretary, 29 May 1943. CHAR 20/128, CAC.
13. Prime Minister to Field Marshal Smuts, 4 June 1943. CHAR 20/112/54/5, CAC.
14. Bryant, op. cit., p.624.
15. Lord Simon, the Lord Chancellor; as Sir John Simon he had been chairman of the Simon Commission, which had reported on the Indian constitutional problem in 1931. Clement Attlee, the Labour Party leader, now also in the Cabinet, had endorsed this opinion.
16. Lord Chancellor to Prime Minister, 13 July 1945. PRO. PREM 4/46/11.
17. Leopold Amery (1873–1955), former First Lord of the Admiralty, Secretary of State for the Colonies and for Dominion Affairs; Secretary of State for India and Burma, 1940–45.
18. Alfred Milner (1854–1925), Oxford classical scholar, Governor of the Cape of Good Hope, 1897–1901; of the Orange River Colony and of the Transvaal, 1901–5; High Commissioner for South Africa, 1897–1905; Secretary of State for War, 1919–21.
19. PRO. PREM 5/532.

20. Secretary of State for India to House of Commons, 8 October 1942.

21. Memorandum from Sir Alec Lascelles (Private Secretary to the King) to King George VI, 24 April 1943. RA PS/GVI/C/200/03.

22. Prime Minister to Viceroy, 9 June 1943. PRO. PREM 5/532.

23. *The Viceroy's Journal.*

24. Amery Papers, AMEL 7/37, CAC.

25. *The Viceroy's Journal.*

26. Amery Papers, AMEL 1/6/21, CAC.

27. Wavell to Churchill, 17 June 1943. PRO. PREM 5/332.

28. For reference details of Henry Channon, see Chapter 10, above.

29. Channon had published a novel, *Joan Kennedy*; a book on life in Chicago, *Paradise City*; and a biography, *The Ludwigs of Bavaria.*

30. Henry Channon diary, 2 April 1943. Private collection.

31. Peter Quennell, *Customs and Characters*, Weidenfeld & Nicolson, London, 1982.

32. Robert Rhodes James, *Chips: The Diaries of Sir Henry Channon*, Weidenfield & Nicholson, London, 1967. The Marchioness of Willingdon was a former Vicereine of India; R.A. 'Rab' Butler was a Conservative MP and a minister at the Board of Education; Virginia Cowles was a writer and journalist; Lord Kemsley was a press baron whose empire at that time included *The Sunday Times*; Oscar Solbert was an American soldier-diplomat; Lady Colefax was a well-known London hostess in the 1930s and 1940s. 'Peter' referred to Peter Coats.

33. George Mallaby, *From My Level*, Hutchinson, London, 1965. 'Nancy' was properly Florence Anne, and 'Molly' was Lillian Mary.

34. Ibid.

35. Channon diary, 30 May 1943. Emerald Cunard famously remarked that 'the trouble with Wavell is that he is riddled with idealism'.

36. James Pope-Hennessy.

37. See James Lees-Milne, *Ancestral Voices*, Faber & Faber, London, 1984.

38. Channon diary, 22 June 1943. Lord Kelmsley's dinner was attended by the Archbishop of Canterbury, Dr Temple, and by a large number of diplomats and politicians. Channon's reference to Lord Curzon concerned the celebrated dinner given by fellow-Old Etonians to Curzon on the eve of his departure to India to begin his term as Viceroy in 1898.

39. Channon diary, 15 June 1943.

40. Ibid., 31 May 1943.

41. Sir Alan Lascelles diary. LASL 1/2/2, CAC. 'Bet Asquith' was Hon.

Elizabeth Manners; she married Hon. Arthur Asquith, son of the former Prime Minister H.H. Asquith (later the Earl of Oxford and Asquith). 'Eny Strutt' was Baroness Irene de Brienen, at one time married to Vice-Admiral Hon. Arthur Strutt.

42. Coats, op. cit., p.205.

43. The King's Assistant Private Secretary until July 1943, when he took over from Sir Alec Hardinge as Private Secretary. Hardinge was not in favour of Wavell, and vainly tried to block his appointment as Viceroy.

44. Channon diary, 23 June 1943.

45. Mrs Joan Bright Astley to author.

46. Channon diary, 19 July 1943.

47. See 'Race Basis in Indian Politics', *The Contemporary Review*, May 1890, p.757.

48. Prime Minister, House of Commons, 10 September 1942.

49. See Professor Peter Clarke, *The Last Thousand Days of the British Empire*, Allen Lane, 2007.

50. Leopold Amery diary, 1 July 1943. AMEL 7/37, CAC.

51. Wavell, *Allenby in Egypt*.

52. Ibid.

53. Ibid.

54. 6 January 1944.

55. Ibid.

56. Ibid., and see Orwell's *Complete Works*, ed. Peter Davison, vol.xvi, p.53.

57. Amery diary, AMEL 7/37, CAC.

58. *The Viceroy's Journal*, p.14.

59. Later Sir Evan Jenkins. He had previously been Chief Commissioner of Delhi and Secretary to the Department of Supply. Subsequently a much-respected governor of the Punjab, 8 April 1946–14 August 1947.

60. Mohandas K. Gandhi (1869–1948). Educated at University College, London, and called to the Bar by the Inner Temple. He developed a civil-rights movement in South Africa before returning to India, where he became the leading agitator for self-rule (Swaraj), which he argued should be sought by non-violent means. M.A. Jinnah (1876–1948). Called to the Bar by Lincoln's Inn, became a successful lawyer in Bombay. He turned to politics, joining the Indian National Congress in 1896. In due course he became the leader of the All India Muslim League, whose cause was helped by *Dawn*, the newspaper he founded in 1941.

61. PRO. PREM 4/46/3.
62. A moderate and experienced leading Congress politician, formerly Prime Minister of Madras. Wavell described him as pleasant and intelligent, but not apparently a forceful character.
63. James Grigg, *Prejudice and Judgment*, Jonathan Cape, London, 1948.
64. 1st Quebec Conference, 13–24 August 1943.
65. RA GVI/PRIV/01/24/740.
66. Prime Minister's Directive to Viceroy, 8 October 1943. PRO. CAB 66/41/50.
67. Amery Papers, AMEL 7/37, CAC.
68. Prime Minister's speech, Claridge's Hotel, 6 October 1943.
69. Amery Papers, AMEL 7/37, CAC.
70. Lady Doreen Prior-Palmer, interview with Capt. R.H. Fox, RN, 27 January 1993. Wavell arrived in Delhi on 18 October wearing 'a crumpled blue suit'; two days later, looking very dignified, and more smartly attired in a grey frock-coat, he was sworn in as Viceroy. (Diary of Capt. P.G. Carter, ADC to Lord Linlithgow, 1941–43. Prior-Palmer collection.)

Chapter 16: Indian Summer

1. The Viceroy customarily had three ICS secretaries: a Private Secretary, a Deputy and an Assistant; the initials PSV, DPSV and APSV were well-known designations in Delhi official circles.
2. Rudyard Kipling: 'The White Man's Burden', from *The Complete Verse of Rudyard Kipling*, Kyle Cathie, London, Revised Edition, 2002.
3. Wavell to Amery, 1 November 1943. BL/IOR/L/PO/10/25. India Office Papers, British Library.
4. Viceroy to Secretary of State, 29 December 1943.
5. Viceroy to King George VI, 4 January 1944. RA PS/GVI/Co52A/01.
6. At this time the British Army had 2.71 million men, and the Japanese 2.58 million.
7. Paymaster General to Prime Minister, 3 August 1943. Cherwell Papers H290, Nuffield College, Oxford.
8. Nearly £23 billion at current purchasing power.
9. Wavell to Joan Bright, 26 March 1944. Private collection.
10. Sir George Abell, writing in the *Aberdeen University Review*, vol.XXXIII, no.103, Autumn 1950.

11. Wavell to Freya Stark, 3 May 1944. John Murray Archive.

12. See Chapter 15, above. Jenkins' appearance was rather that of Neville Chamberlain when young.

13. Sir Olaf Caroe (1892–1981) was appointed Governor of the North-West Frontier Province in September 1945. He did not enjoy cordial relations with Wavell, although they were both Wykehamists. Sir George Abell (1904–89) was Private Secretary to both Wavell and Mountbatten, and subsequently a director of the Bank of England. He was a good games player, being awarded Blues at Oxford for cricket, rugger and hockey; he later played cricket for Worcestershire. Ivor Jehu was subsequently editor of *The Times of India*.

14. Wavell to Freya Stark, 3 August 1944. John Murray Archive.

15. Ditty popular among Wavell's staff: Sir Edward Ford to author.

16. Cecil Beaton diary. Private collection.

17. *The Viceroy's Journal*, p.40.

18. In 1919 General Dyer caused great indignation in India by firing on a crowd in an enclosed space in Amritsar.

19. Note by the Viceroy on the political situation in India, April 1944. PRO. WP (44) 250.

20. Presidential address to the All India Muslim League, Lahore, March 1940. Quoted in *The Partition of India: Policies and Perspectives, 1935–1947*, ed. C.H. Philips and Mary Wainwright, Allen & Unwin, London, 1970.

21. M.A. Jinnah explained his views in detail at a meeting with the British MP, Harold Macmillan, in February 1947. A copy of Macmillan's report is in CHAR 2/43A, CAC.

22. Sir Gilbert Laithwaite to Marquess of Linlithgow, 23 December 1943. Hopetoun House Archive.

23. Viceroy to the King-Emperor, 31 December 1945. Quoted in *Transfer of Power*, vol. vi.

24. *The Viceroy's Journal*, p.314.

25. RA PS/GVI/Co52A/01.

26. BL/IOR/L/PO/10/21.

27. Prime Minister to War Cabinet, 13 August 1944. PRO. PREM 4/46/3.

28. Wavell to Amery, 10 August 1944. BL/IOR/L/PO/10/25.

29. Wavell to Amery, 23 August 1944. Ibid.

30. Wavell to Freya Stark, 3 August 1944. John Murray Archive.

31. Viceroy to Prime Minister, 24 October 1944. PRO. PREM 4/46/6.

32. Ibid.

33. Dame Frances Campbell-Preston to author.

34. *The Viceroy's Journal*, 26 April 1945.

35. Ibid., p.126.

36. Ibid., 26 May 1945.

37. Interview between James Cameron and Muhammad Ali Jinnah, quoted on Granada TV, 1955. Rhodes House Archive. Cuff-links seemed to possess a certain importance for Jinnah, who had more than sixty pairs.

38. RA PS/GVI/Co52A/19.

39. In July 1945. The results were announced three weeks after polling day in Britain, to allow for the collection of voting slips from servicemen overseas; in the event, their vote was thought to have boosted Labour's success, partly because of a very successful brainwashing exercise by the Education Corps officer (and subsequently Labour minister) George Wigg, via political lectures to the troops, organised by the Army Bureau of Current Affairs.

40. A most successful Minister of Labour in the wartime coalition government; formerly General Secretary of the powerful Amalgamated Transport and General Workers Union.

41. Formerly Mayor of Stepney, and a lecturer at Ruskin College and the LSE. Pipe-smoking and of unassuming appearance (Churchill described him as 'a sheep in sheep's clothing'), Attlee yet had a steely resolve, a healthy contempt for the press and the ability to manage government business with speed and efficiency.

42. On hearing this news, Wavell commented, 'Now for the horrors of peace.' At least the drabness of London after the war's end was occasionally contrasted with colour: Chips Channon gazed happily at the sight of one ballroom, filled with dancers in jewels and finery: '*This* is what we've been fighting for,' he remarked to Lady Cunard. 'Why, dear?' she replied, 'Are they all Poles?'

43. Wavell to Freya Stark, 26 September 1945. John Murray Archive.

44. The trials began on 5 November 1945; there was a strong demand for leniency from both politicians and populace, and Wavell agreed to the commander-in-chief, Auchinleck, reducing the charges and the subsequent sentences for those found guilty. The trials turned out to be of considerable importance in that, during their course, revelations as to the state of mind of many Indian soldiers made the exhausted British

realise that they could no longer rely on the sepoys' loyalty to maintain their authority.

45. A mixed bunch, of moderate abilities: Cripps was a very clever Wykehamist, but shared few other characteristics with Wavell. Pethick-Lawrence, who had considerable standing in India and was known and trusted by many Indian politicians – hence his appointment as Secretary of State for India – was educated at Eton and Cambridge. Alexander was a former goalkeeper of Bristol City Football Club. It was considered important that preparations for the Mission should not be made public: for example, clothing coupons for tropical kit were issued in false names. For a discussion of the reasons for the Mission see Kenneth Harris, *Attlee*, Weidenfeld & Nicolson, 1982.

46. Horace Alexander and Agatha Harrison, from the India Conciliation Group; each very much the type of self-righteous, blinkered 'do-gooder' who in fact did so much harm to the Empire. Cripps also had two hangers-on: Major John McLaughlin Short and Major Woodrow Wyatt, whose job was to help smooth relations with the Sikhs and with the Muslim League. Great embarrassment was caused by the expenses that they incurred along the way, especially drink bills – strangely, as most Muslims did not touch alcohol.

47. In February 1946.

48. See Penderel Moon, *Divide and Quit*, OUP, London, 1961/1998.

49. Stafford Cripps diary, 7 April 1946. Quoted in Peter Clarke, *The Cripps Version*, Penguin, London, 2002.

50. Ibid.

51. *The Viceroy's Journal*, p.285, entry for 2–3 June 1946.

52. Viceroy to Cabinet, 3 June 1946, 'Appreciation of Possibilities in India'.

53. *The Viceroy's Journal*, 23 June 1946. The minister was originally called Frederick Lawrence, but he expanded his name after marrying the suffragette firebrand Emmeline Pethick. After attending Eton and then Cambridge, where he became President of the Union, Lawrence was called to the Bar. He declined the government's invitation to fight for his country during the First World War; instead, claiming protection as a conscientious objector, he worked on a farm.

54. Ibid., p.314.

55. Op. cit., 1961, p.54.

56. F.F. (later Sir Frank) Turnbull, a high-flying civil servant from the India

Office, and at that time Principal Private Secretary to the Secretary of State for India. Wavell called him 'the official minder'.

57. William Roger Louis, *The Ends of British Imperialism*, I.B. Tauris, New York, 2006.

58. After Lewis Carroll's 'Jabberwocky'; see *The Viceroy's Journal*, p.316.

59. Lt Gen. Sir Francis Tuker, *While Memory Serves*, Cassell, London, 1950, p.160.

60. Wavell to Governor of the Punjab, November 1946. IOR/L/PO/10/23.

61. Nehru to Wavell, 15 October 1946. Quoted in *Transfer of Power*, vol.ix, no.462.

62. Professor Peter Clarke, *The Last Thousand Days of the British Empire*, Allen Lane, London, 2007.

63. Sir Ian Scott, Deputy Private Secretary to the Viceroy; conversation with Viceroy, August 1946. MSS. Brit. Emp.s.527, Rhodes House Archive, Oxford.

64. Channon diary. Rattigan had another lifelong friend in the well-known dandy Bunny Roger, whose louche but entertaining qualities were exemplified by the occasion when, while walking down a London street in rather a tight-fitting suit, he was jeered by a cab driver who called out, 'Watch out, luv, you've dropped your diamond necklace.' Roger at once retorted, 'Diamonds with tweed? Never!'

65. About £38 billion in today's money.

66. *Transfer of Power*, vol.viii, no.26.

67. Louis, op.cit. Britain finally evacuated Palestine in 1948, ceding its influence there to the United States. In the same year the welfare state was established in Britain.

68. Their loyalty would be all the more necessary in such circumstances as the number of British troops stationed in India was falling sharply. In the 1930s the ratio of British troops to Indian was more than one in two; after the war that ratio fell to about one in six.

69. *Transfer of Power*, vol.ix, no.390, 13 February 1947.

70. A hugely controversial disturbance that took place in 1919 and was perhaps seminal for the future of the Indian Empire, when the British, under General Dyer, fired on a hostile crowd that had gathered in an enclosed space, see note 18, above.

71. Guy Wint, *The British in Asia*, Faber & Faber, London, 1947. Wint served on Wavell's staff for a time.

72. BL/L/P&J/10/111.

73. See Irial Glyn, 'An Untouchable in the Presence of Brahmins', *Modern Asian Studies* 41(3), 2007, pp.639–63.

74. Minutes of Indian Conference in London, 5 December 1946. *Transfer of Power*, vol.ix, no.157.

75. Including the Reforms Commissioner, V.P. Menon, who played a large part in the arrangements for transferring power. He was long a 'trusted confidant' of the Viceroy, but many other advisers felt that he was too close to the Congress leaders, who thus, unfairly, had a better idea of British intentions than did the Muslims.

76. Enclosure to Doc. no.316, 27 December 1945, quoted in *Transfer of Power*, vol.vi.; for Wavell's definition of areas for Pakistan, dated 6 February 1946, see BL/IOR/L/PJ/8/525; f.103.

77. *Transfer of Power*, vol.ix, no.199, 17 December 1946.

78. *Transfer of Power*, op. cit., vol.ix: No. 236, Bevin to Attlee, 1 January, 1947; No. 243, Attlee to Bevin, 2 January 1947.

79. Minutes of the India Committee meeting, 3 January 1947. Ibid., no.245.

80. Wavell to Lascelles, 1 January, 1946. RA PS/GVI/C052A/31B.

81. Wavell to Attlee, 22 July 1946. *Transfer of Power*, vol.viii, no.64.

82. Known to many Americans as 'Save England's Asian Colonies'.

83. *The Viceroy's Journal*, 31 December 1946, p.402.

84. Attlee to Wavell, 31 January 1947. *Transfer of Power*, no.331.

85. To Captain Peter Longmore, MC, son of Air Chief Marshal Sir Arthur Longmore, Wavell's erstwhile colleague in the Middle East.

86. See Hansard, vol.433, 1946–7, cols1398–1401, House of Commons proceedings on 20 February 1947, and House of Lords announcement on the same day.

87. Ibid.

88. The Granada Historical Records Interview, Panther Record, 1967.

89. Wavell Papers.

90. Rhodes House, Oxford, mss Brit Empire. 527/6.

91. Mrs Jaya Thadani to author. Her father was Kanwar Sir Dalip Singh, a judge in the High Court at Lahore.

92. Col. F.J. Burnaby-Atkins, erstwhile ADC to the Viceroy, to author.

93. Viceroy to King George VI, 24 February 1947. RA PS/GVI/C052A/47.

94. Ibid.

95. BBC report, above.

96. The Mountbattens arrived at 3.45, accompanied by the Military Secretary, Col. Douglas Currie, and the new Viceroy was sworn in two days later. See Alan Campbell-Johnson, *Mission with Mountbatten*, Hale, London, 1951.
97. *The Viceroy's Journal*, 28 March 1947.

Chapter 17: Distance Run

1. Wavell to Dover Wilson, 30 April 1947. John Dover Wilson Papers, National Library of Scotland, MS14314/17.
2. Lord Braybrooke to Dover Wilson, 12 May 1947. National Library of Scotland, MS14314/44.
3. Maj. Gen. Andrew Watson to author.
4. Dame Frances Campbell-Preston to author.
5. Wavell to Freya Stark, 8 June 1947.
6. Field Marshal Haig, another chronically silent man, overcame his difficulty far less well than Wavell, and his speeches could be acutely embarrassing, if sometimes amusingly maladroit. On one occasion he addressed the winners of an inter-regimental cross-country race: 'I congratulate you on your running. You have run very well. I hope you will run as well in the presence of the enemy.'
7. The Geographical Magazine, vol. 22, December 1949, No.8, p.295.
8. Wavell to T.S. Eliot, 13 December, 1948. T.S. Eliot Archive.
9. *The Viceroy's Journal*, p.438.
10. Ibid., p.444.
11. See David Gilmour, *Curzon*, Papermac, London, 1995, p.586.
12. CIGS to Auchinleck, 26 June 1941. Dill Papers, 3/22, LHCMA.
13. Comment by the Australian Prime Minister, War Cabinet no.26 of 1941, 7 March 1941, Confidential Annex, Cabinet papers. PRO. CAB 65/22, quoted in Sir Martin Gilbert, *Winston S. Churchill*, vol. VI, p.1030.
14. T.S. Eliot to Lord Ballantrae. Quoted in the *Times Literary Supplement*, 1980.
15. Wavell, *Allenby: A Study in Greatness*.
16. Mallaby op. cit.

SOURCES

PRIMARY sources for this book have included interviews and discussions with people who knew Lord Wavell or who have personal knowledge of matters relevant to his life story, many of whom are referred to in the Acknowledgments (see page 431).

I have also drawn information from manuscript papers, diaries and similar primary sources, including those of the following:

Birmingham University Library: Earl of Avon
Bodleian Library: T.E. Lawrence
British Library, India Office Papers: Donnison Papers, Sir Reginald Dorman-Smith, De Chazal MSS, correspondence between the Viceroy and the Secretary of State for India, and between the Viceroy and governors of provinces
Churchill Archives Centre: Sir Leopold Amery, Lawrence Burgis, Sir Winston Churchill, Sir James Grigg, Lord Ismay, Sir Ian Jacob, Sir Alan Lascelles, Ronald Lewin
T.S. Eliot Archive: T.S. Eliot
Hopetoun House Archive: Sir Gilbert Laithwaite, Marquess of Linlithgow
Imperial War Museum: Brigadier G.S. Brunskill, Field Marshal Lord Chetwode, Brigadier D.W. Clarke, Lt Gen. N.M.S Irwin, Gen. Sir Richard O'Connor, Lt Gen., A.E. Percival, Capt. O.C. Williams
Liddell Hart Centre for Military Archives: Lord Alanbrooke, Lord Allenby, Sir Robert Brooke-Popham, Sir John Burnett-Stuart, Sir John Dill, Sir Thomas Hutton, Sir Basil Liddell Hart

McMaster University: John Connell
John Murray Archive: Freya Stark
National Library of Scotland: Lord Ballantrae, John Dover Wilson, Sir Aylmer Haldane
Nuffield College, Oxford: Viscount Cherwell
Private collections: Joan Bright Astley, Cecil Beaton, Alexander Reid Scott
Reading University Library: Peter Fleming
Rhodes House, Oxford: Hailey Papers
St Antony's College, Oxford: Lord Killearn, Sir Edward Spears.

I also consulted many journals and books (published in London except where stated), including the following:

The Army Quarterly, Blackwood's Magazine, The Contemporary Review, European Studies Review, Horizon, House and Garden, Journal of Commonwealth Political Studies, Journal of the History of Strategic Studies, Journal of Modern History, Journal of the RUSI, The Listener, The London Gazette, Middle East Journal, Modern Asian Studies, The National Review: Foreign Affairs, the Nineteenth Century and After, The Quarterly Review, The Red Hackle, The Round Table, The Spectator.

Aldrich, Richard, *Intelligence and the War Against Japan*, CUP, 2000.
Aldridge, Nicholas, *Time To Spare?*, Talboys, Oxford, 1989.
Ansprenger, Franz, *The Dissolution of the Colonial Empires*, Routledge, 1989.
Arnold, H.H., *Global Mission*, Hutchinson, 1951.
Astley, Joan Bright, *The Inner Circle*, Hutchinson, 1971.
Avon, Earl of, *The Eden Memoirs: The Reckoning*, Cassell, 1965.
Bagnold, Ralph, *Sand, Wind and War*, University of Arizona Press, Tucson, 1990.
Barnett, Correlli, *The Audit of War*, Pan, 1996.
Barnett, Correlli, *The Collapse of British Power*, Pan, 2002.
Barnett, Correlli, *The Desert Generals*, Cassell, 1999.
Barnett, Correlli, *Engage the Enemy More Closely*, Penguin, 2000.
Bayly, Christopher and Harper, Tim, *Forgotten Armies*, Allen Lane, 2004.
Baynes, John, *The Forgotten Victor: General Sir Richard O'Connor*, Brassey's, 1989.
Bence-Jones, Mark, *The Viceroys of India*, Constable, 1982.

Bennett, Ralph, *Ultra and Mediterranean Strategy, 1941–45*, Hamish Hamilton, 1989.

Bierman, John and Smith, Colin, *Fire in the Night*, Pan, 2000.

Bix, Herbert P., *Hirohito and the Making of Modern Japan*, Duckworth, 2000.

Bond, Brian, ed., *Chief of Staff: The Diaries of Lt-Gen Sir Henry Pownall*, Leo Cooper, 1972.

Bond, Brian and Kyoichi Tachikawa, eds., *British and Japanese Military Leadership in the Far Eastern War, 1941–45*, Frank Cass, 2004.

Brendon, Piers, *Decline and Fall of the British Empire*, Jonathan Cape, 2007.

Bryant, Arthur, *The Turn of the Tide, 1939–1943*, Collins, 1957.

Burns, Sir Alan, *In Defence of Colonies*, George Allen & Unwin, 1957.

Burrows, Sir Bernard, *Diplomat in a Changing World*, Memoir Club, Spennymoor, 2001.

Butler, J.R.M. and Howard, Michael, *Grand Strategy*, HMSO, 1956–76.

Byron, Robert, *Essay on India*, Routledge, 1931.

Callahan, Raymond, *The Worst Disaster*, University of Delaware, Newark, 1977.

Carver, Lord, *Dilemmas of the Desert War*, Spellmount, Staplehurst, 2002.

Carver, Lord, *Wavell and the War in the Middle East, 1940–41*, Ransom, Texas, 1993.

Casey, Maie, *Tides and Eddies*, Michael Joseph, 1966.

Cassidy, Martin, *Inniskilling Diaries, 1899–1903*, 2001.

Cave Brown, Anthony, *Bodyguard of Lies*, W.H. Allen, 1976.

Churchill, Winston S., *The Boer War*, Mandarin, 1990.

Churchill, Winston S., *My Early Life*, Mandarin, 1990.

Churchill, Winston S., *Their Finest Hour*, and *Grand Alliance*, Penguin, 2005.

Clarke, Dudley, *Seven Assignments*, Jonathan Cape, 1948.

Clarke, Peter, *The Cripps Version*, Allen Lane, 2002.

Clarke, Peter, *The Last Thousand Days of the British Empire*, Allen Lane, 2007.

Close, H.M., *Attlee, Wavell, Mountbatten and the Transfer of Power*, National Book Foundation, Islamabad, 1997.

Close, H.M., *An Essay on Wavell*, National Book Foundation, Islamabad, 1999.

Coats, Peter, *Of Generals and Gardens*, Weidenfeld & Nicolson, 1976.

Coats, Peter, *Of Kings and Cabbages*, Weidenfeld & Nicolson, 1984.

Collier, Basil, *Leader of the Few*, Jarrolds, London, 1957.

Collins, R.J., *Lord Wavell*, Hodder & Stoughton, 1947.

Connell, John, *Wavell: Scholar and Soldier*, Collins, 1964.

Connell John, *Wavell, Supreme Commander 1941–43*, Collins, 1969.

Cooper, Artemis, *Cairo in the War*, Hamish Hamilton, 1989.

Cooper, Pamela, *A Cloud of Forgetting*, Quartet, 1993.

Cornwall-Marshall, Sir James, *Wars and Rumours of Wars*, Leo Cooper, 1984.

Cruikshank, Charles, *Deception in World War II*, OUP, 1981.

Cunningham, Andrew, *A Sailor's Odyssey*, Hutchinson, 1951.

Danchev, Alex, *Establishing the Anglo-American Alliance*, Brassey's, 1990.

Danchev, Alex, *Very Special Relationship*, Brassey's, 1986.

Danchev, A. and Todman D., *War Diaries 1939–1945: Field Marshal Lord Alanbrooke*, Weidenfield & Nicolson, 2001

Davin, D.M., *History of New Zealand in the Second World War 1939–45*, War History Branch, Wellington, 1953.

De Guingand, Frederick, *From Brass Hat to Bowler Hat*, Hamish Hamilton, 1979.

Dewey, Clive, *Anglo-Indian Attitudes*, Hambledon, 1993.

Dilke, Christopher, *Dr Moberly's Mint-Mark*, Heinemann, 1965.

Emerson, Rupert, *From Empire to Nation*, Harvard, Cambridge, Mass., 1959.

Farrell, Brian, *The Defence and Fall of Singapore*, Tempus, 2005.

Fergusson, Bernard, Lord Ballantrae, *Trumpet in the Hall*, Collins, 1970.

Fergusson, Bernard, Lord Ballantrae, *Wavell, Portrait of a Soldier*, Collins, 1961.

Fforde, J.S., *The Bank of England and Public Policy, 1941–58*, CUP, 1992.

Fieldhouse, D.K., *The Colonial Empires*, Weidenfeld & Nicolson, 1966.

Fischer, Louis, *The Essential Gandhi*, Vintage, 1983.

Fort, George Seymour, *Alfred Beit*, Nicholson & Watson, 1932.

Fraser, Gen. Sir David, *Alanbrooke*, Collins, 1982.

French, David, *Raising Churchill's Army*, OUP, 2000.

French, Patrick, *Liberty or Death*, HarperCollins, 1997.

Freyberg, Paul, *Bernard Freyberg, VC*, Hodder & Stoughton, 1991.

Gandhi, Mahatma, *Collected Works*, Government of India, 1958–84.

Gardner, Howard, *Extraordinary Minds*, Weidenfeld & Nicolson, 1997.

Garewal, S.M., ed., *Jinnah–Wavell Correspondence, 1943–47*, Research Society of Pakistan, University of the Punjab, Lahore, 1986.

Gaunson, A.B., *The Anglo-French Clash in Lebanon and Syria, 1940–45*, Macmillan, 1987.

Gilbert, Sir Martin, *The Churchill War Papers*, Heinemann, 1993.

Gilbert, Sir Martin, *Winston S. Churchill*, vol.vi, Heinemann, 1993.

Gilmour, David, *The Long Recessional*, John Murray, 2002.

Graecen, Lavinia, *Chink*, Macmillan, 1989

Grigg, Sir Edward, *The Faith of an Englishman*, Macmillan, 1936.

Grigg, James, *Prejudice and Judgment*, Jonathan Cape, 1948.

Hailey, Lord, *The Future of Colonial Peoples*, OUP, 1943.

Harriman, Averell, *Mission to the Middle East*, Hutchinson, 1976.

Haupt, Werner and Bingham, J., *North African Campaign*, Macdonald, 1969.

Hetherington, John, *Blamey*, Cheshire, Melbourne, 1954.

Hinsley, F.H., *British Intelligence in the Second World War*, HMSO, 1993.

Hobson, J.A., *Imperialism: A Study*, Allen & Unwin, 1988.

Hodson, H.V., *The Great Divide*, OUP, 1997.

Horne, Alastair, *The Price of Glory*, Penguin, 1993.

Horner, David, *Blamey*, Allen & Unwin, St Leonard's, Australia, 1998.

Horrocks, Brian, *A Full Life*, Leo Cooper, 1974.

Irvine, A.L., *College in the Nineties*, Wykeham Press, Winchester, 1947.

Izzard, Molly, *Freya Stark*, Hodder & Stoughton, 1993.

Jackson, W.G.F., *The North African Campaign, 1940–3*, Batsford, 1975.

Jolliffe, John, ed., *Raymond Asquith, Life and Letters*, Collins, 1980.

Kennedy, *The Business of War*, Hutchinson, 1957.

Kiernan, R.H., *Wavell*, Harrap, London, 1946.

Kiernan, W., *The Lords of Human Kind*, Little, Brown, Boston, 1969.

King, Robert and Kilson, Robin, eds., *The Statecraft of British Imperialism*, Frank Cass, 1999.

Kipling, Rudyard, *Something of Myself*, Tauschnitz, 1938.

Kirby, S.W., *The War Against Japan*, HMSO, 1957–65.

Lamb, Alastair, *Incomplete Partition*, Roxford, Hertingfordbury, 1997.

Lash, Joseph, *Roosevelt and Churchill, 1939–1941*, Andre Deutsch, 1976.

Latrides, John O., *Ambassador McVeagh Reports, Greece 1933–47*, Princeton University Press, Princeton, 1980.

Lee, Raymond E., *The London Journal, 1940–41*, Little, Brown, Boston, 1971.

Lewin, Ronald, *The Chief*, Hutchinson, 1980.

Lewin, Ronald, *Ultra Goes to War*, Penguin, 2001.

Liddell Hart, Sir Basil, *The Other Side of the Hill*, Hamish Hamilton, 1956.

Liddell Hart, Sir Basil, ed., *The Rommel Papers*, Collins, 1953.

Long, Gavin, *Australia in the War of 1939–1945*, Australian War Memorial, Canberra, 1953.

Longmore, Sir Arthur, *From Sea to Sky*, Bles, 1946.

Louis, William Roger, *Ends of British Imperialism*, I.B. Tauris, 2006.

Louis, William Roger, *Imperialism at Bay, 1941–1945*, Clarendon Press, Oxford, 1977.

MacDonald, Callum, *The Lost Battle: Crete 1941*, Pan, 2002.

Mack, Edward, C., *Public Schools and British Opinion*, New York, 1973.

Mallaby, George, *From My Level*, Hutchinson, 1965.

Mansergh, Nicholas, ed., *The Transfer of Power in India, 1942–7*, HMSO, London, 1970–82.

March Phillipps, Lisle, *With Rimington*, Edward Arnold, 1901.

Marshall, George C., *The Papers of George Catlett Marshall*, Johns Hopkins Press, 1991.

Mason, Philip, *The Men Who Ruled India*, Jonathan Cape, 1953.

Mason, Philip, *A Shaft of Sunlight*, Vikas, New Delhi, 1978.

Masters, Brian, *Great Hostesses*, Constable, 1982.

Mayo, Katherine, *Mother India*, Jonathan Cape, 1927.

Meintjes, J., *De La Rey*, Keartland, Johannesburg, 1966.

Minney, R.J., ed., *The Private Papers of Hore-Belisha*, Collins, 1960.

Mockler-Ferryman, A.F., *Annals of Sandhurst*, Heinemann, 1900.

Moon, Penderel, *Divide and Quit*, OUP, 1998.

Moore, R.J., *Churchill, Cripps and India*, Clarendon Press, Oxford, 1979.

Moore, R.J., *Escape from Empire*, Clarendon Press, Oxford, 1983.

Mott-Radclyffe, Charles, *Foreign Body in the Eye*, Leo Cooper, 1975.

Muggeridge, Malcolm, ed., *Ciano's Diary, 1939–1943*, Heinemann, 1947.

Mure, David, *Master of Deception*, Kimber, 1980.

Neame, Sir Philip, *Playing With Strife*, Harrap, 1947.

Page, David, *Prelude to Partition*, OUP, 2002.

Papagos, Alexander, *The German Attack on Greece*, Greek Office of Information, London, 1946.

Papagos, Alexandros, *The Battle of Greece, 1940–1941*, J.M. Scazikis, Athens, 1949.

Pitt, Barrie, *Crucible of War*, Macmillan, 1986.

Playfair, I.S.O., *The Mediterranean and the Middle East*, HMSO, 1954.

Porter, Bernard, *The Absent-Minded Imperialists*, OUP, 2004.

Reid, Miles, *Last on the List*, Leo Cooper, 1974.

Rhodes James, Robert, ed., *'Chips': The Diaries of Sir Henry Channon*, Weidenfeld & Nicolson, London, 1967.

Roberts, Andrew, *Eminent Churchillians*, Weidenfeld & Nicolson, 1994.

Rolo, Charles, *Wingate's Raiders*, Harrap, 1944.

Rooney, David, *Stilwell the Patriot*, Greenhill, 2005.

Rose, David, *Off the Record*, Staplehurst, 1976.

Sadat, Anwar, *Revolt on the Nile*, Wingate, 1957.

Scott, Ian, *Memoirs*, ed. Denis Judd, Radcliffe Press, 1999.

Seeley, Sir John, *The Expansion of England*, University of Chicago Press, 1971.

Slim, Field Marshal Sir William, *Unofficial History*, Cassell, 1959.

Slim, Field Marshal Sir William, *Defeat Into Victory*, Cassell, 1956.

Smyth, Sir John, *Leadership in War, 1939–1945*, David & Charles, 1971.

Smyth, Sir John, *Milestones*, Sidgwick & Jackson, 1979.

Spears, Sir Edward, *Fulfilment of a Mission*, Leo Cooper, 1977.

Stark, Freya, *Dust in the Lion's Paw*, Century, 1985.

Sweet-Estcourt, Bickham, *Baker Street Irregular*, Methuen, 1965.

Tedder, Lord, *With Prejudice*, Cassell, 1966.

Thorne, C., *Allies of a Kind*, OUP, 1979.

Thornton, A.P., *The Imperial Idea and Its Enemies*, Macmillan, 1959.

Trocki, Carl, *Opium, Empire and the Global Political Economy*, Routledge, 1999.

Tuchman, Barbara, *Sand Against the Wind*, Macmillan, 1971.

Tuker, F., *While Memory Serves*, Cassell, 1950.

Wauchope, A.G., *A Short History of the Black Watch*, Edinburgh, 1908.

Wavell, A.P., *Allenby: A Study in Greatness*, Harrap, 1940.

Wavell, A.P., *Allenby in Egypt*, Harrap, 1943.

Wavell, A.P., *Generals and Generalship*, Times Publishing Co. 1941.

Wavell, A.P., *The Good Soldier*, Macmillan, 1948.

Wavell, A.P., *Other Men's Flowers*, Jonathan Cape, 1944.

Wavell, A.P., *The Palestine Campaigns*, Constable, 1928.

Wavell, A.P., *Soldiers and Soldiering*, Jonathan Cape, 1953.

Wavell, A.P., *Speaking Generally*, Macmillan, 1946.

Wavell, Earl, *The Viceroy's Journal*, ed. Penderel Moon, OUP, 1973.

Wheeler, Capt. Owen, *The War Office Past and Present*, Methuen, 1914.

Wilson, Angus, *The Strange Ride of Rudyard Kipling*, Secker & Warburg, 1977.

Winant, John, *A Letter from Grosvenor Square*, Hodder & Stoughton, 1947.

Wint, Guy, *The British in Asia*, Faber & Faber, 1947.

Winton, Harold, *To Change an Army*, Brassey's, 1985.

Wohlpert, Stanley, *Shameful Flight*, OUP, 2006.

Woollcombe, Robert, *The Campaigns of Wavell, 1939–43*, Cassell, 1959.

Ziegler, Philip, *Mountbatten*, Collins, 1985.

INDEX

attends Chungking conference with
Chiang Kai-shek, 255-7; Chiang
offers Chinese troops to, 256-8; as
commander of ABDACOM area,
259-60, 267-9, 277; and defence of
Singapore, 262-3, 265-7, 275-6;
directs control in Malaya, 266;
strategy in South-East Asia and
Pacific, 269-72, 278-80; injured in
fall, 275; Order of the Day to
Singapore troops, 275-6; and
surrender of Singapore, 276-7;
resumes post as C.in C. in India,
277, 290; and Burma campaign,
281-6, 294; on irresolution of
forces against Japanese, 282;
underestimates Japanese soldiers,
282, 422; positive effect on morale,
283; revises estimate of Japanese
soldiers, 286, 312; and Indian
independence movement, 287-90;
relaxations and pastimes, 291-2;
writes verse, 291-2, 295, 319, 326,
344, 396; keeps Churchill informed
from India, 293; keeps
Commonplace Book, 293; plans to
reconquer Burma, 295-6, 298-300,
304, 306-11, 317-20; relations with
Stilwell, 297, 310; and anti-British
campaign in India, 301; attends
conferences with Churchill in
Cairo and Moscow (1942), 301-2;
requests and receives promotion to
Field-Marshal, 302-3; encourages
special operations in Burma, 304-6,
312-13; and Arakan campaign,
311-16; and Japanese defence
tactics, 314-16; distracted by
civilian administrative demands,
316; restructures India's Eastern
Army, 316; attends Washington
Conference with Churchill (1943),
320-4; confers in London (April
1943), 320; fatigue, 321; Churchill
loses confidence in, 324-5;

compiles anthology of poetry
(*Other Men's Flowers*), 327-10;
appointed Viceroy of India, 333-4,
337-9, 345, 348-9, 357-8, 361;
expects appointment as Supreme
Commander in East Asian theatre,
338; and London society, 340-4,
426; viscountcy, 345; and
constitutional settlement of India,
346-7, 349-50, 352-8, 375-6, 382-6,
392-3, 396, 413, 422-3; liberal
political views, 349, 376; role and
duties as Viceroy, 359-60; and
Indian famine (1943), 362-8; and
administration of India, 365-6,
368-9, 374-6; differences with
Cabinet and India Committee over
Indian affairs, 366-7, 379-80, 383,
385; staff and organisation in India,
369-71; lifestyle in India, 370-3;
manner, 372; dealings with
Gandhi, 377-80; visits England
from India (March 1945), 383; sits
for Epstein bust, 385; conference
with Indian leaders (June/July
1945), 387-8; and Labour
Government (1945), 389-90; and
Cripps's 1946 mission to India,
391-5; and proposals for British
withdrawal from India ('Breakdown
Plan'), 394, 404-6, 408, 413;
opposes formation of Pakistan,
397; and rioting and killings in
India, 399-400; attends London
conference (December 1946), 401,
404; loses confidence of Labour
government, 406-8; replaced as
Viceroy by Mountbatten, 408-10,
414; returns to England from
India, 414-15; earldom, 416;
honorary degrees, 416; post-India
activities, 416-18; speechmaking,
418; despondency at decline of
Empire, 419-21; achievements
assessed, 421-6; uneasy relations